Good Faith in European Contract Law

For some Western European legal systems the principle of good faith
has proved central to the development of their law of contracts, while
in others it has been marginalised or even rejected. This book starts by
surveying the use or neglect of good faith in these legal systems and
explaining its historical origins. The central part of the book takes
thirty situations which would, in some legal systems, attract the
application of good faith, analyses them according to fifteen national
legal systems and assesses the practical significance of both the principle of good faith and its relationship to other contractual and non-
contractual doctrines in each situation. The book concludes by
explaining how European lawyers, whether from a civil or common law
background, may come to terms with the principle of good faith. This is
the first completed project of The Common Core of European Private
Law launched at the University of Trento.

Reinhard Zimmermann is Professor of Private Law, Roman Law and
Comparative Legal History at the University of Regensburg and Fellow
of St John's College, Cambridge.

Simon Whittaker is Lecturer in Law at the University of Oxford and
Fellow of St John's College, Oxford.

GU00758526

The Common Core of European Private Law Project

For the transnational lawyer the present European situation is equivalent to that of a traveller compelled to cross legal Europe using a number of different local maps. To assist lawyers in the journey beyond their own locality 'The Common Core of European Private Law Project' was launched in 1993 at the University of Trento under the auspices of the late Professor Rudolf B. Schlesinger.

The aim of this collective scholarly enterprise is to unearth what is already common to the legal systems of European Union member states. Case studies widely circulated and discussed between lawyers of different traditions are employed to draw at least the main lines of a reliable map of the law of Europe.

Books in The Common Core of European Private Law Project

General editors
Mauro Bussani and Ugo Mattei

Good Faith in European Contract Law
edited by Reinhard Zimmermann and Simon Whittaker

The Enforceability of Promises in European Contract Law
edited by James Gordley

Good Faith in European Contract Law

edited by

Reinhard Zimmermann
and Simon Whittaker

CAMBRIDGE
UNIVERSITY PRESS

CAMBRIDGE UNIVERSITY PRESS
Cambridge, New York, Melbourne, Madrid, Cape Town, Singapore, São Paulo, Delhi

Cambridge University Press
The Edinburgh Building, Cambridge CB2 8RU, UK

Published in the United States of America by Cambridge University Press, New York

www.cambridge.org
Information on this title: www.cambridge.org/9780521771900

First published 2000
This digitally printed version 2008

A catalogue record for this publication is available from the British Library

Library of Congress Cataloguing in Publication data

Good faith in European contract law / edited by Reinhard Zimmermann
and Simon Whittaker
        p.   cm. – (Cambridge studies in international and comparative
law; 14)
ISBN 0 521 77190 0 (hardbound)
    1. Contracts – Europe.   2. Good faith (Law) – Europe.
I. Zimmermann, Reinhard, 1952–   .   II. Whittaker, Simon.
III. Title: European contract law.   IV. Series: Cambridge studies in
international and comparative law (Cambridge, England: 1996); 12.
KJC1720.G66   2000
341.7′53 – dc 21   99–37679   CIP

ISBN 978-0-521-77190-0 hardback
ISBN 978-0-521-08803-9 paperback

Contents

General editors' preface

This is the first book in the series 'The Common Core of European Private Law' which will publish its results within Cambridge Studies in International and Comparative Law. The project was launched in 1993 at the University of Trento under the auspices of the late Professor Rudolf B. Schlesinger. We welcome this inaugural volume edited by Reinhard Zimmermann and Simon Whittaker as offering a significant step forward not only in our understanding of the notion of 'Good Faith' but, more generally, in our knowledge of comparative contract law. The methodology used in the Trento project is novel. By making use of case studies it goes beyond mere description to detailed inquiry into how most European Union legal systems resolve specific legal questions in practice, and to thorough comparison between those systems. It is our hope that these volumes will provide scholars with a valuable tool for research in comparative law and in their own national legal systems.

We must thank not only the editors and contributors to these first published results but also all the participants who continue to contribute to The Common Core of European Private Law project. It would be impossible to thank each and every one by name. An exception must be made for Professors Barry Nicholas and Rodolfo Sacco, both of whom were present together with the General Editors and Professor Zimmermann when the project was launched in Trento in 1993. With a sense of deep gratitude we also wish to recall our late Honorary Editor, Professor Rudolf B. Schlesinger. We are sad that we have not been able to present him with the results of a project in which he believed so firmly. No scholarly project can survive without committed sponsors. The Dipartimento di Scienze Giuridiche of the University of Trento, its past and present directors and its excellent staff must first be thanked. The Istituto Trentino di Cultura made possible the organisation of the annual General Meetings. The Consiglio Nazionale delle Ricerche, the Istituto Subalpino per l'Analisi e l'Insegnamento del Diritto delle Attivatà

Transnazionali, the University of Torino, the Fromm Chair in International and Comparative Law at the University of California, the Hastings College of Law, the TMR Network on Common Principles of European Private Law, the University of Regensburg and the Leibniz programme of the German Research Association have all contributed to the funding of this project. Last but not least we must encourage all those involved in our ongoing Trento projects in contract law, property, tort and other areas whose results will be the subject of future published volumes. Our home page on the internet is at http://www.jus.unitn.it/dsg/common-core. There you can follow our progress in mapping the common core of European private law.

General Editors:

Mauro Bussani (Università di Trento)
Ugo Mattei (Università di Torino – University of California, Hastings)

Late Honorary Editor:

Rudolf B. Schlesinger (Cornell University – University of California, Hastings)

Preface

When this project was conceived, in June 1994, the topic chosen was somewhat unconventional. 'Good Faith' appeared to be insufficiently specific, conceptually, to lend itself to comparative analysis. At the same time, the topic was widely regarded as unsuitable for a truly European inquiry in view of its distinctly civilian flavour. In the meantime, however, there has been a surge of interest, both in civil law and common law jurisdictions. This may be due, at least partly, to the implementation of the Directive on Unfair Terms in Consumer Contracts in the member states of the European Union; for, as a result of this Directive, every legal system within the European Union now faces the practical challenge of coming to terms with a general notion of good faith. Significantly, also, the draftsmen of the Principles of European Contract Law appear to have regarded 'good faith' as part of the common core of European contract law, for they included in their Principles a general provision according to which 'in exercising his rights and performing his duties each party must act in accordance with good faith and fair dealing'. Thus, we think, our project no longer requires any specific justification.

The intellectual objectives pursued, and the method adopted, in the present study are set out in chapter 1 ('Good faith in European contract law: surveying the legal landscape'). By focusing on the comparative analysis of specific case studies we have attempted to go beyond the merely doctrinal. Our aim has been to explore the practical significance of the notion of good faith, to put it into its context and, perhaps most importantly, to clear away some of the misunderstanding and misinformation which has often prevented an unbiased comparative evaluation.

We are very grateful to the contributors to this volume for preparing their reports and discussing their findings at the Regensburg symposium in July 1997. We would also like to thank our friends and colleagues in

Trento where the project originated, and Finola O'Sullivan at Cambridge
University Press who so kindly and efficiently helped to bring it to a good
end. For a variety of reasons which will be obvious to the reader the
present volume was more difficult to edit than any other with which we
have been involved. Without the assistance received from Gabriele
Schmitt, secretary at the Lehrstuhl in Regensburg, and Martin Laing, B.A.,
LL.B. (Stellenbosch), research assistant at the Lehrstuhl in Regensburg in
1998/9, it would have been impossible. To them we owe a particular debt
of gratitude.

Simon Whittaker   Reinhard Zimmermann
St John's College, Oxford   St John's College, Cambridge

March 1999

Contributors

ISMENE ADROULIDAKIS-DIMITRIADIS, Dr. iur., is Professor of Private Law in the University of Athens

KATE BENNET is a solicitor and was Research Assistant in Private Law in the University of Glasgow

ANGEL CARRASCO PERERA, Dr. iur., is Professor of Private Law in the University of Castilla-La Mancha

JAMES GORDLEY, LL.D., is Professor of Law in the University of California, Berkeley

MICHELE GRAZIADEI, Dr. iur., is Professor of Comparative Law in the University of Insubria, Como, and Professor of Anglo-American Law in the University of Torino

VIGGO HAGSTRØM, Dr. iur., is Professor of Private Law in the University of Oslo

TORGNY HÅSTAD, Dr. iur., is Justice in the Supreme Court in Stockholm

HANNU TAPANI KLAMI, Dr. iur., Cand. hum., is Professor of Jurisprudence and Private International Law in the University of Helsinki

HELMUT KOZIOL, Dr. iur., is Professor of Private Law in the University of Vienna

HORATIA MUIR-WATT is Professor of Law in the University of Paris I

DECLAN MURPHY is Lecturer in Law in the University College, Dublin

DIARMUID ROSSA PHELAN, Ph.D., is a barrister and a lecturer in Trinity College, Dublin

STÉPHANE REIFEGERSTE is Doctor of Law from the University of Paris–Sud XI

MARTIN JOSEF SCHERMAIER, Mag., Dr. iur., is Professor of Roman Law and Private Law in the University of Münster

RUTH SEFTON-GREEN, M.A. (Oxon.), is Doctor of Law, a solicitor, an advocate in France and a lecturer in law in the University of Paris I

MATTHIAS E. STORME is Professor of Private Law in the University of Ghent

ROBERT S. SUMMERS, Ph.D., Dr. iur. (h.c.), is McRoberts Research Professor of Law, Cornell Law School

JOSEPH M. THOMSON is Regius Professor of Law in the University of Glasgow

J. H. M. VAN ERP, Dr. iur., is Professor of Civil Law and European Private Law in the University of Maastricht

DIRK A. VERSE, Dr. iur., M.Jur. (Oxon.), is Research Assistant in Private Law, Roman Law and Comparative Legal History in the University of Regensburg

KLAUS VOGEL, Mag. iur., is Research Assistant in Private Law in the University of Vienna

SIMON WHITTAKER, B.C.L., M.A., D.Phil. (Oxon.), of Lincoln's Inn, barrister, is Lecturer in Law in the University of Oxford and Fellow of St John's College, Oxford

REINHARD ZIMMERMANN, Dr. iur., LL.D., LL.D. (h.c.), is Professor of Private Law, Roman Law and Comparative Legal History in the University of Regensburg

Table of legislation

Austria

Civil Code (ABGB)

7	51, 496
418	519
601	261
861	238–9
863	534
866	176 n. 23
870	215–16, 364, 560
871	215, 364–5, 518, 560, 582–3
872	215, 216, 365, 560
877	216
878	176 n. 23
879	406
883	261
903	323–4
904	323
914	50, 324, 405, 422, 641
915	381
918	641
920	423
922 ff.	365–6, 582
932	366, 582
932 II	422
934	214
976	380
1062	323
1118	309
1152	283

Denmark

Denmark and Norway

England

Norway

Portugal

Scotland

Spain

Sweden

Switzerland

PART I · SETTING THE SCENE

Abbreviations

ABGB	*Allgemeines bürgerliches Gesetzbuch*
AC	Appeal Cases, Law Reports
AcP	*Archiv für die civilistische Praxis*
AGBG	*Gesetz zur Regelung des Rechts der Allgemeinen Geschäftsbedingungen (AGB-Gesetz)*
al.	*alinéa*
ALR	Australian Law Reports
Areopagus	*Areios Pagos*
art.	article
Ass. plén.	*Assemblé plénière* of the *Cour de cassation*
B & S	Best and Smith's Reports, Queen's Bench
BGB	*Bürgerliches Gesetzbuch*
BGH	*Bundesgerichtshof*
BGHZ	*Entscheidungen des Bundesgerichtshofes für Zivilsachen*
Bos & Pul	Bosanquet and Puller's Reports, Common Pleas
Bull. civ.	*Bulletin des arrêts des Chambres civiles de la Cour de cassation*
Burr	Burrow's Reports, King's Bench
BVerfGE	*Entscheidungen des Bundesverfassungsgerichts*
B.W.	*Burgerlijk Wetboek*
C.	Justinian's Code
c.	*canon*
CA	Court of Appeal
cap.	*caput*
C.B.	Chief Baron
c.c.	*Codice civile*
C. civ.	*Code civil*
C. cons.	*Code de la consommation*
Ch	Law Reports, Chancery Division
chap(s).	chapter(s)

Civ.	*Cour de cassation, Chambre civile*
Civ. (1)	First civil chamber of the *Cour de cassation*
Civ. (3)	Third civil chamber of the *Cour de cassation*
col(s).	column(s)
Com.	Commercial chamber of the *Cour de cassation*
concl.	*conclusions*
D	*Recueil Dalloz* or *Dalloz Sirey*
D.	Justinian's Digest
Digesto sez. civ.	*Digesto delle discipline privatistiche - sezione civile*
Doug	Douglas' Reports, King's Bench
DP	*Recueil Dalloz périodique*
DS	*Dalloz Sirey*
dub.	*dubitatio*
E I	First draft of the German Civil Code (BGB)
E.C.	European Community
edn	edition
ed(s).	editor(s)
Einf. v.	*Einführung vor* (introduction to)
Einl.	*Einleitung* (introduction)
Einl. v.	*Einleitung vor* (introduction to)
ERPL	European Review of Private Law
fasc.	fascicle
FIRA	*Fontes Iuris Romani Anteiustiniani*
Gai.	Gaius' Institutes
GP	*Gazette du Palais*
Hare	Hare's Reports, Chancery
Harvard LR	Harvard Law Review
HL	House of Lords
I.	Justinian's Institutes
ibid.	*ibidem*
J.	Justice
JBl	*Juristische Blätter*
JCP	*Jurisclasseur périodique* (otherwise known as *La Semaine Juridique*), *édition générale*
JLH	Journal of Legal History
JZ	*Juristenzeitung*
KB	Law Reports, King's Bench Division
l.	*loi*
lib.	*liber*
liv.	*livre*
L.J.	Lord Justice
Lloyd's Rep	Lloyd's Law Reports
LQR	Law Quarterly Review

LRQB	Law Reports, Queen's Bench
M & W	Meeson and Welsby's Reports, Exchequer
M.R.	Master of the Rolls
n.	note, number
NJW	*Neue Juristische Wochenschrift*
NoB	*Nomikon Vima*
OGH	*Österreichischer Oberster Gerichtshof*
OJ EC	Official Journal of the European Communities
OR	*Schweizerisches Obligationenrecht*
Oxford JLS	Oxford Journal of Legal Studies
p.	page
Pap.	Papinian
PD	Law Reports, Probate, Divorce, and Admiralty Division
Peake	Peake's Reports, Nisi Prius
pr.	*principium*
Prob.	*De notis iuris fragmenta Valerio Probo vulgo tributa* (FIRA II 454 ff.)
QB	Queen's Bench
qu.	*quaestio*
RabelsZ	*Zeitschrift für ausländisches und internationales Privatrecht*
RE	*Paulys Realencyclopädie der classischen Altertumswissenschaft* (G. Wissowa, W. Kroll, K. Mittelhaus, K. Ziegler, 1893 ff.)
RGZ	*Entscheidungen des Reichsgerichts in Zivilsachen*
RIDC	*Revue internationale de droit comparé*
RTDCiv	*Revue trimestrielle de droit civil*
S	*Sirey*
s.	section
SC (HL)	Session Cases, House of Lords
sect.	*section*
Stark	Starkie's Reports, Nisi Prius
s.v.	*sub voce*
SZ	*Entscheidungen des österreichischen Obersten Gerichtshofes in Zivil- und Justizverwaltungssachen*
t.	*tomus*
tit.	*titulus, titre*
tom.	*tomus*
Tulane LR	Tulane Law Review
UCC	Uniform Commercial Code
Ulp.	Ulpian
vol.	volume
vulg.	Vulgate (or Latin: *vulgata*)
WLR	Weekly Law Reports
X	*Liber Extra* (*Corpus Juris Canonici*)

ZEuP   *Zeitschrift für Europäisches Privatrecht*
ZGB   *Zivilgesetzbuch*
ZSS   *Zeitschrift der Savigny-Stiftung für Rechtsgeschichte, Romanistische*
               Abteilung

1   Good faith in European contract law:
     surveying the legal landscape

SIMON WHITTAKER AND REINHARD ZIMMERMANN

Note: Sections I–IV and VII have been drafted by *Reinhard Zimmermann*, sections V and VI by *Simon Whittaker* and section VIII jointly. In writing sections V and VII we have drawn on information kindly supplied by the country reporters for the case studies printed in the present volume.

I. A change in perspective

Private law in Europe is in the process of reacquiring a genuinely European character.[1] The Council of the European Communities enacts directives deeply affecting core areas of the national legal systems of the member states.[2] The European Court of Justice develops rules and concepts transcending national legal borders and constituting an embryonic general part of European contract and liability law.[3] The so-called Lando Commission has produced Part I of a Restatement of European Contract Law,[4] is in the process of publishing the second part and has started work on the remaining areas of general contract law.

---

[1] See generally, e.g., Jochen Taupitz, *Europäische Privatrechtsvereinheitlichung heute und morgen* (1993); Ivo E. Schwartz, 'Perspektiven der Angleichung des Privatrechts in der Europäischen Gemeinschaft', ZEuP 2 (1994) 559 ff.; Reinhard Zimmermann, 'Civil Code and Civil Law – The Europeanization of Private Law within the European Community and the Re-emergence of a European Legal Science', (1994/95) 1 *Columbia Journal of European Law* 63 ff.; Martin Gebauer, *Grundfragen der Europäisierung des Privatrechts* (1998); Jürgen Basedow, 'The Renascence of Uniform Law: European Contract Law and its Components', (1998) 18 *Legal Studies* 121 ff.; the contributions in Peter-Christian Müller-Graff (ed.), *Gemeinsames Privatrecht in der Europäischen Gemeinschaft* (1993), Nicolò Lipari (ed.), *Diritto Privato Europeo* (1997), and Arthur Hartkamp, Martijn Hesselink *et al.*, *Towards a European Civil Code* (2nd edn, 1998).

[2] For overviews, see Schwartz, ZEuP 2 (1994) 559 ff.; Zimmermann, (1994/95) 1 *Columbia Journal of European Law* 68 ff.; Peter-Christian Müller-Graff, 'EC Directives as a Means of Private Law Unification', in: Hartkamp/Hesselink *et al.* (n. 1) 71 ff.; Marian Paschke, Constantin Iliopoulos (eds.), *Europäisches Privatrecht* (1998); concerning contract law see, most recently, Stefan Grundmann, *Europäisches Schuldvertragsrecht* (1999).

[3] On the role of the European Court of Justice, see Ulrich Everling, 'Rechtsvereinheitlichung durch Richterrecht in der Europäischen Gemeinschaft', RabelsZ 50 (1986) 193 ff.; Christian Joerges, Gert Brüggemeier, 'Europäisierung des Vertragsrechts und Haftungsrechts', in: Müller-Graff (n. 1) 233 ff.; the contributions by David A. O. Edward and Lord Mackenzie Stuart, in: David L. Carey Miller, Reinhard Zimmermann (eds.), *The Civilian Tradition and Scots Law: Aberdeen Quincentenary Essays* (1997) 307 ff., 351 ff.; Nicola Scannichio, 'Il diritto privato europeo nel sistema delle fonti', in: Lipari (n. 1) 58 ff.; Walter van Gerven, 'The ECJ-Case Law as a Means of Unification of Private Law?', in: Hartkamp/Hesselink *et al.* (n. 1) 91 ff.; for general background on legal unification by means of appeal court decisions in states with several legal systems see the symposium edited by Klaus Luig, ZEuP 5 (1997) 762 ff. (with contributions by Antonio Padoa-Schioppa, Filippo Ranieri, Herbert Kronke, Michael Rainer, Klaus Luig, Barbara Pozzo and Ulrich Everling).

[4] Ole Lando, Hugh Beale (eds.), *Principles of European Contract Law*, Part I (1995); for comment, see Reinhard Zimmermann, 'Konturen eines Europäischen Privatrechts', JZ 1995, 477 ff.; Hugh Beale, 'The Principles of European Contract Law and Harmonisation of the Law of Contract', in: *Festskrift til Ole Lando* (1997) 21 ff.; Ralf Michaels, 'Privatautonomie und Privatkodifikation', RabelsZ 62 (1998) 580 ff. Generally, cf. also the contributions in Hans-Leo Weyers (ed.), *Europäisches Vertragsrecht* (1997).

International groups of academics are busy drafting European principles of delictual liability[5] and of trust law.[6] Textbooks are being written which analyse particular areas of law under a European perspective and deal with the rules of English, French or German law as local variations of a common theme.[7] At least two legal periodicals are competing for the attention of lawyers interested in the development of European private law.[8] The Commission of the European Communities has increased the mobility of law students through its immensely successful Erasmus (now Socrates) scheme.[9] More and more law faculties in Europe try to obtain a 'Euro'-profile by establishing integrated courses and programmes on an undergraduate and postgraduate level.[10] Chairs are established for European Private Law, European Legal History or Comparative Legal Culture. Interest has been rekindled in the 'old' European *ius commune* and legal historians are busy recognising, once again, the European perspective of their subject, rediscovering the common historical foundations of the modern law and restoring

[5] This group is referred to as the 'European Group on Tort Law' (formerly 'Tilburg-group'); see Jaap Spier (ed.), *The Limits of Liability* (1996); Spier (ed.), *The Limits of Expanding Liability* (1998); H. Koziol (ed.), *Unification of Tort Law: Wrongfulness* (1998); for general background, see Ulrich Magnus, 'Elemente eines europäischen Deliktsrechts', ZEuP 6 (1998) 602 ff. with further references.

[6] This group has been established by the *Onderzoekcentrum Onderneming & Recht* of the University of Nijmegen. The 'Principles of European Trust Law' (eds. D. J. Hayton, S. C. J. J. Kortmann, H. L. E. Verhagen, 1999) have recently been published and discussed at a conference in The Hague on 15 January 1999. The historical background is explored in Richard Helmholz, Reinhard Zimmermann (eds.), *Itinera Fiduciae: Trust and Treuhand in Historical Perspective* (1998).

[7] Cf. the programme sketched by Hein Kötz, 'Gemeineuropäisches Zivilrecht', in: *Festschrift für Konrad Zweigert* (1981) 498, and now implemented in Hein Kötz, *Europäisches Privatrecht*, vol. I (1996), and Christian von Bar, *Gemeineuropäisches Deliktsrecht*, vol. I (1996). The first chapter of *Europäisches Vertragsrecht*, vol. II, is published in ZEuP 5 (1997) 255 ff.: Axel Flessner, 'Befreiung vom Vertrag wegen Nichterfüllung'.

[8] *Zeitschrift für Europäisches Privatrecht* (ZEuP), since 1993; *European Review of Private Law* (ERPL), also since 1993. Cf. also the *Maastricht Journal of European and Comparative Law* (which is, however, not confined to Private Law), since 1994; *Contratto e Impresa/Europa*, since 1996; *Uniform Law Review* (published by Unidroit), since 1996; *Europa e diritto privato*, since 1998.

[9] Cf. the presentations by J. A. Dieckmann, ZEuP 1 (1993) 615 ff. (Erasmus) and U. Caspar, ZEuP 5 (1997) 910 ff. (Socrates).

[10] For discussion on the Europeanisation of Legal Training, see Bruno de Witte, Caroline Forder (eds.), *The Common Law of Europe and the Future of Legal Education* (1992); Hein Kötz, 'Europäische Juristenausbildung', ZEuP 1 (1993) 268 ff.; Roy Goode, 'The European Law School', (1994) 13 *Legal Studies* 1 ff.; Filippo Ranieri, 'Juristen für Europa: Wahre und falsche Probleme in der derzeitigen Reformdiskussion zur deutschen Juristenausbildung', JZ 1997, 801 ff.

intellectual contact with comparative and modern private lawyers.[11] Attention is paid to models of legal harmonisation in other parts of the world, such as the United States of America (here, in particular, the Uniform Commercial Code and the Restatements),[12] Latin America,[13] or the mixed legal systems in South Africa,[14] Scotland,[15] Louisiana,[16] Quebec[17]

[11] Reinhard Zimmermann, 'Roman and Comparative Law: The European Perspective', (1995) 16 *JLH* 21 ff.; Zimmermann, 'Savigny's Legacy: Legal History, Comparative Law, and the Emergence of a European Legal Science', (1996) 112 *LQR* 576 ff.; cf. also, e.g., Reiner Schulze, 'European Legal History – A New Field of Research in Germany', (1992) 13 *JLH* 270 ff.; Schulze, 'Allgemeine Rechtsgrundsätze und europäisches Privatrecht', *ZEuP* 1 (1993) 442 ff.; Rolf Knütel, 'Rechtseinheit in Europa und römisches Recht', *ZEuP* 2 (1994) 244 ff.; Eugen Bucher, 'Recht – Geschicklichkeit – Europa', in: Bruno Schmidlin (ed.), *Vers un droit privé commun? – Skizzen zum gemeineuropäischen Privatrecht* (1994) 7 ff.; John Blackie, Niall Whitty, 'Scots Law and the New Ius Commune', in: Hector MacQueen (ed.), *Scots Law into the 21st Century: Essays in Honour of W. A. Wilson* (1996) 65 ff.; and see the symposium on the Teaching of Legal History at the University of Cape Town, published in *ZEuP* 5 (1997) 366 ff. (with contributions by Hector MacQueen, Peter Stein, Willem Zwalve, Klaus Luig, Gerhard Lubbe and Alfred Cockrell). Two series of monographs, both published by Duncker & Humblot, Berlin, have been founded with the aim of re-establishing the European dimension of legal history: *Comparative Studies in Continental and Anglo-American Legal History*, since 1985; *Schriften zur Europäischen Rechts- und Verfassungsgeschichte*, since 1992.

[12] Cf., e.g., Mathias Reimann, 'Amerikanisches Privatrecht und europäische Rechtseinheit – Können die USA als Vorbild dienen?', in: Reinhard Zimmermann (ed.), *Amerikanische Rechtskultur und europäisches Privatrecht – Impressionen aus der Neuen Welt* (1995) 132 ff.; Melvin A. Eisenberg, 'Why is American Contract Law so Uniform? – National Law in the United States', in: Weyers (n. 4) 23 ff.; Richard Hyland, 'The American Restatements and the Uniform Commercial Code', in: Hartkamp/Hesselink *et al.* (n. 1) 105 ff.; Thomas Schindler, 'Die Restatements und ihre Bedeutung für das amerikanische Privatrecht', *ZEuP* 6 (1998) 277 ff.

[13] Jurisprudence in Latin America has never been completely reduced to a national legal science. Particularly under the auspices of *Mercosur* attempts are now being made to unify commercial law. See the contributions in the new journal *Roma e America, Diritto Romano Comune: Rivista di Diritto in Europa e in America Latino*, Roma, since 1996; and see Thilo Scholl, *ZEuP* 5 (1997) 1180 ff.; Scholl, *Die Rezeption des kontinental-europäischen Vertragsrechts in Lateinamerika am Beispiel der allgemeinen Vertragslehre in Costa Rica* (1999).

[14] Reinhard Zimmermann, Daniel Visser (eds.), *Southern Cross: Civil Law and Common Law in South Africa* (1996).

[15] Cf., e.g., the contributions in Robin Evans-Jones (ed.), *The Civil Law Tradition in Scotland* (1995); Alan Rodger, 'Thinking About Scots Law', (1996) 1 *Edinburgh Law Review* 3 ff.; Niall R. Whitty, 'The Civilian Tradition and Debates on Scots Law', 1996 *Tydskrif vir die Suid-Afrikaanse Reg* 227 ff. and 442 ff.; David Carey Miller, Reinhard Zimmermann (eds.), *The Civilian Tradition and Scots Law – Aberdeen Quincentenary Essays* (1997).

[16] Cf., e.g., Joachim Zekoll, 'Zwischen den Welten – Das Privatrecht von Louisiana als europäisch-amerikanische Mischrechtsordnung', in: *Amerikanische Rechtskultur und europäisches Privatrecht* (n. 12) 11 ff.

[17] On the new civil code cf., e.g., Pierre Legrand, 'Civil Law Codification in Quebec: A Case of Decivilianization', *ZEuP* 1 (1993) 574 ff.; Bernd von Hoffmann, 'Le nouveau Code civil

or Israel.[18] The internationalisation of private law is also vigorously pro-
moted by the uniform private law based on international conventions
which cover large areas of commercial law.[19] The United Nations
Convention on Contracts for the International Sale of Goods, in particular, has been adopted by close to fifty states (among them ten of the
member states of the European Union)[20] and is starting to give rise to a
considerable amount of case law.[21] The International Institute for the
Unification of Private Law has published a set of Principles of
International Commercial Contracts.[22] Somewhat surprisingly, in view
of widespread scepticism expressed in the 1960s and '70s, the idea of
codification has been regaining ground internationally.[23] The new Dutch
Burgerlijk Wetboek (B.W.) has aroused considerable interest but it is
neither the only nor even the latest recent codification.[24] The academic
lawyer today does indeed live in a golden age.[25]

There can no longer be any question about the change in perspective we
are experiencing at the moment: we cannot stop, or wish away, the re-emergence of a European (as opposed to merely national) private law. We can,
however, influence both the speed and scope of the development. One of

du Québec – modèle d'une harmonisation du droit privé européen?', in: *Études
Québécoises: Bilan et perspectives* (1996) 15 ff.
[18] Cf., e.g., Alfredo Mordechai Rabello (ed.), *Essays on European Law and Israel* (1996).
[19] Cf., e.g., Jan Ramberg, *International Commercial Transactions* (1997) and the contributions
in Franco Ferrari (ed.), *The Unification of International Commercial Law* (1998).
[20] It has not been implemented by Greece, Portugal, Belgium, Great Britain and
Luxembourg; concerning Great Britain, see the comments by Barry Nicholas, *The United
Kingdom and the Vienna Sales Convention: Another Case of Splendid Isolation?* (1993).
[21] Cf. Michael R. Will, *International Sales Law under CISG: The First 284 or so Decisions* (1996);
Ulrich Magnus, 'Stand und Entwicklung des UN-Kaufrechts', *ZEuP* 3 (1995) 202 ff.;
Magnus, 'Das UN-Kaufrecht: Fragen und Probleme seiner praktischen Bewährung', *ZEuP*
5 (1997) 823 ff. Cf. also the new *Review of the Convention on Contracts for the International Sale
of Goods*, since 1996.
[22] Rome, 1994. Cf. also Michael Joachim Bonell, *An International Restatement of Contract Law*
(2nd edn, 1997); Bonell, 'The Unidroit Principles – A Modern Approach to Contract Law',
in: Weyers (n. 4) 9 ff.; Arthur Hartkamp, 'Principles of Contract Law', in:
Hartkamp/Hesselink *et al.* (n. 1) 105 ff. with further references.
[23] For details, see Reinhard Zimmermann, 'Codification: History and Present Significance
of an Idea', (1995) 3 *ERPL* 95 ff. For a historical evaluation see, most recently, Pio Caroni,
Saggi sulla storia della codificazione (1998); for a comparative appraisal, see the symposium
'Codification in the Twenty-First Century', (1998) 31 *University of California Davis Law
Review* 655 ff.
[24] Even as far as England is concerned, the draft of a Contract Code, drawn up on behalf of
the English Law Commission by Harvey McGregor, was uncovered and published in Italy.
The discovery was hailed as 'sensational' by Professor Gandolfi in his preface.
[25] Kenneth G. C. Reid, 'The Third Branch of the Profession: The Rise of the Academic
Lawyer in Scotland', in: *Scots Law into the 21st Century* (n. 11) 39.

the most important issues discussed in this respect today is whether European private law (or at least the law of obligations) should be codified. The European Parliament, for instance, has repeatedly called for such a step to be taken.[26] Academic lawyers have, by and large, received this idea with considerable reservation; the opinion seems to prevail that, even if a European Civil Code may ultimately be desirable, the time is not yet ripe for it. But whether one inclines towards the bold proposition of a Thibaut *redivivus* or subscribes to the more cautious attitude of a modern Savigny,[27] it is clearly desirable to take stock of the situation *de lege lata*: to ascertain the amount of common ground already existing between the national legal systems and to identify discrepancies on the level of specific result, general approach and doctrinal nuance. This is what the present comparative study attempts to do for one specific topic within the general law of contract.

II. Good faith: common core or imposition?

The topic chosen is, no doubt, somewhat unconventional. So is the method adopted. Both points therefore need some explanation. It is hardly accidental that neither the second part of *Zweigert/Kötz*, 'An Introduction to Comparative Law',[28] nor *Kötz*, 'Europäisches Vertragsrecht'[29] contain a chapter on 'good faith'. Comparative studies normally focus on specific subject matters, problem areas and real life sit-

---

[26] Cf., e.g., Winfried Tilmann, 'Entschließung des Europäischen Parlaments über die Angleichung des Privatrechts der Mitgliedsstaaten vom 26.5.1989', ZEuP 1 (1993) 613 ff.; Tilmann, 'Eine Privatrechtskodifikation für die Europäische Gemeinschaft?', in: Müller-Graff (n. 1) 485 ff.; Tilmann, 'Zweiter Kodifikationsbeschluß des Europäischen Parlaments', ZEuP 3 (1995) 534 ff.; Tilmann, 'Artikel 100 a EGV als Grundlage für ein Europäisches Zivilgesetzbuch', in: *Festskrift til Ole Lando* (n. 4) 351 ff.; Giuseppe Gandolfi, 'Pour un code européen des contracts', *RIDC* 1992, 707 ff.; Jürgen Basedow, 'Über Privatrechtsvereinheitlichung und Marktintegration', in: *Festschrift für Ernst-Joachim Mestmäcker* (1996) 347 ff. The question was discussed at a symposium in The Hague on 28 February 1997; cf. René de Groot, 'European Private Law between Utopia and Early Reality', (1997) 4 *Maastricht Journal of European and Comparative Law* 1 ff.; Winfried Tilmann, 'Towards a European Civil Code', ZEuP 5 (1997) 595 ff.; and the contributions in (1997) 5 *ERPL* 455 ff.

[27] Cf. (1996) 112 *LQR* 576 ff. for a discussion drawing on Savigny's programmatic writings. Cf. also Marcel Storme, 'Lord Mansfield, Portalis of von Savigny? Overwegingen over de eenmaking van het recht in Europa, i.h.b. via vergelijkende rechtspraak', *Tijdschrift voor privaatrecht* 1991, 849 ff.; Ole Lando, 'The Principles of European Contract Law after Year 2000', in: Franz Werro (ed.), *New Perspectives on European Private Law* (1998) 59 ff.

[28] Konrad Zweigert, Hein Kötz, *Einführung in die Rechtsvergleichung* (3rd edn, 1996); the work has been translated into English by Tony Weir: *An Introduction to Comparative Law* (3rd edn, 1998).   [29] Cf. n. 7 above.

uations, or on relatively well-defined legal institutions like mistake, agency or *stipulatio alteri*. 'Good faith' fits into neither of these categories. At the same time, however, it is at least in some legal systems regarded as a vitally important ingredient for a modern general law of contract.[30] That immediately raises the question how other legal systems cope without it. This inquiry appears to be all the more topical since all member states of the European Union have implemented the Directive on Unfair Terms in Consumer Contracts and will thus have to come to terms with a general notion of 'good faith' in a central area of their contract law.[31] Moreover, both the Principles of European Contract Law as proposed by the Lando Commission and the Principles of International Commercial Contracts as published by Unidroit contain general provisions according to which 'in exercising his rights and performing his duties each party must act in accordance with good faith and fair dealing'.[32] At least the Principles of

[30] Concerning German law, Werner F. Ebke and Bettina M. Steinhauer describe the doctrine of good faith as having ripened from little more than a legislative acorn 'into a judicial oak that overshadows the contractual relationship of private parties': 'The Doctrine of Good Faith in German Contract Law', in: Jack Beatson, Daniel Friedmann (eds.), *Good Faith and Fault in Contract Law* (1995) 171.

[31] For England, see Hugh Collins, 'Good Faith in European Contract Law', (1994) 14 *Oxford JLS* 229 ff.; Hugh Beale, 'Legislative Control of Fairness: The Directive on Unfair Terms in Consumer Contracts', in: Beatson/Friedmann (n. 30) 231 ff.; Jack Beatson, 'The Incorporation of the EC Directive on Unfair Consumer Contracts into English Law', ZEuP 6 (1998) 957 ff.; for Germany, see Oliver Remien, 'AGB-Gesetz und Richtlinie über mißbräuchliche Verbrauchervertragsklauseln in ihrem europäischen Umfeld', ZEuP 2 (1994) 34 ff.; Helmut Heinrichs, 'Das Gesetz zur Änderung des AGB-Gesetzes', NJW 1996, 2190 ff.; for France: Claude Witz, Gerhard Wolter, 'Die Umsetzung der EG-Richtlinie über mißbräuchliche Klauseln in Verbraucherverträgen', ZEuP 3 (1995) 885 ff.; cf. also the comparative analyses in (1995) 3 *ERPL* 211 ff. The Directive on Unfair Terms in Consumer Contracts was not the first E.C. directive to use the standard of good faith; see, seven years earlier, the Directive on Self-Employed Commercial Agents (OJ EC 1986 L 382/17), arts. 3 I and 4 I.

[32] Art. 1:201 Principles of European Contract Law; Art. 1.7 Principles of International Commercial Contracts. For comment, see Zimmermann, JZ 1995, 491 f.; Basedow, (1998) 18 *Legal Studies* 141 f. In this context it must also be noted that according to Art. 1.107 Principles of European Contract Law and Art. 5.3 Principles of International Commercial Contracts '[e]ach party owes to the other a duty to co-operate in order to give full effect to the contract'. In most European legal systems this rule is regarded as flowing from the principle of good faith. Peter Schlechtriem has recently drawn attention to the fact that 'similar to the irresistible force of fundamental laws of nature such as the law of gravity, the principle that . . . the evaluation of the relations, rights and remedies of the parties, should be subject to the principles of good faith and fair dealing has found its way into the Convention [on Contracts for the International Sale of Goods], its understanding by the majority of legal writers and its application by the courts', even though the draftsmen of the Convention ultimately refrained from adopting a respective provision: *Good Faith in German Law and in International Uniform Laws* (1997) 3.

European Contract Law, however, profess to be inspired by the idea of a European Restatement of Contract Law. Their draftsmen expressly refer to a common core of contract law of all member states of the European Union which has to be elaborated – even though they concede that this may be a somewhat more 'creative' task than the one tackled by the draftsmen of the American Restatements.[33] Does 'good faith', as embodied in a rule like Art. 1.106 of the Principles of European Contract Law, constitute part of the common core of European contract law,[34] or is it a notion to be found in one or several legal systems and artificially imposed on others? Until very recently, the question has not attracted much scholarly attention.[35]

[33] Lando/Beale (n. 4) xx f.

[34] Cf., e.g., ibid., 56: 'The principle of good faith and fair dealing is recognised or at least appears to be acted on as a guideline for contractual behaviour in all EC countries'; Otto Sandrock, 'Das Privatrecht am Ausgang des 20. Jahrhunderts: Deutschland – Europa – und die Welt', JZ 1996, 9: 'Es gibt . . . einige allgemeine Rechtsgrundsätze, die allen Rechtskreisen dieser Welt gemeinsam sind, wie z.B. der Grundsatz pacta sunt servanda oder die Verpflichtung, Verträge bona fide zu erfüllen'; BGH NJW 1993, 259 (263): the principle of good faith is 'als übergesetzlicher Rechtssatz allen Rechtsordnungen immanent' (inherent in all legal systems as pre-positive law). According to Basedow, good faith is a general principle of E.C. contract law: (1998) 18 Legal Studies 137. For support of this proposition, he draws attention to the case law of the European Court of Justice (more specifically, to two judgments interpreting the Brussels Judgments Convention (on which, see also Jürgen Basedow, in: Münchener Kommentar zum Bürgerlichen Gesetzbuch, vol. I (3rd edn, 1993) § 12 AGBG, n. 29)) and to the directives on self-employed commercial agents and unfair terms in consumer contracts. Cf. also, in this context, the observations by Van Gerven (n. 3) 102 ff.

[35] Cf. also Schlechtriem (n. 32) 5 who states: 'If the principle of good faith and fair dealing is indeed common to all legal systems based on the values of western civilization, then it should be easy to find a common core of concrete rules derived from this principle . . . But I have looked in vain for a monograph comparable to, say, Ernst Rabel's "Recht des Warenkaufs", which would report and compare in detail the various manifestations of the principle and its applications and understanding in the legal systems of the Western world . . .'. As far as modern comparative literature is concerned, cf., in particular, Beatson/Friedmann (n. 30); J. M. Smits, Het vertrouwensbeginsel en de contractuele gebondenheid (1995); Hans Jürgen Sonnenberger, 'Treu und Glauben – ein supranationaler Grundsatz?', in: Festschrift für Walter Odersky (1996) 703 ff.; Martijn Hesselink, 'Good Faith', in: Hartkamp/Hesselink et al. (n. 1) 285 ff.; Filippo Ranieri, 'Bonne foi et exercice du droit dans la tradition du civil law', RIDC 1998, 1055 ff. (building on a number of previous studies on more specific topics by the same author); Hein Kötz, 'Towards a European Civil Code: The Duty of Good Faith', in: Peter Cane, Jane Stapleton (eds.), The Law of Obligations: Essays in Celebration of John Fleming (1998) 243 ff. Mention should also be made of the essays collected in La bonne foi (Journées louisianaises), (1992) 43 Travaux de l'Association Henri Capitant, and in Alfredo Mordechai Rabello, Aequitas and Equity: Equity in Civil Law and Mixed Jurisdictions (1997); and of the fact that no less than four out of the twenty-four booklets published, so far, under the auspices of the Centro di studi e ricerche

At first sight, one might be inclined to agree with the latter proposition. Moreover, we appear to be dealing with a rather clear-cut civil law/common law divide. 'Scots law based its system of consensual contracts on the *ius commune* but . . . it has not accepted the civilian doctrine that the exercise of contractual rights is subject to the principles of good faith. The better view is that like English law it requires strict adherence to contracts': this is how a prominent lawyer from a mixed jurisdiction has recently restated the apparent dichotomy.[36] And indeed, statements to the effect that English contract law does not recognise a general concept of good faith are legion. It tolerates 'a certain moral insensitivity in the interest of economic efficiency'[37] and values 'predictability of the legal outcome of a case' more highly 'than absolute justice'.[38] Common law lawyers have traditionally tended to regard 'good faith [as] an invitation to judges to abandon the duty of legally reasoned decisions and to produce an unanalytical incantation of personal values'; and they point out that it 'could well work practical mischief if ruthlessly implanted into our system of law'.[39] A duty to negotiate in good faith has even been described as 'inherently repugnant to the adversarial position of the parties when involved in negotiations' and as 'unworkable in practice'.[40] Closer inspection, however, shows that matters are more complex. The position in English law appears to be much less unequivocal than a continental lawyer faced with some of these general propositions might be led to expect. Conversely, the civilian approach is much less uniform than a common law lawyer might be led to believe.[41] This, we hope, will become apparent in the main section of this book which seeks to investigate the

di diritto comparato e straniero in Rome are dealing with the topic of good faith: Roy Goode, *The Concept of 'Good Faith' in English Law* (no. 2); Allan Farnsworth, *The Concept of Good Faith in American Law* (no. 10); Denis Tallon, *Le concept de bonne foi en droit français du contrat* (no. 15); and Peter Schlechtriem, *Good Faith in German Law and in International Uniform Laws* (no. 24); cf. also Arthur S. Hartkamp, *Judicial Discretion under the New Civil Code of the Netherlands* (no. 4).

36 Niall Whitty, as quoted by David Carey Miller, 'A Scottish Celebration of the European Legal Tradition', in: Carey Miller/Zimmermann (n. 15) 45.
37 Barry Nicholas, 'The Pre-contractual Obligation to Disclose Information, English Report', in: Donald Harris, Denis Tallon (eds.), *Contract Law Today: Anglo-French Comparisons* (paperback reprint 1991) 187.
38 Roy Goode, *The Concept of 'Good Faith' in English Law* (1992) 7.
39 M. G. Bridge, 'Does Anglo-Canadian Contract Law Need a Doctrine of Good Faith?', (1984) 9 *Canadian Business Law Journal* 412 f., 426.
40 *Walford v. Miles* [1992] 2 AC 128, 138, *per* Lord *Ackner*. But see the comparative observations by Kötz, in: *Essays Fleming* (n. 35) 253 f.
41 Cf., as far as Germany and France are concerned, the comparative remarks by Sonnenberger (n. 35) 703 ff.

ways in which European legal systems deal with cases which, in the view of some of them, attract the application of a general principle of good faith. Before explaining how this section was put together, we will offer a few introductory remarks attempting to set the scene.

III. *Bona fides*

The notion of 'good faith', or *bona fides*, finds its origin in Roman law.[42] In relation to *iudicia stricti iuris* (claims which have to be adjudicated upon according to strict law) it gained its influence as a result of a specific standard clause, inserted at the request of the defendant into the procedural *formula* which defined the issue to be tried by the judge. This clause was known as the *exceptio doli* and it was worded in the alternative: 'si in ea re nihil dolo malo A^i A^i factum sit neque fiat' (if in this matter nothing has been done, or is being done, in bad faith by the plaintiff).[43] It was particularly the second alternative (*neque fiat* – or is being done) that made the *exceptio doli* such a powerful instrument in bringing about a just solution, for it invited an answer which located *dolus* not so much in personal misconduct, but rather in an inequity or injustice that would flow from the action being allowed to succeed.[44] Ultimately, therefore, it gave the judge an equitable discretion to decide the case before him in accordance with what appeared to be fair and reasonable.[45] This, essentially, was the regime applicable to one cornerstone of the Roman contractual system, the stipulation, for it was governed by the *iudicium stricti iuris par excellence*, the *condictio*.[46] The other cornerstone was the consensual contracts. A specific device in the form of an *exceptio doli* was here not necessary in order to check the improper exercise of contractual rights.[47] The judge had this discretion anyway for he was, according to the *formulae* applicable to these kinds of contracts, instructed to condemn the defendant into 'quidquid ob eam rem N^m N^m A^o A^o dare facere oportet ex fide bona' (whatever on

---

[42] For all details, see the study by Martin Schermaier in the present volume.

[43] Gai. IV, 119.

[44] Geoffrey MacCormack, 'Dolus in the Law of the Early Classical Period (Labeo-Celsus)', *Studia et documenta historiae et iuris* 52 (1986) 263 f.

[45] On *bona fides* and *dolus* and on the meaning of *dolus* in the present context, see Reinhard Zimmermann, *The Law of Obligations: Roman Foundations of the Civilian Tradition* (paperback edn, 1996) 667 ff.   [46] For details, see ibid., 68 ff.

[47] Cf. D. 30, 84, 5: '. . . quia hoc iudicium fidei bonae est et continet in se doli mali exceptionem'.

that account the defendant should give to, or do for, the plaintiff in good faith).[48] The substantive content of the *exceptio doli*, in other words, was absorbed into the requirement of good faith according to which the dispute had to be decided.

Bona fides was one of the most fertile agents in the development of Roman contract law. In the contract of sale, for instance, it paved the way for the reception of the aedilitian remedies into the *ius civile*.[49] The harsh principle of *caveat emptor* was thus largely abandoned. Similarly, the buyer was granted an action to claim his positive interest in cases of eviction.[50] On a more general level, *bona fides* allowed error (mistake) and *metus* (duress) to be taken into account in determining whether an *actio empti* or *venditi* could be granted.[51] Equally, the judge was able to consider a counterclaim arising from the same transaction and to condemn the defendant only in the difference between the two claims.[52] Liability for latent defects, the rules relating to the implied warranty of peaceable possession, rescission of contracts on account of mistake and *metus*, set-off: these and many other institutions of modern contract law can be traced back to the *iudicia bonae fidei* of Roman law. They were retained in spite of the fact that decline, and eventual abolition, of the formulary procedure had led to an absorption of the concept of *bona fides* into the broader notion of *aequitas* (equity).[53] Throughout the Middle Ages, and in the early modern period, *aequitas* remained in the forefront of discussion as a counterpoise to the *ius strictum* (strict law),[54] but it was commonly identified with *bona fides*.[55] *Bona fides* and/or *aequitas* also dominated relations between merchants and became a fundamental principle of the medieval and early modern *lex mercatoria*.[56] 'Bona fides est primum mobile ac

---

[48] The respective claims therefore came to be designated *iudicia bonae fidei* (claims which have to be adjudicated upon in terms of the requirements of good faith).

[49] See *Law of Obligations* (n. 45) 320 ff. The aedilitian remedies had been created by the magistrates responsible for the conduct and regulation of the Roman markets and dealt with defects in slaves and certain livestock bought on these markets.

[50] Ibid., 296 ff.   [51] Ibid., 587 ff., 658.   [52] Ibid., 761 ff.

[53] See Alexander Beck, 'Zu den Grundprinzipien der bona fides im römischen Vertragsrecht', in: *Aequitas und bona fides – Festgabe für August Simonius* (1955) 24 ff.

[54] Cf., e.g., Gunter Wesener, 'Aequitas naturalis, "natürliche Billigkeit", in der privatrechtlichen Dogmen- und Kodifikationsgeschichte', in: *Der Gerechtigkeitsanspruch des Rechts* (1996) 81 ff.; Jan Schröder, 'Aequitas und Rechtsquellenlehre in der frühen Neuzeit', *Quaderni Fiorentini* 26 (1997) 265 ff.

[55] For all details, see the contribution by James Gordley to the present volume.

[56] Rudolf Meyer, *Bona fides und lex mercatoria in der europäischen Rechtstradition* (1994) 61 ff.

spiritus vivificans commercii' (good faith is the prime mover and lifegiving spirit of commerce) as *Casaregis* put it; and in the same vein *Baldus* had stated 'bonam fidem valde requiri in his, qui plurimum negotiantur' (good faith is much required of those, who trade most).[57] As in Roman law, *bona fides* significantly contributed to the kind of flexibility, convenience and informality required by the international community of merchants.

IV. *Treu und Glauben*

1. *'Baneful plague' or 'queen of rules'?*

In Germany, *bona fides* could conveniently be blended with the indigenous notion of *Treu und Glauben* (literally: fidelity and faith): a phrase which we find in a number of medieval sources and which was used, in the context of commercial relations, as a synonym for *bona fides*.[58] *Treu und Glauben* also, of course, was ultimately destined to find its way into the famous § 242 of the German Civil Code of 1900: 'Der Schuldner ist verpflichtet, die Leistung so zu bewirken, wie Treu und Glauben mit Rücksicht auf die Verkehrssitte es erfordern.'[59] This is not the only place where the BGB refers to *Treu und Glauben*; for according to § 157 BGB 'contracts shall be interpreted according to the requirements of good faith, ordinary usage being taken into consideration'.

In view of its subsequent interpretation, the wording of § 242 BGB is surprisingly narrow. It merely relates to the manner in which performance must be rendered.[60] Determination of the content of a contract is regulated in § 157 and is regarded as a matter of interpretation. It is not entirely clear whether the draftsmen of the BGB really intended to give the principle of good faith such a restricted field of operation. The first draft had still contained one comprehensive clause according to which 'the contract obliges the contracting party to whatever results from the

---

[57] Both quotations taken from ibid., 62.
[58] Ibid., 64 ff.; Adalbert Erler, 'Treu und Glauben', in: *Handwörterbuch zur deutschen Rechtsgeschichte*, 34th part (1992) cols. 317 ff.; Okko Behrends, 'Treu und Glauben: Zu den christlichen Grundlagen der Willenstheorie im heutigen Vertragsrecht', in: Gerhard Dilcher, Ilse Staff, *Christentum und modernes Recht* (1984) 277 ff.; Hans-Wolfgang Strätz, *Treu und Glauben*, vol. I (1974).
[59] (The debtor is bound to perform according to the requirements of good faith, ordinary usage being taken into consideration.)
[60] Case 8 provides a typical example. It is based on Rudolf Henle, *Treu und Glauben im Rechtsverkehr* (1912) 30 f.

provisions and the nature of the contract according to law and ordinary usage and with reference to good faith, as content of his obligation'.[61] This had come closer to the *exceptio doli generalis* as it had been recognised in pandectist legal literature and applied by nineteenth-century courts.[62] The term *exceptio doli*, of course, no longer had the procedural implications of the Roman formulary procedure and was retained, predominantly, as a convenient label. The four consensual contracts, after all, were *bonae fidei iudicia*; and since they provided the historical foundation of the modern general concept of contract law,[63] the latter was bound to be subject to the regime of *bona fides*, too.[64] Use of the term *exceptio doli*, in other words, was tantamount to a recourse to the idea of good faith except that the matter was seen, naturally enough, from the point of view of the defendant.

Soon after the BGB had been adopted, a debate flared up as to whether the *exceptio doli* was still applicable, be it on the basis of § 242 BGB or as a result of 'the grace of God'.[65] Judicial practice, without much ado, opted for the former alternative and continued to operate as it had done before the promulgation of the code. The Imperial Court, in particular, did not hesitate to grant protection against the improper exercise of legal

[61] § 359 E I; on which see 'Motive', in: Benno Mugdan, *Die gesammten Materialien zum Bürgerlichen Gesetzbuch für das Deutsche Reich*, vol. II (1899) 109. There is no indication that the draftsmen of the BGB, when revising § 359 E I and splitting up its content into what were to become §§ 157 and 242 BGB, intended a substantial change of the law; cf. 'Protokolle', in: Mugdan, ibid., 521 ff. For all details, see the discussion by Jürgen Schmidt, in: Staudinger, *Kommentar zum Bürgerlichen Gesetzbuch* (13th edn, 1995) § 242, nn. 19 ff.
[62] For all details, see Wendt, 'Die exceptio doli generalis im heutigen Recht oder Treu und Glauben im Recht der Schuldverhältnisse', AcP 100 (1906) 1 ff.; cf. also the references in Bruno Huwiler, 'Aequitas und bona fides als Faktoren der Rechtsverwirklichung', in: Bruno Schmidlin (ed.), *Vers un droit privé européen commun? – Skizzen zum gemeineuropäischen Privatrecht* (1994) 59 ff. and the discussion by Ranieri, RIDC 1998, 1058 ff., 1064 ff.
[63] For an account of this development, see Helmut Coing, *Europäisches Privatrecht*, vol. I (1985) 398 ff.; *Law of Obligations* (n. 45) 508 ff., 537 ff.; and the contributions to John Barton (ed.), *Towards a General Law of Contract* (1990).
[64] Cf., e.g., Ferdinand Regelsberger, *Pandekten*, vol. I (1893) 686; Heinrich Dernburg, *Pandekten*, vol. I (5th edn, 1896) § 138, 4; Bernhard Windscheid, Theodor Kipp, *Lehrbuch des Pandektenrechts* (9th edn, 1906) § 47, n. 7. Windscheid/Kipp refer to the *exceptio doli* as being 'unpraktisch' (which may mean 'impractical' or 'no longer used in practice'). On the use of *bona fides* and the *exceptio doli* in Roman-Dutch and modern South African law, see Reinhard Zimmermann, 'Good Faith and Equity', in: Zimmermann/Visser (n. 14) 217 ff.
[65] The various points of view are set out by Wendt, AcP 100 (1906) 1 ff.; cf. also, e.g., Paul Oertmann, *Das Recht der Schuldverhältnisse* (vol. II of a commentary to the German Civil Code edited by Biermann, von Blume and others), (2nd edn, 1906) § 242, 4.

rights.[66] The Court thus tried to steer a middle course: neither was it regarded as sufficient if the plaintiff merely acted inequitably nor was judicial intervention to be confined to the extreme case where the only purpose of exercising a right had been to cause damage to another.[67] The application of § 242 BGB soon became a bone of contention in the great methodological disputes of the first part of this century (positivism, free law movement, jurisprudence of interests).[68] Strong language was used. The good faith provision was seen, on the one hand, as 'the source of the baneful plague gnawing in a most sinister manner at the inner core of our legal culture';[69] on the other hand, it was celebrated as the 'queen of rules'[70] which could be used to unhinge the established legal world.

2. Adjusting exchange rates

These hopes and fears concerning the judicial function did not, at first, have any impact on mainstream legal literature and practice. Sooner or later, however, the potential conflict between Imperial Supreme Court and Imperial Parliament inherent in this issue was bound to become politically and practically relevant. In Germany this happened on 28 November 1923 when the Imperial Court decided, effectively, to abandon the principle of the nominal value with regard to the *Reichsmark*.[71] Inflation, by that time, had reached hitherto unimaginable

---

[66] See the references in Wendt (n. 65) or in: *Das Bürgerliche Gesetzbuch mit besonderer Berücksichtigung der Rechtsprechung des Reichsgerichts (Reichsgerichtsrätekommentar)*, vol. I (6th edn, 1928) § 242, 4. And see the discussion by Ranieri, *RIDC* 1998, 1065 ff. who also emphasises the continuity of development ('la réalisation du principe de la bonne foi et de l'idée de l'exceptio doli generalis dans la doctrine et la pratique allemande . . . a été constante de l'époque de l'usus modernus pandectarum jusqu'à la jurisprudence du Bundesgerichtshof': 1081). Generally on the development of the interpretation of § 242 BGB since 1900, see *Staudinger/J.* Schmidt (n. 61) § 242, nn. 51 ff.

[67] The latter case, incidentally, is covered by a special rule: § 226 BGB. In view of the wide interpretation of § 242 BGB, it does not have much practical significance ('weitgehend leerlaufend': Helmut Heinrichs, in: Palandt, *Bürgerliches Gesetzbuch* (57th edn, 1998) § 226, n. 1). On the historical background of § 226 BGB (*aemulatio*), see Huwiler (n. 62) 57 ff. and Antonio Gambaro, 'Abuse of Right in Civil Law Tradition', in: *Aequitas and Equity* (n. 35) 632 ff.

[68] For an overview of these methodological positions, see Peter Raisch, *Juristische Methoden* (1995) 107 ff.; Franz Wieacker, *A History of Private Law in Europe with particular reference to Germany*, translated by Tony Weir (1995) 363 ff., 453 ff.   [69] Henle (n. 60) 3.

[70] Cf. the (critical) discussion by Justus Wilhelm Hedemann, *Die Flucht in die Generalklauseln: Eine Gefahr für Recht und Staat* (1933) 10 f.

[71] For details of what follows cf., in particular, the discussion by Bernd Rüthers, *Die unbegrenzte Auslegung: Zum Wandel der Privatrechtsordnung im Nationalsozialismus* (paperback edn, 1973) 64 ff.

dimensions: one gold mark was traded in November 1923 for 522 billion paper marks. The association of judges of the Imperial Supreme Court had submitted, and published, draft legislation to deal with the problem but the Imperial Parliament remained impassive. It was in this situation that the Court refused to allow a debtor to discharge an obligation incurred before the First World War, and secured by means of a mortgage, by paying the nominal value of the debt in paper marks.[72] The creditor, in the opinion of the Court, could not be compelled to consent to a deletion of the mortgage from the register. Moreover, the Court considered itself entitled to fix a new exchange rate. Obviously, the judges found themselves in a grave moral dilemma: they regarded the inaction of the legislature as intolerable and gravely detrimental to the general respect for law and justice. But the Court attempted to disguise the fundamental issues by using § 242 BGB as a positivistic peg. The unforeseeable devaluation of the mark, so it was argued, had given rise to a conflict between what the principle of nominal value, as embodied in contemporary currency legislation, required and what could in good faith be expected of a debtor concerning the discharge of his obligations. In this conflict, preference had to be given to § 242 BGB which, after all, governed all legal transactions. The currency laws had to be disregarded in so far as they could not be reconciled with the precepts of good faith.[73]

This decision hit the German legal community like a bombshell.[74] Here was finally a case where the Court could indeed be said to have unhinged the established legal world. The fixing of exchange rates was certainly not the business of the courts and it was irreconcilable with the *exceptio doli generalis* even in its most extended version. If general legal provisions could be used to justify this kind of judicial interventionism, anything seemed possible. Perspicacious critics started to realise that this conceivably entailed grave 'dangers for State and law'.[75] These misgivings were fully confirmed by what happened after 1933. The general provisions were one of the most convenient points of departure for imbuing the legal

---

[72] RGZ 107, 78 ff. Differently still RGZ 101, 141 ff.

[73] Cf. also the discussion and further references in *Reichsgerichtsrätekommentar* (n. 66) § 242, 5 b)–d) (pp. 368 ff.).   [74] Rüthers (n. 71) 66 (with references).

[75] Cf. the subtitle of the booklet published by Hedemann (n. 70) on the eve of the Nazi regime. Hedemann himself, incidentally, soon became a leading proponent of the idea to replace the BGB by a 'people's code' better suited to a national spirit emanating from the 'community of blood and soil'. For details, see Heinz Mohnhaupt, 'Justus Wilhelm Hedemann als Rechtshistoriker und Zivilrechtler vor und während der Epoche des Nationalsozialismus', in: Michael Stolleis, Dieter Simon (eds.), *Rechtsgeschichte im Nationalsozialismus: Beiträge zur Geschichte einer Disziplin* (1989) 107 ff.

system with the spirit of the new, 'national' (*völkisch*) legal ideology.[76] A study of the history of private law of this period reveals the frightening flexibility of the methodological tools available to lawyers inspired by ideological premises and preconceptions. The 'unlimited interpretation' was an important key to the insidious perversion of the legal system by those charged with its preservation.[77]

3. Domesticating the monster

Today we have still not managed to find a magic formula which defines the line to be drawn between what may properly be classified as 'interpretation' and what is usually referred to as 'judicial development' of the law.[78] The latter phenomenon is not merely tolerated but very widely regarded as indispensable. As long as judicial law-making *contra legem* is not (openly) permitted, the parliamentary prerogative remains substantially unaffected.[79] But even if great advances have not been made at a general methodological level, the modern German situation is different in two very significant respects. Most importantly, of course, it is no longer the fascist ideology of the 1930s and early '40s which sustains and informs the German legal system. Reacting to the totalitarianism of the Nazi regime, the draftsmen of the Basic Law entrenched respect for human dignity and the right to personal freedom, very prominently, in its first two articles. These articles constitute part of a comprehensive Bill of Rights which does not only provide the individual citizen with protection against the activities of the state but also constitutes a system of basic values permeating the legal system as a whole.[80] Thus, for example, the entire body of private law has to be interpreted in the spirit of the fundamental rights,[81] and the general provisions contained in the BGB are par-

[76] The seminal publication on this subject is the book by Bernd Rüthers (n. 71).
[77] Generally on the perversion of law after 1933 cf. Reinhard Zimmermann, 'An Introduction to German Legal Culture', in: Werner F. Ebke, Matthew W. Finkin (eds.), *Introduction to German Law* (1996) 22 ff. with references to the abundant literature.
[78] Cf., e.g., Karl Larenz, Claus-Wilhelm Canaris, *Methodenlehre der Rechtswissenschaft* (3rd edn, 1995) 133 ff. as opposed to 187 ff.
[79] Cf., e.g., Fritz Ossenbühl, 'Gesetz und Recht – Die Rechtsquellen im demokratischen Rechtsstaat', in: Josef Isensee, Paul Kirchhof (eds.), *Handbuch des Staatsrechts der Bundesrepublik Deutschland*, vol. III (1988) § 61, nn. 35 ff.
[80] Of fundamental importance was the *Lüth* decision of the Federal Constitutional Court: BVerfGE 7, 198 ff.; on which see, e.g., David P. Curry, *The Constitution of the Federal Republic of Germany* (1994) 27 ff.; Ernst-Wolfgang Böckenförde, *Zur Lage der Grundrechtsdogmatik nach 40 Jahren Grundgesetz* (1989) 25 ff.
[81] The concept of *mittelbare Drittwirkung*, or indirect effect, of fundamental rights in the

ticularly malleable tools in this process. They have greatly facilitated the constitutionalisation of private law and have thus, on the whole, performed a very beneficial function.

In the second place it must be noted that German lawyers have become accustomed to thick layers of case law emerging from the interstices of their Code[82] and that they have learnt to cope with this phenomenon. Since the enactment of the Civil Code, countless decisions have relied, in one form or another, on § 242 BGB; and one attempt to record the relevant case law as comprehensively as possible has led to what many consider as the hypertrophy of legal commentary.[83] But despite appearances, the modern German lawyer is not faced with an impenetrable wilderness of single instances.[84] This is due to the endeavours by legal writers, operating in close interaction with the Federal Supreme Court, to discern the different functions of § 242, to categorise its various fields of application and to establish typical 'groups of cases' (*Fallgruppen*). This process of domestication (or 'concretisation'[85]) was stimulated by an influential study of the great legal historian *Franz Wieacker*[86] and it has led, generally speaking, to a more orderly and rational analysis.[87]

area of private law was developed by Günter Dürig, 'Grundrechte und Zivilrechtsprechung', in: *Festschrift für Hans Nawiasky* (1956) 158 ff. For a brief summary in English on the 'constitutionalization of private law', see Basil S. Markesinis, *A Comparative Introduction to the German Law of Torts* (3rd edn, 1994) 27 ff. See also Johannes Hager, 'Grundrechte im Privatrecht', JZ 1994, 373 ff. Generally on interpretation in conformity with the Constitution, see Robert Alexy, Ralf Dreier, 'Statutory Interpretation in the Federal Republic of Germany', in: D. Neil MacCormick, Robert S. Summers (eds.), *Interpreting Statutes: A Comparative Study* (1991) 73 ff.

[82] John P. Dawson has referred to Germany's 'case-law revolution'; cf., in this context, the remarks in Ebke/Finkin (n. 77) 16 ff. and Zimmermann, (1994/95) 1 *Columbia Journal of European Law* 89 ff.; and see Reinhard Zimmermann, Nils Jansen, 'Quieta Movere: Interpretative Change in a Codified System', in: Cane/Stapleton (n. 35) 285 ff.

[83] Wilhelm Weber, in: Staudinger, *Kommentar zum Bürgerlichen Gesetzbuch* (11th edn, 1961) § 242, a volume of more than 1,500 pages.

[84] Kötz, in: *Essays Fleming* (n. 35) 250.

[85] Hesselink (n. 35) 289. *Staudinger*/J. Schmidt (n. 61) refers to a 'Binnensystem' (inner system).

[86] *Zur rechtstheoretischen Präzisierung des § 242 BGB* (1956). Generally on the chances, and on the ways and means, of specifying the content of general provisions, see Franz Bydlinski, 'Möglichkeiten und Grenzen der Präzisierung aktueller Generalklauseln', in: Okko Behrends, Malte Diesselhorst, Ralf Dreier (eds.), *Rechtsdogmatik und praktische Vernunft – Symposium zum 80. Geburtstag von Franz Wieacker* (1990) 189 ff. See also, in this context, the remarks by John P. Dawson, 'The General Clauses, Viewed from a Distance', *RabelsZ* 41 (1977) 441 ff.; Ernst Zeller, *Treu und Glauben und Rechtsmißbrauchsverbot* (1981) 5 ff.

[87] This emerges very clearly from the way in which standard commentaries like Max Vollkommer, in: Jauernig, *Bürgerliches Gesetzbuch* (8th edn, 1997); *Palandt*/Heinrichs (n. 67); Olaf Werner, in: Erman, *Handkommentar zum Bürgerlichen Gesetzbuch*, vol. I (9th edn, 1993) and Günter H. Roth, in: *Münchener Kommentar zum Bürgerlichen Gesetzbuch*, vol. II (3rd edn,

Thus, it is generally recognised today that § 242 BGB operates *supplendi causa* (so as to supplement the law).[88] It specifies the way in which contractual performance has to be rendered and it gives rise to a host of ancillary, or supplementary, duties that may arise under a contract: duties of information, documentation, co-operation, protection, disclosure, etc.[89] These duties can also apply in the precontractual situation[90] and they may extend after the contract has been performed (*post contractum finitum*).[91] In the second place, § 242 BGB serves to limit the exercise of contractual rights.[92] German commentators, in this context, very widely use the term *unzulässige Rechtsausübung*[93] (inadmissible exercise of a right) as a *nomen collectivum* but they also frequently refer to *Rechtsmißbrauch* (abuse of a right).[94] Thus, for instance, going against one's own previous conduct

1994) analyse and classify the case material. Ebke/Steinhauer (n. 30) and Schlechtriem (n. 32) follow, essentially, the same pattern. A different theoretical approach is adopted by *Staudinger/*J. Schmidt (on which, see n. 143 below). Cf. also Hesselink (n. 35) 290 ff. who refers to the trichotomy of functions usually assigned to good faith (interpretative, supplementative and limitative) as constituting the European 'common core' (that the trichotomy adopted in German law, following Franz Wieacker, is slightly different, is a consequence of the fact that interpretation, according to the principles of good faith, is not based on § 242 but on § 157 BGB); and see the discussion by *Staudinger/*J. Schmidt (n. 61) nn. 113 ff. and Ranieri, *RIDC* 1998, 1070 ff.

[88] Cf. Wieacker (n. 68) 21 ff. (who alludes to the description of the (praetorian) *ius honorarium* in classical Roman law: 'Ius praetorium est, quod praetores introduxerunt adiuvandi vel supplendi vel corrigendi iuris civilis gratia propter utilitatem publicam': Pap. D. 1, 1, 7, 1).

[89] *Jauernig/*Vollkommer (n. 87) § 242, nn. 10 ff.; *Palandt/*Heinrichs (n. 67) § 242, nn. 23 ff.; *Erman/*Werner (n. 87) § 242, nn. 50 ff.; *Münchener Kommentar/*Roth (n. 87) § 242, nn. 109 ff.; cf. also Ebke/Steinhauer (n. 30) 177 ff.

[90] This is the field of application of *culpa in contrahendo*; on which cf. the German report to case 1.

[91] *Jauernig/*Vollkommer (n. 87) § 242, nn. 28 ff.; *Palandt/*Heinrichs (n. 67) § 276, n. 121; *Erman/*Werner (n. 87) § 242, n. 58; *Münchener Kommentar/*Roth (n. 87) § 242, n. 117 and *passim*.   [92] Wieacker (n. 68) 24 ff.

[93] *Jauernig/*Vollkommer (n. 87) § 242, nn. 32 ff.; *Palandt/*Heinrichs (n. 67) § 242, nn. 38 ff.; *Erman/*Werner (n. 87) § 242, nn. 73 ff.; *Münchener Kommentar/*Roth (n. 87) § 242, nn. 255 ff.

[94] Abuse of a right (*abus de droit*), therefore, does not in German law constitute a special defence outside the range of application of § 242 BGB but constitutes a sub-category of cases covered by this general provision. Since it does not have a specific technical significance, use of the term *Rechtsmißbrauch* differs considerably (cf., e.g., *Münchener Kommentar/*Roth (n. 87) § 242, nn. 280 ff. who refers to 'Rechtsmißbrauch im engen Sinne' (abuse of a right in the narrow sense)). See also § 226 BGB as an emanation of the idea that a right must not be abused (n. 67 above) and see, on abuse of rights in general, the contributions by Paul A. Crépau, Antonio Gambaro, Ergun Özsunay, Shmuel Shilo, Fritz Sturm and A. N. Yiannoloulos, in: *Aequitas and Equity* (n. 35) 583 ff. Even though *Rechtsmißbrauch* is the German translation of *abus de droit*, it has a different significance; see, in particular, Ranieri, *RIDC* 1998, 1082 ff. The Swiss Civil Code contains both a good

(*venire contra factum proprium*) is frowned upon[95] and so is relying on a right which has been dishonestly acquired (*nemo auditur turpitudinem suam allegans*),[96] demanding something which has to be given back immediately (*dolo agit qui petit quod statim redditurus est*),[97] proceeding ruthlessly and without due consideration to the reasonable interests of the other party (*inciviliter agere*),[98] or reacting in a way which must be considered as excessive when compared with the event occasioning the reaction (*Übermaßverbot*).[99] Lapse of time may also lead to a loss of right even before the relevant period of prescription has expired (*Verwirkung*).[100] We are dealing here with the core area of application of the old *exceptio doli*. Many rules and legal maxims of the *ius commune* thus continue to apply under the guise of § 242 BGB. Finally, and most problematically, § 242 BGB has also been used to interfere in contractual relations in order to avoid grave injustice.[101] The modern German version of the *clausula rebus sic stantibus*, the doctrine of the collapse of the underlying basis of the transaction (*Wegfall der Geschäftsgrundlage*),[102] owes its origin to this corrective function

faith clause (Art. 2 I ZGB) and a separate provision dealing with the abuse of a right (Art. 2 II ZGB). For background discussion, see Huwiler (n. 62) 57 ff.; Pio Caroni, *Einleitungstitel des Zivilgesetzbuches* (1996) 189 ff. and the contributions by Sturm and Gambaro mentioned earlier in this note.

[95] *Jauernig/Vollkommer* (n. 87) § 242, nn. 48 ff.; *Palandt/Heinrichs* (n. 67) § 242, nn. 55 ff.; *Erman/Werner* (n. 87) § 242, n. 79; *Münchener Kommentar/Roth* (n. 87) § 242, nn. 322 ff. The prohibition of *venire contra factum proprium* has recently been investigated in depth by Reinhard Singer, *Das Verbot widersprüchlichen Verhaltens* (1993).

[96] *Jauernig/Vollkommer* (n. 87) § 242, n. 45; *Palandt/Heinrichs* (n. 67) § 242, nn. 42 ff.; *Erman/Werner* (n. 87) § 242, n. 80; *Münchener Kommentar/Roth* (n. 87) § 242, nn. 286 ff.

[97] *Jauernig/Vollkommer* (n. 87) § 242, n. 39; *Palandt/Heinrichs* (n. 67) § 242, n. 52; *Erman/Werner* (n. 87) § 242, n. 81; *Münchener Kommentar/Roth* (n. 87) § 242, nn. 435 ff. The rules on set-off are an emanation of this principle: see Reinhard Zimmermann, 'Die Aufrechnung: Eine rechtsvergleichende Skizze zum europäischen Vertragsrecht', in: *Festschrift für Dieter Medicus* (1999) 715 f.

[98] *Jauernig/Vollkommer* (n. 87) § 242, n. 43; *Palandt/Heinrichs* (n. 67) § 242, nn. 50 f.; *Erman/Werner* (n. 87) § 242, n. 83; *Münchener Kommentar/Roth* (n. 87) § 242, nn. 280 ff.

[99] *Jauernig/Vollkommer* (n. 87) § 242, n. 40; *Palandt/Heinrichs* (n. 67) § 242, nn. 53 f.; *Erman/Werner* (n. 87) § 242, n. 71; *Münchener Kommentar/Roth* (n. 87) § 242, nn. 438, 442 ff.

[100] *Jauernig/Vollkommer* (n. 87) § 242, nn. 53 ff.; *Palandt/Heinrichs* (n. 67) § 242, nn. 87 ff.; *Erman/Werner* (n. 87) § 242, nn. 84 ff.; *Münchener Kommentar/Roth* (n. 87) § 242, nn. 360 ff. On *Verwirkung*, see also Gerhard Kegel, 'Verwirkung, Vertrag und Vertrauen', in: *Festschrift für Klemens Pleyer* (1986) 513 ff.; Ranieri, *RIDC* 1998, 1066 ff. ('. . . sans doute l'un des développements jurisprudentiels les plus importants que les juges allemands ont effectués dans l'interprétation du § 242 du BGB, comme norme générale pour tout le droit privé').   [101] Wieacker (n. 68) 36 ff.

[102] On which see Rüthers (n. 71) 38 ff.; for the historical background, see *Law of Obligations* (n. 45) 579 ff.; and see the German report to case 25.

of § 242 BGB. It is obvious, however, that by arrogating to themselves the right to adjust the contract, the courts are also interfering with the law as laid down by the draftsmen of the BGB.[103] Not unlike the Roman *praetor*, they have thus acted to *correct* the civil law (*iuris civilis corrigendi causa*).[104]

4. *Doctrinal innovations*

This is, of course, merely the roughest survey as to how the require-ments of § 242 BGB have been specified over the years. *Wegfall der Geschäftsgrundlage* has become a sophisticated doctrine in its own right even though it is still discussed, for the sake of convenience, under the umbrella of § 242 BGB.[105] Both the consequences of the Second World War and of the reunification of Germany[106] have provided opportunities for its deployment. But *Wegfall der Geschäftsgrundlage* is not confined to the cata-clysmic events in the history of a nation: cases of hardship resulting from an unforeseeable change of circumstances have come before the courts at all times and quite independently of war, inflation and change of politi-cal system. Judicial revaluation of the type undertaken by RGZ 107, 78[107] (not, strictly speaking, a case of *Wegfall der Geschäftsgrundlage* since the Imperial Court based its decision directly upon § 242 BGB) has remained a very exceptional *cause célèbre*; it is today, as one of the leading commen-taries puts it reassuringly, of only historical significance.[108] Closely related to *Wegfall der Geschäftsgrundlage* is the right to terminate a long-term contractual relationship 'for an important reason' without the necessity to observe a period of notice.[109] This is specifically laid down with regard to leases of accommodation (§ 554 a BGB), contracts of service (§ 626 BGB)

---

[103] They, after all, had decided not to adopt the *clausula rebus sic stantibus* (nor Bernhard Windscheid's doctrine of tacit presupposition).   [104] Cf. n. 88 above.

[105] *Jauernig/*Vollkommer (n. 87) § 242, nn. 64 ff.; *Palandt/*Heinrichs (n. 67) § 242, nn. 110 ff.; *Erman/*Werner (n. 87) § 242, nn. 166 ff.; *Münchener Kommentar/*Roth (n. 87) § 242, nn. 496 ff. See also the excellent discussion, in English, by Werner Lorenz, 'Contract Modification as a Result of Change of Circumstances', in: Beatson/Friedmann (n. 30) 357 ff.; Ebke/Steinhauer (n. 30) 180 ff. Both the Principles of European Contract Law (Art. 2.117) and the Principles of International Commercial Contracts (Arts. 6.2.1 ff.) contain specific provisions dealing with hardship as a result of change of circumstances and have thus separated the matter from the general issue of good faith in contract law; for comment, see *JZ* 1995, 486 f.

[106] *Palandt/*Heinrichs (n. 67) § 242, nn. 152 a ff.; *Münchener Kommentar/*Roth (n. 87) § 242, nn. 626 ff.   [107] Cf. n. 72 above.   [108] *Palandt/*Heinrichs (n. 67) § 242, n. 172.

[109] See, e.g., *Palandt/*Heinrichs (n. 67) § 242, n. 120; *Münchener Kommentar/*Roth (n. 87) § 242, nn. 583 ff.; *Staudinger/*J. Schmidt (n. 61) § 242, nn. 1383 ff.; cf. also, in this context, the explanation in the German report to case 7.

and partnership agreements (§ 723 BGB), but also applies, as a general rule, in other cases. The general rule is usually 'derived from' § 242 BGB.[110] Or, to put it slightly differently: §§ 554 a, 626, 723 BGB have come to be seen as specific statutory emanations of the principle of good faith which may be extended *per analogiam*. *Positive Forderungsverletzung* (positive breach of contract), a judge-made doctrine of central importance for the modern law relating to breach of contract,[111] has occasionally been based on § 242 BGB.[112] In fact, however, the precepts of good faith are only relevant for determining the range of ancillary duties infringement of which leads to a liability in damages. The doctrinal pegs originally used to justify the introduction of the doctrine were other rules of the BGB.[113] *Culpa in contrahendo*[114] extends these ancillary duties into the precontractual area; it entered modern German law under cover of fictitious precontractual contracts, later, equally unconvincingly, on the basis of a general analogy to §§ 122, 179 and 307, 309 BGB. In a way, of course, liability for *culpa in contrahendo* can also be seen as an emanation of § 242 BGB since it is the close relationship between the negotiating parties which is held, in good faith, to give rise to special duties.[115]

The most important and far-reaching doctrinal development over the past forty years based directly on § 242 BGB was the overt judicial control

---

[110] Alternatively, or in addition, it may be based on an analogy to §§ 554a, 626, 723 BGB; see, e.g., *Palandt*/Heinrichs (n. 67), Einl. v. § 241, n. 18.

[111] See the German report to case 16.

[112] Cf. BGHZ 11, 80 (84) and Ebke/Steinhauer (n. 30) 172 ff.

[113] The Imperial Court had originally based the doctrine on § 276; this rule, however, only determines the standard of liability, not in which situations a debtor is liable. Nevertheless, *positive Forderungsverletzung* is still traditionally discussed *sub* § 276: *Jauernig*/Vollkommer (n. 87) § 276, nn. 46 ff.; *Palandt*/Heinrichs (n. 67) § 276, nn. 104; Robert Battes, in: Erman, *Handkommentar zum Bürgerlichen Gesetzbuch*, vol. I (9th edn, 1993) § 276, nn. 85 ff.; but see Volker Emmerich, in: *Münchener Kommentar zum Bürgerlichen Gesetzbuch*, vol. II (3rd edn, 1994) Vor § 275, nn. 218 ff. Later, the doctrine was predominantly founded on a general analogy to §§ 280, 286, 325, 326 BGB. Today, a doctrinal basis in the BGB is regarded as dispensable since *positive Forderungsverletzung* is widely held to constitute *Gewohnheitsrecht* (customary law).

[114] On which see the German report to case 1.

[115] See *Jauernig*/Vollkommer (n. 87) § 276, nn. 69 ff.; *Palandt*/Heinrichs (n. 67) § 276, nn. 65 ff.; *Münchener Kommentar*/Emmerich (n. 113), Vor § 275, nn. 54 ff. In discussing *culpa in contrahendo*, German legal authors do not, however, usually refer to 'good faith' but rather to '[reasonable] reliance'. The link between *culpa in contrahendo* and good faith appears very clearly from the title of the famous article by Friedrich Kessler and Edith Fine, 'Culpa in contrahendo, Bargaining in Good Faith, and Freedom of Contract: A Comparative Study', (1964) 77 *Harvard Law Review* 401 ff. Cf. also Ebke/Steinhauer (n. 30) 172 and, generally on the notion of *Sonderverbindung* in the present context, Hesselink (n. 35) 299.

of standard contract terms.[116] A considerable body of case law was developed by the courts before it was eventually channelled into the provisions of the Standard Contract Terms Act of 1976.[117] According to the core provision of this Act (§ 9), any standard contract term is invalid which unreasonably disadvantages the other party contrary to the precepts of good faith. This is exactly the general guideline which the courts had previously developed on the basis of § 242 BGB. *Ludwig Raiser*[118] celebrated the willingness on the part of the courts to intervene in situations where the contract cannot typically be regarded as the proper expression of the autonomy of both of the contracting parties as a 'page of glory' in the records of German legal development:[119] an evaluation which is widely shared today.[120] Even after the enactment of the Standard Contract Terms Act, the Federal Supreme Court has not been reluctant to subject certain types of contract to judicial control concerning their substantive fairness, in particular notarially authenticated contracts of sale relating to immovable property[121] and certain types of partnership agreements.[122] Similarly successful was the judicial invention of *Einwendungsdurchgriff* with regard to 'connected transactions' like consumer contracts financed by a third party: the purchaser is allowed to raise defences based on his contract of sale against the bank's claim for repayment of the loan. Once again, the courts used to rely on § 242 BGB in this regard; again however, the solution worked out by the courts has now essentially been adopted by the Consumer Credit Act of 1990.[123]

[116] Cf. BGHZ 22, 90 (95 ff.); 38, 183 (184 ff.); 41, 151 (152 ff.); 60, 243 (245 ff.). Judicial control of standard contract terms had been started by the Imperial Supreme Court under the auspices of § 138 I BGB (the *contra bonos mores* clause). The terms were struck down if a monopolist had imposed them on the other party: cf. RGZ 20, 115 (116 f.); 48, 114 (127 f.); 32, 342 (343); 62, 264 (266). For details, see *Staudinger/Weber* (n. 83) 364 ff.; cf. also the overview by Wolfgang Hefermehl, in: Erman, *Handkommentar zum Bürgerlichen Gesetzbuch*, vol. I (9th edn, 1993) Vor § 1 AGBG, nn. 3 ff.
[117] For a comparative discussion of which, see Zweigert/Kötz (n. 28) 325 ff.; *Europäisches Privatrecht* (n. 7) 209 ff.
[118] Who had published in 1935 a monograph of central importance on the topic: *Das Recht der Allgemeinen Geschäftsbedingungen*.   [119] 'Vertragsfreiheit heute', *JZ* 1958, 1 (7).
[120] Hein Kötz, in: *Münchener Kommentar zum Bürgerlichen Gesetzbuch*, vol. I (3rd edn, 1993), Einl. AGBG, n. 7.
[121] BGHZ 101, 350; 108, 164; cf. Dieter Medicus, *Zur gerichtlichen Inhaltskontrolle notarieller Verträge* (1989); Mathias Habersack, 'Richtigkeitsgewähr notariell beurkundeter Verträge', *AcP* 189 (1989) 403 ff.
[122] BGHZ 64, 238 (241); 84, 11 (13 f.); 102, 172 (177). Generally on judicial control of contracts outside the range of application of the Standard Contract Terms Act, see Dagmar Coester-Waltjen, 'Die Inhaltskontrolle von Verträgen außerhalb des AGBG', *AcP* 190 (1990) 1 ff.
[123] Cf., e.g., the references in *Palandt/Heinrichs* (n. 67), Einf. v. § 305, n. 18.

In assessing the comprehensive role of good faith in German contract law, account must also be taken of § 157 BGB. This provision, as has been mentioned,[124] requires the interpretation of contracts to be governed by the precepts of good faith.[125] It is occasionally far from clear whether a particular decision, or even a line of decisions, may be based on § 157 or § 242 BGB. For all practical purposes the distinction does not much matter. Had § 242 BGB not been included in the BGB, the courts would, presumably, have used § 157 BGB much more extensively. Particularly the 'supplementary interpretation' of a contract[126] is situated in the grey area between proper interpretation and the implication of terms based on the normative standard of good faith. The Federal Supreme Court has repeatedly maintained that even the famous contract with protective effect *vis-à-vis* third parties constitutes an example of supplementary interpretation;[127] mostly, however, it is regarded as a case of judicial development of the law based on § 242 BGB.[128]

Finally, it should be noted that a number of startling developments over the last couple of years have been based on § 138 I BGB rather than § 242 BGB. § 138 I ('Ein Rechtsgeschäft, das gegen die guten Sitten verstößt, ist nichtig')[129] is another general provision, and also one with an ancient pedigree.[130] In its requirements it is much stricter than § 242, its legal consequences are much less flexible. § 138 I BGB determines the outermost limits of private autonomy and is a manifestation of a legal system's self-respect.[131] It is this rule that has been invoked to strike down instalment credit transactions on account of excessive rates of

---

[124] Cf. text after n. 59, p. 18 above.

[125] The second rule determining the interpretation of contracts is § 133 BGB: 'In interpreting a declaration of intention the true intention shall be sought without regard to the declaration's literal meaning.' On the coordination of these two rules, see Othmar Jauernig, in: Jauernig, *Bürgerliches Gesetzbuch* (8th edn, 1997) § 133, n. 7; *Palandt/Heinrichs* (n. 67) § 133, nn. 1 f.; Theo Mayer-Maly, in: *Münchener Kommentar zum Bürgerlichen Gesetzbuch*, vol. I (3rd edn, 1993) § 133, nn. 19 f.; Dieter Medicus, *Allgemeiner Teil des BGB* (7th edn, 1997) nn. 319 ff. For historical background of both rules, see *Law of Obligations* (n. 45) 622.

[126] On which see *Jauernig/Jauernig* (n. 125) § 157, nn. 2 ff.; *Palandt/Heinrichs* (n. 67) § 157, nn. 2 ff.; *Münchener Kommentar/Mayer-Maly* (n. 125) § 157, nn. 24 ff.; Medicus (n. 125) nn. 338 ff.; and see the German report to case 19.

[127] Cf., e.g., BGHZ 56, 269 (273); *Palandt/Heinrichs* (n. 67) § 328, n. 14.

[128] *Jauernig/Vollkommer* (n. 87) § 328, n. 21; Peter Gottwald, in: *Münchener Kommentar zum Bürgerlichen Gesetzbuch*, vol. II (3rd edn, 1994) § 328, n. 80.

[129] Literally translated: 'A legal transaction which offends against the good morals is void.' This is the codified version of the old *contra bonos mores* provision.

[130] *Law of Obligations* (n. 45) 706 ff. As far as modern legal systems are concerned, see Zweigert/Kötz (n. 28) 407 ff.; Kötz, in: *Essays Fleming* (n. 35) 235 ff.

[131] Cf., e.g., *Münchener Kommentar/Mayer-Maly* (n. 125) § 138, nn. 1 ff.

interest[132] and also, even more recently, ruinous contracts of suretyship entered into by close relatives of the principal debtor.[133] It is interesting to see that parts of the legal literature had proposed to proceed via § 242 BGB but that this suggestion was not accepted by the courts.[134]

5. An open norm

Nothing has, so far, been said about what good faith actually means. The reason for this is that not much can be said; and what can be said is not very helpful for deciding concrete cases.[135] One thing is clear, however: good faith in the sense of *Treu und Glauben* must be distinguished from good faith in the sense of *guter Glaube*. The latter notion (often dubbed subjective good faith) has to do with knowledge. Thus, a person to whom a non-owner has transferred property can still acquire ownership if he is 'in good faith' (§ 932 I BGB); and he is not 'in good faith' if he knows, or as a result of gross negligence does not know, that the piece of property does not belong to the transferor (§ 932 II BGB). 'Objective' good faith (*Treu und Glauben*), on the other hand, constitutes a standard of conduct to which the behaviour of a party has to conform and by which it may be judged; and our present study is only concerned with good faith in this objective sense.[136] *Treue*, the one element of the German phrase, signifies faithfulness, loyalty, fidelity, reliability; *Glaube* means belief in the sense of faith or reliance. The combination of *Treu und Glauben* is sometimes seen to tran-

---

[132] For all details, see Rolf Sack, in: Staudinger, *Kommentar zum Bürgerlichen Gesetzbuch* (13th edn, 1996) § 138, nn. 227 ff.; Volker Emmerich, 'Rechtsfragen des Ratenkredits', *Juristische Schulung* 1988, 925 ff.; Peter O. Mülbert, 'Das Darlehen in der höchstrichterlichen Rechtsprechung 1989–1991', *JZ* 1992, 291 ff. For a brief overview in English, see Zimmermann/Jansen (n. 82) 295 f.

[133] For all details, see Uwe Blaurock, 'Nahe Angehörige als Sicherheitengeber', *ZEuP* 4 (1996) 314 ff.; Mathias Habersack, Reinhard Zimmermann, 'Recent Developments in German Suretyship Law: Legal Change in a Codified System', (1999) 3 *Edinburgh Law Review* 272 ff. This new development has been triggered off by a decision of the Federal Constitutional Court charging the civil courts with the task of controlling the content of contracts which are unduly burdensome for one of the two parties and which result from structurally unequal bargaining power (BVerfGE 89, 214 ff.).

[134] Harm Peter Westermann, 'Die Bedeutung der Privatautonomie im Recht des Konsumentenkredits', in: *Festschrift für Hermann Lange* (1992) 995 ff., 1008 ff.; Karl Larenz, Claus-Wilhelm Canaris, *Lehrbuch des Schuldrechts*, vol. II/2 (13th edn, 1994) § 60 II 3 b.

[135] According to *Münchener Kommentar*/Roth (n. 87) § 242, n. 9, the terms used in § 242 BGB are 'simply irrelevant'; cf. also Staudinger/J. Schmidt (n. 61) § 242, n. 139.

[136] On the distinction between 'objective' and 'subjective' good faith, see P. van Schilf-Gaarde, 'Over de verhouding tussen de goede trouw van het handelen en de goede

scend the sum of its components and is widely understood as a conceptual entity. It suggests a standard of honest, loyal and considerate behaviour, of acting with due regard for the interests of the other party, and it implies and comprises the protection of reasonable reliance.[137] Thus, it is not a legal rule with specific requirements that have to be checked but may be called an 'open' norm.[138] Its content cannot be established in an abstract manner but takes shape only by the way in which it is applied.[139] This is the reason for developing an 'inner system' of § 242, based upon the existing case law and, at the same time, guiding the courts in deciding future cases.

Many legal institutions 'based on' § 242 BGB have started to lead an independent life. The control of standard contract terms is regulated today by the Standard Contract Terms Act, and the relevant case law thus no longer burdens the commentaries to § 242 BGB.[140] The same applies to the availability of *Einwendungsdurchgriff*.[141] The contract with protective effect *vis-à-vis* third parties, positive malperformance and *culpa in contrahendo* are also generally not discussed *sub* § 242 BGB although they are, in some or other way, taken to be related to this rule. *Wegfall der Geschäftsgrundlage*[142] still finds its place in the commentaries on § 242 but very much as a matter of convenience. For all practical purposes, it has become a self-contained doctrine with its own requirements. It has even been argued that all the rules developed under cover of § 242 BGB should be relegated to that part of the law of contract to which they systematically belong and which they restrict, supplement, change or otherwise modify:[143] the rules relating to

---

trouw van het niet weten', in: *Goed & trouw, Opstellen aangeboden aan prof. mr. W.C.L. van der Grinten t.g.v. zijn afscheid als hoogleraar aan de K.U. Nijmegen* (1984) 57 ff.; and see the comparative remarks by Hesselink (n. 35) who points out that a number of legal systems (such as French or English law) tend to use the same term in both meanings.

[137] See, for instance, *Jauernig/Vollkommer* (n. 87) § 242, n. 3; *Palandt/Heinrichs* (n. 67) § 242, n. 3; *Münchener Kommentar/Mayer-Maly* (n. 125) § 157, nn. 3 f.; *Münchener Kommentar/Roth* (n. 87) § 242, n. 5; *Staudinger/J. Schmidt* (n. 61) § 242, nn. 141 ff. Generally see Zeller (n. 86) 145 ff., 158 f.; Strätz (n. 58) *passim*.

[138] *Palandt/Heinrichs* (n. 67) § 242, n. 3; Hesselink (n. 35) 288 f.

[139] '[T]he character of good faith is best shown by the way it operates': Hesselink (n. 35) 289.

[140] Cf. text after n. 116, p. 28 above. Even before the enactment of that Act, § 242 BGB 'was gradually lapsing into benign neglect': Kötz, in: *Essays Fleming* (n. 35) 251.

[141] Cf. n. 123 above.   [142] Cf. text after n. 104, p. 26 above.

[143] So that, ideally, 'the commentary to § 242 should be limited to a few phrases that good faith is not a norm, and then for the discussion of rules which the courts have adopted mentioning § 242 BGB, refer to the commentary to the rules that were changed by them': see *Staudinger/J. Schmidt* (n. 61) § 242, nn. 236 ff.; Hesselink (n. 35) 306 (from whom the quotation is taken).

Verwirkung to the law of extinctive prescription,[144] the rules concerning rights of termination without notice 'for an important reason' in long-term contracts to the general contractual risk regime,[145] etc. Whilst a radical adoption of this approach would probably go too far, and might also be impractical,[146] the development is heading, in some respects, in this direction. This explains the fact that the most comprehensive commentary to § 242 BGB today makes do with a comparatively modest total of 539 pages, as opposed to the more than 1,500 pages in a previous edition.[147] § 242 BGB is often needed merely for a transitory phase until a new rule is sufficiently well established to be able to stand on its own legs: so that 'figuratively speaking, the statutory foundation of § 242 could be withdrawn without any risk of having the judge-made edifice collapse'.[148] All in all, therefore, § 242 BGB is neither 'queen of rules' nor 'baneful plague' but an invitation, or reminder, for courts to do what they do anyway and have always done:[149] to specify, supplement and modify the law, i.e. to develop it in accordance with the perceived needs of their time.

V. *Bonne foi*

1. *The* Code civil *and its background*

It is well known that the provisions of the *Code civil* governing the general law of contract were dominated by the ideas of the French natural law Romanists, *Domat* and *Pothier*. At times *Domat*, the earlier of these two, can be seen to revel in the triumph of contemporary juristic thought over the particular distinctions found in the ancient texts and this is true of his treatment of good faith. So having noted the ancient distinction between contracts *bonae fidei* and *stricti iuris*, he declares that 'by the law of nature and by our customs, every contract is *bonae fidei*, because honesty and integrity hath and ought to have in all contracts the full extent that equity can demand'[150] and gives as expressions of this various obligations

---

[144] *Staudinger/J.* Schmidt (n. 61) § 242, nn. 516 ff.   [145] Ibid., § 242, nn. 1396 ff.

[146] If only because it is useful to have § 242 BGB as a general reference point for principles of an intermediate level of abstractness (like *dolo agit* or *venire contra factum proprium*) which apply across the field of contract law and cannot, therefore, be fitted into any other systematic niche.   [147] Cf. n. 83 above.

[148] Kötz, in: *Essays Fleming* (n. 35) 250.

[149] This point is emphasised by Hesselink (n. 35) 300 ff.

[150] *Les loix civiles dans leur ordre naturel,* Liv. I, Tit. 1, Sect. III, § XIV, at 26, as translated by William Strahan, *The Civil Law in its Natural Order: Together with the Publick Law,* vol. I (London, 1722) 45.

imposed on sellers, including those respecting liability for latent defects,[151] but also vitiation of the contract on the ground of precontractual *dol*.[152]

While the *Code civil* itself included *dol* as a ground of vitiation of contracts (together with *violence* (duress) and a fairly narrow provision for *erreur* (mistake)),[153] its final version provided by art. 1134 al. 3 that contracts 'doivent être exécutées de bonne foi' (should be performed in good faith),[154] but made no general statement as to their creation. Article 1135 continued that '[l]es conventions obligent non seulement à ce qui est exprimé, mais encore à toutes les suites que l'équité, l'usage ou la loi donnent à l'obligation d'après sa nature'.[155]

The *Code civil* also set a more extensive test of 'directness' for remoteness of damage for cases where the defendant's non-performance constituted *dol*, here meaning deliberate non-performance.[156] On the other hand, it ruled out invalidation on the ground of substantive inequality of a bargain (*lésion*) except in specific cases[157] and allowed contractual non-performance to be excused only where performance was impossible by reason of *force majeure*:[158] neither initial nor subsequent gross imbalance were to affect the binding force of contractual obligations.[159]

However, despite the generality of these provisions, at least during the latter part of the nineteenth century, very little recourse was made to either good faith or equity in performance in order to qualify contractual rights or to regulate contractual relationships. Instead, French contract law became dominated by the idea of the *autonomie de la volonté*, and the way in which this idea was interpreted appeared to leave little room for a wide role for good faith in contracts. Thus, the circumstances leading up to the making of an agreement were examined to see if there was any evidence of a 'defect in consent' of one of the parties, annulment on the

---

[151] Ibid.   [152] Liv. I, Tit. XVIII, Sect. III.   [153] Arts. 1109–17 C. civ.

[154] An earlier draft of art. 1134 al. 3 C. civ. stated that '[contracts] must be *contracted* and performed in good faith' (emphasis added, see P. A. Fenet, *Recueil Complet des Travaux Préparatoires du Code Civil*, t. XIII (Paris, 1828) 8). It would seem that the omission of reference to creating contracts in good faith was made on formal rather than substantive grounds: J. Mestre, RTDCiv 1988.340 at 346 citing P. Bonnassies, *Le dol dans la conclusion des contrats* (unpublished thesis, Lille, 1955) 321.

[155] (Agreements oblige a party not only to what is there expressed, but also to all the consequences which equity, custom and the law give to the obligation according to its nature.)   [156] Arts. 1150–1 C. civ.

[157] Art. 1108 C. civ. The original examples included sale of immovable property at a defined undervalue (art. 1674 C. civ.; for historical background, see *Law of Obligations* (n. 45) 264) and contracts under which a joint inheritance is apportioned (art. 887 C. civ.).

[158] Arts. 1147–8 C. civ.   [159] Art. 1134 al. 1 C. civ.

ground of *erreur* in particular being widely interpreted.[160] Furthermore, the Code's insistence that contracts be performed in good faith was seen as meaning no more than that the parties must keep to their agreements and that the latter should be interpreted according to the parties' true intentions rather than the words which they used.[161] Good faith or equity should not be thought of as qualifying the agreement. *Qui dit contractuel dit juste.*[162]

2. The abuse of rights, accessory obligations and the control of unfair contract terms

However, by the end of the nineteenth century and the beginning of the twentieth, there were signs of change in these attitudes[163] and two developments in particular will be mentioned here.

First, it was suggested, apparently in response to provisions enacted in the German[164] and the Swiss Civil Codes,[165] that French law should recognise a general theory of the 'abuse of rights'.[166] This theory was by no means universally welcomed,[167] and even where it was, no juristic agreement was or has yet been reached as to its proper limits. However, two variants became particularly prominent, a person being said to abuse a right if its purported exercise (i) was effected with an intention to harm another person[168] or (ii) was contrary to its economic or social purpose.[169] The latter, much wider view, has met with considerable success in France, even

---

[160] Barry Nicholas, *The French Law of Contract* (2nd edn, 1994) 83 ff.; Jean Carbonnier, *Droit civil, t. IV, Les obligations* (18th edn, 1994) 98 dates this development to around 1870.

[161] V. Marcadé, *Explication théorique et pratique du Code Napoléon*, t. IV (6th edn, Paris, 1869) 396.

[162] (If it is contractual, it is fair.) This aphorism is attributed to *Fouillée* by François Terré, Philippe Simler, Yves Lequette, *Droit civil, Les obligations* (5th edn, 1993) 30.

[163] See generally ibid., 30 ff.   [164] § 226 BGB; on which see n. 67 above.

[165] Art. 2 II ZGB; on which see n. 94 above and n. 273 below.

[166] Although there were a number of theses and articles written on the topic after 1900, this suggestion is generally attributed to Saleilles, first made in his submission to the committee for the reform of the *Code civil*: see Raymond Saleilles, 'De l'abus de droit, Rapport présenté à la 1re. Sous-commission de la Commission de la revision du Code civil', in: *Bulletin de la Société d'études législatives* (1905) 325. For general discussions see Jacques Ghestin, Giles Goubeaux, *Traité de droit civil, Introduction générale* (3rd edn, 1990) 674 ff. and P. Catala, J. A. Weir, 'Delict and Torts: A Study in Parallel, Part II', (1964) 38 *Tulane LR* 221 who cite some nineteenth-century decisions which reflect the idea of the abuse of right: ibid., at 222–4.

[167] Marcel Planiol was a particularly prominent opponent: see his *Traité élémentaire de droit civil* (10th edn, 1926) 297 ff.

[168] Notably, Georges Ripert, *La règle morale dans les obligations civiles* (4th edn, 1949) 157 ff.

[169] This view was most influentially taken by Louis Josserand; see, especially, *De l'esprit de droits et de leur relativité* (2nd edn, 1939).

though it is realised that it strikes at the heart of the liberal conception of individual rights (*droits subjectifs*) and gives rise to considerable uncertainty and judicial discretion.[170] The courts, on the other hand, have consistently refused to accept any one theory of the abuse of rights, but have instead interpreted it to mean different things in different contexts.[171] Thus, the idea of the abuse of *contractual* rights was soon recognised and seen as supported by art. 1134 al. 3's command that contracts be performed in good faith.[172] Moreover, other rights associated with contracts, though not arising from them, were seen as capable of being abused, notably the right to refuse to conclude a contract where this was done in an abrupt fashion after lengthy negotiations.[173] In this situation, the abuse of rights is sanctioned by the imposition of liability in damages based on delictual fault, French courts here being able to rely on the generality of arts. 1382 and 1383 of the *Code civil*.[174] In all, therefore, in the modern law at the stage of the performance of contracts the two ideas of the abuse of rights and of contractual good faith (or rather bad faith) intertwine; and at the stage of negotiation of contracts, these ideas are reinforced by the idea of delictual fault.

Secondly, towards the end of the nineteenth century, a group of French jurists argued that the law of contract should be used so as to enable the victims of accidents at work to recover damages without the need to prove fault in delict.[175] The technique which they suggested for this purpose – the recognition of a strict *obligation de sécurité* (contractual obligation of safety) – was sometimes justified on the basis of implied agreement, but was more generally and more convincingly based on art. 1135's reference to *équité*.[176] While their suggestion was not successful in the context of work accidents, it was later adopted by the courts in relation to accidents suffered in the course of travelling and then somewhat more generally. These developments were not without their critics at the time, being seen by some as a 'forcing' of contract to do a job which was naturally delict's,[177]

---

[170] Ghestin/Goubeaux (n. 166) 700 ff.   [171] Ibid., 719 ff.   [172] Ripert (n. 168) 176 ff.

[173] See the French report to case 3, below. And see generally Simon Whittaker, in: John Bell, Sophie Boyron, Simon Whittaker, *Principles of French Law* (1998) 313–14. Some authors have also seen the idea of the abuse of rights reflected in the various legislative restrictions on a person's right to refuse to enter a contract (*refus de contracter*): see Ghestin/Goubeaux (n. 166) 709.

[174] On liability for delictual fault in general, see Whittaker (n. 173) 357 ff.

[175] See Simon Whittaker, 'Privity of Contract and the Law of Torts: The French Experience', (1995) 15 *Oxford JLS* 327, at 334 ff.

[176] E.g. J.-E. Labbé, 'Note', S 1885.4.25. More recently, Terré/Simler/Lequette (n. 162) 331.

[177] Louis Josserand, 'Note', DP 1929.2.17.

but *obligations de sécurité* are now a settled feature of the modern law,[178] allowing the courts a flexible interplay between contract and delict[179] and providing a major example of the consequences of *équité* in the performance of contracts.

A further French legal development related to good faith has been the gradual recognition of *obligations d'information* (obligations to inform or disclose).[180] These obligations, which at first typically arose in the context of contracts of sale, were often justified by reference to the idea that, despite its absence in the *Code civil*, French law recognised that contracts must be made as well as be performed in good faith. At first, apart from particular legislative contexts, the idea of *obligation d'information* was used principally to determine the question in what circumstances a party to negotiations should disclose information which may be relevant to the other party's decision,[181] but the modern *jurisprudence* is much wider than this, breach of an obligation being also used, for example, to impose liability in damages in cases of failure to warn about the dangers of products.[182] Interestingly, though, the doctrine of *obligation d'information* has attained a degree of independence and unity which has emancipated it from its parent, good faith, an independence which recent legislation which gave it formal recognition in the important context of consumer contracts will serve only to emphasise.[183]

Before looking at the attitudes of modern French jurists to the proper role of good faith as a principle in contract law, we should note French law's treatment of exemption clauses and of 'unfair contract terms' more generally, the latter enjoying the name, redolent of bad faith, of *clauses abusives*. As regards exemption clauses, despite acceptance of the binding force of contracts, French jurists and courts have proved extremely hostile and have found a number of ways in which to invalidate them or reduce their impact.[184] In the case of penalty clauses, legislation in 1975 amended

---

[178] Philippe Malaurie, Laurent Aynès, *Droit civil, Les obligations* (7th edn, 1997), 472–5.
[179] Whittaker (n. 173) *passim*.
[180] In general, see Jacques Ghestin, 'The Pre-Contractual Obligation to Disclose Information', in: Donald Harris, Denis Tallon (eds.), *Contract Law Today, Anglo-French Comparisons* (1989) 151; Muriel Fabre-Magnon, *De l'obligation d'information dans les contrats, Essai d'une théorie* (1992) and Fabre-Magnon, 'Duties of Disclosure and French Contract Law: Contribution to an Economic Analysis', in: Beatson/Friedmann (n. 30) 99.
[181] See the examples given in Christian Larroumet, *Droit civil, t. III, Les obligations, Le contrat* (4th edn, 1998), 309–12. [182] See the French report to case 1.
[183] *Loi* no. 92–60 of 18 January 1992, art. 2, now contained in art. 111–1 C. cons.
[184] First, while such a clause may modify or exclude any contractual liability, it may not do so for delictual liability based on fault, which is *d'ordre public*: art. 6 C. civ. and see Civ.

the *Code civil* so as to allow the courts to reduce or increase the size of a stipulated contractual penalty if it appeared to them to be 'manifestly excessive or derisory'.[185] More generally, legislation was passed in 1978 which gave power to the French administration to make decrees banning particular examples of *clauses abusives* in contracts between businesses and consumers under certain circumstances,[186] but in the absence of the exercise of this power, astonishingly the *Cour de cassation* in 1991 accepted that the courts could themselves take on the job and nullify a clause within the same conditions.[187] Perhaps fortunately for the maintenance of the integrity of the principle of the separation of powers, the need to implement the E.C. Directive on Unfair Terms in Consumer Contracts gave the French legislature an occasion to put these considerable judicial powers of control of unfair contract terms on a proper legal basis.[188]

3. How wide is the impact of good faith in French contract law?

Finally, we should turn to the question of the more general impact of the principles of good faith in the negotiation and performance of contracts, it being clear that it now extends to the former despite the limited terms of the *Code civil*.[189] There is general agreement among the jurists as to the importance of good faith as a legal basis for the construction by the courts of *obligations de loyauté*, and *obligations de co-opération*.[190] However, more

---

17 Feb. 1955, DS 1956.1.7 note Esmein, JCP 1955.II.8951 note Rodière. Secondly, no clause may affect a party's contractual liability for either *dol* or *faute lourde*, the latter being a gross form of fault and including recklessness: Larroumet (n. 181) 741–2. Thirdly, the courts have in particular contexts prevented those in business (*professionnels*) from excluding or limiting their liability. So, notably, while the *Code civil* prevents a seller from excluding his liability for *known* latent defects, the courts extended this to all sellers in business, who are irrebuttably presumed to know of their property's defects: art. 1643 C. civ. and see, e.g., Com. 17 Dec. 1973, GP 1974.1.429 note Planqueel, JCP 1975.II.1792 note Savatier.

[185] Art. 1152 al. 2 C. civ.; *loi* no. 75–597 of 9 July 1975, art. 1.
[186] *Loi* no. 78–23 of 10 January 1978, arts. 35–8.
[187] Civ. (1) 14 May 1991, JCP 1991.II.21763 note G. Paisant, D 1991.449 note Ghestin. Only two *décrets* had been made under the legislation.
[188] Council Directive 93/13/EC; art. L. 132–1.1 C. cons. (as amended by the *loi* no. 95–96 of 1 February 1995).
[189] See Terré/Simler/Lequette (n. 162) 320; Patrice Jourdain, 'Rapport français', in: *La bonne foi* (n. 35) 122.
[190] An example of breach of the *obligation de loyauté*, which applies to contracts generally, may be found in a case where a party to a contract deprives the other of the intended benefit of performance of the contract. *Obligations de co-opération*, on the other hand, are more or less marked in their impact according to the nature of the contract, being particularly prominent in the contract of employment: see Terré/Simler/Lequette (n. 162) 322–3; Malaurie/Aynès (n. 178) 350.

generally, French jurists are somewhat divided. At one extreme, *Flour* and *Aubert* consider art. 1134 al. 3 as 'a technical provision, possessing no significance of substance whatsoever' and they deride attempts to give it a more substantial significance as threatening to certainty and useless given art. 1135's injunction to courts to supplement the parties' agreement with legal, customary and equitable obligations.[191] At the other extreme was *Demogue*, who emphasised the co-operative nature of contracts, in which 'the contractors form a sort of microcosm; [a contract] is a sort of little partnership in which each must work towards a common purpose which is the sum (or more) of individual purposes pursued by each'.[192] Not surprisingly, the majority of jurists, however, find themselves holding more moderate positions. Thus, *Carbonnier* wittily jibes in relation to *Demogue's* position, that 'future commentators would be surprised that, at a time when marriage had already been transformed rather too much into just another contract, others dreamed of transforming all contracts into marriage'.[193] Even those jurists who are generally quite favourable towards good faith accept that it should not be allowed to lead to the idea of an 'absolute altruism negating one's own interests'.[194] As *Patrice Jourdain* concludes: 'In the end good faith remains a hazy notion, which is expressed effectively only when it runs into the legal mould of other concepts with more precise contents. This congenital weakness stems from the vague nature of a notion which in practice remains essentially moral and which has been made into a norm of behaviour governing precontractual relations. But if the notion of good faith appears to be of somewhat restrained utility as an instrument of legal technique, no-one would contest that the idea of good faith inspires many actual solutions to legal problems. For this reason, should one at least raise it to the rank

---

[191] '[U]ne disposition technique, dépourvue de signification substantielle, qui annonce l'article suivant, . . . Fondamentalement, c'est là un principe d'interprétation': Jacques Flour, Jean-Luc Aubert, *Les obligations, L'acte juridique* (6th edn, 1994) 289–90.

[192] 'Les contractants forment une sorte de microcosme; c'est une petite société où chacun doit travailler pour un but commun qui est la somme (ou davantage) des buts individuels poursuivis par chacun': Réné Demogue, *Traité des obligations en général*, t. VI (1931) 9. The French *société* ('partnership') has the significance both of the contract of partnership and of the much wider idea of society itself.

[193] 'On s'étonnera qu'à une époque où le mariage s'était peut-être trop transformé en contrat, d'aucuns aient rêvé de transformer tout contrat en mariage': Carbonnier (n. 160) 195. Cf. A. Bénabent, 'Rapport français', in: *La bonne foi* (n. 35) 293.

[194] '[A]ltruisme absolu négateur de ses propres intérêts': Jacques Mestre, 'Note', RTDCiv 1990.649, at 652, quoted with approval by Terré/Simler/Lequette (n. 162) 320.

of a general principle of law? The debate on this question, though, remains open.'[195]

As for the courts, they certainly do resort both to the idea of performance of contracts in good faith[196] and to the idea of a requirement that rights arising from the creation of contracts must not be exercised abusively[197] and sometimes to both at the same time.[198] And, while resort to good faith has hitherto been somewhat sparing in French practice, particularly in contrast with the German position, for some authors it is growing in importance.[199]

VI. Good faith

1. The absence of a general principle of good faith

English law does not recognise a general duty to negotiate nor to perform contracts in good faith.[200] Indeed, in some judicial utterances, this stark

---

[195] 'Il reste que la bonne foi demeure une notion floue, qui ne s'exprime efficacement qu'en se coulant dans le moule juridique d'autres concepts au contenu plus précis. Cette faiblesse congénitale tient au caractère vague d'une notion qui demeure essentiellement morale dans l'usage qui en est fait comme norme de comportement régissant les relations précontractuelles. Mais si, en tant qu'instrument de technique juridique, la notion semblerait n'être que d'un faible secours, nul ne contestera pas que l'idée de bonne foi inspire bien des solutions de notre droit positif. Pour cette raison, ne pourrait-on au moins l'élever au rang de principe général du droit? Le débat sur cette question reste ouvert': Jourdain (n. 189) 132.

[196] E.g. Civ. (3) 6 Jun. 1984, Bull. civ. III, no. 111; Civ. (1) 31 Jan. 1995, D 1995.389 note Jamin.

[197] E.g. Civ. (3) 11 May 1976, D 1978.269 note Taisne (*clause de dédit*).

[198] E.g. Ass. plén. 1 Dec. 1995, D 1996.13 concl. Jeol, note Aynès in which the *Assemblé plénière* roundly declared that the parties to a long-term supply contract could validly set its future prices by reference to the *supplier's* normal contract rate, subject to this right not being exercised abusively, that court expressly relying on art. 1134 al. 3 C. civ. to this effect.   [199] Malaurie/Aynès (n. 178) 350.

[200] On the significance of good faith and/or fairness in English law, see Bridge, (1984) 9 *Canadian Business Law Journal* 412 ff.; J. F. O'Connor, *Good Faith in English Law* (1990); Goode (n. 38); P. D. Finn, 'Equity and Contract', in: P. D. Finn (ed.), *Essays on Contract* (1987) 104 ff.; H. K. Lücke, 'Good Faith in Contractual Performance', ibid., 155 ff.; J. W. Carter, M. P. Furmston, 'Good Faith and Fairness in the Negotiation of Contracts', (1994) 8 *Journal of Contract Law* 1 ff.; Roger Brownsword, 'Two Concepts of Good Faith', (1994) 7 *Journal of Contract Law* 197 ff.; Staughton L.J., 'Good Faith and Fairness in Commercial Contract Law', (1994) 7 *Journal of Contract Law* 193 ff.; Beatson/Friedmann (n. 30) especially the essays by Jack Beatson and Daniel Friedmann, 'Introduction: From Classical to Modern Contract Law', 3 ff., Nili Cohen, 'Pre-Contractual Duties: Two Freedoms and the Contract to Negotiate', 25 ff. and Ewan McKendrick, 'The Regulation of Long-Term Contracts in English Law', 305 ff.; Reziya Harrison, *Good Faith in Sales* (1997); Hugh Collins, *The Law of Contract* (3rd edn, 1997) chaps. 13 and 15; Roger

if not (to many civil lawyers) startling position represents the very nature of the contractual process. Thus, for Lord *Ackner*, 'the concept of a duty to carry on negotiations in good faith is inherently repugnant to the adversarial position of the parties when involved in negotiations. Each party to the negotiations is entitled to pursue his (or her) own interest, so long as he avoids making misrepresentations. A duty to negotiate in good faith is as unworkable in practice as it is inherently inconsistent with the position of the negotiating parties.'[201]

Similarly, as regards performance, it is clear that parties are entitled to exercise their rights arising under the contract or under the law of breach of contract for whatever reason they choose. As *Potter* L.J. recently remarked in denying the significance of a party's motive in determining the legitimacy of a purported termination of the contract, '[t]here is no general doctrine of good faith in the English law of contract. The plaintiffs are free to act as they wish provided that they do not act in breach of a term of the contract.'[202] An extreme example of the irrelevance of motive to the effectiveness of the exercise of a right arising under a contract may be found in the decision of the Court of Appeal in *Chapman v. Honig*,[203] which upheld the exercise by a landlord of his right to give notice to quit to his tenant, even though this had been exercised because the tenant had given evidence against him in a dispute with another tenant: the fact that the landlord's action in giving notice constituted a criminal contempt of court did not deprive him of the exercise of the right. For, according to *Pearson* L.J., '[a] person who has a right under a contract or other instrument is entitled to exercise it and can effectively exercise it for a good reason or a bad reason or no reason at all'.[204]

Brownsword, 'Contract Law, Co-operation, and Good Faith: The Movement from Static to Dynamic Market-Individualism', in: Simon F. Deakin, Jonathan Michie (eds.), *Contracts, Co-operation and Competition* (1997) 255 ff.; Gunther Teubner, 'Legal Irritants: Good Faith in British Law or How Unifying Law Ends Up in New Divergences', (1998) 61 *Modern Law Review* 11 ff.; P. J. Millett, 'Equity's Place in the Law of Commerce', (1998) 114 *LQR* 214 ff.; Peter Macdonald Eggers, Patrick Foss, *Good Faith and Insurance Contracts* (1998). [201] *Walford v. Miles* [1992] 2 AC 128, 138 (the rest of the House agreed).

[202] *James Spencer & Co. Ltd v. Tame Valley Padding Co. Ltd* (Court of Appeal, 8 April 1998, unreported). It is interesting to note that in the context of sale of goods, this position was changed in 1994: see the Sale and Supply of Goods Act 1994, s. 4, providing for a new Sale of Goods Act 1979, s. 15A(1).

[203] [1963] 3 WLR 19 (Lord *Denning* M.R. dissenting).

[204] Ibid., at 32. See, similarly, *White and Carter (Councils) Ltd v. McGregor* [1962] AC 413, 430 *per* Lord *Reid*, though in the same case Lord *Reid* accepted that a party would not have a right to perform his side of a contract and sue for the price rather than for damages where he had 'no substantial or legitimate interest' in doing so: ibid., at 431.

This example also shows the relationship between English law's exclusion of any general requirement of good faith in the performance of contract and its more general denial of a theory of the abuse of rights,[205] perhaps reflecting a traditionally wide liberal approach to the concept of a right itself. Moreover, at the level of breach, apart from the special context of 'anticipatory breaches' of contract,[206] it remains irrelevant whether or not a breach is deliberate.[207] It is sometimes said that these attitudes as regards contract law reflect English law's focus on large-scale commercial transactions, made between hard-nosed traders, dealing at arm's length.[208] But whatever forms the background to these attitudes, taken at face value, it would seem that the making, performing or breaking of contracts is conducted in a context which is permitted by the law to be nasty and brutish, the parties being entitled to flout all considerations of decency and fair play.

Clearly, though, such a description of the English law of contract must be qualified to such an extent as to make these bald general statements appear little more than caricatures. Indeed, qualifications must be made at two levels, one concerning the historical significance of the notion of good faith or bad faith in English contract law and the other concerning the modern significance of its general irrelevance.

2. The law merchant, Lord Mansfield and a looser approach to 'fraud'

It is by no means clear that the rules or the attitudes as we have so far described them have existed for long in English law, especially in relation to its commercial contract law.

First, it has been noted that English law long accepted the propriety of recourse to broad notions of good faith and commercial expectations which were current throughout Western Europe under the *lex mercatoria* or law merchant.[209] The way in which the central English courts and in particular the courts of common law took over the jurisdiction of the fair courts of the medieval period is by no means a simple

[205] Catala/Weir, (1964) 38 *Tulane LR* 257–78 and see *Bradford Corpn v. Pickles* [1892] AC 25 and *Allen v. Flood* [1897] AC 1, 167.
[206] G. H. Treitel, *The Law of Contract* (9th edn, 1995) 769 ff.
[207] A. G. Guest (gen. ed.), *Chitty on Contracts* (27th edn, 1994) vol. I, § 26–011. As May L.J. observed, 'a deliberate contract breaker is guilty of no more than breach of contract': *Bank of Nova Scotia v. Hellenic Mutual War Risks Association (Bermuda) Ltd* [1990] 1 QB 818, 894.   [208] See, e.g., the comments by Kötz, in: *Essays Fleming* (n. 35) 256 ff.
[209] Goode (n. 38) 1; O'Connor (n. 200) 39. Cf. above, p. 17.

one,[210] but it is clear that by the middle of the seventeenth century, the law merchant was considered to be 'part of the laws of this Realm'[211] and that by the end of the century the common law courts no longer felt the need to take evidence of mercantile custom.[212] Commercial practice clearly dominated the rules of the law merchant, but it also drew on the civil law[213] and on the general canonist notion requiring 'faith to be kept'.[214] Even while in England, unlike other European countries, commercial and maritime law did not form a separate body of law and was 'developed by the machinery and in the technical atmosphere of the courts of law and equity',[215] this does not mean that many of its rules were not drawn from the law merchant. In this respect, we should note Lord *Mansfield's* dictum in *Carter v. Boehm* in 1766 that '[t]he governing principle is applicable to all contracts and dealings. Good faith forbids either party by concealing what he privately knows, to draw the other into a bargain, from his ignorance of that fact, and his believing the contrary.'[216] The context of this statement was the recognition of the status of contracts of insurance as *uberrimae fidei* and this is the proposition for which it is generally remembered.[217] However, one could rather view it as an explicit reflection of an element already present in the sources of English commercial contract law.[218] The fact that such a general approach did not survive

---

[210] See Sir William Holdsworth, *History of English Law*, vol. V (3rd edn, reprint, 1966) 112 ff.
[211] Sir Edward Coke, *The First Part of the Institutes of the Laws of England or A Commentary upon Littleton* (1st edn, 1628; we have used the 7th edn, 1670) 182 a.
[212] Holdsworth (n. 210) 145.
[213] See G. Malynes' popular work, *Consuetudo vel Lex Mercatoria* (1622) and the comments by Holdsworth (n. 210) 134 and in *ZEuP* 1 (1993) 29 ff. (32).
[214] Holdsworth (n. 210) 81 (writing of the law merchant in Europe in general).
[215] Holdsworth (n. 210) 153.
[216] (1766) 3 Burr 1905, at 1910. He added: 'But either party may be innocently silent, as to grounds open to both, to exercise their judgment upon.' See also *Mellish v. Motteux* (1792) Peake 156, 157 *per* Lord *Kenyon* and *Cornfoot v. Fowke* (1840) 6 M & W 358, 379 *per* Lord *Abinger* C.B. (dissenting). See further James Oldham, *The Mansfield Manuscripts and the Growth of English Law in the Eighteenth Century* (1992), vol. I, chapter 8.
[217] See, e.g., *Banque Keyser Ullmann SA v. Skandia (U.K.) Insurance Co.* [1991] 2 AC 249. To say that a contract of insurance is *uberrimae fidei* or 'of the utmost good faith' means in English law that the parties are bound to disclose all facts material to the risk both before the conclusion and during the course of the contract.
[218] It must be noted, moreover, that Lord *Mansfield* was well-versed in civilian legal thought: Holdsworth (n. 210) 147; *ZEuP* 1 (1993) 36. Oldham concludes his study of Lord *Mansfield's* contribution to contract law to the effect that 'Mansfield believed in the importance of certainty in mercantile transactions and in a few other contexts, but fairness, not certainty was his lodestar for the general run of contract cases': (n. 216) vol. I, 242. See also Lord *Mansfield's* use of civil law writers in relation to the enforceability of 'ranson bills' in *Anthon v. Fisher* (1782) 3 Doug 166 on the basis that

so as to appear in the great rationalising textbooks of the later nineteenth century, such as *Anson*[219] or *Pollock*,[220] should not deny that it did play some role at an earlier stage of development.

Secondly, it is clear that in the early part of the nineteenth century a party's bad faith in the making of a contract was a ground of its invalidity, even in the absence of a dishonest statement (and therefore fraud in its usual modern sense[221]), this being clearly visible in *Joseph Chitty's* leading work on commercial contracts first published in 1824.[222] For as part of a discussion on 'how the performance of a contract may be suspended, annulled' etc., *Chitty* notices that in the case of fraud 'courts of law as well as equity will relieve a party in the performance of the contract'.[223] Fraud for this purpose included statements of falsehood, but *Chitty* also cites cases which establish that, at least in certain circumstances, concealment may also constitute fraud, giving as an example a case where the agent of a seller of a picture, knowing that the buyer 'laboured under a delusion with respect to the picture, which materially influenced his judgement, permitted him to make the purchase without removing that delusion' in which the sale was held void.[224]

Even more surprisingly to a modern common lawyer, *Chitty* goes farther in his definition of what constitutes fraud, including cases where the 'fraud appears from the intrinsic nature and subject of the bargain itself'. Here, he concludes that 'though inadequacy of price when standing by itself be not sufficient to induce a court to relieve a party from the performance of his agreement, yet, when connected with other circumstances, it may tend materially to assist a party in equity in making out a case of fraud; and even when standing alone, if the inadequacy of the consideration be so strong, gross, and manifest, that a man of common sense would start at the bare mention of it, a court of equity will consider it a sufficient proof of fraud to set aside the purchase'.[225] Furthermore, '[g]reat weakness

---

Grotius 'lays down that the state is bound, in such a case [of a contract founded on natural law], to oblige private men to keep good faith': Oldham, ibid., 666.

[219] W. R. Anson, *Principles of the English Law of Contract* (1st edn, 1879) especially at 132 ff.

[220] Sir Frederick Pollock, *Principles of Contract at Law and in Equity* (1st edn, 1876).

[221] Though cf. Lord *Browne-Wilkinson's* dictum in *C.I.B.C. Mortgages plc v. Pitt* [1994] 1 AC 200, 209 that '[a]ctual undue influence is a species of fraud'.

[222] *A Treatise on the Laws of Commerce and Manufactures and the Contracts relating thereto*, vol. III, *A Treatise on Commercial Law* (1824).   [223] Ibid., 155.

[224] *Hill v. Gray* (1816) 1 Stark 435; Chitty (n. 222) 157.

[225] Ibid., 158, citing Lord *Eldon's* judgment in *Astley v. Weldon* (1801) 2 Bos & Pul 351, 346 though Lord *Eldon* also stated that 'it appears to me extremely difficult to apply with propriety the word "excessive" to the terms in which parties choose to contract with each other'.

of understanding, although it does not amount to insanity, if coupled with circumstances of fraud, apparent either from the unconscientious bargain, from the exercise of undue influence, from the want of adequate motive, or the like, is a ground for setting aside an agreement, especially in courts of equity'.[226] This very brief look at *Chitty's* work shows how extensive a concept of fraud was at that period recognised, it not being inaccurate to say that this idea was used to describe a range of situations from positive false statement to gross imbalance of bargain in which the courts, whether of law or equity, would intervene.[227]

This historical excursus is not, of course, intended to show that, before the acceptance by English courts of the mid- to late nineteenth century of the ideas both of consensualism and freedom of contract, they recognised in a very developed way a general principle of good faith or bad faith. However, it does show that the position taken by later courts, notably to precontractual nondisclosure in *Smith v. Hughes*,[228] is not simply the logical conclusion of a historical continuum.

3. The modern law

These observations found in *Chitty* raise the question of the role of equity in the modern English law of contract. An orthodox English view would consider this relatively modest, if by equity we refer to those principles or doctrines developed by the Court of Chancery. Clearly, equitable doctrine in this sense does affect general contract law – the law of undue influence, promissory estoppel or the equitable remedies of specific performance or injunction spring immediately to mind – but its influence is not all-pervasive. Moreover, it seems clear that in English law, the impact of equity is felt through the application or extension of particular doctrines,[229] rather than through a notion that equity should be used to temper the rigour of contractual or legal rights by reference to general considerations of fairness or conscience. It should be added, though, that these last few

---

[226] Chitty (n. 222) 159.

[227] Though see, as to the significance of this imbalance, J. L. Barton, 'The Enforcement of Hard Bargains', (1987) 103 *LQR* 118 ff. and Michael Lobban, 'Contractual Fraud in Law and in Equity c. 1750 to 1850', (1997) 17 *Oxford JLS* 441 ff.

[228] (1871) LR 6 QB 597. For a similar attitude in classical Roman law, cf. the case of the grain merchants sailing to famine-stricken Rhodes: *Law of Obligations* (n. 45) 256 f.

[229] E.g. the development of undue influence; cf. also the use of the 'ordinary equitable doctrine of notice' in a new contractual (tripartite) context in *Barclays Bank plc v. O'Brien* [1994] 1 AC 180.

sentences have been careful to refer only to English law, for this is an area where other common law jurisdictions have taken very different routes, giving a much larger role to equity. Particularly striking in this respect is the law of Australia, where relief against unconscionable bargains, in the words of Sir *Anthony Mason*, has been allowed to emerge from its historical shadows.[230]

While, though, it is true that modern English courts have not gone back on leading later nineteenth-century decisions such as *Smith v. Hughes*[231] and have not had recourse to general or even very large equitable doctrines to evade the consequences of contractual unfairness,[232] modern English law is not the hard-hearted Dickensian ogre which this would at first sight lead one to believe, for recourse has been had to 'piecemeal solutions in response to demonstrated problems of unfairness'.[233] These solutions may be seen to have been effected in four main ways.

First, English lawyers have long used recourse to interpretation of the parties' intentions to achieve a variety of normative results. This is not to say that all recourse to the language of intention, whether the construction of express terms or the finding of implied ones, should be dismissed as fictitious, mere window-dressing to give juristic respectability to decisions made on other grounds. Rather, issues of interpretation should be seen as reflecting a continuum, a sliding scale where search for the actual intentions of the parties is found at one end of the scale and direct normative input is found at the other.[234] In between, we find various gradations, including looking at the typical intentions or expectations of parties to the type of contract in question. Clearly, though, interpretation of express contractual terms as reasonable people would understand

---

[230] 'The Place of Equity and Equitable Remedies in the Contemporary Common Law World', (1994) 110 *LQR* 238, 249 and 254; and see, by way of example, the decision by Finn J. in *Hughes Aircraft Systems International v. Airservices Australia* (1997) 146 ALR 1, at 37.

[231] (1871) LR 6 QB 597.

[232] Nowhere is this clearer than in the judicial response to Lord *Denning* M.R.'s attempt to establish a 'principle of inequality of bargaining power': see *Lloyds Bank v. Bundy* [1975] QB 326, 339 and *National Westminster Bank v. Morgan* [1985] 1 AC 686, 708. The orthodox English position on older cases granting relief on grounds of unconscionability either of conduct or bargain is to accept them but to see them as both narrow and somewhat isolated: see Treitel (n. 206) 281–382. See also, *Chitty on Contracts* (n. 207) vol. I, §§ 7–042 – 7–047.

[233] *Interfoto Picture Library Ltd v. Stilletto Visual Programmes Ltd* [1989] 1 QB 433, 439 *per Bingham* L.J.

[234] Cf. *Liverpool City Council v. Irwin* [1977] AC 239, 254, where Lord *Wilberforce* referred to the idea of 'shade[s] on a continuous spectrum'.

them[235] or the implication of terms where one of the parties is held to be responsible to the other for defects in the subject matter of the contract which he has not disclosed before contract[236] lead to some of the legal results which in other systems are dealt with by a general requirement of good faith.[237] Indeed, for Lord *Steyn*, writing extra-judicially, 'there is not a world of a difference between the objective requirement of good faith and the reasonable expectations of the parties'.[238]

Secondly, the law of special contracts is far less hostile to the idea of good faith than is its general counterpart. Various particular contracts involve duties expressly put in terms of good faith, whether this results directly from a rule of law applicable to the contract in question (such as in insurance,[239] suretyship[240] or partnership[241]) or by way of the implication of a term (such as in employment contracts).[242] Moreover, here we should mention the very considerable significance of contracts involving 'fiduciaries'. The notion of a fiduciary is itself very difficult to define satisfactorily for all contexts, but the core idea is that a fiduciary is a person who is held to duties positively to promote another person's interests even at the cost of his own.[243] Apart from trustees, fiduciaries clearly include persons such as lawyers, and agents of all sorts, including brokers and other intermediaries of financial services. Whenever a contract involves a

---

[235] *Prenn v. Simmonds* [1971] 1 WLR 1381 especially at 1383–4; *Wickman Machine Tool Sales Ltd v. Schuler A.G.* [1974] AC 235, 251. Particularly clear is the recent *Cargill International SA v. Bangladesh Sugar and Food Industries Corp.* [1998] 1 WLR 461, 468 per Potter L.J.

[236] S. 14, Sale of Goods Act 1893, confirming the common law in *Jones v. Just* (1868) LR 3 QB 197. See now s. 14, Sale of Goods Act 1979, as amended by the Sale and Supply of Goods Act 1994, s. 1.

[237] Barry Nicholas, 'Rules and Terms – Civil Law and Common Law', (1974) 48 *Tulane LR* 946, 950. For a detailed comparative investigation, see now Wolfgang Grobecker, *Implied Terms und Treu und Glauben* (1999); cf. also Martin Schmidt-Kessel, 'Implied Term – auf der Suche nach dem Funktionsäquivalent', *Zeitschrift für Vergleichende Rechtswissenschaft* 96 (1997) 101 ff.

[238] Johan Steyn, 'Contract Law: Fulfilling the Reasonable Expectations of Honest Men', (1997) 113 *LQR* 446, 450.

[239] *Banque Keyser Ullman v. Skandia (U.K.) Insurance Co. Ltd* [1990] 1 QB 665, affirmed on other grounds [1991] 2 AC 249.

[240] See the discussion in *Chitty on Contracts* (n. 207) vol. II, § 42–020 and the recent decisions at first instance in *Levett v. Barclays Bank plc* [1995] 1 WLR 1260 and *Credit Lyonnaise Bank Nederland v. Export Credit Guarantee Department* [1996] 1 Lloyd's Rep. 200.

[241] R. C. l'Anson Banks, *Lindley & Banks on Partnership* (17th edn, 1995) §16–01; *Blisset v. Daniel* (1853) 10 Hare 493; *Floydd v. Cheney, Cheney, & Floydd* [1970] Ch 602, 608.

[242] *Chitty on Contracts* (n. 207) vol. II, § 37–051.   [243] Ibid., § 31–107.

fiduciary acting in this capacity, that person will owe a very wide range of duties of good faith to the other person simply as a result of the existence of this status.[244]

Thirdly, the common law of contract has been transformed over the last half century or so by statutory intervention, sometimes at a general level but more often at the particular level. The legislation on unfair dismissal of employees[245] and the law protecting residential and commercial tenants from forfeiture[246] should both be seen as examples of particular situations in which controls on the exercise of contractual rights have been imposed. At a general level, the Unfair Contract Terms Act of 1977 introduced important controls on the effectiveness of exemption clauses in both consumer contracts and in standard form contracts between businesses, these controls either being an outright ban or referring to the reasonableness of the term in question.[247]

Fourthly, English courts have developed various legal doctrines which clearly govern the behaviour of those who make contracts and put limits on the absoluteness of contractual obligations (and therefore contractual rights). An example of the former may be found in the relatively recent acceptance by English courts of a doctrine of economic duress,[248] one of whose elements is the improper or illegitimate nature of the pressure which is used.[249] An example of the latter may be seen in the judicial invention in the nineteenth century of the doctrine of frustration, at first tied to the notion of an implied term in the contract, but later freed from this particular juristic baggage.[250]

In conclusion, it should be noted that English judges and legal scholars remain divided on the question whether English law's recourse to piecemeal solutions to achieve many of the results which good faith is perceived to require is satisfactory. Some clearly think that it is,[251] and even Lord *Steyn*, who is clearly not at all hostile to the notion, has observed that there is no need for English law to introduce a general duty of good

---

[244] See, for example, as to liability for profits made in breach of fiduciary duty, J. E. Martin, *Hanbury & Martin, Modern Equity* (15th edn, 1997) 595 ff.
[245] A convenient summary may be found in *Chitty on Contracts* (n. 207) vol. I, § 37–150 ff.
[246] Kevin Gray, *Elements of Land Law* (2nd edn, 1993) 805 ff.
[247] E.g. s. 2(1) (outright ban); s. 3 (reasonableness test).
[248] The first clear case is *North Ocean Shipping Co. Ltd v. Hyundai Construction Co. Ltd* [1979] QB 705.   [249] *Chitty on Contracts* (n. 207) vol. I, § 7–011 ff.
[250] The leading case is *Davis Contractors Ltd v. Fareham U.D.C.* [1956] AC 696.
[251] Cohen (n. 200) 32 (in relation to the conduct of negotiations).

faith as it is unnecessary as long as the courts respect the reasonable expectations of the parties 'in accordance with [English law's] own pragmatic tradition'.[252] Other English writers have argued for an overt and more principled approach based on a 'rule of good faith', itself reflecting a vision of contract as a co-operative venture rather than the traditional individualistic terms of the free market.[253]

VII. More national variations on the common theme

The last three sections have been devoted to a brief survey of the role of good faith in three of the major legal systems of Western Europe: German, French and English law. They are, at the same time, generally considered to be the prime exponents of the three most important 'legal families' of European law.[254] But what about the other jurisdictions? Do they follow the pattern of German, French or English law? In some instances this appears to be undoubtedly the case. Irish courts have, by and large, followed the same approach as their English counterparts.[255] Scots law, too, according to a widely held view, does not recognise any general obligation on the parties to a contract to conform to a standard of good faith.[256] In its general attitude, therefore, it follows English law and it also uses many of the substitute devices developed south of the border. It will, however, become apparent that there are also subtle variations, e.g., concerning the scope of the doctrines of frustration and of undue influence. Yet, at the same time, there is also a different view. According to the late Professor W. A. Wilson, '[t]here is an underlying principle of good faith in the Scottish law of contract although it is difficult to find a clear and comprehensive statement of it'.[257] More recently, 'the broad principle in the field of con-

---

[252] Steyn, (1997) 113 *LQR* 442.   [253] Brownsword, (1994) 7 *Journal of Contract Law* 197 ff.

[254] On the concept of 'legal family', see Zweigert/Kötz (n. 28) 62 ff.; and see Hein Kötz, 'Abschied von der Rechtskreislehre?', *ZEuP* 6 (1998) 493 ff. On the filiations of the modern codes prevailing in Europe, see Zimmermann, (1995) 3 *ERPL* 101 ff.

[255] Yet, in spite of the same starting points in doctrine and approach, Irish and English law have developed different solutions in a surprising number of situations; see p. 655 below.

[256] See, for a representative statement, Whitty, as quoted above (n. 36). There are no relevant entries in the table of contents or indices to W. W. McBryde, *The Law of Contract in Scotland* (1987) or vol. XV (dealing with the law of obligations) of Thomas Smith, Robert Black (eds.), *The Laws of Scotland, Stair Memorial Encyclopedia* (1996).

[257] This statement appeared in the comparative comments to Art. 1.106 of the Principles of European Contract Law: Lando/Beale (n. 4) 58.

tract law of fair dealing in good faith' has even been endorsed by the House of Lords (in a Scottish case concerning suretyship).[258] The matter has now, for the first time, been subjected to more than cursory academic scrutiny at a symposium in the University of Aberdeen.[259] According to *Hector MacQueen, Wilson's* successor as the Scottish representative in the Lando Commission, the principle of good faith does indeed play a substantial role in the Scottish law of contract, even though this role has been 'submerged or subterranean', and the effects have not been as far-reaching as in the Continental systems. This proposition was rejected by *Joseph Thomson*, the Scottish contributor to the present study. What is beyond dispute is that good faith (under the label of *uberrima fides*) applies to insurance contracts and in suretyship transactions. Apart from that, Scots lawyers have started to explore the doctrine of personal bar[260] which, in his contribution to the Aberdeen symposium, was tentatively explained by *John Blackie* in terms of a general notion of good faith.[261]

The German approach is most faithfully reflected in Greek private law.[262] Article 288 of the Greek Civil Code (1940) is a verbatim translation of § 242 BGB and it appears systematically at the very same place within the Code.[263] Good faith also guides the interpretation of contracts: art. 200 Greek Civil Code corresponds to § 157 BGB. The Greek equivalent of § 226 BGB,[264] however, is considerably wider: it is not confined to situations where the only purpose of exercising a right has been to cause

[258] *Smith v. Bank of Scotland* 1997 SC (HL) 111, at 121.
[259] 30/31 October 1998, organised by Angelo Forte. The contributions to this conference are due to be published by Richard Hart in the course of 1999.
[260] Which is also referred to in a number of the Scots case studies in the present volume.
[261] As to the previous paragraphs, see Hector L. MacQueen, 'Good Faith: An Undisclosed Principle?'; J. M. Thomson, 'Good Faith in Contracting – A Sceptical View'; A. D. M. Forte, 'Good Faith and Utmost Good Faith – Insurance and Cautionary Obligations'; and John W. G. Blackie, 'Good Faith and the Doctrine of Personal Bar', all in the Aberdeen volume (n. 259).
[262] On the origin, and the system, of the Greek Civil Code see, e.g., G. Plagiannakos, *Die Entstehung des griechischen Zivilgesetzbuchs* (1963).
[263] For a general comment on its range of application, see Michael P. Stathopoulos, *Contract Law in Hellas* (1995) nn. 50 ff. More specifically on duties, based on good faith, to show consideration to the other party's interest, see Ismene Androulidakis-Dimitriadis, *Ypochreoseis synallaktitis pisteos* (1972). The Greek notion of good faith also has roots in the *pistis* of ancient Greek law; see, e.g., Sp. Troianos, J. Velissaropoulos-Karakostas, *History of Law: From Ancient to Modern Greece* (1997) 89 ff., 186 ff., 341 ff. (in Greek).
[264] Art. 281 Greek Civil Code; on which, see Symeon C. Symeonides, 'The General Principles of the Civil Law', in: Konstantin D. Kerameus, *Introduction to Greek Law* (2nd edn, 1993) 60.

damage to another but declares the exercise of a right to be inadmissible, if it plainly exceeds the limits set by good faith, or the *boni mores*, or the social and economic purposes of the right. Thus, art. 281 Greek Civil Code constitutes a statutory version of the notion of 'abuse of a right' and appears to have been inspired by the doctrinal developments in France since the beginning of the twentieth century.[265] Moreover, the Greek Civil Code contains a special provision dealing with change of circumstances: it gives the judge wide powers to adapt or terminate the contract.[266] Generally speaking, Greek courts have given the standard of good faith, as laid down in these various provisions, a broad application.[267]

Austria, too, forms part of the 'Germanic' legal family. Its Code is considerably older than the BGB and it does not contain a general clause like § 242 BGB. Nor does it refer to *Treu und Glauben*. Instead, honest business usage ('die im redlichen Verkehr geltenden Gewohnheiten und Gebräuche' and 'die Übung des redlichen Verkehrs') is resorted to in order to determine (i) under which circumstances a contract has been concluded (§ 863 II ABGB) and (ii) how contracts have to be interpreted (§ 914 ABGB).[268] The Austrian Supreme Court has used these two rules as a springboard in order to assert, in very general terms, that *Treu und Glauben* and the reliance on honest business usage constitute ethical principles which are so generally acknowledged that they may even be applied, in individual cases, without having been specifically laid down by the legislature.[269] The general principle of good faith is thus widely taken to be inherent in the Austrian Code; and whilst these and similar statements

---

[265] Cf. text after n. 163, p. 34 above. Under cover of art. 281, the Greek courts have, however, also received the German doctrine of *Verwirkung* (deactivation of rights); see the Greek report to case 22.

[266] Art. 388 Greek Civil Code, to which the notion of 'good faith' is also central. Article 388 is regarded as a special application of art. 288: Stathopoulos (n. 263) n. 60.

[267] See Konstantin Kerameus, in: Lando/Beale (n. 4) 58, and referring specifically to Areopagus 927/1982 NoB 31, 214 on the courts' power to change the terms of a contract and Areopagus 433/1953 NoB 1, 747 on the adaptation of money obligations.

[268] In its original version, § 914 ABGB had merely stated that an ambiguous contract has to be interpreted so that it does not contain a contradiction and that it is effective. In tune with contemporary natural law thinking, *Franz von Zeiller*, one of the leading spirits behind the code, had been hostile to the equity of Roman law. For details, see Ranieri, *RIDC* 1998, 1061 ff. In 1916, § 914 ABGB was redrafted; but in spite of the 'suggestive force' of § 242 BGB which undoubtedly played a role in the process of redrafting (Heinrich Klang, Franz Gschnitzer, *Kommentar zum Allgemeinen bürgerlichen Gesetzbuch* (2nd edn, 1955) § 914, I) still no mention was made of the notion of good faith.

[269] OGH in SZ 38/72. In a number of more recent cases, however, the Court has emphasised the lack of a provision corresponding to § 242 BGB and has thus refused to invoke the notion of good faith: see, e.g., OGH in JBl 1982, 426 (428); JBl 1991, 250 (252).

undoubtedly betray considerable influence from German law,[270] it is also often emphasised that not everything acknowledged under § 242 BGB may simply be transported into Austrian law.[271] Concerning the necessary leeway for doctrinal innovations, account must also be taken of the extraordinary provision of § 7 ABGB: when a case cannot be decided on the basis of the words or the natural meaning of a statute or with reference to analogous provisions, the judge may *ultimately* even resort to the principles of natural law. However, this provision has not very much been used in practice since, as *Zweigert/Kötz* put it, 'the judges preferred to make law behind a smokescreen of traditional techniques of construction rather than be openly creative'.[272] The Swiss Civil Code (ZGB) and Law of Obligations (OR), in their entirety, constitute the fourth important codification of private law within the Germanic legal family. The ZGB contains a general good faith provision ('In exercising his rights and in performing his duties everyone has to act in accordance with good faith')[273] which was placed, significantly,[274] in a very prominent position: Art. 2 I. In addition, Art. 2 II ZGB denies legal protection to 'the manifest abuse of a right'. The relationship of these two subsections *vis-à-vis* each other has been much debated by Swiss commentators:[275] are we dealing here with two distinct principles or merely with two emanations of one and the same basic idea? The latter view seems to prevail today, stressing the intrinsic unity of the two rules contained in Art. 2 ZGB. A German observer, at any rate, cannot

---

[270] For a long time, even under the new § 914 ABGB, the Austrian courts adopted a markedly restrictive approach and refused, for instance, to recognise the *exceptio doli generalis*; for critical comment, see, e.g., Armin Ehrenzweig, *System des österreichischen allgemeinen Privatrechts*, vol. I (2nd edn, 1951) 338. The new, more liberal approach, strongly influenced by German jurisprudence, dates back to the 1970s. For details of the development, see Ranieri, *RIDC* 1998, 1074 ff. Cf. also the monograph by Peter Mader, *Rechtsmißbrauch und unzulässige Rechtsausübung* (1994).

[271] Cf., in particular, the discussion by Peter Rummel, in: Rummel (ed.), *Kommentar zum Allgemeinen Bürgerlichen Gesetzbuch*, vol. II (2nd edn, 1992) § 863, n. 2. And see, most recently, the commentary by Peter Apathy, Martin Binder, in: Michael Schwimann (ed.), *Praxiskommentar zum Allgemeinen Bürgerlichen Gesetzbuch*, vol. V (2nd edn, 1997) §§ 863 and 914.

[272] Zweigert/Kötz (n. 28) 162. On the use made of § 7 ABGB in Austrian practice, see Willibald Posch, in: Michael Schwimann (ed.), *Praxiskommentar zum Allgemeinen Bürgerlichen Gesetzbuch*, vol. I (2nd edn, 1997) § 7; and see, in the present context, the references in Ranieri, *RIDC* 1998, 1075, n. 63.

[273] Which was, according to Rudolf Gmür, *Das Schweizerische Zivilgesetzbuch verglichen mit dem Deutschen Bürgerlichen Gesetzbuch* (1965) 50 'most probably . . . decisively influenced' by §§ 157 and 242 BGB.   [274] Cf. Zweigert/Kötz (n. 28) 169 ff.

[275] Cf., e.g., Zeller (n. 86) 160 ff. and the recent discussion by Caroni (n. 94) 191 ff.; and see, on the historical background, the references in nn. 67, 94 above.

fail to be struck by the fact that Art. 2 ZGB appears to perform a very similar function, and to be applied in a very similar way, to § 242 BGB.[276]

The French *Code civil* has been, historically, more influential than any other European codification. Thus, for instance, it applied from the beginning in what is now Belgium. Belgian courts, however, have relied much more extensively than their French counterparts on the principle of good faith in the performance of contracts as contained in art. 1134.[277] This was, at least partly, due to German influence and has led to a substantial body of literature culminating in a comprehensive monograph by *Matthias Storme*.[278] Significantly, 'De goede trouw – Redelijkheid en billijkheid in het Privaatrecht' was also the topic of discussion of the thirty-fourth congress of the Flemish lawyers' association.[279] The Spanish *Código civil* determines that contracts give rise not only to obligations to accomplish what has expressly been agreed upon, but also to all the results which, according to its nature, are in conformity with good faith, custom and the law (art. 1258). Moreover a new art. 7 was introduced in the early 1970s (i) stating very generally that rights must be exercised in conformity with the requirements of good faith and (ii) codifying the doctrine of abuse of right that had, on the French model, been developed by the courts.[280]

The interpreters of the Italian code of 1865 initially followed the French approach and thus were hostile to the notion of an *exceptio doli generalis*.

---

[276] Cf. the discussion by Caroni (n. 94) 199 ff. highlighting, *inter alia*, the role of general provisions like Art. 2 as ports of entry for constitutional rights and referring to *clausula rebus sic stantibus, venire contra factum proprium*, loss of right due to lapse of time (*Verwirkung*) and *nemo auditur turpitudinem suam allegans*. See also the comparative remarks by Ranieri, *RIDC* 1998, 1073 f.

[277] See the comparative statement in Lando/Beale (n. 4) 58. It is pointed out that Belgian courts have used good faith extensively in order to supplement contractual obligations but have used it to limit obligations only in cases of disproportion and abuse of right. Thus, abuse of right and good faith are not distinct notions in Belgian law: abuse of right is an expression of the limitative function of good faith.

[278] M. E. Storme, *De invloed van de goede trouw op de kontraktuele schuldvorderingen* (1990). Cf. also, e.g., W. van Gerven, A. Dewaele, 'Goede trouw en getrouw beeld', in: *Liber Amicorum Jan Ronse* (1986) 103 ff.; P. van Ommeslaghe, 'L'exécution de bonne foi, principe général de droit?', *Tijdschrift voor belgisch burgerlijk recht* 1987, 101 ff.; E. Dirix, 'Over de beperkende werking van de goede trouw', *Tijdschrift voor belgisch handelsrecht* 1988, 660 ff.; J. Périlleux, 'Rapport belge', in: *La bonne foi* (n. 35) 237 ff.

[279] Published under the same title, 1990.

[280] Cf. also art. 57 of the Commercial Code (parties to commercial contracts have to perform in accordance with the standard of good faith). For Portugal (arts. 762 (2) (good faith in the accomplishment of an obligation and in the exercise of a right), 334 (abuse of right) and 437 (1) (change of circumstances) of the Civil Code), see Antonio Menezes-Cordeiro, 'Rapport portugais', in: *La bonne foi* (n. 35) 337 ff.

Since the turn of the century, however, they began to become interested in German legal doctrine.[281] The *Codice civile* of 1942 subjects precontractual negotiations, formation (art. 1337), interpretation (art. 1366) and performance of a contract (art. 1375) to the (objective) standard of good faith (*buona fede*). Apart from that it requires debtors and creditors to behave according to the rules of fairness, or fair dealing ('Il debitore e il creditore devono comportarsi secondo le regole della correttezza'): art. 1175, which forms part of the preliminary provisions on obligations in general. The code also contains a specific provision on change of circumstances which, however, turns around the notion of *eccessiva onerosità* (art. 1467; cf. also art. 1664 as a specific application of the same approach). This provision is a legislative endorsement of the good faith principle which also lies at the roots of other articles of the code. Concerning the application of the standard of good faith in cases not covered by specific articles of the code, Italian scholars have mostly looked for inspiration to German doctrines on good faith. However, German influence appears to have occurred, predominantly, at a fairly abstract level, for some of the more audacious advances of the good faith principle in German law (*Verwirkung*, relaxation of rules prescribing a specific form for legal transactions) have not, so far, filtered into Italian legal practice.[282] The Italian reporter to the case studies in the present volume regards this reluctance of fully accepting the idea of a creative, corrective role of good faith as a legacy of the age of statutory positivism.[283]

Dutch law has traditionally also been counted among the Romanistic legal family: a categorisation which can no longer be maintained today.

---

[281] See Ranieri, *RIDC* 1998, 1077 ff. Generally on good faith in modern Italian law, see the contributions in *Studi sulla buona fede* (1975); *Il principio di buona fede* (1987); *L'abuso del diritto* (1998); and see Mario Bessone, Andrea D'Angelo, 'Buona fede', in: *Enciclopedia giuridica V* (1988); Lina Bigliazzi Geri, 'Buona fede nel diritto civile', Digesto, 4th edn, sez. civ., II (1988) 154; Umberto Breccia, *Diligenza e buona fede nell'attuazione del rapporto obbligatorio* (1968); Domenico Corradini, *Il criterio della buona fede e la scienza del diritto privato* (1970); Adolfo di Majo, 'Delle obbligazioni in generale', in: *Commentario del codice civile di Scialoja e Branca* (1988), arts. 1173–6; Luca Nanni, *La buona fede contrattuale* (1988); Ugo Natoli, 'L'attuazione del rapporto obbligatorio, I, II', in: *Trattatto Cicu-Messineo-Mengoni* (1984); Filippo Ranieri, 'Eccezione di dolo generale', Digesto, 4th edn, sez. civ., VII (1991) 311; Pietro Rescigno, 'L'abuso del diritto', *Rivista di diritto civile* 1965, I, 205 ff.; Rodolfo Sacco, *La buona fede nella teoria dei fatti giuridici di diritto privato* (1949).

[282] See, e.g., L. Nanni, 'L'uso giurisprudenziale dell'exceptio doli generalis', *Contratto e impresa* 1986, 197 ff.; Di Majo (n. 281) art. 1175; Carlo Castronovo, in: *Commentario al Codice civile diretto da Paolo Cendon*, IV, 2 (1991), *sub* art. 1175, 5 ff.; Ranieri, *RIDC* 1998, 1079 ff. with further references; Hesselink (n. 35) 291.

[283] See the Italian report to case 20.

This shift away from French influence is well reflected in the role attributed to good faith. In its art. 1374, the old *Burgerlijk Wetboek* (B.W.) used to contain a good faith provision which was based on art. 1134 *Code civil*[284] and which, like its French model, was for a long time not accorded much practical significance.[285] From about the time of the First World War onwards, however, the attitudes of courts and legal writers started to change, until art. 1374 came to be regarded as one of the practically most important provisions of the entire code. Its application was now comparable to that of § 242 BGB. The new B.W. of 1992,[286] therefore, commences its regulation of the legal consequences of contracts with the following two rules (art. 6:248): (i) a contract does not only have the legal consequences agreed upon by the parties but also those which arise from the nature of the contract, from the law, from general usage, and from the requirements of good faith (*redelijkheid en billijkheid*[287]); (ii) a rule which is valid between the parties as a result of their agreement is not applicable as far as it is, under the circumstances, inappropriate according to the precepts of good faith (*redelijkheid en billijkheid*). A change of circumstances is dealt with by a separate rule (art. 6:258), which is also based on *redelijkheid en billijkheid*. Finally, we have, at the outset of the general part of the law of obligations, a provision (art. 6:2) according to which (i) debtor and creditor have to behave *vis-à-vis* each other in conformity with the require-

---

[284] Article 1375 of the old B.W. corresponded to art. 1135 C. civ. On arts. 1374 f. of the old B.W. see, above all, Piet Abas, *Beperkende werking van de goede trouw* (1972) (also comparative: 221 ff.).

[285] For what follows, see A. S. Hartkamp, *Mr. C. Asser's Handleiding tot de Beoefening van het Nederlands Burgerlijk Recht, Verbintenissenrecht*, Part II (10th edn, 1997) 285 ff. Cf. also Diana Dankers-Hagenaars, 'Rapport néerlandais', in: *La bonne foi* (n. 35) 311 ff.; J. M. Smits, *Het vertrouwensbeginsel en de contractuele gebondenheid* (1995) 81 ff.; H. C. F. Schoordijk, *Redelijkheid en billijkheid aan de vooravond van een nieuw millennium* (1996); Ranieri, *RIDC* 1998, 1076 f.; Hesselink (n. 35) 291.

[286] On the recodification process see, e.g., A. S. Hartkamp, *Aard en opzet van het nieuwe vermogensrecht (Monografieën Nieuw BW)* (2nd edn, 1990). A commented edition of the new B.W. with references to the *travaux préparatoires* and the old code can be found in: J. H. Nieuwenhuis, C. J. J. M. Stolker, W. L. Valk, *Burgerlijk Wetboek, Tekst en Commentaar* (3rd edn, 1998). For an English translation of the provisions of the new code, see P. P. C. Haanappel, Ejan Mackaay, *Nieuw Nederlands Burgerlijk Wetboek, Het Vermogensrecht* (1990).

[287] The concept of *redelijkheid en billijkheid* constitutes a merger of the *billijkheid* contained in the old art. 1375 (i.e. the *équité* of art. 1135 C. civ.) and the *goede trouw* in the old art. 1374, section 3 (i.e. the *bonne foi* of art. 1134 al. 3 C. civ.). In determining what *redelijkheid en billijkheid* require, reference has to be made to 'generally accepted principles of law, to the current legal convictions in the Netherlands, and to the societal and personal interests involved in the given case' (art. 3:12 B.W.). The new code thus attempts to provide certain guidelines as to how to concretize the standard of good faith.

ments of good faith (*redelijkheid en billijkheid*) and (ii) any rule based on the law, general usage or legal act is not applicable as far as it is, under the circumstances, inappropriate according to the precepts of good faith (*redelijkheid en billijkheid*). These sweeping provisions have to be regarded as the culmination of the statutory career of the concept of good faith.[288]

Finally there are the Nordic countries. They are usually taken to form a special legal family which is distinguished by a number of characteristic features. One of them is the close co-operation prevailing among lawyers from Denmark, Norway, Sweden and Finland which, in turn, is based upon the historical, political, economic and cultural ties between those countries.[289] A somewhat schematic distinction may, however, be drawn between West Nordic and East Nordic law. The former consists of Denmark and Norway which were joined in a union until 1814.[290] Finland and Sweden, in turn, also formed a union until 1809, so that it was largely Swedish law that prevailed in Finland. In 1809 the Russian Tsar became Grand Duke of Finland, an event which did not, however, lead to a substantial degree of russification of the law. The very close interrelationship between Finnish and Swedish private law also continued after the former country gained its independence in 1917. Since the seventeenth century Swedish–Finnish law was deeply influenced by the European *ius commune*. Contract law, in particular, was permeated by the Roman principle of *bona*

---

[288] In view of the fact that the new code was only introduced a few years ago, the Dutch reporter to the present volume was faced with specific difficulties in analysing the thirty case studies. In a general preface to his report he points out that 'in view of the introduction of the new civil code, Dutch law has gone through a phase of transition. Whilst the new code often only codified pre-existing case law, it also sometimes adopted a new approach. As a result, it could happen that the Dutch Supreme Court changed its case law if it felt that the draft code offered a better solution than the one hitherto followed. Also, the Supreme Court sometimes adopted a solution provided in the draft code when it was faced with a problem that had not previously been decided. The old law was thus, by way of anticipatory interpretation (see A. M. J. van Buchens-Spapens, *Anticipatie (Monografieën Nieuw BW)* (1986)), brought into line with the new law. Where the code only restates existing law, reference will be made in the case studies to cases decided under the old code. Where, however, a new solution was adopted (as has happened in the area of non-performance of contracts) only a somewhat tentative answer could be given since even for Dutch lawyers it is not entirely clear how the new provisions will be applied in practice. A new civil code also, of course, clarifies many problems that were previously disputed. Some of the Dutch answers to the cases in the present volume can therefore be very brief.'

[289] Cf., e.g., Zweigert/Kötz (n. 28) 270 ff.; Gebhard Carsten, 'Europäische Integration und nordische Zusammenarbeit auf dem Gebiet des Zivilrechts', *ZEuP* 1 (1993) 335 ff.

[290] Iceland also belongs to the West Nordic countries, but its independent contribution to legal development is not significant. On the Icelandic legal system, see Halldór E. Sigurbjörnsson, 'Island – im Nordlicht am Rande der modernen europäischen Rechtsentwicklung', forthcoming in *ZEuP* 8 (2000).

fides, in that most contracts under the old medieval codes were taken to be *contractus bonae fidei*. This is also reflected in the joint Nordic Contracts Act[291] which contains a general requirement of mutual loyalty and honesty in its s. 33: 'A legal act which would otherwise be deemed valid may not be relied upon where the circumstances in which it arose were such that, having knowledge of such circumstances, it would be inequitable to enforce the legal act, and where the party in respect of whom such legal act was performed must be presumed to have had such knowledge.'[292] According to s. 36 of the same Act, contracts may be invalidated or adjusted on the grounds of unconscionability.[293] References to equity are also contained in other enactments, especially in the Sale of Goods Act.[294]

Even if there is, therefore, a substantial degree of uniformity of contract law, it must be kept in mind that the same statute may be interpreted differently in different countries. Thus, for instance, s. 33 of the Contracts Act has been of greater importance in legal usage and theory in Norway than in Denmark, Sweden or Finland. Norwegian courts and legal writers regard it as a mainstay for the requirement of honesty and good faith in contractual relationships whereas in the other countries it is taken to perform a largely supplementary function. On the other hand there is some room, in Swedish law, for invalidity as a consequence of incorrect presuppositions, no matter whether these presuppositions were initially incorrect or turned out to be so at a later stage (*felaktiga förntsättningar*).[295]

---

[291] It was enacted in Sweden, Denmark and Norway between 1915 and 1918, and in Finland in 1929.   [292] Translation supplied by the Swedish Government Chancery.

[293] 'A contract term or condition may be modified or set aside if such term or condition is unconscionable having regard to the contents of the agreement, the circumstances prevailing at the time the agreement was entered into, subsequent circumstances, and circumstances in general. Where a term is of such significance for the agreement that it would be unreasonable to demand the continued enforceability of the remainder of the agreement with the terms unchanged, the agreement may be modified in other respects, or may be set aside in its entirety' (source of translation as above, n. 292).

[294] A modern Sale of Goods Act for the Nordic countries was enacted in Denmark, Norway and Sweden between 1905 and 1907 (but not in Finland). In the meantime, a new uniform sales law has been adopted in Finland, Norway and Sweden between 1982 and 1990 (but not in Denmark).

[295] Or, in German, *Wegfall der Geschäftsgrundlage* (text after n. 104, p. 26 above; cf. also, in this context, *Windscheid's* presupposition doctrine). On the requirements of the Swedish doctrine, see Bert Lehrberg, *Förntsättningslären* (1988) and the Supreme Court cases in *Nytt Juridiskt Arkiv* 1949, p. 134; 1985, p. 178; and 1997, p. 5. Normally each party carries the risk for the presuppositions he makes. A transfer of risk can take place, for instance, when the presupposition is related to circumstances within the other party's sphere, or when it was induced by the other party.

Legal writers sometimes refer to a general duty to be loyal towards the other party, based on an analogy to ss. 6, 30, 33 and 36 of the Contracts Act and on similar provisions in other legislation.[296]

Notice must also be taken of the fact that there is a very close correlation between interpretation in terms of reasonableness and invocation of the general provision contained in s. 36 of the Contracts Act.[297] West Nordic courts, in particular, will do anything they can to avoid unreasonably harsh results by way of interpretation: the parties cannot be presumed to have intended that which is clearly unreasonable. Thus, there is a marked reluctance to accept a contractual right as absolute. A classic example from Norwegian law is *Norsk Retstidende* 1922, p. 308, involving a commercial purchase under the Nordic Sale of Goods Act. According to a specific statutory rule, any delay entitled the buyer to rescind the contract since punctuality was of the utmost importance for these kinds of transactions. Nevertheless, and in spite of the fact that there was no foundation in the contract for assuming that the parties had contracted out of this rule, the Supreme Court held that it had not been the intention of the parties to apply the rescission rule in a situation where the delay in delivery was of no major significance to the buyer whereas rescission would have inflicted very significant losses on the seller.[298]

VIII. The genesis of this book

It is clear from this brief survey that the range of uses of the notion of good faith (and of related concepts, like the abuse of rights) is extraordinarily wide. A comparison confined to a purely conceptual level would not, therefore, take us very far. Instead, it was thought to be more appropriate to look at the way in which a general good faith provision such as § 242 BGB is applied in practice and to compare the solutions for typical sets of facts to those arrived at, for the identical set of facts, in other legal systems. For even if the solutions in different legal systems focus on good faith, that notion may be understood, or applied, quite

[296] See the overview written in Swedish and using material from different Nordic countries by the Finnish author Lars Erik Taxell, *Avtal och rättskydd* (1972). In some contractual relationships the Supreme Court has stated that there is a duty to act loyally; see the Supreme Court case in *Nytt Juridiskt Arkiv* 1992, p. 351 concerning a creditor's liability towards a surety, and see the Swedish report to case 3 concerning *culpa in contrahendo*.
[297] Cf., e.g., *Norsk Retstidende* 1992, p. 22.
[298] See, today, s. 26 of the (new) Nordic Sale of Goods Act and, for Denmark, the decision of the Supreme Court, *Ugeskrift for Retsvæsen* 1995, p. 108.

differently.[299] But these systems may also look to other ideas, doctrines or rules, or may employ different techniques. By focusing on typical applications of good faith we hoped to be able to move beyond stereotypical assertions to the effect that a legal system does or does not require good faith.

The present book forms the result of one of three pilot projects initiated at a meeting of a small group of scholars from various European countries which had been convened in June 1994 by *Ugo Mattei* and *Mauro Bussani* at the University of Trento. Good faith in European contract law was suggested as a potentially promising project by *Reinhard Zimmermann* who had just investigated the way in which *bona fides* and equity had become fused in Roman-Dutch contract law.[300] He undertook to draw up a list of hypothetical cases illustrating the various uses and the potential range of application of good faith in contract law. These cases were discussed at the first general meeting of the Trento 'Common Core of European Private Law' project in July 1995, which devoted considerable time to a discussion of the methodology to be adopted and of its potential problems. In particular, it was generally regarded as important that the choice of cases should not be reflective of the concerns, or conceptions, of a particular legal system, or family of systems. Equally, it was agreed that the conceptual analysis offered by the reporters for their legal systems should not focus on the 'topic' of good faith as such but should explain as broadly as possible the approach to the cases adopted in their respective legal systems.

As a result of these deliberations, it was re-emphasised that the key feature of our project was to be the analysis of sets of facts by a number of reporters from various legal systems: a manner of proceeding which had previously been used by a team of scholars led by the late *Rudolf Schlesinger* in relation to the formation of contracts[301] and which, it was hoped, would also provide interesting insights into the different ways in which the analysis of cases is conducted in the various European states.[302] At the contract

---

[299] Cf., as far as the notions of *bonne foi* and *Treu und Glauben* in art. 1134 al. 3 C. civ. and § 242 BGB are concerned, the comparative study by Sonnenberger (n. 35) 703 ff. Both rules, even though they derive from the same historical source, have been given a very different meaning. More recently, however, there has been a certain *rapprochement* in that art. 1134 al. 3 C. civ. has been given greater significance both on a theoretical and practical level; cf. also sections V, 2 and 3 above, and Martijn Hesselink, 'De opmars van de goede trouw in het Franse contractenrecht', *Weekblad voor Privaatrecht* 1994, 694.

[300] Reinhard Zimmermann, 'Good Faith and Equity', in: Zimmermann/Visser (n. 14) 217 ff.

[301] R. Schlesinger *et al.*, *Formation of Contracts: A Study of the Common Core of Legal Systems*, vols. I and II (1968).

[302] On the concept of legal style, in this context, see Zweigert/Kötz (n. 28) 62 ff.

law working group, chaired by *Simon Whittaker*, it was decided to accept the initial list of twenty hypothetical cases presented to the meeting. Whilst these cases were mainly derived from textbooks and court decisions in German law, German law is generally held to give a particularly wide scope of application to its good faith provision.[303] Thus, it was regarded as the most suitable starting point to mark some of the outer limits to which the notion of good faith can conceivably be taken, so as to cover as broad a range of potentially relevant situations as possible. However, at the suggestion of the participants of the meeting in Trento ten more cases were added to the list, extending it, in particular, to cover precontractual good faith[304] and the law relating to conditions.[305] At the same time, however, it was decided to leave certain topics out of consideration, mainly for the practical reason that analysis of thirty cases already appeared to be a considerable workload for the contributors and that the project had to remain manageable. As a result, the project does not address the use of notions of good faith, or unfairness, in the control of standard terms of contract. While this is certainly a very important issue, it is a very large topic in its own right which, moreover, has now become the subject of E.C. legislation in the form of the Directive on Unfair Terms in Consumer Contracts.[306] For practical reasons, we also reluctantly decided not to include cases on deliberate or malicious breach of contract.

---

[303] See, e.g., Lando/Beale (n. 4) 56.

[304] For recent comparative discussion of precontractual liability cf., e.g., Ewoud H. Hondius (ed.), *Precontractual Liability, Reports to the XIIIth Congress of the International Academy of Comparative Law* (1991) (covering twenty-two different legal systems); *La bonne foi* (n. 35) (covering nine different legal systems); Alfredo Mordechai Rabello in a series of articles: 'The Theory Concerning Culpa in Contrahendo (Precontractual Liability): From Roman Law to the Modern German Legal System', in: Rabello (ed.), *European Legal Traditions and Israel* (1994) 69 ff.; 'Culpa in contrahendo and Good Faith in the Formation of Contract: Precontractual Liability in Israeli Law', in: *Essays on European Law and Israel* (n. 18) 245 ff.; 'Culpa in Contrahendo: Precontractual Liability in the Italian Legal System', in: *Aequitas and Equity* (n. 35) 463 ff.; Stephan Lorenz, 'Die culpa in contrahendo im französischen Recht', *ZEuP* 2 (1994) 218 ff.; Cohen (n. 200) 25 ff. Some codes contain specific provisions to the effect that in the conduct of contractual negotiations the parties have to conduct themselves according to the standard of good faith (art. 197 Greek Civil Code; art. 1337 *codice civile*). In other legal systems good faith and liability for *culpa in contrahendo* are also (indirectly) related to each other (for German law, cf. n. 115 above).

[305] On which see, in comparative and historical perspective, A. B. Schwarz, 'Bedingung', in: Franz Schlegelberger (ed.), *Rechtsvergleichendes Handwörterbuch für das Zivil- und Handelsrecht des In- und Auslandes*, vol. II (1929) 415 ff.; *Law of Obligations* (n. 45) 716 ff.

[306] See above (n. 31). Generally on Unfair Terms in Consumer Contracts see, most recently, Thomas Wilhelmsson, 'Standard Form Conditions', in: Hartkamp/Hesselink *et al.* (n. 1) 255 ff.; Hein Kötz, 'Unfair Terms in Consumer Contracts', in: *Festskrift Lando* (n. 4) 203 ff.

In order to accommodate the methodological concerns voiced at the meeting in Trento, the editors also wrote to all contributors to the project, requesting them to address the cases at three different levels. Thus we asked (i) for a purely legal, or doctrinal, analysis, indicating the practical result (including remedies) and the way in which it is reached, with suitable supporting references,[307] some indication as to significant differences of opinion which might exist within the respective legal system, and a discussion of the underlying policy concerns. But we also asked (ii) that this analysis be placed in its legal context so that the country reporters should explain the reason why one legal analysis was adopted rather than another; and (iii) that account be taken of any institutional, procedural or even cultural features that might be pertinent to a proper understanding of the approach adopted. In addition, the contributors were invited to change the facts slightly, if they thought this to be appropriate for casting light on the core case and/or on the approach characteristic for their legal system. In this way, we hoped to avoid 'missing the point' in a particular legal system by some unfortunate choice of the particular facts. Moreover, we attempted to cover the application of good faith not only in general contract law but also in a number of specific contractual contexts; hence the setting of some of the cases in employment, lease, insurance or medical law.

We invited contract lawyers from twelve Western European jurisdictions (apart from England and Germany which were to be covered by the editors) to participate in the project from the point of view of their national legal systems. The main part of this book contains their reports arranged not country by country but case by case. Within the treatment of any one case, the reports are always listed in the same order, keeping together related legal systems. In view of the very close ties existing between Danish and Norwegian law, it appeared reasonable to have them covered by the same contributor. All in all, therefore, we have fourteen national solutions for each case.[308]

In the course of the early summer of 1997, the editors went through the national contributions that had been handed in and attempted to provide

---

[307] These references were to focus (apart, of course, from legislation and pertinent judicial decisions) on standard works within the jurisdiction and, if possible, also on works accessible to foreign lawyers.

[308] Germany, Greece, Austria, France, Belgium, Spain, Italy, the Netherlands, England, Ireland, Scotland, Denmark and Norway, Sweden, Finland. Unfortunately, the Swiss and Portuguese contributors dropped out of the project at a time when it was no longer practical, without considerable delay, to arrange their replacement.

a comparative analysis for each case. In this book these comparative analyses appear after the national reports dealing with the cases. A general comparative conclusion of the project was then drafted by the editors. At a meeting of all contributors held in July 1997 in Regensburg, and sponsored by the Leibniz programme of the German Federal Research Foundation, the national reports, the comparative analyses and the draft general conclusion were discussed. After the meeting, the contributors were given an opportunity to refine their own reports in the light of the questions raised, and comments made, at the Regensburg meeting.[309]

The case studies in this project deal with the modern, national legal systems as they prevail in Europe today. It was, however, regarded as important also to keep in mind the role which good faith and equity have played in European legal history: for looking backwards, here as always, provides us with an understanding of how we have arrived where we are.[310] Since legal history in Europe can, in significant respects, be described as European legal history, such an inquiry seems to be particularly germane to a 'common core' project like the present one. But just as our cases cannot pretend to present a comprehensive picture of the range of application of good faith, we had to be selective and have focused on Roman law and Canon law. Moreover, the introductory section contains one essay relating the experience in what may be described, for present purposes, as a mixed jurisdiction: the United States of America.[311] They inherited from the common law the English scepticism towards adopting a general notion of good faith but have subsequently recognised it in a particularly important piece of legislation.[312]

Finally, it should be emphasised that while this project forms part of a wider umbrella project entitled 'Common Core of European Private Law', this should not be interpreted as reflecting a particular position on the

[309] We also asked all contributors, if at all possible, to check and discuss their answers with another colleague from their own jurisdiction.

[310] For a particularly crisp statement to this effect, see Alfred Cockrell, 'Studying Legal History in South Africa: The Lesson of Lot's Wife', ZEuP 5 (1997) 436 ff.

[311] On which, see recently E. Allan Farnsworth, 'Good Faith in Contract Performance', in: Beatson/Friedmann (n. 30) 153 ff. Farnsworth also draws attention to Australia as another country within the common law world which has started to support a doctrine of good faith (157 f.); and see above (n. 230).

[312] For the experience of other mixed jurisdictions, see Vernon Palmer, 'The Many Guises of Equity in a Mixed Jurisdiction: A Functional View of Equity in Louisiana'; Paul A. Crépeau, 'Abuse of Rights in the Civil Law of Quebec'; and Reinhard Zimmermann, 'Good Faith and Equity in Modern Roman-Dutch Contract Law', all in: Aequitas and Equity (n. 35) 395 ff., 632 ff., 517 ff.

appropriateness of harmonisation or codification of private law in
Europe, nor a particular expectation as to the results which were anticipated as the conclusion of the project. What it does rightly emphasise is a
concern for going beyond the doctrinal and looking at practical results.
Our aim in the 'good faith project' has been to explore the significance of
this important idea, to put it properly into its functional and comparative
context and, perhaps most importantly, to clear away some of the misunderstanding and misinformation which has often clouded discussion
of this elusive topic.

2   *Bona fides* in Roman contract law

MARTIN JOSEF SCHERMAIER

> *Ut inter bonos bene agier oportet*
> *et sine fraudatione*
> 'One must act well, as among good men,
> and without fraudulence'
> (Cicero, *De officiis* 3, 70)

I. Strict law and equity

At some point in the development of every legal system, the original strict and formal application of rules is supplemented by a freer approach which aims to go beyond the positivist strictures.[1] In some cases the older concepts are merely amended by the newer; in others the new legal principles completely replace the older law by virtue of their intrinsic superiority.[2] This can be seen both in the development of Equity

---

I would like to thank Anya Liversidge, B.A. (Oxon.), and Reinhard Zimmermann for the English translation of this chapter.

[1] The same view has been expressed by Josef Esser, 'Wandlungen von Billigkeit und Billigkeitsrechsprechung im modernen Privatrecht', in: *Summum ius summa iniuria: Individualgerechtigkeit und der Schutz allgemeiner Werte im Rechtsleben* (1963) at 35.

[2] Cf. Henry J. S. Maine, *Ancient Law* (reprint, 1963) at 26.

in England[3] and in the success of the general clauses of the German BGB, especially § 242. These two examples also show, however, that the same phenomenon can have different causes and flourish under different conditions. While the development of Equity in the Court of Chancery was a reaction against the procedural formalism of the writ system, the modern German *Billigkeitsrechtsprechung*, as *Esser* has called it,[4] is used to correct the substantive law of a highly developed and sophisticated legal system. The equitable case law was triggered and influenced by a conceptually different set of rules;[5] the triumph of the general clauses of the BGB, in comparison, is closely linked to the clash between two opposing concepts within the same system of law: *Begriffsjurisprudenz* (conceptual jurisprudence) and *Freirechtsbewegung* (free law movement).[6] Both this and the state of contemporary jurisprudence contributed to the fact that the two developments were accompanied by differing degrees of critical reflection.[7] The intensity of the actual critical reflection, however, says little about the critical potential itself. The strictures of form and doctrine, whether of codification or procedure, were felt similarly both in

[3] See, e.g., Andreas B. Schwarz, 'Equity', in: *Die Zivilgesetze der Gegenwart, vol. II: Das Zivilrecht Englands in Einzeluntersuchungen* (1931) Part 1, 101, 107 ff.; Alfred W. B. Simpson, *A History of the Common Law of Contract: The Rise of the Action of Assumpsit* (1975) 396 ff.; for an overview and further references, see Konrad Zweigert, Hein Kötz, *Einführung in die Rechtsvergleichung* (3rd edn, 1996) 184 ff.   [4] Esser (n. 1) 22 ff.
[5] For a discussion of the influence of Canon law on Equity, see Reinhard Zimmermann, 'Der europäische Charakter des englischen Rechts: Historische Verbindungen zwischen civil law und common law', ZEuP 1 (1993) 21 ff. and 27 ff., with particular reference to developments in contract law; on the theory of contract in Equity see also Simpson (n. 3) 278 f.; for an account of the action of assumpsit see Richard H. Helmholz, 'Assumpsit and fidei laesio', in: Helmholz, *Canon Law and the Law of England* (1987) 282 ff.
[6] The opposing views can be outlined by reference to two leading proponents of these schools. E. Fuchs, 'Verhältnis der Freirechtslehre zum deutschen und ausländischen Rechtsdenken', *Die Justiz* 1 (1925/26) 349 describes § 242 as a 'königliche[n] Paragraphen', the 'archimedische[n] Punkt, von dem aus die alte juristische Welt aus den Angeln gehoben wurde'. Justus W. Hedemann, *Die Flucht in die Generalklauseln* (1933) sees especially in § 242 BGB a 'Gefahr für Staat und Recht' (also the subtitle of his work).
[7] For an analysis of Chr. St Germa(i)n, 'A Dialogue in Englysshe betwyxt a Doctoure of Dyuynytie and a Student of the Lawes of England of the grounds of the sayd Lawes and of Conscyence' and his forerunners, see Simpson (n. 3) 376 ff. Concerning the debate within German jurisprudence in the first half of the twentieth century see, e.g., Karl Larenz, 'Entwicklungstendenzen der heutigen Zivilrechtsdogmatik', JZ 1962, 105 ff. (with further references); for a discussion of the fundamental problems arising from the growing importance of § 242 BGB see, e.g., Esser (n. 1) 22 ff.; Esser, '§ 242 und die Privatautonomie', JZ 1956, 555 ff.; Joachim Gernhuber, 'Die Billigkeit und ihr Preis', in: *Summum ius summa iniuria* (n. 1) 205 ff.; Robert Scheyhing, *Pluralismus und Generalklauseln, betrachtet auf dem Hintergrund gesellschaftlichen Wandels* (1976).

medieval England and modern Germany to pose a contradiction between positive law and justice: a contradiction encapsulated by the Romans in the phrase *summum ius, summa iniuria*.[8]

Roman law also offers the first example of how a legal system is renovated under the influence of equitable ideas.[9] This historical event connects the examples given above, the role of Equity in England and the extensive interpretation of § 242 BGB. In Roman law, similarly to England, the restrictions of formal procedure were overcome by measures taken by the officers responsible for the administration of justice. Alongside the actions provided by the old *ius civile* newer ones were established by the *praetor* in his yearly edict (*ius honorarium*). These, as the late-classical jurist *Papinian* writes, supplemented and corrected the *ius civile* for the good of all.[10] To this phenomenological affinity with English law[11] corresponds a

---

[8] Marcus Tullius Cicero, *De officiis* 1, 33; for an analysis of older versions and possible Greek influences, see J. Stroux, 'Summmum ius summa iniuria: Ein Kapitel aus der Geschichte der interpretatio iuris', in: *Römische Rechtswissenschaft und Rhetorik* (1947) 7 ff.; further Georg Eisser, 'Zur Deutung von "summum ius summa iniuria" im römischen Recht', in: *Summum ius summa iniuria* (n. 1) 1 ff.; Manfred Fuhrmann, 'Philologische Bemerkungen zur Sentenz "summum ius summa iniuria"', in: *Studi Volterra*, vol. II (1971) 53 ff.; Malte Dobbertin, *Zur Auslegung der Stipulation im klassischen römischen Recht* (1987) 31 ff.; more recently (particularly in connection with P. Terentius Afer, *Heautontimorumenos*, 787 ff. and with many further references) Wolfgang Waldstein, 'Aequitas und summum ius', in: *Tradition und Fortentwicklung im Recht, Festschrift für Ulrich von Lübtow* (1991) 23 ff.

[9] B. Huwiler, 'Aequitas und bona fides als Faktoren der Rechtsverwirklichung: zur Gesetzgebungsgeschichte des Rechtsmissbrauchsverbotes (Art. 2 Abs. 2 ZGB)', in: Bruno Schmidlin (ed.), *Vers un droit privé européen commun? – Skizzen zum gemeineuropäischen Privatrecht* (1994) 57, 58 f. points to earlier Greek examples. This is correct in so far as the Roman concept of *aequitas*, often used to characterise *bona fides*, had its origin in the Greek *epieíkeia* (important in this context is, e.g., Aristoteles, *Ethica Nicomachea*, 1137a–1138a); cf. also Fritz Pringsheim, 'Aequitas und bona fides', in: *Conferenze per il XIV centenario delle Pandette* (1931) 185 ff. (= 'Equita e buona fede', 1931 *Giornale dell'avvocato*, fasc. 6, 1 f. and 7, 3). However, in Greece *epieíkeia* was a philosophical and not a jurisprudential concept.

[10] D. 1, 1, 7, 1: 'Ius praetorium est, quod praetores introduxerunt adiuvandi vel supplendi vel corrigendi iuris civilis gratia propter utilitatem publicam.'

[11] For a discussion of the similarity between the dualisms *ius civile/ius honorarium* and common law/equity, see principally William W. Buckland, *Equity in Roman Law* (1911); cf. also Hans Peter, *Römisches Recht und englisches Recht* (1969) 31 ff. (pp. 81 ff. of the *Sitzungsberichte der Wissenschaftlichen Gesellschaft Frankfurt*, vol. VII (1968), Nr. 3) who emphasises that we are dealing here with a case of independent parallel development (26, 76); Peter Stein, 'Equitable Principles in Roman Law', in: R. A. Newman (ed.), *Equity in the World's Legal Systems: A Comparative Study dedicated to René Cassin* (1973) 75 f.; Giovanni Pugliese, 'Ius honorarium a Roma ed equity nei sistemi di common law', *Rivista trimestrale di diritto e procedura civile* 42 (1988) 1105 ff. Remarkable overlaps between Roman and English ideas in the mixed jurisdiction of South Africa have been noted by

genealogical one with modern German law:[12] central to the *praetor's* reforms was the introduction of actions based on *bona fides*, a term usually translated, with recourse to § 242 BGB, as *Treu und Glauben*.[13] These *bonae fidei iudicia* required the debtor to perform in such a way as good faith demanded,[14] which corresponds to the imperative of § 242 BGB to render performance 'wie Treu und Glauben mit Rücksicht auf die Verkehrssitte es erfordern'.

II. Example: liability for concealed defects

One example of the central role which *bona fides* occupied in the restructuring of Roman law[15] is found in the writings of *Cicero*.[16] 'The augurs were going to take an augury on the citadel, and they ordered *T. Claudius Centumalus*, who had a house on the Caelian hill, to demolish that part of it that was high enough to obstruct the auspices. *Claudius* advertised the block for sale and *P. Calpurnius Lanarius* bought it. The augurs made the same demand of him, and *Calpurnius* pulled down the required bit. When

Reinhard Zimmermann, 'Good Faith and Equity in Modern Roman-Dutch Contract Law', in: Alfredo M. Rabello (ed.), *Aequitas and Equity: Equity in Civil Law and Mixed Jurisdictions* (1997) 517 ff., especially 550 ff.

[12] Interesting phenomenological parallels between the Roman *officium iudicis* and the task of the German judge to specify the general clause of § 242 BGB are noted by Franz Wieacker, *Zur rechtstheoretischen Präzisierung von § 242 BGB* (1956); also in: *Ausgewählte Schriften, vol. II: Theorie des Rechts und der Rechtsgewinnung* (1983) 195 ff.

[13] Cf. the new German translation of the *Corpus iuris civilis* by Okko Behrends, Rolf Knütel, Berthold Kupisch, Hans Hermann Seiler, *Digesten 1–10*, vol. II (1995), e.g. in D. 2, 14, 7, 5–6 and 7–10; D. 2, 14, 27, 2; this corresponds to their chosen 'zielsprachenorientierte Methode' (see Rolf Knütel, 'Einzelne Probleme bei der Übersetzung der Digesten', ZSS 111 (1994) 376 ff.), but is problematical due to the different meanings attributed to the two concepts; preferable is the translation adopted by Max Kaser, *Das Römische Privatrecht*, 1. *Abschnitt* (2nd edn, 1971) at 178 ('gute Treue'); cf. also Kaser, '"Ius honorarium" und "ius civile"', ZSS 101 (1984) 1 ff. at 29.

[14] For a discussion of the nature of the *bonae fidei iudicia* see section III below.

[15] The vast literature on the role of *bona fides* in Roman law has (up to 1985) been collated by Pierre D. Senn, 'Buona fede nel diritto romano', in: *Digesto delle Discipline Privatistiche, sez. civile*, vol. II (1988, reprint 1993) 129 f. Important later works include Sebastiano Tafaro, 'Criteri di imputazione della responsabilità contrattuale e "bona fides": brevi riflessioni sulle fonti romane e sul Codice Civile Italiano', in: *Studi in honore di Arnaldo Biscardi VI* (1987) 311 ff.; Amelia Castresana, *'Fides', 'Bona Fides': Un concepto para la creacion del derecho* (1991); P. Frezza, 'A proposito di "fides" e "bona fides" come valore normativo in Roma nei rapporti dell'ordinamento interno e internazionale', *Studia et documenta historiae et iuris* 57 (1991) 297 ff.

[16] Cicero, *De officiis* 3, 66; the same event is reported by Valerius Maximus, *Facta et dicta memorabilia* 8, 2, 1.

he discovered that *Claudius* had advertised the house after he had been ordered by the augurs to demolish some of it, he compelled him to go before the arbitrator. Could he demand from *Claudius* compensation for his loss?' Under the *ius civile* the seller of a piece of land was only responsible for those defects the existence of which he had expressly denied. *Cicero* traces this liability back to a provision of the Twelve Tables[17] which stated that a seller was liable only in respect of any formal undertakings (*nuncupationes*) he had made.[18] It can be assumed from *Cicero's* reference that such *nuncupationes* could accommodate all manner of assurances about both the factual and legal state of the object of sale.[19] It is true that a promise to the effect that the house was not subject to an order effecting a partial expropriation,[20] as in this case, is difficult to imagine: a buyer would never demand such an assurance unless he had already learnt of the order before entering the contract. The whole point of this case, however, is that *Calpurnius* had no idea and acquired the house at a price which did not take into consideration the reduction in value caused by the demand of the *augures*. Thus, at least according to the (old)[21] *ius civile*, *Calpurnius* had no means of claiming redress for his loss.

Accordingly, the claim finally initiated by *Calpurnius* was based not on the strict law but was conceived as a *bonae fidei iudicium*, therefore requiring the judge to decide the extent of *Claudius'* duties as seller according to *quidquid . . . dare facere oportet ex fide bona.*[22] As *Cicero* explains, *bona fides* demands that the buyer should be told of all defects which are known to

---

[17] XII Tables (*Lex duodecim tabularum*) 6, 1 from Sex. Pompeius Festus, *Epitomae operis de verborum significatu Verrii Flaccii quae extant* 176, 5 (ed. Lindsay): 'Cum nexum faciet mancipiumque, uti lingua nuncupassit, ita ius esto.'

[18] Cicero, *De officiis* 3, 65: 'Nam cum ex duodecim tabulis satis esset ea praestari, quae essent lingua nuncupata . . .'; for a general discussion of *nuncupatio*, see Kaser (n. 13) 47.

[19] In the modern literature this is controversial; the only liability actually verifiable is that for false statements about the size of a piece of land (*actio de modo agri*, Julius Paulus, *Sententiae* 2, 17, 4); for the various arguments see Vincenzo Arangio-Ruiz, *La compravendita in diritto romano* II (1954, reprint 1980) 353 ff.; Antonius L. Olde Kalter, *Dicta et promissa* (1963) 33 ff. and 147 ff.; for the view expressed above, see Raymond Monier, *La garantie contre les vices cachés dans la vente romaine* (1930) 6 ff.; Heinrich Honsell, *Quod interest im bonae fidei iudicium* (1969) 62 ff.; and Honsell, 'Von den aedilizischen Rechtsbehelfen', in: *Gedächtnisschrift für Wolfgang Kunkel* (1986) 55 ff., all with further references.

[20] On the problematical nature of expropriation in Roman law, see Martin Pennitz, *Der 'Enteignungsfall' im römischen Recht der Republik und des Prinzipats* (1991) 63 ff., with references to earlier literature on the subject.

[21] Later the *bonae fidei iudicia* were themselves taken to be part of the *ius civile*; cf. Gaius, *Institutiones* 4, 45 and D. 18, 5, 8; and see Kaser (n. 13) 487; Kaser, *ZSS* 101 (1984) 30 f.; André Magdelain, *Les actions civiles* (1954) 54 ff.   [22] Cf. Cicero, *De officiis* 3, 66.

the seller.[23] If the latter conceals known defects, then he should be liable for any detriment resulting to the innocent buyer. The *arbiter* dealing with the case, *M. Porcius Cato*, did in fact order *Claudius* to compensate *Calpurnius* for the loss which the latter had suffered as a result of his silence.[24]

Cicero was not telling his contemporaries anything new: even at the time the judgement was passed, probably around 100 BC,[25] neither the action nor the result were revolutionary. But with the lack of earlier evidence it is impossible to establish exactly when the *bonae fidei iudicia* emerged.[26] At any rate *Cicero's* account demonstrates that the jurisprudence of the late Republic was still very much aware of the division between the old claims of the *ius civile* and the newer actions introduced by the *ius honorarium*. But *Cicero* was not writing a historical report; the older law was well known during his lifetime[27] and continued to be known for a long time afterwards.[28] Rather it was his aim to show how the work of the jurists led to the ideal of the *vir bonus*, who would not use deceit to gain a contractual advantage,[29] being incorporated into the administration of justice. The example is to demonstrate the progress that was brought about by judicial recognition of the principle of *bona fides*.

Cicero, however, does not stop there. In a further case, which must have taken place at about the same time as the first, he shows that any provision derived from the concept of *bona fides* itself becomes inflexible and unjust if it is not continually tested against the standard of *bona*

---

[23] Ibid., 3, 67: 'Ergo ad fidem bonam statuit pertinere notum esse emptori vitium, quod nosset venditor.'

[24] In Cicero's account (ibid., 3, 66) the seller's silence is merely the basis, not the yardstick, for his liability ('. . . cum in vendundo rem eam scisset et non pronuntiasset, emptori damnum praestari oportere').

[25] *M. Porcius Cato*, grandson of *Cato Censorius* and father of *Cato Uticensis*, a contemporary of *Cicero*, died between 95 and 91 BC; cf. Franz Miltner, *RE* XXII/2, 166 (s.v. 'Porcius', n. 12); quite mistaken therefore is Rudolf Düll, 'Zu Gaius Veronensis, den iudicia der Legisaktionen und zum Vorformularverfahren', *ZSS* 95 (1978) 270 at 278 f., who confuses *Cato Uticensis* with *Cato Censorius* and would date the above case at around 220 BC.

[26] The history of their development is discussed below, section III.

[27] Cicero, *De legibus* 2, 59 reports that as a boy he was required to learn the text of the Twelve Tables by heart.

[28] The most important source for our knowledge of the old *legis actiones* procedure is *Gaius'* 'Institutes' written in the middle of the second century AD (Gaius, *Institutiones* 4, 10–31).

[29] Cicero, *De officiis* 3, 61: 'Ita nec ut emat melius nec ut vendat quicquam simulabit aut dissimulabit vir bonus'; the statement is to be seen in connection with the *actio de dolo*, first granted by the *praetor* (?) *C. Aquilius Gallus*, and with his definition of *dolus malus* as *aliud simulatum aliud actum* (Cicero, *De officiis* 3, 60; similarly *De natura deorum* 3, 74); see Kaser (n. 13) 246 and 627 f.; Heinrich Honsell, in: Wolfgang Kunkel, *Römisches Recht* (4th edn, 1987) 371 f., both with further references.

fides.[30] '*Marius Gratidianus* sold to *C. Sergius Orata* a house that he had bought from the same man only a few years before. It was under a liability, but *Marius* did not state that in the contract of sale. *Sergius* brought the matter to court, although he must have known of the liability as it had existed before he sold the house to *Marius* in the first place.' In court the case was fought out by two of the most famous orators of the time; *M. Licinnius Crassus*[31] represented the plaintiff *Sergius* while *M. Antonius*[32] represented *Marius*. *Crassus* based his claim on *Marius*' breach of duty: a failure to disclose known defects at the time of contracting contravened *bona fides*. In answer to this *Antonius* argued that since it had not been necessary to inform *Sergius* about the servitude, he had not been deceived by *Marius*' silence.[33] Not only *Cicero*[34] but also modern authors are surprised that *Sergius*' views could have been seriously propounded in court.[35] To us it is obvious that a seller is not liable for a defect if it was known to the buyer at time of contracting.[36] *Crassus*' arguments are clearly very formalistic: they lie within the wording of the rule derived from *bona fides* but take no account of the substantive content of good faith itself.[37] *Cicero* here

---

[30] Cicero, *De officiis* 3, 67.

[31] For a biography, see N. Häpke, *RE* XIII/1, 252 ff. (s.v. 'Licinius', n. 55).

[32] For a biography, see Klebs, *RE* I/2, 2590 ff. (s.v. 'Antonius', n. 28).

[33] Cicero, *De officiis* 3, 67: 'quoniam id vitium ignotum Sergio non fuisset, qui illas aedes vendidisset, nihil fuisse necesse dici nec eum esse deceptum, qui id, quod emerat, quo iure esset, teneret'.

[34] Cicero, *De officiis* 3, 67: 'Quorsus haec? Ut illud intellegas, non placuisse maioribus nostris astutos.'   [35] Cf., e.g., Honsell, in: *Gedächtnisschrift Kunkel* (n. 19) 57.

[36] See, for instance, § 460 BGB: 'Der Verkäufer hat einen Mangel nicht zu vertreten, wenn der Käufer den Mangel bei dem Abschlusse des Kaufes kennt'; art. 1642 C. civ. contains a similar provision ('Le vendeur n'est pas tenu des vices apparents et dont l'acheteur a pu se convaincre lui-même'); art. 1482 III c.c. fits the case exactly. The source is D. 19, 1, 1, 1, a decision in which *Ulpian* considers the scope of *bona fides* within the action of sale: 'Haec ita vera sunt, si emptor ignoravit servitutes, quia non videtur esse celatus, qui scit, neque certiorari debuit, qui non ignoravit.'

[37] That *Crassus* should here have stressed the literal meaning is astonishing, since in the so-called *causa Curiana*, which raised a comparable hermeneutical problem, he took the opposite view. That case was concerned with the interpretation of wills, and *Crassus* argued that to rely on the wording alone was insufficient; rather, the testator's true intention should be ascertained and implemented (Cicero, *Brutus: De claris oratoribus* 144 ff., 195 ff.; Cicero, *De oratore* 1, 180; 2, 140 f.; Cicero, *De inventione* 2, 122 etc.). He is alleged to have said 'si verba, non rem sequeremur, convici nihil posset' (Cicero, *De oratore* 1, 243): advocacy was even in Roman times a matter of pragmatism rather than principles. On the problem raised by the *causa Curiana*, see Stroux (n. 8) 42 ff.; Franz Wieacker, (1967) 2 *The Irish Jurist* 151 ff.; G. L. Falchi, 'Interpretazione "tipica" nella "causa Curiana"', *Studia et documenta historiae et iuris* 46 (1980) 383 ff.; Jan W. Tellegen, 'Orators, Iurisprudentes and the "Causa Curiana"', *Revue international des droits de l'antiquité* 30 (1983) 293 ff.

demonstrates that *bona fides* cannot be reduced to a specific *formula* or to legal institutions with specific rules and delimitations but that it constitutes a principle 'das die Pflichten des konkreten Lebensverhältnisses selbst beherrschen will'.[38] It should be noted, however, that *Cicero* does not in fact measure the arguments of plaintiff and defendant against the requirements of *bona fides*, although these were decisive for the decision itself. He rather treats the principle of *bona fides* as an expression of *aequitas*,[39] which has to be used constantly to correct the injustices of the *summum ius*.[40]

III. From the *legis actiones* to the *iudicia bonae fidei*

Although *Cicero* was mainly concerned with the ethical dimension of *bona fides*, his account is also of interest to the legal historian;[41] for it contains a catalogue, directly quoted from Q. M. *Scaevola Pontifex*,[42] of those contractual relationships which in *Cicero's* time were subject to *bona fides*. He includes guardianship (*tutela*), partnership (*societas*), trusts (*fiducia*), mandate (*mandatum*), contracts of sale (*emptio venditio*) as well as hire of a thing or of services and contracts for a piece of work to be done (*locatio conductio*).[43] Similar later catalogues compiled by *Gaius* and *Justinian* do not substantially extend this list.[44] It is however striking that these no longer

---

[38] (That wants to govern the duties of the concrete real life situation itself): Okko Behrends, 'Institutionelles und prinzipielles Denken im römischen Privatrecht', ZSS 95 (1978) 188; Cicero, De officiis 3, 67 is not mentioned by Behrends, but *Sergius'* (*Crassus'*) suggestion is a good example of 'institutional' thinking.

[39] Cicero, De officiis 3, 67 stresses that *Antonius* referred to *aequitas*.

[40] Accurate in this respect is Wolfgang Waldstein, 'Entscheidungsgrundlagen der römischen Juristen', in: *Aufstieg und Niedergang der römischen Welt II (Principat)*, vol. XV (1976) 1 ff. at 76 f., who sees both *fides* and *bona fides* as expressions of a 'natural order', closely related to *aequitas* and *iustitia*.

[41] Similarly Bruno Schmidlin, 'Der verfahrensrechtliche Sinn des ex fide bona im Formularprozeß', in: *De iustitia et iure, Festgabe für Ulrich von Lübtow* (1980) 359 ff. at 365.

[42] For a biography see Friedrich Münzer, RE XVI/1, 437 ff. (s.v. 'Mucius', n. 22).

[43] Cicero, De officiis 3, 70: 'Q. quidem Scaevola, pontifex maximus, summam vim esse dicebat in omnibus iis arbitriis, in quibus adderetur "ex fide bona", fideique bonae nomen existimabat manare latissime, idque versari in tutelis, societatibus, fiduciis, mandatis, rebus emptis, venditis, conductis, locatis, quibus vitae societas contineretur; in iis magni esse iudicis statuere, praesertim cum in plerisque essent iudicia contraria, quid quemque cuique praestare oporteret'; on other catalogues by *Cicero*, see below, section V.

[44] Gaius, Institutiones 4, 62: 'Sunt autem bonae fidei iudicia haec: ex empto vendito, locato conducto, negotiorum gestorum, mandati, depositi, fiduciae, pro socio, tutelae, rei uxoriae'; I. 4, 6, 28: '[B]onae fidei sunt hae: ex empto vendito, locato conducto, negotiorum gestorum, mandati, depositi, pro socio, tutelae, commodati, pigneraticia, familiae erciscundae, communi dividundo ...'

contain the *actio fiduciae*. While the actions granted by the *praetor* for resolving disputes arising out of *tutela, societas, mandatum, emptio venditio* and *locatio conductio* expressly required the judge to assess the claim according to *bona fides*, the *actio fiduciae* was subject to a special clause, which did indeed impose the standard of *bonum*, but did not directly mention *bona fides*. From this important conclusions can be drawn as to the historical development of the law.[45] It is clear from the additional *bonae fidei iudicia* cited by *Gaius* that some actions were not made subject to the requirement of *bona fides* until after *Cicero's* death.[46] *Justinian* even included in his catalogue actions which allowed the judge a similar breadth of discretion as did the *bonae fidei iudicia*, but which did not in fact refer to *bona fides*.[47] This too can be connected to the crucial procedural changes which occurred.[48]

We have little information about legal development before *Cicero's* time, but his account can provide a starting point even for this. *Cicero's* description in the above case of the contrast between the claims that the old *ius civile* provided and the standard of *bona fides* which was inherent in the new *actio empti* relies for its effectiveness on the fact that the dichotomy was still known to his readers. *Wieacker* therefore estimates the emergence of the *bonae fidei iudicia* to have occurred during the second half of the second century BC.[49] *Lombardi*, in contrast, thinks that they did not come into being until 'ai tempi di M. Catone e Q. Mucio', that is until the time of the cases related in *Cicero*, 'De officiis' 3, 66 ff.[50] Others, who would

---

[45] Discussed further below, section IV.

[46] This concerns particularly the *actio negotiorum gestorum* (see Otto Lenel, *Das Edictum Perpetuum – ein Versuch zu seiner Wiederherstellung* (3rd edn, 1927; new edn, 1985) 101 ff.) and the *actio depositi* (see Lenel, ibid., 288 ff.) which were both originally conceived *in factum*; see further below, section III.

[47] Particularly the *actio familiae erciscundae* and the *actio communi dividundo*; the view that these actions contained a *bona fides* clause is rejected by Max Kaser, 'Oportere und ius civile', *ZSS* 83 (1966) 24 f.; for a different view, see Honsell, in: Kunkel (n. 29) 357, n. 4; for further comments see Martin Schermaier, 'Teilvindikation oder Teilungsklage?', *ZSS* 110 (1993) 167 f.

[48] The *cognitio* procedure made it unnecessary for the judge to confine himself to a programme of litigation as contained in the procedural *formula*; the actions of partition contained standards similar to those of the (classical) *bonae fidei iudicia* to enable him to weigh up the claims and counterclaims between the parties; for an account of the classical *cognitio* procedure see Max Kaser, Karl Hackl, *Das römische Zivilprozeßrecht* (2nd edn, 1996) 435 ff. *Justinian's* classicism (for which see, e.g., I. 4, 6, 28) did not alter this; on the post-classical *actio* ibid., 577 ff.

[49] Franz Wieacker, 'Zum Ursprung der bonae fidei iudicia', *ZSS* 80 (1963) 1 ff. at 34.

[50] Luigi Lombardi, *Dalla fides alla bona fides* (1961) 179 ff., quote on p. 180; specifically rejected by Wieacker, *ZSS* 79 (1962) 415.

connect the *bonae fidei iudicia* more closely with the development of the formulary procedure, date their emergence far back into the third century BC.[51] It is not possible to go into this discussion in detail; but in order to understand the procedural role played by *bona fides* a short historical outline is necessary.

The oldest known procedure was later[52] named *legis actio. Lege agere* – literally, act (sue) according to the law – can be understood in two ways. On the one hand, only claims which were recognised by legislation – in the Twelve Tables or by subsequent *plebiscita* – were actionable.[53] On the other hand, the solemn *formulae* through which claims could be laid before the *praetor* were also described as *leges*. There is a close connection between these two interpretations, for the *formulae* were, in general, fixed by statute.[54] Before, by utterance of the correct *formula*, *litis contestatio* could be brought about, and a judge could be appointed to take evidence and decide the case,[55] the *praetor* had to consider whether the law in fact provided a remedy for the plaintiff's grievance. He had no power to create any new actions and was thus tied to the limited number of actions provided for at law. These actions therefore defined which subjective rights were enforceable at law, and together with some rules of customary law[56] they constituted the old *ius civile*.

Probably during the third century BC[57] the *legis actiones* were supple-

---

[51] See, e.g., Mario Talamanca, s.v. 'Vendita (dir. rom.)', *Novissimo digesto italiano* 46 (1993) 303 ff.; Kaser, *ZSS* 101 (1984) 23 ff.; and, following his view, Kaser/Hackl (n. 48) 153 ff.

[52] See Giovanni Pugliese, *Il processo civile romano, vol. I: Le legis actiones* (1961/2) 11 f.

[53] Kaser/Hackl (n. 48) 35.

[54] Though some *legis actiones* may have developed before the introduction of the Twelve Tables; this is certainly true for the *legis actio per pignoris capionem* (cf. Gaius, *Institutiones* 4, 26 f.).

[55] For a detailed discussion of the individual procedural stages, see Kaser/Hackl (n. 48) 64 ff.; also Antonio Guarino, *Diritto privato romano* (7th edn, 1984) 176 ff.

[56] On the contribution of customary law to the *ius civile* see, e.g., Antonio Guarino, 'Mores maiorum', in: *Le origini quiritarie* (1973) 211 ff.; Lucio Bove, *La consuetudine in diritto romano* (1971); Wolfgang Waldstein, 'Gewohnheitsrecht und Juristenrecht in Rom', in: *Festgabe von Lübtow* (n. 41) 106 ff.; numerous references in Walter Selb, in: Kunkel (n. 29) 2, n. 1.

[57] The *lex Aebutia* (Gaius, *Institutiones* 4, 30; Aulus Gellius, *Noctes atticae* 16, 10, 8) admitted actions according to *formulae conceptae* alongside the *legis actiones*; its date of origin is unclear (probably the second century BC). Modern researchers agree that the statute only subsequently recognised the formulary procedure; on the discussion see, e.g., Kaser, *ZSS* 101 (1984) 48 ff. For an account of the formulary procedure before the enactment of the *lex Aebutia*, see Kaser/Hackl (n. 48) 159 f. (with further references); Giovanni Pugliese, *Il processo civile romano, vol. II: Il processo formulare* (1963) 43 ff.; Walter

mented by a new type of procedure: the formulary system.[58] This was no longer reliant on the utterance of ritual phrases by the parties to the dispute; the *agere* of plaintiff and defendant was confined to a free recital of the facts and the submission of both to the procedural *formula* issued by the *praetor*, which established the programme of litigation and appointed a judge to determine the dispute.[59] This judge had to examine the facts of the case as described in the *formula* (*demonstratio*)[60] and pass judgement on the asserted claims and defences (*intentio*). The *formula* also contained instructions as to the judgement (*condemnatio*) should the plaintiff's assertions prove correct. Those *formulae* which superseded the *legis actiones sacramento in personam*[61] were characterised by the fact that the defendant's alleged duty to perform was described as *dare oportere*.[62] This *oportere* referred implicitly to a legal obligation of the defendant; he 'has to' perform, because he is legally obliged to do so. As *Wieacker* states: '[damit wurde] der ritualisierte Klagvortrag der Spruchformel unmittelbar in die objektiv formulierte Urteilsbedingung des Magistrats transponiert'.[63] The *formula* of the *actio certae creditae pecuniae*, the action for the repayment of a specific sum of money, is given[64] as an example of such an *actio civilis*:[65] '*Gaius*[66] iudex esto. Si paret N(umeriu)m N(egidiu)m

---

Selb, 'Zu den Anfängen des Formularverfahrens', in: *Festschrift für Werner Flume I* (1978) 199 ff.; Carlo A. Cannata, 'Introduzione ad una rilettura di Gai. 4, 30–33', in: *Sodalitas, Scritti in onore di Antonio Guarino IV* (1984) 1869 ff.

[58] For a general discussion of the formulary system see Kaser/Hackl (n. 48) 149 ff., especially 172 ff.; Pugliese (n. 57) tom. 1; Franz Wieacker, *Römische Rechtsgeschichte: Quellenkunde, Rechtsbildung, Jurisprudenz und Rechtsliteratur, 1. Abschnitt: Einleitung, Quellenkunde, Frühzeit und Republik* (1988) 447 ff.   [59] But cf. also Selb (n. 57) 199 f.

[60] A *demonstratio* was contained only in actions for a claim the amount of which was still uncertain at the time when the action was brought (actions for an *incertum*).

[61] As this essay is only concerned with contractual claims, only this old *legis actio* is mentioned here, which Gaius, *Institutiones* 4, 16 describes as *generalis*; see Kaser/Hackl (n. 48) 82 and 86 f. For a general discussion as to the modification of the old civil actions by the formulary procedure, see Kaser, *ZSS* 101 (1984) 36 ff.

[62] *Dare oportere* was already a component of the *legis actio sacramento in rem*; cf. Prob. 4, 1.

[63] (The submission of the claim by way of ritualised utterance of the formula was thus transposed directly into the objectively phrased condition for the giving of judgement by the magistrate.) Wieacker (n. 58) 447 f.

[64] See Lenel (n. 46) 237; for the preservation of this formula cf. particularly Gaius, *Institutiones* 4, 41 and 50.

[65] According to the prevailing view the *oportere* is the 'technische Ausdruck für die Obligierung nach *ius civile*': Kaser, *ZSS* 83 (1966) 1; for a different view, see Fritz Sturm, 'Oportere', *ZSS* 82 (1965) 211 ff.

[66] Blanket name for the appointed judge; this was presumably left blank in the *formulae* issued by the *praetor* in his edict.

A(ul)o A(geri)o[67] sestertium decem milia[68] dare oportere, iudex Nm Nm Ao
Ao sestertium decem milia condemna; si non paret, absolve.' (Let *Gaius* be
judge. If it appears that the defendant ought to pay the plaintiff 10,000 *sesterces*, do thou, judge, condemn the defendant to the plaintiff in 10,000 *sesterces*; if it does not appear, absolve.) It was up to the plaintiff to prove the
defendant's obligation to pay the 10,000 *sesterces*. He certainly had to set
forth the source of the obligation (*causa*), although it was not mentioned
in the procedural *formula*. The *formula* was therefore applicable to all
claims for a certain sum of money.[69] As the *dare oportere* indicates, the
causa had to be recognised by statute or customary law in order to ground
an enforceable obligation. If the source of the obligation lay outside the
ius civile then any claims arising could not be enforced by means of this
action. It could not be used, for instance, for lawsuits under a formless
contract of sale. But the arrangement of the *formulae*, which had to be publicly announced each year by the new *praetor*,[70] offered extensive opportunities to expand the list of enforceable actions.

It is not known at what point the edict began to contain actions based
not on the old civil *oportere* but rather on the *oportere ex fide bona*. It can
only be established that in the course of the second century BC, at the
latest, *bona fides* had ceased to be a merely ethical yardstick of contractual
liability and had been incorporated into the praetorian law (*ius honorarium*). It was controversial for a long time whether *bona fides* formed a new
source of obligations[71] or whether it merely supplemented the old civilian
oportere, giving the judge a tool to assess the standard of performance
required.[72] The answer may lie somewhere between these alternatives.[73]
Extra-legal ties based on *fides* undoubtedly existed long before the intro-

---

[67] *Aulus Agerius* is the blanket name for the plaintiff, and *Numerius Negidius* that for the
defendant; the (fictitious) *nomina gentilia* contain the plaintiff's *agere* and the
defendant's denial of the claim (*negare*).

[68] In Gaius, *Institutiones* 4, 41 the alleged debt of 10,000 *sesterces* is contained in the
demonstratio of the *actio certae creditae pecuniae*.

[69] In the form of a *condictio* this *formula* was available for all claims for *certam rem dare*; see
Kaser (n. 13) 592. The *condictio* is the source of modern unjustified enrichment claims.

[70] For an authoritative account of the *praetor*'s office and *iurisdictio*, see Wieacker (n. 58)
429 (with further references).

[71] See especially Wolfgang Kunkel, 'Fides als schöpferisches Element im römischen
Schuldrecht', in: *Festschrift für Paul Koschaker II* (1939) 1 ff., especially 5 ff.

[72] See Wieacker (n. 49) 3, 8, especially 23 ff. (rejecting Kunkel's views (n. 71)) and Antonio
Carcaterra, *Intorni ai bonae fidei iudicia* (1964) 36 ff., 45 ff.; for a critical response to
Carcaterra's views see Franz Wieacker, 'Bonae fidei iudicia', *Labeo* 12 (1966) 250 at 253 f.

[73] Cf. Kaser, *ZSS* 82 (1965) 421 ff.; Kaser (n. 47) 27 f.

duction of the *bonae fidei iudicia*, and so did legal protection for certain older trust relationships. However, for the ideal of *fides* to be legally relevant it had to be set up as the standard of one of the claims protected by a procedural *formula*.[74] That the *praetor* was here merely specifying more closely the civil *oportere* is unlikely given the novelty of the claims.[75] If the *formula* was nevertheless conceived *in ius*, describing the obligation of the plaintiff as *dare facere oportere*,[76] it may be assumed that the *praetor* regarded *fides* as a new source of obligations, separate from the actions of the older *ius civile*.

Cicero's case of the dishonest seller provides a good example of the advantages of the *bonae fidei iudicia* over the strict civil law action. Their procedural requirements appear from the *formula* of the buyer's action, the *actio empti*,[77] as mentioned by *Cicero*: 'Gaius iudex esto. Quod AsAs de NoNo domum qua de agitur emit, qua de re agitur, quidquid ob eam rem NmNm AoAo dare facere oportet ex fide bona, eius iudex NmNm AoAo condemna, si non paret, absolve.' (Let *Gaius* be judge. Whereas the plaintiff bought from the defendant the house which is the object of this action, which sale is the matter involved in this case, whatever on that account the defendant ought in good faith to pay to or do for the plaintiff, in that much do thou judge condemn the defendant to the plaintiff; if it does not so appear, absolve him.) Here, too, judgement against the defendant took the form of a specific sum of money to be paid, since the duty established as owed to the plaintiff was assessed in monetary terms.[78] However, in assessing the value of the performance owed, the judge was bound neither by a specific sum asserted by the plaintiff (as in the *actio certae creditae pecuniae*, described above) nor by a set of pre-established

---

[74] See Kaser, *ZSS* 83 (1966) 28, n. 132; similarly Pringsheim (n. 9) 204 and now also Schmidlin (n. 41) 369.

[75] Gisbert Noordraven, *De fiducia in het Romeinse recht* (1988) 349 ff., for instance, finds no evidence of the *legis actiones* encompassing breach of *fiducia*.

[76] This is, for instance, still controversial in respect of the *actio fiduciae*; cf., e.g., Lenel (n. 46) 291 ff.; Kaser, *ZSS* 83 (1966) 26; Kaser, 'Studien zum römischen Pfandrecht II: Actio pigneraticia und actio fiduciae', *Tijdschrift voor rechtsgeschiedenis* 47 (1979) 319 ff. (= *Studien zum römischen Pfandrecht* (1982) 99 ff.); for different views, see Carcaterra (n. 72) 32 ff.; Alan Watson, *The Law of Obligations in the Later Roman Republic* (1965) 172 ff. (still undecided in: 'The Origins of Fiducia', *ZSS* 79 (1962) 329 at 332 f.); and now Noordraven (n. 75) 363 ff. (reconstruction 413); with whom Felix Wubbe, *ZSS* 108 (1991) 521 agrees.

[77] See Lenel (n. 46) 299.

[78] *Omnis condemnatio pecuniaria*; cf. D. 42, 1, 6, 1; D. 2, 9, 5; on this principle (especially within the formulary procedure) see Kaser/Hackl (n. 48) 371 ff. (with further references).

rules.[79] He was free to consider the claim himself and to assess, according to the principles of good faith, whether and to what extent the claim was substantiated. In this way the *officium* of the judge was extended from fact-finding and merely applying the terms of the *formula* to these facts to an assessment of the legal merits of the case. A significant element of the *praetor's* task was thereby transferred to the judge.[80] He did, of course, have to confine himself to the *formula* issued by the *praetor*, but the *bona fides* clause allowed him to shape its substantive content. Thus, it became possible to soften the old, rigidly formalised actions with reference to equitable considerations in order to achieve just results.[81]

Claims based on *bona fides* could only be enforced through the formulary procedure as they had no statutory basis.[82] The formulary process was therefore an essential precondition to the development of the *bonae fidei iudicia*. That the two evolved simultaneously is, however, unlikely.

---

[79] Such as in those cases where the judge was required to ascertain the value of the object of the claim (*quanti ea res est/erit/fuit*); see Max Kaser, *Quanti ea res est* (1935); and more recently Sebastiano Tafaro, *La interpretatio ai verba 'quanti ea res est' nella giurisprudenza romana* (1980); Kaser/Hackl (n. 48) 317 f.

[80] The *bonae fidei iudicia*, therefore, represent an important landmark in the historical evolution from the procedure *in sacramento* via the older formulary to the *cognitio* procedure. In contract law, one had managed to incorporate *fides* into the *formulae* and thereby integrate it into the normal procedure. The result was merely an extension of the judicial *officium*. The formalism of the law of inheritance made it, however, impossible to enforce an informal appeal to the heir's 'faith' (*fideicommissum*); this led during the early classical period to the development of a second procedural avenue, the *extraordinaria cognitio*. So far the emergence of the *bonae fidei iudicia* has been explained with reference to the need for a more elastic evaluation of an *incertum*: see, for example, Wieacker, *ZSS* 80 (1963) 34; Schmidlin (n. 41) 359 ff. The parallel example of the development of the *cognitio* procedure however shows that Roman lawyers were principally concerned with taking account of the extra-legal fiduciary relationships. For a general account of the *cognitio* procedure, see Kaser/Hackl (n. 48) 435 ff., on its development in connection with *fideicommissum* ibid. 452 f.; and see David Johnston, *The Roman Law of Trusts* (1988) especially 273 ff.

[81] This phenomenon can be compared with the alteration of the medieval writ system by means of Equity, though only the development of the *extraordinaria cognitio* within the framework of the law relating to *fideicommissa* bears a direct comparison to the writ/Equity dualism (cf. n. 80). The reserved attitude adopted by Hans Peter, *Actio und Writ: Eine vergleichende Darstellung römischer und englischer Rechtsbehelfe* (1957) 88 f. is therefore appropriate. The growing strain on the general clauses of the BGB, on the other hand, is independent of procedural prerequisites; see above, section I.

[82] Cicero, *De officiis* 3, 61 expressly refers to the *bonae fidei iudicia* as *iudicia sine lege*; cf., however, Gaius, *Institutiones* 3, 10: 'Quaedam praeterea sunt actiones, quae ad legis actiones exprimuntur, quaedam sua vi ac potestate constant.' For an account of the different views, see Kaser, *ZSS* 83 (1966) 27 and *ZSS* 101 (1984) 24.

Otherwise why would actions have developed that were neither conceived *in ius* nor subject to *bona fides*?[83] Apart from that, it must be noted that different impulses lay behind the introduction of the formulary system and the development of the *bonae fidei iudicia*. Concerning the former, the influx of foreign traders has rightly been emphasised,[84] since *lege agere* was confined to Roman citizens.[85] The *bonae fidei iudicia*, on the other hand, as *Wieacker* has shown,[86] did not originate in legal relations between foreigners and Roman citizens.[87] For while it is true that *bona fides* bound Roman citizens and foreigners equally, and that it was, therefore, a source of obligations according to the *ius gentium* to which all people were subject, this is in itself no reason to place the origin of the *bonae fidei iudicia* in legal proceedings relating to *peregrini* (non-Romans). *Fides* and *bona fides* are just as much Roman concepts as the concept of *ius gentium* itself; they are therefore to be interpreted on the basis of the Roman experience.

IV. From *fides* to *bona fides*

The fact that the application of the new procedural *formula* did not lead to uncertainty and arbitrariness was due to a concrete and uniform understanding of what accorded with both *fides* and *bona fides*. This understanding, central to the use of the *bonae fidei iudicia*, was rooted in Roman social ethics recognising comprehensive duties of fidelity and faithfulness and encompassing both citizens and non-citizens. The way in which these duties were extended from *fides* to *bona fides*, however, is largely unclear.[88]

---

[83] So-called *formulae in factum conceptae* for *rem redditam non esse* as in the case of the *actiones commodati, pigneraticia* and *depositi* (cf. Gaius, *Institutiones* 4, 47); see Lenel (n. 46) 252 ff., 254 ff. and 288 ff. A later *bonae fidei iudicium* was introduced for deposit and probably also for lending (cf. again Gaius, *Institutiones* 4, 47); for a brief discussion, see Max Kaser, *Ius gentium* (1993) 145 f.

[84] On the *praetor peregrinus*, see Wieacker (n. 58) 438 ff.; Feliciano Serrao, *La jurisdictio del pretore peregrino* (1954); Kaser, ZSS 101 (1984) 15 ff.

[85] For further details, see Kaser/Hackl (n. 48) 61 f.; Wieacker (n. 58) 439 f.; Kaser, ZSS 101 (1984) 16 f.

[86] Wieacker, ZSS 80 (1963) 9 ff.; for a reinforcement of his arguments see (n. 58) 442 f.; cf. also André Magdelain, 'Gaius IV 10 et 33: Naissance de la procédure formulaire', *Tijdschrift voor rechtsgeschiedenis* 59 (1991) 239 at 248 f. and also Kaser (n. 83) 143 ff.

[87] For an account of the content and significance of the old Roman fiduciary relationships, see immediately below, section IV.

[88] Even Lombardi's research with its promising title 'Dalla fides alla bona fides' (n. 50) could not provide a historical explanation; cf. also the scepticism expressed by Dieter Nörr, *Die Fides im römischen Völkerrecht* (1991) 43.

Whereas *fides* was understood as remaining faithful to one's word,[89] *bona fides* was applied to ascertain the content of contracts concluded. Faithfulness to one's word is a precondition of any legal intercourse, and *Cicero* therefore describes it as *fundamentum iustitiae*.[90] *Bona fides* in comparison does not demand performance itself, but by requiring the parties to act honestly, influences the way performance is made.

Our efforts to understand the development are not facilitated by the fact that the concept of *fides* carried several different meanings. In Roman (public) international law the subjugation to Roman domination was described as *deditio in fidem*.[91] At the same time, in international treaties and in the law relating to diplomatic relations, *fides* was emphasised as being true to one's word.[92] International treaties were kept in the temple dedicated to the goddess *Fides*,[93] built 'in the middle of the third century'[94] next to that of *Dius Fidius*.[95,96] The *fides* of the (Roman) conqueror in respect

---

[89] Cicero, *De officiis* 1, 23: 'credamus . . . , quia fiat, quod dictum est, appellatam fides'; similarly Cicero, *De republica* 4, 7; Cicero, *Epistulae ad familiares* 16, 10, 2; on the value of keeping one's word Cicero, *De officiis* 3, 102 ff. Still worth reading, in this context, is Fritz Schulz, *Prinzipien des römischen Rechts* (1954) 151 ff.; valuable philological insights are offered by Eduard Fraenkel, 'Zur Geschichte des Wortes fides', *Rheinisches Museum für Philologie* 71 (1916) 187 ff. and Richard Heinze, 'Fides', *Hermes: Zeitschrift für klassische Philologie* 1929, 140 ff.

[90] Cicero, *De officiis* 1, 23 states: 'Fundamentum autem est iustitiae fides, id est dictorum conventorumque constantia et veritas'; ibid., 3, 104 is similar. *Fides* and *iustitia* are also mentioned together in ibid., 3, 79 and 98 and treated as virtually equivalent.

[91] Dieter Nörr, *Aspekte des römischen Völkerrechts: Die Bronzetafel von Alcántara* (1989) 94 ff. describes an example of a *deditio* related in Polybios 20, 9–10; for a discussion of the nature and function of *deditio*, see also Karl-Heinz Ziegler, 'Das Völkerrecht der römischen Republik', in: *Aufstieg und Niedergang der römischen Welt*, vol. I 2 (1972) 68 at 94 ff.; Nörr (n. 88) 13 ff. (both with further references).

[92] References to sources are omitted here; see Nörr (n. 91) 102 ff.

[93] For an account of the *Fides* cult see Kurt Latte, *Römische Religionsgeschichte* (1960) 237; Otto, 'Fides', *RE VI*, 2281 ff.; Giulia Piccaluga, 'Fides nella religione romana di età imperiale', in: *Aufstieg und Niedergang der römischen Welt*, vol. II 17/2 (1981) 703 ff.; cf. also Antonio Carcaterra, 'Dea fides e "fides" – storia di una laicizzazione', *Studia et documenta historiae et iuris* 50 (1984) 199 ff.

[94] Nörr (n. 91) 110 and Latte (n. 93) 237, n. 1; the building is dated at 250 BC by Luigi Amirante, 'L'origine dei contratti di bouna fede', in: *Atti del seminario sulla problematica contrattuale in diritto romano*, vol. I (1988) 81 at 82.

[95] Cf. Cicero, *De officiis* 3, 104 and *De natura deorum* 2, 61; for a full account, see Latte (n. 93) 126 ff.

[96] While *Dius Fidius*, i.e. *Jupiter*, as invoked under oath (cf., for instance, *Ennius* in Cicero, *De officiis* 3, 104: 'O Fides alma apta pinnis et ius iurandum Iovis'; extensive evidence has been collected by Roberto Fiori, *Homo sacer: Dinamica politico-costituzionale di una sanzione guiridico-religiosa* (1996) 155 ff.), harked back to an old cult, *Fides* was probably an

of those who had placed themselves under the protection of that *fides* seems, however, difficult to reconcile with this meaning ('fidelity of contract'). *Beseler* has attempted to reconcile semasiologically 'protection and leniency towards one's subjects' with 'fidelity of contract': he who surrenders is bound by his captor; and this 'binding' was transferred to being bound by one's word.[97] *Lombardi* and *Wieacker* believe that the notion of *fides* as 'protection of one's subjects' preceded that of keeping one's promises,[98] whereas *Nörr*, following *Heinze*, maintains that *fides* always combined two meanings: trust and trustworthiness.[99] These two meanings, one of them active and the other passive, correspond here to the notions of keeping one's word and displaying consideration and leniency towards those under one's protection.

This dualism can also be found within the private law. The protective relationship in public international law described above was repeated, essentially, in the structure of the relationship between a patron and his freed slave,[100] and between a patron and his clients;[101] even the relationship arising out of a letter of recommendation could be described as one of trust.[102] The duties of care and protection characterising these relationships can similarly be found in some of the old fiduciary relationships

---

idolisation of the concept of *fides*; see Nörr (n. 91) 110 f.; conversely: Carcaterra, *Studia et documenta historiae et iuris* 50 (1984) 199, esp. 231 ff.; for the theory that the *Fides* cult developed out of the *Jupiter* cult, see Fiori, ibid., 148 ff.

[97] Georg v. Beseler, 'Fides', in: *Atti del congresso internazionale di diritto romano*, vol. I (1934) 133 ff., esp. 143 ff. Beseler invokes a series of symbols, from the *stipula* in a *stipulatio* to the exchanging of rings in a marriage ceremony; for a critical response, see Wieacker, *ZSS* 80 (1963) 25 f.; for a similar view (without reference to Beseler) see now Carcaterra, *Studia et documenta historiae et iuris* 50 (1984) 199 at 201 ff. (*fides* as *vinculum religionis*).

[98] Lombardi (n. 50) makes a fundamental distinction between 'fides come potere' (47 ff.) and 'fides come promessa' (105 ff.); Wieacker, *ZSS* 80 (1963) 20 ff., esp. 27 ('Schonung des sich Unterwerfenden', 'Schutz für den Hilfesuchenden, ohne welchen auch die frühesten Gesellschaften nicht bestehen können').

[99] Nörr (n. 91) 150; Heinze (n. 89) 140, esp. 150 ff. A similar phenomenon can be observed with respect to the development of the German 'Treu und Glauben': see Hans-Wolfgang Strätz, *Treu und Glauben: Beiträge und Materialien zur Entwicklung von 'Treu und Glauben' in deutschen Privatrechtsquellen vom 13. bis zur Mitte des 17. Jahrhunderts* (1974) 98 ff.

[100] For a recent detailed discussion of the legal relationship between *patronus* and *libertus*, see Wolfgang Waldstein, *Operae libertorum* (1986).

[101] Cf. Schulz (n. 89) 157; Kunkel (n. 71) 5.

[102] For a detailed discussion supported by extensive evidence see Matthias Gelzer, *Die Nobilität der römischen Republik* (2nd edn, 1983) 52 ff., esp. 54 f.; on the connection between *fides* and *amicitia*, and the interpretation even of private friendship as a permanent fiduciary relationship, see Schulz (n. 89) 158 ff.

which later became actionable with the development of the *bonae fidei iudicia*. These include the relationships between guardian and ward (*tutela*), between transferor and transferee under a *fiducia*, between *mandator* and *mandatarius*,[103] and finally the old *societas omnium bonorum*, the partnership that was modelled on a community of heirs.[104] These relationships were not marked by a particular emphasis on 'keeping one's word'. They rather reflected very specific ideas of how the contracting parties should behave towards each other: the *mandatarius* had to endeavour loyally to fulfil his mandate; a *tutor* had to administer his ward's affairs as if they were his own; the transferee under a *fiducia*, although acquiring ownership, had to keep the object according to the terms of the fiduciary agreement and to return it; among the members of a *societas* (*omnium bonorum*) all dispositions of one of them had effect for and against all others which both presupposed and entailed a high degree of honesty among the *socii*. It is remarkable that except for the *fiducia* the duties arising from these relationships were originally not enforceable.[105] One could only place one's reliance in the *fides* of one's partner.[106]

In his address 'Pro Caecina' and in his 'Topica' *Cicero* lists only these four contracts as *contractus bonae fidei*,[107] while the catalogue he cites in 'De

---

[103] There is an obvious similarity between the 'Empfehlungsschreiben' (recommendations) mentioned by Gelzer (n. 102) and the contract of mandate. This is particularly clear in Cicero, *Epistulae ad familiares* 7, 5, 3, where he recommends the jurist *Trebatius* to *Caesar* with the words: 'totum denique hominem tibi ita trado de manu ut aiunt in manum'.

[104] For an account of *tutela* see Kaser (n. 13) 85 ff. and 352 ff.; of *fiducia* 460 ff.; of *mandate* 577 ff., and of *societas* and its various stages of development 572 ff. Wieacker, *ZSS* 80 (1963) 27 f. also counts – with some justification – the obligations arising from *dos* (dowry), among the old fiduciary relationships (28).

[105] A criminal action could be brought against a *tutor* (*accusatio suspecti tutoris*), and a claim for the settling of accounts could be instituted after the end of the *tutela* (*actio de rationibus distrahendis*), but a duty carefully to administer the ward's affairs could not be enforced by the *actio tutelae* until the later Republic. If a *socius* of a *societas omnium bonorum* fell into disagreement with the other members, then his only option was an action of division by means of which the *societas* was dissolved. Only the *actio pro socio* provided an opportunity for a settlement of accounts (later even *manente societate*). No precursor of the *actio mandati* is known; the 'civil law protection' mentioned by Wieacker, *ZSS* 80 (1963) 30 did not, therefore, concern itself with breach of faith.

[106] For an account of mandate see particularly Okko Behrends, 'Die "bona fides" im "mandatum"', in: *Ars boni et aequi, Festschrift für Wolfgang Waldstein* (1993) 33 ff. and Dieter Nörr, 'Mandatum, fides, amicitia', in: Dieter Nörr, Shigeo Nishimura (eds.), *Mandatum und Verwandtes: Beiträge zum römischen und modernen Recht* (1993) 13 ff.; on *fiducia* see, apart from Noordraven (n. 75) and Johnston (n. 80), Béla Kemenes, 'Das "fides"-Prinzip und sein Zusammenhang mit der "fiducia"', in: *Studi Pólay* (1985) 245 ff.

[107] Cicero, *Oratio pro A. Caecina* 3, 7; *Topica* 42, though the latter does also not include *tutela*.

officiis' (mentioned above) and that in 'De natura deorum' also contain *emptio venditio* and *locatio conductio.*[108] By comparing the catalogues it becomes clear, however, that in his philosophical writings *Cicero* was concerned with comprehensiveness, from the legal point of view,[109] while his other lists were written with different aims. In 'Pro Caecina' *Cicero* is seeking to establish a specific duty of loyalty based on the older fiduciary relationships and thus refers back to the original ones. Even more markedly in the 'Topica' he merely wishes to illustrate his argument that if guardians, partners, agents and fiduciaries are under an obligation to act loyally then this should by analogy also be extended to appointed business managers.[110] A further important sign for the special substantive qualification of the fiduciary relationship in trust, mandate, guardianship and partnership was that condemnation for breach of trust involved *infamia.*[111]

The formal duty to keep one's word lacked this specific content with its corresponding sanction. Merely breaking one's word did not lead to *infamia* but triggered a contractual action which, as in the verbal contract[112] *stipulatio,*[113] could be an action *stricti iuris. Fides* as 'fiat, quod dictum est'[114] can therefore hardly have been the only inspiration for the *bonae*

---

[108] Cicero, *De officiis* 3, 70 (cf. above, section II); *De natura deorum* 3, 74. For a discussion of these texts see Amirante (n. 94) 85; and, particularly, Okko Behrends, 'Die Wissenschaftslehre im Zivilrecht des Q. Mucius Scaevola pontifex', in: *Nachrichten der Akademie der Wissenschaft Göttingen, philologisch-historische Klasse* (1976) 263 ff. at 294 ff.

[109] In *De officiis* he cites the jurist Q. Scaevola Pontifex; in *De natura deorum* he reports (through the voice of C. Aurelius Cotta) on the daily work of the *praetor; emptio venditio* and *locatio conductio* are here treated clearly independently of the old *fides*-relationships (*De natura deorum* 3, 74: ' . . . inde tot iudicia de fide mala, tutelae, mandati, pro socio, fiduciae, reliqua, quae ex empto aut vendito aut conducto aut locato contra fidem fiunt . . .').

[110] Cicero, *Topica* 42: 'Sunt enim similitudines quae ex pluribus collationis perveniunt quo volunt hoc modo: Si tutor fidem praestare debet, si socius, si cui mandaris, si qui fiduciam acceperit, debet etiam procurator.'

[111] For an account of the social and legal consequences of *infamia* see Kaser (n. 13) 274 f.

[112] Verbal contracts were formal promises, often reliant on ritual phrases; the most important form was the *stipulatio.* When *Cicero* in his example of the deceitful house-seller stresses that the latter according to the *ius civile* was only liable for express undertakings (Cicero, *De officiis* 3, 65; above, section II), he refers to a pertinent *dictum* that could be made in the course of mancipating a piece of real property, the so-called *lex mancipio dicta*; see, e.g., Valentin-Al. Georgescu, *Essai d'une théorie générale des leges privatae* (1932) 46 ff. and 144 ff.; Olde Kalter (n. 19) 9 ff.

[113] For an account of *sponsio-stipulatio* see Kaser (n. 13) 168 ff. and 661 ff.; Honsell, in: Kunkel (n. 29) 106 ff. and 294 ff.; Reinhard Zimmermann, *The Law of Obligations: Roman Foundations of the Civilian Tradition* (1990, paperback edn, 1996) 117 ff.; Guarino (n. 55) 740 ff. (all with further references) and Piere Cornioley, 'De la "sponsio" à la stipulatio: Procedure et "contrat"', in: *Sodalitas* (n. 57) VI (1984) 2891 ff.

[114] Cf. Cicero, *De officiis* 1, 23.

fidei iudicia. They were rather marked by the fiduciary relationships described above in which a specific standard of behaviour could be expected which was based on the ethical values of society.[115] The qualification of *fides* as *bona fides* emphasises the substantive specificity of that standard of behaviour: it is the *bene agere* of the Roman citizen who acted carefully and prudently and who respected the interests of his contractual partner – who acted as *bonus vir*.[116] That the adjective *bonus* is to be understood as determining the contents of a binding promise[117] is made even clearer by the fact that the old part of the *formula* of the *actio fiduciae* demanded the *bene agere* of the trustee.[118] As this demand corresponded to the classical standard of *bona fides*[119] it seems reasonable to assume that the *actio fiduciae* was a precursor of the *bonae fidei iudicia*. From early times the *arbitrium boni viri* was seen to be an independent verdict of an arbitrator which took into consideration the interests of both parties.[120] As *Schmidlin* has emphasised, the latter point indicates that the *bonae fidei iudicia* were intended to provide the opportunity to weigh up both parties' interests in assessing an enforceable claim.[121]

This brings us back to the historical development of *bona fides*. Research, however, has not yet come up with a satisfactory explanation of how *bona fides* became the basis and the yardstick of praetorian actions. The three central elements of the classical *bona fides*, i.e. the substantive determination of the old fiduciary relationships (*bene agere*), the binding nature of

[115] In this respect Wieacker's view (*ZSS* 80 (1963) 29 ff.) is convincing.
[116] See Schmidlin (n. 41) 362 ff.   [117] Similarly Nörr (n. 91) 153.
[118] Cicero, *De officiis* 3, 70 mentions two parts of the *formula*, one of which refers to *fides* and the other, in the same sense, to *bene agere*: (i) *Uti ne propter te fidemve tuam captus fraudatusve sim*, (ii) *Ut inter bonos bene agier oportet et sine fraudatione*. According to nearly universal opinion only the second sentence was part of the *actio fiduciae*; cf. the literature noted above, n. 76.
[119] Cicero (*De officiis* 3, 70) can therefore count them among the *bonae fidei iudicia* (see too Cicero, *De natura deorum* 3, 74; cf. also Cicero, *De officiis* 3, 61); and see, above all, Nicla Bellocci, *La tutela della fiducia nell'epoca repubblicana* (1974) 61 ff.
[120] See, e.g., M. Porcius Cato, *De agri cultura* 144, 6 and 145, 9; examples in Schmidlin (n. 41) 363 and Gerardo Broggini, *Iudex arbiterve: Prolegomena zum officium des römischen Privatrichters* (1957) 115. The clearest text from the classical period is probably D. 19, 2, 24: 'nam fides bona exigit, ut arbitrium tale praestetur, quale viro bono convenit'.
[121] Characteristic is Gaius, *Institutiones* 3, 137: 'Item in his contractibus alter alteri obligatur de eo quod alterum alteri ex bono et aequo praestare oportet, cum alioquin in verborum obligationibus alius stipuletur alius promittat et in nominibus alius expensum ferendo obliget alius obligetur'; see Schmidlin (n. 41) 365.

even an informal promise, and the *officium* of the judge who had to balance both parties' interests,[122] provided, however, the pattern for the development of the *bonae fidei iudicia*.[123] To what extent their emergence was aided by the need for actions which allowed the judge to consider both parties' claims is particularly difficult to gauge. The fact that they were a conscious creation of the *praetor* covering several types of contracts suggests that they may indeed have been the result of critical reflection and policy interests. The old action of partition,[124] the defences granted by the *praetor*[125] and, particularly, the *actiones fiduciae* and *rei uxoriae*[126] enabled, in fact required, the judge to weigh up both sides of the dispute even in earlier times. Here, it may be presumed, lie the historical roots of the expansion of the *officium iudicis*.[127]

V. Advances in the substantive law

This expansion of the judicial discretion in assessing the merits of a case lay at the heart of the brilliant development of Roman contract law from

---

[122] Worthy of note is Broggini's theory (n. 120) 194, esp. 218 ff., that would trace the free balancing of interests, as permitted by the *bonae fidei iudicia*, back to the proceedings before an elected arbitrator (*arbiter*). For an investigation into the roots of Roman arbitration see André Magdelain, 'Aspects arbitraux de la justice civile archaique à Rome', *Revue international des droits de l'antiquité* 27 (1980) 205 ff.

[123] The same view is taken by Wieacker, ZSS 80 (1963) 40.

[124] Especially the *actio familiae erciscundae* for dissolving a community of heirs and the *societas omnium bonorum* (modelled on the former and regarded by *Cicero* as one of the old fiduciary relationships; cf. above, nn. 103 ff.).

[125] The introduction of the *exceptio doli* may be related to the creation of the *actio de dolo* by C. Aquilius Gallus (cf. Cicero, De officiis 3, 60; De natura deorum 3, 74; D. 4, 3, 1, 2); an earlier form is mentioned in Cicero, Epistulae ad Atticum 6, 1, 15: 'extra quam si ita negotium gestum est, ut eo stari non oporteat ex fide bona'. For a discussion of the age and wording of the *exceptio doli* cf. the literature cited by Kaser (n. 13) 488 f. and Kaser/Hackl (n. 48) 261 ff.

[126] The *actio rei uxoriae* allowed the person who had provided a dowry to reclaim it if the marriage failed; the judge could within his *officium* take into account deduction rights of the husband (or the children). The plaintiff could only recover *quod aequius melius est*; see Kaser (n. 13) 336 ff. On the classification of the *actio rei uxoriae* as a *bonae fidei iudicium* see, above all, Alfred Söllner, *Zur Vorgeschichte und Funktion der actio rei uxoriae* (1969) 135 ff., on its *formula* esp. 137 ff.; it should be noted that Wieacker, ZSS 80 (1963) 28, for instance, also classifies the dotal law among the old *fides* relationships (see n. 104 above).

[127] The *actio fiduciae*, in particular, may – as even Kaser finally admitted – represent an early stage in the development of the *bonae fidei iudicia*; cf. Kaser, *Tijdschrift voor rechtsgeschiedenis* 47 (1979) 320 f. and his later article ZSS 101 (1984) 31, n. 135.

the time of the late Republic until the end of the classical period.[128] Before the introduction of the *bonae fidei iudicia* the judge was confined to determining whether the claim asserted under the procedural *formula* did or did not exist. The *bona fide* clause enabled him to consider the parties' relationship 'in seinem Entstehen und in allen seinen Auswirkungen, im Gesamtrahmen der Umstände und des Verhaltens der Parteien'.[129] This took place under the auspices of a general value system, by means of which the excessive procedural formalism was broken up. At the same time, substantive rules were created which have become an integral part of our modern understanding of the law.

A mere comparison of the wording of the procedural *formula* makes clear the fundamental difference between *bonae fidei iudicia* and the actions *stricti iuris*. In considering whether and to what extent the defendant's duty to perform accorded with *bona fides* the judge would include any defences which the former could raise against the claim. In the actions *stricti iuris*, in contrast, the defendant had to ask in the pre-trial hearing before the *praetor* (*in iure*) that his defences (*exceptiones*) be incorporated into the *formula*.[130] If, for instance, a creditor had given his debtor extra time to pay (*pactum de non petendo*) but then nevertheless started proceedings against him, it was up to the debtor to ensure that the *praetor* added an *exceptio pacti* into the *formula* of the *actio certae creditae pecuniae*. The judge could then not pass judgement against the debtor if it was shown that payment of the debt had indeed been deferred.[131] But if the debtor had neglected to request an *exceptio*, the judge was unable to take his defence into account during the trial (*apud iudicem*). The judge was bound by the wording of the *actio certae creditae pecuniae* which did not direct him to take account of a *pactum de non petendo*.

The approach under a *bonae fidei iudicium* was completely different. Here the judge was required to take account of all arrangements between plaintiff and defendant in assessing the defendant's duty to perform. Informal

---

[128] That the *bonae fidei iudicia* represented a decisive step in overcoming the old formalism as early as the pre-classical period is confirmed by the cases reported by *Cicero* (above, section II); the period in question here thus covers around 300 years, from the beginning of the first century BC to the beginning of the third century AD.

[129] (. . . in its origin and all its effects, within the framework of all surrounding circumstances and the conduct of the parties.) See Alexander Beck, 'Zu den Grundprinzipien der bona fides im römischen Vertragsrecht', in: *Aequitas und bona fides: Festgabe für August Simonius* (1955) 9 ff. at 18.

[130] For the technical details, see Kaser/Hackl (n. 48) 260 ff.

[131] Kaser/Hackl (n. 48) 260 f. therefore describe the *exceptio* as a 'negative Kondemnationsbedingung'; further references are given at 320.

ancillary agreements (*pacta adiecta*), for example the *pactum protimiseos*[132] or a provision for calling off a sale,[133] were even independently actionable with the *iudicium* of the main contract. The same applied where additional obligations were undertaken under the contract; interest, which had to be specifically stipulated for under an obligation *stricti iuris*, was automatically awarded according to the *bona fides*.[134] At the same time *bona fides* also limited the amount of interest which the creditor could claim: thus, for instance, it was *contra bonam fidem* if he demanded interest for the time before the debtor was *in mora*.[135] Within the *bonae fidei iudicia* it was also possible to offset any counterclaims arising out of the same legal relationship against the main award (*compensatio*).[136] This was not permitted in respect of an *actio stricti iuris*; the only option was for the defendant to bring a cross-action. According to a rescript of *Marcus Aurelius* the defendant was allowed, at least, to introduce his counterclaim into the proceedings by means of an *exceptio doli*.[137]

The development of liability for latent defects in the law of sale is a particularly clear illustration of the influence of *bona fides*:[138] the seller was not merely liable for express assurances but also for fraudulently concealing a defect.[139] The *formula* of the *actio empti* also made it possible to integrate the aedilitian remedies into the law of sale and to subject even innocent sellers to a liability involving either redhibition or reduction of the price.[140] This was the basis for *Julian's* distinction between the position of an innocent seller who faced redhibition or a reduction of the price,

---

[132] Compare D. 18, 1, 75; D. 19, 1, 21, 5.

[133] For a general discussion on provisions for calling off a sale, see Kaser (n. 13) 561 f.; Frank Peters, *Die Rücktrittsvorbehalte im römischen Kaufrecht* (1973); Zimmermann (n. 113) 735 ff.

[134] D. 22, 1, 32, 2: 'In bonae fidei contractibus ex mora usurae debentur'; for further comment, see Kaser (n. 13) 487 f.   [135] D. 16, 3, 24.

[136] Gaius, *Institutiones* 4, 61 ff.; on which, see Beck (n. 129) 22 f.; Kaser (n. 13) 644 ff.; Detlev Liebs, *Römisches Recht* (4th edn, 1993) 296 ff.

[137] Cf. I. 4, 6, 30.

[138] Cf. also, in the perspective of doctrinal history, Bruno Huwiler, 'Die Vertragsmäßigkeit der Ware: Romanistische Gedanken zu Art. 35 und 45 ff. des Wiener Kaufrechts', *Wiener Kaufrecht Berner Tage für die juristische Praxis 1990* (1991) 249 ff. at 296 ff.

[139] In the law of sale (D. 19, 1, 4 pr.; D. 19, 1, 6, 9; D. 19, 1, 11, 5 *passim*) as well as in the law of lease (D. 19, 2, 23).

[140] The *actio redhibitoria* and the *actio quanti minoris* were granted by the *aediles curules*, who issued their own edict within their area of responsibility (market police and supervision of the market place). As a result, these claims were only available for market sales of slaves and beasts of burden; for details see Kaser (n. 13) 558 ff.; Zimmermann (n. 113) 311 ff. and 319 ff.

and that of the *venditor sciens* who was liable for consequential loss;[141] in certain cases an assurance was even imputed and a seller held liable despite his ignorance of the defect.[142] A similar expansion of the seller's liability can be observed in the rules relating to liability for eviction. The buyer usually only had a remedy once a third party had successfully asserted his proprietary right over the object of sale,[143] but sometimes a claim for the purchaser's interest in acquiring ownership in the object sold was granted against a seller who had knowingly sold an object which did not belong to him even before eviction.[144]

The *bonae fidei iudicia* were used predominantly to sanction fraudulent behaviour.[145] *Cicero* describes the standard of *bona fides* – the notion of *bene agere* – as the conceptual opposite of fraudulent behaviour.[146] This had two procedural consequences. Any act of *dolus* would usually result in judgement against the guilty party, irrespective of whether it occurred in the process of contracting or was committed by means of instituting the proceedings. In the late classical period the action for *dolus in contrahendo* was even granted when a contract was invalid due to initial impossibility of performance.[147] Conversely, the judge would not allow a contractual action brought by the fraudulent party to succeed. The *exceptio doli* was

[141] D. 19, 1, 13 pr.; this corresponds to §§ 463, 480 II BGB; the provisions of §§ 932 I, 1295 I ABGB, on the other hand, go much further.

[142] For instance the famous case of the sale of a defective vessel, D. 19, 1, 6, 4 (similarly for the lease of a vessel, D. 19, 2, 19, 1); cf. Zimmermann (n. 113) 320 f.; Peter Apathy, 'Sachgerechtigkeit und Systemdenken am Beispiel der Entwicklung von Sachmängelhaftung und Irrtum beim Kauf im klassischen römischen Recht', ZSS 111 (1994) 95 ff.

[143] The so-called 'eviction principle'; for an overview, see Kaser (n. 13) 353 ff.; Zimmermann (n. 113) 293 ff.

[144] D. 19, 1, 30, 1; this decision, too, can be traced back to *Julian*; cf. Frank Peters, 'Die Verschaffung des Eigentums durch den Verkäufer', ZSS 96 (1979) 197 ff.; also Liebs (n. 136) 271 ff., who refers to D. 19, 1, 43 and 45.

[145] For instance D. 19, 1, 6, 9 ('. . . aestimari oportet dolum malum eius, quem semper abesse oportet in iudicio empti, quod bonae fidei sit'); D. 19, 1, 37 ('Sicut aequum est bonae fidei emptori alterius dolum non nocere, ita non est aequum eidem personae venditoris sui dolum prodesse').

[146] Cicero, *De officiis* 3, 61 (for instance: 'aut cum dicitur "inter bonos bene agier", quicquam agi dolose aut malitiose potest?').

[147] The model case is D. 18, 1, 62, 1, one of the crucial texts for *Jhering's* theory of *culpa in contrahendo*; cf. Rudolf v. Jhering, 'Culpa in contrahendo oder Schadensersatz bei nichtigen oder nicht zur Perfection gelangten Verträgen', *Jherings Jahrbücher für die Dogmatik des Bürgerlichen Rechts* 4 (1861) 1 ff. at 8 ff. See also Dieter Medicus, 'Zur Entdeckungsgeschichte der culpa in contrahendo', in: *Festgabe für Max Kaser* (1986) 169 ff. at 170 ff.

inherent in the *bonae fidei iudicia*,[148] and so the judge would always implicitly consider whether the plaintiff's claim or the bringing of the action was based on *dolus*. This antithesis was pursued so far that even actions *stricti iuris* which required the insertion of an *exceptio doli* were described as *bonae fidei iudicia*.[149] It is in keeping with this that a precursor of the praetorian *exceptio doli* mentioned by *Cicero* was concerned with whether a transaction was valid according to *bona fides*.[150]

In its role as the conceptual opposite to fraudulent behaviour[151] the ethical dimension of *bona fides* becomes especially clear. The Roman jurists were careful, however, not to extend the concept of *bona fides* beyond the sphere of the *bonae fidei iudicia*.[152] Where the *ius civile* was in need of correction, equivalent notions like *aequitas* or *bonum et aequum* were employed. A good parallel to the rule that only an innocent buyer could bring the *actio empti* in case of latent defects[153] is provided by D. 21, 1, 48, 4: according to *Pomponius* it is *aequum* to grant a defence to a seller who is sued by a buyer who knew about the defect. This defence was necessary as the aedilitian actions for redhibition or reduction of the price were not *bonae fidei iudicia*.[154] Conversely, one did not hesitate to describe contractual *bona fides* as part of a comprehensive 'equity', although it was stressed that its application required *summam aequitatem*.[155] In some late classical

---

148 *Julian* states in D. 30, 84, 5: '. . . quia hoc iudicium [i.e. the actio venditi] fidei bonae est et continet in se doli mali exceptionem'; further references in Carcaterra (n. 72) 150 ff.; Kaser (n. 13) 488, n. 35.

149 For instance D. 39, 6, 42 pr.; D. 5, 1, 41 does not fit in here (though see Beck (n. 129) 24, n. 66), as it seems to be concerned with the *actio rei uxoriae* (cf. Lenel (n. 46) 834).

150 Cicero, *Epistulae ad Atticum* 6, 1, 15: '. . . extra quam si ita negotium gestum est ut eo stari non oporteat ex fide bona'.

151 *Dolus* and *bona fides* are mentioned in antithesis in, for instance, D. 18, 1, 68; cf. also the contrast between *bona fides* and *fraus* highlighted in D. 3, 3, 34 and D. 19, 2, 25; see Carcaterra (n. 72) 144 f.; Emilio Betti, 'Der Grundsatz von Treu und Glauben in rechtsgeschichtlicher und vergleichender Betrachtung', in: *Studien zum kausalen Rechtsdenken: Festgabe für Müller-Erzbach* (1954) 7 ff. at 15 ff.

152 More generalised applications were not, however, unknown; for instance D. 19, 1, 50 and D. 19, 1, 11, 18 (on the justification of the 'functional synallagma': if one party to a reciprocal contract does not perform, the other party may refuse to counterperform) or D. 50, 17, 57 (discussing the grounds for the principle *ne bis in idem*).

153 Cf. the example in Cicero, *De officiis* 3, 67 (above, section II); this decision is, substantially, reflected in D. 19, 1, 21 pr. (*cum id emptor ignoraverit*) and D. 19, 1, 1, 1.

154 *Actio quanti minoris* and *actio redhibitoria*; cf. Kaser (n. 13) 558 ff. and Zimmermann (n. 113) 311 ff.

155 D. 16, 3, 31 pr.: 'Bona fides quae in contractibus exigitur aequitatem summam desiderat.'

texts *bona fides* is even linked to the moral category of the *boni mores*.[156] *Aequitas* also combines the two basic meanings of *fides*, keeping one's word and observing a certain standard of behaviour:[157] thus, it is stated at one place in the Digest that *aequitas naturalis* required a breach of promise (*fidem fallere*) to be sanctioned.[158]

VI. A return or revival of *bona fides*?

Out of the mass of decisions based on *bona fides* there slowly crystallised a body of general rules which played a vital role in the reception of Roman law into modern legal systems. *Venire contra factum proprium* and *turpitudo sua neminem allegat*[159] may be mentioned as examples. Principles such as these continue to influence the modern administration of justice through the general clauses incorporated into the national codifications.[160] The evidence collected by *Pringsheim* regarding the rule *nemo cum alterius detrimento fieri locupletior* shows, however, that even during the classical period *bona fides* was being drawn into a melting pot of similar notions. The rule was traced back to both *bona fides* (D. 17, 1, 10, 3) and *aequum et bonum* (D. 23, 3, 6, 2), or was justified merely by a short reference to *aequius* or *benignius*.[161] The degree of abstraction to which contractual *bona fides* was carried is best demonstrated by D. 50, 17, 57, where it forms the basis of the prohibition *ne bis idem exigatur*. These principles all find their roots in

[156] D. 16, 3, 1, 7; D. 22, 1, 5 and D. 50, 17, 116 pr.; cf. Theo Mayer-Maly, 'Contra bonos mores', in: *Festgabe für Max Kaser* (1988) 151 at 158. D. 17, 1, 12, 11 (*adversus bonam fidem*) does not probably belong here; cf. Sandro-Angelo Fusco, '"Adulescens luxuriosus": Ulp. D. 17, 1, 12, 11 – ein Mandat contra bonos mores?', in: *Mandatum und Verwandtes* (n. 106) 387 ff.
[157] Correct, in this respect, is Waldstein (n. 40) 77 f.
[158] D. 13, 5, 1 pr. is concerned with the *praetor's* promise to grant legal protection in cases of a *constitutum debiti*: an informal promise which was therefore based merely on good faith in the sense of keeping one's word. *Aequitas naturalis* and *fidem servare* are mentioned with almost exactly the same meaning in D. 2, 14, 1 pr.
[159] Both are embedded in the *exceptio doli generalis* of the *ius commune*; for their classical roots cf., for instance, D. 39, 5, 29, 2 (here in the context of *contra bonos mores*) and D. 18, 1, 8 pr. (prevention of a condition from materialising).
[160] See Wieacker, in: *Ausgewählte Schriften II* (n. 12) 209 ff.; for further examples, see Rolf Knütel, 'Rechtseinheit in Europa und römisches Recht', *ZEuP* 2 (1994) 244 at 251 ff., and his more recent article 'Ius Commune und Römisches Recht vor Gerichten der EU', *Juristische Schulung* 1996, 768, esp. 772 f.; Reinhard Zimmermann, 'Civil Code and Civil Law', (1994/95) 1 *Columbia Journal of European Law* 94 ff.
[161] D. 5, 3, 38 (*aequius*); D. 11, 7, 14, 1 (*melius*); D. 20, 5, 12, 1 (*aequius*); D. 14, 4, 5, 6 (*aequissimum*) etc.; cf. Fritz Pringsheim, 'Bonum et aequum', *ZSS* 52 (1932) 78 at 145 ff.

the requirement of fair dealing, but it is scarcely possible to trace each one separately back to the contractual standard of *bona fides*.

From the end of the classical period *bona fides* gradually lost ground to a reasoning based on *(naturalis) aequitas*.[162] There were undoubtedly several reasons for this, the most important one being that the fate of *bona fides* was closely linked to that of the classical formulary procedure. As the latter fell into disuse *bona fides* was left to face the direct competition of general ethical categories such as *aequitas, humanitas* and *benignitas*.[163] These proved to be more flexible and comprehensive than the concept of *bona fides*, confined as it was to the ideas of loyalty and fair dealing between contracting parties. However, the legal institutions it had shaped and the finely nuanced considerations to which it had given rise became part and parcel of the civilian heritage on which the modern legal systems are based.

In addition, the ethical principles which formed the basis of the classical notion of *bona fides* are today enjoying a renaissance. This has to do with the fact that within a framework of general concepts the modern lawyer has to resolve legal issues which have always been measured against the ideals of the *bonus vir* and *bene agere*; i.e. the main pillars of *bona fides* itself. Two examples take us back to *Cicero*, who was unmatched in blending the jurisprudential[164] and the practical points of view. The theme of the first example[165] is that of remaining faithful to one's word. 'A man receives a sword as a deposit and is thus obliged to return it whenever the depositor so requires. The latter requests its return at a time when he has obviously become insane.' For *Cicero*, unlike modern civil lawyers, the problem is not whether the mentally ill person can make a valid declaration of intention, but rather whether the contractual duty to return the deposited item is stronger than the duty to protect a lunatic from harming himself or others. Veracity and honesty (*veritas* and *fides*) demand that a promise should be kept. But *Cicero* does not hesitate to subordinate this duty to another one of greater priority under the circumstances: not to harm anybody and to consider the interests of the community. As the

---

[162] 'Die Aequitas, nicht die bona fides, ist es gewesen, der im Mittelalter bis in die Neuzeit die führende Rolle in der Rechtswissenschaft zukam': Beck (n. 129) 25.

[163] See generally Beck (n. 129) 24 ff.

[164] At least the second of the following examples was a case often discussed by the Stoic philosophers; as Cicero reports, it allegedly goes back to *Diogenes* and *Antipater* (*De officiis* 3, 51).   [165] Cicero, *De officiis* 3, 30 ff.

situation changes, the duty also changes.[166] This example, demonstrating
the tension between contractual fidelity and the general principle of not
harming others, stands at the cradle of the modern civil law doctrine
of the collapse of the underlying basis of a contract (*Wegfall der
Geschäftsgrundlage*). The historical connections were established by *St
Augustine, Thomas Aquinas*, the late Scholastics and *Grotius*.[167] The essentials
of the modern discussion, conducted in Germany mainly within the
framework of § 242 BGB, were already mentioned by *Cicero*: a promisor is
released from his promise if its performance is no longer of use to the promisee, or if the loss suffered by the promisor as a result of performance
exceeds the advantage gained by the promisee.[168] *Cicero* is clearly balancing the interests of the contracting parties against each other, in the same
way as the judge was required to do by the *bonae fidei iudicia*.[169] Although
no equally pointed example has come down to us from Roman legal practice,[170] a comparable conflict of interests is to be found in the issue of

---

[166] Cicero, *De officiis* 1, 31: 'Referri enim decet ad ea, quae posui principio fundamenta
iustitiae [though cf. *De officiis* 1, 23: "fundamentum autem est iustiae fides!"], primum
ut ne cui noceatur, deinde ut communi utilitati serviatur. Ea cum tempore
commutantur, commutatur officium et non semper est idem.'

[167] Augustine, *Ennarationes in psalmos* 5, 7; Thomas Aquinas, *Summa Theologica* II–II qu. 120,
art. 1 *responsum*; Leonardo Lessius, *De iustitia et iure*, lib. II, cap. XVIII, dub. X; Hugo
Grotius, *De iure belli ac pacis*, lib. II, cap. XI, § VI 1 (e.g. in the law relating to mistake); the
discussion after Grotius has tended to focus on the notion of *condictio tacita*, even up to
Bernhard Windscheid, *Die Lehre von den Voraussetzungen* (1850) 88 ff. For a history of the
clausula rebus sic stantibus and the modern German doctrine of the collapse of the
underlying basis of a transaction see, e.g., Robert Feenstra, 'Impossibilitas and Clausula
rebus sic stantibus: Some Aspects of Frustration of Contract in Continental Legal
History up to Grotius', in: Alan Watson (ed.), *Daube Noster: Essays in Legal History for David
Daube* (1974) 74 ff.; Margarethe Beck-Mannagetta, 'Die Clausula Rebus Sic Stantibus und
die Geschäftsgrundlage in der Dogmengeschichte', in: *La formazione Storica del Diritto
Moderno in Europa*, vol. III (1977) 1263 ff.; Beck-Mannagetta, 'Geschäftsgrundlage,
Voraussetzung und "causa"', *Index* 3 (1972) 512 ff.; Michael Rummel, *Die 'clausula rebus
sic stantibus': Eine dogmengeschichtliche Untersuchung unter Berücksichtigung der Zeit von der
Rezeption im 14. Jahrhundert bis zum jüngeren Usus Modernus in der ersten Hälfte des 18.
Jahrhunderts* (1991) esp. 95 ff.; Reinhard Zimmermann, '"Heard Melodies are Sweet, but
those Unheard are Sweeter . . ." – Condicio tacita, implied condition und die
Fortbildung des europäischen Vertragsrechts', *Archiv für die civilistische Praxis* 193 (1993)
134 ff.; Zimmermann (n. 113) 579 ff.; Klaus Luig, 'Dogmengeschichte des Privatrechts
als rechtswissenschaftliche Grundlagenforschung', *Ius Commune* 20 (1993) 193 ff.

[168] Cicero, *De officiis* 3, 32.

[169] A good modern parallel can be found in the possibility of judicial modification of
suretyship obligations undertaken by consumers under § 31 a V of the Austrian
Consumer Protection Law (KSchG).

[170] But cf. D. 12, 6, 66; D. 12, 4, 3, 7; D. 39, 5, 2, 1 (concerning cessation of *causa*); and cf. D.
23, 3, 10, 4; 23, 3, 21 and 68 (*condicio tacita*).

whether an innocent seller should be liable for consequential loss resulting to the buyer from a defect in the object of sale.[171]

The second case is concerned not with contractual risk allocation but
with honesty and fairness in performing a contract.[172] 'A *vir bonus* brings
a cargo of corn from Alexandria to Rhodes, a place which is stricken by
famine at the time. He knows that several other corn merchants have set
sail from Alexandria heading for Rhodes, but the Rhodians are not aware
of this. May he keep silent in order to sell his own produce at as high a
price as possible?' *Cicero* does not consider whether the economic principle of low supply and great demand should here be allowed to bring about
an unlimited price rise;[173] he is only concerned with the seller's informational advantage. Is he allowed to keep silent about the fact that other
ships are on their way to Rhodes? That *bona fides* should provide a limit is
evidenced not only by the pointed description of the grain merchant as a
vir bonus, but also by the fact that *Cicero* regards the case as on a par with
that of not disclosing defects in an object of sale,[174] discussed in close
vicinity. Modern lawyers do not, however, entirely agree with *Cicero's* line
of thought. The defining limits which we today find in our provisions
dealing with the problem of equality[175] in exchange were set less tightly
by the Roman jurists. One text states that it was naturally permitted for
both contracting parties to overcharge each other.[176] This included the
right to remain silent about factors affecting the value of the object concerned, as long as disclosure was not positively required.[177] *Cicero*, on the

---

[171] D. 19, 1, 6, 4 in comparison with D. 19, 1, 13 pr.   [172] Cicero, *De officiis* 3, 50 ff.

[173] The notion of *iustum pretium* was first recognised as a problem by the Scholastics and
Canonists; cf. Udo Wolter, *Ius canonicum in iure civili* (1975) 113 ff. For a general
discussion of the problem of a fair price see Theo Mayer-Maly, 'Der gerechte Preis', in:
Erlebtes Recht in Geschichte und Gegenwart: Festschrift für Heinrich Demelius (1973) 139 ff.; for
further references Zimmermann (n. 113) 255 ff.

[174] Cicero, *De officiis* 3, 54: 'Vendat aedes vir bonus, propter aliqua vitia, quae ipse novit,
ceteri ignorent . . .'; the parallel to *De officiis* 3, 66 (above, section II) is obvious.

[175] § 138 II BGB; § 879 II 4 ABGB.

[176] D. 4, 4, 16, 1: 'Pomponius ait in pretio emptionis et venditionis naturaliter licere
contrahentibus se circumvenire'; along the same lines D. 19, 2, 22, 3; see, above all,
Andreas Wacke, 'Circumscribere, gerechter Preis und die Arten der List', ZSS 94 (1977)
184 at 185 ff.

[177] This was how *Diogenes* argued: Cicero, *De officiis* 3, 51; and he added that one might as
well give the object away, if one were not permitted to sell at as high a price as possible
(*De officiis* 3, 53). It appears from the sources that the Roman jurists, too, did not regard
the concealment of defects as an act of *circumvenire* that was permitted; see Theo Mayer-
Maly, 'Privatautonomie und Vertragsethik im Digestenrecht', *IURA: Rivista internazionale
di diritto romano e antico* 6 (1955) 128 at 130. In this respect Cicero's examples (*De officiis* 3,
50 and *De officiis* 3, 54) do not fit well together; see Mayer-Maly, ibid., 133.

other hand, thought it more proper that the people of Rhodes should be informed about the impending arrival of other ships.[178]

The discrepancy between the legal and moral–philosophical points of view reveals a dilemma still relevant today: when may a contracting party remain silent and when is he under a duty to disclose? Was Desdemona's profitable purchase[179] only the 'clever exploitation of an advantageous situation' or was it a 'deceitful machination'?[180] What *Cicero* fails to address determines the solution today: the modern codifications disapprove of an informational advantage only if it manifests itself in a grave imbalance between performance and price. Compared with *Cicero's* point of view this solution appears to be a pragmatic one; the question of honest behaviour becomes tied up with the aspect of *iustum pretium*.[181] A Roman judge would have decided differently, probably even in Desdemona's case. Against the background of liberal economic thinking, i.e. quite independently of considerations concerning adequacy of consideration, Roman *bona fides* did not entail a general duty to disclose.

This transformation from *invicem se circumvenire* to legal rules limiting the extent to which parties may overcharge each other is an example of the way in which the same ethical principle, emphatically postulated by *Cicero* the philosopher – not *Cicero* the jurist – as being part of Roman law, can be shaped and altered as historical and social conditions change. Concern about informational advantage is today complemented by the issue of equality of exchange, on the one hand, and by a modern sensitivity to the effects of social and economic superiority in contractual relations, on the other. The principles of *bona fides*, as incorporated into the general clauses, render a substantial contribution to the adaptation of the codified law to changing social values. They thus contribute, as *Stammler* has said, to the realisation of a social ideal.[182] Without this constant regard for fairness and justice Roman law would not have survived throughout the ages; and the modern codifications, too, would soon have become useless and outdated, had they not provided space for the operation of *bona fides*.

---

[178] Cicero, *De officiis* 3, 57.   [179] Case 2 of the present project.

[180] Cf. Zimmermann (n. 113) 257.

[181] Cf. Christoph Becker, *Die Lehre von der laesio enormis in der Sicht der heutigen Wucherproblematik: Ausgewogenheit der Vertragsverhältnisse und § 138 BGB* (1993) 57 ff.

[182] Rudolf Stammler, *Das Recht der Schuldverhältnisse in seinen allgemeinen Lehren* (1897) 43 ff. The Roman (or rather Ciceronian) influence on Stammler's thinking can be seen in his definition of the content of good faith (41): 'Es ist die Idee einer Menschengemeinschaft, in der ein Jeder die Zwecke des Anderen zu den seinigen macht'; cf. Cicero, *De officiis* 3, 52: '. . . debes et servire humanae societati . . . ut utilitas tua communis sit utilitas vicissimque communis utilitas tua sit'.

3   Good faith in contract law in the medieval *ius commune*

JAMES GORDLEY

I. Introduction

Many modern legal systems require the contracting parties to act according to 'good faith' or 'equity'. These concepts are notoriously difficult to define. Some say they cannot be defined at all, or at least, not in the same way as other legal concepts.[1] Jurists can only list different situations or *Fallgruppen* in which courts have found this requirement to be violated. The list seems long and heterogeneous. It is hard to say what these situations have in common.

   The medieval jurists who wrote about Roman and Canon law also spoke of 'good faith' and 'equity' in contract law.[2] Unfortunately, their academic

---

[1] See nn. 123 and 124, below.
[2] This study is limited to Roman and Canon law. For a study of good faith in medieval German law, see Hans-Wolfgang Strätz, *Treu und Glauben*, vol. I (1974). For a study of good faith in the medieval law merchant, see Rudolf Meyer, *Bona fides und lex mercatoria in der europäisches Rechtstradition* (1994).

literature does not tell us much about the *Fallgruppen* to which they applied these concepts. We cannot know much without archival studies of the records of medieval courts. This study will be limited to what the medieval academic literature can tell us.

It can tell us that the medieval jurists, like ourselves, found it difficult to define 'good faith' and 'equity'. As we will see, only *Baldus de Ubaldis*, the last great medieval jurist, gave a relatively coherent account of what these terms meant. His account depended heavily on ideas he had borrowed from *Aristotle* and *Thomas Aquinas*.

The jurists before *Baldus*, whether they were writing about Roman or Canon law, used the terms 'good faith' or 'equity' to describe three types of conduct expected of the contracting parties.[3] First, each party should keep his word. Second, neither should take advantage of the other by misleading him or by driving too harsh a bargain. Third, each party should abide by the obligations that an honest person would recognise even if they were not expressly undertaken.

While the medieval jurists said that, in these situations, the parties must act according to good faith and equity, they did not analyse the concepts of good faith and equity in order to determine how the parties should act. Instead, in each situation, they described how the parties should act by building a rudimentary system or schema to classify their Roman legal texts. As we will see, each of the three systems or schema seems quite independent of the others and of the general concepts of equity and good faith.

In the field of contract law, then, good faith and equity remained amorphous concepts. That conclusion is rather surprising. One might have expected a clear statement from the Canon lawyers of what Christian morality required. The Canon lawyers identified 'good faith' with a good conscience.[4] They even identified 'faith' in the religious sense with 'good faith' in the legal sense. A decree of the Fourth Lateran Council collected in the 'Decretals' of *Gregory IX* began by quoting St *Paul*[5] on faith and ended by condemning a Roman rule that allowed a possessor in bad faith to acquire title by prescription: 'Since everything that is not from faith is a

---

[3] Of course, 'good faith' mattered in contexts other than contract law although they will not be described in this study. For a summary, see H. E. Troje, 'Guter Glaube', in: *Handwörterbuch zur deutschen Rechtsgeschichte*, vol. I (1971) 1866 ff.

[4] Hostiensis (Henricus de Segusio), *In Decretalium Commentaria* (1581) to X 2, 26, 17 no. 11. Because the *Decretals* of Pope Gregory IX were known as the *Liber Extra*, they are usually cited by the abbreviation 'X'. That convention will be used here in citing commentaries on the *Decretals*.   [5] Romans 14:23: 'Omne autem, quod non est ex fide, peccatum est.'

sin . . . prescription counts for nothing without good faith in matters of Canon law and civil law alike.'[6] One might have expected that the Canonists would be equally bold in declaring what 'good faith' required of the contracting parties. Instead, as we will see, they passively accepted the conclusions that the civil lawyers had reached on the basis of Roman texts.

Very likely, one reason the Canonists acted so circumspectly is that the civil lawyers had taught them what a tricky area of law they were dealing with. It was easy enough to enunciate general principles: one should keep one's word; deceive no one; honour even implicit obligations. But, as we will see, at every turn, the civilians had encountered difficulty reconciling these general principles with specific rules of Roman law. Their experience may have convinced the Canonists of the need to be careful.

We will examine the pragmatic if inconclusive efforts of the jurists before *Baldus*, and then look at his attempt to find an overarching principle.

II. Medieval Roman and Canon law before *Baldus*

As mentioned, according to the jurists before *Baldus*, 'good faith' and 'equity' meant that a party must keep his word, refrain from deceit and overreaching, and honour obligations that are only implicit in his contract.

1. Keeping one's word

First, one must keep one's word.[7] According to the medieval jurists, one must do so as a matter of 'faith', 'equity' and the *ius gentium*, a law binding upon all peoples.[8] The jurists founded these conclusions on their Roman

---

6 'Decretales Gregorii IX', in: Emil Friedberg (ed.), *Corpus iuris canonici*, vol. II (1876) 2, 26, 20: 'Quoniam omne quod non est ex fide peccatum est. Synodali iudicio diffinimus, ut nulla valeat absque bona fide prescriptio, tam canonica quam civilis.' On good faith in the Canon law governing prescription, see Luigi Lombardo, *Il concetto di buona fede nel diritto canonico* (1944).

7 For a study devoted entirely to good faith in this sense, see Okko Behrends, 'Treu und Glauben: Zu den christlichen Grundlagen der Willenstheorie im heutigen Vertragsrecht', in: Luigi Lombardi Vallauri, Gerhard Dilcher (eds.), *Christianesimo, secolarizzazione e diritto moderno*, vol. II (1981) 957 ff. On ancient Roman law, see the contribution by Martin Schermaier to this volume, text at nn. 89–99.

8 In discussing contract law, the medieval jurists consistently identified good faith and equity. See also nn. 35, 51, 52 and 74, below. For that reason it is misleading to try to compare the significance of the two concepts in shaping medieval contract law:

96   JAMES GORDLEY

texts. A text ascribed to *Ulpian* linked *fides* in the sense of keeping one's word with 'natural equity' (*aequitas naturalis*). It said that a praetorian edict[9] that enforced certain types of agreements rested on 'natural equity' 'for what is so much in accord with human faith as to observe that which men have agreed upon among themselves?'[10] The text added that consent or agreement is to be found in all contracts whether or not they were enforceable merely upon consent.

Another text, ascribed to *Triphoninus*, linked *fides* to 'equity' and also to the *ius gentium*. It said that 'the good faith that is required in contracts calls for the greatest degree of equity (*aequitas*)'. But, it asked, should that equity be evaluated by looking only to the law of nations (*ius gentium*) or by looking to civil and praetorian law as well? Suppose someone received a deposit of 100 *sesterces* from a man who has been convicted on a capital charge and whose property is forfeit to the state. If we look to the *ius gentium* only, the money should go to the depositor, but as a matter of civil law, the money should be paid to the state.[11]

Early on, the medieval jurists concluded that as a matter of faith, equity and the *ius gentium*, agreements must be kept.[12] At that point, however, the conclusions they drew from these very general texts seemed to collide

Alexander Beck, 'Zu den Grundprinzipien der bona fides im römischen Vertragsrecht', in: *Aequitas und Bona Fides: Festgabe zum 70. Geburtstag von August Simonius* (1955) 9 at 25 (greater role played by the concept of equity). On the Roman jurists' identification of good faith and equity in this and other contexts, see Schermaier (n. 7) text at nn. 152–3, 158, 161–2. Since the medieval jurists were blind to the historical development of Roman law, it will not be described here.

[9] The edict 'pacta conventa . . . servabo': D. 2, 14, 7, 7. See Max Kaser, *Das Römische Privatrecht, 1. Abschnitt* (2nd edn, 1971) 527.

[10] Ulp. D. 2, 14, 1 pr.: 'Huius edicti aequitas naturalis est, quid enim tam congruum fidei humanae, quam ea quae inter eos placuerunt servare?' See C. 2, 4, 20.

[11] D. 16, 3, 31.

[12] Irnerius, in: Enrico Besta, *L'opera d'Irnerio, vol. II, Glosse inedite d'Irnerio al Digestum vetus* (1896) 31, to D. 2, 14: 'Pacta servari aequitas est, non eius qua pro tempore seu loco postulat, conveniens dicitur, sed eius quae natura dictante semper et in cunctis se optinet. Namque ipsum genus eius est natural: hoc est fidem praestare. fides autem est eorum quae dicta sunt constantia et veritas. dictat vero partim ratio sola, partem noster consensus et, is cogimur servare superiorem partem, quanto magis inferiorum.' *Summa trecensis*, published as: H. Fitting (ed.), *Summa Codicis des Irnerius* (1894) 2, 3, 3: 'Equitas seu ratio qua pacta servantur tum iudicium proprium est, cui resistendum non est: hoc enim varii et inconstantis hominis est, quia quod semel nobis placuit, id postea displicere non debet. tum fides qua a uno promittitur [et?] ab altero separatur, hoc suadet, ut eas que comlacita sunt serventur, cum veritati hoc debemus ne fallamur, et hoc naturaliter in nobis inest ut verum dicamus.' The observance of 'natural equity' was mandated by the *ius gentium*. Accursius, *Glossa ordinaria* (1581) to D. 2, 14, 1 pr. to *Huius edicti*: 'quod dicit naturalis, dic, id est naturali ingenio vel industria hominum introducta: quod est iurisgentium'.

with Roman contract law. In Roman law, only certain contracts, the so-called contracts *consensu*, were binding by consent. *Justinian's* 'Institutes' mentioned sale, lease, partnership and mandate, which was a gratuitous agency.[13] Others, the contracts *re*, were binding when an object was delivered. *Justinian's* 'Institutes' mentioned gratuitous loans of the object for consumption or use, pledges and deposits.[14] Still others were binding only on completion of a formality. Contracts that fell into none of these categories (the so-called innominate contracts) were not binding at all until one party had performed. Roman law, it would seem, contradicted the *ius gentium*.

The medieval jurists solved this problem formalistically. They said that the obligations arising from consent or mere agreement under the *ius gentium* were 'natural obligations' as distinguished from 'civil obligations'. According to the Roman jurists, a 'natural obligation' arose when a contract could not be enforced but nevertheless had certain legal consequences. For example, a contract made by a slave or by a father with his son was not enforceable. Nevertheless, if a third party guaranteed performance of the obligation, the guarantee could be enforced. Moreover, a party who performed such an obligation could not demand his performance back.[15] These obligations, according to *Accursius*, had a 'natural root' only. To be enforceable, they had to have a 'civil root' as well.[16] In the generation after *Accursius*, the 'ultramontane' jurists *Iacobus de Ravanis* and *Petrus de Bellapertica* explained that underlying the formal contract of the civil law was a natural obligation arising under the *ius gentium* which was based on consent. The civil law gave the formal contract its 'form' or 'substance' by prescribing an 'intrinsic solemnity'. In contrast, the natural obligation was 'naturally invented'. The civil law did not 'introduce' it but merely gave 'approbation'.[17]

---

[13] I. 3, 13, 22–6.   [14] I. 3, 14.

[15] D. 46, 1, 17. See Kaser (n. 9) 480; Kaser, *Das Römische Privatrecht*, 2. *Abschnitt* (2nd edn, 1975) 245.   [16] Accursius (n. 12) to I. 3, 14 pr. to *necessitate*.

[17] Petrus de Bellapertica, *Lectura Institutionum* (1536) to I. 1, 2, 1 no. 30: 'Dico in obligationibus iurisgentium nulla est obligatio nisi naturali inventione cum non necessarium fuit obligationem civilem introducere . . . Non necessarium fuit obligationem civilem introducere [cit. omitted] sed approbatione sic, quia ius civile approbat [cit. omitted] naturalem.' Iacobus de Ravanis, 'Super Institutionibus commentaria', published under the name of Bartolus de Saxoferrato, in: *Omnia quae extant opera* (1615) to I. 3, 14, 1 no. 3: 'Nam iure gentium erat quis naturaliter obligatus, tamen contractus, et omnes obligationes fuerunt introducti de iure gentium . . . sed ius civile dabat istis obligationibus efficaciam agendi . . . Et istam naturalem . . . posse dici approbationem civilem.' On the authorship, see E. M. Meijers, *Etudes d'histoire du droit*, vol. III: *Le Droit romain au moyen âge* (1959) 68–9.

This formal reconciliation did not explain why Roman civil law refused to enforce natural obligations. After all, they arose under the *ius gentium*, and one would expect them to be binding as a matter of equity and good faith. This difficulty was noted by *Iacobus de Ravanis* who gave a rather unsatisfactory explanation: 'If I agree that you give me ten for my horse there is an action on the agreement. But if I agree that you give me your ass for my horse there is no action on the agreement. If a layman were to ask the reason for the difference it could not be given for it is merely positive law. And if you ask why the law was so established, the reason can be said to be that the contract of sale is more frequent than that of barter. And more efficacy is given to sale than barter.'[18]

A second difficulty was that, according to one Roman text, the distinction between contracts that are and are not enforceable upon consent is rooted in the *ius gentium*. 'By the *ius gentium*, some agreements give rise to actions and others to exceptions.'[19] According to the text, the distinction depended on the 'name' of the agreement in question.[20] *Bartolus* concluded that by the *ius gentium* itself, and not merely by Roman positive law, some contracts are binding upon consent and others are not, and that the reason is a difference in 'name'. Contracts such as sale are binding on consent because they take their name from an act a party performs by agreeing. I can sell you my house today by so agreeing even if I do not put you in possession until next month. Contracts such as deposit are not binding on consent because they take their name from an act a party performs by delivering. I cannot say I am depositing an object with you unless I am actually depositing it right now.[21] At one point, *Baldus* adopted this solution.[22]

Thus, while the medieval jurists concluded that good faith, equity and the *ius gentium* required one to keep one's word, they never convincingly reconciled this principle with the rules of Roman law. *Bartolus* systematised the Roman rules in the way just described, but the system did not

---

[18] Iacobus de Ravanis, *Lectura super Codice* (published under the name of Petrus de Bellapertica (1519)) to C. 4, 64, 3: 'Si ego conveni quod pro equo meo dares michi x potest agi ex ista conventione. Sed si ego conveni quod pro equo dares michi asinum ex ista conventione agi non potest. Si laicus querat rationem diversitatis reddi non potest nam hoc est mere ius positivum. Et si tu queras quare sic fuit constitutum, potest dici quod illa fuit ratio, quia contractus venditionis frequentior est permutatione. et ideo maior efficacia data est venditioni quam permutationi.' On the authorship, see Meijers (n. 17) 72–7.   [19] D. 2, 14, 7 pr.   [20] D. 2, 14, 7, 1.

[21] Bartolus de Saxoferrato, 'Commentaria in Corpus iuris civilis', in: *Omnia quae extant opera* (n. 17) to D. 2, 14, 7 no. 2.

[22] Baldus de Ubaldis, *Commentaria in Corpus iuris civilis* (1577) to C. 2, 3, 27.

follow in any obvious way from the principle that one should keep one's word. It seemed in tension with that principle.

In Canon law, *Gratian's* 'Decretum' contained two examples of promises which were said to be binding even though, the Canon lawyers observed, they would not have been enforceable at Roman law.[23] The 'Decretals' of *Gregory IX* stated the principle that agreements must be kept.[24] The Canonists concluded that agreements were enforceable in Canon law courts without regard to the Roman distinctions between contracts *consensu* and *re* and between nominate and innominate contracts.[25] They quoted the maxim that 'God doesn't distinguish between mere speech and an oath.'[26] Their conclusion was less innovative than some modern scholars[27] have supposed. As we have seen, the Roman lawyers had already said that agreements were binding under the *ius gentium* and some of them regarded the Roman distinctions as mere matters of Roman positive law.

Moreover, the Canon lawyers did not say that every agreement was enforceable even in Canon law.[28] As *Astuti* notes, they said little about the matter because, unlike the civilians, their prime concern was not whether an agreement was actionable but whether breach was a sin.[29] As late as the fourteenth century, *Baldus* could still claim that the Roman distinction

---

[23] According to one text, if remuneration is promised to someone for doing something for the Church, the promise should be kept. *Decretum, Causa* 12, *Quaestio* 2, c. 66 in: *Corpus iuris canonici* (n. 6) vol. I. The Ordinary Gloss notes that in such a case, labour might have been provided and land promised in return: *Glossa ordinaria to Decretum Gratiani* (1595) *Causa* 12, *Quaestio* 2, c. 66, *Casus*. The other text said that when an Archbishop had promised goods to a monastery before he died, his successor should keep the promise: *Decretum, Causa* 12, *Quaestio* 5, c. 3.

[24] *Decretales* (n. 6) 1, 35, 1: 'Aut inita pacta obtineant firmitatem, aut conventus, si se cohibuerat, ecclesiasticam senentiat disciplinam. dixerunt universi: pax servetur, pacta custodiantur.' *Decretales* (n. 6) 1, 35, 3: 'Studiose agendum est, ut ea, quae promittuntur, opere compleantur.'

[25] *Glossa ordinaria* (n. 23) to *Causa* 12, *Quaestio* 2, c. 66 to *promiserint*; *Glossa ordinaria* to *Decretales Gregorii IX* (1612) to 1, 35, 1 to *pacta custodiantur*; Hostiensis (Henricus de Segusio), *Summa aurea* (1556) f. 86vb.

[26] The maxim is found in *Decretum* (n. 23) *Causa* 22, *Quaestio* 5, c. 12, and quoted in *Glossa ordinaria* (n. 25) to 1, 35, 1 to *pacta custodiantur*.

[27] J. Roussier, *Le Fondement de l'obligation contractuelle dans le droit classique de l'Eglise* (1933) 177–216; A. Solmi, 'Elementi del diritto medievale italiano', in: *Contributi alla storia del diritto comune* (1937) 147 at 223; F. Schupfer, *Il diritto delle obbligazioni in Italia nell'età del risorgimento*, vol. I (1920) 151.

[28] Roussier correctly notes that one cannot infer from their silence that they thought all agreements were enforceable: Roussier (n. 27) 179–81.

[29] Astuti, 'I principii fondamentali dei contratti nella storia del diritto italiano', *Annali di storia del diritto* 1 (1957) 34–7.

between contracts *consensu* and *re* was part of Canon law.[30] Since he agreed with *Bartolus* that this distinction belonged to the *ius gentium*, he concluded it must belong to Canon law as well. Later, we will see that *Baldus* proposed another limitation and one which was accepted by later Canonists: to be enforceable in Canon law, a promise must have a *causa*.

2. Fraud or unfairness

According to the medieval jurists, good faith and equity also meant that neither party should mislead or take advantage of the other.[31] A text attributed to *Ulpian* said that everything contrary to good faith is considered in an action of sale: for example, selling property without revealing it is subject to a servitude.[32] A text attributed to *Pomponius* said that because sale gave rise to an action of good faith, there should be no deceit (*dolus*). Therefore, a seller would be liable to the buyer if he knowingly sold another person's property while disclaiming liability should it belong to another.[33] The medieval jurists concluded that good faith meant there could be no *dolus* or deceit. They read this conclusion into a text that said: 'it is equitable to take account of good faith in contracts'.[34] The text meant that the victim of *dolus* had a remedy.[35]

As before, the medieval jurists did not define good faith or equity and then use the definition to explain the concept of *dolus*. They explained *dolus* by a system or schema that was supposed to reconcile their Roman texts but which had no clear link to the concept of good faith. Moreover, as before, tensions remained with the technical rules of Roman law.

This schema had been developed early on by the Glossators.[36] *Dolus* or

---

[30] Baldus (n. 22) to C. 2, 3, 27.

[31] See Reinhard Zimmermann, *The Law of Obligations: Roman Foundations of the Civil Law Tradition* (1990, paperback edn, 1996) 664–71. On the development of this idea by the Roman jurists, see Schermaier (n. 7) text at nn. 145–7.

[32] D. 19, 1, 1, 1: 'Venditor si, cum sciret deberi, servitutem celavit, non evadet ex empto actionem, si modo eam rem emptor ignoravit: omnia enim, quae contra bonam fidem fiunt, veniunt in empti actionem.' On the duty to disclose defects in Roman law, see Schermaier (n. 7) text at nn. 15–40, 138–44.

[33] D. 19, 1, 6, 9: 'Si venditor sciens obligatum aut alienum vendidisset et adiectum sit neue eo nomine quid praestaret, aestimari oportet dolum malum eius, quem semper abesse oportet in iudicio empti, quod bonae fidei sit.'

[34] C. 4, 10, 4: 'Bonam fidem in contractibus considerari aequum est.'

[35] Accursius (n. 12) to C. 4, 10, 4; Odofredus, *Lectura super Codicem* (1552) to C. 4, 10, 4; Bartolus (n. 21) to C. 4, 10, 4.

[36] Vacarius, *Liber pauperum*, edited by: F. de Zulueta (1927) 4, 51 to D. 19, 2, 23, 3; Rogerius, 'Summa Codicis', in: A. Gaudentius (ed.), *Scripta anecdota glossatorum* (1913) to C. 4, 44; Azo Portius, 'Summa Codicis', in: Azo, *Summa aurea* (1557) to C. 2, 20 no. 9; Accursius (n.

'fraud' was classified as 'causal' or 'incidental'. 'Causal fraud' leads a person to contract who would not have done so otherwise. For example, the seller of a horse might tell some lie to make the buyer think he would soon lose his own horse. 'Incidental fraud' leads a person to contract on more disadvantageous terms. For example, the seller might lie about the age of the horse to get a better price. The remedies for the two types of fraud are correspondingly different. The victim of causal fraud can escape his contract entirely. The victim of incidental fraud can demand the price he would otherwise have obtained as long as he was the victim of fraud in the normal sense, that is, as long as the other party had deceived him deliberately (*ex proposito*).

Again, however, these general principles conflicted with the technicalities of Roman law. Roman law distinguished between contracts of good faith and those of strict law.[37] In the latter but not the former, a party's defence of fraud would be considered only if he raised the matter specially as a defence.[38] The medieval jurists therefore qualified their conclusion. The victim of causal fraud could always escape the contract. But a contract of good faith was void *ipso iure* for causal fraud. In contrast, a contract of strict law was not void but the victim could raise fraud as a defence.

Suppose, however, that a person had not been deceived deliberately but nevertheless, like the victim of incidental fraud *ex proposito*, had contracted on disadvantageous terms. According to the medieval jurists, he was the victim of 'fraud that appears from the transaction itself' (*dolus ex re ipsa*). *Dolus ex re ipsa* was not fraud in the normal sense. The victim had not been deliberately misled. He simply had paid more or less than the just price.

The medieval jurists created this category by conflating two texts. One, a very famous text in the Code, ascribed to *Diocletian* but possibly interpolated by *Justinian*, gave a remedy to one who had sold an estate for less than half the just price. The buyer had the option of either returning the estate or paying the just price in full.[39] At an early date, the medieval jurists concluded that the same remedy should be given to sellers as well as buyers, and not only in sales of land but in analogous transactions.[40] They

---

12) C. 4, 10, 4; Odofredus (n. 35) to C. 4, 10, 4; Bartolus (n. 21) to C. 4, 10, 4; see Gérard Fransen, *Le Dol dans la conclusion des actes juridiques* (1946) 49–55.

[37] See Schermaier (n. 7) text at nn. 57–144; Franz Wieacker, 'Zum Ursprung der bonae fidei iudicia', ZSS 80 (1980) 1 ff. at 29–37.   [38] See Schermaier (n. 7) text at nn. 130–2.

[39] C. 4, 44, 2.

[40] *Corpus legum sive Brachylogus iuris civilis* (1743) III, xii, 8; Hugolinus de Presbyteris, *Diversitates sive dissensiones dominorum super toto corpore iure civilis*, edited by: G. Haenel (1834) § 253.

described the just price as the market price, a price that could differ from day to day and from region to region.[41] The label *dolus ex re ipsa* was suggested by a Roman text that said that in the case of the formal contract of *stipulatio*, a contract of strict law, a party could have an *exceptio doli* even if there was 'no *dolus*' but 'the transaction itself had deceit within it' (*res ipsa in se dolum habet*).[42] The medieval jurists interpreted this text to apply to transactions at more or less than half the just price. It meant that a party would have the same remedy even if the contract was one of strict law rather than one of good faith.[43]

It is important to note that in speaking of *dolus ex re ipsa*, the medieval jurists were not advancing a theory of why relief should be given for an unjust price. They knew that this type of *dolus* was not *dolus* in the ordinary sense. They were simply noting that the effect of *dolus ex re ipsa* was the same as that of incidental *dolus ex proposito*: the victim received a less favourable price. Thus here, as in the other situations we have examined, one cannot really say that the medieval jurists had a theory. They recognised as a general principle that good faith meant there should be no deceit or overreaching. But to explain good faith or overreaching, they developed a system for classifying Roman texts that was dimly linked to the concept of good faith.

Again, Canon lawyers borrowed the conclusions of the civilians. They said that good faith was the contrary of *dolus*.[44] They borrowed the civilian's classification of *dolus*.[45] The 'Decretals' of *Gregory IX* incorporated the Roman remedy for *dolus ex re ipsa*. One who paid more or received less than half the just price could force the other party either to rescind the transaction or to pay the difference between the just price and the contract price.[46]

---

[41] Accursius (n. 12) to D. 13, 4, 3 [vulg. 13, 4, 4] to *varia*; to C. 4, 44, 4 to *auctoritate iudicis*.

[42] D. 45, 1, 36: 'Si quis, cum aliter eum convenisset obligari, aliter per machinationem obligatus est, erit quidem suptilitate iuris obstrictus, sed doli exceptione uti potest: quia enim per dolum obligatus est, competit ei exceptio. idem est si nullus dolus intercessit stipulantis, sed res ipsa in se dolum habet: cum enim qui petat ex ea stipulatione, hoc ipso dolo facit, quod petit.'

[43] Accursius (n. 12) to D. 45, 1, 36; Odofredus (n. 35) to D. 45, 1, 36; Petrus de Bellapertica, *Commentaria in Digestum Novum Repetitiones variae* (1571) to D. 45, 1, 36; Bartolus (n. 21) to D. 45, 1, 36.

[44] *Glossa ordinaria* (n. 25) to X 3, 16, 2 to *rebus tuis salvis*: 'si bona fides abest, dolus adesse praesumitur. nam contraria sunt'; Hostiensis (n. 4) to X 3, 16, 2: 'Bona fides et dolus contraria sunt.'

[45] *Glossa ordinaria* (n. 25) to X 3, 17, 3 to *deceptione*; Hostiensis (n. 25) ff. 218ra–19vb.

[46] *Decretales* (n. 6) 3, 17, 3; 3, 17, 6.

3. Tacit obligations

Finally, good faith meant doing whatever else could be expected of an honest person engaged in a given type of transaction.[47] One Roman text explained that 'nothing is more in accord with good faith than to do what was agreed by the contracting parties. If nothing was agreed, one should perform what naturally is included according to the decision of the judge.'[48] These obligations are what a modern jurist would call the implied terms of a contract, terms that are read into it when the parties are silent. The text just mentioned gave as an example what a modern lawyer would call the seller's warranty against eviction.

Here again, the medieval jurists identified the requirements of good faith with those of equity and the *ius gentium*. According to *Odofredus*, these obligations were said to belong to a contract 'naturally' because they were 'introduced by natural reason by the *ius gentium*'.[49] As we have seen, another text said: 'it is equitable to take account of good faith in contracts'.[50] According to the jurists, this text meant, not only that the parties must avoid deceit, but also that they are bound by terms to which they had not agreed,[51] indeed, by terms which they had never contemplated.[52]

Here again, however, the medieval jurists do not define good faith or equity and then try to show how the terms to be read into a contract followed from the definition. Instead, they fit the Roman texts into a different system or schema in which the key words were not 'good faith' and 'equity' but 'nature', 'substance' and 'accident'. They never explained the relationship between these concepts and good faith or equity. Moreover, their system did not resolve certain tensions within the Roman rules.

They said that the terms to be read into an agreement absent express provision came from the 'nature' of the contract.[53] They rested this conclusion on the text just mentioned that said that these terms belonged to

---

[47] On the development of this idea by the ancient Roman jurists, see Schermaier (n. 7) text at nn. 57–90.

[48] D. 19, 1, 11: 'nihil magis bonae fidei congruit quam id praestari, quod inter contrahentes actum est. Quod si nihil convenit, hunc ea praestabuntur quae naturaliter insunt huius iudici potestate.'

[49] Odofredus (n. 35) to D. 19, 1, 11: 'naturaliter insunt, id est, naturali ratione iure gentium introducta'.   [50] C. 4, 10, 4.

[51] Odofredus (n. 35) to C. 4, 10, 4: 'multa veniunt de quibus non est actum'.

[52] Albericus de Rosate, *Commentaria in primam Digesti veteris partem* (1585) to C. 4, 10, 4: 'veniunt ea . . . de quibus non est cogitatum, aequum est, tamen, ut veniunt'. Bartolus (n. 21) to 4, 10, 4: 'veniunt ea de quibus non est actum nec cogitatum'.

[53] Odofredus (n. 35) to D. 19, 1, 11: 'de natura contractus insunt'; Bartolus (n. 21) to D. 19, 1, 11: 'veniunt ex natura contractus'.

the contract 'naturally'. They contrasted these natural terms with those that belonged to the 'substance' of a contract. Their source for this distinction was a text that said that since 'the substance of a sale consists in the price', parties who agree on a different price are not modifying their contract but making a new one.[54] *Accursius* explained that the 'substance' of a contract includes those matters 'without which it cannot be': in a sale, the price and the object sold.[55]

The terminology was a bit unfortunate because even before the rediscovery of *Aristotle's* works on physics and metaphysics, the terms 'nature' and 'substance' had roughly the same meaning philosophically. *Accursius* tried to explain: 'we say an agreement is of the nature [of a contract] that is beyond what is natural'.[56] The explanation sounds confusing but, nevertheless, the underlying idea was fairly clear. Each type of contract had a nature or substance. The substantial terms defined that type of contract and so the parties could not change them without making a different contract. The natural terms belonged to a contract of a particular type, and, in that sense, they followed from its nature or substance but did not define it. They would be read into the contract if the agreement was silent though, if they wished, the parties could agree not to be bound by them.

The substantial and the natural terms were contrasted with the 'accidental' terms of a contract. They were 'extraneous' to its nature. They were only binding if the parties expressly agreed to them. Examples were an agreement that the seller can reclaim his goods if the price is not paid by a certain day or that a church will or will not be built on land that is purchased.[57]

The jurists concluded, then, that every kind of contract had its natural terms, and that a party must observe them as a matter of 'good faith' and 'equity' and the *ius gentium*. But they never explained the relationship

---

[54] D. 18, 1, 72.
[55] Accursius (n. 12) to D. 18, 1, 72 to *ex pretio*: 'Quia sine pretio esse venditio non potest [cit. omitted]. Item si fiat super re vendita augenda vel minuenda [cit. omitted] cum res similiter sit de substantia emptionis, nec sine ea esse possit.'
[56] Azo (n. 36) to C. 4, 54 no. 2: 'Sed nos dicimus pactum esse de natura quod sit super eo quod est naturalis contractus, ut de evictione praestanda certo mode vel nullo modo'; Accursius (n. 12) to D. 18, 1, 72 to *nova emptio*: 'Sed nos pactum de natura dicimus esse quod sit super id quod est naturale, ut de evictione praestanda.'
[57] Azo (n. 36) to C. 4, 54 no. 1: 'Quaedam sunt accidentalia sive extranea. ut de dando codice exemplaris loco ut aliquo simili non attingenti venditioni. ut puta si venditor restituat emptori pretium intra certum diem reddatur ei res vel ut emptor praestat venditori usuram pretii tardius soluti vel ut emptor faciat vel ut non faciat monumentum vel ecclesiam in fundo vendito.'

between the 'nature' or 'substance' of a contract on the one hand, and 'equity', 'good faith' and the *ius gentium* on the other.

Moreover, once again, their efforts to state a general principle ran up against the rules of Roman law. As already noted, Roman law distinguished between contracts of good faith and those of strict law. The text quoted earlier, according to which 'if nothing was agreed, one should perform what naturally is included', had been speaking of 'good faith *iudicia* such as sale'.

As before, the jurists' reconciliation of rule and principle seems wooden. Good faith was required, they said, in both contracts of good faith and those of strict law. That, they claimed, was the meaning of the text that called it 'equitable to take account of good faith in contracts'. But, in Roman law, only the parties to a contract of good faith were bound to terms to which they had not expressly agreed.[58] The jurists did not explain why Roman positive law should be in seeming conflict with the *ius gentium*.

The end result therefore resembles the jurists' treatment of the duty to keep one's word or to avoid deceit and overreaching. They announced a general principle resting on good faith, equity and the *ius gentium*. They made a schema or system to explain the Roman texts – here one based on distinctions between the 'substance', 'nature' and 'accidents' of a contract. They did not explain the relationship between this system and the general principle. And they did not fully resolve the tension between the principle and the system and the technical rules of Roman law.

The Canonists repeated the civilians' conclusion that in contracts of good faith, unlike those of strict law, the parties are bound to the unexpressed terms that good faith requires.[59] They often describe the difference between contracts of good faith and strict law in the same way as the civilians without any hint that the distinction does not matter in Canon law.[60] *Baldus* finally said that in Canon law, all contracts were of good faith, but he was careful to say that he was merely giving his own opinion.[61]

---

[58] Odofredus (n. 35) to C. 4, 10, 4; Albericus (n. 52) to C. 4, 10, 4; Bartolus (n. 21) to C. 4, 10, 4.

[59] *Glossa ordinaria* (n. 25) to X 3, 17, 6: 'in contractibus bonae fidei multa veniunt de quibus nec est dictum nec cogitatum'; to X 2, 25, 6 to *bonae fidei*: 'in bona fidei actionibus quandoque veniunt ea de quibus nihil est cogitatum'.

[60] *Glossa ordinaria* (n. 25) to X 3, 17, 3 to *deceptione*; Hostiensis (n. 25) ff. 218ra–219vb; Innocent IV, *Commentaria super libros quinque Decretalium* (1570) to X 3, 17, 6.

[61] Baldus de Ubaldis, *In Decretalium volumen commentaria* (1595) to X 2, 11, 1 no. 12: 'ego puto quod de aequitate canonica omnes contractus mundi sit bonae fidei'.

Thus in this instance, as in the others, the Canon lawyers took longer than one might expect to jettison the technicalities of Roman law. Perhaps that explains why, here as elsewhere, they did not go further. As we have seen, the Canon law was bolder in dealing with the requirement of good faith to obtain title to property by long continued possession. The 'Decretals' of *Gregory IX* declared that '[s]ince everything that is not from faith is a sin' a person who possessed in bad faith could never gain title, and that this rule had to be respected in civil law as well as Canon law courts.[62] In contrast, even those Canon lawyers who thought that Canon law courts should ignore Roman distinctions between innominate and nominate contracts or between contracts of good faith and strict law did not claim civil courts should do so. In dealing with contracts, the Canonists did not show the same commitment to abstract principle.

III. The coming of *Aristotle* and the work of *Baldus*

Like earlier jurists, *Baldus* thought his task was to explain the Roman texts. Unlike them, he developed a coherent idea of good faith or equity. He seems to have done so by drawing on the philosophical ideas of *Aristotle* and *Thomas Aquinas*. To understand his work we must therefore say something about theirs.

1. Aristotle *and* Thomas Aquinas

In the late twelfth and early thirteenth centuries, *Aristotle's* works on metaphysics, physics, politics and ethics became available in the West for the first time. They touched off the kind of intellectual revolution we associate with *Newton* or *Darwin*. The thirteenth-century theologian *Thomas Aquinas* used *Aristotle's* ideas to construct a systematic moral philosophy. Some of these ideas concerned contracts.

In the 'Ethics', *Aristotle* described exchange as a type of commutative justice. While distributive justice secured for each citizen a fair share of whatever wealth and honour the society had to divide, commutative justice preserved his share.[63] Thus, according to *Aristotle*, each party to an exchange had to give something of equivalent value to what he received.[64] In another passage in the 'Ethics', *Aristotle* discussed the virtue of 'liberal-

---

[62] See n. 6, above.   [63] Aristotle, *Nicomachean Ethics*, V.ii.   [64] Ibid., V.iv–v.

ity': the liberal person disposed of his money wisely, giving 'to the right people the right amounts and at the right time'.[65] In still another passage, he discussed the virtue of promise-keeping. A promise breaker was like a liar: the words of the promise breaker did not match his acts just as the words of a liar did not match his thoughts.[66]

Thomas Aquinas put these ideas together. Promises should be kept, as *Aristotle* had said, because of the virtue of fidelity to one's word.[67] Promises, however, could be used to enter into two different types of arrangements. When one person transferred a thing to another, either it was an act of commutative justice that required an equivalent or it was an act of liberality.[68]

Thomas classified various contracts familiar from Roman law as either acts of commutative justice or acts of liberality. For example, a donation is an act of liberality in which a thing was transferred and nothing is asked in return. Sale and lease are acts of commutative justice in which a party transfers, respectively, a thing and the use of a thing.[69]

In Aristotelian and Thomistic philosophy, defining is the first step towards understanding. Each thing has an 'essence' or 'nature' or 'substantial form' that makes it what it is. The essence can be captured by a definition. The definition can then be used to explain the structure and characteristics of the thing. If a particular contract can be defined as an act of commutative justice, then one should be able to move from this definition to the rules appropriate to such a contract.[70]

Thomas did so when he discussed 'cheating which is committed in buying and selling'.[71] Sale is an act of commutative justice. Each party must therefore receive something equivalent in value to what he gave. That principle, according to *Thomas*, explains the Roman law remedy for an unfair price. Though an equivalent is always required, for practical reasons, civil law remedies only large deviations.[72] *Thomas* used the same principle to explain some of the rules that governed sale: for example, that the seller is liable for defects in the goods he sold. Defective goods are not equal in value to the price paid for sound ones.[73]

---

[65] Ibid., IV.i 1119a–1120a.   [66] Ibid., IV.vii 1127a–1127b.
[67] Thomas Aquinas, *Summa theologiae* II–II, qv. 88, art. 3; qv. 110, art. 3 ad 3.
[68] Ibid., II–II, qv. 61, art. 3.   [69] Ibid., II–II, qv. 61, art. 3.
[70] James Gordley, *The Philosophical Origins of Modern Contract Doctrine* (1991) 15–23.
[71] Thomas Aquinas (n. 67) II–II, qv. 77.   [72] Ibid., II–II, qv. 77, art. 1, ad 1.
[73] Ibid., II–II, qv. 77, art. 2.

2. Baldus

Like the jurists who preceded him, *Baldus* identified good faith with equity[74] and with conscience.[75] But he gave special attention to one particular requirement of equity and good faith: the requirement that no one should be enriched at another's expense.[76] This principle looks like the principle of equality which, according to *Aristotle* and *Thomas Aquinas*, is the foundation of commutative justice. *Baldus* called it 'the rule of rules in the life of conscience'.[77]

For *Baldus*, this principle was explicit in some Roman texts and implicit in others. He called it 'natural equity',[78] or 'general'[79] or 'generic equity'.[80] By using these terms, he linked it to such Roman maxims as 'by the law of nature it is equitable that no one should be enriched through another's expense or injury',[81] and 'it is equitable to take account of good faith in contracts'.[82]

Speaking of this principle as one of 'equity', however, created some terminological confusion which *Baldus* then had to clear up. *Thomas Aquinas* had used the term 'equity' for *Aristotle's epieíkeia*. Since laws are framed generally, circumstances can always arise in which the lawmaker himself would not wish the law to be followed. 'Equity' or *epieíkeia* means that under such circumstances, the law should not be applied.[83] *Baldus* avoided confusion by explaining that the word 'equity' had two meanings, which he called 'specific' and 'generic' equity (*aequitas in specie* and *aequitas in genere*). He defined 'specific equity' much as *Aristotle* and *Aquinas* had defined 'equity': it meant deviating from the law when the circumstances require. In contrast, 'generic equity' meant reaching a just result: 'correct judgment' taking account of 'both substance and circumstances'.[84] In this

---

[74] Baldus (n. 61) to X 1, 29, 3: 'bona fides aequitatem desiderat'; Baldus (n. 22) to D. 16, 3, 31 (*bona fides* and *aequitas* used interchangeably).

[75] Baldus (n. 61) to X 1, 29, 3 nos. 6, 7: 'voco bonam fidem id est bonam mentis qualitatem et conscientiam quae etiam in contractibus stricti iuris requiritur'; to X 1, 6, 24 no. 24: 'Quaero unde proveniat bona fides. dicit glossa quod non proveniat mere a iure, sed ab hominis conscientia.'

[76] On the identification of good faith and equity with this principle by Roman jurists, see Schermaier (n. 7) text at nn. 161, 180.

[77] Baldus (n. 61) to X 1, 2, 8 no. 1: 'Regula regularum in via conscientie est, non locupletari cum aliena iactura.'   [78] See nn. 87 and 88, below.   [79] See n. 87, below.

[80] See n. 85, below. On *Baldus'* identification of these terms with the maxim of D. 50, 17, 206, see Norbert Horn, *Aequitas in den Lehren des Baldus* (1968) 115.   [81] D. 50, 17, 206.

[82] C. 4, 10, 4.   [83] Thomas Aquinas (n. 67) II–II, q. 120, a. 1.

[84] Baldus (n. 22) to D. 1, 1, 1 pr. no. 5: 'Tertio oppono quod ius non sit ars boni et equi. nam quedam iura non sunt equa, sed rigorosa. Est autem rigor generalis ordinatio, habens

passage, *Baldus* does not say on what principles the justice of this result depends. Elsewhere, however, he identifies 'generic equity' with the principle that no one should be enriched at another's expense.⁸⁵

There was another source of terminological confusion. The medieval jurists had said that 'equity' and 'good faith' were violated by breaking one's word and by causal fraud. Yet in these situations, the violator might not be enriched at the victim's expense. Indeed, as we have seen, for *Aristotle* and *Thomas*, these violations concerned, not commutative justice, but other virtues. Not to break a promise pertained to the virtue that *Thomas* called 'fidelity'. Not to lie pertained to the closely related virtue that *Aristotle* and *Thomas* called 'truth'.

Accordingly, *Baldus* distinguished several kinds of good faith. The judge, he said, might take account of 'good faith' in contracts for two purposes: first, to know whether contracts are binding or not, and second, to know what the parties' obligations are and whether they have been fulfilled. For this second purpose, good faith had two meanings. It means the absence of *dolus*. It also means 'the observation of that to which the parties are committed according to natural equity and the ordination of the law. Attention is to be paid to natural equity when doubt arises as to those things that are not expressed in the law, and attention is to be paid to the law's ordination in things that it does express.'⁸⁶ For *Baldus*, then, 'natural

eandem vim in differentibus in ratione [cit. omitted]. Item quedam sunt equa in quibus destruuntur regula et principia sic non sunt bona [cit. omitted]. Est autem equitas applicatio animi seu iudicium in quo circumscripta iuris regula aliquid de mente singulari ex propria ratione statuitur loquor de equitate in specie. sed equitas in genere est applicatio animi ad directum iudicium intellectu non errante in substantia nec in circumstantiis facti. Sicut dicitur quod equum est iudicium ecclesie clave non errante.'

⁸⁵ Baldus (n. 22) to D. 12, 6, 13: 'Nota neminem locupletari debere ex alieno: verum est sine causa, sed cum causa approbata iure civili sic: quia rigor in specie vincit aequitatem in genere.'

⁸⁶ Baldus (n. 22) to C. 4, 10, 4 nos. 1–2: 'Ad intellectum huius legis quaero, ad quem finem debet iudex considerare bonam fidem. Ad hoc respondeo quod ad duos fines: quia duo sunt actus circa contractum, qui recipit duos fines: primus est in contrahendo, secundus vero in adimplendo. In primo actu consideratur bona fides, ut per hoc diiudicetor, et cognoscatur, an contractus sit servandus vel non, et hoc tangit glossa hic posita. Circa secundum consideratur bona fides ut in eo casu quo servandus est contractus, diiudicetur an satisfaciat, sicut satisfieri debet et intelligitur primo bona fides per abnegationem, scilicet sui contrarii, id est, privationem doli [cits. omitted], unde bona fide cessante, id est, dolo interveniente, de iure contractus non est servandus; sicut factus per eum, qui dolum passus est; et si contractus bonae fidei incipit a traditione, habet locum actio de dolo propter dolum [cits. omitted], et si credebat se teneri, locum habet condictio indebiti secundum Nic[olaus] de Mat[arellis]. In secundo autem actu intelligitur bona fides et observatio eius, quod actum est inter

equity' is a type of good faith distinct from faithfulness to one's promises and the mere absence of *dolus*. 'Natural equity' determines what the parties' obligations are when their contract and the law are silent as to a particular matter.

In other passages, *Baldus* expressly identified 'natural equity' with the principle that no one should be enriched at another's expense.[87] He also said that 'natural equity' requires that a person who received an unjust price should have a remedy.[88] In discussing that remedy, he maintained that 'equity or equality is to be served in contracts both in interpreting them and in justifying them'.[89]

Thus *Baldus'* conclusions parallel those of *Aristotle* and *Thomas*. *Baldus* identified a fundamental principle which is much like the Aristotelian principle of equality. Like *Aristotle* and *Thomas*, he distinguished violations of this principle from other wrongful actions: from breaking one's word and deceiving the other party. Like *Thomas*, he used the principle to explain why relief is given when the price is unfair. Like *Thomas*, he used it to explain why the parties are bound to certain obligations which they did not expressly assume.

A further parallel is the way *Thomas* and *Baldus* discussed the implied obligations of the parties. For *Thomas*, as we have seen, the principle of equality is the source of the implied obligations of the parties because a contract of exchange is defined in terms of equality. It is an act of commutative justice. The terms that will preserve equality therefore followed from the nature, substantial form or essence of a contract of exchange.

Baldus also said that the implied obligations of the parties followed from the nature of their contract. As we have seen, this terminology had been

---

contrahentes secundum naturalem aequitatem, et iuris ordinationem. naturalis enim aequitas est attenda, cum dubitatio oritur circa ea, quae non sunt in iure expressa, et per hoc intelligitur iudici committi [cits. omitted] aut ordinatio attenditur in his, quae in iure sunt expressa [cits. omitted]. Ex praedictis modis suadet equitas bonam fidem servari, quod comprehendit et tradit haec lex.'

[87] Baldus (n. 22) to D. 4, 32, 2 no. 3: 'et fundantur in ratione, naturali aequitate, que est quod quis non locupletetur cum aliena iactura'. See n. 88, below. That principle, according to Baldus, is the basis of the law of unjust enrichment. Ibid. to C. 4, 44, 1 no. 3: 'non debet quis praetextu metus sibi illati lucrari cum aliena iactura [cit. omitted] et in ista equitate generali fundatur omnia remedia in integrum restitutionis'.

[88] Ibid. to C. 4, 44, 2 nos. 17–18: C. 4, 44, 2 applies to all contracts *bonae fidei* 'quia omnium contractuum bonae fidei eadem est equitas et ratio: ergo idem debet ius esse. Dico etiam quod equitas huius legis extendit se ad contractus stricti iuris, in quibus hicinde par debet nasci obligatio secundum naturalem equitatem.'

[89] Ibid. to C. 4, 44, 2 no. 48: 'in contractibus, est servanda aequitas, vel aequalitas, tam in interpretandis, quam in ipsis iustificandis'.

used by medieval jurists long before *Baldus*. Initially, at least, these jurists could not have known much about the meaning of terms such as 'nature' or 'substance' in Aristotelian philosophy. They could not have read the 'Physics' or 'Metaphysics' and knew Aristotelian metaphysics only as trivialised by *Boethius*.[90] *Baldus* not only continued to use their terminology. He seems to have been using it in its Aristotelian sense.

As already noted, he said not only that the implied obligations of the parties are natural to the contract, but also that the contract is to be interpreted according to the principle that no one should be enriched at another's expense. That is close to the Thomistic and Aristotelian idea that the nature of a contract of exchange is defined in terms of equality.

Moreover, *Baldus* spoke of 'nature', 'substance' and 'accident' in a way that shows an appreciation of the Aristotelian meaning of these terms. The 'essential' or 'substantial' terms are the 'original root' of a contract to which it is 'principally ordered'. The natural terms are 'an extension of this root to the production of mere qualities' to which the contract is 'consecutively ordered'.[91] While the natural terms are 'according to the nature of a contract', the accidental terms are 'beyond its nature'.[92] They are a 'form [that] can be added or subtracted without a substantial change in the subject'.[93] Ordered as they are to the nature of the contract, the natural terms belong to it 'tacitly'.[94] The parties can modify them by express agreement, but there is a limit to the extent to which they can do so. If the parties added a provision that would remove the 'natural effect' of the contract, the provision is void since to remove the 'natural effect is to remove the species'.[95] Indeed, 'agreements that cannot attain their due

---

[90] Hermann Kantorowicz, William Buckland, *Studies in the Glossators of the Roman Law* (1938) 41. On the knowledge of *Aristotle* of the later Glossators, see Gordley (n. 70) 33–4.

[91] The substance of a contract is its 'radix originalis'. The natural terms are an 'extensio illius radicis ex mera qualitate producta'. Accidental terms are not included 'virtute contractus' because 'nec principaliter nec consecutive ordinabatur ad hoc': Baldus (n. 22) to C. 4, 38, 13 no. 8. Since he had just distinguished essential and natural terms, presumably he meant that the former are principally ordered and the latter are consecutively ordered to the contract.

[92] Baldus (n. 22) to D. 18, 1, 72, 1 no. 4: 'Conclude ergo quod accidentalia sunt praeter naturam: naturalia sunt secundum naturam.'

[93] Ibid. to C. 4, 38, 13 nos. 6–7: 'aliud vocatur accidens, quod est forma quaedam superaddita supra substantiam et naturam ex aliquo speciali modo, vel pacto: et quae forma potest adesse et abesse sine substantiali transmutatione subiecti'.

[94] Ibid. to D. 18, 1, 72: 'quaedam naturalia, quae tacite insunt'.

[95] Ibid. to C. 4, 38 (rubric) no. 19: 'quaeritur, quid si apponatur pactum, quod removet a contractu naturalem eius effectum . . . ? Respondeo non tenet venditio, quia a quo removetur naturalis effectus, removetur species.'

end according to the nature given them are deemed to be imperfect'[96] and cannot be enforced until the imperfection is removed.[97] For example, a contract cannot fail to provide that a party would not be liable for *dolus* committed in the future.[98]

There is a further parallel. *Aristotle*, as we have seen, discussed the virtue of commutative justice in one part of the 'Nicomachean Ethics' and the virtue of liberality in another. *Thomas* concluded that when one person transferred a thing to another, he was either performing an act of commutative justice or an act of liberality. *Baldus* formulated the famous doctrine that every contract must have a *causa*, and the *causa* can be either 'liberality' or the receipt of something in return for what one gave. This distinction resembles the one *Thomas* drew between acts of liberality and acts of commutative justice.

This distinction is not contained in the Roman texts that mention *causa*.[99] It was not drawn by the Glossators, who were unfamiliar with *Aristotle's* 'Ethics'. In the late thirteenth century, *Petrus of Bellapertica*, who was familiar with *Aristotle*, distinguished contracts made *causa onerosa* and *causa lucrativa*.[100] In the fourteenth century, *Bartolus*, who admired *Aristotle* and *Aquinas*, said that a contract must have a *causa*,[101] and seems to have thought the *causa* might be liberality.[102]

With *Baldus* the parallel to the ideas of *Aristotle* and *Aquinas* became closer still. *Baldus* explained that 'without a *causa* equity will not say that an action arises lest one party use his substance badly and the other be unjustifiably enriched'.[103] That statement makes sense only if one thinks of the distinction between the two kinds of *causa* exactly as *Aristotle* and *Aquinas* thought of the distinction between liberality and commutative justice. An act of commutative justice enriches neither party at the other's

---

[96] Ibid. to C. 4, 38, 13 no. 5: 'unde conventiones, quae non possunt attingere debitum finem secundum naturam eis datam, reputant imperfectae'.

[97] Ibid. to C. 4, 38, 13 nos. 24–5.

[98] Ibid. to D. 4, 3, 7 no. 9: 'Dolus futurus per pactum remitti non potest.'

[99] One Roman text said that 'when there is no *causa*, no obligation can be constituted by an agreement'. D. 2, 14, 7, 1. Accursius said that *causa* means *datio vel factum*, something given or done: Accursius (n. 12) to D. 2, 14, 7, 1 to *causa*. Another text said that a *stipulatio* must have a *causa*. Accursius said that *causa* means *re vel spe*, a thing or the hope of a thing: Accursius (n. 12) to D. 44, 4, 2, 3 to *idoneam*.

[100] Petrus de Bellapertica (n. 43) to D. 44, 7, 53 [vulg. 44, 7, 52]; to D. 44, 7, 54 [vulg. 44, 7, 53].

[101] Bartolus (n. 21) to D. 12, 47, 2: 'nulla subest causa, scilicet impleta, sed conventio bene fuit ob causam'.   [102] See ibid. to D. 44, 4, 2, 3.

[103] Baldus (n. 61) to X 1, 4, 11 no. 30: 'non enim debet esse nudum causam quia sine causa aequitas non dictat actionem nasci, ne qui male utatur substantia sua, et alius immerito locupletetur'.

expense. An act of liberality does so, but in a sensible manner. As *Aristotle* said, liberality meant not merely giving wealth away but giving 'to the right people, the right amounts, and at the right time'.[104] Therefore, one who performs an act of liberality is not using his substance badly. And indeed, elsewhere *Baldus* presumes that if one gives wealth away, either it is an act of liberality or it is foolishness. For example, if the notarial document (a formality that had become the accepted substitute for *stipulatio*) did not state the *causa* for which wealth was given away, one should presume the contract was made out of 'foolishness' rather than 'liberality'.[105] If a rustic or ignorant person has renounced the remedy for *laesio enormis*, the judge should assume he did so 'more from stupidity than from liberality'.[106] If the seller might have known he was receiving less than the just price, and there is doubt as to his intentions, we should 'rather presume mistake than liberality'.[107]

Baldus concluded that a contract without a *causa* was unenforceable even in Canon law.[108] As modern scholars have noted, he was the first to formulate this doctrine which then became standard among Canon lawyers.[109]

The extent to which *Baldus* drew upon *Aristotle* and *Aquinas* has sometimes been overlooked. *Norbert Horn*, in his excellent work on the philosophical ideas of *Baldus*, noted only one of the parallels we have seen: the

---

[104] Aristotle (n. 63) IV.i 1119b–1120a.

[105] Baldus (n. 22) to C. 4, 30, 13 no. 14: 'sicut ergo nulla inserta causa presumiter stultia, non liberalitas'.

[106] Ibid. to C. 4, 44, 2 no. 21: One who knows he is selling for less than half the just price is treated as one who renounces the remedy. 'Sed Nic[olaus] de Mat[arellis] intelligit hoc verum, nisi personae simplicitas vel rusticitas, quae arbitrio iudicis committitur, suadet potius esse processum ex facilitate, quam ex liberalitate.'

[107] Ibid. to C. 4, 44, 2 no. 24: If it is uncertain whether the seller knew he was receiving less than half the just price, proof of the matter depends on conjectures; 'si autem de talibus coniecturis nihil est probatum, presumitur potius error quam liberalitas, ubi est tantae laesionis enormitas, secundum Nic[olaus] de Mat[arellis]'.

[108] Ibid. to C. 3, 36, 15 no. 3: 'iure canonico oritur actio ex nudo pacto, dummodo habeat causam'; see also Baldus (n. 61) to X 1, 35, 1.

[109] A. Söllner, 'Die causa im Kondiktionen- und Vertragsrecht des Mittelalters bei den Glossatoren, Kommentoren und Kanonisten', ZSS 77 (1960) 182 at 250; K. Nanz, *Die Entstehung des allgemeinen Vertragsbegriffs im 16. bis 18. Jahrhundert* (1985) 54. Roussier claimed that *Baldus* could not have been the first because the tradition of Christian morality would never have enforced an 'abstract act' without regard to whether there was a 'duty in conscience' to perform the promise: Roussier (n. 27) 179–81. That argument suggests that even prior to *Baldus* the Canon law courts would not enforce any promise whatever, but it does not show that anyone before *Baldus* formulated the requirement of *causa*.

resemblance between *Baldus' aequitas in specie* and *Aristotle's epieíkeia*. He doubted that *Baldus* was drawing directly on *Aristotle* for the sole reason that *Baldus* did not cite him.[110] That is not a powerful argument. *Baldus'* purpose was not to show the inspiration for his ideas but rather that these ideas could be supported from Roman texts. It is not surprising he only cites these texts. Moreover, *Baldus* often does not cite *Aristotle* or *Aquinas* even when his debt to them is evident: for example, when he notes that 'that which removes the potency removes the act',[111] or identifies the efficient, material, formal and final causes of a human act,[112] or tells us that 'the final cause is the first principle in intention although it is the last in execution'.[113] One could give dozens of similar examples. Moreover, the number of instances in which *Baldus* seems to be drawing on *Aristotle* or *Thomas* is too great to be explained any other way.

Whatever the influence of *Aristotle* and *Thomas*, *Baldus'* treatment of good faith and equity in contracts is remarkably different from that of earlier jurists. As we have seen, the earlier jurists thought that good faith meant keeping one's word, avoiding deceit and overreaching, and respecting obligations that were implicit in the transaction in which one is engaged. But they did not propose a definition of equity or good faith that would help in analysing these situations. *Baldus* identified a critical principle of 'equity' or 'good faith': no one should be enriched at another's expense. This was not all that equity or good faith required. One should also keep one's word and refrain from deceit. But, for *Baldus*, this principle helped to place a limit to one's duty to keep one's word. One need only do so when there was a *causa*: either liberality or the exchange of things of equivalent value. It explained the remedy for the kind of unfairness his predecessors had called *dolus ex re ipsa*. And it was the source of the obligations which the parties must respect but to which they had not expressly agreed.

IV. Conclusion

1. *After* Baldus

Paradoxically, although the new Aristotelian learning helped *Baldus* to clarify the concepts of good faith and equity, ultimately, it made recourse

---

[110] Horn (n. 80) 48.
[111] Baldus (n. 22) to C. 4, 32, 2 no. 5: 'a quo removetur potentia, removetur actus'.
[112] Ibid. to C. 4, 6, 8 nos. 10–11: 'Debes scire, quod quattuor sunt causae cardinales, ut sic dixerim. causa efficiens, finalis, formalis et materialis.'
[113] Ibid. to C. 5, 12, 6 no. 24: 'causa finalis est primum principium intentionis, licet sit ultimum executionis'.

to these concepts less necessary. In the sixteenth and early seventeenth centuries, a school of jurists centred in Spain and known to historians as the 'late Scholastics' self-consciously tried to synthesise Roman law with the moral philosophy of *Aristotle* and *Aquinas*. *Baldus* had borrowed from that philosophy interstitially. The late Scholastics rebuilt Roman law on an Aristotelian and Thomistic ground plan. Many of their conclusions were borrowed and popularised by the Natural law school of the seventeenth and eighteenth centuries founded by *Hugo Grotius* and *Samuel Pufendorf*, and by those the Natural lawyers influenced, such as the French jurists *Jean Domat* and *Robert Pothier*.[114]

The late Scholastics and the northern Natural lawyers discussed the various duties which, according to *Baldus*, arise from 'equity' and 'good faith'. Unlike *Baldus*, however, they were not trying to pin their conclusions to the wording of particular Roman texts. Therefore, they used the expressions 'equity' or 'good faith' much less frequently. Typically, they spoke about faithfulness to promises, about *dolus*, about gratuitous contracts and contracts of exchange, about equality in exchange, and about the terms which the nature of a contract called for.[115]

There were exceptions. According to *Domat*, a person who enters into an agreement of a given type is bound 'not only by what is expressed but also to everything that is required by the nature of the agreement and to all the consequences that equity, statute and usage give to the obligation one has undertaken'.[116] According to differences in their needs, the parties could modify these provisions as they saw fit.[117] But they could not do so in a way that would violate law, good morals or the 'equity' that ought to prevail in an onerous contract. For example, absent agreement by the parties, the seller must guarantee his goods against defects since otherwise the buyer would have paid the fair price for non-defective goods and received defective ones instead. If they wished, *Domat* explained, the parties could agree that the seller will not be liable for defects, but they could do so only if the seller reduces the price to preserve equality.[118] For *Domat*, as for *Baldus*, 'equity' meant equality in exchange.

His words were preserved in art. 1135 of the French Civil Code which provides: 'Agreements are obligatory not only as to that which is expressed in them but also as to all the consequences that equity, usage or statute give the obligation according to its nature.' By the nineteenth century, however, Aristotelian notions of equality in exchange had fallen out of

[114] Gordley (n. 70) 69–111.   [115] Ibid.
[116] Jean Domat, *Les Loix civiles dans leur ordre naturel* (1713) I.i.iii.1.
[117] Ibid., I.i.4; Jean Domat, *Traité des loix* (1713) vi.9.   [118] Domat (n. 116) I.i.2.

fashion. Commentators on the French Civil Code defined contract in terms of the will of the parties. According to *Laurent*, the implied terms of the parties' agreement were merely terms the parties themselves would have willed. The law read them into the agreement merely 'to dispense the parties from writing them into their instruments . . .'.[119] The judge should carefully refrain from interfering with the parties' decision in the name of equity.[120] The will had become the source of all the parties' obligations, and there was no higher standard by which the will itself could be criticised or supplemented.

Nineteenth-century German jurists defined contract in terms of *Willenserklärungen*, the expressions of wills of the parties. They had as little use for concepts of equality in exchange as the French. For them, as for the French, the implied obligations of the parties arose from the parties' will.[121] Thus, as has often been remarked, when the German jurists placed a requirement of good faith in § 242 of the German Civil Code, it seemed innocuous. 'Good faith' no longer meant there were obligations of substantive fairness which the parties must respect. The committee that initially approved the words 'good faith' thought they were adopting 'less a legal norm proclaiming a duty to perform the contract than a general rule of interpretation'.[122] Yet the genie was still in the bottle, ready to come forth when it was summoned.

2. Retrospective

Seeing how jurists once approached a problem can sometimes help us to understand it better. In this instance, the guidance the past gives us is not clear.

According to some modern jurists, the concept of good faith is inherently undefinable. Some German jurists have warned that we should not expect to find a clear rule.[123] We must be content with a list of *Fallgruppen*.

---

[119] François Laurent, *Principes de droit civil français*, vol. XVI (3rd edn, 1869–78) § 182.
[120] Ibid., 178.
[121] E.g., Georg Puchta, *Pandekten* (2nd edn, 1844) § 58; Bernhard Windscheid, *Lehrbuch des Pandektenrects*, vol. I (7th edn, 1891) § 75 n. 1a; Ludwig Enneccerus, *Rechtsgeschäft, Bedingung und Anfangstermin* (1889) 17–19.
[122] 'Protokolle der [1.] Kommission zur Ausarbeitung eines bürgerlichen Gesetzbuchs', in: Horst Jakobs, Werner Schubert (eds.), *Die Beratung des Bürgerlichen Gesetzbuchs in systematischer Zusammenstellung der unveröffentlichten Quellen, Recht der Schuldverhältnisse*, vol. I (1978) 47.
[123] E.g., Günter Roth, in: *Münchener Kommentar zum Bürgerlichen Gesetzbuch*, vol. II (3rd edn, 1994) § 242, n. 1 ('§ 242 ist seiner heutigen Bedeutung nach keine Rechtsnorm in dem

Similarly, the American jurist *Robert Summers* had described 'good faith' as an 'excluder': a concept that cannot be defined but excludes heterogeneous instances of bad faith.[124] Those who hold this view might well point to the experience of the medieval jurists. Before *Baldus*, they never defined good faith in a way that helped to resolve cases. Instead, they described discrete situations in which good faith was required. They explained what good faith required in these situations with systems or schema which seem quite independent of any general conception of good faith. When *Baldus* tried to give 'good faith' a more definite meaning, he drew on Aristotelian philosophical ideas that are now quite out of fashion. Perhaps the medieval experience suggests that we will always need an expression like 'good faith' but we will never be able to define it. We should remain content with our list of *Fallgruppen*.

Or perhaps the medieval experience at least suggests how we could usefully classify our *Fallgruppen*. As we have seen, to the jurists before *Baldus*, good faith meant (i) keeping one's word, (ii) neither (a) deliberately deceiving the other party nor (b) driving an overly harsh bargain, and (iii) respecting those obligations which are not expressly undertaken but belong to the contract as a matter of fair interpretation. This list is simpler than the one typically found in commentaries on § 242 of the German Civil Code. Moreover, it is striking how many of the case studies on which this book is based fall within one of these categories.

Or could it be that the principle of equality in exchange is only temporarily out of fashion?[125] Perhaps *Baldus* was right, and the principle can explain when the parties are bound by obligations they did not expressly undertake or are not bound by those they did. If so, we could again speak of an underlying principle and not merely of *Fallgruppen*. Indeed, like the jurists after *Baldus*, we might find ourselves speaking more often of equality and less often of good faith.

Sinn, daß unter seinen Tatbestand ein Sachverhalt subsumiert werden und aus seiner Rechtsfolgeaussage dann ein konkretes Ergebnis entnommen werden könnte').

[124] Robert S. Summers, '"Good Faith" in General Contract Law and the Sales Provisions of the Uniform Commercial Code', (1968) 54 *Virginia Law Review* 185 ff.

[125] See James Gordley, 'Equality in Exchange', (1981) 69 *California Law Review* 1587 ff.; Gordley, 'Enforcing Promises', (1995) 83 *California Law Review* 547 ff.

4   The conceptualisation of good faith in American contract law: a general account

ROBERT S. SUMMERS

I. Historical introduction

Each state of the United States has its own separate and relatively self-sufficient body of general contract law. In a given state, most of this law consists of common law opinions of the highest court of that state. This means the United States has fifty bodies of general contract law. Each state legislature has also adopted the Uniform Commercial Code, a body of statute law that applies to contracts for the sale of goods, negotiable instruments, certain relations between banks, and between banks and their depositors, letters of credit, bulk sales, warehouse receipts, bills of lading, investment securities, and security interests in personal property. In addition, each state legislature has adopted various isolated statutes of its own which deal with one or more aspects of contract law. A few federal statutes also address issues of contract law.

Before the 1960s, it could not be said that the American states acknowledged any *general* obligation of good faith in their contract law. A tiny handful of states might have been viewed as exceptions to this generalisation, but in none of those states was the obligation of good faith at all explicitly developed. The major contract treatises by *Samuel Williston* and by *Arthur L. Corbin* did not recognise any general obligation of good faith in the American case law, nor did any other leading scholars. But in research for an article that I published in 1968, I discovered that it was possible to identify many important types of American judicial decisions which could be construed to exemplify a general obligation of good faith in contractual relations. I also discovered that many of these decisions actually invoked not merely concepts of good faith, but also this very terminology.[1]

In the 1960s, the Uniform Commercial Code was being introduced in, and adopted by, the American state legislatures. That Code included section 1–203 which provides: 'Every contract or duty within this Act imposes an obligation of good faith in its performance or enforcement.' This provision, however, was applicable only to contracts covered by the Code such as sale of goods contracts, letters of credit and security agreements. It did not apply to contracts generally, and therefore did not apply to construction contracts, land sale contracts, real estate mortgage contracts, insurance contracts and many other types of contracts.

Apart from UCC section 1–203, above, it was not until 1979 (with official promulgation in 1981) that there was any kind of official acknowledgement of a widespread general obligation of good faith in major types of contractual relations in American contract law, and that acknowledgement came in the form of the new 'Restatement of Contracts Second' in its section 205, which provides as follows: '§205. Duty of Good Faith and Fair Dealing. Every contract imposes upon each party a duty of good faith and fair dealing in its performance and its enforcement.'

The American concept of a 'Restatement' is a very special type of 'law'. It is not statute law adopted by a state legislature or by Congress. Nor is it common law made by the highest court of any given state. It is not even an attempt to restate the actual case law of every state, state by state. Instead, a Restatement represents an attempt by the American Law Institute, a private organisation of scholars, judges and practitioners, to formulate with some precision the leading rules and principles in major

---

[1] Robert S. Summers, '"Good Faith" in General Contract Law and the Sales Provisions of the Uniform Commercial Code', (1968) 54 *Virginia Law Review* 195 ff.

fields of American law, 'in the aggregate', so to speak, as if the United States consisted of only one, rather than fifty, state jurisdictions. Where the actual legal rules and principles in the various states are in conflict, or are not well developed, the Restatements frequently purport to formulate rules and principles that represent 'the better view'. The American Restatements began in the 1920s. The first Restatement in contract law was promulgated in 1932, and as I have said, the second Restatement officially appeared in 1981. There were several major changes between the first and second Restatements of Contracts, and the entirely new section 205, above, represents one of the three or four most significant changes. Section 205 in the second Restatement was based mainly on the accumulation of cases identified in the article I published in 1968, on UCC section 1–203, and on an important earlier article by Professor *Farnsworth* in 1963.[2]

The American Restatements have had and continue to have substantial influence on the courts within each state of the United States. Thus, by the 1980s, not only had the 'Restatement of Contracts Second' incorporated section 205, above, but the state court systems of many American states had explicitly adopted or acknowledged a general obligation of good faith applicable to contractual relations, and all the American state legislatures had adopted the Uniform Commercial Code with its section 1–203, set forth above.

One American treatise published in 1995 which deals exclusively with good faith, states that: 'In all the years before 1980, there were perhaps 350 reported cases interpreting the obligation to perform a contract in good faith. In the dozen years following 1980, there were another 600 or more.'[3]

II. Some concrete examples of contractual bad faith

Merely to lend concreteness to this article, and to provide meaningful background for the general discussion which follows, several specific examples of contractual bad faith will now be set forth. All are based on actual American case law, although it cannot be said that every American State Supreme Court would certainly treat each as a prohibited form of bad faith.

First, I will offer two examples of behaviour in the *negotiation and formation* of contracts that would fail to satisfy a general requirement of contractual good faith, in so far as adopted and applicable, in the jurisdic-

---

[2] E. Allan Farnsworth, 'Good Faith Performance and Commercial Reasonableness Under the Uniform Commercial Code', (1963) 30 *University of Chicago Law Review* 666 ff.

[3] Steven J. Burton, Eric G. Andersen, *Contractual Good Faith – Formation, Performance, Breach, and Enforcement* (1995) 20 ff.

tion, to the negotiation and formation stage.[4] (i) *The withdrawing negotiator*: A negotiator tells the other party that if the other party will make certain expenditures, then the negotiator will enter a contract with the other party; but after the other party makes the expenditures, the negotiator entirely refuses to negotiate further, and there is no change of circumstances. (ii) *The non-disclosing negotiator*: A prospective purchaser of real property, by trespassing on the owner's land, learns that the land contains valuable minerals unknown to the owner, but does not disclose this to the owner and contracts to buy the land from the owner at a lower price.

Secondly, I offer two illustrative examples of behaviour in the purported performance of a contract that would fail to satisfy a general requirement of contractual good faith. (iii) *The diverting lessee*: A lessee who leases business premises from lessor A at a rental that is a percentage of lessee's gross sales on lessor A's premises, later leases other business premises from lessor B nearby at a rental that is a lower percentage of gross sales, and lessee then diverts customers away from lessor A's premises to the premises leased from lessor B. (iv) *The uncooperative buyer*: A buyer contracts to buy land from the seller which the buyer knows the seller does not then own but plans to acquire from a third party at a public auction, yet the buyer himself also attends the auction, and outbids his seller and thus himself takes the land from the third party.

Thirdly, I present two examples of behaviour in the purported enforcement of contract rights that would fail to satisfy a general requirement of contractual good faith. (v) *The opportunistic employer*: An employer in a contract terminable 'at will' exercises his general legal power to terminate the employment of an employee–salesman, but this is to avoid having to pay the employee a contractually specified commission on a sale that the employee previously had made on behalf of the employer, but which was not yet payable to the employee on the date of termination. (vi) *The dishonest compromiser*: A party pretends to be dissatisfied with the other's performance in order to secure a 'compromise' that, in effect, reduces the contract price that the dishonest compromiser must pay.

III. The variant conceptualisations of good faith

Here, I will identify and discuss several different conceptualisations of good faith in American law and in scholarly writings. These conceptualisations appear in: (1) UCC 1–203, (2) Restatement (Second) of Contracts

---

[4] Neither UCC § 1–203 nor Restatement § 205 apply the good faith requirement to the negotiation and formation stage.

sec. 205, (3) writings of Professor *Robert S. Summers*, (4) writings of Professor *Steven J. Burton*, and (5) writings of Professor *E. Allan Farnsworth*. Each is distinctive in some way. There are judicial decisions following each.

1. The UCC Section 1–203 conceptualisation

The Uniform Commercial Code, section 1–203 does not apply to the negotiation or formation stage. The section provides that: 'Every contract or duty within this Act imposes an obligation of good faith in its performance or enforcement.' UCC section 1–201(11) defines good faith at least to mean 'honesty in fact in the conduct or transactions concerned'. This is a narrow definition. Indeed Professor *Farnsworth* argued that this narrow definition 'enfeebled' UCC 1–203.[5] UCC section 2–103(1)(b) also includes a broader definition of good faith applicable at least within Article Two of the Code on sales of goods: 'In this article, unless the context otherwise requires ... good faith in the case of a merchant means honesty in fact and the observance of reasonable commercial standards of fair dealing in the trade.'

It may be that the Code drafters intended this broader definition to apply only when a specific provision in Article Two on the sale of goods uses the phrase 'good faith'. On this reading, the scope of the broader definition would be highly narrow because only thirteen sections in Article Two use the words 'good faith'.[6] Another limiting feature of the special definition of good faith in Article Two is that it applies only 'in the case of a merchant'. UCC section 2–104(1) says: '(1) "Merchant" means a person who deals in goods of the kind or otherwise by his occupation holds himself out as having knowledge or skill peculiar to the practices or goods involved in the transaction or to whom such knowledge or skill may be attributed by his employment of an agent or broker or other intermediary who by his occupation holds himself out as having such knowledge or skill.'

The broader definition of good faith in UCC section 2–103(1)(b) can operate only in so far as there are commercial standards of fair dealing in a given trade which are reasonable. It may be difficult to determine what a trade is, and a given trade may not have any standards at all; it may be a jungle. In that event, the only forms of bad faith ruled out would be those

---

[5] See Farnsworth, (1963) 30 *University of Chicago Law Review* 674 ff.
[6] UCC §§ 2–305(2), 2–306(1), 2–31(1), 2–323(2)(b), 2–328(4), 2–402(2), 2–403(1), 2–506(2), 2–603(3), 2–615(a), 2–703(3), 2–706(1), 2–706(5) and 2–712(1).

excluded by the narrow 'honesty in fact' language of UCC section 1-201(19). Thus, for example, forms of bad faith involving carelessness or recklessness would not be ruled out. Nor would openly taking unfair advantage, openly abusing a power to specify terms, openly acting capriciously, or openly undercutting another's performance.

The Uniform Commercial Code's various sections also have accompanying 'Official Comments' which the courts take seriously as guidelines to construing the Code. Numerous comments expressly require some form of contractual good faith.[7]

There is now a large body of case law interpreting and applying the Uniform Commercial Code's provisions on good faith.[8] Nearly all of these cases are consistent with the conceptualisations of good faith in the Code.

In 1994, the Permanent Editorial Board of the Uniform Commercial Code promulgated an addition to the Official Comment to UCC section 1-203 on good faith:[9] 'This section does not support an independent cause of action for failure to perform or enforce in good faith. Rather, this section means that a failure to perform or enforce, in good faith, a specific duty or obligation under the contract, constitutes a breach of that contract or makes unavailable, under the particular circumstances, a remedial right or power. This distinction makes it clear that the doctrine of good faith merely directs a court towards interpreting contracts within the commercial context in which they are created, performed, and enforced, and does not create a separate duty of fairness and reasonableness which can be independently breached.'

A further proposed revision of UCC section 1-201(19) states that good faith means 'honesty in fact and the observance of reasonable standards of fair dealing in the conduct of the transaction concerned'.[10]

2. The Restatement (Second) of Contracts conceptualisation

As we have seen, the text of section 205 of the Restatement provides: '§205. Duty of Good Faith and Fair Dealing. Every contract imposes upon each party a duty of good faith and fair dealing in its performance and its enforcement.' This conceptualisation is accompanied by a formal

---

[7] See Summers, (1968) 54 *Virginia Law Review* 214 ff.
[8] *Uniform Commercial Code Case Digest, Volume 1–201 through 1–203*, Clark/Boardman/Callaghan, (1997) 708–831 ff.
[9] *Uniform Commercial Code Reporting Service Findex, PEB Commentary No. 10* (1997).
[10] Richard E. Speidel, 'The Duty of Good Faith in Contract Performance and Enforcement', (1996) 46 *Journal of Legal Education* 537 ff., n. 19, 540 ff.

comment that, in subsections a, d and e, provides as follows (and for the full text, see the appendix to this chapter):

'a. *Meanings of "good faith".* Good faith is defined in Uniform Commercial Code § 1–201(19) as "honesty in fact in the conduct or transaction concerned". "In the case of a merchant" Uniform Commercial Code § 2–103(1)(b) provides that good faith means "honesty in fact and the observance of reasonable commercial standards of fair dealing in the trade". The phrase "good faith" is used in a variety of contexts, and its meaning varies somewhat with the context. Good faith performance or enforcement of a contract emphasizes faithfulness to an agreed common purpose and consistency with the justified expectations of the other party; it excludes a variety of types of conduct characterized as involving "bad faith" because they violate community standards of decency, fairness or reasonableness. The appropriate remedy for a breach of the duty of good faith also varies with the circumstances . . .

'd. *Good faith performance.* Subterfuges and evasions violate the obligation of good faith in performance even though the actor believes his conduct to be justified. But the obligation goes further: bad faith may be overt or may consist of inaction, and fair dealing may require more than honesty. A complete catalogue of types of bad faith is impossible, but the following types are among those which have been recognized in judicial decision: evasion of the spirit of the bargain, lack of diligence and slacking off, willful rendering of imperfect performance, abuse of a power to specify terms, and interference with or failure to cooperate in the other party's performance.

'e. *Good faith in enforcement.* The obligation of good faith and fair dealing extends to the assertion, settlement and litigation of contract claims and defenses. See, e.g., §§ 73, 89. The obligation is violated by dishonest conduct such as conjuring up a pretended dispute, asserting an interpretation contrary to one's own understanding, or falsification of facts. It also extends to dealing which is candid but unfair, such as taking advantage of the necessitous circumstances of the other party to extort a modification of a contract for the sale of goods without legitimate commercial reason. See Uniform Commercial Code § 2–209, Comment 2. Other types of violation have been recognized in judicial decisions: harassing demands for assurances of performance, rejection of performance for unstated reasons, willful failure to mitigate damages, and abuse of a power to determine compliance or to terminate the contract. For a statutory duty of good faith in termination, see the federal Automobile Dealer's Day in Court Act, 15 U.S.C. §§ 1221–25 (1976).'

Thus, Restatement section 205 does not apply to the negotiation stage, but only to the performance and enforcement of contracts actually entered. Comment a, above, sets forth three purposes of the duty of good faith and fair dealing: (i) 'faithfulness to an agreed common purpose', (ii) 'consistency with the justified expectations of the other party', and (iii) consistency with 'community standards of decency, fairness or reasonableness'. Plainly all these categories overlap.

Section 205 was incorporated into the then evolving draft of the Restatement at the May 1970 meeting of the American Law Institute in Washington D.C. The transcript of the 1970 Proceedings includes the following statement by Professor *Robert Braucher* of the Harvard Law School who was then the chief drafter of the Restatement:[11] 'Now, the trouble with this section, of course, is that it's very general, very abstract, and it needs specification the worst way, and specification is not to be had. I am indebted for its formulation here in the comments – formulations in the comments – to Professor *Summers* in a piece cited on page 100. He made considerable effort and collected this very large number of cases in which judicial opinions had insisted on some obligation of good faith and fair dealing in the performance and enforcement of contracts. And then he tried to categorize them, and I have borrowed heavily from his classification scheme in giving a little more detail about this.'

Section 205 and its comments thus rely *partly* on what may be called an 'excluder' conceptualisation of good faith. That type of conceptualisation is explained below.

3. The Summers 1968 'excluder' conceptualisation of good faith

The article I wrote on which Professor *Braucher* based part of the American Law Institute's excluder conceptualisation of good faith appeared in volume 54 of the 'Virginia Law Review' at page 195 in April 1968. The key portion of the article is quoted below (footnotes omitted) and appears at pages 200–6: 'One of the principal theses of this article is that in cases of doubt, a lawyer will determine more accurately what the judge means by using the phrase "good faith" if he does not ask what good faith itself means, but rather asks: What, in the actual or hypothetical situation, does the judge intend to rule out by his use of this phrase? Once the relevant form of bad faith is thus identified, the lawyer can, if he wishes, assign a

[11] 1970 Proceedings of the American Law Institute, (1970) 47 *American Law Institute Proceedings* 489–91 ff.

specific meaning to good faith by formulating an "opposite" for the species of bad faith being ruled out. For example, a judge may say: "A public authority must act in good faith in letting bids." And from the facts or the language of the opinion it may appear that the judge is, in effect, saying: "The defendant acted in bad faith because he let bids only as a pretense to conceal his purpose to award the contract to a favored bidder." It can be said that "acting in good faith" here simply means: letting bids without a preconceived design to award the contract to a favored bidder.'

If good faith had a general meaning or meanings of its own – that is, if it were either univocal or ambiguous – there would seldom be occasion to derive a meaning for it from an opposite; its specific uses would almost always be readily and immediately understood. But good faith is not that kind of doctrine. In contract law, taken as a whole, good faith is an 'excluder'. It is a phrase without general meaning (or meanings) of its own and serves to exclude a wide range of heterogeneous forms of bad faith. In a particular context the phrase takes on specific meaning, but usually this is only by way of contrast with the specific form of bad faith actually or hypothetically ruled out. *Aristotle* was one of the first to recognise that the function of some words and phrases is not to convey general, 'extractable' meanings of their own, but rather is to exclude one or more of a variety of things. He thought 'voluntary' was such a word. And the late Professor *J. L. Austin* of Oxford made much of 'excluders'. His discussion of the term 'real' is instructive.

That is, a definite sense attaches to the assertion that something is real, a real such-and-such, only in the light of a specific way in which it might be, or might have been, *not* real. 'A real duck' differs from the simple 'a duck' only in that it is used to exclude various ways of being not a real duck – but a dummy, a toy, a picture, a decoy, etc.; and moreover I do not know just how to take the assertion that it is a real duck unless I know just what, on that particular occasion, the speaker has it in mind to exclude. This, of course, is why the attempt to find a characteristic common to all things that are or could be called 'real' is doomed to failure; the function of 'real' is not to contribute positively to the characterisation of anything, but to exclude possible ways of being not real – and these ways are both numerous for particular kinds of things, and liable to be quite different for things of different kinds. It is this identity of general function combined with immense diversity in specific applications which gives to the word 'real' the, at first sight, baffling feature of having neither one single 'meaning' nor yet ambiguity, a number of different meanings.

But it is not only because good faith is an 'excluder' that the case analyst will be wise to focus on what the phrase rules out, rather than on what it means. It is also because the typical judge who uses this phrase is primarily concerned with ruling out specific conduct, and only secondarily, or not at all, with formulating the positive content of a standard.

Good faith, then, takes on specific and variant meanings by way of contrast with the specific and variant forms of bad faith which judges decide to prohibit. From the cases it would be possible to compile a list of forms of bad faith, with an opposite for each listed as the corresponding specific meaning of good faith. The beginnings of such a list might look like this:

Form of bad faith conduct	Meaning of good faith
1. seller concealing a defect in what he is selling	fully disclosing material facts
2. builder wilfully failing to perform in full, though otherwise substantially performing	substantially performing without knowingly deviating from specifications
3. contractor openly abusing bargaining power to coerce an increase in the contract price	refraining from abuse of bargaining power
4. hiring a broker and then deliberately preventing him from consummating the deal	acting co-operatively
5. conscious lack of diligence in mitigating the other party's damages	acting diligently
6. arbitrarily and capriciously exercising a power to terminate a contract	acting with some reason
7. adopting an overreaching interpretation of contract language	interpreting contract language fairly
8. harassing the other party for repeated assurances of performance	accepting adequate assurances

This list could run on and on, but it is unnecessary to extend it for present purposes. As it stands, it shows how specific meanings for good faith can be derived and that this phrase rules out radically heterogeneous forms of bad faith.

Given the specific meanings of good faith in the foregoing right-hand column, it may seem all the more natural to suppose, contrary to our 'excluder' analysis, that there must be some single word or concise phrase which faithfully unifies all such specific meanings into one general meaning of the term. What about 'honesty'? Is not acting in good faith equivalent to acting honestly? Numerous judges appear to have thought so, but this is wrong unless, of course, the definition of honesty is stretched beyond recognition. Honesty only rules out dishonesty in its various forms. But good faith, as used by many judges, excludes numerous forms of contractual bad faith besides dishonesty. For one thing, dishonesty is necessarily immoral, but in the eyes of many judges contractual bad faith is not necessarily immoral at all. A party may, for example, abuse his bargaining power, undercut the other party's efforts to perform, or act capriciously without having the 'guilty mind' that would make his actions immoral – indeed, a party might even think this conduct is in the other party's own best interest. And despite this purity of mind, many judges could be counted on to say that such conduct conflicts with requirements of contractual good faith. As one judge stated, '[g]ood faith in law . . . is not to be measured always by a man's own standard for the observance of all men in their dealings with each other'.

Even if it were conceded that conduct must be subjectively immoral before it can constitute bad faith, it still would not follow that dishonesty is the only form of contractual bad faith. Thus when a man openly and straightforwardly gives another a 'raw deal', he does not necessarily act dishonestly. That is, he does not undertake to mislead or deceive. Consider, for example, the conduct of a buyer who openly seizes upon trivial defects to justify his rejection of goods under a rule requiring perfect tender, admitting all along that he is rejecting the goods because the price has gone down and he wishes to buy more cheaply elsewhere. Such conduct is not dishonest. But it may well be thought immoral, and it is certainly commercial bad faith. In truth, good faith cannot be defined in terms of honesty. As numerous judges use the phrase, it excludes many forms of bad faith which a requirement of honesty alone does not.

It is submitted that any but the most vacuous general definition of good faith will similarly fail to cover all the many and varied specific meanings that it is possible to assign to the phrase in light of the many and varied forms of bad faith recognised in the cases. Of course, a particular judge might declare that for him good faith does have a general, invariant meaning which he always intends when he uses the phrase. But if such a judge should have to pass on very many of the different forms of bad faith, it is most unlikely that he could stand by his definition for long.

To summarise, general definitions of good faith either spiral into the Charybdis of vacuous generality or collide with the Scylla of restrictive specificity. Moreover, the analyst who puts general definitions aside and tries to focus on the form of bad faith which a given judge intends to exclude by his use of the term is likely to get closer to that judge's meaning, for good faith functions as an 'excluder', and judges are more interested in what they are proscribing than in characterising what is generally allowed.

In 1982, in a further article, *Summers* added these methodological remarks:[12] 'In my view, a judge in a novel case posing an issue of good faith under section 205 with its excluder conceptualization is far from lacking meaningful guidance of the kind legitimately to be demanded in the name of the rule of law. He should start with the language of the section. Second, he should turn to the purposes of section 205 as set forth mainly in Comment a. These purposive rationales will infuse the excluder analysis with meaning in all the ways that purposive interpretation is known generally to provide guidance to judges (as in the case of statutes). Third, after completing this, he should seek guidance by the time-honored common-law method of reasoning by analogy, not only from past cases, but from the various illustrations set forth in the Comments to section 205. Such reasoning, particularly that which is done with an eye to the *reasons* given by prior judges, can provide substantial insight into how novel cases should be decided. Fourth, also in light of the purposes of section 205 and any general analogies, he can analyse the relevant facts – alleged or proven – to see what specific reasons these facts, and the values they implicate, generate for and against characterising the action or inaction in question as bad-faith behavior. Fifth, because of the very nature of the problem, the excluder analysis is not only faithful to the reality involved, but it is itself a distinctive source of illumination. It does not focus on some presumed positive and unitary element or cluster of elements called "good faith"; instead, it focuses on whether the alleged form of bad-faith behavior really is, in the context, ruled out by section 205, when considered in light of its purposes and in relation to the facts of the case. The foregoing factors do not exhaust all the forms of guidance that section 205 provides, but they are more than sufficient to rebut the charge that a section in which good faith is conceptualized as an excluder leaves the judges at sea and the "law" merely whatever the judges say it is.'

4. The Burton *conceptualisation of good faith*

In an important article in the 'Harvard Law Review' in 1980, Professor *Steven Burton* offered and defended still another conceptualisation of good

---

[12] Robert S. Summers, 'The Duty of Good Faith – Its Recognition and Conceptualization', (1982) 67 *Cornell Law Review* 810 ff., 823–4 ff.

faith performance:[13] ' "Good faith performance" occurs when a party's discretion is exercised for any purpose within the reasonable contemplation
of the parties at the time of formation – to capture opportunities that
were preserved upon entering the contract, interpreted objectively.'

The essence of the *Burton* approach is as follows.[14] One of the two
parties will always have what Professor *Burton* calls 'forgone opportunities' (to that party, a 'cost' of contracting). Bad faith contractual activity
is then defined as 'exercising discretion' to recapture one or more of the
opportunities forgone upon entering a contract. To determine whether
an opportunity was in fact forgone, it is necessary to inquire into the reasonable expectations of the 'dependent party' (the other party). The party
with discretion to perform acts in good faith if he does not attempt to
recapture a forgone opportunity. Professor *Burton* also argues that
'whether a particular discretion-exercising party acted to recapture
forgone opportunities is a question of subjective intent' – a 'subjective
inquiry'. Moreover, the 'objective inquiry' into the dependent party's reasonable expectations is not alone 'dispositive'. Indeed, Professor *Burton*
stresses that instead the inquiry into state of mind is 'of central importance'.

We may adopt one of Professor *Burton's* illustrations to try to demonstrate his model at work. Assume that L and T entered into a lease providing that T was to pay rentals as a percentage of the gross receipts of T's
business on the premises. T also had another store in the same town. From
time to time, he diverted customers to that other store (where he owned
the premises), thereby reducing the rentals otherwise payable to L. For
this, L sued T, claiming that T's diversionary tactics were in bad faith.
Here, according to Professor *Burton*, a court should presumably find (i) that
a reasonable person in L's position expected to receive rentals not depleted
by T's diversionary acts, and (ii) that T acted with the subjective intention
of recapturing a forgone opportunity.

Professor *Burton*, unlike many who have criticised general requirements
of good faith, does believe in them and has sought to direct his efforts
largely to making them more effective. Moreover, he does not ultimately
seek to resolve issues of good faith through a general definition of some
presumed positive content of that phrase. He also concedes that what a

---

[13] Steven J. Burton, 'Breach of Contract and the Common Law Duty To Perform in Good
Faith', (1980) 94 *Harvard Law Review* 369 ff., 373 ff.
[14] These remarks are drawn, with some modification, from pp. 830–4 of Summers, (1982)
67 *Cornell Law Review* 810 ff.

general good faith requirement rules out varies to some extent depending on the context. And he generally seeks to focus on the reasons for ruling out claimed forms of bad faith. In all these respects, despite some misleading protestations to the contrary, his approach is itself generally consistent with the spirit of section 205, including its excluder conceptualisation.

Professor *Burton* makes a number of claims on behalf of his approach, as opposed to what he calls the 'traditional' approach (born not so long ago in the history of the common law and including, presumably, that of section 205). First, he says that his approach provides more analytical focus. It isolates 'with greater particularity the factors that must be considered in determining good or bad faith performance'. Instead of an 'amorphous totality of factual circumstances', we have an inquiry into reasonable expectations of the 'dependent party' and the subjective intent of the 'discretion-exercising' party – all to determine precisely whether the discretion-exercising party has acted to recapture forgone opportunities so as to constitute bad faith. Is this analysis necessarily any more focused than that of section 205 in a novel good faith performance case? Does it focus on the right things? Does it go far enough? These are large questions, and I cannot now do full justice to them. I have already tried to show here that section 205 provides judges with considerable guidance, not merely in novel performance cases but in performance and enforcement cases generally. It is true that Professor *Burton's* model introduces new terminology and appears to reduce to two questions; but I do not see that anything turns on this. Why, for example, should it 'advance the analysis' to inquire whether the discretion-exercising party is seeking to 'recapture forgone opportunities', rather than whether his actions fall outside the reasonable expectations of the dependent party in light of the various factors in the circumstances that legitimately shape those expectations? Or why does it help (if it does) in our foregoing lease illustration to inquire whether the tenant, in diverting customers, was trying to recapture costs incurred in entering the contract, rather than whether what the tenant did was, all things considered, contrary to the spirit of the deal?

One may also question whether the *Burton* model really focuses on the right things. For example, does the subjective inquiry into the discretion-exercising party's state of mind really have the central importance that is claimed? Part of the claim, as I understand it, is that this inquiry is *typically* relevant, not just contingently so. This does not accord with section 205. Moreover, in a great many well-decided performance cases, courts give little or no consideration to this factor. Indeed, its independent significance in the *Burton* model is at least in some areas problematic. Consider, again, the lease illustration. If the court decides that the reasonable expectations of the landlord rule out the tenant's acts of diverting customers to his other store, what if anything would it add to inquire into the tenant's state of mind? It is said (a) that the 'traditional analysis' focuses mainly on benefits due the promisee under the agreement and (b) that this is inadequate because the promisor may be 'entitled' to withhold something in good faith. Whether or not (a) is true, (b) does not follow. If what is due the promisee really does exclude what the promisor wants to withhold, then that will be dispositive. What one is 'entitled' to withhold depends on what is due the promisee. (This is not to say that an inquiry into the promisor's state of mind can never have independent significance in good faith performance cases.)

Further, in my view the *Burton* model does not go far enough. That is, it does not provide as much focus as section 205 of the Restatement Second and the general case law now permit. I suspect that it is now possible to develop useful lists of factors generally relevant to the determination of good faith performance in a number of different performance contexts. Professor *Burton* seems content, for example, to leave the general test of reasonableness of expectations relatively unanalysed. Nothing in the excluder conceptualisation embodied in section 205 is inconsistent with the articulation of such criteria. A general requirement of good faith can rule out forms of bad faith identifiable by reference to these criteria. Indeed, as I have already suggested, some such criteria in some contexts may now be ripe for formulation in rules.

Professor *Burton* claims that, in addition to more focus, his model provides more generality than other approaches and thus is more 'lawlike'. In particular, he thinks it is less a 'licence' for the exercise of *ad hoc* judicial intuition. Again, I fail to see why there is any less generality in the Restatement Second approach. Certainly each 'context' to which Professor *Braucher* referred in the Comments consists of more than 'the discrete case'. Indeed, he adopted a number of *general* categories for the classification of general types of bad faith – categories well populated with actual decisions. Moreover, there is no reason why the legal generalities emergent in these contexts cannot take account of factors which vary with the stage in the contracting process at which the issue of good faith arises.

Finally, Professor *Burton* claims that his model provides a useful new 'perspective and policy framework' within which good faith performance issues are more manageable. Close analysis suggests, however, that it is less general than Professor *Burton* makes it seem, and that it introduces economic ideas and terminology that may breed uncertainty or confusion. I will say something further only about the first of these observations. The model is less general because it is in truth drawn mainly from those cases in which contracting parties have in fact conferred on one of the parties some genuine discretionary power in matters of performance. Many good faith performance cases are not of this kind; they do not confer *discretion* to perform in some way. It is not difficult to discern the likely motive here behind the *Burton* model. The manoeuvre of adopting a conceptual framework in which one party is always considered to have discretion felicitously generates the *possibility* that the 'discretion-exercising' party might have failed to perform in good faith, and thus seems to give pervasive point to the 'subjective-inquiry' of such central importance in the model. After all, 'a party with discretion may withhold all benefits for good reasons'. In many cases posing issues of good faith performance, however, there will be no such discretion and therefore no such possibility. And even when this is not so, the subjective inquiry may lack independent significance.

5. *The* Farnsworth *conceptualisation of good faith*

As I noted earlier, Professor E. Allan *Farnsworth* in 1963 wrote the first major article on good faith under the Uniform Commercial Code, and argued persuasively that the Code's general 'honesty in fact' conceptualisation 'enfeebled' UCC 1–203.[15] In his influential treatise, 'Farnsworth on Contracts', published in 1990, he states: 'The concept of good faith has, in a relatively few years, become one of the peculiarly American cornerstones of our common law of contracts.' In his treatise, Professor *Farnsworth* does not offer an explicit general conceptualisation of good faith. He does emphasise that '[c]ertainly many of the uses to which the new concept of good faith is put today do not go beyond those to which the traditional techniques of interpretation and gap filling were put in yesteryear'.[16]

Professor *Farnsworth* includes a great many good faith cases in the section of his treatise headed 'Deciding Omitted Cases'. There, he offers some general remarks on the duty of good faith and fair dealing in Restatement 205. He says: 'This duty is based on fundamental notions of fairness, and its scope necessarily varies according to the nature of the

---

[15] See Farnsworth, (1963) 30 *University of Chicago Law Review* 666 ff.
[16] E. Allan Farnsworth, *Farnsworth on Contracts*, vol. II (1990) 328 ff.

agreement. Some conduct, such as subterfuge and evasion, clearly violates the duty. However, the duty may not only proscribe undesirable conduct, but may require affirmative action as well. A party may thus be under a duty not only to refrain from hindering or preventing the occurrence of conditions of the party's own duty or performance of the other party's duty, but also to take some affirmative steps to co-operate in achieving these goals . . .'[17]

IV. Scope of the requirement of good faith

The Restatement and the Uniform Commercial Code limit the duty of good faith to the performance and the enforcement of a contract already made. Section 2–209(1) of the Uniform Commercial Code and some case law require that contract modifications be made in good faith.

In general, the requirement of good faith in American law does not apply to contract negotiations. Of course, the parties may contract to negotiate in good faith. And there are specific instances where it might be said that the general requirement applies even at the negotiating stage. Professor *Farnsworth* gives the example of the 'closed-mouth negotiator' – a prospective buyer of land learns that the land contains valuable minerals, unknown to the owner, but says nothing of this to the owner during negotiations prior to making a contract to buy the land. Professor *Farnsworth* says: 'at least under the Restatement Second of Contracts, sec. 161, nondisclosure may amount to a misrepresentation unless remaining silent is consistent with good faith and reasonable standards of fair dealing'.[18]

V. A note on remedies for bad faith

The appropriate remedy for bad faith in American law depends on the nature of the bad faith and the stage at, or context in which, it occurs. Bad faith may simply amount to a breach of a contractual promise or term, giving rise to damages, as where a buyer rejects non-conforming goods in bad faith in a falling market, and becomes liable for the contract–market

---

[17] Farnsworth (n. 16) 311 ff. See also E. Allan Farnsworth, 'Good Faith in Contract Performance', in: Jack Beatson, Daniel Friedmann (eds.), *Good Faith and Fault in Contract Law* (1995) 153 ff.

[18] E. Allan Farnsworth, 'Comment on Michael Bridge's: Does Anglo-Canadian Contract Law Need a Doctrine of Good Faith?', (1984) 9 *Canadian Business Law Journal* 426 ff., 427–8 ff.

differential. But if a seller secures a contract modification in bad faith, the appropriate remedy may only be to invalidate the modification. If a party's duty is conditioned on being satisfied with the other party's performance, and if the party is not satisfied in bad faith, the appropriate remedy may be to excuse the non-occurrence of the condition altogether, thereby rendering the party acting in bad faith liable (or whatever) as if the condition were satisfied. And there are still other possibilities that similarly reveal how the appropriate remedy depends on the stage at which, or the context in which, bad faith occurs.

VI. Conclusion

In a contract world, there are still other possible forms of generally applicable law besides a requirement of good faith. These other possible forms of law include more specific rules of law such as those dealing with fraud, custom and usage, course of dealing, 'implied' terms, and general principles of interpretation, as well as detailed terms of the contract. Could these other possible forms of law, alone or together, satisfy any essential need for a general requirement of contractual good faith? Is good faith redundant?

No. And there are several reasons for this. First, the world of contract law is an imperfect world inhabited by imperfect lawmakers and contracting parties who cannot foresee and provide in advance against all forms of contractual bad faith that may subsequently arise.

Second, it would unduly stretch the concept of contract interpretation to use it as a complete substitute for a general requirement of good faith. For instance, interpretation cannot really apply to cases of bad faith in negotiation. As my examples make clear, in many cases where a contract has been formed, interpretation as such cannot, strictly speaking, yield a genuine meaning of the parties. Among other things, the parties may not have addressed the matter at all.

Third, good faith analysis calls for a distinctive type of substantive reasoning. The overall rational justification for the recognition in a legal system of a general requirement of contractual good faith is a two-step analysis. Initially, it must be shown that other legal means are not an adequate substitute. Then, it must be shown that there are good affirmative reasons for a legal system to adopt such a requirement of good faith.

I believe there are such reasons. A general requirement of contractual good faith requires that parties do not deal dishonestly or contrary to standards of fair dealing in contract negotiations. Furthermore, in regard to contracts already negotiated and formed, a general requirement of contractual good faith requires as well that parties observe the fundamental rightness norm of *pacta sunt servanda*. A specific contract, of course, brings this norm into play, and good faith (among other things) helps to particularise its meaning and thus enforce what may be the unspecified 'inner logic' of the transaction or arrangement. At the same time, good faith also requires that there be no dishonesty or unfairness, notions which may even qualify or limit express terms of the contract, at least where any such dishonesty or unfairness is also ruled out by the unspecified inner logic of the contract. Good faith serves other contractual ends as well.

Some of the foregoing rationales may be reformulated in terms of protection of justified expectations of the parties, too. One or more of the above rationales can be deployed to justify applying the general requirement of good faith to each of my six examples, in section II above.

Appendix

§205. Duty of Good Faith and Fair Dealing

Every contract imposes upon each party a duty of good faith and fair dealing in its performance and its enforcement.

Comment:

a. Meanings of 'good faith'. Good faith is defined in Uniform Commercial Code § 1–201(19) as 'honesty in fact in the conduct or transaction concerned'. 'In the case of a merchant' Uniform Commercial Code § 2–103(1)(b) provides that good faith means 'honesty in fact and the observance of reasonable commercial standards of fair dealing in the trade'. The phrase 'good faith' is used in a variety of contexts, and its meaning varies somewhat with the context. Good faith performance or enforcement of a contract emphasizes faithfulness to an agreed common purpose and consistency with the justified expectations of the other party; it excludes a variety of types of conduct characterized as involving 'bad faith' because they violate community standards of decency, fairness or reasonableness. The appropriate remedy for a breach of the duty of good faith also varies with the circumstances.

b. Good faith purchase. In many situations a good faith purchaser of property for value can acquire better rights in the property than his transferor had. See, e.g., § 342. In this context 'good faith' focuses on the honesty of the purchaser, as distinguished from his care or negligence. Particularly in the law of negotiable instruments inquiry may be limited to 'good faith' under what has been called 'the rule of the pure heart and the empty head'. When diligence or inquiry is a condition of the purchaser's right, it is said that good faith is not enough. This focus on honesty is appropriate to cases of good faith purchase; it is less so in cases of good faith performance.

c. *Good faith in negotiation.* This Section, like Uniform Commercial Code § 1–203, does not deal with good faith in the formation of a contract. Bad faith in negotiation, although not within the scope of this Section, may be subject to sanctions. Particular forms of bad faith in bargaining are subjects of rules as to capacity to contract, mutual assent and consideration and of rules as to invalidating causes such as fraud and duress. See, for example, §§ 90 and 208. Moreover, remedies for bad faith in the absence of agreement are found in the law of torts or restitution. For examples of a statutory duty to bargain in good faith, see, e.g., National Labor Relations Act § 8(d) and the federal Truth in Lending Act. In cases of negotiation for modification of an existing contractual relationship, the rule stated in this Section may overlap with more specific rules requiring negotiation in good faith. See §§ 73, 89; Uniform Commercial Code § 2–209 and Comment.

d. *Good faith performance.* Subterfuges and evasions violate the obligation of good faith in performance even though the actor believes his conduct to be justified. But the obligation goes further: bad faith may be overt or may consist of inaction, and fair dealing may require more than honesty. A complete catalogue of types of bad faith is impossible, but the following types are among those which have been recognized in judicial decision: evasion of the spirit of the bargain, lack of diligence and slacking off, willful rendering of imperfect performance, abuse of a power to specify terms, and interference with or failure to cooperate in the other party's performance.

Illustrations:

1. A, an oil dealer, borrows $100,000 from B, a supplier, and agrees to buy all his requirements of certain oil products from B on stated terms until the debt is repaid. Before the debt is repaid, A makes a new arrangement with C, a competitor of B. Under the new arrangement A's business is conducted by a corporation formed and owned by A and C

and managed by A, and the corporation buys all its oil products from C. The new arrangement may be found to be a subterfuge or evasion and a breach of contract by A.

2. A, owner of a shopping center, leases part of it to B, giving B the exclusive right to conduct a supermarket, the rent to be a percentage of B's gross receipts. During the term of the lease A acquires adjoining land, expands the shopping center, and leases part of the adjoining land to C for a competing supermarket. Unless such action was contemplated or is otherwise justified, there is a breach of contract by A.

3. A Insurance Company insures B against legal liability for certain bodily injuries to third persons, with a limit of liability of $10,000 for an accident to any one person. The policy provides that A will defend any suit covered by it but may settle. C sues B on a claim covered by the policy and offers to settle for $9,500. A refuses to settle on the ground that the amount is excessive, and judgement is rendered against B for $20,000 after a trial defended by A. A then refuses to appeal, and offers to pay $10,000 only if B satisfies the judgement, impairing B's opportunity to negotiate for settlement. B prosecutes an appeal, reasonably expending $7,500, and obtains dismissal of the claim. A has failed to deal fairly and in good faith with B and is liable for B's appeal expense.

4. A and B contract that A will perform certain demolition work for B and pay B a specified sum for materials salvaged, the contract not to 'become effective until' certain insurance policies 'are in full force and effect'. A makes a good faith effort to obtain the insurance, but financial difficulty arising from injury to an employee of A on another job prevents A from obtaining them. A's duty to perform is discharged.

5. B submits and A accepts a bid to supply approximately 4,000 tons of trap rock for an airport at a unit price. The parties execute a standard form of 'Invitation, Bid, and Acceptance (Short Form Contract)' supplied by A, including typed terms 'to be delivered to project as required', 'delivery to start immediately', 'cancellation by A may be effected at any time'. Good faith requires that A order and accept the rock within a reasonable time unless A has given B notice of intent to cancel.

6. A contracts to perform services for B for such compensation 'as you, in your sole judgement, may decide is reasonable'. After A has performed the services, B refuses to make any determination of the value of the services. A is entitled to their value as determined by a court.

7. A suffers a loss of property covered by an insurance policy issued by B, and submits to B notice and proof of loss. The notice and proof fail to comply with requirements of the policy as to form and detail. B does not point out the defects, but remains silent and evasive, telling A broadly to perfect his claim. The defects do not bar recovery on the policy.

e. Good faith in enforcement. The obligation of good faith and fair dealing extends to the assertion, settlement and litigation of contract claims and defenses. See, e.g., §§ 73, 89. The obligation is violated by dishonest conduct such as conjuring up a pretended dispute, asserting an interpretation contrary to one's own understanding, or falsification of facts. It also extends to dealing which is candid but unfair, such as taking advantage of the necessitous circumstances of the other party to extort a modification of a contract for the sale of goods without legitimate commercial reason. See Uniform Commercial Code § 2–209, Comment 2. Other types of violation have been recognized in judicial decisions: harassing demands for assurances of performance, rejection of performance for unstated reasons, willful failure to mitigate damages, and abuse of a power to determine compliance or to terminate the contract. For a statutory duty of good faith in termination, see the federal Automobile Dealer's Day in Court Act, 15 U.S.C. §§ 1221–25 (1976).

Illustrations:

8. A contracts to sell and ship goods to B on credit. The contract provides that, if B's credit or financial responsibility becomes impaired or unsatisfactory to A, A may demand cash or security before making shipment and may cancel if the demand is not met. A may properly demand cash or security only if he honestly believes, with reason, that the prospect of payment is impaired.

9. A contracts to sell and ship goods to B. On arrival B rejects the goods on the erroneous ground that delivery was late. B is thereafter precluded from asserting other unstated grounds then known to him which A could have cured if stated reasonably.

Reporter's Note

This Section is new. See Farnsworth, Good Faith Performance and Commercial Reasonableness under the Uniform Commercial Code, 30 U. Chi. L. Rev. 666 (1963); Summers, 'Good Faith' in General Contract Law and the Sales Provisions of the Uniform Commercial Code, 54 Va. L. Rev. 195 (1968); 3A Corbin, Contracts §§ 654A-1 (Supp. 1980). As to the development of 'good faith' in German law, see Dawson, The Oracles of the Law 461–502 (1968).

For an important discussion of the concept, see Fortune v. National Cash Register Co., 373 Mass. 96, 364 N.E.2d 1251 (1977), applying it to an employment contract terminable at will. In VTR, Inc. v. Goodyear Tire & Rubber Co., 303 F. Supp. 773 (S.D.N.Y. 1969), it was held that particular conduct that would have been barred by the duty of good faith could be expressly consented to in the contract. Some of the limits of the duty are discussed in Sessions, Inc. v. Morton, 491 F.2d 854 (9th Cir. 1974); see also Commercial Contractors, Inc. v. United States F. & G. Co., 524 F.2d 944 (5th Cir. 1975) (discussing good faith, custom of trade and a general contractor's lack of duty to help a subcontractor keep his work force intact when another subcontractor offers higher wages).

Comment b. See Gilmore, The Commercial Doctrine of Good Faith Purchase, 63 Yale L. J. 1057 (1954).

Comment c. See Kessler & Fine, Culpa in Contrahendo, Bargaining in Good Faith, and Freedom of Contract: A Comparative Study, 77 Harv. L. Rev. 401 (1964); Cox, The Duty to Bargain in Good Faith, 71 Harv. L. Rev. 1401 (1958); Summers, Collective Agreements and the Law of Contracts, 78 Yale L. J. 525 (1969).

Comment d. Illustration 1 is based on Western Oil & Fuel Co. v. Kemp, 245 F.2d 633 (8th Cir. 1957); cf. Fort Wayne Corrugated Paper Co. v. Anchor Hocking Glass Corp., 130 F.2d 471 (3d Cir. 1942); Uniform Commercial Code § 2–306(1). Illustration 2 is based on Daitch Crystal Dairies, Inc. v. Neisloss, 8 A.D.2d 956, 190 N.Y.S.2d 737 (1959), aff'd mem., 8 N.Y.2d 723, 201 N.Y.S.2d 101, 167 N.E.2d 643 (1960); Carter v. Adler, 138 Cal. App.2d 63, 291 P.2d 111 (1955); see Annots., 170 A.L.R. 1113 (1947), 38 A.L.R.2d 1113 (1954); cf. Food Fair Stores, Inc. v. Blumberg, 234 Md. 521, 200 A.2d 166 (1964) (good faith of lessee); Uniform Commercial Code § 2–306(2) (obligation to use best efforts in cases of exclusive dealing in goods); Bloor v. Falstaff Brewing Corp., 601 F.2d 609 (2d Cir. 1979) (discussion of scope of 'best efforts'); Riess v. Murchison, 503 F.2d 999 (9th Cir. 1974), cert. denied, 420 U.S. 993 (1975) (buyers of land required by implied obligation of good faith to produce, save and sell water on which sellers' adjoining lands were dependant); Center Garment Co. v. United Refrig. Co., 369 Mass. 633, 341 N.E.2d 669 (1976) (franchisor required to make at least some effort to find supplies for franchisee when previous source was cut off). Compare Sessions, Inc. v. Morton, 491 F.2d 854 (9th Cir. 1974) (no implied obligation on lessors to agree to dedicate significant portion of land to public use even though dedication might be necessary to permit lessee to develop land). Illustration 3 is based on Brassil v. Maryland Cas. Co., 210 N.Y. 235, 104 N.E. 622 (1914); see Annot., 69 A.L.R.2d 690 (1960); cf. Annot., 40 A.L.R.2d 168 (1955) (insurer's duty to settle); Keeton, Ancillary Rights of the Insured Against His Liability Insurer, 13 Vand. L. Rev. 837 (1960); Spindle v. Travelers Ins. Cos., 66 Cal. App.3d 951, 136 Cal. Rptr. 404 (1977), discussed below in connection with Comment *e.* Illustration 4 is based on Omaha

Pub. Power Dist. v. Employers' Fire Ins. Co., 327 F.2d 912 (8th Cir. 1964). Illustration 5 is based on Sylvan Crest Sand & Gravel Co. v. United States, 159 F.2d 642 (2d Cir. 1945); cf. Uniform Commercial Code § 2–309(3). Illustration 6 is based on Pillois v. Billingsley, 179 F.2d 205 (2d Cir. 1950); see also In re Estate of Hollingsworth, 88 Wash.2d 322, 560 P.2d 348 (1977); cf. California Lettuce Growers, Inc. v. Union Sugar Co., 45 Cal.2d 474, 484, 289 P.2d 785, 791 (1955) (power to fix price of goods); Uniform Commercial Code § 2–305(2) (same). Illustration 7 is based on Johnson v. Scottish Union Ins. Co., 160 Tenn. 152, 22 S.W.2d 362 (1962); cf. Uniform Commercial Code § 2–311 (cooperation in sale of goods).

Comment e. See Kessler & Brenner, Automobile Dealer Franchises: Vertical Integration by Contract, 66 Yale L. J. 1135 (1957). Several courts have found that an express power to terminate a contract at will was modified by a duty of good faith. See, e.g., Fortune v. National Cash Register Co., 373 Mass. 96, 364 N.E.2d 1251 (1977) (salesman's employment contract); Spindle v. Travelers Ins. Cos., 66 Cal. App.3d 951, 136 Cal. Rptr. 404 (1977), 26 Drake L. Rev. 883 (1976–77) (termination of physician's malpractice insurance allegedly as part of scheme to intimidate the profession to accept higher premiums; court analogized from the insurer's duty to settle claims in good faith, see Illustration 3, supra); L'Orange v. Medical Protective Co., 394 F.2d 57 (6th Cir. 1968) (termination of dentist's malpractice insurance as retaliation because he testified against other dentist insured by same carrier); Shell Oil Co. v. Marinello, 63 N.J. 402, 307 A.2d 598 (1973), cert. denied, 415 U.S. 920 (1974) (termination of service station franchise; court reasoned both from dominant position of franchisor and from Legislature's enactment of franchising statute not applicable to particular transaction). Illustration 8 is based on James B. Berry's Sons Co. v. Monark Gasoline & Oil Co., 32 F.2d 74 (8th Cir. 1929); cf. Uniform Commercial Code §§ 1–208, 2–609. Illustration 9 is based on Fielding v. Robertson, 141 Va. 123, 126 S.E. 231 (1925); cf. § 248; Uniform Commercial Code § 2–605(1)(a).

PART II · THE CASE STUDIES

Contributors to the Case Studies

The case studies have been prepared

for Germany by *Reinhard Zimmermann* and *Dirk A. Verse*, Regensburg

for Greece by *Ismene Androulidakis-Dimitriadis*, Athens[1]

for Austria by *Helmut Koziol* and *Klaus Vogel*, Vienna

for France by *Horatia Muir-Watt, Ruth Sefton-Green* and *Stéphane Reifegerste*, Paris[2]

for Belgium by *Matthias E. Storme*, Ghent

for Spain by *Angel Carrasco Perera*, Toledo

for Italy by *Michele Graziadei*, Como/Torino[3]

for the Netherlands by *J. H. M. van Erp*, Maastricht

for England by *Simon Whittaker*, Oxford

for Ireland by *Declan Murphy* and *Diarmuid Rossa Phelan*, Dublin

for Scotland by *Joseph M. Thomson* and *Kate Bennet*, Glasgow

for Denmark and Norway by *Viggo Hagstrøm*, Oslo

for Sweden by *Torgny Håstad*, Stockholm

for Finland by *Hannu Tapani Klami*, Helsinki

comparative observations by *Simon Whittaker*, Oxford, and *Reinhard Zimmermann*, Regensburg

---

[1] I would like to thank *Evangelia Karvouni*, Athens, and *Dimitra Gelti*, London, for their contributions to the Greek report.

[2] With thanks to *Jerome Kullman* for his contribution on insurance law.

[3] I am indebted to *Rodolfo Sacco, Aldo Frignani, Mauro Bussani, Alberto Musy, Roberto Caso* and *Umberto Izzo* for their helpful comments on a previous draft of this paper. I am very grateful also to *Simon Whittaker* for his suggestions and to *Martin Laing* for his revision of my text. The usual disclaimer applies.

Abbreviations

Germany

AcP	*Archiv für die civilistische Praxis* (law journal)
AP	*Arbeitsrechtliche Praxis* (reference work for decisions of the Federal Labour Court)
Art.	*Artikel*
AtomG	*Atomgesetz* (Atomic Energy Act)
BAG	*Bundesarbeitsgericht* (Federal Labour Court)
BB	*Betriebs-Berater* (law journal)
BGB	*Bürgerliches Gesetzbuch* (German Civil Code)
BGH	*Bundesgerichtshof* (Federal Supreme Court)
BGHZ	*Entscheidungen des Bundesgerichtshofs für Zivilsachen* (Decisions of the Federal Supreme Court in Private Law Matters)
ECJ	European Court of Justice
Einf. v.	*Einführung vor* (introduction to)
GG	*Grundgesetz* (Basic Law)
HaftpflG	*Haftpflichtgesetz* (Legal Liability Act)
HGB	*Handelsgesetzbuch* (Commercial Code)
JA	*Juristische Arbeitsblätter* (law journal)
JBl	*Juristische Blätter* (law journal, published in Austria)
JR	*Juristische Rundschau* (law journal)
JuS	*Juristische Schulung* (law journal)
JZ	*Juristenzeitung* (law journal)
KE-BGB	*Kommissionsentwurf zur Überarbeitung des Schuldrechts* (Draft of the Commission charged with the revision of the law of obligations)
LM	*Lindenmaier-Möhring, Nachschlagewerk des BGH* (reference work for decisions of the Federal Supreme Court)
LuftVG	*Luftverkehrsgesetz* (Air Traffic Act)

NJW	*Neue Juristische Wochenschrift* (law journal)
NJW-RR	*NJW-Rechtsprechungs-Report Zivilrecht* (supplement to law journal with case reports in private law)
NZA	*Neue Zeitschrift für Arbeitsrecht* (law journal)
OLG	*Oberlandesgericht* (Regional Appeal Court)
PflVersG	*Pflichtversicherungsgesetz* (Compulsory Insurance Act)
ProdHG	*Produkthaftungsgesetz* (Product Liability Act)
RGZ	*Entscheidungen des Reichsgerichts in Zivilsachen* (Decisions of the Imperial Court in Private Law Matters)
SGB V	*Sozialgesetzbuch* (Social Security Code) fifth part
StGB	*Strafgesetzbuch* (Criminal Code)
StVG	*Straßenverkehrsgesetz* (Road Traffic Act)
Überbl. v.	*Überblick vor* (overview to)
VersR	*Zeitschrift für Versicherungsrecht* (law journal)
Vorbem.	*Vorbemerkung* (preliminary note)
VVG	*Versicherungsvertragsgesetz* (Contracts of Insurance Act)
WM	*Wertpapiermitteilungen* (law journal)
WuM	*Wohnungswirtschaft und Mietrecht* (law journal)

Greece

Areopagus	*Areios Pagos* (Greek Supreme Court in Civil and Criminal Matters)
Arm	*Armenopoulos* (law journal)
art.	article
BGB	*Bürgerliches Gesetzbuch* (German Civil Code)
ch.	chapter
Dni	*Dikaiosyni* (law journal)
EED	*Epitheorissis Emporikou Dikaiou* (law journal)
EEN	*Ephimeris Hellinon Nomikon* (law journal)
EllDni	*Helliniki Dikaiosyni* (law journal)
ErmAK	*Ermineia tou Astikou Kodica* (commentary)
Gr. C.C.	Greek Civil Code
L.	Law
L.D.	Law Decree
MonProt	*Monomeles Protodikeion* (Court of First Instance)
n.	note
no(s).	number(s)
NoB	*Nomikon Vima* (law journal)
PolProt	*Polymeles Protodikeion* (Court of First Instance)
RGRK	See bibliography

Austria

ABGB	*Allgemeines bürgerliches Gesetzbuch* (Austrian Civil Code)
BGBl	*Bundesgesetzblatt* (Government Gazette)
EheG	*Ehegesetz* (Marriage Act)
EvBl	*Evidenzblatt der Rechtsmittelentscheidungen* (included in the *Österreichische Juristen-Zeitung*, ÖJZ) (case reports)
GlUNF	*Sammlung von zivilrechtlichen Entscheidungen des k. k. Obersten Gerichtshofes, herausgegeben von Glaser/Unger, Neue Folge* (case reports of the Imperial Supreme Court)
HGB	*Handelsgesetzbuch* (Austrian Commercial Code)
JBl	*Juristische Blätter* (law journal)
JZ	*Juristenzeitung* (law journal, Germany)
KSchG	*Konsumentenschutzgesetz* (Consumer Protection Act)
MietSlg	*Sammlung mietrechtlicher Entscheidungen* (collection of decisions relating to lease law)
MRG	*Mietrechtsgesetz* (Protection of Tenants Act)
NZ	*Österreichische Notariats-Zeitung* (law journal)
NZwG	*Notariatszwangsgesetz* (Statute on official recording of a contract)
ÖBA	*Österreichisches Bankarchiv* (law journal)
OGH	*Österreichischer Oberster Gerichtshof* (Austrian Supreme Court)
ÖJZ	*Österreichische Juristen-Zeitung* (law journal)
ÖRZ	*Österreichische Richterzeitung* (law journal)
RdW	*Recht der Wirtschaft* (law journal)
sent.	sentence (*Satz*)
SZ	*Entscheidungen des österreichischen Obersten Gerichtshofes in Zivil- und Justizverwaltungssachen* (Decisions of the Austrian Supreme Court in Matters relating to Private Law and Administration of Justice)
VVG	*Versicherungsvertragsgesetz* (Contracts of Insurance Act)
ZBl	*Zentralblatt für die juristische Praxis* (law journal)
ZEuP	*Zeitschrift für Europäisches Privatrecht* (law journal, Germany)
ZVR	*Zeitschrift für Verkehrsrecht* (law journal)

France

al.	*alinéa*
art(s).	*article(s)*
Ass. plén.	*Assemblé plénière* of the *Cour de cassation*
Bull. civ.	*Bulletin des arrêts des Chambres civiles de la Cour de cassation* (a selection of the decisions of the various civil

	chambers of the *Cour de cassation* which are reported in four different sections, designated by the appropriate Roman numeral)
Bulletin Joly	*Bulletin mensuel d'information des sociétés* (legal periodical)
C. civ.	*Code civil*
C. cons.	*Code de la consommation* (Consumer Law Code)
CE	*Conseil d'Etat*
Civ.	*Cour de cassation*
Civ. (1)	First civil chamber of the *Cour de cassation*
Civ. (2)	Second civil chamber of the *Cour de cassation*
Civ. (3)	Third civil chamber of the *Cour de cassation*
Com.	Commercial chamber of the *Cour de cassation*
Comm. gouv.	*Commissaire du gouvernement*
concl.	*conclusions*
Cont., Conc., Cons.	*Contrats, concurrence, consommation* (legal periodical)
C. trav.	*Code du travail* (Labour Code)
D	*Recueil Dalloz* or *Dalloz Sirey* (this legal periodical is divided into different sections: 'Chron.' refers to the *Chronique*; 'Somm.' to the *Sommaires* and 'I.R.' to the *Informations Rapides*)
Def.	*Répertoire du notariat Defrénois* (legal periodical)
DP	*Recueil Dalloz périodique* (legal periodical, prior to its amalgamation with *Sirey* in 1965 to form *Dalloz Sirey* ('D'))
Droit sociétés	*Droit des sociétés* (legal periodical)
GP	*Gazette du Palais* (chiefly law reports; includes a section *Panorama de jurisprudence* ('Pan.jur.')).
JCP	*Jurisclasseur périodique* (chiefly law reports; otherwise known as *La Semaine Juridique*), *édition générale*
JCP (éd. N.)	*Jurisclasseur périodique* (chiefly law reports; otherwise known as *La Semaine Juridique*), *édition notariale*
L.	*loi*
Leb.	*Recueil Lebon* or *Recueil des décisions de la Conseil d'Etat* (chiefly reports of decisions of the *Conseil d'Etat*)
obs.	*observations*
Rec. gén. des ass. terr.	*Recueil générale des assurances terrestres* (chiefly law reports)
Req.	*Chambre des requêtes* of the *Cour de cassation*
Rev. sociétés	*Revue des sociétés* (legal periodical)
RTDCiv	*Revue trimestrielle de droit civil* (legal periodical)
S	*Sirey* (legal periodical, prior to its amalgamation with *Recueil Dalloz* in 1965 to form *Dalloz Sirey* ('D'))
Soc.	*Chambre sociale* of the *Cour de cassation*

t.	*tomus*
TGI	*Tribunal de grande instance*
Trib. civ.	*Tribunal civil*

Belgium

AJT	*Algemeen jurisch tijdschrift* (law journal)
Arr.	*Arresten van het Hof van cassatie / Bulletin des arrêts de la Cour de cassation* (law reports)
art.	article
BGB	*Bürgerliches Gesetzbuch* (German Civil Code)
Cass.	*Hof van cassatie / Cour de cassation* (Supreme Court)
C.C.	*Code civil* (Belgian Civil Code)
Civ.	Civil Court of First Instance
CJEC	Court of Justice, European Community
Comm.	Commercial Court of First Instance
DAOR	*Droit des affaires / Ondernemingsrecht* (law journal)
E.C.	European Community
JL	*Jurisprudence de Liège* (law reports)
JT	*Journal des Tribunaux* (law journal)
JTT	*Journal des Tribunaux du Travail* (law journal)
Pas.	*Pasicrisie belge* (law reports)
RCJB	*Revue critique de jurisprudence belge* (law review)
RGAR	*Recueil général des assurances et responsabilités* (law review)
RW	*Rechtskundig weekblad* (law review)
sec.	section
T. Aann.	*Tijdschrift voor aannemingsrecht / L'Entreprise et le droit* (law review)
TBBR	*Tijdschrift voor belgisch burgerlijk recht / Revue générale de droit civil* (law review)
TBH	*Tijdschrift voor belgisch handelsrecht / Revue de droit commercial belge* (law review)
TPR	*Tijdschrift voor privaatrecht* (law review)

Spain

ADC	*Anuario de Derecho Civil* (law journal)
art.	*artículo* (article)
BOE	*Boletín Oficial del Estado* (law reports)
C. Civ.	*Código Civil Español* (Spanish Civil Code)
CCJC	*Cuadernos Civitas de Jurisprudencia Civil* (law journal)
Col. Leg.	*Colección Legislativa de España, Repertorio de Jurisprudencia del Tribunal Supremo* (law reports)
E.C.	European Community
RJA	*Repertorio Jurisprudencia Aranzadi* (law reports)

Italy

App.	*Corte d'Appello* (Appeal Court)
Arch. civ.	*Archivio civile* (legal periodical)
art(s).	article(s)
BGB	*Bürgerliches Gesetzbuch* (German Civil Code)
BGH	*Bundesgerichtshof* (German Federal Supreme Court)
BGHZ	*Entscheidungen des Bundesgerichtshofs für Zivilsachen* (Decisions of the German Federal Supreme Court in Private Law Matters)
Cass.	*Corte di Cassazione*
c.c.	*Codice civile* (Italian Civil Code)
C.E.E.	*Comunità Economica Europea* (European Economic Community)
Com.	Commercial chamber of the French *Cour de cassation*
Contr. e impr.	*Contratto e impresa* (legal periodical)
Corte cost.	*Corte costituzionale* (Constitutional Court)
c.p.c.	*Codice di procedura civile* (Code of Civil Procedure)
Digesto sez. civ.	*Digesto delle discipline privatistiche – sezione civile* (legal encyclopaedia)
Digesto sez. comm.	*Digesto delle discipline privatistiche – sezione commerciale* (legal encyclopaedia)
Dir. giur.	*Diritto e giurisprudenza* (legal periodical)
Dir. prat. lav.	*Diritto e pratica del lavoro* (legal periodical)
d.lgt.	*decreto legislativo* (legislative enactment)
d.m.	*decreto ministeriale* (ministerial decree)
d.p.r.	*Decreto del Presidente della Repubblica* (Decree of the President of the Republic)
Fam. dir.	*Famiglia e diritto* (legal periodical)
Foro it.	*Il foro italiano* (legal periodical)
Giur. comm.	*Giurisprudenza commerciale* (legal periodical)
Giur. it.	*Giurisprudenza Italiana* (legal periodical)
Giust. civ.	*Giustizia civile* (legal periodical)
G.U.	*Gazzetta Ufficiale della Repubblica* (Official Gazette of the Republic)
JCP	*La Semaine Juridique* (French legal periodical)
l.	*legge* (law)
n.	*numero* (number)
Nuova giur. civ. comm.	*La nuova giurisprudenza civile commentata* (legal periodical)
obs.	*observations*
O.J.	Official Journal of the European Communities
ord.	*ordinanza* (ordinance)
Pret.	*Pretura* (District Court)
Rass. dir. civ.	*Rassegna di diritto civile* (legal periodical)
Riv. crit. dir. priv.	*Rivista critica del diritto privato* (legal periodical)

Riv. dir. civ.	*Rivista di diritto civile* (legal periodical)
Riv. giur. lav.	*Rivista giuridica del lavoro* (legal periodical)
Riv. not.	*Rivista del notariato* (legal periodical)
Riv. pen.	*Rivista penale* (legal periodical)
Società	*Le Società* (legal periodical)
Trib.	*Tribunale* (Court of First Instance)

The Netherlands

art.	article
B.W.	*Burgerlijk Wetboek* (Dutch Civil Code)
HR	*Hoge Raad* (Supreme Court)
jo.	*juncto* (read in conjunction with)
NJ	*Nederlandse Jurisprudentie* (law journal)
par.	paragraph
RvdW	*Rechtspraak van de Week* (law reports)

England

AC	Appeal Cases, Law Reports
All ER	All England Law Reports
App Cas	Law Reports, Appeal Cases, House of Lords
B & Ad	Barnewall and Adolphus's Reports, King's Bench
B & Ald	Barnewall and Alderson's Reports, King's Bench
B & C	Barnewall and Cresswell's Reports, King's Bench
Beav	Beavan's Reports, Rolls Courts
Bing NC	Bingham's New Cases, Common Pleas
Burr	Burrow's Reports, King's Bench
CA	Court of Appeal
CB	Common Bench
Ch	Law Reports, Chancery Division
Ch D	Law Reports, Chancery Division
CLR	Commonwealth Law Reports
Com Cas	Commercial Cases
Co Rep	Coke's Reports
DF & J	De Gex, Fisher and Jones' Reports, Chancery
E & E	Ellis and Ellis' Reports, Queen's Bench
Eq	Law Reports, Equity
FLR	Family Law Reports
Hare	Hare's Reports, Chancery
HLC	Clark's Reports, House of Lords
J.	Justice
KB	Law Reports, King's Bench Division
L.J.	Lord Justice

Lloyd's Rep	Lloyd's Law Reports
LR	Law Reports
LT	Law Times
M.R.	Master of the Rolls
Oxford JLS	Oxford Journal of Legal Studies
PD	Law Reports, Probate, Divorce, and Admiralty Division
Price	Price's Reports, Exchequer
pt	part
QB	Queen's Bench
QBD	Law Reports, Queen's Bench Division
reg.	regulation
s(s).	section(s)
sch.	schedule
SI	Statutory Instrument
Taunt	Taunton's Reports, Common Pleas
TLR	The Times Law Reports
TR	Term Reports
V.-C.	Vice-Chancellor
Ves Jun	Vesey Junior's Reports, Chancery
WLR	Weekly Law Reports

Ireland

AC	Appeal Cases, Law Reports
App Cas	Law Reports, Appeal Cases, House of Lords
Ch D	Law Reports, Chancery Division
DF & J	De Gex, Fisher and Jones's Reports, Chancery
Hare	Hare's Reports, Chancery
ILR	Irish Law Reports
ILRM	Irish Law Reports Monthly
IR	Irish Reports
IR CL	Irish Reports, Common Law
KB	Law Reports, King's Bench Division
Lloyd's Rep	Lloyd's Law Reports
LR Ir	Law Reports (Ireland), Chancery and Common Law
LRQB	Law Reports, Queen's Bench
NI	Northern Ireland Law Reports
QB	Queen's Bench
QBD	Law Reports, Queen's Bench Division
reg.	regulation
s(s).	section(s)
Ves Jun	Vesey Junior's Reports, Chancery
WLR	Weekly Law Reports

Scotland

AC	Appeal Cases, Law Reports
Ad & El	Adolphus and Ellis's Reports, King's Bench and Queen's Bench
All ER	All England Law Reports
App Cas	Law Reports, Appeal Cases, House of Lords
BLR	Building Law Reports
CA	Court of Appeal
D	Dunlop's Session Cases
DLR	Dominion Law Reports (Canada)
EAT	Employment Appeal Tribunal
F	Fraser's Session Cases
GWD	Green's Weekly Digest
HL	House of Lords
ICR	Industrial Cases Reports
IRLR	Industrial Relations Law Reports
IT	Industrial Tribunal
KB	Law Reports, King's Bench Division
LR Ex	Law Reports, Court of Exchequer
M	Macpherson's Session Cases
Macq	Macqueen's House of Lords Reports
OH	Outer House
PC	Judicial Committee of the Privy Council
pt	part
QB	Law Reports, Queen's Bench Division
R	Rettie's Session Cases
reg.	regulation
S	Shaw's Session Cases
s(s).	section(s)
SC	Session Cases
sch.	schedule
SC (HL)	House of Lords cases in Session Cases
SCLR	Scottish Civil Law Reports
Sh Ct	Sheriff Court
SI	Statutory Instrument
SLR	Scottish Law Reporter
SLT	Scots Law Times
SLT (Sh Ct)	Scots Law Times, Sheriff Court Reports
WLR	Weekly Law Reports

Denmark and Norway

CISG	United Nations Convention on Contracts for the International Sale of Goods

H	*Højesteret* (Danish Supreme Court Decisions)
JT	*Juridisk Tidskrift* (law journal)
NJA	*Nytt Juridiskt Arkiv* (Swedish Supreme Court Reports)
Rt.	*Norsk Retstidende* (Norwegian Supreme Court Reports)
s(s).	section(s) (Danish/Norwegian: *ledd*)
TfR	*Tidsskrift for Rettsvitenskap* (law journal)
U	*Ugeskrift for Retsvæsen* (Danish Court Reports, with B indicating the section containing legal literature)

Sweden

ch.	chapter
CISG	United Nations Convention on Contracts for the International Sale of Goods
ECE	United Nations Economic Commission for Europe
NJA	*Nytt Juridiskt Arkiv* (Swedish Supreme Court Reports)
NL	*Nordiska Leveransvillkor* (Standard form for the supply of machines and electrical equipment, issued by the industrial organisations of Denmark, Finland, Norway and Sweden)
RH	*Rättsfall från hovrätterna* (Swedish Appeal Court Decisions)
Rt.	*Norsk Retstidende* (Norwegian Supreme Court Reports)
s(s).	section(s)
SOU	*Statens Offentliga Utredningar* (Official reports series of legislative and investigation commissions)
U	*Ugeskrift for Retsvæsen* (Danish Court Reports)
WLR	Weekly Law Reports

Finland

E.C.J.	European Court of Justice
E.C.R.	Report of Cases before the Court of Justice of the European Communities
KKO	*Korkein oikeus* (Yearbook of the Finnish Supreme Court)
Ma, Ra, Si, Ty, Yr	Abbreviations of the Chapters in the Finnish statute-book
s(s).	section(s)

Bibliographies

Germany

Adolf Baumbach, Klaus Hopt, *Handelsgesetzbuch* (29th edn, 1995).

David P. Currie, *The Constitution of the Federal Republic of Germany* (1994).

Malte Diesselhorst, 'Die Geschäftsgrundlage in der neueren Rechtsentwicklung', in: Ulrich Immenga (ed.), *Rechtswissenschaft und Rechtsentwicklung* (1980) 153 ff.

Heinrich Dörner, '"Mängelhaftung" bei Sperre des transferierten Fußballspielers?', JuS 1977, 225 ff.

Günter Dürig, 'Grundrechte und Zivilrechtsprechung', in Theodor Maunz (ed.), *Vom Bonner Grundgesetz zur gesamtdeutschen Verpassung: Festschrift zum 75. Geburtstag von Hans Nawiasky* (1956) 157 ff.

Werner Ebke, Bettina Steinhauer, 'The Doctrine of Good Faith in German Contract Law', in: Jack Beatson, Daniel Friedmann (eds.), *Good Faith and Fault in Contract Law* (1995) 171 ff.

Volker Emmerich, 'Rechtsfragen des Ratenkredits', JuS 1988, 925 ff.

Erman, *Handkommentar zum Bürgerlichen Gesetzbuch, Band I* (9th edn, 1993).

Johannes Hager, 'Grundrechte im Privatrecht', JZ 1994, 373 ff.

Rudolf Henle, *Treu und Glauben im Rechtsverkehr* (1912).

Tony Honoré, *The Quest for Security: Employees, Tenants, Wives* (1982).

Othmar Jauernig, *Bürgerliches Gesetzbuch* (8th edn, 1997).

'Trennungsprinzip und Abstraktionsprinzip', JuS 1994, 721 ff.

Rudolf von Jhering, 'Culpa in contrahendo, oder Schadensersatz bei nichtigen oder nicht zur Perfektion gelangten Verträgen', *Jherings Jahrbücher für die Dogmatik des bürgerlichen Rechts* 4 (1861) 16 ff.

Theodor Kipp, 'Über Doppelwirkungen im Recht', in: *Festschrift für Ferdinand von Martitz* (1911) 211 ff.

Rolf Knütel, 'Zur sogenannten Erfüllungs- und Nichterfüllungsfiktion bei der Bedingung', JBl 1976, 613 ff.

Hein Kötz, *Europäisches Vertragsrecht*, vol. I (1996).

Karl Larenz, *Geschäftsgrundlage und Vertragserfüllung* (3rd edn, 1983).

Werner Lorenz, 'Reform of the German Law of Breach of Contract', (1997) 1 *Edinburgh Law Review* 317 ff.

Peter Marburger, *20 Probleme aus dem Schuldrecht, Besonderer Teil I* (3rd edn, 1985).

B. S. Markesinis, *The German Law of Torts: A Comparative Introduction* (3rd edn, reprint 1997).

B. S. Markesinis, W. Lorenz, G. Dannemann, *The German Law of Obligations*, vol. I
    (1997).
Dieter Medicus, *Allgemeiner Teil des BGB* (6th edn, 1994).
    Bürgerliches Recht (17th edn, 1996).
    'Der Grundsatz der Verhältnismäßigkeit im Privatrecht', AcP 192 (1992) 35 ff.
    Schuldrecht, Band I, Allgemeiner Teil (9th edn, 1996), *Band II, Besonderer Teil* (8th
    edn, 1997).
    'Zur Entstehungsgeschichte der culpa in contrahendo', in: *Festgabe für Max
    Kaser* (1986) 169 ff.
Münchener Handbuch zum Arbeitsrecht, Band I, Individualarbeitsrecht (1992).
Münchener Kommentar zum Bürgerlichen Gesetzbuch, Band I, Allgemeiner Teil (§§ 1–240)
    (3rd edn, 1993), *Band II, Schuldrecht Allgemeiner Teil (§§ 241–432)* (3rd edn, 1994),
    Band V, Schuldrecht Besonderer Teil III (§§ 705–853) (3rd edn, 1997), *Band VII,
    Familienrecht I (§§ 1297–1585), VAHRG, VAÜG, EheG* (3rd edn, 1993).
Paul Oertmann, *Die Geschäftsgrundlage: Ein neuer Rechtsbegriff* (1921).
Palandt, *Bürgerliches Gesetzbuch* (56th edn, 1997).
Soergel, *Bürgerliches Gesetzbuch, Band I, Allgemeiner Teil (§§ 1–240)* (12th edn, 1987),
    Band II, Schuldrecht I (§§ 241–432) (12th edn, 1990).
Staudinger, *Kommentar zum Bürgerlichen Gesetzbuch, Einleitung zu §§ 241 ff., §§241–243*
    (13th edn, 1995), *§§ 244–8 (Geldrecht)* (13th edn, 1997), *§§ 255–292* (13th edn,
    1995), *§§ 293–327* (13th edn, 1995), *§§ 535–563* (13th edn, 1995), *§§ 616–619* (13th
    edn, 1997), *Einleitung zu §§ 854 ff., §§ 854–882* (13th edn, 1995).
Olaf Werner, 'Die Quantitätsabweichung beim Handelskauf', BB 1984, 221 ff.
Johannes Wertenbruch, 'Die "Gewährleistungsansprüche" des übernehmenden
    Bundesligavereins bei Transfer eines nicht einsetzbaren DFB-Lizenzspielers',
    NJW 1993, 182 ff.
Harm Peter Westermann, 'Zum Vertragsrecht im bezahlten Fußballsport', JA
    1984, 394 ff.
Franz Wieacker, *Zur rechtstheoretischen Präzisierung des § 242 BGB* (1956).
Udo Wolter, *Mietrechtlicher Bestandsschutz* (1986).
Reinhard Zimmermann, 'Extinctive Prescription in German Law', in: Erik Jayme
    (ed.), *German National Reports in Civil Law Matters for the XIVth Congress of
    Comparative Law* (1994).
    'An Introduction to German Legal Culture', in: Werner F. Ebke, Matthew W.
    Finkin (eds.), *Introduction to German Law* (1996) 1 ff.
    'Konturen eines Europäischen Vertragsrechts', JZ 1995, 477 ff.
    'Sittenwidrigkeit und Abstraktion', JR 1985, 48 ff.
    The Law of Obligations: Roman Foundations of the Civilian Tradition (1990, paperback
    edn, 1996).
Reinhard Zimmermann, Nils Jansen, 'Quieta Movere: Interpretative Change in a
    Codified System', in: Peter Cane, Jane Stapleton (eds.), *The Law of Obligations:
    Essays in Celebration of John Fleming* (1998) 285 ff.
Konrad Zweigert, Hein Kötz (tr. Tony Weir), *An Introduction to Comparative Law* (2nd
    edn, paperback edn, 1992).

Greece

Ismene Androulidakis-Dimitriadis, 'The Effect of Unmarried Cohabitation by a
    Former Spouse upon His or Her Right to Continue to Receive Alimony', in:
    Festschrift für Georges Michaelides-Nouaros, vol. A (1987) 65 ff.
    Exogami symviosi [Extra-marital Cohabitation] (1984).
    'Griechenland', in: Gerhard Hochloch (ed.), *Internationales Scheidungs- und
    Scheidungsfolgenrecht* (1998) 105 ff.
    'Persönlichkeitsschutz nach griechischem und deutschem Recht', in: *Festschrift
    für Johannes Karakatsanes* (1998) 35 ff.
    *Ypochreoseis synallaktikis pisteos [Obligations arising from Good Faith in the Law of
    Contract]* (1972).
    Ypochreosi enimerosis tou asthenous [The Obligation to Inform the Patient] (1993).
K. Asprogerakas-Grivas, *Genikes Arches tou Astikou Dikaiou [General Principles of Civil
    Law]* (1981).
G. Balis, *Genikai Archai [General Principles of Civil Law]* (8th edn, 1961).
A. Chiotellis, *Rechtsfolgenbestimmung bei Geschäftsgrundlagenstörungen in
    Schuldverträgen* (1981).
Ludwig Enneccerus, Hans Nipperdey, *Allgemeiner Teil des Bürgerlichen Rechts* (15th
    edn, 1960).
ErmAK, *Ermineia tou Astikou Kodika [Article by Article Interpretation of the Greek Civil
    Code]*, *Genikes Arches [General Principles]*, vol. I (1971); *Enochiko Dikaio [Law of
    Obligations]*, vol. II (1949).
P. Filios, *Enochiko Dikaio, Eidiko Meros [Law of Obligations, Special Part]* (1997).
Werner Flume, *Allgemeiner Teil des Bürgerlichen Rechts, Band II* (3rd edn, 1979).
C. Fragistas, 'Der Rechtsmißbrauch nach dem griechischen Zivilgesetzbuch', in:
    Festschrift für Martin Wolff (1952) 49 ff.
L. Georgakopoulos, *Dikaion Diarkon Enochon [The Law of Standard Obligations]* (1979).
A. Georgiadis, *Empragmato Dikaio [Law of Property]*, vol. I (1991).
    *Nees Morphes Symvaseon [New Forms of Contracts: Leasing, Factoring, Forfeiting,
    Franchising]* (2nd edn, 1995).
    'Standpunkt und Entwicklung des griechischen Deliktsrechts', in: *Festschrift
    für Karl Larenz* (1983) 175 ff.
A. Georgiadis, M. Stathopoulos, *Astikos Kodix [Civil Code]*, vol. I (1978), vol. II (1979),
    vol. III (1980), vol. IV (1982), vol. VII (1991), vol. VIII (1993).
J. Karakostas, *Euthini tou Paragogou gia Elattomatika Proionta [Producers' Liability for
    Defective Products]* (1995).
    Prostasia tou Katanaloti [Consumer Protection] (1997).
M. Karassis, *Culpa in contrahendo im griechischen Recht* (1987).
K. Kerameus, *Studia Juridica*, vol. III (1995).
G. Koumantos, *Ypokeimeniki Kali Pistis [Subjective Good Faith]* (1958).
E. Kounougeri-Manoledaki, 'Ektasi kai synepeies tis akyrotitas tis aischrokerdous
    dikaiopraxias', Arm 1975, 9 ff.

C. Ladas, *Akyrotis tis dikaiopraxias logo antitheseos sta christa ithi [Annulment of Immoral Transactions]* (1979).

Karl Larenz, *Allgemeiner Teil des deutschen Bürgerlichen Rechts* (7th edn, 1989).

Karl Oftinger, 'Betrachtungen über die Laesio im Schweizerischen Recht', in: *Xenion Zepos*, vol. II (1973) 544 ff.

M. Papaloukas, *Dioikisi kai Athlitiko Dikaio [Government and Athletic Law]* (1996).

P. Papanikolaou, *Katapleonektikes Dikaiopraxies [Unconscionable Contracts]* (1983).
Peri ton orion tis prostateutikis paremvaseos tou dikasti stin symvasi [The Limits of the Protective Interference of the Judge with the Contract] (1991).

N. Papantoniou, *Genikes Arches [General Principles of Civil Law]* (3rd edn, 1983).
Kali Pistis eis to Astikon Dikaion [Good Faith in Civil Law] (1957).

A. Pouliadis, *Culpa in contrahendo und Schutz Dritter* (1981).

RGRK, *Das Bürgerliche Gesetzbuch, Kommentar, herausgegeben von Reichsgerichtsräten und Bundesrichtern, Band I* (12th edn, 1982).

K. Simantiras, *Genikes Arches tou Astikou Dikaiou [General Principles of Civil Law]* (4th edn, 1988).

Soergel, *Bürgerliches Gesetzbuch, Band I, Allgemeiner Teil (§§ 1–240)* (12th edn, 1987).

J. Spyridakis, *Akyrosis tis Empragmatis dikaiopraxias [Annulment of Real Property Contracts]* (1981).
'Gedanken über einen allgemeinen privatrechtlichen Aufopferungsanspruch', in: *Festschrift für Joannis Sontis* (1977) 241 ff.
Note, NoB 25 (1977) 762 ff.

M. Stathopoulos, *Contract Law in Hellas* (1995).

M. Stathopoulos, A. Chiotellis, M. Avgoustianakis, *Europaiko Astiko Dikaio [European Community Civil Law]*, vol. I (1995).

S. Symeonides, 'The General Principles of the Civil Law', in: K. Kerameus, P. Kozyris (eds.), *Introduction to Greek Law* (2nd edn, 1993) 49 ff.

C. Taliadoros, *English Translation of the Greek Civil Code* (1982, supplement 1983).

K. Triantaphyllopoulos, in: *Materials for the Draft of the Greek Civil Code, vol. II, Enochiko Dikaio [Law of Obligations]* (1935, reprint 1989).

E. Vousikas, *Agogi adikaiologitou ploutismou [Unjust Enrichment]* (1948).

P. Zepos, *Enochikon Dikaion [Law of Obligations]*, vol. II (2nd edn, 1965).

P. Zepos, F. Christodoulou, 'Professional Liability', in: *International Encyclopedia of Comparative Law, vol. XI: Torts* (1983).

Reinhard Zimmermann, *The Law of Obligations: Roman Foundations of the Civilian Tradition* (1990, paperback edn 1996).

Austria

Peter Apathy, 'Gewährleistung für bedungene Eigenschaften und den verabredeten Gebrauch', JBl 1975, 572 ff.

Peter Avancini, Gert M. Iro, Helmut Koziol, *Österreichisches Bankvertragsrecht*, vol. I (1987), vol. II (1993).

Wolfgang Berger, 'Gesetzliche Formvorschriften für Rechtsgeschäfte nach
österreichischem Recht', in: *Gutachten für die Fachveranstaltungen des 3.
Österreichischen Notariatskongresses 1986 '175 Jahre ABGB'* (1986) 41 ff.

Franz Bydlinski, *Juristische Methodenlehre und Rechtsbegriff* (2nd edn, 1991).
'Lohn- und Kondiktionsansprüche aus zweckverfehlenden Arbeitsleistungen',
in: *Festschrift zum 60. Geburtstag von Walter Wilburg* (1965) 45 ff.
Privatautonomie und objektive Grundlagen des verpflichtenden Rechtsgeschäftes (1967).
System und Prinzipien des Privatrechts (1996).
'Über listiges Schweigen beim Vertragsabschluß', JBl 1980, 393 ff.
'Vergleichsverhandlungen und Verjährung, Anlageschäden und überholende
Kausalität', JBl 1967, 130 ff.
'Zum Kontrahierungszwang der öffentlichen Hand', in: *Auf dem Weg zur
Menschenwürde und Gerechtigkeit, Festschrift für Hans R. Klecatsky* (1980) 129 ff.

Claus-Wilhelm Canaris, 'Ansprüche wegen "positiver Vertragsverletzung" und
"Schutzwirkung für Dritte" bei nichtigen Verträgen', JZ 1965, 475 ff.

Gunter Ertl, *Inflation, Privatrecht und Wertsicherung* (1980).

Dieter Giesen, *Arzthaftungsrecht* (4th edn, 1995).

Monika Gimpel-Hinteregger, 'Der Unterhaltsanspruch des geschiedenen
Ehegatten bei Eingehen einer Lebensgemeinschaft', in: Friedrich Harrer,
Rudolf Zitta (eds.), *Familie und Recht* (1992) 633 ff.

Franz Gschnitzer, Christoph Faistenberger, Heinz Barta, *Allgemeiner Teil des
bürgerlichen Rechts* (2nd edn, 1992).

Franz Gschnitzer, Christoph Faistenberger, Heinz Barta, Bernhard Eccher,
Österreichisches Schuldrecht, Allgemeiner Teil (2nd edn, 1985).

Ludwig Häsemeyer, *Die gesetzliche Form der Rechtsgeschäfte* (1971).

Gert M. Iro, 'Versuch eines harmonischen Verständnisses der Bestimmungen
über Willensmängel bei Verkehrsgeschäften', JBl 1974, 225 ff.

Peter Jabornegg, *Das Risiko des Versicherers* (1979).

Heinrich Klang, Franz Gschnitzer (eds.), *Kommentar zum Allgemeinen bürgerlichen
Gesetzbuch*, vols. I/1 (2nd edn, 1964), II/2 (1st edn, 1934), IV/1 (2nd edn, 1968),
IV/2 (2nd edn, 1978), V (2nd edn, 1954), VI (2nd edn, 1951).

Rolf Knütel, 'Zur sogenannten Erfüllungs- und Nichterfüllungsfiktion bei der
Bedingung', JBl 1976, 613 ff.

Helmut Koziol, 'Delikt, Verletzung von Schuldverhältnissen und
Zwischenbereich', JBl 1994, 209 ff.
'Generalnorm und Einzeltatbestände als System der Verschuldenshaftung:
Unterschiede und Angleichungsmöglichkeiten', ZEuP 1995, 359 ff.
'Grenzen des Zurückbehaltungsrechts bei nicht gehöriger Erfüllung', ÖJZ
1985, 737 ff.
Österreichisches Haftpflichtrecht, vol. I, *Allgemeiner Teil* (3rd edn, 1997), vol. II,
Besonderer Teil (2nd edn, 1984).

Helmut Koziol, Rudolf Welser, *Grundriß des bürgerlichen Rechts*, vol. I (10th edn,
1995), vol. II (10th edn, 1996).

Ernst Kramer, *Arbeitsvertragsrechtliche Verbindlichkeiten neben Lohnzahlung und Dienstleistung* (1975).

Gerhard Kramer, 'Verwirkung und Anspruchsverlust durch stillschweigenden Verzicht', JBl 1962, 540 ff.

Karl Krückl, 'Der Anspruch des Patienten auf Einsicht in seine Krankengeschichte', ÖJZ 1983, 281 ff.

Peter Mader, *Rechtsmißbrauch und unzulässige Rechtsausübung* (1994).

'Verjährung und außergerichtliche Auseinandersetzung', JBl 1986, 1 ff.

Heinrich Mayrhofer, *Schuldrecht, Allgemeiner Teil* (1986).

Rudolf Reischauer, *Der Entlastungsbeweis des Schuldners* (1975).

Peter Rummel, 'Anmerkungen zum gemeinsamen Irrtum und zur Geschäftsgrundlage', JBl 1981, 1 ff.

'Wegfall des Rechtsgrundes und Zweckverfehlung als Gründe der Kondiktion nach § 1435 ABGB', JBl 1978, 449 ff.

Peter Rummel (ed.), *Kommentar zum Allgemeinen bürgerlichen Gesetzbuch*, vol. I (2nd edn, 1990), vol. II (2nd edn, 1992).

Martin Schauer, *Das österreichische Versicherungsvertragsrecht* (3rd edn, 1995).

Josef von Schey, *Die Obligationsverhältnisse*, vol. I/2 (1895).

Wilhelm Schlesinger, 'Das Wesen der positiven Vertragsverletzungen', ZBl 1926, 721 ff.

Michael Schwimann (ed.), *Praxiskommentar zum Allgemeinen Bürgerlichen Gesetzbuch*, vols. I, V (2nd edn, 1997).

Manfred Straube, *Kommentar zum Handelsgesetzbuch*, vol. I (2nd edn, 1995).

Theodor Tomandl (ed.), *Treue- und Fürsorgepflicht im Arbeitsrecht* (1975).

Bea Verschraegen, *Die einverständliche Scheidung in rechtsvergleichender Sicht* (1991).

Rudolf Welser, 'Das Verschulden beim Vertragsabschluß im österreichischen bürgerlichen Recht', ÖJZ 1973, 281 ff.

Vertretung ohne Vollmacht (1970).

Georg Wilhelm, *Die Vertretung der Gebietskörperschaften im Privatrecht* (1981).

'Der Verzug mit der Verbesserung als Problem der Gesetzeskonkurrenz zwischen Gewährleistung und Nichterfüllung', JBl 1975, 113 ff.

'Zur Formalität verdeckter Schenkungen von GmbH-Anteilen', NZ 1994, 250 ff.

France

A. Bénabent, 'La bonne foi dans l'exécution du contrat, Rapport Français', in: *La bonne Foi, Travaux de l'Association Henri Capitant*, t. XLIII (1994) 291.

J. Carbonnier, *Droit civil, 4. Les obligations* (18th edn, 1995).

Flexible droit (8th edn, 1995).

J. Ghestin, *Traité de droit civil, La formation du contrat* (3rd edn, 1993).

J. Ghestin, C. Jamin, M. Billau, *Traité de droit civil, les effets du contrat* (2nd edn, 1994).

P. Jourdain, 'Le devoir de "se" renseigner', D 1983.Chron.139.

A. Kassis, *Théorie générale des usages de commerce, droit comparé, contrats et arbitrages internationaux, lex mercatoria* (1984).

P. Le Tourneau, 'De l'allégement de l'obligation de renseignements ou de conseil', D 1987.Chron.101.

P. Le Tourneau, L. Cadiet, *Droit de la reponsabilité* (1996).

P. Malaurie, L. Aynès, *Cours de droit civil, Les obligations* (8th edn, 1998).

J. Mestre, 'D'une exigence de bonne foi à l'esprit de collaboration', RTDCiv 1986.101.

Y. Picod, 'La clause résolutoire et la règle morale', JCP 1990.I.3447.

Le devoir de loyauté dans l'exécution du contrat (1989).

'L'exigence de bonne foi dans l'exécution du contrat', in: *Le juge et l'exécution du contrat, Colloque I.D.A. Aix-en-Provence, 28 mai 1993* (1993) 57.

'L'obligation de co-opération dans l'exécution du contrat', JCP 1988.I.3318.

B. Starck, H. Roland, L. Boyer, *Obligations, 2. Contrat* (6th edn, 1998).

F. Terré, P. Simler, Y. Lequette, *Droit civil, Les obligations* (6th edn, 1996).

G. Viney, *Introduction à la responsabilité* (2nd edn, 1995).

'Responsabilité civile', JCP 1997.I.4025.

G. Virassamy, *Les contrats de dépendance, thèse* (1986)

Belgium

F. Bouckaert, *De handelszaak* (1989).

R. O. Dalcq, 'Expertises civiles et secret professionnel des médecins', in: *Liber amicorum Krings* (1991) 502 ff.

W. De Bondt, 'Redelijkheid en billijkheid in het contractenrecht', TPR 1984, 95 ff.

R. Kruithof, H. Bocken, 'Overzicht van rechtspraak, Verbintenissen', TPR 1994, 171 ff.

P. Lambert, *Le secret professionnel* (1985).

L. Neels, 'Mededinging na overdracht van handelszaak', RW 1980–1981, 2133 ff.

D. Philippe, *Changement de circonstances et bouleversement de l'économie contractuelle* (1986).

J. Ronse, 'Marginale toetsing in het privaatrecht', TPR 1977, 211 ff.

'Overzicht van rechtspraak, Vennootschappen', TPR 1978, 681 ff.

G. Schrans, 'De progressieve totstandkoming der contracten', TPR 1984, 1 ff.

K. Schutyser, 'Eigendomsrecht en medische dossiers', RW 1984–1985, 3044 ff.

M. E. Storme, 'De bepaling van het voorwerp van een verbintenis bij partijbeslissing', TPR 1988, 1259 ff.

De invloed van de goede trouw op kontraktuele schuldvorderingen (1990).

'Kontraktuele kontrolerechten en bewijsovereenkomsten', in: *De behoorlijke beëindiging van overeenkomsten – La fin du contrat* (1993) 57 ff.

'Onhandelbare gedachten over de toekomst van het verhandelbaar vermogensrecht', 25 DAOR 1992, 137 ff.

'Rechtszekerheid en vertrouwensbeginsel in het Belgisch verbintenissenrecht', in: *Vertrouwensbeginsel en rechtszekerheid in België, Vereniging voor de Vergelijkende Studie van het Recht in België en Nederland* (1997) 1 ff.

M. L. Storme, 'Het schuldeisersverzuim, Proeve van rechtsvinding naar belgisch recht', in: *Op de grenzen van komend recht, Opstellen aangeboden aan prof. mr. J. H. Beekhuis* (1969) 231 ff.

M. L. Storme, M. E. Storme, 'De bindende derdenbeslissing naar belgisch recht', TPR 1985, 713 ff.

W. van Eeckhoutte, 'De goede trouw in het arbeidsovereenkomstenrecht', TPR 1990, 971 ff.

T. Vansweevelt, *Civielrechtelijke aansprakelijkheid van de geneesheer en van het ziekenhuis* (1992).

'De toestemming van de patiënt', TPR 1991, 285 ff.

Spain

Alberto Bercovitz, 'Note', 41 CCJC 1996, 530 ff.

A. Cabanillas, 'La mora del acreedor', 40 ADC 1987, 1342 ff.

E. Gomez Calle, *Los deberes precontractuales de información* (1994).

J. M. Miquel, 'Comentario sub art. 7', in: R. Bercovitz, L. Diez-Picazo, C. Paz-Ares, P. Salvador (eds.), *Comentario del Código Civil*, vol. I (1991).

A. M. Morales, 'El dolo como criterio de imputación al vendedor por los defectos de la cosa', 35 ADC 1982, 602 ff.

El error en los contratos (1988).

Italy

Guido Alpa, 'Italy', in: Ewoud H. Hondius (ed.), *Precontractual Liability – Reports to the XIIIth Congress International Academy of Comparative Law, Montreal, Canada, 18–24 August 1990* (1991) 195 ff.

Guido Alpa, Mario Bessone, Vincenzo Zeno-Zencovich, 'I fatti illeciti', in: *Trattato di diritto privato diretto da Rescigno XIV* (2nd edn, 1995).

Roberto Baldi, *Il contratto di agenzia, la concessione di vendita il franchising* (6th edn, 1997).

Alessandro Bellavista, 'Abbigliamento del dipendente e poteri del datore di lavoro', Riv. giur. lav., 1994, II, 226 ff.

Augusto Bellero, 'Assicurazioni contro i danni (III. Assicurazioni agricole)', Digesto, 4th edn, sez. comm., I (1987) 423 ff.

Francesco Benatti, 'Culpa in contrahendo', Contr. e impr., 1987, 287 ff.

'Doveri di protezione', Digesto, 4th edn, sez. civ., VII (1991) 221 ff.

Mario Bessone, *Adempimento e rischio contrattuale* (1969).

Cesare Massimo Bianca, *Diritto Civile, III Il contratto* (1987), *IV L'obbligazione* (1990).

'La vendita e la permuta', in: *Trattato di diritto civile diretto da Vassalli VII, 1* (2nd edn, 1993).

Giovanni Bonilini, Ferruccio Tommaseo, 'Lo scioglimento del matrimonio', in: *Il codice civile – Commentario diretto da Schlesinger* (1997).

Fabio Bortolotti, *I Contratti di subfornitura* (1998).

Umberto Breccia, 'Le obbligazioni', in: *Trattato di diritto privato a cura di Iudica e Zatti* (1991).

Francesco Donato Busnelli, 'Itinerari europei nella "terra di nessuno" tra contratto e fatto illecito: La responsabilità da informazioni inesatte', Contr. e impr., 1991, 539 ff.

Mauro Bussani, *La colpa soggettiva* (1991).

Fabrizio Cafaggi, *Profili di relazionalità della colpa* (1996).

Oreste Cagnasso, Maurizio Irrera, *Concessione di vendita, Merchandising, Catering* (1993).

Ezio Capizzano, 'Miglioramenti agrari', Digesto, 4th edn, sez. civ., XI (1994) 343 ff.

Daniela Caruso, *La culpa in contrahendo: L'esperienza statunitense e quella italiana* (1993).

Roberto Caso, 'Subfornitura industriale: analisi giuseconomica delle situazioni di disparità contrattuale', Riv. crit. dir. priv., 1998, 243 ff.

Carlo Castronovo, 'Obblighi di protezione', in: *Enciclopedia giuridica XXI* (1990).

Giovanni Cattaneo, 'Mora del creditore', Digesto, 4th edn, sez. civ., XI (1994) 432 ff.

Angelo Chianale, *Diritto soggettivo e tutela in forma specifica* (1992).
Obbligazione di dare e trasferimento della proprietà (1990).

Giovanni E. Colombo, 'L'azienda e il mercato', in: *Trattato di diritto di diritto civile e commerciale diretto da Galgano* (1979).

Francesca Coraggio, 'Abuso di posizione dominante e obblighi legali di contrarre', Nuova giur. civ. comm., 1997, II, 179 ff.

Giorgio de Nova, 'Franchising', Digesto, 4th edn, VI (1991) 100 ff.
'Il divieto di concorrenza nella vendita di azienda e nella vendita di studio professionale', Giur. it., 1974, I, 1, 2045 ff.

Anna de Vita, 'La reforme de la responsabilité médicale: responsabilité ou assurance?', in: *Rapports nationaux Italiens au XIIIe Congrès international de droit comparé* (1990) 95 ff.

Adolfo di Majo, 'Dell'adempimento in generale, artt. 1177–1200', in: *Commentario del Codice Civile Scialoja-Branca a cura di Galgano* (1994).

Franco di Sabato, *Manuale delle società* (5th edn, 1995).

Massimo Franzoni, 'Dei fatti illeciti, artt. 2043–2049', in: *Commentario del Codice Civile Scialoja-Branca a cura di Galgano* (1993).

Aldo Frignani, *Il franchising* (1990).

Enrico Gabrielli, 'Tipo negoziale, prevedibilità dell'evento e qualità della parte nella distribuzione del rischio contrattuale', Giur. it, 1986, I, 1, 1705 ff.

Francesco Galgano, *Diritto civile e commerciale, II, Le obbligazioni e i contratti, 1* (1st edn, 1990; 2nd edn, 1993).

Paolo Gallo, *Sopravvenienza contrattuale e problemi di gestione del contratto* (1992).

Antonio Gambaro, 'Abuso del diritto (Diritto comparato e straniero)', in: *Enciclopedia giuridica I* (1988).

Lina Bigliazzi Geri, Umberto Breccia, Francesco Busnelli, Ugo Natoli, *Diritto civile* (1987).

Alberto Germanò, 'Prelazione agraria', Digesto, 4th edn, sez. civ., XIV (1996) 178 ff.

Gino Gorla, *Il contratto, I* (1955).

Giuseppe Grisi, *L'obbligo precontrattuale di informazione* (1990).

Attilio Guarneri, 'L'azione di nullità, Riflessioni sistematiche e comparatistiche', Riv. dir. civ., 1993, I, 41 ff.

Federico Introna, Alberto Colafigli, Massimo Tantalo, *Il codice di deontologia medica 1995: commentato con leggi e documenti* (1996).

Marco Lipari, 'La risoluzione del contratto per eccessiva onerosità: la struttura del giudizio di prevedibilità e la rilevanza dell'inflazione', Giust. civ., 1985, I, 2795 ff.

Angelo Luminoso, 'La lesione dell'interesse contrattuale negativo (e dell'interesse positivo) nella responsabilità civile', Contr. e impr., 1988, 792 ff.

Luigi Mengoni, 'I poteri dell'imprenditore', in: Luigi Mengoni, *Diritto e valori* (1985) 387 ff.

Pier Giuseppe Monateri, *Cumulo di responsabilità contrattuale e extracontrattuale* (1989).

'La responsabilità civile', in: *Trattato di diritto civile diretto da Sacco* (1998).

Alberto Musy, 'Responsabilità precontrattuale (culpa in contrahendo)', Digesto, 4th edn, sez. civ., XVII (1998) 391 ff.

Roberto Pardolesi, *I contratti di distribuzione* (1979).

'Subfornitura industriale e diritto: un rapporto difficile', in: Gobbi (ed.), *L'artigianato nell'economia e sul territorio, analisi delle tendenze evolutive, I* (1985) 133 ff.

Guido Patti, Salvatore Patti, 'Responsabilità precontrattuale e contratti standards, artt. 1337–1342', in: *Il codice Civile – Commentario diretto da Schlesinger* (1993).

Salvatore Patti, 'Abuso del diritto', Digesto, 4th edn, sez. civ., I (1987) 1 ff.

Denis M. Philippe, *Changement de circonstances et bouleversement de l'economie contractuelle* (1986).

Alfredo Mordechai Rabello, 'Culpa in Contrahendo: Precontractual Liability in the Italian Legal System', in: Alfredo Mordechai Rabello (ed.), *Aequitas and Equity: Equity in Civil Law and Mixed Jurisdictions* (1997) 463 ff.

Filippo Ranieri, 'Eccezione di dolo generale', Digesto, 4th edn, sez. civ., VII (1991) 311 ff.

Rinuncia tacita e Verwirkung, Tutela dell'affidamento e decadenza da un diritto (1971).

'Verwirkung et renonciation tacites: Quelques remarques de droit comparé', in: *Mélanges en l'honneur de Daniel Bastian, I* (1974) 427 ff.

Pietro Rescigno, 'L'abuso del diritto', Riv. dir. civ., 1965, I, 205 ff.

Carlo Rossello, 'Responsabilità contrattuale e aquiliana: il punto sulla giurisprudenza', Contr. e impr., 1996, 664 ff.

Domenico Rubino, Giovanni Iudica, 'Dell'appalto – artt. 1655–1677', in: Commentario del Codice Civile Scialoja-Branca a cura di Galgano (3rd edn, 1992).

Rodolfo Sacco, 'Il possesso', in: Trattato di diritto civile e commerciale già diretto da Cicu e Messineo, continuato da Mengoni, VII (1988).

'Purezza del consenso, elementi perfezionativi del contratto, effeti del negozio: i cento articoli delle leggi, e la regola unica preterlegale', in: Nozione, formazione e interpretazione del diritto dall'età romana alle esperienze moderne – ricerche dedicate al Professor Filippo Gallo, IV (1997) 449 ff.

'Rapport italien', in: La bonne foi – Travaux de l'Association Henri Capitant, XLIII (1992).

Rodolfo Sacco, Giorgio de Nova, 'Il contratto', in: Trattato di diritto civile diretto da Sacco I, II (1993).

Mario Sanino, 'Sport', in: Enciclopedia giuridica XXX (1993).

Giuseppe Terranova, 'L'eccessiva onerosità nei contratti', in: Il codice civile – Commentario diretto da Schlesinger (1995).

Giuseppe Vettori, Anomalie e tutele nei rapporti di distribuzione fra imprese (1983).

Giovanna Visintini, La reticenza nella formazione dei contratti (1972).

Reinhard Zimmermann, The Law of Obligations: Roman Foundations of the Civilian Tradition (1990, paperback edn, 1996).

The Netherlands

P. P. C. Haanappel, E. Mackaay, Nieuw Nederlands Burgerlijk Wetboek, Het vermogensrecht (New Netherlands Civil Code, Patrimonial law/Nouveau Code Civil Néerlandais, Le droit patrimonial) (1990).

A. S. Hartkamp, Aard en opzet van het nieuwe vermogensrecht (Monografieën Nieuw BW) (2nd edn, 1990).

Mr C. Asser's Handleiding tot de Beoefening van het Nederlands Burgerlijk Recht, Verbintenissenrecht, Deel I, De verbintenis in het algemeen, Asser-serie 4 (10th edn, 1996), Deel II, Algemene Leer der Overeenkomsten, Asser-serie 4 (10th edn, 1997).

J. M. M. Menu, De toezegging in het privaatrecht: een intern rechtsvergelijkende analyse met de toezegging in het bestuursrecht (1994).

J. H. Nieuwenhuis, C. J. J. M. Stolker, W. L. Valk, Burgerlijk Wetboek, Tekst & Commentaar (3rd edn, 1998).

W. H. M. Reehuis, E. E. Slob, Parlementaire geschiedenis van het Nieuw Burgerlijk Wetboek: parlementaire stukken systematisch gerangschikt en van noten voorzien, Invoering boeken 3, 5 en 6, Boek 3: Vermogensrecht in het algemeen (1990), Boek 6: Algemeen gedeelte van het verbintenissenrecht (1990).

J. M. Smits, Het vertrouwensbeginsel en de contractuele gebondenheid: beschouwingen omtrent de dogmatiek van het overeenkomstenrecht (1995).

R. P. J. L. Tjittes, De hoedanigheid van contractspartijen: een rechtsvergelijkend onderzoek *naar de betekenis van de (onderlinge) hoedanigheid van partijen voor de totstandkoming en de vaststelling van de inhoud van rechtshandelingen* (1994).

J. M. van Dunné, *Verbintenissenrecht, Deel 1 (Contractenrecht)* (1997).

J. H. M. van Erp, *Contract als rechtsbetrekking: een rechtsvergelijkende studie* (1990).

C. J. van Zeben, J. W. du Pon, *Parlementaire geschiedenis van het nieuw burgerlijk wetboek: parlementaire stukken systematisch gerangschikt en van noten voorzien, Boek 3: Algemeen gedeelte van het verbintenissenrecht* (1981), *Boek 6: Vermogensrecht in het algemeen* (1981).

J. B. M. Vranken, *Mededelings-, informatie- en onderzoeksplichten in het verbintenissenrecht* (1989).

England

P. V. Baker, P. St J. Langan, *Snell's Equity* (29th edn, 1990).

R. C. l'Anson Banks, *Lindley & Banks on Partnership* (17th edn, 1995).

J. Bell, 'The Effect of Changes in Circumstances on Long-Term Contracts, I: English Report', in: D. Harris, D. Tallon (eds.), *Contract Law Today* (1989) 195 ff.

Peter Birks, 'In Defence of Free Acceptance', in: A. Burrows (ed.), *Essays on the Law of Restitution* (1995) 105 ff.

An Introduction to the Law of Restitution (1985).

A. Burrows, *The Law of Restitution* (1993).

Sir Edward Coke, *The First Part of the Institutes of the Laws of England or A Commentary upon Littleton* (1st edn, 1628; 7th edn, 1670 used).

John Stuart Colyer (cons. ed.), 'Landlord and Tenant', in: Lord Hailsham of St Marylebone (ed.), *Halsbury's Laws of England*, vol. 27(1) (4th edn, reissue, 1994).

S. M. Cretney, J. M. Masson, *Principles of Family Law* (6th edn, 1997).

Christine Davis, 'Estoppel: An Adequate Substitute for Part Performance?', (1993) 13 *Oxford JLS* 99 ff.

J. Dewar, *Law and the Family* (2nd edn, 1992).

E. P. Ellinger, E. Lomnicka, *Modern Banking Law* (2nd edn, 1994).

Robert Goff, Gareth Jones, *The Law of Restitution* (5th edn, 1998).

K. Gray, *Elements of Land Law* (2nd edn, 1993).

A. G. Guest (gen. ed.), *Benjamin's Sale of Goods* (4th edn, 1992).

Chitty on Contracts, vols. I and II (27th edn, 1994).

A. H. Hudson, Norman Palmer, 'Confidence and Data Protection', in: Lord Hailsham of St Marylebone (ed.), *Halsbury's Laws of England*, vol. 8(1) (4th edn, reissue, 1996).

E. R. Hardy Ivamy, 'Insurance', in: Lord Hailsham of St Marylebone (ed.), *Halsbury's Laws of England*, vol. 25 (4th edn, reissue, 1994).

I. Kennedy, A. Grubb, *Medical Law, Text with Materials* (2nd edn, 1994).

Ewan McKendrick, 'The Regulation of Long-Term Contracts in English Law', in: Jack Beatson, Daniel Friedmann (eds.), *Good Faith and Fault in Contract Law* (1995) 305 ff.

Norman Palmer, *Bailment* (2nd edn, 1991).

Norman Palmer, Alison Powell, 'Bailment', in: Lord Hailsham of St Marylebone
    (ed.), *Halsbury's Laws of England*, vol. 2 (4th edn, reissue, 1991).
Günter Treitel, *The Law of Contract* (9th edn, 1995).
Richard Whish, 'Trade, Industry and Industrial Relations', in: Lord Hailsham of
    St Marylebone (ed.), *Halsbury's Laws of England*, vol. 47 (4th edn, reissue, 1994).

Ireland

R. C. l'Anson Banks, *Lindley & Banks on Partnership* (17th edn, 1995).
J. Brady, A. Kerr, *The Limitation of Actions* (2nd edn, 1994).
J. Breslin, *Banking Law in the Republic of Ireland* (1998).
R. Clark, *Contract Law in Ireland* (3rd edn, 1992).
R. J. Friel, *The Law of Contract* (1995).
R. Keane, *Equity and the Law of Trusts in the Republic of Ireland* (1988).
A. Shatter, *Family Law in Ireland* (3rd edn, 1986).
D. Tomkin, P. Hanafin, *Irish Medical Law* (1995).
G. H. Treitel, *The Law of Contract* (8th edn, 1991).
J. Wylie, *Irish Land Law* (3rd edn, 1997).

Scotland

Joseph Bell, *Principles of the Law of Scotland* (10th edn, 1899).
William M. Gloag, *The Law of Contract* (2nd edn, 1929).
Nigel Morrison, 'Loan', in: Thomas Smith, Robert Black (eds.), *The Laws of Scotland,
    Stair Memorial Encyclopaedia*, vol. 13 (1992).
John Rankine, *A Treatise on the Law of Personal Bar in Scotland* (1921).
Günter Treitel, *Frustration and Force Majeure* (1994).
D. M. Walker, *The Law of Contracts and Related Obligations in Scotland* (3rd edn, 1995).
W. A. Wilson, Angelo Forte (eds.), *Gloag & Henderson, The Law of Scotland* (10th edn,
    1995).

Denmark and Norway

Lennart Lynge Andersen, Palle Bo Madsen, Jørgen Nørgaard, *Aftaler og
    mellemmænd* (3rd edn, 1997).
Carl Jacob Arnholm, *Privatrett I & II* (1964).
    Tre utsnitt av den almindelige privatrett (1975).
Per Augdahl, *Den norske obligasjonsretts almindelige del* (5th edn, 1978).
Erling Borcher, 'Om ophør af agentur- og forhandleraftaler', U 1993 B, 97 ff.
Kirsti Strøm Bull, *Avtaler mellom ektefeller* (1993).
Børge Dahl, *Produktansvar* (1973).
Bernhard Gomard, *Almindelig kontraktsret* (2nd edn, 1996).
    Forholdet mellem erstatningsregler i og utenfor kontraktsforhold (1990).
    Obligationsret 1. del (2nd edn, 1989), *2. del* (1995), *3. del* (1993).

Viggo Hagstrøm, 'Brist i loven eller etikken', *Lov og Rett* 1997, 385 ff.
  Fragmenter fra obligasjonsrett I (1992).
  'Kjøpsrettskonvensjon, norsk kjøpslov og internasjonal rettsenhet', TfR 1995,
    561 ff.
  'Regnskapsmessig estimering og privatrettslig bundethet og ansvar', *Lov og
    Rett* 1995, 375 ff.
  'Urimelige avtalevilkår', *Lov og Rett* 1994, 131 ff.
Stub Holmboe, *Foreldelse av fordringer* (1946).
Henning Jakhelln, *Oversikt over arbeidsretten* (1996).
Asbjørn Kjønstad, Steinar Tjomsland, *Foreldelsesloven* (1983).
Jan Kleineman, 'Avtalsrättsliga formföreskrifter och allmänna
    skadeståndsrättsliga ansvarsprinciper', JT 1993/1994, 433 ff.
Kai Krüger, *Pengekrav* (2nd edn, 1984).
Preben Lyngsø, *Dansk Forsikringsret* (6th edn, 1989).
Ola Mestad, *Om force majeure og risikofordeling i kontrakt* (1991).
Jacob Nørager-Nielsen, Søren Theilgaard, *Købeloven med kommentarer* (2nd edn,
    1993).
Nils Nygaard, *Skade og ansvar* (4th edn, 1994).
Knut Selmer, *Forsikringsavtaleloven* (1990).
Erling Selvig, *Knophs Oversikt over Norges Rett* (10th edn, 1993).
Lasse Simonsen, *Prekontraktuelt ansvar* (1997).
Michael H. Svendsen, 'Goodwill-erstatning in eneforhandlingsforhold', U 1994 B,
    252 ff.
  'Om beregning af godtgørelse efter § 25 i lov om handelsagenter og
    handelsrejsende', U 1993 B, 227 ff.
Henry Ussing, *Aftaler* (3rd edn, 1950).
Bo von Eyben, Jørgen Nørgaard, Hans Henrik Vagner, *Lærebog i erstatningsret* (2nd
    edn, 1993).
Morten Wegener, '"Goodwill-erstatning" til eneforhandlere', U 1994 B, 350 ff.
  'Kompensation til eneforhandlere for mistet kundekreds', *Juristen* 1992,
    361 ff.
  'Mere om ophør af agentur- og forhandleraftaler', U 1994 B, 20 ff.

Sweden

Torgny Håstad, *Den nya köprätten* (4th edn, 1998).
Jan Hellner, 'Rådighetsinskränkningar vid köp av lös egendom', in: *Festskrift till
    Jan Ramberg* (1997) 209 ff.
  Skadeståndsrätt (5th edn, 1995).
Hjalmar Karlgren, *Passivitet* (1965).
Jan Kleineman, *Ren förmögenhetsskada* (1987).
Folke Schmidt (Tore Sigeman, gen. ed.), *Löntagarrätt* (1988).
Lennart Vahlén, *Fastighetsköp* (1971).

Finland

Aulis Aarnio, 'Muodon merkitys oikeudellisessa käyttäytymisessä [The Relevance of Form in Legal Behaviour]', in: *Oikeustiede-Jurisprudentia I* (1972) 185 ff.

Tuula Ämmälä, 'Ns. negatiivisesta sopimusedusta [On the so-called Negative Interest in Contract]', in: *Turun Yliopiston oikeustieteellinen tiedekunta 30 vuotta* (1991) 547 ff.

Jouko Halila, Matti Ylöstalo, *Saamisen lakkaamisesta [On the Termination of Obligations]* (1966).

Mika Hemmo, *Sopimusoikeus [The Law of Contracts]*, vol. I (1997).

Vahingonkorvauksen määräytymisestä sopimussuhteissa [Fixing Damages in Contract Law] (1994).

Osvi Lahtinen, *Oikeustoimen muoto-ongelmasta [The Problem of the Form of a Legal Act]* (1957).

Juha Laine, *Rakennusvirheistä [On Construction Defects]* (1991).

P. J. Muukkonen, *Muotosäännökset [Formal Provisions]* (1958).

Lars Erik Taxell, *Avtal och rättsskydd [Contracts and Remedies]* (1972).

K. A. Telaranta, *Sopimusoikeus [The Law of Contract]* (1990).

Thomas Wilhelmsson, *Vakiosopimus [Standard Contract]* (1985).

Case 1: Courgettes perishing

Case

Barchester Chemicals Ltd is a producer of agricultural and domestic fertilisers. Cecil is a market gardener and buys directly from Barchester's a quantity of one of their products, 'Growright 100', for use on his courgettes. Owing to the high content of salt in this product, the plants' vegetation perishes: it is clear that this would not have happened if Cecil had been advised to give the plants large quantities of water at the time of administering the product. What claims does Cecil have against Barchester?

Discussions

GERMANY

The case may, in the first place, be seen as giving rise to liability for latent defects under §§ 459 ff. BGB. §§ 459 ff. BGB constitute the modern statutory version of the aedilitian remedies of Roman law.[1] If the subject matter of the sale is defective, the purchaser may either demand cancellation of the sale (*Wandelung*, i.e. the German equivalent of the *actio redhibitoria*) or reduction of the purchase price (*Minderung*, i.e. the German equivalent of the *actio quanti minoris*). A claim for damages is available only if a promised quality in the object sold was absent or if the vendor has fraudulently concealed a defect (§ 463 BGB). An object is regarded as defective if it is not suited for its ordinary use or for the use provided in the contract (§ 459 I BGB). In the present case, however, Barchester's fertiliser does not seem to

---

[1] Zimmermann, *Obligations* 305 ff., 327 f.

171

have been defective. It is assumed that the fertiliser was as good as could be produced at the time of sale. It was also suitable for watering Cecil's courgettes, provided Cecil gave the plants large quantities of water at the time of administering the product, and provided Cecil knew that he had to do so.

Yet, a claim will lie on the ground of *culpa in contrahendo*. The doctrine of *culpa in contrahendo* was formulated first by *Rudolf von Jhering* in a celebrated article published in 1861.[2] Contractual *diligentia*, he postulated, is owed not only where the contract has come into existence but also where it is still *in statu nascendi*. With the commencement of their negotiations, the parties enter into a special relationship giving rise to rights and duties which go beyond the compass of the law of delict. Infringement of the duties *in contrahendo* by one of the parties entitles the other to claim the damages. The liability is of (quasi-)contractual nature and it is based on *culpa* (in the sense of fault); compensation is limited to the negative (reliance) interest. *Culpa in contrahendo* has become a firmly established feature of the legal landscape of German private law, albeit *praeter legem*, i.e. by way of judge-made law.[3] Over the years, courts and legal writers have worked out specific criteria for liability for typical groups of cases.[4] In the present situation, Barchester would be liable if failure to inform Cecil of the need for watering the plants constitutes breach of a precontractual duty of information. Generally speaking, no such duty to inform exists in view of the natural conflict of interests between the parties. A person who concludes a contract, in principle, has the responsibility to decide to what uses the subject matter of the contract can be put. Thus, a buyer must discern what dangers the article may hold for him. If he does not possess the necessary technical knowledge, he will have to inform himself. On the other hand, if a party to a contract is inexperienced in technical, economic or business questions he may, in view of the requirement of good faith (*Treu und Glauben*), expect to be informed of material circumstances as long as the other party knows of the inexperience of his target group and is himself conscious of the risks and dangers flowing from the trans-

---

[2] *Jherings Jahrbücher für die Dogmatik des bürgerlichen Rechts* 4 (1861) 16 ff.

[3] The BGB only contains certain traces of recognising the *culpa in contrahendo* doctrine for special situations; cf. § 307, or § 122 (but in the latter case, liability is not based on fault!). For details, see Medicus, in: *Festgabe Kaser* 169 ff.; Zimmermann, *Obligations* 244 f. and the references given there. *Culpa in contrahendo*, in German law, is seen as falling on the contractual side of the contract/delict divide and has in fact been used to remedy certain deficiencies of the German law of delict; cf. Zimmermann, *Obligations* 11 ff.; Zweigert/Kötz 674 ff.

[4] Cf., e.g., the overview in *Jauernig/Vollkommer* § 276, nn. 74 ff.; *Palandt/Heinrichs* § 276, nn. 72 ff.

action. Hence, Barchester Chemicals Ltd, who knew about the specific risk arising from the use of the fertiliser and who had the necessary know-how that Cecil lacked, should have informed the latter that much watering was necessary for effective use of the fertiliser. A duty has been breached and Cecil may therefore claim damages in the form of negative interest, i.e. the value of his perished plants.

The case is very much a borderline situation. If the fertiliser were seen to be defective, Cecil would have no claim for damages under §§ 459 ff., since there was neither fraud nor a specific promise on the part of Barchester. Cancellation or reduction, of course, does not help Cecil in the present case. A claim for *culpa in contrahendo* would then also be excluded since it should not be used to undercut the evaluations on which §§ 459 ff. BGB are based. This is why, according to the prevailing view, *culpa in contrahendo* is not available, if Barchester's duty to inform related to a quality of the object sold.[5] Arguably, however, this does not apply as far as consequential loss is concerned.[6] Loss of the vegetables, in the present case, constitutes consequential loss (*Mangelfolgeschäden*) as opposed to damages pertaining to the object of the sale itself (*Mangelschäden*). To make matters even more complicated, the borderline between *culpa in contrahendo* and positive malperformance (*positive Forderungsverletzung*)[7] is rather difficult to draw and the case might therefore also be analysed in terms of a duty to inform the other party arising (as an ancillary duty) under the contract of sale rather than the precontractual relationship. Here it is very widely recognised that a claim for consequential loss may be brought in spite of the restrictive provisions of §§ 459 ff. BGB.[8] The considerations as to when such a duty to inform may be seen to exist are very much the same as under *culpa in contrahendo*.[9]

In the present case it is arguable that a duty to inform does not exist in view of the fact that Cecil was himself a market gardener, i.e. not a layman. It would seem preferable, however, to reduce Cecil's claim for damages under § 254 I BGB on account of contributory fault.

§ 242 BGB, the general good faith clause, is only referred to in the present case when it comes to establishing the range of precontractual (or contractual) duties under *culpa in contrahendo* (or positive malperformance).[10] Apart from that, § 254 BGB ('If any fault of the injured party has

---

[5] Cf. *Palandt*/Heinrichs § 276, n. 80 and Vorbem. v. § 459, n. 7.
[6] Cf. *Jauernig*/Vollkommer § 459, n. 47; for a detailed analysis of the different views and arguments exchanged, see Marburger 88 ff.
[7] On which see below, the German report to case 16.
[8] Cf., e.g., *Jauernig*/Vollkommer § 459, n. 48.   [9] *Palandt*/Heinrichs § 433, n. 17.
[10] Cf., e.g., *Jauernig*/Vollkommer § 242, nn. 16 ff.

contributed to causing the damage, the obligation to compensate the injured party and the extent of the compensation to be made depends upon the circumstances, especially upon how far the injury has been caused predominantly by one or the other party') is often regarded as a statutory emanation of the good faith principle.[11]

Moreover, Cecil will have a product liability claim in terms of the German law of delict. According to § 823 I BGB,[12] a person who negligently and unlawfully injures the property of another is bound to compensate him for the damage arising. In the present case, Barchester has caused damage to Cecil's courgettes. This was unlawful in view of Barchester's duty to inform Cecil.[13]

Finally, Cecil may claim compensation under § 1 Product Liability Act (*Produkthaftungsgesetz* = ProdHG). The fertiliser was defective within the meaning of § 3 I a ProdHG since it did not measure up to the standards which a buyer could reasonably expect in view of the way in which it was presented. Lack of proper instruction is generally regarded as being covered by the term 'presentation' (*Darbietung*) in § 3 I a ProdHG. However, application of § 1 I 2 ProdHG excludes liability if the courgettes are not intended to be used for private purposes.

GREECE

In this case Cecil, a market gardener, will try to establish a claim against Barchester Chemicals Ltd, a producer of agricultural and domestic fertilisers. Cecil will try to argue that the product given by Barchester Chemicals Ltd was defective as it killed his plants.

The question concerns the area of the law in which Cecil might have a claim. According to Greek law liability arising from precontractual negotiations cannot be applied in this case because Cecil has already bought the 'Growright 100' and the contract is valid. On this point the Greek law differs slightly from the German theory concerning precontractual liability.[14]

(i) It is clear from the case that the plants' vegetation perished. If Cecil had been advised to give the plants large quantities of water at the time of administering the product, this would not have happened. Barchester

---

[11] BGHZ 34, 355 (363); 56, 163 (169); *Palandt/*Heinrichs § 254, n. 2; *contra: Münchener Kommentar/*Grunsky § 254, n. 2.
[12] For background discussion, see Zweigert/Kötz 638 ff.; Zimmermann, *Obligations* 1036 ff.; Markesinis, *Torts* 35 ff.   [13] Cf. *Palandt/*Thomas § 823, n. 207.
[14] Stathopoulos, *Contract* no. 88, p. 85.

Chemicals Ltd, therefore, in performing its duties, specified as implied terms in the contract, has not acted in good faith and according to fair dealing *per se* (art. 288 Gr. C.C.). This situation therefore entitles Cecil to claim compensation for the damages suffered on the basis of breach of contract.[15]

(ii) Cecil has a second, alternative claim for compensation against Barchester Chemicals Ltd, under art. 914 Gr. C.C. (unlawful acts or tort liability), if he can prove the existence of a fault.[16]

(iii) A new law (L. 2251/1994, art. 5 I) dealing with producers' liability will provide Cecil with a third possibility for claiming compensation from Barchester Chemicals Ltd. According to this article 'in every sale the producer is under a duty to provide the consumer in writing, in the Greek language, or by writing established in the natural symbols, clear directions for the safe use, preservation, conservation and right exploitation of the product and information about the dangers arising from its use or preservation. Products which are simple in their construction, use and preservation are excluded.'

Furthermore according to art. 1 IV of the same law a consumer is defined as the final recipient of goods (products and services), a natural or legal entity, regardless of whether he uses the product for his own personal needs or for his profession. In comparison with E.C. Council Directive 85/374/EEC the above-mentioned art. 1 IV expands the notion of consumer and includes also the use of the product for professional reasons, provided the consumer is the final user. Therefore it could be said that Cecil is a consumer, as long as he was the final user of the fertiliser. Cecil as a consumer has the right to know about all effects which use of the product can cause, as in this case the 'Growright 100' had to be used with plenty of water in order not to harm the plants.

To claim compensation under L. 2251/1994 Cecil has to prove that (a) he has not been properly informed about the dangers arising from the use of the 'Growright 100', (b) he suffered damage and (c) the damage he suffered was causally related to the defectiveness of the product (lack of expected safety of the product, art. 6(5)). He does not have to prove fault.[17]

According to the above, Cecil, if utilising the claims he has under L. 2251/1994, which concerns the liability of a producer, is in a favourable

[15] Stathopoulos, in: *Astikos Kodix II* art. 288, no. 46; Androulidakis-Dimitriadis, *Ypochreoseis* 96, 121, 149 ff.
[16] Stathopoulos, *Contract* nos. 5, 39–41, pp. 47–9; Georgiades, in: *Festschrift Larenz* 175 ff.
[17] Karakostas, *Euthini tou Paragogou* 162; Karakostas, *Prostasia tou Katanaloti* 95; Stathopoulos/Chiotellis/Avgoustianakis 39.

position to claim compensation. It has to be pointed out that the meaning of defectiveness used by L. 2251/1994 is quite different from the meaning of actual defect used in the law of obligations, especially in sale contracts.[18]

The establishment of liability for producers by L. 2251/1994, following the incorporation of the European Community Directives (E.C. Council Directive 85/374/EEC, etc.) in Greek law, resolved issues of ambiguity by the application of the term 'good faith'. A producer's liability under L. 2251/1994 is strict liability and arises irrespective of the existence, nonexistence, validity or non-validity of the contract.

AUSTRIA

Since Barchester Chemicals Ltd has performed its contractual duties in conformity with the terms of the contract, this case does not give rise to a claim by Cecil for damages for non-performance. On the other hand, a claim in delict based on damage to Cecil's property (namely the perishing of his courgettes) may be considered;[19] indeed one Austrian legal scholar has maintained that this is the only possibility in a situation such as this.[20]

However, the prevailing view would treat this case rather differently, and would look instead to the existence of special duties to provide information or to take care which arise whenever people come into 'lawful contact' with a view to entering into a contract.[21] These duties correspond to those which arise between the parties to a contract once it has been concluded, no matter whether the contract is valid or not.[22] By contrast, however, it is clear that these *precontractual* duties do not arise from any agreement between the parties, but as a matter of law by way of analogous application of several provisions in the Austrian Civil Code.[23] Applying this approach, it can be seen that Barchester Chemicals Ltd has failed in its duty to provide appropriate information to Cecil: it ought to have advised him of the dangerous properties of the product and of its dangers in use, which it either knew or ought to have known as its producer. Barchester could not expect a purchaser to be aware of all the properties of its product and it is clear that any such purchaser would have a strong interest in knowing what they were.

[18] Appeal Court of Athens 647/1994 NoB 43, 395.
[19] The question of strict product liability will not be discussed here.
[20] Reischauer, in: *Rummel, ABGB I* vor §§ 918–33 nn. 4, 5, 14.   [21] Welser, *Vertretung* 57.
[22] Canaris, JZ 1965, 475.
[23] E.g. §§ 866, 878 ABGB. Also Welser, *Vertretung* 59 ff.; OGH in SZ 52/135 (1979).

Recognition of duties such as these which arise from 'lawful contact' give an injured person a wider protection than is provided by the law of delict, this being justified by the special relationship existing between the parties. In this respect it should be noted that the claims which arise from breach of such duties are taken to be contractual in nature. This is important in view of the significant differences actually existing between contractual and delictual claims although § 1295 I ABGB appears to treat breach of contract and delict in the same way.[24] Thus, for example, in contractual relations a person is strictly liable for any fault of a person whom he employs in performing his obligations,[25] whereas under the law of delict, a person is liable for those who assist him only if they are incompetent or dangerous.[26] A second difference between the two liability regimes relates to the burden of proof as to fault: a person who fails to perform his contract is liable unless he proves the absence of fault on his part,[27] whereas a person allegedly injured by another's delict must establish that person's fault in order to recover.[28] Thirdly, pure economic loss is recoverable in an action for breach of contract, but is not in general recoverable in delict. Finally, contractual obligations entail much more extensive duties to take care than exist in the law of delict, particularly as regards duties to act in order to avoid harm to the other party.

It may well be that these advantages of contractual liability were one of the reasons for recognising the existence of special precontractual duties, it being thought that the inadequacy of liability in delict should be remedied by the imposition of special obligations arising at the point of 'lawful contact' between the parties. At a more general level, such a development may be explained by reference to the idea that there is a sliding scale between breach of contract and delict and that the application of the legal rules governing contractual or non-contractual liability ought to depend on the intensity of the legal relationship between the parties concerned.[29]

FRANCE

Cecil has a claim against Barchester Chemicals Ltd for breach of a duty to inform (*obligation d'information*) which is incumbent upon it as producer and seller. This obligation applies here during performance and not formation of the contract. The information given under this duty to inform

---

[24] Koziol, JBl 1994, 209 ff.   [25] § 1313a ABGB.   [26] § 1315 ABGB.   [27] § 1298 ABGB.
[28] § 1296 ABGB.   [29] Koziol, JBl 1994, 214 ff.; Koziol, ZEuP 1995, 359.

is not a determining factor inducing Cecil to enter into the contract, but relates to the conditions in which the product should be used.

In French law the duty to inform is the product of case law, created by an extensive interpretation of the contract's content, based on the duty of performance in good faith found in art. 1134 al. 3 and in art. 1135 of the French Civil Code, which provides that contracts 'obligate a party not only as to what is there expressed, but also to all the consequences which equity, custom and the law give to the obligation according to its nature'. Moreover, in contracts of sale, the courts have extended the seller's obligations to deliver the property (under art. 1604 of the Civil Code) to include information concerning the product (*obligation de livre une chose conforme*). Such an obligation is particularly extensive when the seller is *professionnel*, that is, acting in the course of business. As a seller acting in the course of business, Barchester Chemicals Ltd must give Cecil all the essential information he needs to use the product. A seller must draw a buyer's attention to drawbacks inherent in the product. He must also tell him about precautions to be taken in the use of the product and so in one case the court held that '[the seller] had failed to perform the obligation which it had undertaken in its capacity as a *professional* seller, to inform the buyer about the conditions of use of new *material* when necessary, when proposing to substitute new material for the product chosen by him' (our italics).[30] A seller must also find out about the needs of the buyer and inform his client of the fitness of the material proposed for the use envisaged.[31] This obligation of advice is implied from art. 1135 of the Civil Code.

The principle of a duty of information, developed by the courts, has been incorporated into art. 2 of the *loi* of 18 January 1992.[32] However, as Cecil is a market gardener, he is probably also acting in the course of business and does not fall within the definition of a consumer. He cannot therefore claim the benefit of this legislative duty of information.

In the event that both Barchester Chemicals Ltd and Cecil are classified by French law as 'professionals', the duty to inform on the seller may be less onerous for Barchester Chemicals Ltd since Cecil has a duty to ask for information. Thus the duty may vary according to a number of factors: whether the product is dangerous, complex or new and on the relative status of the parties. In a recent case,[33] the *Cour de cassation* held that the seller was under an obligation to inform a professional buyer about the technical restrictions inherent in the object sold and its fitness to attain

---

[30] Com. 11 Jan. 1988, Bull. civ. IV, no. 250.   [31] Civ. (1) 5 Dec. 1995, Bull. civ. I, no. 453.
[32] Art. L. 111–1 C. cons.   [33] Com. 1 Dec. 1992, Bull. civ. IV, no. 391.

the desired objective, thus quashing the court of appeal's decision which had taken into consideration the conditions under which the contract had been made (i.e. at a fair), and the fact that the buyer was incapable of knowing how to regulate the machine, just as the seller was unaware of the conditions of use by the buyer's staff, thus not inferring a duty on the seller to advise the buyer. The legal reasoning behind this case is somewhat unsatisfactory as in order to quash the court of appeal's decision, reference was made to art. 1604 of the Civil Code, which concerns a seller's contractual obligation of delivery. Here, however, the duty to inform arises in order for the sale to be concluded with knowledge of the circumstances and therefore arises before contract.

Cecil might want to argue that the fertiliser sold by Barchester Chemicals Ltd is dangerous since it killed off his courgettes and that this factor should be taken into consideration. However, in relation to dangerous products the *Cour de cassation* has held[34] that as between professional sellers and buyers, the seller was not under a duty to include instructions for use since the buyer ought himself to know how to use the product or himself be able to find this out.

This rule is modified by two special considerations: firstly, the novelty of the product and, secondly, the status of the parties as 'traders in the same type of business' (*professionnels de même spécialité*). The novelty of the product does not appear to be an issue on the facts of case 1, although in this respect a recent case of the *Cour de cassation*[35] held that 'the seller of a product marketed very recently had an obligation to give to the user all the information necessary for its implementation'. The status of the parties as 'professionals' of a different speciality is the argument which Cecil could rely on most usefully. Thus, it was held in one case that a manufacturer of vegetable compost should inform the buyer (a market gardener producing melons) of the degree of humidity that should be maintained and that even if the buyer might have an insight into the question, he was not fully informed.[36] This case provides a perfect analogy with the facts stated, and suggests that Cecil would be able to succeed in his claim for breach of a duty to inform by Barchester Chemicals Ltd.

In the event that Cecil is able to prove that Barchester Chemicals Ltd breached its duty to inform, he may claim damages. According to case law such an obligation is generally considered to be a duty to take reasonable

---

[34] Com. 8 Jan. 1973, Bull. civ. IV, no. 16.   [35] Civ. (1) 4 May 1994, Bull. civ. I, no. 163.
[36] Civ. (1) 9 Dec. 1975, the 'punctured melon' case, Bull. civ. I, no. 361, JCP 1977.II.18588 note Ph. Malinvaud, D 1978.205 note R. Savatier.

care (*obligation de moyens*).[37] His damages would be limited to foreseeable losses, pursuant to art. 1150 of the Civil Code, as any allegation of deliberate non-performance (*inexécution dolosive*) on the part of Barchester Chemicals Ltd does not arise on the facts.

The existence of the duty to inform in contracts of sale derives from the courts' interpretation of arts. 1134, 1135 and 1604 of the Civil Code. The duty to inform, based on the principle of performing contracts in good faith, and more explicitly imposing a duty on the contracting parties to co-operate, is a means of giving protection to the buyer and, as such, is based on policy considerations. However, the intensity of the duty to inform incumbent upon the seller is the subject of academic controversy. Some authors are in favour of an onerous duty on the part of the seller, whereas others suggest that a certain duty lies on the buyer to explain clearly what he expects or requires. Originally based on a professional/non-professional distinction, this has now been recognised by legislation in the law of 18 January 1992. Since the duty depends on the status of the parties, case law has developed fine distinctions as to the speciality of the parties. This development has raised the issue of the relevance of the distinction. In sales between professionals the extent of protection afforded to buyers presently appears to be settled on a case-by-case basis. In this respect, the concept of good faith provides a useful tool for the courts to take moral factors into consideration.

BELGIUM

Case 1 concerns a frequently encountered problem. The rule is quite clear. The practical solution, on the other hand, is much less clear since the rule is open-ended and its application depends on the circumstances of the case.

(i) Belgian law has developed rules concerning (a) the duty of the debtor (here the seller) to inform the creditor (here the buyer) and (b) the duty[38] of the creditor (the buyer) to inform himself. Whether Cecil has a claim against Barchester depends on an evaluation of these duties in the present situation.

---

[37] Civ. (2) 23 Apr. 1985, Bull. civ. I, no. 125, D 1985.558 note S. Dion.
[38] More correctly, this is not a duty, but a 'burden' (German *Obliegenheit*, Dutch *last*, French *charge* or *incombanc*), but this distinction is not often clearly made in Belgian doctrine (see M. E. Storme, *De invloed* no. 196 ff.).

Belgian law recognises extensive duties of the seller – especially the professional seller – to inform the buyer about the possible risks of his product. However, this presupposes that use on courgettes is a normal use for this product or that the seller knew that Cecil was going to use the product for this purpose.[39] Strictly speaking, this duty on the part of the seller is based on the fact that it is incumbent upon him to have sufficient – especially professional – knowledge before entering into a contract.[40]

On the other hand, there is no duty to inform to the extent that the disputed characteristic of the product should have been known to the buyer. To a certain extent, a duty of the buyer to inform himself is recognised. This duty, however, does not completely neutralise the seller's duty to inform the buyer, unless the buyer is more professionally experienced with respect to the goods than the seller (take, for example, a buyer who is an agricultural engineer). The relative position of the parties, especially their professional position, will often be the determining factor. This element is, however, evaluated *in concreto* (except for very specific provisions in consumer law). There is no abstract rule, distinguishing, for example, professionals of the same branch from professionals of different branches. Generally speaking, the seller is judged more strictly than the buyer, because, after all, he is the one who has to deliver the goods and who purports (expressly or impliedly) to deliver goods of a certain quality.

(ii) The legal basis for the process of balancing the duties of buyer and seller, and the appropriate systematic niche, depends on an evaluation of the facts of the present case.

Strictly speaking, this is a case where nothing is wrong with the product itself. The damage would have been avoided if the seller had informed the buyer. The product, therefore, is defective. Moreover, the damage would have been avoided even if the seller had informed the buyer only after the conclusion of the contract. Thus, the problem in this case is not a precontractual, but a contractual one (see the discussion under (c)).

If, however, Cecil could prove that he would not have bought the product if he had known that it was necessary to use so much water, or that he would have bought it only for a lower price (both of which appear to be improbable), there may also be (a) a remedy based on mistake (error) and/or *culpa in contrahendo* or (b) a remedy based on latent defects. The position concerning product liability rules is referred to under (d),

[39] See Cass. 18 Nov. 1971, *Aquacoat*, Arr. 274 = RCJB 1973, 609 note Ph. Gerard.
[40] This may explain the possible difference from case 2 below.

whereas situations in which the seller's liability may be excluded are considered under (e). In so far as the case is considered to raise the issue of non-performance of a contractual duty, liability in delict (including precontractual liability) is excluded.[41]

(a) Mistake can give rise to a right to avoid the contract, and thus to claim restitution of the price. According to art. 1108 C.C., mistake only gives rise to avoidance where it relates to the 'substance' of the subject matter of the contract – but according to case law, 'substance' means any element without which that party would not have concluded the contract.[42] If such mistake has not occurred, only damages can be awarded on the basis of *culpa in contrahendo* (precontractual fault) of the other party. *Culpa in contrahendo* is not specifically regulated in Belgian law, but is an application of the general rules of the law of delict. Violation of a duty to inform certainly must be taken to constitute *culpa in contrahendo*. Whether such a duty has been violated depends on the considerations sketched under (i).

Generally speaking, however, Cecil would have no interest in avoiding the contract for mistake or claiming damages on the ground of *culpa in contrahendo*, since the rules concerning latent defects are more advantageous to him.

(b) According to art. 1641 C.C. the seller has to guarantee that the product does not have latent defects. These rules derive from the aedilitian liability in Roman law. In case of 'bad faith', the seller is also liable for all damage caused, in case of 'good faith' only for the negative interest without any consequential loss (i.e. only the costs incurred by the buyer); see art. 1644 C.C. 'Good faith' in this provision was certainly meant in a subjective sense (*guter Glauben*, not *Treu und Glauben*; see however below how a deliberate 'misinterpretation' has given rise to an enlarged liability for the seller). In the case of bad faith, the positive interest is awarded. This shows that these rules, although certainly having a precontractual origin, notably as *leges speciales* in cases of mistake, are treated nowadays in Belgian law as a specific form of contractual liability, thus allowing for compensation of the positive interest instead of merely the negative one.[43]

---

[41] See further the Belgian report in case 16 below.

[42] Cass. 31 Oct. 1966, Arr. 301; Cass. 27 Oct. 1995, RW 1996–1997, 298.

[43] The distinction between positive and negative interest has been drawn explicitly only in recent years in Belgium (see e.g. Kruithof/Bocken, TPR 1994, 434 ff.; one of the first authors to use it was Ronse, TPR 1978, 744), but it has traditionally been implicit in Belgian decisions (hidden behind considerations of causation).

In case 1, however, the difference between positive and negative interest probably[44] plays no role, as the damage is consequential damage.

Result: where the seller is liable on the basis of latent defects, his liability will normally be a full liability for all harm suffered by the buyer (except for the harm the buyer should have avoided according to the rules concerning mitigation of damage[45]), unless the seller proves that he could not have known of the defect ('state of the art' defence). In the latter situation, the seller is only liable for restitution of the price (plus other expenses incurred as a result of the contract).

The application of rules relating to latent defects in the present case is doubtful. It is true that Belgian law has interpreted the notion of 'defect' in an enlarged sense, notably by not restricting it to 'inherent defects' in a naturalistic sense (defects of the object compared to what an object of this 'nature' should normally be like) and by making it cover 'functional defects' (the object is not suitable for its intended use);[46] none the less, the application remains doubtful for the above-mentioned reason, namely that the product was suitable for its intended use, provided large quantities of water were administered. Still, the warranty for latent defects is discussed here because, although it is theoretically incorrect to include informational deficiencies in the notion of 'defect', this is sometimes done in practice (case law). The rules concerning warranty for latent defects should also be kept in mind in order to understand how the real basis for the claim, i.e. the duty to inform, has developed in Belgian law. Both have often been linked together or even been mixed up. The reason may be that there is a firm and precise statutory basis for the warranty for latent defects but not for the duty to inform: and lawyers still tend to clutch at the life-line of a statutory provision, when they venture into a sea of case law.

Finally, because in Belgium the aedilitian remedies have been applied by analogy to contracts other than sales contracts, it is doubtful whether they can still be considered as specific rules for sales law; they have tended to become part of the general law of obligations.

(c) As stated above, the legal basis of Cecil's claim will normally be a

---

[44] Theoretically, with the standard of positive interest, the damage could be assessed taking into account the crop which would normally have grown in the case of correct use of the product, and with the negative interest only the crop which would have grown without the use of the product at all. In this case, however, it is very difficult to make that distinction in practice.   [45] See the discussion in (ii) (e) below.

[46] See Cass. 18 Nov. 1971, *Aquacoat*, Arr. 274 = RCJB 1973, 609 note Ph. Gerard.

contractual duty to inform. The seller should have known of the conditions for the use of the product he sells, and he has a duty to communicate this knowledge to the buyer. In case of violation of such a duty, the normal remedies for non-performance are available, which may include damages (for the consequential loss; in principle limited to foreseeable damages (art. 1150 C.C.) but in this case the damage was foreseeable) and possibly termination of the contract with restitution of the price.

Such a duty to inform is especially prominent in consumer law. For example, art. 30 of the Trade Practices and Consumer Protection Act of 14 July 1991 provides that the buyer has to give the consumer sufficient information concerning the characteristics of the product, taking into account the need for information expressed by the consumer and the normal use or the intended use communicated by the consumer, or the reasonably foreseeable use of the product. This rule as such is not applicable to the present case, as Cecil is not a consumer in relation to his crop. Furthermore, even without these special rules, similar results would probably be reached under the general law of obligations (as stated above, the professional position of the parties is often of decisive importance).

Commentators often relate duties to inform to the general principle of good faith (in Belgium more so than in France); studies on good faith are traditionally divided into two parts, dealing with the precontractual applications of good faith and the contractual ones respectively.[47] In the case law of the *Hof van cassatie*, however, it is dealt with as a traditional rule (which survived codification even though not incorporated into the Civil Code), according to the adage *spondet peritiam artis*.[48] This rule is used, especially, to explain the duty of the seller to examine the goods offered for sale (precontractual duty of the seller, contractual duty in the case of sale of generic goods). But apart from this, there is also a duty to inform, even after conclusion of the sale.[49]

This duty to inform has been linked to the warranty in respect of latent defects (aedilitian remedies) in a peculiar way. Violation of the duty to inform, so it is argued, deprives the seller of the right to invoke his 'good faith' even in the subjective sense (*guter Glauben*). Thus, he is treated as someone who knew of the defects, with the consequence that his non-performance will normally be considered intentional and his liability not be

---

[47] For example, De Bondt, TPR 1984, 95 ff.

[48] See Cass. 4 May 1939, *sa Ateliers du Kremlin v. Ingersoll-Rand*, Pas. I 223.

[49] See e.g. Cass. 28 Feb. 1980, *pvba gymnastiekwerktuigen international v. asbl Arts & métiers d'Erquelinnes, asbl Centre intercommunal de loisirs actifs d'Erquelinnes v. Picart*, JT 1981, 241 note M. Fallon, RCJB 1983, 228 note J. L. Fagnart.

restricted to foreseeable damages. Parties therefore often base their claim on the warranty, although they could (and should, more correctly) base it on a duty to inform as such.

As under the general law of obligations, the debtor's duty to inform has, in the meantime, been considerably developed by Belgian law. However, the link with the aedilitian remedies has been criticised in recent times, because it results in a stricter (i.e. more far-reaching) liability on the basis of the aedilitian rules compared to the general law of obligations. The difference does not so much consist in a stricter duty to examine or inform (there is no longer a difference on this point), but in the consequences of the equation of the seller's negligence with intentional non-performance, thus excluding the possibility of a valid exclusion clause and setting aside the limitation of compensation to foreseeable damages. Despite the criticism, this assimilation, which rests on a (perhaps deliberate) confusion between subjective and objective good faith, is still frequently encountered in the case law.

On the other hand, this frequent assimilation of the duty to inform with the aedilitian remedies also has the effect that the short limitation period for the latter claims (usually a maximum of one year after appearance of the defect) applies.

(d) The specific rules on product liability, i.e. the Product Liability Act of 25 February 1991, do not apply (they do not, however, make a big difference between contracting parties; in implementing E.C. Council Directive 85/374/EEC, Belgium has opted for the 'state-of-the-art' exception and has not, therefore, implemented a regime of strict liability in the full sense of the word; the difference with general sales law is small). Article 5 defines, in accordance with the E.C. Directive, a defect in terms of a lack of the safety one may expect, taking into account all circumstances. In the present case, the defect (in so far as there is one) is not a defect in safety, but a 'functional' defect. The Product Liability Act is also not applicable, because Cecil's damage is not 'private' damage.

(e) The warranty against latent defects does not apply to cases where the defect is not 'hidden' (art. 1642 C.C.). This is the case where the disputed characteristic of the product should have been known to the buyer. Legal writers usually state that the duty to inform only exists in so far as the buyer did not know and should not have known of the characteristic or defect. As was pointed out above, this implies that, to a certain extent, a duty of the buyer to inform himself is recognised. The effect of such a duty differs according to the legal basis of the claim. If it is based on the warranty, there is no liability at all if the buyer should have known of the defect. The result is normally 'all or nothing'. If the claim is based on (the violation of) a duty to inform as such (which would appear to be so in the present case) the fault of the buyer does not completely neutralise the fault of the seller, but will result in a reduction of the claim on the basis of contributory negligence.

(iii) The development of the duty to inform can be rationalised in economic terms. The risk concerning deficiencies in information should be borne by the party to whom such information is most easily available. This, at least, is the case where the contract is not a zero game (where parties have opposite goals and the advantage of the one is the disadvantage of the other, see for example case 2), but where the success of the transaction is normally their common concern. In the present case, the basic question is whether the seller should have known of the problem or not, and not whether or not he had to inform the buyer (for, given the function of this information, he had a duty to communicate his knowledge). The seller is being reproached not for taking advantage of his knowledge, but for his professional incompetence. A strict duty to examine the goods and inform the other party enhances the quality of products and professional services on the market.

SPAIN

In Spanish law, Barchester is liable in damages to Cecil for the damage suffered by the plants. This liability may be based either on (i) breach in the law of contract or (ii) the law of delict.

(i) Articles 1484–6 of the Spanish Civil Code of 1889 provide that a seller is liable to a buyer for any latent defects in the property sold, provided that they render it useless for the agreed or intended purpose of the buyer. This liability arises whether or not the seller knew of the defects in question, but it does not do so where the purchaser ought to have known or to have discovered the defects owing to his profession or business. The Spanish High Court of Justice has repeatedly affirmed that this particular strict liability covers compensation for damage to other property owned by the buyer which is caused by the property which the seller supplies, as long as that damage is a reasonably foreseeable consequence of the seller's delivery of property with the defects in question.[50] Spanish courts have interpreted the meaning of 'defect' broadly for the purposes of these

---

[50] Judgements of 6 May 1911 (Col. Leg. vol. 121, nº 53), 15 June 1973 (RJA 1973, 2539), 10 June 1983 (RJA 1983, 3454).

provisions and so, notably, a lack of warning or instructions as to the proper way in which to use the property sold has been held to constitute a defect in it.[51]

Articles 1484–6 are special legal provisions which govern contracts of sale. None the less, since the Civil Code came into force, the Spanish High Court has imposed liability on sellers on the basis of the general law of liability for breach of contract, as provided for by arts. 1101, 1107 and 1124 of the Civil Code. Article 1101 enshrines the general position as regards liability for breach of contract and provides that liability is imposed on a debtor where 'in any way' (*de cualquier modo*) he fails to fulfil his duties under the contract. This rule is interpreted broadly by the courts so as to cover any case in which a creditor does not in fact receive what was intended as long as this was caused by the debtor's fault (fault for this purpose being breach of an obligation, deceit, non-disclosure etc.). This general law governing liability for breach of contract applies to all contracts except those special contracts to which special rules apply.

The purpose of this second basis of liability in a context like the present one has been to allow a buyer to avoid the short period of six months[52] within which he may bring the special action arising under the law of sale, and to make clear that a seller's liability extends to damage caused by the property sold to other property belonging to the buyer. Apart from these differences, the results reached by the general law of contract and by the special rules of sale are substantially alike.

In 1994 the Products Liability Act was enacted in order to implement in Spanish law the E.C. Council Directive on liability for defective products.[53] Under this Act, a manufacturer is liable for the damage which its defective products cause to property other than the defective product itself as long as that other property was of a type intended for private use or consumption.[54] On the facts of the present case, the latter condition is problematic, for Cecil has grown the courgettes as part of his business rather than for his private use. Apart from this particular difficulty, it should be noted that for the purpose of this liability, a defect exists where the product does not offer the safety which is to be expected taking into account all the circumstances, especially its foreseeable use.[55] Once it is shown that a defect in the product has caused the plaintiff harm, a manufacturer cannot escape liability even if he proves that he neither could know of nor could have prevented the existence of the defect. Liability

---

[51] High Court judgements of 20 October 1983 (RJA 1983, 5334), 3 October 1991 (RJA 1991, 6902).   [52] Art. 1490 C. Civ.   [53] 85/374.   [54] Arts. 2 and 10.   [55] Art. 3.

under the 1994 Act ceases ten years after the product was put onto the market or three years after the plaintiff suffers the damage.

On facts like those of this case, there are often no relevant differences between these three bases of liability, viz., the general law of contract, the special rules applicable to sale and the law relating to liability for defective products. Indeed, since the scope of their protection often seems to be the same, Spanish courts have not found occasion to distinguish between liability based on contract and that based on the Product Liability Act. Thus, in all contract cases, the courts have proved willing to apply the long prescription period of the general law of contract (fifteen years, according to art. 1964 of the Civil Code), rather than the short prescription period of six months in the law of sale. On the other hand, no case has yet made clear whether in future Spanish courts will allow a purchaser the benefit of the long prescription period of the general law of contract even if his claim is based on product liability.

In conclusion, it can be seen that Spanish law possesses overlapping legal provisions governing a case like this and grants the purchaser an option between them to obtain the same result.

(ii) Even though the damage to Cecil's plants is caused by Barchester's defective performance of the contract, the Spanish High Court has held that a buyer in such a case is entitled to compensation under the general law of liability for delictual negligence[56] because he has suffered harm to property other than that which is the subject matter of the contract, a position which holds good even if the damage is caused by the property which has been sold.[57] Although there is some inconsistency of approach in the courts, in most cases it can be concluded that the courts allow an injured party in this sort of situation to elect between claiming in contract or in delict. In fact, recourse to the general law of delict confers no special advantage on a purchaser. Thus, for example, the amount of any damages recoverable is calculated in accordance with the criteria laid down by the law of contract, and the prescription period applicable to claims in delict expires one year after the injured party receives knowledge of the existence of his harm. Finally, it should be noted that there is no judicial authority which helps to determine whether the approach which we have described with respect to the general law of liability for delictual fault needs to be changed as a result of the enactment of the Products Liability Act in 1994.

---

[56] Art. 1902 C. civ.
[57] Judgements of 9 March 1983 (RJA 1983, 1463), 19 June 1984 (RJA 1984, 3250), 16 December 1986 (RJA 1986, 7447), 10 June 1991 (RJA 1991, 4434).

ITALY

Under Italian law, fertilisers must be sold accompanied by technical information concerning their composition and instructions for their use,[58] both of which must be clear and intelligible.[59] The Italian legislation which makes these requirements implements Council Directive 76/116 of 18 December 1975, on the Approximation of the Laws of the Member States Relating to Fertilisers,[60] and any failure to obey these requirements is punishable by an administrative fine and may constitute a crime. If Barchester Chemicals has supplied the product accompanied by the information which this legislation requires and which is both correct and complete, it is unlikely that Cecil will recover compensation for the damage to property which he has suffered. The information provided with the fertiliser shields the producer from liability for the destruction of the crop.

Considering the possible outcome of an action in contract against the producer, except proof of a latent defect of the fertiliser,[61] the assumption is that the courgettes perished because the gardener failed to take notice of the producer's instructions regarding the correct use of the fertiliser. Although there is no Italian case in point, our judges would probably approach the question like the French *Cour de cassation* did in *Société de Protection de l'Agriculture (S.O.P.R.A.) c. Richard*.[62] That case involved potatoes rather than courgettes, which had perished following treatment with the fertiliser manufactured by the defendant.[63] The grower who suffered loss as a result claimed that the producer had violated the duty to inform him of the correct use of the fertiliser. Apparently, the grower had relied on instructions concerning the use of the product communicated to him on previous occasions. Such instructions differed from those supplied with the latest version of the same product which had caused the damage. The *Cour de cassation* quashed the decision of the lower court which had awarded damages to the gardener on the basis of latent defects with respect to the fertiliser. The *Cour de cassation* declared the lower court's

[58] L. 19 Oct. 1984, n. 708.   [59] Ibid., art. 3.   [60] O.J. 1976, L 241.
[61] The circumstance that the fertiliser contained a high percentage of salt will not trigger the remedies for latent defects provided by the Civil Code provisions on sale (arts. 1490–1493 c.c.) if that percentage is not due to an anomaly of the product. Lack of a quality in the thing sold supports a claim for rescission of the contract and damages where such a quality is essential for its use or where it was promised, provided that this failure exceeds the limits of tolerance established by usage (art. 1497 c.c.). Here again, however, the product is not lacking any quality; it should just be employed in conformity with the seller's instructions. On the current notion of 'defect' or 'lack of quality' with respect to sales see Bianca, in: *Trattato Vassalli* 1,2 884 ff.
[62] Com. 16 Oct. 1973, JCP 1974.II.17846 obs. Ph. Malinvaud.
[63] The issue relating to privity need not be examined here.

finding of latent defects erroneous because the grower 'complains not of an internal defect in the thing, but of a lack of warning'.[64] The same Court also noticed that the lower court had not examined how the grower had used the product. The case was therefore remitted to the lower court with the instruction to examine whether or not the grower's use of the product had been according to the instructions and warnings delivered with the fertiliser at the time of the sale. From this decision, it appears that the success of the grower's claim would have been certain had the crop perished despite compliance with the producer's instructions and warnings concerning the mode of employment of the fertiliser, but not otherwise.

An action in tort against Barchester Chemicals Ltd would have a similar result. Supposing the producer sold the fertiliser with the required information on its composition and employment, the gardener's claim in tort against him would be rejected.

Cecil may try to establish Barchester's liability under the general provision of art. 2043 of the Italian Civil Code: '[a]ny fraudulent, malicious or negligent act that causes an unjustified injury to another obliges the person who has committed the act to pay damages'.[65] It seems, however, that if the seller provided the information required by the law concerning the composition and the mode of employment of the fertiliser he could not be held to have been negligent.

Moreover, a claim against Barchester based on the Italian legislation implementing E.C. Council Directive 85/374 on liability for defective products[66] which establishes the liability of producers is also barred in the circumstances. Under the present regime the product is defective where it does not measure up to the standard of safety one may reasonably expect considering all the circumstances.[67] In the evaluation of such an issue all the circumstances of the case are relevant, including the way in which the product was offered on the market, its presentation, its obvious characteristics, the instructions and warnings supplied with it, the use for which it may reasonably be employed and the behaviour in relation to it which one can reasonably foresee.[68] Once more, however, supposing the producer sold the fertiliser with the required information, there will be no ground to hold the product defective. In any case, by art. 11(1)1b of this legislation liability is not imposed on producers for damage to things not intended to be used for private use or consumption.

---

[64] '... se plaint non d'un vice interne de la chose, mais d'un défaut de mise en garde.'
[65] For in-depth commentary on this norm see Monateri, in: *Trattato Sacco, passim*; Alpa/Bessone/Zeno-Zencovich, in: *Trattato Rescigno* 239 ff.; Franzoni, in: *Commentario Scialoja-Branca, passim*.   [66] D.p.r. 24 May 1988, n. 224.   [67] Ibid., art. 5.   [68] Ibid.

On the other hand, if the producer did not sell the fertiliser together with the information required by the legislation concerning agricultural fertilisers the buyer will certainly recover damages for breach of contract, or in tort.

Barchester's contractual duty to inform Cecil is established by art. 1374 of the Civil Code, which provides that '[a] contract binds the parties not only as to what it expressly provides, but also to all the consequences deriving from it by law [legge], or in its absence, to usage and equity'. The legislature has established the duty to provide the information required to make proper use of the fertiliser to prevent harm such as that suffered by the plaintiff. Hence, one of the seller's obligations under the contract was to inform the buyer about how to employ the product. This approach is consistent with art. 1477 of the Civil Code, which obliges the seller to deliver to the buyer the documents pertaining to ownership and use of the thing sold.[69]

Barchester's failure to provide the information required by the legislation on fertilisers is also relevant from the point of view of delictual liability. The violation of this duty to inform the buyer can be considered fault for the purposes of art. 2043 of the Civil Code, the general provision on delictual liability. For the same reason the product would be judged defective according to the law regulating product liability.[70]

If this hypothetical case were approached from a broader perspective, to discover how Italian law deals with the question of whether or not (and to what extent) the parties to a contract should exchange information which may influence their choices during the precontractual phase, one may note that the duty to negotiate in good faith enacted by art. 1337 of the Civil Code does not provide a general answer to the question except in cases where it is clear to one party that the other party is contracting under a misapprehension. In this particular case the requirement of good faith is satisfied only if the party to the contract who is aware of the other party's misapprehension communicates to the latter the relevant information.[71] Italian law is by no means hostile to the idea that one party may be obliged to disclose to the other party information which may influence a decision whether or not to conclude a contract, but it has not yet developed a broad rule on this issue. Instead, there are several rules enacted by the legislature which point towards the following principle: those contractors who possess special information for reasons related to their trade or profession must pass on to the 'non-professionals' with whom they contract any

---

[69] On the interpretation of this provision see Bianca, in: *Trattato Vassalli 1,1* 435 ff.
[70] See p. 190, above.   [71] Sacco/De Nova, in: *Trattato Sacco I* 434–40.

information of this kind which is needed to make an informed decision about the contract; if these professionals have a personal relationship with their customers they should also be aware of the possible mistakes or mis-apprehensions of which the customers may be victim and speak out so as to dispel them.[72]

THE NETHERLANDS

First, this case is not so much a case about precontractual negotiations, as about whether the sales contract compelled Barchester to give informa-tion about the use of the product to the buyer. There is nothing wrong with the product itself, it is just that if adequate information had been given this type of damage would not have arisen. Therefore this is a case about non-performance of a sales contract (arts. 6:74 ff., jo. 7:17 B.W.). Here the expectations of the buyer are relevant. Because the contract does not provide any explicit guidance as to whether Barchester should have given any information, it depends upon what good faith requires of the seller under these circumstances (arts. 6:1, 6:248, jo. 3:12 B.W.; this is the so-called 'supplementary role' of good faith). What 'good faith' means in a given case will have to be established by case law. Cases decided under the old Civil Code show that the *Hoge Raad* will look at several factors, as for example the relative level of knowledge of the parties, their skill and their status in society (e.g. trader, consumer).[73] If it is clear that the product will not have its intended effect, but instead will damage plants, if certain (essential) information is not provided by the producer, the latter will be held responsible to give such essential information. As Barchester Chemicals did not inform the buyer at all, they will be held liable for non-performance of the contract (arts. 6:74 ff. B.W.).

Secondly, in regard to 'good faith', Dutch law distinguishes between subjective and objective good faith. Subjective good faith (*goede trouw*) means that a person is subjectively acting to the best of his knowledge or according to what he should have known (art. 3:11 B.W.). *Goede trouw* is con-sidered to be a doctrine belonging more to the law of property (e.g. protec-tion of good faith acquirers of movables) rather than to the law of obligations. Objective good faith (*redelijkheid en billijkheid*) means an objec-tive standard by which the behaviour of parties to an obligation is judged. The two, however, are not completely separate doctrines, as personal 'good

---

[72] Ibid., 436 ff., at 439–40, with a full review of this legislation, mostly enacted to comply with E.C. directives.   [73] Tjittes, *passim*.

faith' might have an impact on what objective good faith (*redelijkheid en bil-lijkheid*) requires of a party.[74] In this report, which deals with the law of obligations, I focus on good faith in its objective meaning.

Objective good faith can supplement a contract (where no express contractual provision exists and no statutory provision or custom gives guidance) or derogate from a contractual provision (meaning that under specific circumstances an express contractual – or even a mandatory statutory – provision cannot be relied upon).

Concerning the role of good faith in precontractual negotiations it is not really clear if this is the same good faith that applies in contractual situations or if good faith here is a specific emanation of the tort of negligence.[75] This tort, under Dutch law, is extremely broad in its reach (cf. art. 6:162) and encompasses any unlawful act in a very wide sense. What 'unlawful' means is established by case law.[76]

Thirdly, the Civil Code is seen as a system of rules, complete in itself. These rules consist of two types: technical rules (such as on offer and acceptance) and open-ended rules which can be used to adapt the system to changing conditions in society. One of these open-ended rules is good faith.

Good faith functions at several levels and in several ways. Within each *obligation* (a relationship where the duty of one party corresponds with the right of another and which must have as its object anything of economic value)[77] the parties to that obligation are bound to act according to good faith. Within each *contract* (whether unilateral or reciprocal) good faith can supplement the obligations agreed upon. At *both levels* good faith may demand that a duty (irrespective of its origin: statutory, customary or agreed upon) is discarded. Furthermore good faith is seen as the *leading principle* at the heart of the law of obligations; it allows the various technical rules to be supplemented in areas which have not been expressly regulated by the Code. The prime example here is the legal treatment of broken-down negotiations.

There is also a constitutional side to the matter. The technical rules have been elucidated during the parliamentary deliberations leading to the enactment of the B.W. by the Ministry of Justice (including the experts

---

[74] Asser-Hartkamp, *Verbintenissenrecht I* nr. 53 ff.; Asser-Hartkamp, *Verbintenissenrecht II* nr. 300 ff.   [75] Cf. HR 18 June 1982, NJ 1983, 723 [*Plas v. Valburg*] and subsequent case law.
[76] Cf. HR 31 January 1919, NJ 1919, 161 [*Lindenbaum v. Cohen*]. See with respect to precontractual liability Van Dunné 219 ff.
[77] Asser-Hartkamp, *Verbintenissenrecht I* nr. 6 ff.

who assisted the Ministry in the drafting work) in its written *travaux pré-paratoires* as well as by debates in parliament (which are also published).[78] As to the open-ended rules the parliamentary debate touched upon the relationship between parliament and the judiciary. It is the democrati-cally elected parliament which accepted – by adopting the Code with its various open-ended rules at its respective levels – that the technical rules were of great importance, but could never be seen as always giving the correct answer. However, the judiciary, which is not democratically elected, has to implement these open-ended rules. This means that the courts apply 'good faith' by parliamentary command and permission, in other words, by endorsement of the democratic legislature. That endorse-ment is based on the deep trust parliament has in the integrity and inde-pendence of the Dutch judiciary. The only more substantial direction given by parliament as to the application of good faith is to be found in art. 3:12 B.W.: the court has to take into account (i) generally recognised principles of law, (ii) general legal convictions that are alive in the Netherlands, and (iii) the general, societal as well as the personal interests involved in the case at hand.

ENGLAND

There are two possible legal bases for Cecil to claim against Barchester Chemicals Ltd: (i) for breach of the implied terms in the contract of sale between the parties as to the satisfactory quality of the product and its reasonable fitness for purpose and (ii) in the tort of negligence.

(i) From Cecil's point of view, the more attractive basis of claim is for breach of the implied terms in the contract of sale of goods which he has concluded with Barchester Chemicals Ltd. While the common law recog-nised similar implied terms in contracts of sale of goods,[79] since 1893 these terms have possessed a statutory basis, this now being found in s. 14 of the Sale of Goods Act 1979 (as amended by the Sale and Supply of Goods Act 1994, s. 1). Section 14(1) starts by stating the original and general approach at common law that 'except as provided by this section . . . there is no implied term about the quality or fitness for any particular purpose

---

[78] The so-called 'parliamentary history' of the new Civil Code has been collected in consolidated form. See e.g. Van Zeben/Du Pon, *Parlementaire geschiedenis, Boek 3*; Van Zeben/Du Pon, *Parlementaire geschiedenis, Boek 6*. See also Reehuis/Slob, *Parlementaire geschiedenis, Boek 3*; Reehuis/Slob, *Parlementaire geschiedenis, Boek 6*.

[79] See *Jones v. Just* (1868) LR 3 QB 197.

of goods supplied under a contract of sale'. However, s. 14 creates two important and very large exceptions to this general approach. Section 14(2) provides that '[w]here the seller sells goods in the course of a business, there is an implied term that the goods supplied under the contract are of satisfactory quality'. The 'quality of the goods includes their state and condition and . . . [their] fitness for all the purposes for which goods of the kind in question are commonly supplied'.[80] Secondly, s. 14(3) of the 1979 Act provides that '[w]here the seller sells goods in the course of business and the buyer, expressly or by implication, makes known . . . to the seller . . . any particular purpose for which the goods are being bought, there is an implied term that the goods supplied under the contract are reasonably fit for that purpose, whether or not that is a purpose for which such goods are commonly supplied. . .'. It is to be noted that there is no restriction as to the type of buyer (consumer or trader) who may rely on these implied terms.

On the facts of case 1, it would seem more appropriate for Cecil to claim for breach of the implied term as to the goods' 'satisfactory quality' in s. 14(2A) in that, owing to its lack of proper instructions, the product is not fit for the purpose for which goods of this kind were supplied, viz. use as a fertiliser on vegetables etc. There would, therefore, be no need for Cecil to show that his particular intentions as to his own use had been known by Barchester Chemicals Ltd. The lack of proper instructions for the use of goods may go to the issue of their fitness for purpose.[81] The implied terms in s. 14 are very strict: breach consists simply in failing to supply goods of a satisfactory quality etc., and there is no need for the buyer to prove fault nor even any possibility for the seller to escape liability on proof of no fault.

Once breach of this implied term in the contract is established, Cecil can recover damages for breach of contract. In principle, he may recover such an amount as would put him into the position as though the contract (including the implied term) had been performed. On the facts, Cecil could therefore recover damages for the loss of the courgette plants, and for the profits which he would have made on the sale of the courgettes which he would have grown on the assumption that the fertiliser would have increased their productiveness (to the extent to which it is likely that Barchester Chemicals Ltd would have advertised and thus subject to a test of remoteness).

---

[80] Sections 14(2A) and (2B).   [81] *Wormell v. R.H.M. Agriculture (East) Ltd* [1987] 3 All ER 75.

Even if it could be said that Cecil as a market gardener ought to have known better than to have administered this sort of fertiliser without watering, his claim for damages could not be met with any defence of his own contributory negligence in relation to the damage to the courgette plants, since English law allows a defence of contributory negligence to an action for breach of contract only where that action is for breach of a contractual obligation of reasonable care concurrent with a liability in the other party in tort for negligence.[82] On the other hand, if it can be said that Cecil ought to have known of the goods' 'defect' it would seem that he may be denied the benefit of reliance on the implied terms in s. 14 altogether.[83]

(ii) On the facts as presented in case 1, Cecil has an alternative claim against Barchester Chemicals Ltd in the tort of negligence. To succeed, Cecil must show that Barchester failed to take reasonable care in relation to the provision of warnings or instructions for use of the product and that its negligence in this respect caused him damage to property.[84] It is to be noted that a claim in the tort of negligence could not be brought where the product was merely ineffective or qualitatively defective and thereby caused purely financial loss, rather than (as here) causing damage to property. On the other hand, a claim in tort can exist where there is a contract between the parties.[85]

If he could show negligence, Cecil would be able to recover an award of damages to put him in the position as though the tort had not been committed, which would allow him to recover for his perished crop and (reasonably foreseeable) consequential lost profits on that crop.[86] Even if significant, no recovery for any lost bargain on the purchase could be recovered. Cecil's claim in the tort of negligence could be met with a defence of contributory negligence, this allowing the court to reduce any damages to be awarded accordingly.[87]

In practice, Cecil would claim in tort only where the incidental rules of the 'tort regime' made it advantageous to do so.

It is to be noted that the common law set its face against any general application of a rule of good faith by the middle of the nineteenth century,

---

[82] *Forsikringsaktieselskapet Vesta v. Butcher* [1988] 3 WLR 565.

[83] Guest, *Chitty on Contracts* § 41–319 *arguatur* from the clear case of denial of the benefit of reliance where the buyer knows of the defect.

[84] *Muirhead v. Industrial Tank Specialities Ltd* [1986] QB 507.

[85] *Henderson v. Merrett Syndicates Ltd* [1995] 2 AC 145.

[86] *Spartan Steel and Alloys Ltd v. Martin & Co. (Contractors) Ltd* [1973] 1 QB 27.

[87] Law Reform (Contributory Negligence) Act 1945, s. 1.

also denying as a matter of principle any general duty to disclose information on one party to a contract to the other.[88] These general denials apply
to sales of goods as to other contracts: formally, therefore, the rule
remains *caveat emptor.* On the other hand, English law, both common law
and statute, has made very considerable use of the technique of *particular*
implied terms in *particular* types of contract (here, sale of goods), as a result
of which one of the parties to a contract is made contractually responsible
for a particular issue or state of affairs. So, on these facts, while Barchester
Chemicals Ltd is said not to be under any duty to explain, disclose or warn
its buyer of the consequences of failing to water when using its product,
if it fails to do so and loss results, damages may be recovered for breach of
contract. Moreover, it should be noted that any clause attempting to
exclude the seller's liability for breach of the implied terms in s. 14 of the
Sale of Goods Act would be void as against a person dealing as a consumer
and subject to a reasonableness test as against all others.[89] While some of
the later amendments of s. 14 of the Sale of Goods Act have clearly been
aimed at the protection of consumer buyers, this was not the original
orientation of the provision, which was a commercial one (this being
clearest in the use in 1893 of the test of 'merchantable quality' rather than
the 1994 test of 'satisfactory quality'). Appeal to the implied intentions of
the parties may be accused of fictitiousness, but may be supported to an
extent by reference to the typical expectations of parties to this type of
contract. Clearly though, both the courts and the legislature have been
concerned to develop a policy of protection for buyers (whether commercial or consumer) who purchase on trust (i.e. without inspection or sale by
sample) as to the quality and utility as well as to the safety of the goods.

IRELAND

Cecil on the facts before us would have a choice of remedies, (i) in contract
and (ii) in tort.

(i) Where the seller sells goods in the course of his business, the Sale of
Goods Act implies a condition that the goods are of merchantable quality,
goods being defined as being of merchantable quality 'if they are fit for
the purposes for which goods of that kind are commonly bought'.[90]

---

[88] *Smith v. Hughes* (1871) LR 6 QB 597, *Bell v. Lever Bros. Ltd* [1932] AC 161.
[89] Unfair Contract Terms Act 1977, ss. 6(2) & (3).
[90] Sections 14(2) and (3) of the Sale of Goods Act 1893, as inserted by s. 10 of the Sale of
Goods and Supply of Services Act 1980.

Although there is no Irish case in point, it would be difficult to describe the fertiliser in question as being fit for the purposes for which it would commonly be bought if it were normally to cause damage to, or death of, the fertilised plants should the purchaser not take further steps of which he has not been advised.

The measure of damages would include the physical damage to the plants and also the profits which have been lost to Cecil as a result of the breach of contract. The lost profits would take account of the extra yield which would probably have resulted from the fertiliser if it had been fit for the purpose for which it was intended. However, this might be difficult to prove in the absence of particular claims by the manufacturer as to the efficacy of the product.

In Irish law, it would be possible for the seller to seek a reduction of the damages by reason of the contributory negligence of the purchaser, on the ground that a commercial gardener should have looked at the contents of the fertiliser, or alternatively should have asked the producer/seller as to any steps that were required to be taken in the administration of the product.

Under s. 34 of the Civil Liability Act 1961, a defence of contributory negligence is available in breach of contract actions. Case law shows that damages may be reduced where the extent of the injury is affected by contributory fault on the part of the plaintiff,[91] although *Friel*[92] argues that s. 34 was misunderstood in that case and that only where the breach of the contract was due in part to the contributory fault will damages be reduced. *Friel*, however, seems to have misread s. 34 of the Act which says '[w]here it is proved that the damage suffered by the plaintiff was caused partly by the negligence or want of care of the plaintiff' then the court may reduce damages having regard to the respective degrees of fault.

(ii) The producer and supplier of a product owe a duty of care to the ultimate consumer where there is no possibility of the plaintiff ascertaining the qualities of the product through examination.[93] Accordingly, where the producer/supplier could reasonably have foreseen the likelihood of injury if he should fail to take reasonable steps in the production, description or presentation of, or affixing of necessary information or warnings to, the product, then liability will be imposed.

The object of an award of damages in tort is to place the plaintiff in the position he would have been in if the tort had not been committed.

---

[91] *Lyons v. Thomas* [1986] IR 666.   [92] *The Law of Contract*, at 311.
[93] *Keegan v. Owens* [1953] IR 267 (Supreme Court).

Accordingly, physical damage to the plants, together with the loss of profits directly consequential on such physical damage, is recoverable in Irish law.[94] That portion of expected profits which arise from the improved yield expected from the use of the fertiliser would not be considered a loss directly consequential on the physical damage to the courgettes and hence not recoverable. Under s. 34 of the Civil Liability Act 1961, damages for tortious injury may be reduced by the court for contributory negligence. But, as it has been said already, it is unlikely that contributory negligence would be found on the facts of the present case.

SCOTLAND

This scenario would not be analysed in the UK as a precontractual problem. Purchase signals the formation of the contract: *Carlill v. Carbolic Smokeball Co. Ltd.*[95] The contract has been formed, so the issue here surrounds the quality of 'Growright 100'.

The question is whether Barchester is in statutory breach of contract in that they have breached the implied terms as to quality and fitness of their product as stipulated by the Sale of Goods Act 1979 as amended by s. 1 Sale and Supply of Goods Act 1994. Section 14 of the Act, which applies 'to goods sold under a contract of sale', states that goods must be of 'satisfactory quality' where sold in the course of business[96] (as is the case here). Satisfactory quality infers that they must meet the standard a reasonable person would regard as satisfactory, taking account of any description of the goods, the price and all other relevant circumstances. The quality of goods embraces their state and condition including, among others, fitness for all the purposes for which goods of that kind are commonly supplied: *Ashington Piggeries v. Christopher Hill Ltd.*[97] 'Fitness for purpose' means that the goods supplied must be reasonably fit for that purpose, where the seller sells goods in the course of a business and the buyer, expressly or by necessary implication, makes known to the seller the purpose of use of the goods.[98] Hence a product could be of satisfactory quality but will not pass the test of fitness for purpose. In order for Cecil to avail himself of the protection of this term it is necessary to show that he, either expressly or by necessary implication, indicated the particular purpose for which the fertiliser was required.

---

[94] *Spartan Steel and Alloys Ltd v. Martin & Co. (Contractors) Ltd* [1973] 1 QB 27 is thought to be good law in Ireland.   [95] [1893] 1 QB 256.   [96] Section 61, Sale of Goods Act 1979.
[97] [1972] AC 441.   [98] Section 14(3), Sale of Goods Act 1979.

In determining whether the goods are of the requisite quality, the container or other packaging, the instructions, or foreign material inadvertently supplied with the goods contracted for may be relevant. With regard to instructions, in the case of *Wormell v. R.H.M. Agricultural (East) Ltd*,[99] a farmer argued that the inadequacy of the instructions on a packet of weedkiller rendered it unfit for its purpose. The English High Court observed that the goods included not just the weedkiller but also its packaging and instructions.

Section 14 imposes strict liability. In terms of remedies, the new section 15B[100] provides that where the seller is in breach of any term of a contract, whether express or implied, the buyer shall be entitled to claim damages, and if the breach is material, to reject the goods and treat the contract as repudiated. This section places remedies for breach of sale in the scheme of Scots contract law. If Cecil could sustain such a claim for statutory breach of contract, he could claim damages for the loss of his courgettes.

Delictual liability may be imposed on Barchester under the Consumer Protection Act 1987, Part I.[101] The Act introduced a regime of strict liability on manufacturers of products which prove to cause harm by reason of a defect.[102] While liability is strict, it is not absolute, in that the pursuer must prove that he has been injured or his property has been damaged, that the defendant manufacturer was the producer of the product, and that it was the manufacturer's product that caused the injury. The strict liability regime is concerned only with safety of the product, not with shoddiness, and safety is relative: the question being, when is the degree of safety not such as persons generally are entitled to expect?[103] 'All circumstances shall be taken into account',[104] and this includes any instructions for or warnings with respect to doing or refraining from doing anything with the product. In terms of warnings, where the danger of a product is a matter of common knowledge a warning will not be necessary; *Yachetti v. John Duff & Son Ltd*.[105] But, where warnings should be given, they should be adequate, precise and appropriately placed. Persons who may be held liable under the 1987 Act are the producer, own-branders, importers or suppliers. However, liability for damage is limited; s. 5(3) states that property must be 'of a description of property ordinarily

---

[99] [1986] 1 All ER 769.
[100] Inserted in the Sale of Goods Act 1979 by the Sale and Supply of Goods Act 1994.
[101] This implements E.C. Council Directive 85/374/EEC, 25 July 1985 on Product Liability.
[102] This applies only to injuries sustained after 1 March 1988.
[103] Section 3(1), Consumer Protection Act 1987.   [104] Section 3(2), ibid.
[105] [1943] 1 DLR 194.

intended for private use, occupation or consumption' and 'intended by the person suffering the loss or damage mainly for his own private use, occupation or consumption'. Thus as Cecil is a market gardener and the courgettes are non-consumer property, he cannot rely on this statutory protection. Had the courgettes been for his own consumption, he could have relied on the provisions of the 1987 Act.

Where the 1987 Act does not apply, common law liability remains[106] and the pursuer may bring an action based on the *Donoghue v. Stevenson*[107] principles. The basis of product liability is laid down in this case; a manufacturer owes a duty of care to the ultimate consumer. The onus is on the pursuer to prove that there has been a breach of this duty, but he will have to prove negligence if he is to be successful.

Has Barchester been negligent in failing to issue a warning? A delictual claim exists if Cecil can establish that his loss is attributable to Barchester's negligence in failing to provide a warning regarding the high content of salt in their product. Various hurdles must be overcome before a claim can be established. For delictual liability to be established, it must be shown that there is a duty of care owed by the defender to the pursuer, that there must be a breach of that duty, and as a result of that breach, the pursuer must have suffered loss.

Accordingly, there must be a sufficient relationship of proximity or neighbourhood between Barchester (B) and Cecil (C), so that B owes C a duty of care not to injure him or his property. The contract between B and C provides a sufficient contractual nexus or proximity to establish B owed a duty of care to C. The nature of that duty is to take reasonable care to avoid acts or omissions which you could reasonably foresee would be likely to injure your neighbour. This test of reasonable foreseeability extends from the concept of the reasonable man. Would the reasonable man in the shoes of B have contemplated the harm the product could cause and what reasonable steps would he have taken to avoid this harm? If it is decided that the reasonable man would have issued a warning with 'Growright 100' then B is in breach of its duty and liable to C for losses incurred.

DENMARK AND NORWAY

The buyer would in this instance base his claim against the seller either (i) on a breach of contract under the rules concerning defects contained in sale of goods law or (ii) on the rules concerning the law of damages.

---

[106] Section 2(6), Consumer Protection Act 1987.   [107] 1932 SC (HL) 31, 1932 SLT 317.

(i) Under the joint Nordic law on the sale of goods (Norwegian Sale of Goods Act No. 27 of 13 May 1988), Cecil could have a claim against Barchester on account of a defect. The deficient advice given by Barchester could be seen as a defect in his delivery. Where the seller fails to give adequate instructions, so that the product becomes unsuitable, it may be said that he has not supplied goods of generally good merchantable quality. A defect must therefore be taken to exist. In order for the seller to be liable for damages, there must, however, be an additional basis for liability. Negligence on the part of the seller would appear to provide a natural basis in the present case.[108]

(ii) In an instance such as this, the seller may also be held responsible under the rules relating to the law of damages. If the seller may be said to have been negligent in that he failed to give the buyer adequate advice, there will be liability for the loss suffered. According to West Nordic law, the distinction between liability within and outside of a contractual relationship will not be of decisive importance. What matters is whether a claim may reasonably be advanced, rather than the formal classification of the relationship; see Rt. 1974, p. 41, concerning deficient instructions regarding the use of an extensible ladder, and NJA 1987, p. 47, concerning the absence of a warning as to the harmful effects of closing off the insulation of a roof when it was covered with roofing felt. The most obvious classification will probably be, in the present case, that there is liability for damages under a contract. But even in a contractual relationship, recovery of damages may follow rules relating to the law of wrongful acts if the type of damage most closely resembles damage under the law of wrongful acts.

Negligence in West Nordic law is thus regarded as a general head of liability, no matter whether a contract has been concluded or not, and it allows recovery even of purely economic loss.

Finally, the damage in this case could be seen to lie in an area bordering on product liability where, to a varying degree, liability would be imposed independently of fault, provided the product contains a defect affecting its safe use.

SWEDEN

The product sold seems not to have been fit for its general use, or at least not fit for the use the buyer had in mind, unless it was applied in a special

---

[108] Dahl 373 ff.; Nørager-Nielsen/Theilgaard 764 f.

way (together with large quantities of water). However, the seller did not provide this necessary information. Therefore, s. 17 of the Sale of Goods Act of 1990 (corresponding to art. 35(2)(b) CISG) seems to apply. If the seller knew of the special purpose and it was not unreasonable for the buyer to rely on the seller's judgement, the buyer could reclaim the price.

However, the destruction of the courgettes (property other than the goods bought) falls outside of the ambit of the Sale of Goods Act. Liability is, pursuant to tort law, in principle dependent on fault or a warranty, but a warranty may be implied. This was the case in NJA 1968, p. 285, where a party, who recommended a weed control and employed it on crops (i.e. under a contract of service) was held liable. Provided the seller knew of the intended use but did not instruct the buyer to use large quantities of water, he would probably have to compensate the buyer also for the damage sustained on the basis of an implied warranty. Also, he seems to have been negligent, not having advised the buyer Cecil to use large quantities of water. As it is a tort case, contributory negligence on Cecil's side may reduce the award of damages.

FINLAND

According to Finnish statutory law (Fertilisers Act of 1993 (Ma 121), s. 6) the contents of the fertiliser and the instructions for use must be indicated on the package, and for this reason (i) if the high content of salt and the instructions were not mentioned there, product liability *per se* exists, or (ii) if they were mentioned, Cecil bears the risk as a professional who should have taken the information into consideration and should have acted accordingly (see also s. 70 of the Sale of Goods Act of 1987 (Si 501): the injured party shall take reasonable measures to mitigate his damage; if he neglects to do so, he shall bear a corresponding share of the loss). In this case the contributory negligence of Cecil excludes the responsibility of the producer. It seems, therefore, that according to Finnish law this case falls both under the notion of 'failure to warn' and under the specific product liability regime. There may, however, be ancillary obligations that are not derived directly from statutory law.

Editors' comparative observations

I. All legal systems under consideration give a remedy in damages for the loss caused to Cecil as a consequence of the damage to his plants on the facts of case 1. But there are considerable doctrinal differences as to the

legal bases on which recovery is allowed. Some legal systems rely on doctrines general to contract law as a whole (*culpa in contrahendo, obligation
d'information*, though as to the latter, it should be noted that the contract
of sale, in practice, provided for a long time the main context in French
law), whereas those which apply the aedilitian remedies tend to rely on an
analysis special to the law of sale. English, Irish and Scots law, in a sense,
sit astride this particular divide, for formally the law stems from statutory
provisions special to the contract of sale of goods, but the technique of
implied term which these provisions use is much wider than this context
and is indeed usually regarded as a common law one.

The following observations may be made in relation to the principles
behind the various doctrinal analyses which have been provided.

(i) The approach of German law can be seen to combine the application
of the principle of good faith with the independent notion of *culpa in
contrahendo*: good faith is the legal basis for the recognition of a duty to
inform the buyer in the relevant manner, but *culpa in contrahendo* provides
the legal basis for the remedy of its breach.

(ii) In those legal systems which rely on aedilitian liability, this is
thought of as possessing a legal independence from other more general
notions, such as good faith, owing to its specific inclusion in the civil
codes. While some systems accept that 'informational deficiencies' (such
as a failure to give proper instructions) can be included in the notion of
defectiveness for this purpose (Spanish law), others do not (German law,
Austrian law).

(iii) French law and Belgian law rely on the notion of good faith, or its
cousin *équité*, as a legal basis for the imposition of *obligations d'information*,
whether these are contractual (giving rise to liability under the general
law of contract) or precontractual (giving rise to liability under the
general law of liability for delictual fault). Nevertheless, in juristic and
judicial discussions the notion of good faith is by no means prominent,
compared to concerns as to the proper ambit and content of the
'autonomous' notion of *obligation d'information*. As regards French law, the
placing in 1992 of the vast majority of these duties on their own legislative basis, which itself makes no reference to good faith, makes it likely
that this independence will be accentuated, for there is no longer the
need to appeal to the general provisions of the Civil Code (arts. 1134 al. 3
and 1135 C. civ.) to give authoritative respectability to these obligations.
Similar observations may be made concerning Italian law. In Belgian law
the *obligations d'information* appear to have been conflated, in a peculiar
way, with the aedilitian remedies.

(iv) Dutch law relies on a principle of good faith in the supplementing of the terms of the contract or particular legislative rules applicable to the contract, so as to require adequate information to be given in order to avoid damage being caused. Where such information is not given, liability is imposed for non-performance of the contract.

(v) The common law systems, and Scotland, rely instead on implied terms, a technique which (at least in its inception) is formally interpretative of the intentions of the parties to the type of contract in question, even though it has played a role which is substantially normative, even outside those important situations (such as sale of goods) where the legal basis for the implication is a statutory one. In general, implied terms (other than those which are genuinely factual according to the so-called 'bystander test') rest on a judgement of the reasonable expectations of parties to the type of transaction in question, even though the *test* for implication is not reasonableness, but necessity. The example of sale of goods (as in case 1) also illustrates that the reasonable expectation of the parties may also be relevant to the application of the term on the facts: for the question whether goods are 'reasonably fit for their purpose' refers to any purpose for which goods are 'commonly supplied'.

Finally, the legal systems under consideration take differing views as to the possibility of resort to delict to ground a claim for damages where a contract exists between the parties, their views following more general positions as to this issue of concurrence. Thus French and Belgian law both reject concurrence in principle (the rule of *non-cumul*), though a distinction is made for this purpose where the delictual liability which is claimed is classified as *pre*-contractual. On the other hand, for Greek law recent legislation implementing but going beyond the E.C. directive on product liability of 1985 has created special liabilities in respect of defective products which covers the situation in case 1, applying to damage to property used by a non-consumer as well as by a consumer.

II. However, while the same result would be reached on the particular facts of case 1, differences of result could arise in slightly different circumstances owing to the differences resulting from the various legal approaches taken by the systems. These differences may be grouped into three.

(i) The legal systems under consideration adopted different views as to the basis of liability, this often reflecting the relative strictness of liability.

(a) Some legal systems based liability on fault, as under the doctrine of *culpa in contrahendo* in German law, in which fault is to be found in the breach of a duty to inform Cecil as to the proper use of the product. Similarly, French law may see non-performance of an *obligation d'information* as constituting a 'fault', though it is clear that the *content* of such an obligation may vary, this being more or less strict following the well-known distinction between *obligations de moyen* ('obligations to take care') and *obligations de résultat* ('obligations of accomplishment'). Some of the Nordic legal systems employ a very broad notion of negligence.

(b) Those systems, such as Spanish law, which base liability in circumstances such as those which arise in case 1 on a modern version of aedilitian liability require proof by the buyer of a latent defect.

(c) The contractual approach to liability taken by English, Irish, Scots and the Nordic laws – based on an obligation that the goods must be fit for normal use – is particularly strict, in that it rests neither on proof of a 'defect', nor on proof of fault.

(ii) On the facts of case 1, it is more than arguable that the buyer as a market gardener was in a position in which he ought to have known better than to use the product in the way in which he did, quite apart from any warnings or instructions accompanying the product. Clearly, one way in which this circumstance may be taken into account would be to characterise the buyer's failure to act in a way in which a (reasonably well-informed) market gardener would act as a fault contributing to his own loss. However, the legal systems under consideration differ on this issue. This difference reflects more general approaches to the significance of the injured party's contributory negligence in relation to claims for damages for breach of contract. The disagreement cuts across the divide between the civilian and common law systems: German, French and Irish law admit a possible reduction of the injured party's damages in these circumstances, while English law does not.

(iii) The issue of the appropriate measure of damages does not arise on the facts of the present case, since the legal systems agreed in allowing compensation for the damage to the courgette plants plus any consequential loss of profits. On the other hand, it is clear that some legal systems would as a matter of principle allow the recovery of damages based on a 'positive interest' (or 'expectation interest'), i.e. to put the buyer in the position as though the fertiliser had done its job properly (English law, Scots law, Spanish law), whereas others would limit recovery to 'negative interest' (or 'reliance' or '*status quo ante* interest'), i.e. to put the buyer in the position as though he had not entered the contract of sale (German law, Austrian law). Other systems, such as French law, do not as a general rule use the distinction between these two measures of recovery; indeed, for French law the issue of the quantum of damages is one for the 'sovereign power of assessment' of the lower courts and this means that it is often not clear precisely on what basis recovery is awarded.

Case 2: Degas drawing

Case

Desdemona is a dealer in fine art and sees what she considers to be a rare and valuable drawing by Degas at the house of Othello, a retired physics professor who has asked her to look at his possessions with a view to purchase. Desdemona asks him about the drawing and he tells her that he knows that it is old and that he has always liked it, but has no idea of its value. Desdemona offers him £1,200 for it, which he accepts. The picture is later authenticated by art experts and Desdemona resells it for £85,000.

Discussions

GERMANY

The contract for the sale of the drawing concluded between Desdemona and Othello may be void under § 138 II BGB. This rule declares legal transactions to be void whereby a person exploiting the distressed situation, inexperience, lack of judgemental ability or grave weakness of will of another, causes to be promised or granted to himself or to a third party in exchange for a performance pecuniary advantages which exceed the value of the performance to such an extent that, under the circumstances, the pecuniary advantages are in obvious disproportion to the performance. We are dealing here with the German version of statutory unconscionability;[1] the Code considers this rule as a special case of a legal transaction *contra bonos mores*.[2] There is an obvious disproportion, in the present case,

---

[1] See generally Zimmermann, *Obligations* 175 ff.
[2] § 138 II BGB reads: 'A legal transaction is also void . . .'. The 'also' refers to § 138 I BGB ('A legal transaction which is *contra bonos mores* is void').

between the drawing and the price paid by Desdemona, since the value of the former exceeds the price by far more than 100 per cent. But the strict subjective requirements relating to the position of Othello (exploitation of a distressed situation, inexperience, lack of judgemental ability or grave weakness of will) have not been met. More particularly, Othello cannot be taken to have been 'inexperienced', since lack of experience in a specialist area such as art dealing does not count for the purposes of § 138 II BGB.

Where the strict requirements of § 138 II BGB are not complied with, German courts have fallen back on the general clause of § 138 I BGB.[3] Again, however, an obvious imbalance between the value of the performance and the price paid will not *per se* avoid the contract. Additional factors, such as a reprehensible attitude, will have to be shown. A particularly outrageous imbalance, however, is taken to create the presumption that a reprehensible attitude exists. A margin of 200 per cent or more may be regarded as particularly outrageous.[4] The requirements of § 138 I BGB may thus, in the present case, be seen to have been met. Since the invalidity affects only the contract of sale itself, the transfer of ownership remains valid.[5] Hence, the rules of the law of unjustified enrichment govern the return of performances (§§ 812 ff. BGB). The developments sketched in this paragraph have effectively heralded a renaissance of the idea of *laesio enormis* which, in turn, is part of a rediscovery of equality in exchange.[6]

It is also conceivable that the contract is voidable under § 123 BGB ('Whoever has been induced to make a declaration of intention by fraudulent deception . . . may rescind the contract').[7] Such voidability will not be excluded on account of the fact that the contract of sale is already void under § 138 I BGB. It is generally agreed today that even a void contract may be rescinded since the consequences resulting from rescission may be more advantageous to the disadvantaged party.[8] Thus, voidability

---

[3] This has happened, particularly, with regard to instalment credit transactions; for the relevant case law, see Emmerich, JuS 1988, 925 ff.; *Münchener Kommentar*/Mayer-Maly § 138, nn. 98 ff.; Zimmermann/Jansen, in: *Essays Fleming* 295 f. (overview in English).

[4] BGH NJW-RR 1990, 1199; *Jauernig*/Vollkommer § 138, n. 16.

[5] This is a consequence of the famous 'principle of abstraction': the transfer of a very valuable drawing does not, *per se*, constitute an infringement of the *boni mores*; see Jauernig, JuS 1994, 721 ff.; Zimmermann, JR 1985, 48 ff.; Zweigert/Kötz (1st edn) chapter 15; Markesinis/Lorenz/Dannemann 19 ff.

[6] See Zimmermann, *Obligations* 268 ff.; Kötz 198 ff.

[7] Thus, it is not the court, but the party's act that rescinds the contract according to German law.   [8] Kipp, in: *Festschrift von Martitz* 211 ff.; Medicus, *Allgemeiner Teil* nn. 728 f.

under § 123 BGB is generally taken also to affect the transfer of owner-ship.[9] As a result the disadvantaged party may avail himself of the *rei vindicatio* (§ 985 BGB) in order to recover his property. This is (i) an *actio in rem* which (ii) is not subject to the defence of change of position. Fraudulent deception under § 123 BGB requires one party by some act or omission and with *animus decipiendi* to induce or maintain a mistake on the part of the other party. Desdemona may have deceived Othello by omission. Nondisclosure of facts will only be regarded as a deception by omission if a duty to disclose exists. This depends on whether Othello could reason-ably expect disclosure according to the principles of good faith and with due regard to generally accepted standards of honest behaviour.[10] Disclosure may reasonably be expected if one party, in view of his eco-nomic position and his know-how, acts like an adviser and the other party relies on his expert advice.[11] Othello had asked Desdemona to make him an offer. Thus, he relied on her technical know-how as an art dealer to value the painting and could, according to the principles of good faith, expect a true valuation of the painting. If Desdemona acted intentionally, her behaviour may be taken to constitute fraudulent deception. Othello may therefore rescind both the contract of sale and the transfer of the painting (§ 123 BGB).

Alternatively, the contract may also be set aside on the basis of *culpa in contrahendo* in conjunction with §§ 249 ff. BGB because of the nondisclo-sure of the true value of the painting.

Whether Othello also has the option of rescinding the contract on account of mistake depends on whether he has been labouring under a mistake as to one of those characteristics of a thing which are generally regarded as essential (§ 119 II BGB) – such as the age of the drawing or by whom it was done – or whether he was merely mistaken about the value of the drawing. In the latter case he would not be able to rescind the con-tract.[12] In any event, however, rescission under § 119 II BGB is less advanta-geous than rescission under § 123 BGB in view of the rescinding party's obligation to compensate the other party for the damage that he has suf-fered by relying on the validity of the contract (§ 122 BGB).

---

[9] *Palandt*/Heinrichs, Überbl. v. § 104, n. 23.
[10] BGH NJW 1989, 764; *Palandt*/Heinrichs § 123, n. 5; *Jauernig*/Jauernig § 123, nn. 3 ff.
[11] *Münchener Kommentar*/Kramer § 123, nn. 13 ff.; *Soergel*/Hefermehl § 123, nn. 9 ff.
[12] *Palandt*/Heinrichs § 119, n. 27. Concerning valuable drawings, however, a mistake as to the price would usually seem to be based on a mistake as to its age or authorship.

GREECE

(i) In the first place it is obvious that the behaviour of Desdemona is contrary to morality (*contra bonos mores*) in terms of arts. 178–9 Gr. C.C.[13] *Contra bonos mores* in the case of Othello and Desdemona means lack of fairness in business transactions.

In so far as art. 178 Gr. C.C. states that '[a]n act which is contrary to morality shall be null and void', this article could be applicable. In terms of this sale the invalidity normally affects only the contract of sale itself. The transfer of ownership of the painting remains valid (cf. art. 1034 Gr. C.C.), with the result that the rules of unjustified enrichment govern the return of the performances (arts. 904 ff. Gr. C.C.).[14]

The fact that Desdemona, a dealer in fine art, considered the drawing to be a rare and valuable drawing by Degas and at the same time knew that Othello, a retired physics professor, had knowledge only that the drawing was old and had no knowledge regarding the real value and the creator of the drawing, may have the effect that the contract for the sale of the drawing concluded between Desdemona and Othello is void not only under art. 178 Gr. C.C. but also under art. 179 Gr. C.C. This latter rule declares legal transactions to 'be null as contrary to morality whereby the freedom of a person is hampered excessively or whereby through an exploitation of the need, the levity of character or the lack of experience of the other party are stipulated or received for one's own benefit or for the benefit of a third party and in consideration of something furnished pecuniary advantages which in the circumstances are obviously out of proportion to the consideration furnished'. The Greek Civil Code considers this rule as a special case of a legal transaction *contra bonos mores*.[15] Since the value of the drawing and the price paid by Desdemona exceeds the real price by far, the pecuniary advantages for Desdemona are in obvious disproportion to the performance.[16]

The next question is whether the other necessary requirements of art. 179 Gr. C.C. exist.[17] In the present case there is *in concreto* inexperience on

---

[13] In general Papanikolaou, *Katapleonektikes Dikaiopraxies, passim*; Papantoniou, *Genikes Arches* § 44; Ladas, *passim*.

[14] Simantiras § 44, nos. 795–810; Papantoniou, *Genikes Arches* § 73 III b.

[15] On the question of *iustum pretium*, in this context, Zimmermann 255–70.

[16] Cf. Simantiras § 44, no. 812, p. 601; Papanikolaou, *Katapleonektikes Dikaiopraxies* § 7, pp. 179 ff.; Areopagus 855/1979 NoB 28, 252; Areopagus 196/1984 NoB 33, 259 (obvious disproportion but no longer direct application of *laesio enormis* in Greek law).

[17] Papanikolaou, *Katapleonektikes Dikaiopraxies* 225 ff.; Simantiras § 44, no. 812; Papantoniou, *Genikes Arches* § 73 III b 3; Karassis, in: *Astikos Kodix I* art. 179, no. 3.

the side of Othello, because while Othello is not completely inexperienced, it is clear from the case that he has no idea about the real value and
the real origin of his drawing. This is contrary to the predominant opinion
in German legal theory.[18]

Greek academic writing and the judiciary support the theory which
maintains that the requirement of 'inexperience', within the meaning of
art. 179 Gr. C.C., is to be found even in cases concerning a lack of experience in a special area, as in the case of Othello.[19] Thus, the requirements
of art. 179 Gr. C.C. have been met in the case of Othello, and the contract
of sale between him and Desdemona can be taken to be contrary to morality and therefore void according to art. 179 Gr. C.C.

In Greek law it is held that invalidity in cases of acts being contrary to
morality under art. 179 Gr. C.C., as an exception to the general principle
of abstraction (see art. 1034 Gr. C.C.), affects not only the contract of sale
itself but also the transfer of ownership from Othello to Desdemona.[20]
This view is supported by the words 'are stipulated or received' as contained in art. 179 Gr. C.C.[21]

In this respect it must be noted, however, that it is only the transfer of
the ownership of the drawing from Othello to Desdemona which is void.
The transfer of the ownership of the money from Desdemona to Othello
is valid.[22] As a result, therefore, Othello has against Desdemona the *rei vindicatio* (arts. 1094 ff. Gr. C.C.) or an action for unjustified enrichment
because the cause is void, while Desdemona has against Othello only an
action for unjustified enrichment (arts. 904 ff. Gr. C.C.).[23]

(ii) Othello has also the possibility of suing Desdemona for damages for
her negative interest under arts. 197–8 Gr. C.C. (a statutory version of the
culpa in contrahendo doctrine), because of the nullity of the contract in
terms of art. 179 Gr. C.C.[24]

---

[18] *Soergel*/Hefermehl § 138, nn. 70 ff.; RGRK § 138, n. 61; Flume § 18, 7b; Larenz § 22 III d;
BGH NJW 1979, 758; cf. Enneccerus/Nipperdey § 192 II 1b n. 5.
[19] Papanikolaou, *Katapleonektikes Dikaiopraxies* 229; Areopagus 416/1973 NoB 21, 1303; Cf.
Oftinger, in: *Xenion Zepos* 535 ff. (544).
[20] Georgiadis, *Empragmato Dikaio* § 48 I, nos. 11, 12; Simantiras § 44, no. 814, p. 605; Ladas
201.   [21] Georgiadis, *Empragmato Dikaio* § 48 I, no. 13.
[22] Cf. Kounougeri-Manoledaki, Arm 1975, 9–10. The matter is disputed.
[23] Cf. Simantiras no. 813, p. 607 and Ladas 203.
[24] According to art. 197 the parties must deal with each other, in the course of contractual
negotiations, according to the dictates of good faith and business usage. Any damage
caused in violation of this duty must be compensated by the party at fault, even if no
contract is eventually concluded (art. 198). See Symeonides, in: *Introduction* 65;
Papantoniou, *Genikes Arches* § 63, p. 343.

(iii) Othello was in error. The legal agreement between him and Desdemona could thus be considered voidable under art. 142 Gr. C.C., if Othello's error can be regarded as substantial, which is debatable. A substantial error has to refer to qualities of a person or a thing which are of such importance with regard to the whole legal act, taking into consideration the agreement of the parties, the requirements of good faith and business usage, that if the person in error had been aware of the true situation he would not have entered into the transaction. In this case the question is whether the essential characteristics of the drawing were its age or by whom it was done, or whether Othello was merely mistaken about the value of the drawing. In the latter case Greek theory does not regard the contract as voidable (arts. 140–5 Gr. C.C.). The matter is different in the case where the mistake about the price is based on a mistake as to the age or the authorship of the drawing, which seems to have occurred here.[25]

The annulment of the act (by the courts: art. 140 Gr. C.C.) refers only to the obligatory contract and does not affect the transfer of the ownership of the movables. Othello, therefore, has only an action against Desdemona for unjustified enrichment (arts. 904 ff. Gr. C.C.).[26]

As in German law, the annulment of the act due to a declaration made in error (art. 145 I Gr. C.C.) is less advantageous for Othello because he may be bound to compensate for any loss arising as a result of the annulment (art. 145 I Gr. C.C.). This danger does not, however, exist for Othello, because according to art. 145 II Gr. C.C. the obligation to compensate shall be excluded if the person injured had knowledge of or ought to have known of the error. In the present case Desdemona at least ought to have known of Othello's error.

(iv) Another possible remedy for Othello against Desdemona is the one provided in art. 147 Gr. C.C. ('declaration prompted by deception'). Othello will have to prove that he had been prompted by Desdemona's fraudulent deception to make his declaration of intention leading to the contract. If the contract is declared void under art. 147 Gr. C.C. Othello has an action based on ownership and one based on unjustified enrichment against Desdemona, because in this case the annulment affects both the obligatory contract and the transfer of ownership.[27]

---

[25] Papantoniou, *Genikes Arches* § 70, pp. 388 ff.; Simantiras no. 735; Areopagus 5/1990 NoB 38, 1318.

[26] Areopagus 910/1981 NoB 30, 628; Georgiadis, *Empragmato Dikaio* § 50, p. 503, no. 57.

[27] Georgiadis, *Empragmato Dikaio* § 48 I no. 10.

(v) As may have become obvious, the case of Othello and Desdemona is influenced by the principle of good faith in many ways, since nearly all the rules applicable (arts. 178, 179, 142, 144, 197, 199 Gr. C.C.) can be regarded as specific emanations of good faith.[28]

AUSTRIA

Austrian law provides Othello with three possible bases of claim.

(i) The first one focuses on the 'objective imbalance between performance and counter-performance' of the parties to the contract. Under § 934 ABGB a party to a contract may rescind it and claim the return of what he has provided under it, if the market value of what he has received by way of performance from the other party does not come to half of what he has provided, such an imbalance being termed *Verkürzung über die Hälfte*, or *laesio enormis*. Where such an imbalance is shown to exist, the disadvantaged party may rescind the contract without more,[29] thereby making this ground of vitiation very straightforward to establish. On the facts of case 2, the value of Desdemona's counter-performance (paying a price of £1,200) is worth less than half of the value of Othello's performance (delivery of a drawing worth £85,000) and Othello is therefore entitled to declare the contract rescinded and to claim restitution of the benefits which Desdemona derived from his performance of the contract under § 1435 ABGB (such a claim for restitution being known as a *condictio ob causam finitam*).[30] However, under § 934 sent. 2 ABGB, Desdemona may avoid rescission and full restitution by declaring that she is prepared to give Othello the difference between the market value of her and his performances under the contract: such reimbursement would also remedy the objective imbalance between the parties of which the law disapproves.

(ii) The second possible basis of claim might arise from the mistake which he has made in concluding the contract. Here it must, however, be said at the outset that a mere mistake as to the value of the object of the sale (which is regarded as a mere error in motive) is irrelevant since otherwise the strict conditions of § 934 ABGB would be circumvented.

---

[28] Koumantos, *Ypokeimeniki* 56 ff.; Papantoniou, *Kali Pistis* 70 ff.

[29] An exception is made where the disadvantaged party was aware of the imbalance inherent in the contract: § 935 ABGB. The remedy of *laesio enormis* does also not apply to commercial transactions entered into by the injured party: § 351a HGB.

[30] As the drawing has already been sold to a third party who, it may be assumed, has gained title of it, Desdemona is liable for restitution of the benefit received by way of price.

According to § 871 ABGB, a party to a contract is able to contest it on the ground of mistake only where that mistake relates to the content of his declaration of intention. In the present case it appears that Othello is mistaken as to an important characteristic of the subject matter of the contract; this is generally regarded as a mistake concerning the content of the declaration. In addition, however, he must establish *one* of three other circumstances: (a) that the other party either caused his mistake or (b) should have noticed it, or (c) that the mistake must have been brought to light in good time (*rechtzeitig*). On the facts of case 2, Desdemona ought to have noticed Othello's mistake.

The question whether Othello's mistake entitles him to render the contract void under § 871 ABGB or merely to have it adjusted under § 872 ABGB, will depend on whether the mistake was on a 'material point'. Here it must be presumed that the parties would have concluded the contract in any event though – without Othello's mistake – at a higher price. The mistake, therefore, does not relate to a 'material point'. In these circumstances the contract has to be adjusted so that it reflects the bargain which the parties would have struck if they had known the true character of the object and taken this reasonably into account.[31]

(iii) Finally, Othello may argue that he has been deceived by Desdemona within the meaning of § 870 ABGB. Apart from conscious fraud, the prerequisite of deceit on her part is also satisfied if she takes advantage of Othello's mistake with an intention to deceive him, where she ought in honesty to have disclosed the true position.[32]

The question whether such a duty of disclosure would be imposed depends on the nature and closeness of the relationship between the parties. A more onerous duty of disclosure would be imposed upon Desdemona on facts such as are found in the present case. For while she is a dealer in fine art, Othello is inexperienced in these matters. Furthermore, Othello has asked her to look at his possessions with a view to seeing what may be worth purchasing and she is for this reason called upon to protect his interests and to establish a special relationship of trust and confidence with him; for Othello relies on Desdemona's advice who, in turn, exercises influence over him. In these circumstances, Desdemona

---

[31] The expression 'adequate compensation' found in § 872 ABGB does not indicate an award of damages, but rather a restoration of the 'subjective balance' of the contract which was disturbed by the party's mistake.

[32] Bydlinski, JBl 1980, 393 ff.; Rummel, in: *Rummel, ABGB I* § 870 n. 4; OGH in SZ 52/22 (= JBl 1980, 424); JBl 1992, 450.

is subjected to a strict duty to take care and to disclose to Othello all those matters which relate to the subject matter of their possible contracts. This means that even though Desdemona may not be totally sure herself that the drawing is indeed by Degas, she must disclose fully her thinking on the issue to Othello: she is aware of Othello's lack of knowledge and that it would be of great importance to him to know the presumed artist of the drawing. This would influence his decision to sell and allow him to avoid a huge loss. On these grounds, Desdemona is under a 'duty to speak', as the Supreme Court has often had occasion to hold.[33]

Since where one party deceives the other he is not worthy of protection, it is arguable that even an error in motive might be relevant. Moreover, § 870 ABGB provides that a party who suffers from the effect of deceit has the right to rescind the contract regardless of whether his mistake was on a 'material point',[34] and he may claim restitution under § 877 ABGB (*condictio sine causa*). On the ground of such a mistake, he is also entitled, alternatively, to claim that the contract be adjusted by analogous application of § 872 ABGB.[35]

FRANCE

Desdemona's silence as to the value of the painting could be considered to be a 'fraudulent or dishonest failure to speak' (*réticence dolosive*). As a dealer in fine art she considered the drawing by Degas to be rare and valuable, she clearly knew that the painting was worth more than she paid for it and failed to inform Othello of this fact. These facts suggest that she did not conclude the sale with Othello in good faith.

Othello could therefore bring a claim against Desdemona on the basis of (i) *dol* (loosely, 'fraud') for annulment of the contract under art. 1116 of the Civil Code and/or (ii) delictual fault for damages under arts. 1382 or 1383 of the Civil Code.

(i) Othello could ask the court to annul the contract of sale on the basis that his consent was vitiated by Desdemona's fraudulent failure to speak.[36] The notion of *réticence dolosive* results from an extensive interpretation of art. 1116 of the Civil Code as developed by the courts and this may be seen as giving rise to a precontractual duty to inform in certain con-

---

[33] E.g. OGH in EvBl 1996/8.
[34] Gschnitzer, in: *Klang, Kommentar* IV/1 113 f.; OGH in JBl 1957, 240.
[35] Rummel, in: *Rummel, ABGB* I § 870 n. 7; Iro, JBl 1974, 233 f.; OGH in SZ 59/126 (1986).
[36] Art. 1117 C. civ. (*nullité relative*).

texts. Othello must prove that the conditions of *dol* are satisfied. According to art. 1116 of the Civil Code '*dol* is a cause of nullity of the contract when the manoeuvres practised by one of the parties are such that it is clear, that in the absence of such manoeuvres, the other party would not have contracted. It is not presumed and must be proved.' In other words, Othello must show that Desdemona's silence as to the value of the Degas induced his consent, that is, he would not have contracted had he known its true value. It is therefore up to Othello to prove Desdemona's bad faith. Case law has established that a failure to speak may constitute a 'fraudulent manoeuvre' for the purposes of art. 1116 since a decision of the *Cour de cassation* in 1958,[37] confirmed on numerous occasions,[38] in which the Court held that a party to a contract who kept secret from the other certain information which if revealed, would have prevented him from consenting to the contract, had committed *réticence dolosive*.

While it is true that Othello was mistaken as to the value of the drawing which he was selling (the subject matter of his own obligation) and that in general mistakes as to value do not give rise to annulment of contracts, on the facts this does not preclude annulment for two reasons. First, while in principle a mistake as to value is not sufficient to annul a contract, this does not remain the case where it is the consequence of a mistake about the 'substantial qualities' of the subject matter.[39] Secondly, the 'fraudulent manoeuvres' of Desdemona justify annulment of the contract, even if the mistake which arose as a result related only to value.[40] As a result, the case law which accepts that a seller can ask for annulment of the contract on the basis of a mistake concerning the subject matter of his own obligation is firmly established.[41] However, such a mistake does not necessarily lead to annulment by a court as there is a further requirement that the claimant's mistake is excusable. Here, the status of the parties (Desdemona being an art expert, Othello a retired physics professor) would often be significant, but in any case the fraudulent nature of Desdemona's conduct suffices to render Othello's mistake excusable.

Annulment of the contract on the grounds of *dol* leads to its retroactive

[37] Civ. (1) 19 May 1958, Bull. civ. I, no. 251, p. 198.
[38] Civ. (3) 15 Jan. 1971, Bull. civ. III, no. 38, p. 25.
[39] See e.g. the final case in the *affaire Poussin*, Versailles 7 Jan. 1987, D 1987.485 note J.-L. Aubert, JCP 1988.II.21121 note J. Ghestin.   [40] Paris 22 Jan. 1953, D 1953.126.
[41] Civ. 17 Nov. 1930, S 1932.1.17 note A. Breton, D 1932.1.161 note J. Ch. Laurent; Civ. (1) 15 Jun. 1960, JCP 1961.II.12274 note R. Vouin, S 1961.1 note R. Savatier and, in the *affaire Poussin*, TGI Paris 13 Dec. 1972, D 1973.410 note J. Ghestin et Ph. Malinvaud, JCP 1973.II.17377 note R. Lindon.

termination and in principle money paid or other property transferred under it is therefore to be restored to the party who transferred it.[42]

(ii) Othello could also claim damages for delictual fault under arts. 1382 or 1383 of the Civil Code. Article 1382 states that 'any human deed whatsoever which causes harm to another creates an obligation in the person by whose fault it has occurred to compensate it', and art. 1383 adds that '[e]veryone is liable for the harm which he has caused not only by his deed, but also by his failure to act or his lack of care'. Desdemona's liability is considered delictual in French law because it is incurred before the contract (precontractual liability) and therefore does not arise under the contract.

If both the claims for annulment and damages are well founded, Othello has the choice to exercise either of or both these remedies.[43] He could therefore recover the drawing so as to be able to resell it at a more advantageous price and obtain damages for any losses caused by Desdemona's bad faith.

As we can see, the idea of *réticence dolosive* implies for French lawyers the existence of a precontractual duty to inform. The imposition of such a duty is based on a duty of co-operation owed by the parties to the contract (compare what has been said in relation to case 1). In general, French law has a marked tendency to protect parties to contracts who are the victims of mistake and where *réticence dolosive* has induced the mistake, the moral arguments are reinforced. Although the legal basis of the claim here derives from rules of law designed to remedy vitiated consent (the question to what extent the remedy of annulment is truly protective being more open to dispute), these rules are underlined by the existence of a general principle of good faith during precontractual negotiations. This principle is implicitly derived from art. 1134 al. 3 of the Civil Code (which actually refers to *performance* in good faith) by the filling of what is seen as a historical gap in its drafting and this has enabled both courts and jurists to approve the inclusion of good faith in the precontractual phase. Moreover, moral considerations, illustrated by the adage *fraus omnia corrumpit*, are reinforced by the remedies available under arts. 1382 and 1383 of the Civil Code, which allow the courts to sanction a party's wrongful conduct by awarding compensation to the other, innocent party. Thus good faith is used to deter or to sanction

---

[42] Starck/Roland/Boyer 376 ff. (*nullité* in general).

[43] Civ. (1) 4 Feb. 1975, JCP 1975.II.18100 note Ch. Larroumet; Com. 18 Oct. 1994, D 1995.180 note Ch. Atias.

certain behaviour in the formation of a contract which is considered socially unacceptable by the law.

BELGIUM

(i) Case 2 poses a well-known problem, although it is not common in practice. Its outcome is not very certain, due to the fact that the role of duties to inform the other party who is labouring under a mistake is not clearly settled. Possible solutions to the problem may be provided by the doctrines of (a) mistake, (b) fraud, and (c) *laesio enormis* or abuse of circumstances.

(a) This case would be discussed under Belgian law as a case of *error* (mistake). Whether Othello can avoid the contract (and claim back the drawing) depends on a number of factors.

The error must not merely relate to the 'value' of the object but it must turn around the 'substance' of the object (art. 1108 C.C.). According to case law, 'substance' means any element which was determining for that party, i.e. without which that party would not have concluded the contract.[44] The condition is probably met in this case, where there is a mistake concerning the artist of the work.

Further, no avoidance is possible where the error is due to the negligence of the party in error ('inexcusable error'). In more recent times, matters tend to be judged not only from the point of view of the mistaken party (i.e. in terms of mistake) but also in terms of whether the other party was under a duty to provide information. This duty has been developed on the basis, *inter alia,* of the principle of good faith as applied to precontractual relationships. As a result of this, the possibility of avoiding the contract will also depend on the extent of the seller's duty to inform the buyer as opposed to the duty (or rather burden) of the buyer to inform himself.

The extent of these duties will depend, *inter alia*, on the parties' position as professionals or laymen. Normally, a professional has a duty to give whatever information he has or should have, to the other party who does not have such information. However, this rule has its origin in a different context, namely in cases where not informing the other party is a sign of professional incompetence. The duty to inform as an autonomous notion has been developed mainly in the context of latent defects. As was pointed

---

[44] Cass. 31 Oct. 1966, Arr. 301; Cass. 27 Oct. 1995, RW 1996–1997, 298.

out in case 1, the problem there is not one of taking advantage of one's own knowledge, but of professional incompetence and/or carelessness about one's products and the damage they may cause to the other party. In that context, the availability of information serves the common goal of the parties and the duty to inform can thus be seen as an aspect of the duty to co-operate. In case 2, however, the situation is entirely different: the question here is whether one party may benefit from information which the other party does not have. The basic problem here is not whether the professional buyer should have known of the information, but whether he was obliged to communicate it to the other party; it is not his professional quality which is at stake, but the question whether he may take advantage of it.

It would certainly be an exaggeration to say that under Belgian law, as a rule, a party to a contract may benefit from information he possesses. That this is not always the case can be seen from the rules on insider trading. Apart from the question of whether the rules on insider trading are not very specific rules for a very specific market, a distinction probably has to be drawn between information which a party has obtained by chance, and information which results from deliberate efforts and specific skills. Information of the latter kind – such as that acquired by an art dealer, does not have to be communicated to the other party, who does not have the information precisely because he did not invest time and money to acquire such information.[45] Otherwise, parties would no longer have an incentive to acquire such specific information. Whereas in case 1 it is clear that an economic advantage is to be gained by imposing rather strict duties of information, this is different in the present case.

A duty of information is not used as an autonomous cause of action, but as an element to judge whether the mistake of the seller was caused by his own negligence or by the negligence (or intention) of the buyer. That the application of the rules on mistake is influenced by the evaluation of duties to inform, however, can be seen (and is seen by academic writers) as a consequence of the use of the general principle of good faith in interpreting the rules relating to mistake. Since the parties are still in a pre-contractual phase, it is not possible to base duties to inform the other party on the contract (as ancillary obligations). Thus, it is essentially the expansion of the principle of good faith which has given rise to the development of a precontractual duty to inform (outside the context of the war-

---

[45] See M. E. Storme, 25 DAOR 1992, *sub* nos. 14 and 17.

ranty for latent defects) and has thereby influenced the way in which the rules on mistake are being interpreted.

Applying these considerations to the present case, some specific circumstances have to be taken into consideration such as, particularly, the behaviour of the parties and the expectations which were mutually expressed as to each other's role. The art dealer, for example, might argue that she was contacted as a possible purchaser, and not as an expert to assist the seller (in which case the result would be entirely different). She could also argue that the seller was free to ask advice from an expert before selling. If the seller had asked the buyer to give *information* about the estimated quality or value of the work or about the author, and not merely to make an *offer* to buy the painting, he would normally be able to avoid the contract. If not, avoidance is doubtful, unless there is sufficient indication of some abuse of the ignorance of the other party (an art dealer who is specifically 'trained' in obtaining works of art from intellectually weaker parties, an art dealer forcing the other party to accept his offer immediately, etc.).

A judge, in evaluating the case, will certainly take into account the usages in the art trade. In lines of business where it is normal to ask the advice of an expert before concluding a transaction, avoidance will normally not be awarded.

(b) The notion of fraud found in art. 1116 C.C. has been interpreted extensively in Belgian law, thus also covering fraud by omission (*bedrog door verzwijging, dol par réticence*).[46]

Fraud by omission also requires a duty to inform, the existence of which has to be judged in the same way as in the case of mistake (once again, the duty is not seen in an autonomous way, but as an element of fraud). Fraud requires an additional element of intent. If this element can be proven, the aggrieved party is in a stronger position than in the case of mistake: his own negligence becomes irrelevant, and so does the inquiry whether the mistake concerns the 'substance' or the 'value' of the performance.

In the present case, the additional element of intent is probably not difficult to prove. But the existence of a duty to inform the seller remains questionable under Belgian law.

(c) *Laesio enormis* can only lead to avoidance of the contract in cases specifically regulated by statute (art. 1118 C.C.; such specific cases concern, e.g., the sale of land: art. 1674 C.C.).

---

[46] See Cass. 8 June 1978, RCJB 1979, 525.

Case law, however, has developed a remedy (avoidance) in cases where there is not merely a disproportion between the performances, but a disproportion resulting from an abuse of circumstances. The doctrine is found in some specific contracts, especially loans (see art. 1907 *ter* C.C., as inserted by the Royal Decree of 18 March 1935), where the type of circumstances which can give rise to abuse are enumerated (notably need, weakness, passion or ignorance). The legal basis for this doctrine, also called 'qualified lesion' (*gekwalificeerde benadeling, lésion qualifiée*), is found, first, in the general principle of the abuse of rights, applied to freedom of contract, or second, in the concept of 'illicit cause' as a ground for nullity (or avoidance) of a contract in art. 1131 C.C.[47] Apart from other possible meanings or functions of the notion of cause,[48] in this context it is understood in the sense of the consideration given by the stipulator (creditor): where the absence of equivalence of performances is the result of the free will of the parties, the law does not normally intervene (no *iustum pretium* doctrine as such); where, however, it is the result of immoral behaviour on the part of the creditor, he is deprived of the result of his acts by nullifying the contract.

The description of case 2 however, reveals insufficient elements to establish such an abuse by the buyer, unless one accepts fraud on his part; in this case, however, the remedies for fraud are available and they are more favourable for the seller. But, as explained above, the element of 'abuse' can be an element in evaluating the buyer's duty to inform (and thus the possibility of avoiding the contract, whether on the basis of mistake or another ground).

(ii) In case of avoidance, the drawing and the purchase price are subject to restitution (as the drawing is a specific object and as Belgian law has no principle of abstraction, the drawing remains the property of the seller so that a retransfer of ownership is unnecessary).

In contrast to German law (§ 122 BGB), there is no general rule that the mistaken party, after rescinding the contract, has to compensate the other

---

[47] Sometimes, the legal basis is even seen to lie in tort law (*culpa in contrahendo*). However, *lésion qualifiée* entails avoidance of the contract rather than a claim for damages.

[48] The notion of 'illicit cause' is used not only where the promise or the performance of an act are illicit *per se*, but where they must be regarded as illicit in the context of the contract as a whole, especially in relation to the promise, or performance, of the other party. Thus, it is never illicit *per se* to pay a sum of money or to promise to pay a sum of money, but the contract must be regarded as illicit if the sum of money is promised in exchange for an illicit act (such as a murder) or even for a licit act which may not, however, be commercialised (e.g. sexual relationships).

party for the damage the latter has sustained by relying upon the validity of the contract. But the seller has a claim for damages in case of fraud, abuse of circumstances or negligence (violation of a precontractual duty to inform) as possible forms of *culpa in contrahendo* if there is a distinct damage which is not yet made up for by the avoidance. Such distinct damage will often be hard to prove.

(iii) If avoidance is admitted, the question arises whether the buyer should be compensated for his efforts in researching the origin of the work. After all, it is probably only due to these efforts that the seller is able to sell his painting for a much higher price.

This question has rarely been dealt with in Belgian law, and compensation for the professional buyer is quite improbable, unless the seller sells the painting within a short period of time after he has learnt of its true value for a considerably higher price. Even then, compensation is doubtful, as an action for enrichment under Belgian law requires an impoverishment of the other party – which is difficult to argue in this case.

SPAIN

In Spanish law the dispute arising from this case belongs entirely to the law of contract and concerns the availability of rescission of the contract for mistake or for deceit under arts. 1266 and 1269 of the Civil Code respectively. Thus, a party to a contract (and therefore the seller in case 2) may rescind it where he has been labouring under a mistake as to the essential features of the subject matter for which he has contracted (the drawing in case 2) as long as he would not have entered into the contract if he had known the real position. The High Court of Justice has held that a mistake is operative only (i) when it was caused by a misrepresentation concerning a substantial attribute of the property sold and (ii) when it is excusable. A mistake is inexcusable when it may be 'causally imputed' to the party labouring under it, viz. where he should have known or recognised the true situation, or where it would otherwise be unfair to make his contractual partner bear the risk of his ignorance. An exception is made to this approach, however, where a party's mistake was caused by the other's deceit, for here the mistaken party may choose to treat the contract as void, regardless of whether he could have discovered the truth by exercising more care: deceit excuses the other party's lack of care.[49]

---

[49] High Court judgement of 26 October 1981 (RJA 1981, 4001); see the High Court doctrine in Morales, *El error* 263 ff.

In this respect, nondisclosure, by one party to the contract, of circumstances with respect to which the other party is mistaken or ignorant is deemed to be deceit for the purposes of these provisions where the first party owed a duty to disclose the circumstances in question and thereby correct the other's mistake. The real problem on the facts of case 2 is to decide whether there is such a duty to disclose, given the lack of any legislative provision to this effect apart from that in relation to consumer law as provided by art. 13 of the Consumer Protection Act of 1984. In general, the High Court has accepted rescission on account of deceit where good faith or commercial custom required a duty to speak or to give relevant information.[50]

While there is no Spanish decision dealing specifically with facts like the ones in case 2, the following factors would be taken into account in determining whether a duty of disclosure exists.

(i) Should Othello, in view of his profession, recognise the artist of the picture? In one case, the High Court has held that an expert cannot rescind the contract when it is later discovered that the picture was a forgery or a copy: market risks in the art business, so the Court argued, should be borne by an expert who fails to discover a picture's true hand.[51]

(ii) Should Desdemona have informed Othello of the identity of the picture's artist? If Desdemona had spent money and used special means to discover its true artist and so to obtain this information, it is doubtful that there would be a duty to communicate it to the other party. For any information acquired by Desdemona as a result of her particular skill, or at a cost, would increase the value of the picture, and to require its disclosure would result in the transfer of this value to the other party.

(iii) If Desdemona buys the picture *without knowing* its hand, and thereby assumes herself the risk that the picture will not be attributed to a famous artist, it is clear that good faith does not impose on her any duty to inform the other party of her views.

ITALY

Desdemona's silence about the possible identity of the artist responsible for the drawing constitutes fraud in Italian law.

According to the Civil Code, it is fraud for a person to resort to trickery (*raggiri*) to induce another either to enter into a contract or to enter it on

---

[50] Judgement of 27 March 1989 (RJA 1989, 2201).
[51] Judgement of 28 February 1974 (RJA 1974, 742).

less favourable terms than he would otherwise have accepted.[52] Both courts and legal scholars hold that the relevant provisions of the Code apply to 'reticent behaviour' as well, i.e. where a party to a contract knowingly keeps silent on a significant matter.[53] This interpretation is supported by reference to art. 1337 of the Civil Code which expressly establishes a duty on parties to a contract to negotiate in good faith.[54] The fact that Desdemona was a professional (i.e. both an expert and in business) and that Othello asked her to look over his possessions lends extra weight to this approach on the facts. Although Othello did not realise that the drawing was a true Degas, Desdemona cannot set up Othello's mistake as a defence, because in order to satisfy the requirement of good faith she should have disclosed her suspicions as to who drew the drawing when she visited Othello's house.

A contract which is vitiated by fraud is not void, but may be annulled by a court at the instance of the deceived party.[55] Such a judicial annulment in principle results in title to the picture automatically revesting in its transferor. However, an exception to this proprietary effect of annulment is made where the object was sold to a third party purchaser in good faith;[56] and in these circumstances the transferor of property may at his choice recover the value of the thing or the price paid for it by the third party.[57] He may also claim damages for any harm caused to him by the fraudulent behaviour of the other party.[58] In the alternative, a party to a contract aggrieved by fraud may choose to claim damages in delict under the general provision regulating delictual liability[59] without raising the question of any action to rescind the contract. Article 1440 of the Civil Code accepts this solution for a particular case, stating that '[i]f the deception was not such as to compel consent, the contract is valid, even though

---

[52] Arts. 1439 and 1440 c.c.

[53] Sacco/De Nova, in: *Trattato Sacco I* 430–6; Galgano, *Diritto civile* (1993) 317 ff., at 320; Bianca, *Diritto Civile III* 625; Visintini 251 ff. For two recent cases affirming the same principle see: Cass., 14 Oct. 1991, n. 10779, Giur. it., 1993, I,1, 190; Cass., 12 Jan. 1991, n. 257. Some decisions proclaim that mere silence is irrelevant, while silence coupled with deceitful conduct is equivalent to fraud: Cass., 18 Oct. 1991, n. 11038; Cass., 21 Oct. 1981, n. 5503. Yet, where the *conduct* is deceitful there is fraud anyhow.

[54] Art. 1337 c.c.: 'Parties must behave in good faith during precontractual negotiations.' Cf. Sacco/De Nova, in: *Trattato Sacco I* 430; Sacco, in: *La bonne foi* 137–9; Alpa, in: *Precontractual Liability* 195.   [55] Arts. 1441 ff. c.c.

[56] Art. 1445 c.c. Good faith, in this context, is presumed; the presumption is rebutted by proving gross negligence or fraud (cf. art. 1147 c.c.).

[57] Art. 2038 c.c.   [58] Sacco/De Nova, in: *Trattato Sacco I* 421.

[59] Art. 2043 c.c.; Sacco/De Nova, in: *Trattato Sacco I* 421.

without the deception it would have included different terms; however, the contracting party in bad faith is liable for damages'.

On the other hand, Desdemona may certainly recover from Othello any money paid for the expert advice, commissioned by her, which confirmed indeed Degas' authorship; such expert advice was probably necessary to establish the drawing's authenticity. Recovery will be allowed by way of a claim for damages,[60] or of the rescission of the sale and restitution of the picture (or its value).[61]

THE NETHERLANDS

This is a case of error (art. 6:228 B.W., in particular par. 1, *sub* b). The contract can be annulled (with retroactive effect) by Othello (cf. arts. 3:49 ff.). However, in *Hoge Raad* 19 June 1959, NJ 1960, 59 (*Kantharos van Stevensweert*), the *Hoge Raad* ruled that in a case where both parties were unaware of the value of a very old and precious cup and the buyer only found out about its value through extensive research of his own, the seller could not annul the contract because of error.

Article 6:228 is a codification of case law as developed under the old Civil Code. This case law has been the basis for a more general acceptance of duties of disclosure in other areas of the law, as for example in pre-contractual negotiations.[62]

ENGLAND

This is a striking example of English law's antipathy to broad doctrines of vitiation on the ground of mistake and to duties of disclosure of information, for however the problem is analysed, the contract of sale is valid.

Thus, in the absence of any statement, whether through words or conduct, there can be no vitiation on the ground of misrepresentation. Nor does tacit acquiescence in another's self-deception amount to a misrepresentation, provided that it was not previously caused by a positive misrepresentation.[63] Furthermore, there is no general duty of disclosure of information or opinion by one would-be party to a contract to another, even where the first party knows that the information would affect the latter's decision to contract or the price at which he would contract:

---

[60] According to the doctrine of *compensatio lucri cum damno*.   [61] Cf. arts. 2040, 1150.3 c.c.
[62] Cf. HR 15 November 1957, NJ 1958, 67 (*Baris v. Riezenkamp*). See also Vranken, *passim*.
[63] Guest, *Chitty on Contracts* § 6–009.

duties of disclosure exist only in exceptional cases of which the contract of sale is not one.[64] Desdemona has apparently made no false statement to Othello as to the artist or value of the drawing nor is she under a duty to do so.

While the law of fundamental mistake is far from clear (possessing uncertainties both as to the interpretation of the position at law and the status of supposedly special rules in equity), it would seem clear that case 2 would not attract the application of any law which would allow vitiation on the ground of mistake. First, both the common law doctrine of mistake[65] and its supposed equitable supplement[66] apply to *common* mistakes, i.e. where both the parties are under a mistake as to the substance or fundamental quality of the subject matter of the contract.[67] This is not so in case 2, where the most that could be said is that while Othello is mistaken as to both the hand and the value of his drawing, Desdemona is at most not certain as to these issues. Secondly, it is unlikely that Othello's mistake will count as fundamental at least for the purposes of the common law doctrine, as it was made clear in *Bell's* case that a fundamental mistake was not merely a causal or even an important causal one, but required that the thing was essentially different from the thing as it was believed to be.[68] While there is authority to suggest the contrary, the force of this decision suggests that a mistake as to who drew a drawing or even a very considerable difference in its value would not be 'fundamental enough'.[69] Moreover, it could be argued that Othello's *mistake* was only as to the value of his drawing (considering it quite modest given the amount he accepted): he was simply *ignorant* of its hand, not having a view at all.

On the other hand, it should be noted that if owing to her relationship with Othello Desdemona had gained some influence over his decision-making, then the contract could be vitiated on the ground of actual or presumed undue influence. However, there is nothing in the facts to suggest circumstances which would give rise either to a presumption of undue influence or actual undue influence by Desdemona.

This stark position denying duties of disclosure and vitiation on the ground of mistake must be seen in the light not merely of the existence of

---

[64] *Smith v. Hughes* (1871) LR 6 QB 597.

[65] As found in the leading decision of the House of Lords in *Bell v. Lever Bros. Ltd* [1932] AC 161.   [66] As found in *Solle v. Butcher* [1950] 1 KB 671.   [67] Treitel 262.

[68] [1932] AC 161, at 218.

[69] But cf. the discussion in Treitel 266–9 in relation to *Nicholson & Venn v. Smith-Marriott* [1947] 177 LT 189 and *Leaf v. International Galleries* [1950] 2 KB 86.

elaborate grounds of both vitiation and damages on the ground of misrepresentation but also of developed use of 'implied terms' in particular contracts, under which responsibility for some state of affairs etc. is legally allocated.[70] However, Othello's case is not one which is regulated by implied term: the buyer is not held to have impliedly promised anything as to the goods sold by the other party. The main justification for the present law is that while parties to contracts should not mislead each other (whether fraudulently or innocently) as to the subject matter of the contract, they should not in general have to act so as to protect the other's interests, but may act in their own interests. This is sometimes buttressed by an economic argument, that information or opinion is a valuable commodity and that it is therefore unjust or inefficient to require that a person (such as Desdemona) should be made to give away this commodity to other people (would-be contractors).

IRELAND

Irish (and English) courts have been reluctant to require disclosure by the parties of information which would be of advantage to the other party. The major exception to this stance is found in insurance contracts, where a rule of disclosure on the part of the insured has long been considered a precondition of the viable existence of insurance markets; without such a rule the markets would unravel by a process of adverse selection. In commerce generally, there is a persuasive argument that a duty of disclosure on the part of buyers would be inefficient, as it would penalise (or at least insufficiently reward) those who invest time and money in the acquisition of information. Such economic arguments have not been expressly used by the courts, although they are implicit in the attitude that it is up to the seller to ascertain the true worth of his own property.

The leading case in Ireland and England on situations such as are found in case 2 is *Smith v. Hughes*,[71] in which a contract for the sale of oats by sample was upheld even though the seller did not disclose to the buyer that the oats were 'new' rather than 'old' as the buyer thought. On the facts of case 2, Desdemona's nondisclosure will not constitute a misrepresentation, and in addition, Othello's self-induced mistake as to the authorship (and value) of the painting will not operate so as to nullify the contract.

---

[70] See the English report to case 1 above.   [71] (1871) LR 6 QB 597.

However, if the sale were still executory, Othello might attempt to resist a claim for specific performance on the basis that Desdemona had acted unconscionably, though it is unlikely that her behaviour would be castigated by courts of equity since the policy of the law is not to require Desdemona to reveal her valuable information.[72]

Even if specific performance were denied, Othello would still be liable in damages at common law.

SCOTLAND

The concept of misrepresentation, whereby a contract will be set aside if it is shown that one of the parties to the contract was induced to enter into it owing to a misrepresentation by the other party, will not get off the ground here. While misrepresentations can take a variety of forms, silence is not a misrepresentation. In fact, one of the most significant departures from the principle of good faith in contractual dealings is the acceptance by Scots law that, as a general rule, a contracting party is under no duty voluntarily to disclose any matter which could be material to the contemplated contract. However, it is a principle of Scots law that where a contract is obtained as a consequence of the exercise of *undue influence* by a person in a position of authority or trust, it is reducible.

It would appear from this case scenario that Desdemona has exercised undue influence to Othello's disadvantage by exploiting his lack of knowledge of art. Undue influence is said to operate between parties whose relationship is one of mutual trust and confidence, for example, parent and child, law agent and client, doctor and patient, and not between parties whose relationship is at arm's length. The essence of the doctrine of undue influence was explained by Lord President *Inglis* in *Gray v. Binny*:[73] 'If . . . the relation of the parties is such as to beget mutual trust and confidence, each owes to the other a duty which has no place as between strangers. But if the trust and confidence, instead of being mutual, are all given on one side and not reciprocated, the party trusted and confided in is bound, by the most obvious principles of fair dealing and honesty, not to abuse the power thus put in his hands.'

---

[72] Specific performance will be denied where the plaintiff induced the defendant to enter into the transaction by a misrepresentation: *Cadman v. Horner* (1810) 18 Ves Jun 10. Here, however, silence on Desdemona's part will not be characterised as misrepresentation. Specific performance may exceptionally be denied if it would be unfair or a hardship on the plaintiff (cf. Keane 249).   [73] (1879) 7 R 332, at 342.

Thus where a person has been induced to enter into a contract as a result of such an abuse of power, grounds exist for an action of rescission or reduction. Desdemona has the expert knowledge in which Othello has confidence and trust. The onus rests on Othello, as the pursuer, to establish undue influence. However, if the relationship of trust is established 'the onus may be shifted with comparative ease',[74] and the defender must show that she has not abused her position of trust. Thus it is crucial to establish that a relationship of trust exists between Desdemona and Othello. Relationships which are recognised as involving trust and confidence have not been liberally extended beyond narrow bounds. However, in *Honeyman's Executors v. Sharp*,[75] Lord *Maxwell* held that where a person, in this instance a fine art adviser, in pursuance of his profession undertook to give advice to another, and as a result a relationship developed between the adviser and the advised where the advised held trust and confidence in the adviser, then the law recognised a moral duty on the adviser not to take advantage of the advised, at least in relation to matters regarding the area to which the advice related, and the law gave moral effect to that duty by applying the principle of undue influence. It should be noted that in this case the relationship between the parties developed through a course of dealings over a period of several years. However, there is nothing to indicate that such a relationship could not evolve after one meeting, and it is submitted that a one-off dealing is probably enough in this instance. In the more recent case of *Merchiston Hearts Social Club v. Nicholson*,[76] it was held that the doctrine could be applied between employer and employee.

A material or gratuitous benefit must have been received by the party who had the dominant influence, and it is up to the pursuer to show this.

Remedies: As undue influence operates as a factor vitiating the obligor's consent it is a ground for the rescission of an *ex facie* valid obligation or the reduction of an *ex facie* valid deed. The remedy of rescission is barred if *restitutio in integrum* (the ability to restore things to the original position) is impossible, or if *bona fide* third parties have relied upon the *ex facie* valid contract.

DENMARK AND NORWAY

In West Nordic law, the case would be regarded as a classic example of the buyer acting contrary to 'honesty or good faith'. The cardinal provision is

---

[74] *Carmicheal v. Baird* (1899) 6 SLT 369, OH, *per* Lord *Pearson*.   [75] 1978 SC 223.
[76] 1994 GWD 8–503, Sh Ct.

s. 33 of the joint Nordic Contracts Acts of 1918 (Norwegian Act No. 4 of 31 May 1918) which states that '[e]ven if a commitment would otherwise be regarded as valid, it is not binding on the person who made it if, on account of circumstances which existed at the time the other party was informed of the commitment and which he must have been aware of, it would be contrary to honesty or good faith for him to invoke the commitment'. Under this provision, a purchase in the circumstances described will undoubtedly be deemed to be invalid, so that the seller is entitled to have the agreement rescinded, alternatively with repayment of the profit which the buyer made from the transaction. The core elements of an evaluation under s. 33 here will be the combination of a professional buyer, a non-professional seller acting as a private individual, and significant ignorance on the seller's part of which the buyer is aware. Under s. 33 of the Contracts Act, the buyer will be deemed to have a duty of information, and the agreement is disallowed because the buyer has failed to draw the seller's attention to his assessment of the object; cf. Rt. 1984, p. 28.[77]

As mentioned previously, the Nordic countries have had since 1918 a joint Contracts Act, and an identical provision in s. 33. Though it has been given greater significance in Norway than in the other countries, it can hardly be doubted that the case in point lies within the core area of the requirement of s. 33 as to honesty or good faith in the West Nordic tradition.

The evolution of strict honesty requirements in contractual relationships did not stop when s. 33 was adopted. In the early 1980s a general clause was introduced into s. 36 of the joint Nordic Contracts Acts which in principle maintains that '[a]n agreement may be set aside wholly or in part or may be amended in so far as it would seem unreasonable or in conflict with good commercial practice to invoke it'. The provision has its main application with regard to the so-called defects in the nature of agreement, but may also be applied to defects in the process of its origin.[78] In the present instance one would clearly say that there are defects on both counts which must in any case lead to a revision of the agreement under s. 36. Of decisive importance will be the same aspects as those warranting the application of s. 33. If, however, the facts of the case are turned around, making the seller a professional art dealer and the buyer a knowledgeable private collector, it would be difficult to envisage that the agreement could be disallowed, under either s. 33 or s. 36.

---

[77] Arnholm, *Privatrett II* 333; Andersen/Madsen/Nørgaard 210 ff.
[78] Andersen/Madsen/Nørgaard 231 ff.; Hagstrøm, *Lov og Rett* 1994, 131 ff.

SWEDEN

Sections in the Contracts Act of 1915 to be contemplated are primarily s. 30 on fraud, s. 31 on usury and s. 33 on good faith. It is of importance that the owner Othello seems to have been generally mentally capable, had himself decided to sell, had asked Desdemona to come as a buyer and not as an adviser, and had invited Desdemona to look at all his possessions. In addition, the buyer Desdemona did not use inside information. On the other hand, Othello had no special knowledge of art whereas Desdemona was a dealer in fine art, and the price agreed upon was only 1.4 per cent of the market value.

Section 31 requires that the promisor lacks judgement, is irresponsible or is in a dependent position. It is not, probably, applicable here.

Section 30 on fraud is seldom used when the promisee passively takes advantage of the promisor being poorly informed.

In this case s. 33 lies most closely at hand.[79] In the preparatory works to this section it was stated that it can be used whenever the promisee in a dishonest way took advantage of the promisor's ignorance of the circumstances. A promisee, however, is permitted to use his superior business skill, though it is contrary to good faith to use inside information. There are no other specific examples in the preparatory works specifying the notion of 'inside information'. Nor do we have easily comparable cases from the Supreme Court. In NJA 1975, p. 152 the seller at an auction knew that a painting was a reproduction and set a low opening price, but as the painting was signed bidders thought it was an original, with the result that the price was eventually seven times the normal price. Since it was an auction, the seller had, in the opinion of the Supreme Court, not been obliged to intervene. Otherwise, a buyer can expect that the goods possess a quality which is in fair relation to the price (ss. 17 and 19, Sale of Goods Act of 1990).

My judgement is that Desdemona's purchase is invalid pursuant to s. 33, due to a combination of (i) Desdemona being a professional and Othello being a non-professional (an inverted consumer case, cf. s. 36, Contracts Act) and (ii) the vast difference between price and value.

---

[79] S. 33 of the Contracts Act of 1915: 'A legal act which would otherwise be deemed valid may not be relied upon where the circumstances in which it arose were such that, having knowledge of such circumstances, it would be inequitable to enforce the legal act, and where the party in respect of whom such legal act was performed must be presumed to have had such knowledge.'

FINLAND

The seller has erred about the real value of the drawing, since the buyer obviously knew at least that the drawing *might* be much more valuable than the seller thought. (This is a matter of evidence, which is set out only briefly in the report.) The contract is thus invalid according to s. 33 of the Contracts Act of 1929 (Si 402): it was dishonest on the part of Desdemona to abuse the ignorance of Othello regarding the real value of the drawing.[80] In KKO 1975 II 92 the seller of real property had erred regarding the right to build on the estate and, consequently, with regard to the value too. The buyer had been cognisant of the real situation, and the Supreme Court invalidated the sale. There is in Finnish law no direct provision regarding a mistake such as encountered here, i.e. *error in motivis*, but it is treated in a rather casuistic manner on the grounds of s. 33, which refers directly to *bona fides* (the Swedish words are in fact 'tro och heder', that is, faith and honour).

Editors' comparative observations

I. All except English and Irish law allow the possibility of rescission of the contract of sale with Desdemona for Othello's benefit. While the doctrinal grounds for doing so are very diverse, they may be grouped into the following.

(i) Some legal systems rely on the notion of good faith either *simpliciter* (as in West Nordic law) or in combination with other doctrines. Thus, for example, French law uses good faith as a rationale for the imposition of an *obligation d'information* and German law relies on good faith as the basis of finding an obligation to disclose facts so as to allow rescission for deception. It should be noted that the Greek and Italian codes contain express provisions enjoining the parties to negotiate in good faith.

(ii) A number of legal systems consider this to be a case of deception even though Desdemona was silent on her suspicions as to the hand of the picture. For some of them, for example French, Spanish, Italian, Belgian and German law, the question whether deception by omission counts as a ground for rescission is coupled with the idea of a duty to inform.

(iii) Scots law (but not English law) allows, on the particular circumstances of case 2, rescission for undue influence, i.e. on the basis of likely improper pressure rather than deception.

---

[80] See Telaranta 56.

(iv) Dutch law would look to the mistake of Othello rather than to any deception in Desdemona. Othello's mistake is also the focus of the response of Belgian law and of English law, though, in the latter case, with a resultant denial of relief on this ground. A number of legal systems (e.g. Austria and Greece) adopt an analysis in terms of error as a viable alternative to other avenues to assist Othello. It is generally agreed, however, that a mere *error* as to the value of the drawing does not allow Othello to rescind the contract.

(v) Austrian law would rely not only on mistake and deceit, but also on a modern legislative (and very general) version of *laesio enormis*, focusing on the gross disparity between the content of the parties' obligations. Greek and German law have developed very similar doctrines, both of them related to the general *contra bonos mores* clause. Swedish law, too, emphasises the gross imbalance, though under the auspices of a legislative 'good faith' provision.

(vi) Occasionally, a claim for damages on account of *culpa in contrahendo* is granted to Othello, whether invoking contractual rules of liability (Germany, Greece) or on the basis of the law of delict (France). This claim can also lead to the contract being set aside (German law).

II. Thus, the key points of focus found in relation to this case, either alone or in combination, are: protecting the quality of the contractor's consent (whether in terms of mistake, deceit or undue influence); sanctioning the other party's wrongdoing; the substantive unfairness of the result for one of the parties; or simply, good faith.

Clearly, Desdemona's expertise is a significant factual circumstance in the responses of many of the legal systems. Mostly, its relevance relates to the enquiry whether it is reasonable, under the circumstances, for her to be under a duty of disclosure as to the artist and whether nondisclosure constitutes deceit. According to some legal systems, such as Belgian and Spanish law, any money spent, or work done, in establishing the attribution of the drawing would weigh against the availability of rescission. The idea that her skill or special knowledge have a monetary value and therefore should not have to be employed or applied for the benefit of another person without remuneration may be thought to lie behind the stark denial of a remedy in English (and Irish) law, which has consistently denied duties of disclosure of information.

Finally, it should be noted that while rescission of the contract, coupled with restitution of money and property transferred under the contract, is the remedy generally granted, and while some systems add a remedy in damages, Austrian law, under its rules relating to *error*, allows the court to modify the contract, with the result that the buyer may keep the drawing though for an increased price.

Case 3: Breaking off negotiations

Case

Falstaff & Co., a large firm of accountants, enters protracted negotiations with the owner of an office block, Hal & Sons, with the view to renting space for their new office in Everdale. In the course of these negotiations, Falstaffs ask for various work to be done on the premises, including the installation of the wiring necessary for their computer and communications systems. Just before an appointment fixed by the parties for signing the contract, Falstaffs find equally suitable premises in Everdale on offer at a lesser rent and refuse to go any further with Hal & Sons. What claim or claims do Hal & Sons have?

Discussions

GERMANY

Hal & Sons cannot demand conclusion of a contract of lease on the basis of a *pactum de contrahendo* (agreement to make a contract). A *pactum de contrahendo* will only come into existence where the parties already have the intention to be bound and where they are *ad idem* on the material aspects of the main contract.[1] These requirements have not been met in the present case.

Falstaff & Co. asked Hal & Sons for various work to be done on the premises. They may thus be taken to have concluded a contract concerning this work. If that were the case, there would be no problem: Falstaff & Co. would owe whatever remuneration has been agreed upon, alternatively the usual remuneration for this kind of work (§§ 612 II, 632 II BGB).

---

[1] BGH NJW 1990, 1234 (1235); *Münchener Kommentar*/Kramer, Vor § 145, n. 37; *Palandt*/Heinrichs, Einf. v. § 145, n. 37.

Alternatively, if it may be assumed that no contract has been concluded but that Falstaff & Co. have induced Hal & Sons to carry out this work in anticipation of the future contract, a claim may lie in terms of *culpa in contrahendo*.[2] Such a claim does not, of course, aim at the conclusion of a contract of lease; it merely constitutes a remedy to recover the reliance interest. The taking up of serious contractual negotiations between the parties created a precontractual relationship entailing special duties (*vor-vertragliches Schuldverhältnis*). Does Falstaffs' refusal to conclude a contract of lease constitute a breach of such special precontractual duties? In principle, of course, freedom of contract entails that every contracting party has the right to withdraw from contractual negotiations before a contract has actually been concluded. Each party incurs expenses at his own risk in the expectation that a contract may eventually be concluded. If, however, conclusion of the contract as a result of the negotiations appears to be virtually certain, these expenses may be claimed in cases where the other party subsequently refuses to conclude the contract without good reason.[3] This flows from the prohibition of *venire contra factum proprium* (going against one's own action) as deduced from § 242 BGB.[4] By requiring structural changes Falstaff & Co. have created the expectation that they intended to conclude the contract with Hal & Sons. Nevertheless, a better offer may be regarded as a good reason for Falstaff & Co. to give preference to a competitor. Generally speaking, the standards for accepting a good reason to break off negotiations must not be pitched too high. But where negotiations have extended over a long period of time and where the one party has requested the other to incur precontractual expenses,[5] a better offer from another party cannot justify termination of the negotiations. Hence, in the present case, a breach of duty has occurred and damages may be claimed. Falstaff can be presumed to have been at fault. Such fault only has to relate to the breaking off of the negotiations, not to the inducement of reliance on the part of the other party (§ 122 BGB *per analogiam*).[6]

---

[2] On the doctrine of *culpa in contrahendo*, see the references in the German report to case 1.

[3] BGH NJW 1996, 1884 (1885) and many other cases; *Münchener Kommentar*/Kramer, Vor § 275, n. 161; *Palandt*/Heinrichs § 276, n. 72; and see the extensive general discussion in *Soergel*/Wiedemann, Vor § 275, nn. 130 ff.

[4] Cf., e.g., *Jauernig*/Vollkommer § 242, nn. 48 ff.; *Palandt*/Heinrichs § 242, nn. 55 ff.

[5] *Palandt*/Heinrichs § 276, n. 74 with further references.

[6] BGHZ 71, 386 (395); BGH WM 1989, 685 (688); an exception is taken to exist where the expected conclusion of the contract requires notarial authentication: cf. BGH WM 1982, 1436. The most recent decision on the breaking off of negotiations that were to lead to the conclusion of a contract requiring notarial authentication is BGH NJW 1996, 1884 ff. (*dolus* required for a claim based on *culpa in contrahendo*).

GREECE

In this case, Falstaff & Co. did not act in accordance with good faith in the course of precontractual negotiations. Falstaff & Co. asked for various work to be done on the premises of the owner of the office block, which involved expenditure. The owner therefore is entitled to damages. There is no valid contract yet. Falstaff & Co. negotiated with the view to renting space for new offices in Everdale. In the case where Falstaff & Co. refuses to go any further with Hal & Sons, the latter have a claim for compensation. Under Greek law, the claim of Hal & Sons arises from the provisions of arts. 197 and 198 of the Greek Civil Code.[7] These provisions are very important. They solve the ambiguity and dispute encountered in the Greek law before their introduction.[8] Before the Greek Civil Code came into force, liability in the course of precontractual negotiations was established, as in Germany, by the theory of *culpa in contrahendo*. Articles 197 f. are now a statutory version of this doctrine; they constitute a special case of liability imposed by law. This liability may arise from the start of precontractual negotiations, and comes to an end when the negotiations are abandoned, whether or not a contract has been concluded, and whether or not any contract which has been concluded is valid.[9]

Liability under arts. 197 f. Gr. C.C. has four requirements: (i) conduct contrary to precontractual good faith and business usages; (ii) culpability (which is effectively merged with the requirement under (i)); (iii) damage; (iv) causal nexus between damage and conduct contrary to good faith and business usages. The claim for damages covers the negative interest.[10] It includes *damnum emergens* as well as *lucrum cessans*.[11]

AUSTRIA

In Austrian law, in general a person owes no duty to conclude a contract merely on account of the fact that negotiations have already taken place and that the other would-be party has started to rely on a contract being concluded. Usually[12] people are not bound to an agreement until they

---

[7] On which see the Greek report to case 2.

[8] On the systematic position of the rules, and on their ambit, see Papantoniou, *Kali Pistis* 165; Koumantos, in: *ErmAK I* arts. 197–8, nos. 3, 44; Simantiras nos. 635–7, 470–5.

[9] Simantiras no. 636; Koumantos, in: *ErmAK I* arts. 197–8, nos. 4, 44.

[10] For details, see Koumantos, in: *ErmAK I* arts. 197–8, nos. 4, 77.

[11] Litzeropoulos, in: *ErmAK II* art. 298, no. 37; PolProt Artas 79/1995 Arm 96, 1319. Regarding literature to the case, see: Simantiras nos. 635–7, pp. 470–5; and *passim* in Pouliadis, and Karassis, *Culpa*.

[12] Exceptions are found, for example, in the case of preliminary contracts (§ 936 ABGB) or where a (legal) obligation to contract exists, but these cases need not be considered here.

have consented to its terms and have thus (expressly or impliedly) concluded it. This is clearly provided by § 861 sent. 2 ABGB.

However, as has already been explained in relation to case 1, the prevailing view in Austrian law is that special duties of care arise as soon as a 'lawful contact' has been established between the parties to negotiations and it is clear that a failure to conclude a contract without reason may constitute a breach of these duties.[13] For, where a party to negotiations has emphasised his definite intention to enter a contract, it is feared that distrust would infect and consequently obstruct the making of legal transactions if he were allowed to alter his earlier decision. On the facts of case 3, it is highly significant that although Falstaff & Co. did not request Hal & Sons to perform in terms of the envisaged contract, they caused the latter to incur expenses, which are apparently of use only if the contract is concluded. Furthermore, it is also significant that the parties have fixed an appointment to sign the contract for Falstaffs have thus engendered in Hal & Sons a reasonable reliance that the contract would go ahead – a reliance which is disappointed in the present case. For these reasons, it can be said that the relationship between the parties has already become so close that a refusal on Falstaffs' part to conclude the contract may be justified only for good cause, such as for a reason which would be significant enough to allow the cancellation of a contract which has actually been concluded.[14]

No such reason exists on the facts of case 3: Falstaff & Co. have simply found a better opportunity elsewhere. Their refusal to conclude the deal with Hal & Sons therefore constitutes a violation of their duty of care and this means that Hal & Sons may recover damages under the doctrine of *culpa in contrahendo* for the expenditure which they have wasted in anticipation of the contract. It is clear, however, that Hal & Sons cannot recover damages based on any failure on Falstaffs' part to perform their side of the would-be contract, for to allow this would be to recognise indirectly, via damages for *culpa in contrahendo*, a duty to perform a contract before it is concluded, a result which § 861 ABGB clearly prohibits.[15]

FRANCE

Hal & Sons may be able to claim damages as a result of Falstaff & Co.'s breaking off negotiations on the ground that their conduct was abusive.

---

[13] Koziol, *Haftpflichtrecht II* 78; OGH in RdW 1996, 306.
[14] E.g. a mistake on a material point or a subsequent impossibility of the performance; see Koziol, *Haftpflichtrecht II* 78.
[15] Bydlinski, in: *Festschrift Klecatsky* 141 f.; Koziol, *Haftpflichtrecht II* 79; Welser, ÖJZ 1973, 285; OGH in SZ 52/90 (1979); JBl 1992, 120.

Such a claim would be based on delictual liability under arts. 1382 and 1383 of the Civil Code,[16] an application of these provisions which has been accepted by the courts since 1883 and constantly thereafter.[17]

The starting point for French law is that, in principle, the parties to a would-be contract are free to break off negotiations without liability at any stage, but it has put a limit on this principle by developing a general 'duty of loyalty' during negotiations, a duty to negotiate in good faith. The *Cour de cassation* has restricted the possibility of actions based on breach of such a duty in order to ensure that freedom to negotiate is not unduly hampered, by declaring that any liability arising from breaking off negotiations derives from 'an abuse of a right to negotiate'.[18] This abuse may be characterised as a fault, if breaking off negotiations is done with malicious intent or bad faith[19] or at the very least an 'attitude amounting to a certain duplicity'.[20] Alternatively, Hal & Sons may be able to rely on the idea that by refusing to accept the offer, Falstaff & Co. had induced in it an 'excessive confidence' that they were going to conclude the contract.[21]

If the parties had made a preliminary agreement concerning the alterations Hal & Sons would be able to claim contractual damages for breach of this agreement. But in the absence of such an agreement, Hal & Sons may claim delictual damages for the expenses incurred in carrying out the negotiations and the cost of the alterations made at Falstaff & Co.'s request. Damages in delict are more generous as they include all damage directly flowing from the breach and not merely foreseeable damages as is the case in principle in contract.[22] Beyond this, it is extremely difficult in French law to analyse how damages would be awarded in a case like this. French lawyers traditionally have not distinguished between different types of interest recoverable in actions for damages (such as the common law 'reliance' and 'expectation' interests) and the quantum of damages is indeed in the 'sovereign power of assessment' of the lower courts, who are the judges on the merits (*juges du fond*). However, it may be possible for Hal & Sons to make out a claim for potential lost profits in a claim for delictual damages if they could show that the parties were just

---

[16] See the French report to case 2 for the text of these provisions.
[17] Paris 13 Feb. 1883, GP 1883.2.414; followed by the *Cour de cassation*, Civ. (1) 4 Feb. 1975, Bull. civ. I, no. 43, p. 41; also Viney, *Introduction* 356 ff.
[18] Civ. (3) 16 Oct. 1973, D 1974.I.R.35.
[19] Civ. (1) 12 Apr. 1976, Bull. civ. I, no. 122, obs. G. Durry, RTDCiv 1977.127.
[20] Com. 30 Jan. 1990, Paris 24 Sep. 1991, RTDCiv 1992.75.
[21] Civ. (1) 19 Jan. 1977, D 1977.593 note J. Schmidt.
[22] Arts. 1150 and 1151 C. civ.

about to conclude a contract (as is suggested by the facts of case 3). In order to succeed, they would have to show how near the negotiations were to being concluded[23] and also that the profits in question would indeed have been made if the contract had gone ahead. Recent case law seems to indicate that such a claim is not impossible, leaving aside the questions of mitigation and the length of time for which such compensation would be awarded.[24]

At a general level, freedom in relation to the conduct of negotiations is an illustration of the principle of freedom of contract and may be supported for economic reasons (competition, a free market economy, etc.). However, in French law this freedom is qualified by the operation of the duty of good faith, which acts as a deterrent, preventing parties from insisting on their strict legal rights, if in doing so this would cause damage to others.

BELGIUM

Case 3 is a rather frequent problem in Belgium; there is a considerable amount of case law. The first question here is whether a contract has been concluded or not.

(i) The fact that it has not yet been signed, does not exclude the possibility of the contract having been concluded already. Further 'negotiation' is only necessary if the parties have not yet agreed on all essential elements of the contract or refuse to conclude the contract as long as certain details, not essential in themselves, are not agreed upon (such is the case when they agree subject to contract). According to Belgian case law, even the clause 'subject to contract' will lose its effect if the parties initiated performance of the contract.[25] Although in general the will theory dominates contract law, recent case law applies the principle of protection of legitimate reliance also in relation to whether a contract has been concluded or not.[26] Thus, it is probable that a Belgian judge would accept a contract in this case.

If it is decided that a contract was already concluded, Hal & Sons can avail themselves of the normal contractual remedies. While specific performance may be considered 'abusive', full compensation will certainly be

---

[23] Com. 7 Jan. 1997 and 22 Apr. 1997, D 1998.45 note P. Chauvel and see P. Chauvel, D 1998.45.   [24] Com. 6 Jun. 1990, Bulletin Joly 768; Paris 1 Jan. 1990, Droit sociétés 1991.8.

[25] Cf. *Hof van Beroep* (Appeal) Brussel 28 Sep. 1979, T. Aann. 1980, 221.

[26] See e.g. *Hof van Beroep* (Appeal) Brussel 26 May 1992, *ARCO*, TBBR 1993, 333.

awarded, including compensation of the costs incurred, in so far as they have not increased the value of the building, and the benefits of the bargain. In practice, this will be (a) the costs to find another tenant and (b) the difference between the rent offered by Falstaff & Co. and the rent which will ultimately be obtained from another tenant (unless Hal & Sons do not find another tenant due to their own negligence – i.e. if they neglect their duty to mitigate damages).

(ii) Should it be decided that the contract has not yet been concluded, the question of precontractual liability arises. Precontractual liability is usually based on the general duty of care recognised by the Belgian law of delict. Evidently, this general duty of care can be analysed in terms of more specific duties (but it is not necessarily limited to specific duties that have already been recognised). In the present case, we may be dealing with the precontractual duty not to put the other party to unnecessary expense.

In the case law of the *Hof van cassatie*, precontractual liability was, until recently, purely a matter of the law of delict. Recently, however, the Court has also accepted that contracts have to be 'concluded in good faith', thus establishing good faith as a basis for precontractual duties, such as a duty to negotiate in good faith.[27] As in France, the Court has thus filled the gap contained in art. 1134 sec. 3 C.C. (good faith principle) on this point. It is not yet clear whether this will give rise to a further extension of precontractual duties. At any rate, legal doctrine had for some time discussed problems of precontractual dealings in the context of the good faith principle.[28]

Liability for *culpa in contrahendo* as a result of a violation of the obligation to negotiate in good faith will probably be accepted in this case, according to Belgian case law, especially because Falstaff & Co. have caused Hal & Sons to incur costs.[29] One of the requirements of good faith (apart from duties to inform etc.) is indeed that one should not put the other party to expense. Moreover, one might recognise a duty not to keep the other party dangling unnecessarily, a duty not to play people off against one another, etc.

Falstaff & Co. will then have to pay for the costs caused to Hal & Sons (negative interest), but normally not for any benefits lost by them. A more

[27] Cass. 7 Feb. 1994, JTT 1994, 208, RW 1994–1995, 121.
[28] See e.g. Schrans, TPR 1984, 2 ff.; De Bondt, TPR 1984, 95 ff.
[29] Cf. Comm. Kortrijk 11 Apr. 1963, RW 1964–1965, 170; *Cour d'appel* (Appeal) Liège 19 Jan. 1965, RGAR 1965, 7423; Comm. Liège 20 Dec. 1984, JL 1985, 149.

far-reaching compensation may be obtained in exceptional cases such as when performance of the contract has commenced with the assent or at least with the knowledge of the other party.[30] In other cases, part of the benefit could possibly be claimed as compensation for the loss of a chance.

There is no explicit case in Belgian law comparable to *Plas v. Valburg* of the Dutch *Hoge Raad*,[31] but it could be argued that since contracts have to be concluded in good faith, a precontractual duty to compensate at least part of the lost benefit may exist under Belgian law, if negotations are broken off. The freedom to break off negotiations does also not exclude the possibility that the specific way in which such negotiations are broken off can be abusive in the sense of being against good faith. But since parties are in principle free not to conclude a contract and thus to break off negotiations, 'mere negligence' is not sufficient for liability; a 'manifest' negligence, i.e. abuse of right, is required.[32]

Reliance on the (conclusion of the) contract as such does not give rise to liability for *culpa in contrahendo*. Either the reliance is protected, and in that case the contract is deemed to have been concluded, or it is insufficient to ground liability.

(iii) A claim based on unjustified enrichment is not excluded. It presupposes, under Belgian law, an enrichment of the defendant related to an impoverishment of the plaintiff, and the claim is limited to the lesser of these two amounts. Moreover, the claim is excluded if there is a 'legal ground' justifying the enrichment, such as a contract. This last requirement may cause difficulty; the fact that a party freely provides certain services is often seen as a sufficient legal ground for the enrichment of the other party; most applications concern cases of kindness or gratuitous services between friends. But case law also refuses to allow compensation for

---

[30] See the already cited *Hof van Beroep* (Appeal) Brussel 28 Sep. 1979, T. Aann. 1980, 221, deciding that even if the contract were not concluded, the price of the services rendered (and thus also the benefits of the bargain) had to be paid as compensation for a *culpa in contrahendo*.   [31] On which, see the Dutch report to case 3 below.

[32] Concerning the relationship between abuse of right and delict in contemporary Belgian law, the following must be kept in mind. As long as a person merely uses his rights, he cannot commit a delict. Abuse of right is a device to show that, in reality, there is no subjective right to behave in a certain way. Thus, it restricts the extent of subjective rights and does, as such, not give rise to any liability. However, once it has been established that a person was abusing his right, an important obstacle for the imposition of delictual liability is removed. Where a person causing damages *prima facie* acted within his right, case law requires that the negligence be manifest in order to lead to delictual liability.

the costs of writing an offer with specifications, unless compensation is (explicitly) agreed upon.[33]

SPAIN

This case belongs in Spanish law to the area of liability for breaking off preliminary negotiations before a contract has been concluded. Although there is no special legislative provision on this subject, Spanish courts have accepted the existence of a duty to carry on preliminary negotiations in good faith. Here, art. 7 of the Civil Code is of special significance, as it establishes a general duty to exercise rights in accordance with the requirements of good faith and prohibits the abuse of rights.[34] In order to establish the existence of such an abuse, it is enough that the person who holds the right acts outside its 'serious and proper scope', without any further need to show in him any intention to harm another.[35] This duty to exercise rights in accordance with good faith is also reflected in the very broad scope given to art. 1258 of the Civil Code, which imposes a duty to perform a contract not only according to its express terms, but also according to all the terms which result from the requirements of good faith.[36]

The leading case on facts like those of the present case is a decision of the High Court in 1988.[37] There the defendant told the plaintiff of his present intention to move him abroad to a better job within the firm and, in reliance on this statement, the plaintiff gave up other opportunities for employment and also incurred expenses in relation to moving his residence abroad. The defendant then changed his mind regarding the plaintiff's move. In these circumstances, the Court held the defendant liable in damages to the plaintiff for his losses.

---

[33] Civ. Antwerpen 19 Mar. 1981, RW 1982–1983, 712; *Cour d'appel* (Appeal) Liège 6 Oct. 1988, JT 1989, 6; Kruithof/Bocken, TPR 1994, 305.

[34] Article 7 states: '(i) Rights must be exercised in conformity with the requirements of good faith. (ii) The law will not recognise the abuse of a right nor its anti-social exercise. Any action or omission which either in the intention of its author, in its purpose or in the circumstances in which it occurs manifestly surpasses the normal limits of the exercise of a right, to the prejudice of a third party, shall give rise to an appropriate compensation or to the adoption of judicial or administrative measures to prevent persistence in the abuse.'

[35] High Court judgements of 14 April 1944 (Col. Leg. 1944, n° 43), 25 October 1974 (RJA 1974, 3974), 22 April 1983 (RJA 1983, 2120).

[36] Article 1258 states: 'Contracts are concluded by agreement alone and moreover give rise to obligations not only to accomplish what has expressly been agreed, but also to all the results which, according to its nature, are in conformity with good faith, custom and the law.'   [37] Judgement of 16 May 1988 (17 CCJC 1988, 513).

It would depend on the circumstances whether the expenses which Hal & Sons have incurred in reliance on the contract going ahead may be recovered. While there is no conclusive authority on the question of the legal basis of such a claim (whether in delict or contract) and while Spanish courts do not indeed attach any importance to this question, most court judgements assume that the basis is delict under art. 1902 of the Civil Code. Hal & Sons would recover the cost of work done on the premises if the negotiations between the parties were so advanced, and the probability of a successful outcome to the bargaining process was so high, that a legitimate confidence arose on their part that the deal would be reached and the contract performed. Recovery is allowed only for expenses incurred by Hal & Sons which were rendered useless by the contract not going ahead, the Spanish courts not allowing recovery of a person's expectation interest under the head of precontractual liability.

The discussion so far has assumed that the two parties have not actually concluded a contract. However, on the facts of case 3, a Spanish court is most likely to be drawn to the conclusion that the parties have already come to an agreement and that an *oral* contract of lease should be held to have been made. In Spanish law, most contracts can be concluded without any written document or other specific form being required for their validity, and Spanish courts prefer to find that an oral contract has been concluded rather than to award damages for breach of the general duty of good faith.

ITALY

This is the classic situation to which the duty to negotiate in good faith, which is proclaimed by art. 1337 of the Civil Code, will apply.[38]

While Italian law accepts that the principle of freedom of contract requires that contractual negotiations may end without the conclusion of a contract (excepting the situation where the parties owe either a contractual or a legislative obligation to negotiate), it takes the view that the duty of good faith is broken where one party induces the other to rely on the contract going ahead, but then refuses to conclude it for no serious reason. In these circumstances, the party withdrawing from the negotiations is held liable to pay damages to the other party who has suffered loss as a result.

---

[38] See Sacco/De Nova, in: *Trattato Sacco II* 229. See also the Italian report to case 2 above.

In this respect, however, it should be noted that the existence of a more attractive deal offered by a third party (as on the particular facts of case 3) may be considered by the courts to be a good reason to refuse to go ahead with a contract to which the negotiations relate.[39] Nevertheless, where a prospective purchaser requests a seller of premises to make structural changes to the property offered for sale, and these changes are punctually carried out, any subsequent refusal to conclude the contract of sale by the prospective purchaser is invariably held to be contrary to good faith[40] and in these circumstances any consequential award of damages protects the reliance interest (*interesse negativo*) of the injured party.[41]

Finally, it should be noted that in Italian law the nature of the liability arising from breach of the duty to negotiate in good faith is generally considered to be delictual.[42]

THE NETHERLANDS

There is no article in the B.W. directly applicable to this situation. The answer is to be found in case law. According to the *Hoge Raad* the process of precontractual negotiations is governed by good faith (*redelijkheid en billijkheid*) and can be divided into three stages. During the initial stage the parties can withdraw from the negotiations without becoming liable. During the intermediate stage, where negotiations have been conducted for some time, a party can still walk away from the negotiating table, but has to bear the expenses of the other party (compensation for losses). During the last stage, where a party could justifiably expect that agreement would be reached, he can claim not only his expenses, but also the profit which he could have made if a contract would have been concluded. Cf. the *Plas v. Valburg* case and subsequent case law, as mentioned

---

[39] App. Venezia, 6 Jul. 1955, abridged in Giust. civ., Massimari annotati delle Corti d'Appello, 1518, n. 308; App. Venezia 1955, 97.

[40] Cass., 17 Jun. 1974, n. 1781; App. Roma, 30 Jan. 1976, Arch. civ., 1976, 1055, obs. Abbamonte.

[41] Cass., 25 Jan. 1988, n. 855; Cass., 12 Feb. 1982, n. 855. This is the prevailing opinion among scholars: Sacco/De Nova, in: *Trattato Sacco II* 256. Some writers hold that the measure of damages should be the expectation interest: Grisi 353; Benatti, Contr. e impr., 1987, 287; or that the reliance interest can be equal to the expectation interest: Luminoso, Contr. e impr., 1988, 792; Caruso 165 ff.

[42] Cass., 11 May 1990, n. 4051, Foro it., 1991, I, 184, obs. D. Caruso; Cass., 4 Mar. 1990, n. 2798, Giur. it., 1991, I,1, 455; Sacco/De Nova, in: *Trattato Sacco II* 255 (arguing that it must be so in view of the broad provision of art. 2043 c.c. on delictual liability). For the contrary opinion which supports the contractual nature of precontractual liability (following the lead of German law) see Rabello, in: *Aequitas* 463 (a particularly useful discussion); App. Milano, 2 Feb. 1990, Giur. comm., 1990, II, 755.

earlier;[43] and see the recent cases of *Hoge Raad* 14 June 1996, NJ 1997, 481 (*De Ruiterij v. MBO*) and *Hoge Raad* 4 October 1996, NJ 1997, 65 (*Combinatie v. De Staat*). This means that the expenses which Hal & Sons have incurred (wiring etc.) are to be paid by Falstaff. It could also mean that Hal & Sons can claim the profit they could have made if the final contract would have been concluded. In the latter case they will have to prove that the loss of profit they claim has been caused by the breakdown of the negotiations. Such a claim for lost profits has, until now, and as far as I know, not been finally awarded, although a preliminary award has been accepted in the *De Ruiterij v. MBO* case.

It is not really clear what constitutes the doctrinal basis for *Plas v. Valburg* and the later cases. It seems that the *Hoge Raad* followed a pragmatic approach, only indicating that in certain fact situations liability might ensue. The same can be said of the legal consequences of promises by, for example, government authorities (e.g. the promise to appoint someone as a civil servant): in certain fact situations liability might follow. No indication was given if the 'promise' by the government authority might be construed as, for example, a unilateral contract. What did appear to happen in the latter type of case is that doctrines developed in administrative law (protection of justified reliance) were in a sense 'transplanted' into civil law. These developments in case law have led to a fundamental debate about what the basis of liability in those situations might be. Is it good faith, tort or simply justified reliance?[44] There is no definite answer yet.

In the final drafting stage of the new Civil Code it was attempted to codify *Plas v. Valburg*. This attempt failed. It became, however, clear from the parliamentary debate that this failure did not mean that Parliament disapproved of the decision. It was thought that the legal consequences of broken-down negotiations were still too much in a state of development. Codification was therefore considered to be impossible; it should be left to the judiciary to develop the law further and to create more certainty in this area. This is what has in fact happened.[45]

ENGLAND

This case raises problems which are both difficult and controversial within modern English law. There are two possible bases on which recovery

---

[43] HR 18 June 1982, NJ 1983, 723, cited in the Dutch report to case 1 above.
[44] Cf. Van Erp; Menu; Smits; Vranken, all *passim*.
[45] See the cases mentioned above, in the first paragraph; and see Asser-Hartkamp, *Verbintenissenrecht II* nr. 158 ff., 160.

may be made by Hal & Sons in respect of the work which they have had done on their premises. A third possibility has been accepted by the High Court of Australia, but does not accord with general English authority.

The first basis of claim for Hal & Sons is to argue that there was a contract between themselves and Falstaff as to the carrying out of the work on the premises, despite the fact that there was no contract of lease of the premises concluded. This was the basis of the decision of the majority of the Court of Appeal in *Brewer Street Investments Ltd v. Barclays Woollen Co. Ltd.*[46] In that case, the defendants were prospective tenants of the plaintiffs' premises and, in the expectation, which was shared by both parties, that a lease would be agreed, had requested that the plaintiffs have certain work done on the premises which was otherwise of no benefit to them (e.g. putting in a new lift door). The defendants had, however, expressly undertaken that they would be responsible for the cost of this work. Before the work had been completed, it became clear that the lease would not be agreed as the parties could not agree upon a particular clause. The plaintiffs therefore stopped the work and sued for the amounts which they had paid to the contractors in respect of it. The Court of Appeal held that their contract to have the work done was not subject to any condition as to the agreement of the lease being concluded, since at the time either party (and in particular the defendant) could have chosen not to do so. It accepted that while there may be a strong argument for refusing recovery if the lease had not been concluded owing to the plaintiffs' fault (such as going for another tenant at a higher rent), this was not the case where it was caused by the defendants' own conduct in insisting on a term which they had known the plaintiffs were unwilling to accept or where neither party was responsible for the failure to make the contract.[47] The Court of Appeal nevertheless awarded recovery on the basis of a contractual *quantum meruit*, i.e. a reasonable sum for the work done (which was set at the amount which the plaintiffs had paid their contractors) as the defendants had agreed to pay for the cost of the work. Clearly, then, the difficulty with a contractual analysis in Hal's case is that there is no evidence of any clear undertaking of responsibility for the paying for the work, whether or not the lease is executed.

The second possible basis for recovery is by way of a claim for restitution. This was the basis of *Denning* L.J.'s decision in the *Brewer Street Investments* case.[48] The leading authority for such a claim is the decision of *Barry* J. in

---

[46] [1954] 1 QB 428.   [47] Ibid., especially at 433–4.   [48] Ibid., at 435 ff.

William Lacey (Hounslow) v. Davis.[49] There the plaintiffs were builders who had been told that they had submitted the lowest tender for work to be done on the defendant's premises and who had been led to believe that they would be offered the contract to do the work. They therefore agreed to do a number of further estimates which caused them considerable work and apparently increased the value of the premises (owing to regulatory provisions then in force). However, the defendants did not conclude a contract to do the building work with the plaintiffs, but instead sold the premises. *Barry J.* allowed the plaintiffs' claim for a *quantum meruit*, not on the basis of a contract, but rather in quasi-contract, i.e. in modern terms, in restitution. The basis for this recovery was that the plaintiffs had been requested by the defendants to do work in relation to the premises which had not been intended to be gratuitous but which was intended to be compensated for out of the profit which they would make out of the future contract, and that this work benefited the defendant.[50] The court allowed a 'fair remuneration' to the builders, but not one 'by reference to professional scales'. As *Burrows* has pointed out,[51] however, the application of such a restitutionary approach to a claim such as Hal's (or the one in *Brewer Street Investments*) faces the hurdle of an apparent absence of any benefit in Falstaff from the doing of the work on Hal's own premises by Hal: Falstaff & Co. have in no sense received the services involved in the doing of the work, even though they requested them. Other commentators, however, argue that cases like this 'do not depend upon the service adding to the defendant's wealth, the service *per se* is treated as a benefit'.[52]

The third possible basis of claim is promissory estoppel. According to this doctrine, a person who promises not to enforce his strict legal rights against another may be prevented from doing so, even where this promise was not supported by consideration.[53] However, in English law it has been made clear that this doctrine will not create a cause of action, but merely prevents the promisor from enforcing his right[54] (though an exception is made where the promise relates to the acquisition of rights in respect of another's land).[55] It is this restriction which means that estoppel will not help Hal & Sons, though it should be noted that the Australian High Court has indeed used estoppel in this way.[56]

---

[49] [1957] 1 WLR 932.   [50] Ibid., especially at 939.   [51] Burrows 297.
[52] Guest, *Chitty on Contracts* § 29–012; Birks, in: *Essays on Restitution* 105; Goff/Jones 671–3.
[53] *Hughes v. Metropolitan Rly Co.* (1877) 2 App Cas 439.   [54] *Combe v. Combe* [1951] 2 KB 215.
[55] *Crabb v. Arun District Council* [1976] Ch 179.
[56] *Walton Stores (Interstate) Ltd v. Maher* (1988) CLR 387, and see Burrows 298.

IRELAND

Hal & Sons' principal claim would be for restitution on the basis of *quantum meruit*. Irish law has gone somewhat further than its English equivalent in allowing a *quantum meruit* for work requested during negotiation, notwithstanding the fact that the work does not accrue to the benefit of the defendant (here Falstaff & Co.). The leading Irish case is *Folens & Co. v. Minister for Education*[57] in which the plaintiff publisher had been left with useless preparations for an encyclopaedia which the Department of Education had planned to publish. The difficulty of the current case from the restitutionary viewpoint is not only that the defendant has not been specifically benefited, but also that the plaintiff is left with *improved* premises. Nevertheless, the reasoning behind the decision in *Folens & Co.* was that the plaintiff would not have undertaken the requested work if the defendant had explicitly denied any liability for it pending the completion of negotiations for a binding contract and this reasoning applies equally to the facts of case 3.

Two further questions arise in the context of a restitutionary claim: (i) can damages be reduced to reflect the benefit accruing to the plaintiff as a result of his improved premises and (ii) may the plaintiff claim for some element of lost profits in addition to any expenditure made?

As to the first, there is Irish authority to suggest that any benefit conferred on a claimant for a restitutionary remedy will not reduce the award,[58] although the case in question may be distinguishable on the grounds that it did not deal with a *quantum meruit*, but with an action for recovery for total want of consideration of money paid under a contract which had failed. Since the decision in *Folens & Co.* marks the outer boundaries of the law of restitution, in that the defendant was in fact in no way enriched (whether justifiably or unjustifiably), it is highly probable that some allowance might be made for the general improvement to the plaintiff's position as a result of the requested alterations. It would, of course, be a question of fact as to whether and how much the premises would be improved for future letting by the work done by Hal & Sons.

As to the second question, *Folens & Co.* suggests that a claim for a *quantum meruit* in the context of unsuccessful negotiations towards contract may also include an element of lost profits, although the correctness of this aspect of the decision has been questioned.[59]

---

[57] [1984] ILRM 265.   [58] *United Dominions Trust (Ireland) v. Shannon Caravans Ltd* [1976] IR 225.
[59] Clark 491.

Apart from the claim in restitution, a second type of claim might relate to the enforcement of the seemingly complete but unsigned contract. In Irish law it is possible that a contract which was intended to be reduced to writing and signed, may none the less be enforceable notwithstanding the fact that signature of the final contract never took place. It is considered to be a matter of fact whether a contract arose before the signature of the final contract or whether the parties intended that no liability would be created until their agreement had been reduced to written form.[60] This factual question will look to the completeness of the negotiations and the understanding of the parties as regards their legal relations pending signature. However, analysis in terms of a complete but unsigned contract runs into difficulties on the facts of case 3, because contracts to grant leases of certain durations require to be in written form[61] or require to be evidenced in writing and to be signed by the person to be charged.[62]

SCOTLAND

It is questionable whether a contract exists in this case, as the words 'protracted negotiations' suggest that no *consensus in idem* has been reached. Falstaffs' requests regarding the work on the premises constitute a qualified acceptance of the original offer which has the effect of cancelling the original offer, so that the contract will only be formed if the counteroffer is met by an unqualified acceptance; *Wolf & Wolf v. Forfar Potato Co. Ltd.*[63] Hal & Sons must accept the counteroffer before the contract is concluded. Without their acceptance there is no contract. The principle of Scots law applies, that the offer (albeit a counteroffer) may be withdrawn at any time before acceptance; each party has the right to exercise *locus poenitentiae* (the opportunity of withdrawing).

However, in *Avintair Ltd v. Ryder Airline Services Ltd*,[64] the pursuers argued that a contract could be implied, based on part performance. The pursuers sought declarator of the existence of a contract and the debate centred on the question of whether the contract had yet to be performed or whether it had been executed to some extent. The alleged contract was for services and it was held that there was a distinction between a case where the alleged contract had yet to be performed and the case where services had

---

[60] *Pernod Ricard & Comrie plc v. FII Fyffes plc* (unreported, Supreme Court, 11 November 1988).
[61] Deasy's Act 1860, s. 4.
[62] Statute of Frauds (Ireland) 1695, s. 2 together with the rule in *Walsh v. Lonsdale* (1882) 21 Ch D 9.   [63] 1984 SLT 100.   [64] 1994 SLT 613.

been rendered. Furthermore, where one party performed his part without agreement having been reached as to remuneration, the law would imply from the conduct of the parties, a contract that a reasonable sum be paid. The appropriate claim, based on the implied contract, was one for *quantum meruit*; where services have been rendered or work has been performed without prior contractual agreement as to the amount to be paid for it, an action will lie for payment *quantum meruit* – a fair remuneration. This claim is based on the principle of unjustified enrichment which will be discussed below.[65] Thus it could be argued that an action on implied contract, involving a claim for *quantum meruit*, could lie here based on the part performance of the contract, i.e. the work done in the office space by Hal & Sons.

On the other hand, if it is shown that there is an agreement, then unless this lease is for a period of less than one year, this type of contract requires to be constituted in writing. If the requisite formalities are not complied with neither party is bound and each has *locus poenitentiae*. At first sight, as the lease has not been signed it would appear that Falstaff are legitimately exercising *locus poenitentiae* and Hal & Sons have no legal redress.

Under old Scots law (prior to the Requirements of Writing (Scotland) Act 1995), if such a contract had not been constituted in writing in the statutory prescribed way, the contract could be validated by the operation of the doctrines of personal bar known as *rei interventus* and *homologation*. The exception arises in that performance has followed on the agreement, i.e. the party acts on the strength of the agreement even though the necessary formalities have not been completed. The doctrine of personal bar is an equitable one and prevented a party from exercising *locus poenitentiae*.

With the passing of the Requirements of Writing (Scotland) Act 1995, with effect from 1 August 1995, these doctrines are abolished by s. 1(5) and have been replaced by a statutory form of *rei interventus*.[66] The new statutory rule stipulates that where there are contracts which ought to have been constituted in writing but were not, and one of the parties to the contract has acted or refrained from taking action in reliance on the contract with the knowledge and acquiescence of the other party to the contract, then the latter will not be entitled to withdraw from the contract and it will not be regarded as invalid for lack of formalities. But this

---

[65] See the Scottish report to cases 4, 14, 15, 17 and 26 below.

[66] The plea of personal bar, based on *rei interventus* and homologation, still remains at common law regarding those contracts to which the Requirements of Writing (Scotland) Act 1995 does not apply.

applies only if the position of the person in reliance has been affected to a material extent and if his position would be adversely affected to a material extent as a result of withdrawal by the other party. The operation of this principle hinges on there being an agreement. The problem is pre-contractual in a technical sense in that while the conduct of the party wishing to withdraw from the contract must be *after* the agreement, it takes place *before* the contract is constituted.

In other words, if Hal & Sons acted in reliance on negotiations with Falstaff and Falstaff knew of such actings, and furthermore, Hal & Sons have been affected to a material extent and will be adversely affected to a material extent by Falstaff & Co. backing out of taking on the lease, then Falstaff & Co. will not be able to withdraw as the new form of statutory bar will come into operation.

DENMARK AND NORWAY

The starting point must be that as long as no binding agreement of lease has been concluded, the lessor makes investments to render the premises suitable for an intended lessee at his own risk. West Nordic law does, however, recognise that liability for damages may arise also in a pre-contractual phase, in keeping with the principles of *culpa in contrahendo*.[67] A claim for damages may not be based merely on the fact that somebody, who responds to an offer to lease office premises, eventually turns to another lessor. Since, however, the parties here appear to have become involved with each other to such an extent that the intended lessee has asked for repairs to be done to the premises, the break-off of the negotiations will have to occur in a loyal manner. If the lessor had not been clearly told that the lessee was about to conclude a contract with another party, and had not been given a reasonable opportunity to make an offer in order still to have a chance of winning the contract, there is much to be said in favour of liability to compensate for the investments made.

A doctrine of precontractual liability for damages appears to be gaining wider acceptance in the West Nordic countries. Central court rulings here are two judgements by the Swedish *Högsta Domstolen* (Highest Court) in NJA 1963, p. 105 and NJA 1990, p. 745. The earlier case involved a Swedish businessman who stated his interest in the post of day-to-day manager of a Colombian company. Negotiations were held with the main shareholder

---

[67] Simonsen 149 ff.

of the company. On 30 June the main shareholder sent a cable in which he asked the Swedish businessman to report to the company in Colombia on 1 July of the same year. Under Colombian law, however, this required approval by the General Meeting which could only be obtained on the 15th of that same month. Relying on what had occurred, the Swedish businessman moved to Colombia and took up the post. Due to disagreements between the two main groups of shareholders, approval of the General Meeting was never given. The Swedish businessman claimed reimbursement from the main shareholder for his expenses in moving to Colombia, a claim that was accepted by the *Högsta Domstolen*. The judgement places substantial emphasis on the cable being sent by the main shareholder at a time when he was in considerable doubt as to whether the General Meeting would approve the appointment.

The ruling in NJA 1990, p. 745, continues this line of argument. The judgement reinforces the notion of duties owed by the parties in the precontractual stage reasonably to take account of each other's interests. The ruling presupposes that there is a requirement of loyal behaviour also prior to the conclusion of binding agreements. In Norwegian law it is in particular Rt. 1981, p. 462 which shows that justified reliance may enjoy protection in general liability law. In addition to this there are a number of decisions in contract law where non-compliance with the rules concerning competitive bids in invitations to tender has given rise to claims for damages.

As mentioned initially, precontractual liability has not yet found a firm basis in legal usage in the West Nordic countries. Recently, however, a major doctoral thesis has been published by *Lasse Simonsen*[68] which must be expected to be of importance to the further development of the law in this field.

SWEDEN

Of interest in Swedish Supreme Court practice is, in the first place, NJA 1963, p. 105. Here, a 50 per cent shareholder of a company encouraged a person to leave his business in another country to start working as a central executive officer of that company, although the shareholder knew that an appointment required a majority among the shareholders and that it was most unlikely that his partner, who also held 50 per cent of the shares, would agree to the appointment. Damages were awarded.

---

[68] *Prekontraktuelt ansvar* (1997).

In NJA 1978, p. 147 the owner of certain real estate and a company, which was looking for a place to start a grocer's shop, agreed orally that a new building should be erected according to the wishes of the company, and that the parties were to agree later on the terms of the lease. The company changed its plans after a market investigation, which allegedly showed that the business would be less profitable than expected. According to the Supreme Court there was no binding lease agreement, since too many details were left open (the lower courts had ruled that written form had been agreed upon). Nor was there an agreement to compensate for costs incurred, or a usage to the same effect. Therefore, the oral agreement had created only a duty to co-operate towards the conclusion of a contract of lease, with due consideration of the other party's interests. The Supreme Court then stated that both parties knew that the contract was dependent on a number of uncertainties and that their co-operation therefore involved a risk, especially on the owner's side when he adjusted the building to the company's wishes. The company had certainly been obliged to act loyally in giving a definite decision before the owner incurred considerable costs, and to keep the owner informed about how the matter progressed on the company's side. In other respects, however, the company could presuppose that in a business relationship of this kind the other party could safeguard his own interests. The only obligation on the company was to negotiate effectively and to inform the other party without delay when it had decided not to contract. The company was not deemed to have breached these duties. It ought to be noted that the company was not taken to have been obliged to rent the premises unless the conditions offered would be unreasonable, and that the risk for changed market conditions was not transferred to the company by way of the oral agreement. See also NJA 1973, p. 175 and 1990, p. 745.

As I understand the present case, it is presupposed that Falstaff & Co. was not bound, by agreement or otherwise, to rent until a written contract was signed. Hal & Sons incurred their expenses before Falstaff & Co. changed their plans and before they had any reason to believe that they might not rent the premises. It is not established that Hal & Sons incurred considerable costs due to the fact that Falstaff & Co. negligently prolonged their deliberations. Falstaff & Co. informed Hal & Sons without delay after having received the better offer. Hence, Hal & Sons are entitled neither to the conclusion of a contract of lease nor to compensation.

The doctrine of compensation for expenses due to *culpa in contrahendo* is narrowly construed in Swedish law. It should be noticed, however, that the law is more protective in holding a party bound to a contract, who has taken part in negotiations which have led to the other party mistakenly believing the contract to have been concluded and who now, being aware of this mistake, observes the other party acting in reliance on his mistaken belief. This rule is based on s. 6 of the Contracts Act of 1915.[69]

It might also be added that, under Swedish law, a negligent person has to pay compensation for damage to goods or persons, whereas non-criminal negligence causing pure economic loss *in contrahendo*, as a rule, does not result in damages.[70]

FINLAND

This is a case the outcome of which would depend on facts that are not fully supplied in the report. An offer (e.g. to rent) is binding. A Finnish court would perhaps consider that an *oral agreement* (this would be sufficient) had already been reached and would therefore let Falstaff & Co. pay damages, i.e. the costs of installation minus the value of the installation for Hal & Sons. Otherwise Hal & Sons have acted at their own risk: if there is no contract so far but only negotiations are under way, there is no liability. It is also possible that a court would seriously consider the possibility that the investment was the final incentive intended to make Falstaff & Co. conclude the contract. In such a situation it is even more evident that Falstaff & Co. are not liable.

As for the line to be drawn between binding and non-binding discussions I refer to the Finnish discussion in cases 20 and 21. Even if there were no binding contract, there might be reasons justifying some kind of recompense (*negatives Interesse*). See my comments in the Finnish discussion of cases 4 and 5.

Editors' comparative observations

All the legal systems under consideration except for Swedish (and possibly Finnish) law give to the owners (Hal & Sons) some recourse in respect of the work which they have done. Were the facts of this case to be altered slightly, Sweden would also grant some recourse. The measure of recovery allowed in those legal systems which allow an award of damages is the 'negative interest,' i.e. an award whose aim it is to put the owner in the position as if he had not relied on a contract coming into existence. Only

---

[69] See, e.g., NJA 1977, p. 92 (investments in reliance on a distribution agreement).
[70] See Hellner, *Skadeståndsrätt* 66 ff., and Kleineman, *passim*.

the law of the Netherlands allows the *possibility* of recovery on the basis of the 'positive interest', i.e. to put the owner in the position as though the contract had been made and had been performed (though the possibility of damages for loss of the chance of the contract going ahead has also been raised in the Belgian report). Various doctrinal analyses are used to come to these results.

(i) Austrian, German and West Nordic law rely on the notion of *culpa in contrahendo*, whose key element in the present circumstances is the protection of reliance by the owners. In the case of German law, good faith defines the duties whose breach is remedied by *culpa in contrahendo*. Greek law grants a claim on the basis of a statutory version of *culpa in contrahendo*. Swedish law (which denies recovery on the facts of case 3) does recognise *culpa in contrahendo* as a basis of recovery of damages, but takes a very narrow view of its ambit.

(ii) Dutch law and Italian law would see this case as a straightforward example of a requirement of good faith in negotiations. The Italian and the Greek codes contain a specific provision extending the principle of good faith to the stage of precontractual negotiation. Dutch law proceeds from the same premises, though it regarded codification as premature.

(iii) French and Spanish law both rely on a combination of the notion of the abuse of rights and general provisions governing liability in delict. The French approach concentrates in this respect either on the wrongdoing of the would-be lessee *or* the reliance on the contract going ahead by the owners.

(iv) English, Irish and Scots law rely on restitutionary recovery, though in English law concern has been expressed that it is inappropriate to allow recovery on this ground given that it is measured by the reasonable cost of the work done rather than by any apparent benefit to the 'recipient' of the services.

(v) A Belgian court may well see the contract as formed in the circumstances of case 3, but, if so, an attempt to enforce it would be considered abusive with the result that only damages would be recoverable by the owners, these being based on the costs incurred by them to the extent to which they have not increased the value of the building and any lost bargain. Spanish courts may also come to the conclusion that a contract has already come into existence.

Case 4: Formalities I

Case

Paul, a pensioner who does not have much experience in business trans-actions, wants to acquire a piece of property with a house on it. He invests all his savings in this transaction. Eric, an entrepreneur, concludes a con-tract in writing with Paul and explains to Paul that no further formalities are required. After Paul has paid the purchase price, Eric refuses to trans-fer the property. He argues that the contract is null and void in view of the lack of notarial authentication. According to § 313 BGB, such authentica-tion was indeed required.

Discussions

GERMANY

The contract of sale suffers from a formal defect since it has not been notarially authenticated in terms of § 313, 1 BGB. Normally, a contract that does not comply with the formalities prescribed by statute is void (§ 125, 1 BGB). Nevertheless, Eric has to transfer the property in compliance with the contract if § 242 BGB prevents him from invoking the lack of notarial authentication. Transfer of the property would 'cure' the formal defect (§ 313, 2 BGB: 'A contract concluded without observance of [the required form] becomes valid in its entirety if transfer and registration in the land register have taken place').

According to the prevailing view recourse may indeed be had to § 242 BGB if the result would otherwise not only be unfair but totally unbear-able (*schlechthin untragbar*). Legal certainty which normally requires strict compliance with the prescribed formalities may then be sacrificed in the interests of individual justice.[1] The requirement of a totally unbearable result has been seen to be met especially in two types of cases: where the existence of the one party would be destroyed or substantially endangered, or where the other party would gravely offend against good faith by invoking the formal defect.[2]

Paul has an enrichment claim arising under § 812 I 1, first alternative BGB for repayment of the price. His existence is, accordingly, not endangered.[3]

A grave infringement of the precepts of good faith is seen to exist where one party intentionally, i.e. in the knowledge that the contract had to be authenticated, prevented the other from complying with that formality so as to ensure that he could later on invoke the defect.[4] It may be accepted that Eric, an entrepreneur, had the necessary experience to know about the formal requirement. He is therefore barred by § 242 BGB from relying on the invalidity of the contract and will have to transfer the property to Paul.

If, however, Eric had only caused the non-compliance with the formal requirement, and hence the invalidity of the contract, negligently, a claim in terms of *culpa in contrahendo* may lie against him. In contradistinction to other *culpa in contrahendo* cases, Paul could, according to the prevailing opinion, claim the positive interest if the contract, but for Eric's negligence, would have complied with the necessary formalities.[5] That does not, however, mean that Paul may demand conclusion of a valid contract (by way of restoration in kind according to § 249 BGB); only damages may be claimed.[6]

GREECE

According to Greek law, notarial authentication is required for a contract of sale of land (art. 369 Gr. C.C.). If the contract does not comply with this formality, it is void according to art. 159 Gr. C.C. Therefore, Paul cannot

---

[1] BGHZ 29, 6 (10); 48, 396 (398); 85, 315 (318 f.); BGH NJW 1987, 1069 (1070); *Palandt*/Heinrichs § 125, n. 16; *Münchener Kommentar*/Förschler § 125, n. 50.

[2] BGHZ 85, 315 (318 f.); BGH NJW 1987, 1069 (1070); and see *Münchener Kommentar*/Förschler § 125, nn. 55 ff. This approach has predominantly been criticised in legal literature; cf. the discussion in: Medicus, *Bürgerliches Recht* nn. 181 ff. At the same time, relatively few authors argue that § 242 may not be resorted to at all in cases of invalidity due to § 125 BGB: cf. the references in *Münchener Kommentar*/Förschler § 125, nn. 52 ff.

[3] Cf. *Palandt*/Heinrichs § 125, n. 25.   [4] Cf. BGHZ 29, 6 (12).

[5] *Münchener Kommentar*/Förschler § 125, n. 48 with further references; for a different view, see Medicus, *Bürgerliches Recht* n. 184.   [6] *Münchener Kommentar*/Förschler §125, n. 48.

demand transfer of the property. Nor, of course, has he become owner, since transfer of ownership of land must comply with the formal requirements of art. 1033 Gr. C.C. However, Paul was a pensioner who did not have experience in business transactions, and who has invested all his savings in this transfer of property. Eric, on the other hand, was an entrepreneur, who knew the formal requirements and nevertheless concluded his contract with Paul in writing only. Moreover, he specifically pointed out to Paul that no further formalities were required. Although Paul paid the purchase price, Eric subsequently refused to transfer the property. According to art. 281 Gr. C.C., Eric's conduct could constitute an abuse of right.

Courts and academic writers in Greece are predominantly opposed to the application of art. 281 Gr. C.C. to cases of a contract being void for lack of notarial authentication.[7] However, it is accepted that there are a few cases where non-compliance with the prescribed formalities does not lead to nullity.[8] In our case, Eric's conduct is so evidently abusive (*venire contra factum proprium*), that he must be compelled by the courts to transfer the property.[9] It should also be noted that in Greek law no equivalent of § 313, 2 of the German BGB[10] exists. This means that the registration of a transfer of land in the land register on the basis of a contract of sale merely in writing is not possible: the registration office would not accept such contract. So Paul has to obtain a court decision which he might then submit to the registration office.

All in all, therefore, Paul has (i) a claim to have the property transferred to him, based on art. 281 Gr. C.C.; or (ii) a claim to recover what he paid as purchase price (art. 904 Gr. C.C.) (enrichment claim). In addition, there might be (iii) a claim for compensation on the basis of *culpa in contrahendo* (arts. 197–8 Gr. C.C.) and (iv) a claim for compensation in terms of the law of torts (arts. 914 ff. Gr. C.C.).[11]

AUSTRIA

By way of preliminary observation to the following discussion, it must be noted that in general there are no formal requirements for contracts in

---

[7] See Areopagus 107/1961 NoB 9, 889; Areopagus 224/1966 NoB 14, 1104.

[8] Areopagus 1274/1989 EEN 57, 503.   [9] Cf. Areopagus 1274/1989, ibid.

[10] On which, see the German report, above.

[11] For literature regarding the case, see: Simantiras no. 687, pp. 511–12. See also the following leading cases: Areopagus 203/1971 NoB 19, 729; Areopagus 241/1963 NoB 11, 1068; Areopagus 464/1969 NoB 18, 49 (*venire contra factum proprium*); Areopagus 764/1996 EllDni 38, 575.

Austrian law,[12] these resulting therefore only from special legislative provisions or as a result of the agreement of the parties to the contract in question. More particularly, and in contrast to the position in Germany, in Austrian law the sale of real property is not subject to any formal requirements. Nevertheless, the legal problems which are raised by the facts of case 4 do arise in Austrian law where it does exceptionally lay down some requirement of form. The following discussion will, therefore, proceed on the basis that contracts for the sale of real property *do* indeed require a special form, this discussion drawing on the positions reached in relation to other formal requirements.

First, it should be noted that defects of form in general lead to the invalidity of the contract. Although this result is not expressly provided for by the law in relation to all contracts,[13] it does none the less always follow unless the law otherwise provides.[14] For this reason, we should assume that any defect of form in case 4 invalidates the contract.

Secondly, defects of form may be remedied by subsequent performance of the contract under § 1432 ABGB. However, this rule does not help Paul in case 4, for where a contract is by its nature bilateral, any defect in it may be cured only if *both* the parties to it have rendered performance. While an exception is made to this requirement of double performance where the formal requirement in question serves solely to protect one of the parties to the contract, were Austrian law to require a specific form for the purchase of land, this would certainly protect the seller as well as the buyer. Since Eric has not yet performed his side of the contract, the conditions for the application of § 1432 ABGB are not satisfied.

However, it should be added that some scholars take the view, in line with the German position, that a party to a contract should not be allowed to invoke a defect of form, if the formal requirement is aimed solely at protecting his interests and if this party, being aware of the requirement of form, nevertheless concludes an informal contract so as to put the other party at a disadvantage.[15] This view is supported by the argument that the formal requirement does not aim at protecting a person who deceives the other. Even though any formal requirement in case 4 would be aimed not

---

[12] § 883 ABGB.
[13] Cf. e.g. § 1 NZwG (Statute on official recording of a contract); §§ 601, 1346 sec. 2 ABGB.
[14] Cf. §§ 24, 32 sec. 1 KSchG (Consumer Protection Act): the violation of the form provided for instalment plan transactions does not affect the validity of the contract, but leads to the imposition of an administrative penalty.
[15] Berger, in: *Gutachten* 80 f.; Wilhelm, *Vertretung* 190 ff. In the same sense, Gschnitzer/Faistenberger/Barta, *Allgemeiner Teil* 742, who expressly argue on good faith.

only at protecting the interests of the seller, but also those of the buyer, such an approach would probably entitle Paul to claim performance of the contract on the basis that he already performed his side of the agreement and therefore 'cured the defect of form' on his side within the meaning of § 1432 ABGB.

The prevailing view[16] in Austria does not accept this line of argument, pointing out that, quite apart from their main purpose in protecting the parties to contracts, formal requirements often also serve other specific aims, for example, the provision of evidence on which third party interests may be established or, more generally, the support of legal certainty. According to this view, a contract suffering from a defect in form must be held invalid even in the case of deceit by one of its parties.

Thirdly, however, even if this strict view is accepted, Paul would not be without protection, for Eric will be liable to him on the basis of *culpa in contrahendo* if he was aware or should have been aware of the formal requirement and therefore culpably misled Paul in relation to it. In the case of deceit, Eric would be liable for the losses which he has caused by acting *contra bonos mores*. Moreover, even where the parties would, if duly informed of the formal requirement, have concluded the contract as required, the dominant view holds that he may recover damages only in respect of losses incurred in reliance on the validity of the contract.[17] For if Paul were entitled to claim damages so as to put him into the position as though the contract had been performed, this would amount in effect to the recognition of the existence of a valid contract via the mechanism of damages and would thus ignore the purpose of the formal requirement.

In conclusion, therefore, according to the prevailing Austrian view, Paul could only claim (i) restitution of the purchase price which he has paid on the ground of Eric's unjust enrichment and (ii) compensation for expenses incurred in reliance on the validity of the contract on the ground of Eric's wrongful behaviour in relation to the formalities.

FRANCE

Eric's argument is that there is no valid contract of sale since it has not been authenticated by a notary. This is not true in French law since, as a

---

[16] Koziol/Welser, *Bürgerliches Recht I* 152; Mader, *Rechtsmißbrauch* 267; in the same sense now Wilhelm, NZ 1994, 251 f.; cf. also Häsemeyer 294 ff.

[17] Berger, in: *Gutachten* 84 ff.; Wilhelm, *Vertretung* 192 ff. Mader, *Rechtsmißbrauch* 268 ff. considers compensation for the non-performance of the contract in exceptional cases.

general principle, no formal requirements are made for the conclusion of a contract of sale[18] although a formal document is required for the buyer of immovable property to obtain full title, good against third parties.[19] It follows that any formal requirements which must be fulfilled in order for Paul to obtain good title against third parties do not affect the validity of a simple written document between the parties as a contract of sale. Eric is therefore obliged to transfer the property to Paul.

Despite the lack of formality as required by law, Paul and Eric have made a contract called a promise of sale (*promesse de vente*). Such a contract is deemed bilateral, if, as is the case here, both the seller (Eric) and the buyer (Paul) have undertaken to sell and buy respectively. Provided that the parties have agreed upon the essential elements of the sale (the subject matter, the property, and the price pursuant to art. 1583 of the Civil Code), the promise constitutes, in principle, a valid sale.[20] This rule is the result of case law.[21]

On the facts, therefore, Paul has a choice between two remedies, namely, (i) specific enforcement of the contract of sale by asking for a court order which is equivalent to a notarially authenticated act of sale (*acte authentique*) or, if this is no longer possible, (ii) termination of the contract and restitution of his savings paid over to Eric. In both cases Paul can claim, in addition, damages for breach of contract. If Paul successfully obtains the court order he will become full owner of the property from the date on which he paid the purchase price to Eric.[22] If Eric's disloyal behaviour has no effect on Paul's title to the property then it is unnecessary for his behaviour to be legally sanctioned. If, however, Paul suffers a loss due to the non-registration of the transfer which would not have occurred had he and Eric signed a notarially authenticated document upon payment of the price, he may claim damages from Eric.

French law does not directly use the principle of good faith to solve the problems created by an unscrupulous use of knowledge of legal formalities against an intellectually weaker party. Theoretically, a remedy would be available to Paul on the grounds of *réticence dolosive*[23] but this would not provide him with a satisfactory solution as it could lead only to annulment of the contract and/or damages. Formal requirements for contracts for the sale of land are aimed at providing protection for purchasers

---

[18] Art. 1583 C. civ.   [19] *Décret* no. 55–22 of 4 January 1955, art. 4.   [20] Art. 1589 C. civ.
[21] Civ. 9 Dec. 1930, DP 1931.1.118 confirmed recently in Civ. (3) 5 Jan. 1983, *Steinlen*, D 1983.617 note P. Jourdain; Civ. (3) 14 Jan. 1987, D 1988.80 note J. Schmidt.
[22] Art. 1589 al. 3 C. civ.   [23] Art. 1116 C. civ. and see the French report to case 2 above.

against third parties, but paradoxically they enable a stronger contracting party to take advantage of the other and so defeat this protective purpose. In this respect, the principle of good faith in the creation of a contract is perhaps not sufficiently developed by French courts to be of any help in supplementing existing legal remedies. In the event of a seller's bad faith leading to a second sale, a dilemma arises as to whether the law should protect the original promisee or the third party who has acquired the land. This more frequent situation is raised only by inference on the facts of case 4. In French law, priority is given on the basis of the good faith of the third party. In the sort of situation found in case 4, the seller's good faith is not at issue since its absence is self-evident. French law does not appear to have recognised the need to develop a particular remedy or sanction to reinforce the protection of a purchaser not only against third parties but also directly against the seller. This case illustrates the insufficiency of the remedy of annulment as a protective measure for the innocent party.

BELGIUM

(i) Belgian law does not require notarial authentication for a contract of sale, not even of a house. The formalities prescribed by statute have nothing to do with the sales contract (*Verpflichtungsgeschäft*), but only with the transfer of property (*Verfügungsgeschäft*) (in Belgian law seen as performance of the obligation of the seller). More specifically, formalities are only relevant in case of conflict with third parties who also claim to have rights with respect to the same goods.

There are only a few cases where the conclusion of a contract is subject to formalities. The only one which is similar to case 4 concerns contributions to a corporation or company.[24] Even here, it may well be possible that there is a valid promise to contribute; the formality is a problem of company law (capital) rather than contract law.

In contracts of employment, formalities are imposed for the validity of certain types of clauses, e.g. non-competition clauses. Moreover, there is a growing number of formalities in consumer protection legislation (but not relating to the sale of land or houses).

(ii) Where there are formalities in Belgian contract law, they are nearly always specifically imposed for the protection of one of the parties; only

---

[24] Co-ordinated Statutes on Companies of 30 November 1935, art. 4, art. 2 as amended by an Act of 20 July 1991, and art. 11 *bis*, as inserted by an Act of 6 March 1973.

that party may then invoke the invalidity of the contract. Thus, we are dealing with cases of a 'relative invalidity' rather than an 'absolute invalidity' (as we find them with regard to formalities imposed for reasons of 'public order'). If there were such a formality for the sale of a house, it would be necessary to analyse whether it is imposed for the protection of the seller or the buyer, or both ('relative' invalidity), or in the interest of public order ('absolute' invalidity). Such a formality could also form part of consumer protection legislation; in that case, only the consumer could invoke the lack of form. This position probably differs from the one adopted in German or Dutch law, where the lack of formality is normally sanctioned with 'absolute' invalidity.

One of the consequences of the relativity of invalidity is that the contract may be confirmed by the protected party from the moment when the reason for his protection has fallen away. Thus, for example, an employee can confirm agreements which were not binding because of the lack of formality, from the moment when he is no longer an employee. In other cases, parties are protected against precipitate promises which have to be performed only later; the protection ceases when the promise is voluntarily performed (thus, for example, formless promises of gift are in principle not binding; however, once the promise has been performed, the donor cannot invoke the lack of formality any longer).

Where a contract is void, this will evidently give rise to a claim for restitution of any payment already effected. Eric would then certainly have to restore the price.

(iii) Moreover, the invalidity of a contract does not exclude a precontractual liability of one of the parties, e.g. for misrepresentation (as a form of *culpa in contrahendo* or, more precisely, as part of the duty to inform, which implies also a duty not to give incorrect information). Eric, being a professional, will normally be held liable to Paul for all damages caused to Paul by his misrepresentation (consisting of his explanation that no further formalities are required). However, he could argue that there was contributory negligence on the part of Paul; this would lead to a reduction in the amount of compensation. This is only different in cases of fraud. Fraud requires that Eric intentionally provided incorrect information.

In this case, there seems to be misrepresentation as to whether notarial authentication is necessary. In other cases, the purchaser may simply rely on the seller's willingness to honour his promise, even though it is not binding. Here there would be no precontractual liability.

In the case of precontractual liability on the part of Eric, Paul will be compensated for his negative interest only.

(iv) Theoretically, it can constitute an abuse of right and thus be contrary to good faith to invoke the invalidity because of a lack of formality. But compared to German case law, Belgian law seems rather restrictive. The problem does not so much concern the question as to when there is an abuse of right; here the normal standards apply. Thus, it is certainly abusive if one party prevents the other from complying with the formalities required, or induces the other not to comply with these formalities and then to invoke the invalidity of the contract. The main problem lies in the way in which this abuse is sanctioned.

A decision of the *Hof van cassatie* in 1994[25] dealt with a limitation of rights of an employee under a labour contract, which could only be agreed upon in writing and before the commencement of the labour contract. The employee himself asked for it and telephoned the employer abroad, who agreed. Later the employee refused to recognise the validity of the clause, which had been put into writing only after the beginning of performance. The *Hof van cassatie* did not refuse to acknowledge the abuse of right on the part of the employee but found it inappropriate to sanction the abuse by simply accepting the clause as valid. This was based on an incorrect reasoning, proceeding from a correct rule. The correct rule, as found in the case law of the Court itself, states that the sanction of an abuse of right must not extend beyond what is necessary to remedy the abuse; thus, the sanction should consist in restricting the use of the right to a use which is not abusive. In the 1994 case, however, the Court decided that, as the sanction of an abuse of right consists in restricting the right, it may not consist in setting aside the right as such. The abuse therefore remained unsanctioned.

We must not forget, however, that Belgian case law has rarely been obliged to think about the sanction of such an abuse because, as pointed out above, there are only few cases where formalities are imposed (with the exception of a growing number of formalities for the protection of consumers).

(v) Even for an inexperienced person, it must be regarded as very careless to pay the price for a house to the other party before transfer of property has occurred. Although the sale is binding, there evidently is a risk for the buyer as long as the formalities for the transfer of property (*erga omnes*) are not fulfilled (particularly the prospect of the seller's insolvency). Hardly any Belgian buyer would pay more than a small advance.

---

[25] Cass. 7 Feb. 1994, JTT 1994, 208.

Abuses of the kind contemplated in the present case have arisen mainly where the seller still had to build the house, and eventually never did so (or did not complete it). Parliament has intervened to protect acquirers of houses, apartments, etc. who paid before completion of the house or apartment.[26] No payment whatsoever may be asked for by the contractor before a written contract has been signed (but the invalidity can only be invoked by the protected buyer; the contractor cannot refuse to perform the contract for lack of a written instrument); criminal and administrative sanctions are provided by law. Moreover, the contractor has to provide security in the form prescribed by law.

SPAIN

Article 1280.5 of the Civil Code requires that contracts whose object is the transfer of title to land should be notarially authenticated, but Spanish courts have always taken the view that this formal requirement does not go to the validity of the contract.[27] Thus, contracts of this type are completed by the sole agreement of the parties, and so create contractual duties as soon as one party's offer has been accepted. Formal requirements become significant only at the stage of the performance of the contract with the result that either party may require the other to have their contract (which is already valid!) authenticated in proper notarial form. If a party fails to do so when requested, the other, 'innocent' party may apply to the court for an order to this effect.

This approach is taken more generally, so that when formal requirements bring about inequitable consequences for a party who acts in good faith, Spanish courts usually refuse to view these requirements as essential conditions going to the validity of the contract and therefore allow the contract in question to be made by simple oral offer and acceptance. There are, however, a few situations in which, as a matter of law, formal requirements clearly go to the validity of the contract. In these types of cases, the courts hold that it is contrary to good faith for a party to an agreement to take advantage of its lack of proper form where (i) he was himself responsible for this deficiency, (ii) he fails to remedy the

---

[26] Act of 9 July 1971, as amended by an Act of 3 May 1993; the legislation will also be adapted to implement the E.C. Directive on the protection of acquirers of timeshares, viz. 94/47/EEC of 26 October 1994.

[27] High Court judgements 4 July 1899 (Col. Leg. 1899, nº 128), 19 October 1901 (Col. Leg. 1901, nº 87), and a great number of later judgements.

informality by executing the proper form when required to do so by the other party, or (iii) he voluntarily performs the obligations arising from the contract even though he is aware of the defect.[28] Finally, in cases where the invalidity of a contract is caused by the failure of a party to give written notice to the other, the courts consider it contrary to good faith for that other party to complain of this lack of form where he has had knowledge of the contents of such a notice by some other means.[29]

ITALY

In Italian law putting a contract for the sale of land in signed writing is in principle a sufficient formality to effect the transfer of title from seller to buyer.[30] Nevertheless, registration of the contract of sale with the land registry remains highly significant,[31] for while it is neither necessary nor sufficient to pass title, where registration is not effected the title to the property which the buyer receives is defeasible by registration of a subsequent sale of the same property by the same seller to another buyer.[32] Moreover, only notarised sales and contracts in signed writing in which the parties' signatures are authenticated by a notary can be registered immediately in the land register,[33] though the possibility exists for 'private' documents bearing the signature of the parties to be authenticated by way of judicial proceedings which establish in law their authenticity.[34] Not surprisingly, most sales of immovables in Italy are made in the notarial form in order to obtain a quick registration of the transaction.

In the result, in Italian law the contract between Paul and Eric does indeed transfer title to Paul, though he will not be able to register it in the

---

[28] High Court judgements of, *inter alia*, 23 May 1987 (RJA 1987, 3557), 22 December 1990 (RJA 1990, 10364), 6 April 1996 (RJA 1996, 2881).

[29] High Court judgement of 25 October 1993 (RJA 1993, 7657).   [30] Arts. 1350 ff. c.c.

[31] Arts. 2643 ff. c.c.

[32] Art. 2644 c.c. The Italian system of land registration derives from the French model. For further analysis of differences between the two models, see Chianale, *Obbligazione* 149 ff., 178 ff. A different system of land registration, based on the Austrian law, still operates in some Italian provinces which were formerly under Austrian rule (Bolzano, Trento, Trieste, Gorizia). Note that art. 3.1 of d.lgt. 31 Dec. 1996, n. 699, converted into l. 28 Feb. 1997, n. 30, introduced into the Civil Code art. 2645 *bis*. This article allows the registration of contracts which make it binding upon the parties to conclude a subsequent sale of land, thus enhancing the protection of the promisee *vis-à-vis* the promisor's creditors and other third parties.   [33] Cf. art. 2657 c.c.

[34] Art. 2652, n. 3 c.c. Here interim protection for the buyer may be provided by registration of the action pending.

land register because it was neither notarised nor authenticated by a notary. This means that Paul's ownership of the land is liable to be defeated by Eric's subsequent sale of the same land to another buyer, though such a risk will materialise only if that subsequent buyer registers his contract before Paul. In order to minimise this risk, Paul should start judicial proceedings promptly to have the sale document authenticated, as well as make sure that he registers this pending action without delay.

Having said all this about the actual legal position in Italian law on the facts as they are described in case 4, it remains useful to indicate what the position would be in Italy if the contractual sale between Paul and Eric lacked whatever form were required for its validity.

In this respect, the relevant provisions of the Civil Code are quite clear. First, the defect of form results in invalidity of the contract of sale.[35] Secondly, any subsequent performance of the contract does not cure the defect, though the law on acquisitive prescription may help a person in possession of the land in question to establish title after the passing of a considerable period of time.[36] Thirdly, any money paid pursuant to such an invalid contract can be recovered with interest.[37]

A more controversial question is whether Paul can claim the land, or at least damages, on some ground other than the contract itself.

A starting point here is that Paul did not know that the contract was void, whereas Eric, who is in business, either was in fact, or ought to have been, aware of the problem of formality. The result of these circumstances is that Eric ought to have informed Paul of the need to comply with the requirement of form, a duty which is expressly recognised and the breach of which is expressly sanctioned by art. 1338 of the Civil Code. This provision states that '[a] party who knows or ought to know the existence of a reason for the invalidity of the contract and who does not give notice to the other party is bound to compensate any harm suffered by the latter in relying, without fault, on the validity of the contract'. This article obviously is a specific expression of the general provision in the Code which proclaims the duty to negotiate in good faith.[38] Traditionally, Italian

---

[35] Arts. 1325, 1350 c.c.
[36] The relevant term is twenty years (art. 1158 c.c.). Shorter terms apply in other cases regulated by the Code.
[37] By an action *in ripetizione dell'indebito* pursuant to art. 2033 c.c. The notion of invalidity under the Civil Code provisions relating to contracts in general corresponds with the German notion of *Nichtigkeit*, rather than with the French concept of *nullité absolue*. The claimant will not have to go to court to annul the contract. For comparative remarks on this topic: Guarneri, Riv. dir. civ., 1993, I, 41.   [38] Art. 1337 c.c.

courts have considered that ignorance of formal requirements laid down by legislation by a party to a contract is in itself blameworthy (and there-fore 'fault' for the purposes of art. 1338) and undeserving of relief[39] under this provision and, while this position has been criticised by scholars,[40] this approach would without more leave Paul without a remedy other than restitution of the money paid. In the present case, however, there is more, for Eric did not simply omit to inform Paul about the need to comply with the requirement of form, but positively stated to him that the contract was valid, a statement upon which Paul relied. While there is no case which establishes beyond doubt that in these sort of circumstances a person in a position such as Paul would have a right to claim specific per-formance of the contract, Paul may nevertheless seek such a remedy arguing that it should be granted to him on one or other of two grounds.

First, Paul could start by arguing that the court would be in a position to condemn Eric to pay damages for the harm caused by the latter's delict, such a delict coming squarely within the general provision governing delictual liability in the Civil Code: put simply, Eric's misleading state-ments would entitle Paul to recover damages under art. 2043 of the Civil Code.[41] The next stage in Paul's argument would be to point to the general rule applicable to delictual liability which allows an injured person to obtain specific relief in respect of the defendant's obligation to compen-sate his harm as long as such a remedy is not too onerous for the defen-dant,[42] such a remedy being thought of as relating to an 'obligation to repair the harm in kind'. If this line of reasoning were followed, a court could compel Eric to transfer the house to Paul (though the success of such action would be rather uncertain, this being in some respects a case of first impression).

Secondly, and in the alternative, Paul could try to obtain specific relief

[39] See, e.g., Cass., 10 May 1950, n. 1205, Foro it., 1950, I, 1307 (sale of land). But see also the cases cited below, in n. 41, which, on the contrary, hold that lack of the required form of the contract does not bar an action in damages for precontractual liability.
[40] See e.g. Sacco/De Nova, in: Trattato Sacco II 573–4; Sacco, in: Nozione 449; Musy, Digesto, 4th edn, sez. civ., XVII, 1998, 404–5.
[41] Trib. Napoli, 30 Apr. 1984, n. 3877, Dir. giur., 1984, 1010; Cass., 14 Mar. 1975, n. 1411; Cass., 18 May 1971, n. 1499. All these cases establish the defendant's precontractual liability (in accordance with art. 1337 c.c.) for damages up to the reliance interest, where the plaintiff had reached a verbal agreement for the conclusion of a sale of land. On liability for deceptive statements see, in general, Monateri, in: Trattato Sacco 575, Alpa/Bessone/Zeno-Zencovich, in: Trattato Rescigno 239 ff.; Franzoni, in: Commentario Scialoja-Branca 167 ff.; Busnelli, Contr. e impr., 1991, 539, 557 ff., 566 ff.
[42] Art. 2058 c.c. Cf. Chianale, Diritto, passim. See, however, Patti/Patti, in: Il codice Civile 227–8.

in contract by establishing the existence of special circumstances which in practice, if not in theory, relax the need for exact compliance with the relevant formal requirement. A recent case before the *Corte di Cassazione* may illustrate this approach.[43] There, the defendant building company acquired from a local authority the right to build apartments on public land under a contract which required the building company to sell or to lease any apartments built to certain categories of persons by legislation eligible to be housed under such a scheme. Having completed the building work, while the building company allowed such eligible people to occupy the apartments, it made no written contract with them. The occupants paid money to the building company for which it issued receipts which purported to be accepted on account of the purchase price of the apartment. On a claim by the occupiers of the apartments against the building company in order to obtain the transfer of title in their apartments, the *Corte di Cassazione* held that: (i) the written contract between the local authority and the defendant company operated in favour of the plaintiffs, being a contract for the benefit of third parties[44] and this contract's use of the necessary form satisfied the relevant formal requirements even as regards the plaintiffs; (ii) the defendant's representations to the plaintiffs amounted to a valid 'manifestation of intention' to undertake the obligation to transfer ownership of the apartments to them.

While this decision is by no means isolated,[45] it is hard to predict under what exact circumstances a court will enforce an informal agreement reached by the parties, or will compel one party to act consistently with his words: the cases which deal with issues of this kind still wait to be collected systematically and analysed in a broader perspective. The possibility of correcting the strictness of legislative provisions governing form by resorting to the principle of good faith so as to protect a person's legitimate reliance on the validity of a contract still waits to be fully explored.[46]

THE NETHERLANDS

As there is no valid contract, a contractual claim is impossible. The case law on precontractual liability could certainly be applied here, albeit only

[43] Cass., 9 Jul. 1997, n. 6206, Giust. civ., 1998, I, 105.   [44] Arts. 1411–13 c.c.
[45] See, on different facts, Cass., 12 Jun. 1986, n. 3898, Giur. it., 1987, I,1, 1015, obs. C. Scognamiglio; Cass., 23 Jun. 1994, n. 6032, Foro it., 1995, I, 1268, obs. Lenoci.
[46] Sacco/De Nova, in: *Trattato Sacco II* 573 ff. Italian scholars point to the difference between the Italian and the German experience in this respect: Di Majo, in: *Commentario Scialoja-Branca, passim*; Ranieri, Digesto, 4th edn, sez. civ., VII, 1991, 324; and see the Italian report to case 14 below.

by analogy. Good faith requires that Eric should explain to Paul the various legal provisions which apply to a transaction of the type under discussion. Since he has not done so, he will have to compensate Paul for the loss which Paul has incurred in reliance on – what he thought was – a valid contract. It is unlikely that a court would award loss of profit, as this would in fact mean that the contract, though invalid, would in terms of economic (monetary) value be valid after all.

Another approach could be for Paul to argue that Eric negligently did not inform him about this requirement. Liability would then arise on the basis of the provisions on delict and Paul could thus claim the above-mentioned loss.

Whatever the source of liability (contract, tort, precontractual good faith), arts. 6:95 ff. B.W. (provisions on damages) will apply. The law of damages has been unified, irrespective of the source from which the obligation arises to indemnify another. This means, for example, that problems concerning causation are solved on the basis of the same theory, whatever the source of liability (see art. 6:98 – theory of reasonable imputation). The court has a wide discretion as to what is considered to be caused by a person's negligence. The article only states policy factors which 'among other circumstances' the court should consider. It seems reasonable to assume that the court will look at the source of the liability as one of the 'other' relevant circumstances of the case.

This unified approach to the law of damages is completely new. Under the old Civil Code different rules (including a different theory of causation) applied to claims for contractual and delictual damages.

ENGLAND

Two issues arise in relation to these facts: first, can the circumstances of the case avoid or even override the nullity of contract on the ground of the lack of required formality and, secondly, if not, can Paul get his money back?

As to the first question, the law on the formal requirements necessary for contracts for the sale or other disposition of an interest in land was changed in 1989 by the Law of Property (Miscellaneous Provisions) Act 1989, s. 2, which required that such contracts be 'made in writing and only by incorporating all the terms which the parties have expressly agreed' and signed by both the parties. This provision also made radical changes to the effect of failure to comply with formal requirements in the context, any contract affected being no longer merely unenforceable (as under the earlier law), but a nullity.[47] However, while the 1989 Act abolished the old equitable doctrine of 'part performance' under which a failure to comply with formal requirements may not be relied on by one party where the other has partly performed the contract (which could be satisfied by making a payment under it as Paul has done), it specifically retained the possibility of a party to such a contract relying on constructive or implied trust[48] and this was clearly intended to preserve also the law on proprietary estoppel. Indeed, the Law Commission, whose work led to the passing of the 1989 Act, took the view that any potential injustice to which the new stricter formal requirements could give rise could be dealt with in particular by the doctrine of proprietary estoppel and that the courts might well use this doctrine so as to achieve similar results to the old law of part performance.[49] While somewhat elusive of definition, this doctrine of proprietary estoppel has been described by one author as 'applicable where some action is taken by a person ... in reliance on a mistaken belief as to his rights in or over land, or in reliance on expectations relating to land, where the landowner stands by or encourages the action in such circumstances that it would be unconscionable for him later to seek to enforce his strict legal rights'.[50] It is to be noted that this effect of proprietary estoppel in creating rights is to be contrasted with cases outside the context of land where this does not occur.

It could be argued that Paul has taken some action (the paying of the purchase price) in the mistaken belief as to his rights under the putative contract to sell him the land and that Eric has encouraged this belief in circumstances which are indeed unconscionable. If this were the case, then the court possesses the power under the doctrine of proprietary estoppel to require the conveyance of the legal title of the property to Paul,[51] though the remedies available are extremely flexible, the courts being concerned to 'do what is equitable in all the circumstances'.[52] However, although the doctrine of proprietary estoppel is not restricted to cases of the improvement of land in reliance on the proposition that it is or will become one's own, it is by no means clear that the courts would consider the mere payment of money under the contract a sufficient ground for its operation. Put another way, in the absence of special

---

[47] See Gray 257.   [48] Section 2(5), 1989 Act.
[49] Law Commission No. 164 (1987), § 3.105 to § 3.114 and § 5.4.
[50] Davis, (1993) 13 *Oxford JLS* 101, 103; and see Gray chap. 11.
[51] See, e.g., *Dillwyn v. Llewelyn* (1862) 4 DF & J 517.
[52] *Roebuck v. Mungovin* [1994] 2 AC 224, at 235 *per* Lord *Browne-Wilkinson*.

circumstances (such as a significant change in value of the property between the time of Paul and Eric's original agreement and Eric's refusal to complete) a court could take the view that equity would be satisfied by allowing restitution rather than ordering performance of the (void) contract.

Secondly, quite apart from any possible application of proprietary estoppel, can Paul recover his money paid under the void contract on the basis of restitution? The traditional view was that such money was recovered only if Paul shows that the consideration for the payment of his money has failed, consideration bearing here a special meaning distinct from that borne in relation to the conditions for the existence of a contract and referring to the absence of enjoyment of the benefit of any part of what he bargained for under the failed transaction.[53] There is indeed on the facts of case 4 no evidence of any benefit having been conferred on Paul (such as allowing him into possession before transfer of the property). Another interpretation of the notion of 'failure of consideration' argues that consideration is the basis on which the payment was made, here the existence of the contract of sale of the land.[54] On this view, the mere receipt of a benefit would not prevent recovery of the money paid under the void contract of sale of land. In *Westdeutsche Landesbank Girozentrale v. Islington L.B.C.*[55] the Court of Appeal moved further away from the traditional approach and held that recovery of money paid under a void contract is allowed because there is no legal basis for such a payment, the right not being defeated merely because the other party has wholly or in part done what he has promised to do under the void contract. On this basis, Paul would certainly recover his money back under the contract.

Finally, whatever the outcome as to proprietary estoppel or restitutionary recovery, on these facts, Eric has committed a fraud, i.e. a dishonest statement, and this is actionable in damages in the tort of deceit for all direct losses suffered by Paul caused by the fraud.[56]

In conclusion, therefore, it can be seen that the doctrine of proprietary estoppel (and also of constructive trust) has been used by modern English courts in the context of informal transactions relating to land to remedy injustices caused by a party relying unconscionably on formal requirements. The reform in 1989 of the formal requirements for the sale or other disposition in land was undertaken principally in the interests of creating a greater certainty in transactions of this sort, the old doctrine of part

---

[53] See Guest, *Chitty on Contracts* § 29–034.   [54] Birks 219–21.   [55] [1994] 1 WLR 938.
[56] *Derry v. Peek* (1889) 14 App Cas 337.

performance being both inherently vague and uncertain in its actual legal requirements. However, despite espousing a generally strict approach, the Law Commission (and the legislature) accepted that these rules should not be allowed to cause injustice. To the extent, however, that the retention of doctrines such as proprietary estoppel allow the avoidance of the new requirements, their practical certainty in effect is to be doubted.

IRELAND

This case can be analysed only somewhat speculatively, as no equivalent notarial requirement exists in Irish law. Instead, contracts for the sale of interests in land must be evidenced in writing and signed by the party to be charged thereunder, but these evidentiary requirements go only towards the enforcement and not to the validity of the contract. They derive from s. 2 of the Statute of Frauds (Ireland) 1695 and judges have from the earliest stages been keen to ensure that a statute to prevent fraud should not itself become a means of the perpetration of fraud. Accordingly, a number of judicial exceptions to the requirement of writing have been carved out. The most relevant of these is estoppel, according to which a person who gives an assurance will not be allowed to resile from it if the person to whom the assurance has been made has acted on it to his detriment. It has been held by the High Court that an estoppel will arise if, as on the facts of case 4, a party expressly accepts the adequacy of an otherwise inadequate memorandum for the purposes of the Statute of Frauds.[57] In the result, therefore, the courts would decree specific performance of the contract.

A second relevant exception to the requirement of writing concerns part performance of the contract.[58] Payment of the money under the contract by Paul could constitute such an act of part performance if it were established on the balance of probabilities that it referred to the contract as alleged by him. If this were the case, then part performance would also be a ground for allowing the contract to be enforced.[59]

If Irish law did require notarial authentication as a condition for the

---

[57] *Black v. Grealy* (unreported, High Court, 10 November 1977).
[58] *Lowry v. Reid* [1927] NI 142.
[59] In the past, payment of money was not considered a sufficient act of part performance, but there is evidence that Irish courts are likely to follow the more liberal approach to this issue found in the decision of the House of Lords in *Steadman v. Steadman* [1976] AC 536: see, e.g., *Re Irish Commercial Society* (unreported, High Court, 12 February 1987).

validity of a contract, it is unlikely that arguments of estoppel or part performance would mitigate the rigour of the statute; although this would
depend on a construction of the statute in the light of its presumed
purpose or purposes. Estoppel is allowed to operate in relation to requirements of the Statute of Frauds under the fiction that the legislature could
not have intended the requirement of writing to be an engine of fraud;
this liberal reading is helped by the fact that the statute is very old and
that it is not in any real sense undemocratic to modify the application of
such an old statute. It is less likely, however, that the same cavalier attitude would apply to the interpretation of a modern statute, particularly
one passed under the current constitution where the creation of laws is
the prerogative of the *Oireachtas* (parliament). Irish courts are wary of
allowing estoppels to alter the results which were intended by statute.

If the contract were held to be invalid, the question would arise as to
the treatment of the payment of the purchase money paid by Paul. It is
probable that restitution of the money paid would be ordered, on the
basis that the contract was not expressly an illegal contract. Illegal contracts are those where a course of action is actually prohibited and
usually subjected to criminal sanction. While the courts are reluctant to
help the parties who involve themselves in such an illegality, relief may
be awarded if the intention of the legislature is construed as being to
assist one of the parties, or alternatively, where one party is more to
blame for the breach of the prohibition than the other. In the circumstances of case 4, it is most likely that the contract would merely be made
void and accordingly, restitution could be ordered on the basis of a total
failure of consideration.[60]

SCOTLAND

Where parties enter into a contract for the sale of heritage (an interest in
land), provided the requisite formalities have been complied with, the
buyer has a contractual right to have the seller implement the obligation.
However, the ownership of the property (*dominium*) is not transferred to
the buyer unless and until a disposition has been drawn up and recorded
in the Register of Sasines or registered in the Land Register. Until the disposition is recorded or registered, the buyer only has a personal right *vis-
à-vis* the seller for the performance of his obligation. Accordingly, Paul

[60] Cf. *Chartered Trust Ireland Ltd v. Healy & Commins* (unreported, High Court, 10 December
1985).

only has a personal right against Eric and even this is tenuous because the contract may well be invalid.

The first point to note is that there is no need for notarial execution for such a contract in Scotland. For the contract to be valid, all that is required is the signature of the grantor. The first question to ask is whether the contract has been validly executed according to the Requirements of Writing (Scotland) Act 1995, which sets out the rules of constitution for contracts that require to be in writing; notably contracts for the creation, transfer, variation or extinction of an interest in land (including leases for a period of more than one year). If the formalities required by the 1995 Act have not been complied with, the contract is invalid, neither party is bound and each has *locus poenitentiae*, subject to the personal bar exception.[61] If the formalities have been complied with, Eric has no *locus poenitentiae* and must transfer the property to Paul.

It appears that the contract was concluded, but the conveyance has not taken place. Assuming that the contract is valid, the problem is that Paul has performed his part of the contract by handing over his savings in consideration of the property. This means that Eric is in breach of contract and Paul can sue Eric for damages for breach. Alternatively, he could sue for specific implement to force Eric to perform his obligation under the contract.

If the contract is not valid, and if Eric keeps the money, Paul could found an action on the basis of *unjustified enrichment*.[62] Stair in his classification of obligations distinguished clearly between actions founded on unjust or unjustified enrichment and those founded on contract or delict. As there is no valid contract here an action for restitution on the basis of unjust enrichment exists. Emphasis lies on the defender's (Eric) duty to restore or return a gain to which he is not entitled as well as on the pursuer's (Paul) right to recover. Strictly speaking, the remedy concerning the recovery of money is called *repetition*, but it is sometimes regarded as merely a subdivision of restitution, because the term 'restitution' is used in a broad sense to cover actions for the return of money as well as corporeal movables. The remedy of repetition is defined by *Gloag and Henderson* as follows: 'The plea of repetition allows recovery of money which has been paid in circumstances where it would be unjust for the defender to keep the money.'[63]

Another issue to consider here, in the light of Paul's age and inexperience in conveyancing matters, is whether there has been an element of

---

[61] See the Scottish report to case 3 above.
[62] See the Scottish report to cases 14, 15, 17 and 26 below.   [63] Wilson/Forte § 29.2.

facility and circumvention. Scots law recognises that a party to a contract may take advantage of the weak-mindedness of the other contracting party. Where loss or harm has been caused to a person who at the time was in a weak or facile state of mind, and was induced to enter into an obligation by someone taking unfair advantage of his condition, the obligation is open to annulment. The recognition of facility and circumvention developed from the common law concept of fraud. The onus is on Paul to establish that when he entered into the contract, he was in a weak or facile state of mind. The state is less than insanity; it involves a state of mental weakness, arising from, for example, old age; *Munro v. Strain*,[64] *Horsburgh v. Thomson's Trustees*.[65] Owing to this weakness, the person must be seriously liable to be influenced by advice, persuasion or intimidation so as to be unable to form an independent and balanced judgement. Loss or harm must be suffered as a result of the fraud, or circumvention must be averred; *Clunie v. Stirling*.[66] Proof of facility or circumvention is a ground for rescission of an *ex facie* valid obligation, or the reduction of an *ex facie* valid deed, and the principle of restitution would come into play whereby Eric must give Paul his money back.

Eric has clearly misrepresented the conveyancing requirements to Paul. The misrepresentation occurred after the contract was formed, but misrepresentations do not have to be precontractual for the law to recognise them. Eric asserts that no further formalities are required and then tries to rely on the fact that such formalities have not been complied with. As such misrepresentations are fraudulent (Eric knows his misrepresentations are false), the remedy is available to Paul to sue in delict and claim damages. Paul must show that Eric had the requisite *mens rea* for fraud. Scots law in this area has been largely influenced by the English law of tort of deceit. The observations of Lord *Herschell* in *Derry v. Peek*[67] would apply: 'First, in order to sustain an action of deceit (fraud), there must be proof of fraud, and nothing short of that will suffice. Secondly, fraud is proved when it is shown that a false representation has been made (1) knowingly, or (2) without belief in its truth, or (3) recklessly, careless whether it be true or false . . .'.

DENMARK AND NORWAY

In West Nordic law, there are no requirements of formality relating to contracts involving the transfer of land. Under West Nordic law, freedom of

---

[64] (1874) 1 R 522.   [65] 1912 SC 267, 1912 1 SLT 73.   [66] (1854) 17 D 1184.
[67] (1889) 14 App Cas 337, HL.

contract applies in the sense that the parties do not have to comply with a specific form. Thus, the problems dealt with in cases 4 and 5 could not arise in Denmark and Norway.[68] In East Nordic law, however, there are requirements as to formalities, especially relating to the sale of real property. According to traditional regulations in the law on real estate, a promise to conclude a contract of sale involving real property is not binding as long as the formal requirements of the Act have not been met.[69]

In certain minor areas there can be formal requirements also in Denmark and Norway. In such instances, liability for damages may be imposed in cases like the present one. This would be a kind of precontractual liability. It has been said in Swedish academic discussion that the policy considerations justifying the sanction of invalidity in case of non-compliance with the formal requirements have to be weighed up against those supporting a claim for damages of a person who has, for instance, been misled by means of incorrect information. It has been said that the formal requirements ensure that the transfer only takes place after having been well considered. There should, consequently, also be grounds for imposing liability for damages in cases when one party has disloyally misled the other.[70] This line of argument would be acceptable also in Denmark and Norway.

SWEDEN

According to Swedish law,[71] the sale of real estate must be made in writing and the contract has to be signed by both parties and has to state the price. No notarial authentication is needed for the sale to be valid. However, the written form is indispensable. The purpose of the formal requirement is that the parties should have the opportunity thoroughly to deliberate upon the matter, i.e. the transfer. In addition, writing facilitates registration, which creates a presumption for the buyer to be owner, and it is used for purposes of taxation, based on the price.

On the assumption that Eric, the entrepreneur, convinced the pensioner Paul that an oral agreement was sufficient, the contract would be void. Of course, Paul is entitled to receive his purchase money back. But there is no room for exceptions as to the invalidity, due to reasonableness or good faith. Normally, a buyer in this situation is not entitled to compensation for loss of profit. However, in the present case the fraudulent

---

[68] Gomard, *Almindelig kontraktsret* 133.   [69] *Jordabalken*, 1970:994, chapter 4, s. 1.
[70] Kleineman, JT 1993/1994, 437.   [71] 1970 Real Estate Code, ch. 4, s. 1.

statements by Eric as to the requirements of the law may possibly support such claim.

According to NJA 1987, p. 845 II, a buyer is entitled to compensation for improvements made by him on real estate, when the sale is invalid because of a defect as to its form (in the reported case, a false price was stated in the deed), although the buyer ought to have known of the invalidity; since both parties had been in bad faith, no one should benefit from the invalidity.

FINLAND

Due to the lack of notarial confirmation the contract is absolutely void (Land Act of 1995 (Si 601), 2:1; Land Act Proposal 1989/53, p. 86). Already before the new Land Act there was an established judicial practice: if there was an informal agreement regarding a sale of land, the party that refused to comply with it was obliged to reimburse the costs of the other party. The contract was invalid, but there was usually at least a claim for the negative interest (*negatives Interesse*). This practice was taken over into the new Land Act (2:8).

Accordingly, Paul would get the price back and be reimbursed for his expenses (negotiation costs, etc.).

In Finland the principle of equity, or the requirement that the defect must be of material importance, has not been extended to the invalidity of a contract resulting from lack of formality. Certain suggestions by scholars to that effect[72] have not found support in judicial practice.[73] In earlier times even the question concerning *negatives Interesse* was answered in the negative but this has changed as a result of the case KKO 1971 II 51.[74]

Editors' comparative observations

These may be found, together with those relating to case 5, at the end of the next section (p. 289).

---

[72] Lahtinen 134 ff., and later Aarnio, in: *Oikeustiede-Jurisprudentia* 196 ff.
[73] See Muukkonen 212 ff., Hemmo, *Sopimusoikeus* 124 ff. and the cases quoted there.
[74] See with respect to the scope of the costs involved Ämmälä, in: *Turun Yliopiston* 557 ff.

Case 5: Formalities II

Case

Hilary is a recent immigrant. She takes a lease of Imogen's farm; the farm is completely run down. Hilary and Imogen agree that after eight years Hilary may demand transfer of title. Hilary manages to convert the farm into a flourishing enterprise. After eight years she requests Imogen to transfer the farm to her. Imogen refuses since the contract lacks notarial authentication (which is necessary for a contract of sale concerning land).

Discussions

GERMANY

This is an illustration of the first type of case, mentioned above,[1] where German courts are prepared to invoke § 242 BGB in order to prevent a 'totally unbearable' result.

Hilary has built up the farm and she has derived her existence from it for eight years. It may be assumed that she has given up other opportunities for earning a living in the expectation of the transfer of the farm; and that her existence would be endangered if Imogen were not bound by the contract.[2] Under these circumstances, it would be totally unbearable to deprive Hilary, on account of the formal defect, of a right to demand transfer of the property. § 125 BGB, which provides that a contract which fails to comply with statutory formalities is void, is overridden by the principle of good faith. Hilary may ask for specific performance of the contract.

---

[1] See the German report to case 4.
[2] This is an issue of fact; BGHZ 23, 249 therefore referred a similar case back to the court below.

GREECE

Between Hilary and Imogen no valid contract has been concluded. However, there have been negotiations concerning a future transfer of property. Hilary has relied on the statements made by Imogen and may thus have a claim under arts. 197–8 of the Greek Civil Code.

It must also be added that if Imogen's conduct can be interpreted as being contrary to the principle of good faith under art. 281 Gr. C.C., Hilary may ask for specific performance of the contract. The law would thus assist Hilary in order to prevent an extreme and unbearable result.[3]

AUSTRIA

On these facts, the same approach to the question of the validity of the contract must be taken as was explained in relation to case 4. Even if her behaviour has to be evaluated as deceit, Imogen may invoke the invalidity of the contract. The question of liability in damages would also be similarly treated: Imogen would be liable to compensate Hilary for her losses incurred in reliance on the validity of the contract on the ground that she has culpably misled her.

On the other hand, the question of the availability of a claim for restitution in respect of Imogen's unjustified enrichment as a result of Hilary's expenditure in improving the farm requires some further discussion. For Hilary incurred this expenditure principally because she expected to receive title to the farm after a period of eight years and thereby benefit from the results of her own efforts. If, therefore, the contract to transfer title of the farm is invalid and on this basis Imogen refuses to transfer title, she, Imogen, would thereby obtain an advantage without legal reason. On this ground, therefore, Hilary is entitled to claim restitution in respect of her expenditure under § 1435 ABGB in that she is not able to take the benefit of the results of her own efforts as she had expected.[4] Such a claim would focus on compensating her for the increase in value of the farm which resulted from her work, which was done only with the view to receiving title to the farm in the future. But as Imogen has obstructed the transfer of the property which Hilary expected, under Austrian law the latter's claim for restitution does not depend on any actual economic

---

[3] For literature concerning this case scenario, see: Simantiras nos. 683, 688–9, p. 475. See also the following leading cases: Areopagus 1609/1984 EEN 52, 672; Areopagus 336/1969 NoB 17, 1189.

[4] Wilburg, in: *Klang, Kommentar VI* 466 ff.; Rummel, JBl 1978, 449; OGH in JBl 1985, 679.

advantage on the part of Imogen. On the analogy of § 1152 ABGB, Imogen has to pay for the objective value of Hilary's work.[5]

FRANCE

There may be two remedies available to Hilary under French law. She could either (i) bring an action to compel Imogen to transfer the property to her or (ii) claim damages for breach of her promise (*promesse de vente*).

(i) Hilary has managed to convert the farm she was leasing from Imogen into a flourishing enterprise. As a result, she would probably prefer to compel Imogen to transfer the property to her, rather than merely receive damages. The same arguments apply as are set out in the French analysis in case 4. The contract is valid as between the parties but is unenforceable against third parties until the formalities are effected.

(ii) Alternatively, if Hilary decides not to compel Imogen to transfer the property to her, or does not succeed in obtaining a court order, she could claim damages for breach of contract under art. 1147 of the Civil Code for Imogen's failure to transfer the property as she promised.

BELGIUM

Again, a similar case cannot arise under Belgian law, since no formalities exist in such a case or in any case sufficiently similar.

Provided there would be such a formal requirement, the same considerations apply as in case 4. The difference concerns only the amount of damages which would be due on the basis of *culpa in contrahendo*.

The fact that Hilary is a recent immigrant does not make much of a difference, except that this will play a role when judging her possible ignorance about the necessity of formalities. Liability for Imogen on the basis of *culpa in contrahendo* (duty to inform) is more likely in such cases.

Although in the hypothesis of a lack of formalities, Hilary would probably not obtain transfer of title, there are other remedies.

(i) The contract of lease could be avoided on the basis of error, if the possibility of becoming owner of the farm was a substantial element for Hilary in concluding the contract (art. 1108 C.C. – compare here cases 1 and 2 above). An avoidance on the basis of 'qualified lesion' (abuse of circumstances) is also possible.[6] Hilary can then claim restitution of the

---

[5] Bydlinski, in: *Festschrift Wilburg* 45; Bydlinski, *System* 284; Rummel, JBl 1978, 454; OGH in SZ 61/16 (1988).   [6] On this ground of avoidance see the Belgian report to case 2.

rent paid, after having compensated Imogen for the estimated value of the use of the farm she has enjoyed. The enrichment of Imogen thanks to Hilary's activity will be taken into account.

(ii) When the contract is not avoided, compensation could be claimed on the basis of *culpa in contrahendo* or the duty to act in good faith. A Belgian judge would normally decide that Imogen has a duty to warn Hilary that, when investing in the farm, she should be aware of the fact that there was not yet a binding contract of sale. Such a duty to warn is more frequently found in consumer law (which does not apply here since Hilary is not a consumer in relation to the farm), but also in other cases of inequality of bargaining power.

SPAIN

In Spanish law, the same considerations apply here as were discussed in relation to case 4.

ITALY

The facts of this case differ somewhat from those in the previous one, for it does not appear that Imogen reassured Hilary about the validity of the contract, or that she was aware (or ought to have been aware) of the relevant legislative requirement of form. However, leaving aside for the moment any issue relating to the existence of the agricultural lease between the parties, this case raises at a general level the same problems and therefore is governed by the same rules as were discussed in relation to case 4. In the result, if Imogen's behaviour did not infringe her duty to negotiate in good faith,[7] any claim to specific performance of the sale agreement by Hilary would be hopeless and she would do better to seek to recover in respect of any unjust enrichment by Imogen at her expense. Given the current judicial interpretation of art. 1338 of the Civil Code this second possibility seems more likely in the circumstances.[8]

However, case 5 also raises more particular questions relating to the impact of the special legislation concerning agricultural leases. Exceptions apart, in Italian law the minimum duration of leases of this type is fifteen years;[9] the tenant has a statutory right of first refusal if the

---

[7] Arts. 1337, 1338 c.c.   [8] See the Italian report to case 4 above.
[9] L. 22 Jul. 1966, n. 606, art. 1, as amended by l. 11 Feb. 1971, n. 11, art. 17. See also l. 3 May 1982, n. 203, art. 22.

landlord later decides to sell the land[10] and when the lease expires special rules concerning improvement to the property ensure better protection of the agricultural tenant than would the general law governing leases.[11] This being so, it seems that Hilary would at least be adequately compensated for the improvements which she has effected to the farm and would be able to decide whether or not she wants to buy the land should it be offered for sale.

THE NETHERLANDS

The same reply applies here as under the Dutch report to case 4. However, as this has been a long-standing relationship it could very well be that if Hilary (the lessee) would claim damages *in natura* (art. 6:103), she could oblige Imogen (the lessor) to transfer title.

ENGLAND

In English law a lease at a full market rent for a period not exceeding three years may be created either orally or in writing.[12] Other tenancies must be created by deed. However, whatever the legal status of the lease, the formal requirements, and the techniques for their circumvention which apply to the agreement by Imogen subsequently to transfer the title to the property, are the same as in case 4. Assuming, therefore, that the formal requirements made by s. 2 of the Law of Property (Miscellaneous Provisions) Act 1989 have not been fulfilled on the facts, any contract to convey the property is a nullity.

However, these facts are typical of the sort of case in which English courts have had recourse to the equitable doctrine of proprietary estoppel,[13] in that they involve considerable expenditure by Hilary on another's land in the expectation of the conveyance of an interest in the land at a future date: see e.g. *Dillwyn v. Llewelyn*.[14] As has been said, the courts here sometimes order conveyance of the legal title, but have at other times ordered a compensatory award of money instead, though it has been said that such an award is particularly appropriate where expenditure on

[10] For an overview of the relevant legislation, see Germanò, Digesto, 4th edn, sez. civ., XIV, 1996, 178 ff.
[11] For an overview of the relevant legislation, see Capizzano, Digesto, 4th edn, sez. civ., XI, 1994, 343.
[12] Law of Property Act 1925, ss. 52(1), 54(1) and (2); *Crago v. Julian* [1992] 1 WLR 372, at 376.
[13] See the English report to case 4 above.   [14] (1862) 4 DF & J 517.

improvements is not substantial.[15] As was said earlier, the courts in this sort of case possess a wide discretion to make the order appropriate to achieve an equitable readjustment of the parties' proprietary interests.

IRELAND

By s. 2 of the Statute of Frauds (Ireland) 1695 an option for the conveyance of the legal interest in land must be evidenced in writing and signed by the party against whom performance is being sought. As we have seen in relation to case 4, this statutory requirement is a condition precedent to the enforcement, but not to the validity, of the contract.

Courts of equity have allowed a limited exception to the statutory requirement where there exists satisfactory proof of the contract by means of part performance: the Statute of Frauds should not be an 'engine of fraud' itself.[16] There are twin rationales for the doctrine of part performance; first, and most obviously, the contract may be enforced despite the absence of formality where the action of one of its parties by performing makes it unfair for it not to be enforced; secondly, the act of part performance may provide unequivocal evidence of the contract despite the lack of formality. The current position of the Irish courts is to require the plaintiff to establish that the acts of part performance refer unequivocally to the type of contract which is alleged by the party seeking to enforce the contract.[17] A successful claim of part performance is unlikely as it is difficult to sustain an argument that Hilary's action in taking up the lease is unequivocally referable to the grant of an option by Imogen to transfer her reversionary interest in the property.

While estoppel may also act as a bar to the reliance on the Statute of Frauds, as we have noted in relation to case 4, it requires an express or an implied representation by one of the parties that he will not invoke the statute.[18] However, a distinct form of estoppel may apply to the facts of case 5: proprietary estoppel. Such an estoppel arises when a person has expended money on land on the basis of a promise of its future conveyance, and the decision in *Dillwyn v. Llewelyn*[19] is a leading authority for the proposition that estoppel may in appropriate circumstances allow the promisee to enforce the promise made to convey the interest. However, the

---

[15] Gray 384, citing *Cushley v. Seale*, unreported, CA, 28 October 1986.
[16] See the Irish report to case 4 above.
[17] *Silver Wraith Ltd v. Sivicre Eireann Ltd* (unreported, High Court, 8 June 1989, *per Keane* J.).
[18] *Black v. Grealy* (unreported, High Court, 10 November 1977).   [19] (1862) 4 DF & J 517.

court has a wide discretion, and may provide a lesser remedy if this satisfies its 'conscience'. The leading, recent Irish case on proprietary estoppel
is *Cullen v. Cullen*[20] in which the Court refused to order the conveyance of
the property promised, but nevertheless prevented the promisor from
recovering possession of his land. The Court ventured the curious and
unorthodox opinion that after twelve years of an arrangement under
which title had been promised, the promisee would acquire title by
adverse possession. The position in case 5 is quite like that found in *Cullen
v. Cullen*, although Hilary entered the land under a lease, whereas the pro-
misees in *Cullen v. Cullen* did so as mere licensees (i.e. under a mere permission). Thus, on the facts of case 5 an Irish court would probably deem the
lease to have determined and would prevent Imogen from recovering possession, leading to Hilary's acquisition in time of the promised interest in
land.

Later cases have suggested that the courts have a wide discretion to
achieve equity in these circumstances,[21] although no Irish court has yet
ordered the conveyance of the full promised interest in land.

SCOTLAND

Again we have an alleged contract for the transfer of heritage, thus it must
be constituted according to the formalities stipulated by the Requirements of Writing (Scotland) Act 1995. Assuming these formalities have not
been complied with, the contract is invalid. However, the statutory doctrine of personal bar[22] will operate as a form of protection for Hilary.
Imogen will not be able to withdraw from the agreement.

Hilary has acted in reliance on Imogen's agreement to transfer the title
to the property after eight years. Where a contract, unilateral obligation
or trust ought to have been constituted in writing but was not, but one of
the parties has acted or refrained from acting in reliance on the contract
with the knowledge or acquiescence of the other party to the contract,
then the latter will not be entitled to withdraw from the contract and it
will not be regarded as invalid. But this will operate only if the position of
Hilary, in reliance on the contract, has been affected to a material extent,
and if her position would be adversely affected to a material extent and as
a result of the withdrawal of Imogen from the agreement.[23] In *Cumming v.*

---

[20] [1962] IR 268.   [21] See *In Re J.R.* [1993] ILRM 657.
[22] See the Scottish report to case 3 above.
[23] See s. 1(3), (4), Requirements of Writing (Scotland) Act 1995.

Brown,[24] for example, after the effective tender of performance had been made by the purchasers, the seller was no longer entitled to exercise his right to resile from the contract.

It should be noted that Hilary's immigrant status has no significance. Scots law does not afford any extra protection to immigrants despite any language difficulties they may have, and however naively versed they may be in the law of Scotland.

Other thoughts: Could both cases 4 and 5 be analysed as a promise? Would the promise now require to be constituted in writing according to s. 1(2)(a)(ii) of the 1995 Act? Has there been a breach of promise? See *Stone v. MacDonald*[25] where the grant of an option to purchase land was a promise to sell on agreed terms if the grantee chose later to exercise his option. It would still be necessary to invoke the statutory plea of personal bar.

DENMARK AND NORWAY

See the discussion for Denmark and Norway concerning case 4.

SWEDEN

An agreement to transfer land in the future is not binding, and the same applies to options to buy in the future.[26]

The rule is ancient. It is related to a provision in the Real Estate Code of 1734 invalidating a term, which obliges the buyer to retransfer the property if certain events occur. *Inter alia* it was assumed that bonds on real estate could adversely affect the interest of the owner to take good care of the land. Nowadays real estate is often indirectly sold and leased back with an option to repurchase. In such cases the estate must first be sold to a company. Then the shares etc., which encompass the real estate, are sold with an option for the seller to buy them back at a fixed price within a certain time.

As to Hilary's improvements exceeding the standard the lessor was entitled to expect under the lease agreement or supplementary law, the general rule on lease of land is that the owner need not pay compensation for measures he did not order. If the owner does not voluntarily compensate the lessee, the latter may, where possible, remove houses, equipment

---

[24] 1994 SLT (Sh Ct) 11.   [25] 1979 SC 363.   [26] See e.g. Vahlén 133 ff.

etc. when the lease terminates. Otherwise, the equipment after some time will become the property of the lessor.

The problem in the present case is whether in view of the invalid agreement to sell Imogen is under an obligation to compensate Hilary for her costs (not her loss of profit). The case NJA 1987, p. 845 II probably applies, as we are dealing, once again, with an invalidity founded on public policy. Hence, Hilary will be entitled to compensation.

FINLAND

Hilary does not get the farm (no notarial confirmation; see the Finnish report to case 4 above), but at the end of the lease she will get compensation for costs incurred in improving the farm. This is not due to the invalid contract of sale but follows directly from s. 63 of the Lease Act of 1966 (Si 629).

Editors' comparative observations

A striking aspect of the analyses of cases 4 and 5 are the divergences in the legal systems as to the existence and effects of formal requirements in relation to contracts for the transfer of land.

(i) As to the existence of formal requirements in the present context, there is a wide range from the firm denial of any formal requirement (as in Austrian, Belgian and West Nordic law) to the requirement of signed writing and witnesses (as in English law) or notarial authentication (as in German, Greek or Spanish law). The details of the requirements need not detain us here.

(ii) Even more surprising, perhaps, is the range of significance given to whatever formalities are required.

(a) At one extreme, legal systems sometimes see formal requirements as irrelevant to the validity of the contract between its parties. Thus, for example, in French law any failure to fulfil formal requirements in this context is not considered as going to the validity of the contract between the parties, even though it would affect their position as regards third parties. This being the case, French law allows performance to be ordered in the normal way as the contracts relating to the land are valid. Spanish courts have even taken the view that lack of notarial authentication concerning contracts for the sale of land does not affect the validity of the contract.

(b) Of those legal systems which accept that a failure to comply with the formal requirements, at least in the cases under discussion, does indeed go to the validity of the contract (such as German, Greek, English or Scots law; Irish law retains the former approach of English law according to which a failure to comply with formal requirements in relation to contracts for the sale of land goes to the enforceability but not to the validity of the contract), all possess doctrines for the avoidance of hardship in special circumstances and under them allow the possibility of awarding Paul specific enforcement of the contract, some intermediate solution or damages.

A considerable variety of ideas lie behind these doctrines. Thus, Irish law relies on the doctrine of 'part performance' of the contract (part payment being enough), this itself resting on the principle that 'equity will not allow statute to be an engine of fraud'. In this way, conduct by a party to an agreement which indicates its existence may in a sense stand in for the absent formality. This underlines the essentially evidentiary concern of the formal requirements in question. Where the doctrine applies, the informal agreement takes effect as a contract and may be enforced. While English law used to take this approach, since the introduction in 1989 of more stringent formal requirements which nullify any non-conforming agreement, it has had to rely instead on the equitable doctrine of proprietary estoppel, whose central element is detrimental reliance but whose conditions and effects are suffused with general 'equitable' concern. As a result of this last feature, the English doctrine does not necessarily lead to the enforcement of what was promised: for general considerations of fairness mould the remedy available.

German law distinguishes two exceptional situations where good faith requires intervention: where the 'economic existence of a party to the contract would otherwise be destroyed or substantially endangered' and, alternatively, where one party has committed a particularly grave infringement of the precepts of good faith, notably, where he has induced the other party not to be concerned with the execution of the proper formality. These two situations are those found on the sets of facts in cases 4 and 5 respectively. While German courts are often prepared to order the enforcement of the promise, there is also one type of situation where they restrict the disadvantaged party's remedy to damages (though based on its 'positive interest').

Greek law appeals to the notion of the 'abuse of a right' (to rely on the formal invalidity) so as to validate the contract and would allow either the enforcement of the contract or damages.

The change of facts in case 5 does not make any substantial difference to the analyses taken by this group of systems, with the exception of English and Scots law. According to English law the facts of case 5 are ones which much more clearly attract an order for the enforcement of the agreement rather than simply restitution or compensation. Scots law would rely on the statutory doctrine of personal bar in case 5 and thus regard the contract as valid. Dutch law, too, might be prepared (in view of the long-standing relationship between the parties) to oblige Imogen (case 5) to transfer title (though *via* granting a claim of damages which would entail restoration in kind), but not Eric in case 4. Italian courts, on the other hand, might grant Paul (case 4) a right to enforce the invalid contract (quite possibly by allowing him to claim damages in kind), whereas Hilary (case 4) may only recover on the basis of unjustified enrichment.

(c) At the other end of this particular spectrum lies Swedish law. For in no circumstance does Swedish law allow 'inequitable behaviour' (even if this is dishonest) to justify the *enforcement* of a contract for the sale of land which fails to fulfil the relevant formalities. In case 4, Paul could therefore only get his money back and recover damages whereas Hilary in case 5 could recover her costs but would not be able to claim compensation for her improvements.

Case 6: One bag too few

Case

George owes Harry fifty heavy bags of flour. On the appointed day he drives to Harry in order to deliver them. After he has unloaded the bags, it turns out that he has only brought forty-nine rather than fifty of them. Will he be able to deliver the fiftieth bag later that day or will he have to reload and take back the forty-nine bags in order to deliver all fifty bags at one and the same time?

Discussions

GERMANY

In principle, a debtor is not allowed to make part performance (§ 266 BGB). This rule, however, only constitutes *ius dispositivum*. The parties are therefore free to agree otherwise. Such agreement, however, is lacking in the present case.

Yet, according to the general view,[1] the application of § 266 BGB is restricted by § 242 BGB. The creditor may not refuse part performance if acceptance can reasonably be expected of him, taking account of the debtor's position and of his own interests, as far as they are worthy of protection. His behaviour would otherwise constitute an abuse of right. Abuse of right (*mißbräuchliche Rechtsausübung*) in German law does not constitute an independent doctrine but is one of the subcategories elaborated

---

[1] BGH VersR 1954, 297 (298) and consistent practice; *Münchener Kommentar*/Keller § 266, n. 16; *Palandt*/Heinrichs § 266, n. 9; *Jauernig*/Vollkommer § 266, n. 10; *Erman*/Kuckuk § 266, n. 7; *Staudinger*/Selb § 266, n. 12.

within the general framework of § 242 BGB, specifying the requirements of good faith in contractual dealings.[2]

In the present case, it would cause grave inconvenience for George if he had to reload forty-nine heavy bags of flour. No interest of Harry is apparent that would be worthy of protection. The problem here, after all, only concerns one bag that is to be delivered soon. In this case the restriction that § 242 BGB places on § 266 BGB prevails and Harry is obliged to accept part performance. It has to be kept in mind that George will come back with the fiftieth bag that same day so that even that bag will be delivered in time. Harry is not expected to accept late performance.

GREECE

This is a case of part performance (art. 316 Gr. C.C.) which is not allowed under Greek law. But the principle of good faith, as it is stated in art. 288 Gr. C.C., demands that the debtor has to perform his obligation according to the principles of good faith and business usage. At the same time, it is not expected of the creditor to accept performance if it is not in accordance with these standards.

In this case George, without fault, took with him forty-nine bags instead of fifty to deliver to Harry. If George intends to deliver also the fiftieth bag within the time originally agreed upon to Harry and if the circumstances do not require simultaneous delivery of all the bags, he will not be in default (*mora debitoris*) as a result of only delivering forty-nine bags.[3] Basically, the spirit of art. 288 Gr. C.C. pervades the entire law of obligations. It requires conduct in good faith and in accordance with business usage from both parties. Greek law, to that extent, follows German theory, based on § 242 BGB.

AUSTRIA

§ 1415 sent. 1 ABGB provides that a creditor is not obliged to accept performance[4] by instalments. Thus, he may refuse tender of part performance by the debtor without legal sanction. The purpose of this rule is to spare

---

[2] Cf. *Jauernig*/Vollkommer § 242, nn. 37 ff.
[3] Cf. Stathopoulos, in: *Astikos Kodix II* art. 288, no. 49; and see Areopagus 975/75 NoB 24, 278.
[4] This provision applies not only to money payments (as would seem to be indicated by its wording), but to all divisible performances.

the creditor the trouble involved in having to accept delivery a number of times, when he has not agreed to do so.[5] This suggests that George would have to reload and take back the forty-nine bags in order to deliver all fifty bags at one and the same time.

On the other hand, all legal entitlements are subject to limitations based on the idea of the abuse of rights,[6] a principle which also applies to the particular example of a creditor's right to refuse tender of part performance. This general limitation actually finds a statutory basis in § 1295 II ABGB.[7]

According to the now prevailing view,[8] abuse of a right refers to the situation where there is an extreme imbalance between the interests of the person purporting to exercise the right and the person whose interests would be impaired as a result. In the view of the present writer, on the facts of case 6, Harry's refusal to take delivery of the forty-nine bags would constitute an abuse of rights on his part. For to require George to reload and take back the forty-nine bags and deliver fifty bags all at once later would place a heavy burden on him, whereas Harry has nothing ultimately to gain from his refusal, as he must later anyway accept another delivery. Indeed, Harry's refusal is even disadvantageous for himself since he cannot use the flour in the meantime.

In the result, therefore, Harry is not entitled to refuse to accept delivery of the forty-nine bags, being 'in default of acceptance' (*mora creditoris*) if he did so.

FRANCE

Although George is in breach of his obligation to deliver the property,[9] it is unlikely that Harry could force him to reload and deliver the whole lot at one and the same time. Two explanations can be given. First, in assessing whether either specific enforcement (*exécution en nature*) or termination of the contract (*résolution judiciaire*) is appropriate under art. 1184 of

---

[5] Gschnitzer, in: *Klang, Kommentar VI* 381; Reischauer, in: *Rummel, ABGB II* § 1415 n. 6; Harrer, in: *Schwimann, ABGB V* § 1415 n. 1.
[6] Koziol, *Haftpflichtrecht II* 99; Mader, *Rechtsmißbrauch* 116 ff.
[7] Bydlinski, *Methodenlehre* 496 f.; Bydlinski, *System* 138 f.
[8] There is a difference of opinion, however, as to whether § 1295 II ABGB may be applied directly and whether reference should be made to the underlying legal purposes of a right in holding that it has been abused; Bydlinski, *Methodenlehre* 497 fn. 244; Koziol, *Haftpflichtrecht II* 99; Koziol, *ÖJZ* 1985, 741; Mader, *Rechtsmißbrauch* 160 ff.; cf. also Reischauer, in: *Rummel, ABGB II* § 1295 n. 59 and § 1415 n. 7; see also OGH in JBl 1990, 250 with commentary by Robert Rebhahn; EvBl 1995/155.   [9] Art. 1604 C. civ.

the Civil Code, the courts attempt to ensure that the remedy is proportionate to the breach and here it is clear that George has committed a minor breach. Secondly, if Harry wants to insist on exercising his strict contractual rights, he can do so only in moderation, in proportion to George's non-performance.

On the facts, the harm suffered by Harry appears to be fairly minor, since the last bag can be delivered later the same day. Therefore Harry would be considered to be in malicious bad faith if he were to refuse to accept the delivery, for it would be extremely onerous for George to reload the forty-nine heavy bags in order to deliver them again all at the same time. If Harry were to refuse to take delivery, his refusal to perform would be disproportionate to George's minor breach. As a consequence, Harry will only be entitled to claim damages for George's breach under art. 1147 of the Civil Code. Any loss Harry suffers as a result of late performance which is a direct result of the breach is recoverable under art. 1150 of the Civil Code.

This case therefore illustrates the 'bilateral' role of the duty of performance of contracts in good faith, as set out in art. 1134 al. 3 of the Civil Code. Originally the duty of good faith was imposed on the debtor of an obligation, but this concept has been expanded so as to impose on creditors an obligation to exercise their contractual rights in good faith.

BELGIUM

This case is rather extreme and thus very rare. Although, as a rule, a creditor is not obliged to receive partial performance (art. 1244 sec. 1 C.C.), this will be different where otherwise agreed upon (art. 1244 sec. 1 is not mandatory), or where refusal to receive performance would be unreasonable or abusive.

The case presents a manifest 'abuse of right' (limitative function of good faith), according to the standard of disproportionality (between the cost for the debtor in having to deliver, and the benefit to the creditor in receiving, all fifty bags at one and the same time). On the other hand, if part delivery causes the creditor any costs (e.g. the opening of his warehouse for a second time), the debtor will have to be responsible for them. Furthermore, the rule of art. 1244 sec. 1 C.C. has probably already been abrogated by custom (reasoning on the basis of abuse of right would then not even be necessary), depending on the trade concerned.

With respect to remedies, the following must be considered. (i) Damages: George may perform the contract as Harry requires him to do and claim compensation for any additional costs incurred; (ii) termination with damages: George may terminate the contract without any formalities on the basis of art. 1657 C.C. (this rule being more flexible than the general rules on termination of contracts) and claim compensation for (a) any costs incurred and (b) loss of profit if the flour cannot be sold soon at the same price; and (iii) performance: George could simply claim payment of the price, informing Harry that the goods are at his disposal. But he may not simply leave the bags in front of Harry's door. Moreover, he may be under a duty to sell the flour to a third party if the goods are perishable or if their price is fluctuating.

SPAIN

Article 1169 of the Civil Code provides that a creditor of an obligation does not have to accept partial performance tendered by the debtor, and that the creditor is therefore entitled to refuse an offer of incomplete performance (the so-called rule of 'integrity of due performance').

Case 6 raises an issue of fact, for the question whether a refusal to accept partial performance is a violation of the rule against the abuse of rights[10] depends on the circumstances. While there is no Spanish decision on facts such as those found in case 6, it can nevertheless be said that such a rejection would be considered an 'abuse' if (i) Harry has no immediate need to make use of all fifty bags of flour, and if (ii) Harry is able to take some advantage of each bag individually, and (iii) the cost to George of delivering all fifty of the bags together is disproportionate to the loss which Harry would suffer by not receiving all bags together on time.

ITALY

A party to a contract may reject partial performance by the other party even though performance is divisible, as long as neither law nor custom provide to the contrary.[11] The Italian Civil Code states this rule in absolute terms, but scholars note that the provision in question should be interpreted in accordance with the principle of good faith in the performance of obligations and contracts,[12] which forbids chicanery.[13] This means that

---

[10] Art. 7 C. Civ.; see the Spanish report to case 3 above.   [11] Art. 1181 c.c.
[12] Arts. 1175, 1375 c.c.
[13] Di Majo, in: *Commentario Scialoja-Branca* 91, fn. 11; Breccia, in: *Trattato Zatti* 402.

Harry should have had a good reason for refusing to accept delivery of the forty-nine bags. Yet, the facts as they are described do not disclose why Harry behaved as he did. In the absence of a good reason, however, his refusal to take delivery of the bags is unjustified, and will be considered an example of *mora creditoris*.[14]

Given the fact that the creditor's refusal to accept the forty-nine bags was unjustified, he will not be allowed to rescind the contract and claim the full measure of contractual damages.[15] The creditor will only recover damages suffered as a consequence that one bag out of fifty was not delivered on time.

If George had not unloaded the bags, Harry could have refused to accept delivery because under the current interpretation of the Italian Civil Code, in most cases the creditor has a right to obtain performance, but he is not obliged to accept it.[16]

THE NETHERLANDS

There is partial non-performance if Harry only delivers forty-nine bags. If, however, he delivers the fiftieth bag on the same day, performance is complete. Harry has to accept this performance in two parts, unless the contract stated that the fifty bags should be delivered at the same time or Harry has a particular interest in receiving the fifty bags together. See art. 6:38 ff. B.W. (time for performance) and art. 6:74 ff. B.W. (non-performance of obligations).

This case raises a problem of contractual interpretation. According to art. 6:248 B.W. parties to a contract are not only bound by what they have agreed upon, but also by what is required, according to the nature of the contract, by statutory law, custom and good faith. It is within this framework that the contract will have to be interpreted.

---

[14] See the Italian report to case 8 below. [15] Art. 1455 c.c.

[16] This is the opinion of the majority of Italian scholars; see, e.g., Galgano, *Diritto civile* (1990) 81 ff.; Bianca, *Diritto Civile IV* 374 ff., who notes that there is no article in the Italian Civil Code similar to art. 1650 of the French Civil Code, or to § 433 II of the German BGB; Breccia, in: *Trattato Zatti* 413. There are, however, some cases which do not fall under the general rule and should therefore be considered separately (e.g. the actor who hopes to become a celebrity by starring in a certain movie, or the worker who wants to return to the working place after a wrongful dismissal). In any case, the debtor does not lose his rights under the contract simply because the creditor refused to accept performance.

ENGLAND

The case says simply that George 'owes Harry fifty bags of flour'. Such an obligation would typically arise under a contract of sale of flour from George to Harry, but could arise in other ways, such as if Harry owned land which George farmed, the terms of the lease requiring payment of rent in kind by the flour.[17]

If the obligation arises from a contract of sale, the effect of delivery by George as the seller of the wrong quantity of goods is governed by the Sale of Goods Act 1979, s. 30, as recently amended by the Sale and Supply of Goods Act 1994, s. 4(2). As a result, in principle, a buyer may reject goods where the wrong quantity is delivered and the seller cannot escape the consequences of short delivery by promising the rest in due course.[18] However, rejection of the goods under s. 30 does not mean that the buyer is *ipso facto* entitled to terminate the contract and it would be open to the seller to withdraw the defective tender and substitute conforming goods, provided that he can do so in the time limited for delivery.[19] Of course, if Harry accepts the goods as tendered, subject to subsequent delivery of the last bag, no problem arises; but if Harry wishes to reject the goods as tendered, in principle George must reload and redeliver the stipulated quantity later.

However, this principle giving Harry a right of rejection is subject to two important qualifications. First, the rule allowing rejection of the wrong quantity of goods is subject to the maxim *de minimis non curat lex*, so that a trifling or minute deviation does not entitle the buyer to reject the goods.[20] However, it would seem that the omission of one bag of flour out of fifty may well not come within this qualification, it being held in *Harland v. Burstall*[21] that a deficiency of thirty loads out of 500 did not do so.

Secondly, in 1994 these rules were qualified as regards sales of goods by a seller to a buyer who deals otherwise than as a consumer, with the effect that such a buyer 'may not . . . reject the goods . . . if the shortfall . . . is so slight that it would be unreasonable for him to do so', it being for the *seller* to show that a shortfall or excess falls within this proviso so

---

[17] *Coke on Littleton* sect. 213, p. 142; *Doe d. Tucker v. Morse* (1830) 1 B & Ad 365 (rent payable in part by delivery of culm).

[18] Sale of Goods Act 1979, s. 31(1); Guest, *Chitty on Contracts* § 41–197.

[19] Guest, *Benjamin's Sale of Goods* §§ 8–046, 12–025, 12–044.

[20] *Shipton, Anderson & Co. v. Weil Brothers & Co.* [1912] 1 KB 574; Guest, *Chitty on Contracts* § 41–196.   [21] (1901) 6 Com Cas 113.

as to qualify the buyer's right to reject under s. 30(1).[22] A person 'deals as consumer' for this purpose where he neither makes the contract in the course of a business nor holds himself out as doing so, where the other party does make the contract in the course of business and the goods are of a type ordinarily supplied for private use or consumption.[23] Given the facts as presented in case 6, especially the quantity of the flour, it appears that Harry is not dealing as a consumer and therefore it would be for him to show that it was reasonable for him to reject the forty-nine bags on the ground that one was missing. This seems most unlikely in the abstract, though special circumstances could allow it. If Harry has no right to reject the forty-nine bags of flour, then George can simply deliver the final one later in the day.

If the obligation arises other than under a contract of sale, then similar rules as to rejection would be applied as are found in the Sale of Goods Act, as the Sale of Goods Act 1893 put into statute the position at common law.[24] The courts would also, no doubt, apply the same approach as to the application of the maxim *de minimis non curat lex*. On the other hand, no rules analogous to those found in the Sale and Supply of Goods Act 1994, s. 4 could be applied as its provisions are innovative and restricted to contracts for the sale or supply of goods.

In all, then, while the common law position was very strict in its approach to the tender of non-conforming goods, the reforms of 1994 have softened this strictness, appeal being made to a concept of the 'reasonableness' of the behaviour of the party in question.

IRELAND

Under s. 30(1) of the Sale of Goods Act 1893 a buyer of goods may reject delivery by the seller of a quantity less than the contractual amount. Similarly, under s. 31(1) a buyer is not bound to accept delivery by instalments. Accordingly, Harry may require George to re-tender delivery of all fifty bags unless George can prove that by any usage of trade or previous course of dealing his right of rejection is curtailed.[25] Legal policy here puts a premium on certainty in relation to business dealings, despite the occasional inconvenience caused to the parties, although extremely small or

---

[22] Sale of Goods Act 1979, s. 30 (2A) and (2B) as inserted by Sale and Supply of Goods Act 1994, s. 4(2) (emphasis added).
[23] Sale of Goods Act 1979, s. 61(5A); Unfair Contract Terms Act 1977, s. 12.
[24] *Shipton v. Casson* (1826) 5 B & C 378, at 382–3.   [25] Sale of Goods Act 1893, s. 30(4).

wholly trivial shortfalls in any delivery might attract the application of the maxim *de minimis non curat lex* (e.g. 55lb in a delivery of 4950 tons).[26]

This result according to which Harry may reject the forty-nine sacks which George has tendered would probably apply even if this case did not involve the sale of goods, for George's obligation to deliver the fifty sacks 'owed' would probably be construed as an entire and not a severable obligation.

SCOTLAND

The question of whether a contract has been performed or not will depend upon the consideration of the terms, express or implied, of the contract and also upon the manner in which performance has been rendered. A mutual onerous contract obliges the parties to the contract to perform their part of the bargain, and according to the principle of mutuality either both parties are bound to perform or neither. Where a party fails to perform his obligation, or defectively performs his obligation under the contract, it will be in breach of contract. The law regarding breach of contract is based on the two interrelated principles of *mutuality* and *materiality*: *Turnbull v. McLean & Co.*[27] The materiality of a breach of contract describes the degree of seriousness or importance of the breach and is relevant to the effect which the breach has on the contract and further the choice of remedies (other than damages) available to the innocent party, i.e. remedies depend on whether a breach is serious or trivial. A material breach is one that goes to the root of the contract: *Wade v. Waldon.*[28] Materiality is irrelevant in a claim for damages because even where a breach is non-material or very trivial, it is still a breach of the obligation and must be recognised as such: *Webster & Co. v. Crammond Iron Co.*[29]

Has George adequately performed his obligations under the contract? In principle, for adequate performance the law requires complete and exact compliance with all the terms of the contract: *Arcos v. Ronassen & Son.*[30] However, this principle is subject to the *de minimis* qualification, so that performance is not deemed defective by reason of merely trivial or wholly unimportant deviations from exact compliance. On the face of it, George's breach is a very minor one – he has delivered one sack less than required. According to the *de minimis* principle, a party who has substantially performed his obligation, or performed it except for some elements

---

[26] *Shipton, Anderson & Co. v. Weil Bros. & Co.* [1912] 1 KB 574.   [27] (1874) 1 R 730, at 738.
[28] 1909 SC 571, *per* Lord *Dunedin* at 576.   [29] (1875) 2 R 752.   [30] [1933] AC 470.

of minor importance, may be treated as having performed his obligation and may be permitted to enforce the counterpart obligations, subject to the claim of damages in respect of the defect/deficiencies in his performance. Of course, whether performance is substantial or not is a question of fact. For example, if Harry had an obligation to pass the fifty sacks on to another party and could not fulfil this obligation owing to the shortfall, the defective performance would be deemed material as it goes to the root of the contract. George would have to know about Harry's obligation to pass on the goods. It would seem unlikely though that such a minor breach as this case presents would warrant Harry taking on the financial outlay involved in vindicating his rights in a court of law. George's defective performance can easily be rectified and it is unlikely that Harry would insist on George taking all the sacks back with him only to redeliver them as the correct amount.

If the contract falls into that category governed by the Sale of Goods Act 1979 (the goods have been sold in the course of a business), George is protected by statute: s. 30(2D) Sale of Goods Act 1979 as amended by the Sale and Supply of Goods Act 1994 s. 5(2), which states that while goods must correspond to the description given to them and bulk goods must correspond to the quality of a previous sample, where there is either a shortfall or an excess in the quantity of the goods, this will not entitle the buyer to reject these goods unless the shortfall is material.

DENMARK AND NORWAY

According to the joint Nordic Sale of Goods Act of 1988, the general rule is that the buyer is not under a duty to accept an inadequate quantity of the goods purchased. Thus, it is commonly held that an attempt at part performance is of no relevance, so that the matter must be judged as if the seller had done nothing. An exception is made to this general rule if the shortfall is quite insignificant. In such case, the buyer may not refuse to take delivery of the part performance. If he refuses, he is placed in *mora accipiendi* (default of accepting). In the present case the buyer is not therefore entitled to refuse to receive the forty-nine bags and demand delivery of all fifty bags simultaneously.

One of the central areas of common Nordic regulation in the realm of contract law has traditionally been the law relating to the sale of goods. It has been subject to uniform regulation since the adoption of the joint Nordic Acts on the Sale of Goods in 1905–7. When the United Nations Convention on Contracts for the International Sale of Goods (CISG) was introduced into Nordic law, Norway, Sweden and Finland chose to reform the Nordic law relating to the sale of goods, in that new legislation was imposed for domestic and Nordic sales of goods which is substantially in accordance with the CISG.[31] Denmark has retained its Sale of Goods Act of 1906. Neither in the joint Nordic Sale of Goods Acts of 1905–7 nor in the new legislation from 1988 are there any rules concerning the issue dealt with in the case at hand. The answer must therefore take its basis in general principles of contract law which in most of the Nordic countries are not codified. It has been fairly firmly established that a creditor, be it for goods, services or money, cannot object to part delivery in an instance such as the present case.[32]

As has been pointed out, there is no direct foundation in law for the notion that the buyer is here under a duty to assist and take delivery of the goods. The introduction of a general clause in s. 36 of the joint Nordic Contracts Acts of 1918 must be said to have provided substantial support for the idea that rights under contract law must not be exercised in an unreasonable manner. A good example here is a ruling by Denmark's *Højesteret* (Supreme Court) relating to a lease between businessmen.[33] Here the lessee granted a loan to the lessor against a mortgage on the real property. Later, a dispute arose concerning the lease. Before the dispute was resolved, it became necessary to split the property into separately owned units, and the mortgage bond was inconvenient in this context. The lessor therefore offered to exchange the mortgage security for a banker's guarantee, but the creditor refused to accept this. He was, however, held by the *Højesteret* to be obliged to accept the 'swap' of security rights by way of reference to s. 36 of the Contracts Act. It was stated that the debtor had a considerable interest in having the mortgage bond removed whereas the creditor, who had no objections to the nature or to the extent of the security offered, had stated no reasonable grounds for objecting to the exchange. On the contrary, his refusal had apparently only had the purpose of prompting the debtor to accept settlement of the dispute out of court.

SWEDEN

This case concerns a partial delay in delivery. Pursuant to s. 43 of the Sale of Goods Act of 1990 the rules on delay are applied to the delayed part only,

---

[31] Hagstrøm, TfR 1995, 561 ff.   [32] Augdahl 56 ff.; Nørager-Nielsen/Theilgaard 179.
[33] U 1981, p. 300.

unless the delayed part is of essential importance for the whole delivery. The latter does not seem to be the case. Therefore, George can deliver forty-nine bags. He may also deliver the fiftieth afterwards, unless the delay regarding this bag is of essential importance.

FINLAND

The buyer has to accept the partial delivery, but the seller has to deliver the missing part within a reasonable time which is in this case short:[34] 'tolerance limit' is required.[35] According to s. 43 of the Sale of Goods Act of 1987 a partial breach of contract entitles the buyer to 'terminate the contract in its entirety only if the breach of contract is of material importance to him with regard to the entire contract and the seller realised or should have realised this'. The requirement of 'material importance' is employed in several provisions, e.g. s. 25 I regarding delay.

Editors' comparative observations

All the legal systems under consideration except for Irish law give the same result on these particular facts, viz. that the buyer is not entitled to reject delivery of the forty-nine bags even though the contract provides for fifty. The doctrinal bases of this rejection and their contours are somewhat different.

(i) German law again appeals to the principle of good faith, seeing any attempted rejection as an example of an abuse by the buyer of his right to reject. This exemplifies its use in this context of the notion of abuse of rights, for the latter describes a certain sub-category of situations within the overall category of intervention on the grounds of good faith. The Belgian analysis equates abuse of right and the 'limitative function' of good faith. Greek law and Italian law, too, invoke the notion of good faith in order to limit Harry's right of rejection of part performance.

(ii) Austrian, Belgian and Spanish law rely on the notion of the abuse of rights directly and without reference to good faith as such.

(iii) Dutch law considers that interpretation of the contractual stipulation in good faith permits slight deviation, in the absence of express provision to the contrary. Toleration of a *very* slight deviation from an express stipulation is also found in English, Irish and Scots laws' acceptance of the

---

[34] Hemmo, *Vahingonkorvauksen* 50 ff.   [35] See also KKO 1982 II 78.

de minimis maxim in this sort of context, though this is not formally linked to interpretation nor to good faith.

(iv) French law looks rather to general restrictions on the availability of judicial termination of the contract on the grounds of non-performance, though good faith may be relevant to their application.

(v) English and Scots law (but not Irish law) rely in these particular circumstances on recent legislation governing the contract of sale of goods which subjects the party's decision to reject to a test of reasonableness. The legislation distinguishes between consumer sales in which the buyer is (bar *de minimis*) entitled to keep the seller to the strict contractual stipulation, and commercial sales (such as appears to be the situation in case 6) where a buyer must prove that his rejection is reasonable in the circumstances.

Case 7: Late payment of rent

Case

Emily has rented an apartment from Frances. According to the terms of the contract, Frances is entitled to give notice to Emily, if the latter has not paid her rent for two consecutive months. Emily, being in a momentary financial crisis, cannot pay the October rent. In the course of the following weeks she manages to raise enough funds to pay both the October and November rent. The payment, however, is two days late. Frances terminates the lease.

Discussions

GERMANY

German law distinguishes between a notice to quit as an ordinary remedy to terminate a contract of lease (it is only applicable in cases where the lease has been entered into for an unlimited period of time, does not have to be based on a specific reason and is always subject to a period of notice; the German term is *ordentliche Kündigung*) and a notice to quit as an extraordinary remedy (*außerordentliche Kündigung*: it may be used to terminate any contract of lease for a specific reason – usually breach of obligation by the other party – and is in many cases not subject to a period of notice, i.e. takes effect immediately).[1] In the present case we are dealing with the lease of living accommodation which the lessor seeks to terminate. The lessor's ordinary remedy of giving notice to quit has, however, effectively been abolished in the early 1970s with regard to living

---

[1] Cf. the overview in Medicus, *Schuldrecht II* nn. 212 ff.

accommodation.[2] Frances may therefore only avail herself of her 'extra-ordinary' right to terminate which means that she has to provide a specific ground for termination. The lease would then instantly be terminated. Such a ground may, as in the present case, be based upon the contract. The agreement between Frances and Emily is not invalid under § 554 II n. 3 BGB since it does not modify the statutory rule of § 554 I n. 1 BGB (lessor may give notice to quit if lessee is in default in paying the rent, or a not insignificant part of it, for two successive instalments) to the disadvantage of the lessor.

Emily has failed to pay her rent for two consecutive months. She is in *mora debitoris* since a special warning is not required where a time for performance is fixed by the calendar (§ 284 II 1 BGB). In principle, therefore, Frances was entitled to terminate the lease. If the actual termination only took place after belated payment had been received, the termination would be ineffective under § 554 I 2, II n. 3 BGB. If not, a restriction of the right to terminate may be based on § 242 BGB.

Termination which is not subject to a period of notice is, as has been pointed out above, an extraordinary remedy. To an even greater extent than other remedies, its exercise is subject to the precepts of good faith (*Treu und Glauben*) according to § 242 BGB. When termination conflicts with good faith in a particular case, the contract will continue even if the requirements for that termination are, strictly speaking, met.[3] Such a conflict with the principles of good faith may exist, where the delay has been minimal, especially in cases where the contract of lease has been running for a long time.[4] The precepts of good faith, on the other hand, are not infringed, if the opportunity to terminate the lease suits the lessor, for instance because he has found a lessee who is prepared to pay a higher rent. The lessor is fully entitled to utilise this opportunity.[5]

This is a borderline case. On the one hand the lease apparently has not existed for very long. On the other hand the delay has been short and arises only from a temporary financial crisis on the part of Emily. In the final instance the case will probably sway in favour of Emily. The lease is of great importance for her as it provides her with a roof over her head.

---

[2] § 564 b BGB; cf. Medicus, *Schuldrecht II* nn. 250 ff. and the commentaries to this section. On the development of notice protection in order to provide security of tenure, cf. Wolter, *passim*; Honoré 34 ff.; Zimmermann, *Obligations* 342 ff., 382 f.

[3] *Staudinger/Emmerich* § 554, n. 48.

[4] Cf. OLG Frankfurt WuM 1975, 53 (55) where this conclusion was reached in the case of a lease that had run for twenty years and where the debtor had been in default for one day.   [5] *Staudinger/Emmerich* § 554, n. 50.

Moreover, it does not appear as if Frances has made any other arrangement with regard to the leased property (such as a new lease with a third party) that would leave her open to a third party claim for damages on breach.

Generally speaking, the principle of proportionality (*Verhältnismä-ßigkeitsgrundsatz*), recognised as a central feature of German constitutional law,[6] permeates the entire legal system; through general clauses like § 242 BGB it may even affect the relationships between private individuals. A minor misdemeanour, breach of obligation, or defect in performance may not be used to trigger off far-reaching legal consequences.[7] The exercise of a legal right infringes the precepts of good faith, if it has to be regarded as an excessive reaction. The issue is determined by balancing the insignificance of the debtor's breach of obligation and the reasonable interests of the creditor in strict compliance with the terms of the contract. Finally, § 554 II n. 2 BGB must be kept in mind concerning the lease of residential space. It provides for a kind of *purgatio morae*, if the lessor is paid up to one month after an action for eviction on the grounds of the rent due has been brought. Under these circumstances the termination becomes ineffective.

GREECE

Under Greek law (art. 595 Gr. C.C.) rent shall be paid at the agreed or usual times. In the absence of agreement or usage, rent shall be paid at the expiration of the lease; if shorter intervals have been agreed rent has to be paid at the expiration of such intervals. According to the terms of the contract between Emily and Frances, Emily has to pay her rent every month and Frances is entitled to give notice to Emily if the latter has not paid her rent for two consecutive months. This agreement is valid under Greek law. Here Emily did not pay the October rent but has paid both the October and November rent two days late. Frances terminates the lease. As it appears from the case this contract has been entered into for an unlimited period of time. For this case art. 597 Gr. C.C. provides that the lessor shall be entitled to rescind the lease by giving advance notice of ten days. Every other agreement providing for the reduction of the time periods laid down by art. 597 Gr. C.C., or for immediate dissolution of the contract in the event

---

[6] For a comprehensive analysis of the principle of proportionality and its impact on private law, see Medicus, AcP 192 (1992) 35 ff.

[7] Cf., e.g., Jauernig/Vollkommer § 242, n. 40.

of a default of the lessee, or an agreement granting such right to the lessor, shall be null and void according to art. 598 Gr. C.C. In the case of Emily and Frances, Frances is entitled by the contract to give notice to Emily, if Emily has not paid the rent for two consecutive months. This agreement is valid, on the presupposition that Frances gives to Emily ten days' prior notice.

Greek scholars and the courts have accepted that delay in payment of the rent alone does not entitle the lessor to rescind the contract, but that the non-performance on the part of the lessee must be due to his fault.[8]

In our case Emily was in a financial crisis but she managed to raise enough funds to pay the October and November rent two days late. Under these circumstances Frances' action of rescinding the lease (even if she should have given notice ten days before) seems to be contrary to the principle of good faith, as an abuse of her rights within the meaning of art. 281 Gr. C.C.[9]

It must also be pointed out that according to art. 597 II Gr. C.C. the rescission shall become inoperative if the lessee before the expiration of the time period (in our case ten days) paid the arrears of rent together with any expenses relating to the notice. In our case Emily has paid the rent before the expiration of that ten-day period. In so far as the termination of the lease, under Greek law, is not valid, Emily has the right to continue to stay in the rented apartment.

It should also be noted that statutory restrictions for the protection of lessees enacted after the Second World War have mainly been repealed. A new law (L. 2479/1997) orders, in art. 662 A of the Greek Code of Civil Procedure, a very quick hearing for matters concerning rented immovables, if the lessor has already given notice to quit to the lessee at least one month before the hearing by the courts. In accordance with this law, Frances has no right to terminate the lease immediately. She has to follow the statutory provisions.[10]

Apart from that, in terms of various statutory provisions (cf. L. 2235/1994) which are still valid, every contract of lease lasts for three years, even when the parties have not mentioned the time of termination of the contract. Under these provisions, notice of rescission has to be given to Emily fifteen days before and is valid up to the end of the month.[11]

---

[8] Filios 111.   [9] Cf. Areopagus 908/1985 EEN 53, 343.
[10] See also Rapsomanikis, in: *Astikos Kodix III* art. 597, no. 1.
[11] Filios § 52, B, p. 1 and § 44, pp. 200 ff. (206 ff.).

AUSTRIA

In Austrian law, most contracts of tenancy are governed by the Protection of Tenants Act (*Mietrechtsgesetz* = MRG). This legislation restricts a landlord's right to terminate the tenancy for the purpose of the protection of tenants.[12] As regards the facts of case 7, it is important to note that a landlord can terminate a tenancy on the grounds of his tenant's failure to pay the rent only after having reminded that tenant to pay.[13] Furthermore, the Protection of Tenants Act requires that the tenancy must be terminated by the court.[14] Thus, even if Frances had terminated the lease after an earlier demand for payment, Emily could nullify this termination by paying the outstanding amount before the court gives judgement on the case, as long as the delay in paying does not result from grossly negligent behaviour on Emily's part. Moreover, it must be noted that the creditor can remind the debtor to pay only after the date for performance has arrived, and the debtor has an additional period of reasonable length for performance. Thus, even if Frances did indeed remind Emily immediately her rent fell due, the latter's payment would be considered as having been made within a reasonable period of time and therefore would be effective in nullifying Frances' purported termination.

The same result would be reached if the Civil Code, rather than the Protection of Tenants Act, applied to the contract of tenancy between the parties. For while the Civil Code does not recognise the nullifying effect of late payment of the rent on a purported termination by a landlord, under § 1118 a landlord may terminate a tenancy for non-payment of rent only after he has reminded the tenant to pay[15] and he has to give the tenant an additional period of reasonable length to do so.[16] In the result, therefore, even if Frances had reminded Emily to pay immediately after she failed to pay the November rent, Frances could not validly have terminated the contract and, as it transpired, in any event Emily effected payment within a reasonable period of time of any such reminder. Of course, if Frances had not reminded Emily to pay before receipt of her payment, she could no longer terminate the tenancy, for the ground of her doing so (her default in payment) no longer applied.

---

[12] §§ 29 ff. MRG.
[13] § 29 sec. I no. 5 MRG in connection with § 1118 ABGB and § 30 sec. II no. 1 MRG.
[14] § 33 sec. I MRG.   [15] See Würth, in: *Rummel, ABGB I* § 1118 nn. 4 and 17.
[16] Würth, in: *Rummel, ABGB I* § 1118 n. 4.

FRANCE

According to case law, the exercise of a right to terminate a contract under a forfeiture clause is subject to the requirements of good faith.[17] If the judges on the merits (*juges du fond*), using their 'sovereign power of assessment' of the facts, believe that the clause is invoked in bad faith, they will refuse to enforce it, and the contract will not be terminated. This case law refusing to give weight to forfeiture clauses in favour of a lessor in bad faith has been constantly reaffirmed.[18]

Beyond a minimal control in which the lessor's obviously 'disloyal attitude' is sanctioned, the judges assess a lessor's behaviour in concrete terms to assess whether or not he acted in good faith. In fact, the courts use the test of good faith as a means to determine the contract's content. Indeed, the courts have interpreted art. 1134 al. 3 of the Civil Code so as to impose a positive duty to act in a loyal and co-operative way, so that it is only when such a manner is established on the part of the lessor that he can duly invoke a forfeiture clause. This means in particular that a lessor has a duty to facilitate the performance of the lessee's contractual obligations and that if he fails to do so, the judge will set the forfeiture clause aside.[19] Moreover, when the lessee has substantially performed the contract and the failure to perform is minor, the lessor will not be allowed to invoke the forfeiture clause, even if in good faith.[20]

Until recently, the courts went even further in their control of the application of such clauses by taking the tenant's behaviour into account, with the result that if the tenant acted 'loyally' and in good faith and if the sanction of termination therefore seemed disproportionate to the breach, any purported exercise of the forfeiture clause could be set aside without direct reference to the bad faith of the lessor. Under this approach, the *Cour de cassation* reversed the decisions of lower courts on the ground that they had not tried to find out whether the debtor's performance in good faith had prevented the application of the forfeiture

---

[17] Civ. (1) 14 Mar. 1956, Bull. civ. I, no. 133, p. 107.

[18] Civ. (3) 27 May 1987, Bull. civ. III, no. 108, Def. 1988.34202, p. 375, obs. J.-L. Aubert, JCP (éd. N.) 1989.II.143 note Y. Picod. Cf. Civ. (3) 8 Apr. 1987, Bull. civ. III, no. 88, RTDCiv 1988.122 obs. J. Mestre and 146 obs. Ph. Rémy, relating to a sale of property in return for rent for life where the creditors of the rent abstained from asking for rent for ten years and then suddenly invoked the forfeiture clause for its non-payment.

[19] Civ. (3) 7 Nov. 1978, GP 1979.1.Pan.jur.14. See also Civ. (3) 27 May 1987, Bull. civ. III, no. 108; Paris 19 Jun. 1990, D 1991.515 note Y. Picod; Picod, JCP 1990.I.3447.

[20] Civ. (1) 14 Mar. 1956, Bull. civ. I, no. 133.

clause.[21] This approach allowed such a clause to be set aside on the ground of the good faith of the debtor, regardless of the creditor's good or bad faith. However, this approach is no longer reflected in the case law. In 1993, referring to art. 1134 of the Civil Code, the *Cour de cassation* quashed a court of appeal's decision which had refused to apply a forfeiture clause, where it had also held that the lessee had failed to pay the whole of his debt within the delay stipulated.[22] This recent case is similar to the facts of case 7. It should not be surprising that Emily should be unable to rely simply on her good faith in attempting to pay the rent, for this cannot be relevant while she is not performing her obligation to pay the rent. Article 1134 is meant to govern the good faith of contracting parties while performing the contract, and not while they are failing to perform!

This case law concerning forfeiture clauses was the subject of academic controversy since it allowed the courts to override the terms of the contract. It illustrates the potential conflict between the first and third *alinéas* of art. 1134 of the Civil Code, the former declaring the binding force of contractual obligation (*force obligatoire des contrats*), the latter that contracts should be performed in good faith. It is a good example of the flexible or 'empirical' role played by the principle of good faith in French law, allowing the courts to protect whichever party is deemed worthy in the circumstances. The recent case law which put a stop to an over-expansive interpretation of the duty of good faith can be justified both on a literal reading of art. 1134 al. 3 and on the binding force of contract. Policy considerations in favour of legal certainty have thus fixed a limit on the expansion of the duty of good faith.

BELGIUM

This is a frequent problem. Although the solution is quite clear, many cases still come to court.

Termination of a contract presupposes that non-performance is fundamental and that a special warning has been given (*mora debitoris*). The parties can normally define in their contract which non-performance they

---

[21] Civ. (1) 22 Jul. 1986, Bull. civ. I, no. 223, p. 212; Civ. (3) 8 Apr. 1987, Bull. civ. III, no. 88, p. 53, RTDCiv 1988.122 obs. J. Mestre.

[22] Civ. (3) 10 Mar. 1993, D 1993.357 note Ph. Bihr, Cont., Conc., Cons. 1993 no. 149 obs. L. Leveneur, RTDCiv 1994.100 obs. J. Mestre.

consider fundamental, as has been done in this case. They can also dispense the creditor from the requirement of giving a warning and agree that the debtor is automatically *in mora* once the debt has fallen due. In most contracts, such clauses are valid and will be enforced, except in cases of abuse of right. Given the disproportion between the advantage gained by Frances and the disadvantage suffered by Emily, Frances' action would probably be classified as an abuse of right by a Belgian court. Expulsion of a tenant is seen as a very serious disadvantage.[23] Although termination is possible by unilateral declaration, without judicial intervention, if the non-performance is fundamental, the factual expulsion of the tenant requires an 'executory title', i.e. a judgement (or, in some cases, a notarial deed). As a consequence, the expulsion of Emily would not be granted by the judge or, where expulsion could be enforced on the basis of an authenticated contract, it would be stopped by the judge in summary proceedings on demand by the tenant.[24]

This is even more so in the case of a contract of lease, because art. 1762 *bis* C.C. (as inserted by an Act of 30 May 1931) provides that a termination clause is invalid under Belgian law, i.e. that it cannot give rise to more extensive rights than the general contract law, which means that non-performance must be fundamental, irrespective of the definition given by the parties.[25] In contrast to some other contracts,[26] there is no specific rule determining which non-performance is fundamental; a delay in payment of several months is usually required. Moreover, rent cases are always dealt with by the 'judge of peace', who traditionally has a tendency to take equity into account more widely than other judges: he is a sole judge, not forming part of a court or tribunal, and in a certain sense is sometimes still the village elder.

Although, in theory, the effectiveness of termination has to be judged at the time the termination is communicated to the debtor, in practice a

---

[23] The Belgian Constitution, moreover, regards the right to housing as a fundamental right (see art. 23). Although this provision has no direct horizontal effect, it does influence case law in the field of private law.
[24] Most contracts for the rent of a house are not authenticated in Belgium, as long as they are made for a maximum of nine years.
[25] Article 1762 *bis* C.C. is frequently even understood as meaning that even in the case of fundamental performance, the intervention of a judge remains necessary. This is not the correct meaning of art. 1762 *bis* C.C., but this interpretation has to be taken into account by practitioners.
[26] See, for example, the Consumer Credit Act of 1991, art. 29: two terms not paid and still no performance within one month after summons to pay.

subsequent payment will often lead a judge to conclude that non-performance was not yet fundamental.

In conclusion, therefore, Belgian law offers protection on the basis of general contract law (namely the requirement of fundamental non-performance – which is sometimes, but not always, seen as an application of good faith), made mandatory by statute for this specific contract.

SPAIN

Spanish law possesses neither legislation nor case law specifically governing a case such as the present one, but the facts of case 7 could be seen as exemplifying conduct which could fall under the prohibition of the abuse of rights found in art. 7 of the Civil Code. Thus, the question would be whether it is contrary to good faith for Frances to insist strictly on her right to payment on time, in circumstances which suggest that (i) Emily's delay in making payment causes no significant harm to Frances and (ii) it did not result from any choice or fault of Emily.

However, rather than relying on the doctrine of good faith in this way, a Spanish court would be more likely to analyse these facts in terms of the scope of the right of rescission granted to the creditor where the debtor fails to perform, as recognised by art. 1124 of the Civil Code. Here the question to be posed is whether the creditor can rescind a contract where the debtor's failure to perform does not clearly show a 'deliberate intention not to perform'.[27] On the facts of case 7, the answer to this question is clearly in the negative with the result that the creditor (Frances) is not entitled to rescind.

ITALY

The specific facts of case 7 are governed by art. 55 of Law no. 392 of 27 July 1978, whose effect cannot be modified or excluded by any express agreement of the parties.[28] The latter provision protects a tenant in arrears from termination of the lease by allowing him to pay any rent due (plus

---

[27] High Court judgements of 2 February 1984 (RJA 1984, 571) and 6 November 1987 (RJA 1987, 8342).

[28] Cass., 27 Nov. 1986, n. 6995. Termination of the contract in general and the *exceptio non adimpleti contractus* are governed by arts. 1453 ff., 1460 c.c. Article 1460 c.c., on the said *exceptio*, makes clear that that remedy is based on good faith.

interests and costs) up to the time when he first meets the landlord before the judge. Even if at that meeting the tenant does not pay the landlord, the judge still possesses a discretion to fix a period of up to ninety days within which the defendant may do so, taking into account in this regard evidence of the tenant's difficult circumstances. This system of protection is available to a tenant up to three times in every four years. If the tenant's poor financial circumstances are caused by supervening illness, unemployment or other serious difficulties, the delay fixed by the judge may be up to 120 days and the protection of the tenant is extended so that he can 'pay the landlord in court' in this way four times in four years without risk of eviction.

On the facts of case 7, therefore, Frances would not simply be able to rely on the express provision for termination of the lease for non-payment of rent, nor would she be able to terminate the lease for a very slightly late payment of rent under the applicable legislation.

THE NETHERLANDS

The termination would probably be considered contrary to good faith, unless the two-month period was meant to be strictly observed (cf. art. 6:83 (a) B.W.).

Any non-performance could lead to termination of a mutual contract, unless the non-performance is insignificant (art. 6:265 B.W.). It is a matter of contractual interpretation to decide when non-performance is insignificant and it is here that good faith will play a very important role (cf. art. 6:248 B.W.[29]). If there is non-performance the debtor must be in *mora*, when performance is not permanently or temporarily impossible, before termination can take place (art. 6:265 (2) and art. 6:81 ff. B.W.). As in the present case the obligation under consideration is the one which has to be performed by the lessee (i.e. the payment of money), it could be argued that performance is still possible. Thus, before the creditor can terminate the contract, the debtor must be in *mora*. This means that the creditor gives notice of the non-performance to the debtor and also grants the debtor a period within which the latter still can pay. Such a notice is not necessary in cases where the debtor has to pay before a date specifically agreed upon, or – though this is stated only in the *travaux préparatoires* and not in the Code – in cases where good faith does not require a notice. Even

---

[29] Discussed in the Dutch report to case 6 above.

when in *mora*, the debtor can still offer to pay; if he does so together with an offer to pay his creditor's expenses the *mora* can be held to be purged (art. 6:86 B.W.), thus preventing termination of the contract.

Please note: As this is a contract for the lease of living premises, special mandatory rules apply as to termination. Cf. on the special contract of lease generally the article 7A:1584 ff.; see especially art. 7A:1623n B.W.

ENGLAND

In English law, contracts of tenancy or lease do not give rise merely to obligations and personal rights between the parties, but also create in the tenant a proprietary interest in the property, a 'leasehold interest', the landlord retaining the 'reversionary interest', though in the modern law there is something of a tension between these proprietary and contractual visions of the relationship.[30]

The term in the lease between Emily and Frances provides that Frances may 'give notice' to Emily if the latter fails to pay her rent for two consecutive months. While it uses the language of 'giving notice', it clearly operates as a forfeiture clause, i.e. a clause under which the tenant would lose her leasehold interest on failure to perform her obligations, rather than as a clause under which one or other party is simply entitled to terminate the tenancy on giving the appropriate period of notice.

Almost all modern well-drafted leases contain stringent forfeiture clauses which provide that in the event of *any* breach by the tenant the lease shall be determined and the landlord have the power to re-enter the premises.[31] However, forfeiture of leasehold interests has long attracted special treatment in equity.[32] This means that the courts relieve against forfeiture by giving tenants time to pay and in the meantime reinstate the lease, assuming that it is just and equitable to do so. Certainly, once a tenant has actually paid any rent owing, relief will be denied only in exceptional circumstances.[33] Thus, as long ago as 1802, Sir *William Grant* M.R. declared that 'considering that the purpose of the clause of re-entry to be only to secure the payment of rent; and that, when the rent is paid,

---

[30] Gray 673 ff.   [31] Gray 805.

[32] See for a discussion of its basis, Lord *Eldon's* judgement in *Hill v. Barclay* (1811) 18 Ves Jun 56.

[33] *Public Trustee v. Westbrook* [1965] 1 WLR 1160, at 1163 (no relief to speculative assignee of tenant who had not paid for twenty-two years).

the end is obtained; and therefore the landlord shall not be permitted to take advantage of the forfeiture'.[34]

On this basis, therefore, Frances' attempted termination of the lease will be of no effect, the express terms of the contract being controlled by the equitable doctrine relieving against forfeiture.

It is to be noted that outside the particular context of leases, the older general approach of English courts to clauses under which a sum of money already paid or property already transferred under a contract is to be forfeited on breach of contract by that party was to hold them valid. However, since the 1950s the courts have proved willing to apply the law governing penalty clauses to forfeiture clauses, this development being recently recognised by the Privy Council.[35] As a result, the courts may give the contract-breaker more time in which to pay the sum he had failed to pay on time, though they will rarely do more.[36]

IRELAND

Under Irish law Emily may seek relief against forfeiture of the lease, not-withstanding her breach in failing to pay the rent on time, as long as she is prepared fully to perform her obligations.[37] For while legal policy will not immunise her entirely from the consequences of her breaches, it will be loath to see her evicted, when a breach is seen as capable of repair.

A contrast is drawn by the courts in this respect between business leases, where the parties are or should be fully advised, and residential leases, where this is not the case. Thus, an Irish court would in general be reluctant to grant relief in the context of business leases, assuming that the parties are in earnest when they specify their mutual obligations and the consequences for their breach. Unsophisticated parties who enter business leases may still attract judicial protection.

SCOTLAND

At common law a lease is a personal contract and as such is governed by the general law of contract. Both the landlord and the tenant have

---

[34] *Wadman v. Calcraft* (1803) 10 Ves Jun 67, at 69.

[35] See *Workers Trust & Merchant Bank Ltd v. Dojap Investments Ltd* [1993] AC 573 approving the approach in *Stockloser v. Johnson* [1954] 1 QB 476 (Court of Appeal).

[36] Guest, *Chitty on Contracts* § 26–070.

[37] See e.g. *Breaden v. Fuller & Son Ltd* [1949] IR 290 and generally Wylie § 17.088.

obligations under the contract of lease. One of the tenant's fundamental obligations is to pay the stipulated rent, which is the payment in return for which the tenant is given possession of the subjects. The landlord has a variety of remedies under Scots law for a monetary breach such as non-payment of rent. One of the most stringent is *conventional irritancy* which allows a landlord to terminate the lease in such circumstances (as Frances has done in this scenario). An irritancy clause will require to be in the contract of lease in order for this remedy to be available. In the scenario the terms of the lease allow Frances to give Emily notice for non-payment of rent and I am treating this as the equivalent of an irritancy clause for the purposes of this exercise.

An irritancy is a right to put an end to contractual relations and, as a consequence, puts an end to any right which depends upon the continuance of those relations. By virtue of an irritancy, a contract is terminated in the event of a specified breach by one of the parties. Furthermore, it does not give the party in breach an opportunity to repudiate his obligations. At common law a conventional irritancy, once incurred, could not be purged by the tenant's payment of the arrears of rent (even if only two days late). The principle was that the breach was not purgeable since it was inserted by the parties' agreement into the contract of lease; *C.I.N. Properties Ltd v. Dollar Land (Cumbernauld) Ltd*,[38] *Dorchester Studios (Glasgow) Ltd v. Stone*.[39] In theory, the court may step in to prevent an oppressive use by the landlord of his irritancy. There are, however, no reported cases of the court exercising this power.

After a series of cases, e.g. *Dorchester Studios*,[40] where the courts declined to allow an irritancy to be purged by the tenant offering to pay rent shortly after the due date, the harshness of the common law was recognised. The law has been modified by statutory provisions affecting both monetary and non-monetary breaches; Law Reform (Miscellaneous Provisions) (Scotland) Act 1985 ss. 4–7. The statute requires the landlord to give adequate notice of irritancy in respect of monetary breaches. The landlord must, after the irritancy has been incurred, give the tenant at least fourteen days written notice to pay the arrears; only on the lapse of that further period without payment may he proceed to enforce the irritancy. Notice must be served by recorded delivery. One cannot contract out of these provisions.[41] The provisions apply to all leases of land except land

---

[38] 1990 SC 351, 1990 SCLR 712, 1991 SLT 341, OH.
[39] 1975 SC (HL) 56, 1975 SLT 153.   [40] Ibid.
[41] Section 6(1), Law Reform (Miscellaneous Provisions) (Scotland) Act 1985.

used wholly or mainly for residential purposes, and would therefore not be applicable in this instance.

Residential leases are expressly excluded because the existing statutory protection in these cases is thought to be sufficient. Since the First World War, lets of dwelling houses by private landlords have been largely subject to a series of statutes, known originally as the Rent Restriction Acts, and more recently as the Rent Acts. Existing legislation was most recently consolidated by the Rent (Scotland) Act 1984, and there have been fundamental changes via the Housing (Scotland) Act 1988. The purpose of the legislation has been to protect tenants of dwelling houses in the private sector from exploitation by landlords, and it has done this mainly by means of rent control and by providing the tenant with security of tenure.

Tenancies of dwelling houses are subject to a system of assured tenancies.[42] The assured tenant's right to remain in occupation of the let will not initially derive from the statutory provisions; rather it depends on the contractual period of the lease. It is only when the landlord attempts to terminate the tenancy by serving a 'notice to quit' that the statutory provisions for security of tenure come into force. Unless the landlord (i.e. Frances) can establish one of the stated grounds of removal, the tenancy will become a statutory assured tenancy which will give the tenant the right to stay in the property indefinitely.

The contractual period of the tenancy can only be terminated by the landlord serving a notice to quit at least four weeks prior to the termination date.[43] The notice will be invalid unless it contains certain specified information informing the tenant of his or her legal rights.[44] The tenant under an assured tenancy, who remains in possession of the house after the contractual period of his lease has been thus terminated, will continue to have the assured tenancy of the house.[45] The tenant can only be removed if the landlord obtains a court order by a sheriff, based on one of the grounds set out in Schedule 5 of the Housing (Scotland) Act 1988.[46] The tenant must also be given notice of repossession proceedings and the notice must state the ground(s) of repossession. The period of notice depends on the grounds being used (either two months or two weeks), and there is a required form of notice.[47] Therefore, two separate notices would

---

[42] There are also short-assured tenancies where security of tenure may be limited to a period of six months.   [43] Section 112, Rent (Scotland) Act 1984.
[44] Assured Tenancies (Notices to Quit Prescribed Information) (Scotland) Regulations 1988, SI 1988/2067.   [45] Section 16(1), Housing (Scotland) Act 1988.   [46] Section 16(2), ibid.
[47] Assured Tenancies (Forms) (Scotland) Regulations 1988, SI 1988/2109.

have to be issued by Frances: a notice to quit, which brings the contractual period of the lease to an end, and a notice intimating her intention to raise proceedings for repossession.

The grounds for repossession set out in Schedule 5 may be either mandatory[48] or discretionary.[49] In terms of non-payment of rent, mandatory grounds for repossession exist for three months' rent arrears (not applicable here). On mandatory grounds the only leeway allowed the tenant is the opportunity to bring the arrears below the three-month level during the period between the service of the landlord's notice to the date of the hearing, which is two weeks. Discretionary grounds for repossession do exist for rent arrears, but the sheriff will not grant an order for possession unless he considers it reasonable to do so.[50] It is submitted that no sheriff would deem it reasonable to grant an order for repossession in this instance given the fact that Emily is able to purge her arrears, and in consideration of the wider housing issues, i.e. Scotland's homeless.

DENMARK AND NORWAY

In West Nordic law, issues of this nature will be deemed to relate to the question of whether a right of termination exists. It is considered a general rule of contract law in the West Nordic countries that termination presupposes a fundamental breach of contract.[51] Thus, an insignificant delay in payment will not normally constitute a ground for termination.

The present case concerns a lease. Here the tenant will, in the West Nordic countries, enjoy greater protection by virtue of mandatory legislation. The details of this legislation are, presumably, of minor interest. It is, however, characteristic of these rules of law that they offer general protection for the tenant as the weaker party, generally, within the contractual relationship, in that special rules are laid down regarding notice to terminate the lease on failure to pay, and in that a notice to terminate may, in any event, be set aside by the courts as being unreasonable.

Quite apart from the fact that the present case attracts the application of special rules protecting the lessee on social grounds, the problem may also well be seen as one concerning the general rules of contract law: under which circumstances may a contract be terminated? Even disregarding the special regulation under lease law, Frances' right to terminate is based on very weak grounds.

---

[48] Schedule 5, Pt I, Housing (Scotland) Act 1988.   [49] Schedule 5, Pt II, ibid.
[50] Section 18(4), ibid.   [51] Hagstrøm, *Fragmenter* 116 ff.

SWEDEN

In Sweden there is legislative regulation concerning the lease of real property which is unilaterally mandatory, i.e. a contractual deviation from such regulation to the disadvantage of the tenant is not permitted. According to the 1970 Real Estate Code, ch. 12, s. 42, a delay for two days gives the landlord a right to terminate the contract. However, the tenant can regain the contract by paying within three weeks from the time he received notice by the landlord, and a termination can never occur if the tenant has paid what he owed (ss. 43–4).

Also, according to the Swedish Consumer Sales Act from 1990 (s. 40) the creditor (seller) may not cancel the contract because of a delay in payment if the consumer has, at a later stage, paid the price in full. This provision is lacking in the Scandinavian Sale of Goods Act for ordinary sales.

FINLAND

Pursuant to s. 61 IV of the Rent Act of 1995 (Si 417–18), Frances cannot terminate any longer, since Emily is no longer in delay. According to this provision, termination is allowed only when the delay continues. This reflects the view of the legislator that the delay was immaterial to the creditor, if she did not react whilst it lasted.

Editors' comparative observations

All the legal systems under consideration give the lessee protection in the circumstances. Most of them treat this case as an example of possible restrictions on the exercise of a contractual right to terminate a contract for non-performance, but there are several sources of this protection.

(i) Many legal systems protect the tenant on the basis of special legislation for tenants of residential property (e.g. Austrian, Italian, Scots and Swedish law).

(ii) Some systems subject the landlord's exercise of his right to terminate the lease to a requirement of good faith (German, Greek, French and Dutch law, as an alternative analysis also Spanish law). Interestingly, the French report makes clear the importance of the role of the *juges du fond* in the application of the notion of good faith in this sort of context, accepting that their approach is 'casuistic'. Belgian law, too, applies an analysis based on good faith, in that it regards termination, in the present case, as abusive.

(iii) English law treats this as a special case for equitable protection, 'relief in equity against forfeiture of the lease'. It distinguishes between forfeiture, whether of an interest under a lease or of money or other property transferred under a contract, and termination for breach in general. In the case of the latter, once the court has accepted that a party to a contract possessed a right to terminate the contract, whether this right arises from the express terms of the contract or from the substantial nature of the breach, then the manner or motive of the exercise of this right will not be examined or successfully challenged. Irish law also provides equitable relief against the forfeiture of the lease.

(iv) Spanish law prefers to approach the problem by way of interpretation: what is the proper scope of the right of rescission?

(v) It should be noted that in some legal systems (Austria, West Nordic) the decision depends on the notion of reasonableness.

(vi) A number of legal systems (German, Austrian, Belgian, Italian, Dutch, Scots, Swedish and Finnish law, mostly by way of special legislation relating to the lease of residential accommodation) recognise the notion of *purgatio morae*, i.e. late payment by the debtor may purge his default (with the effect that the contract may no longer be terminated).

Case 8: Delivery at night

Case

Vernon buys a washing machine from Walter. Walter is supposed to deliver the machine in the course of the same week. One day within that week, at 3.00 in the morning, he arrives with his lorry, wakes up Vernon and proposes to deliver the machine. Vernon refuses in view of the early hour.

Discussions

GERMANY

Vernon and Walter have agreed that the washing machine should be delivered in the course of the week. Walter has complied with this term of the contract.

Yet, it has been deduced from the precepts of good faith (§ 242 BGB) that performance may not take place at an inopportune time.[1] For business transactions this is specified in § 358 HGB: performance may only take place during business hours.

Performance at three o'clock in the morning does not constitute proper performance for the purposes of § 242 BGB. Vernon may therefore refuse to accept the washing machine without fear of falling into *mora creditoris*. This is the kind of case for which § 242 BGB was originally intended to be applied.[2]

GREECE

The principle of good faith covers also the time at which performance has to be made. Business usage will have to be taken into consideration and is,

---

[1] *Palandt*/Heinrichs § 271, n. 3; *Staudinger*/Schmidt § 242, n. 835.   [2] Cf. Henle 30 f.

in fact, of considerable importance in the present context (see art. 288 Gr. C.C.).[3] For the purposes of art. 288 Gr. C.C. three o'clock in the morning is not an appropriate time with respect to the obligation under consideration, and Vernon's refusal to accept the performance at that time does not place him in *mora creditoris* (arts. 349 ff. Gr. C.C.).

AUSTRIA

In this case, the question is whether Vernon failed to accept performance after due tender. Contrary to the wording of § 1062 ABGB, a purchaser is not under an enforceable duty to take delivery and, thus, any default in doing so would not be a case of *mora debitoris*.[4] However, refusal to accept performance may lead to *mora creditoris* with the result that the purchaser has to bear certain 'unfavourable consequences' (*widrige Folgen*[5]). The question whether Vernon has to bear such 'unfavourable consequences' will depend on whether Walter's tender of performance is at the right time, since only in this case will Vernon have to accept the goods;[6] otherwise, he will be able to refuse performance without sanction.[7]

The proper time for performance of a contractual obligation is determined primarily by the agreement of the parties and, in the second place, by the nature and purpose of the performance in question.[8] If neither of these criteria apply, the creditor of the obligation is entitled to claim performance at once, which means without undue delay,[9] and, by the same token, the debtor is entitled to make delivery at once.

Walter and Vernon did not fix a precise day and hour for performance of the contract, but rather agreed upon a short period of time ('the course of the same week') within which it should take place. Taking this literally, Walter could deliver the goods at any time within this period.

If the contract were a commercial one for the recipient of the performance, § 358 of the Commercial Code would apply, which provides that performance may be made only during normal business hours. However, the facts of case 8 do not suggest a commercial transaction. While the Civil Code does not possess a provision equivalent to § 358, the last section of § 903 ABGB provides that a period of time which ends on a Sunday or other non-business day does not expire until the next working day. These are official days of rest during which the parties are not to be disturbed and

---

[3] For general comment, see Androulidakis-Dimitriadis, *Ypochreoseis* 42, 108, 222.
[4] Bydlinski, in: *Klang, Kommentar IV/2* 353 ff.   [5] § 1419 ABGB.
[6] Bydlinski, in: *Klang, Kommentar IV/2* 342.   [7] § 1413 ABGB.   [8] § 1418 ABGB.
[9] § 904 ABGB.

on these days delivery contrary to the wishes of the creditor is not legally allowed; nor is it allowed outside normal business hours.[10]

From this we can deduce that performance must be made during those working hours which are customary in the ordinary course of business and not at an 'inopportune time'.[11] Delivery at three o'clock in the morning, of course, is not within normal working hours. Therefore, Vernon is entitled to refuse to accept delivery of the washing machine.

Another line of reasoning might also be raised. For since no express term as to the time for performance was stated in the contract, the agreement could be supplemented by interpretation under § 914 ABGB. Here, then, the relationship between *ius dispositivum* (i.e. legal rules which apply subject to any contrary agreement of the parties) and supplementary interpretation of the contract comes into play.[12] In this case, the question regarding the proper time of performance does not arise as a result of the particular agreement reached by the parties, but gives rise to a general problem and, as a result, 'dispositive law' must be given preference to interpretation as a means of supplementing the agreement which was reached by the parties.

FRANCE

The general rule set out in art. 1134 al. 3 is that both parties have to perform their contractual duties in good faith. The courts have given a more precise meaning to this rule by subjecting the parties to obligations of loyalty and co-operation.[13] It has been suggested that these obligations require the parties to perform their obligations in a useful manner.[14] Furthermore, in the present case, Vernon could rely on the supplementary interpretation the courts are entitled to give to a contract on the basis of art. 1135 of the Civil Code.[15] French law does not lay down a precise provision in relation to a seller's obligation of delivery, such as is found in

---

[10] Reischauer, in: *Rummel, ABGB I* § 902 n. 8, § 903 n. 7.
[11] Gschnitzer, in: *Klang, Kommentar IV/1* 347; Reischauer, in: *Rummel, ABGB I* § 903 n. 4; Straube, *HGB I* § 358 n. 1; cf. also OGH in SZ 30/5 = EvBl 1957/168; EvBl 1966/309. Reischauer points out that *Treu und Glauben* (good faith) has no application here.
[12] Cf. the Austrian report to case 30 below.
[13] See e.g. Terré/Simler/Lequette 347–51, Starck/Roland/Boyer 494–500.
[14] Bénabent 291; Mestre, RTDCiv 1986.101; Picod, JCP 1988.I.3318; Picod, *Le devoir, passim*; Picod, in: *Le juge* 57.   [15] See the French report in case 1 above.

English law in s. 29(5) of the Sale of Goods Act 1979 according to which 'the tender of delivery may be treated as ineffectual unless made at a reasonable hour; and what is a reasonable hour is a question of fact'. Instead, French courts must use their general powers of interpretation, which may be supplemented by reference to good faith, usage and custom, as set out in arts. 1134 and 1135 of the Civil Code.

In the present case, Walter, by delivering the washing machine at 3 a.m., has not behaved in a reasonable way. This early hour cannot be considered to be usual or normal for the delivery of a washing machine and so Walter has not acted in a co-operative or loyal way towards Vernon. It would not, therefore, be too difficult for Vernon to adduce evidence of Walter's bad faith on the facts under art. 1134 al. 3. As a result, Vernon is entitled to refuse delivery of the machine at 3 a.m. and to pay for it. He could ask for due performance at a reasonable hour of the day. In theory, Vernon could claim damages for being woken up at 3 a.m. but the harm caused may be difficult to prove!

BELGIUM

Although theoretically this is a matter for good faith, in practice it will not give rise to litigation, and if it does, it will be dealt with as a matter of custom and usage. Unless there is a different usage in the trade concerned (e.g. in the case of some international carriers), no creditor is obliged to receive performance outside of normal business hours. Usage forms part of a contract on the basis of art. 1135 C.C.

How would a judge react to such a case? First, Walter cannot claim damages, because there is no fault on the side of Vernon. There is no *mora creditoris* either, because the tender was not in conformity with the obligation (as understood on the basis of interpretation and usage). Walter's claim could be dismissed also on the basis of *nemo auditur turpitudinem suam allegans*. Secondly, Vernon could certainly claim performance, i.e. delivery at a normal hour. But it is improbable that he would obtain damages. The fact of being woken up is probably insufficient for damages; although *de minimis non curat praetor* is not a legal rule, it does play a role in practice. If Vernon can prove that Walter is going to behave in the same way in the future, he could obtain an injunction sanctioned with an *astreinte* (penalty) for each time that Walter wakes him up at night. An *astreinte* is comparable to contempt of court, but the amount is to be paid to the other party, irrespective of actual loss.

SPAIN

This set of facts again attracts the application of the rule requiring good faith found in arts. 7 and 1258 of the Civil Code. The circumstances of the case are somewhat unlikely and there is no Spanish case exactly on the point, but it is clear that a party's duty to perform the contract in accordance with the requirements of good faith would mean that any delivery of property to be made under a contract would have to take place at a reasonable time of day. On the facts, such a reasonable time would have to be within business hours. The same result may be reached as a matter of interpretation, and according to art. 1287 of the Civil Code the terms of the contract should be interpreted according to custom and usage. It is clearly not customary or usual to deliver goods in the middle of the night in the absence of special circumstances.

ITALY

The problem raised by this case is not covered by art. 1183 of the Civil Code which governs in general the time of performance of obligations and so the question whether or not Vernon's refusal to accept delivery at three o'clock in the morning was justified depends on the interpretation of the Code's provisions on *mora creditoris*.[16] Italian law does not impose an obligation on the creditor of a contractual obligation to accept performance,[17] but an unjustified failure to do so will expose him to the adverse consequences which are gathered under the doctrine of *mora creditoris*.[18] Article 1206 of the Civil Code states that *mora creditoris* does not occur where the creditor has a legitimate reason to reject a tender of performance and such a reason may indeed be found in a breach by the debtor of his duty to perform in good faith.[19] Italian law would consider that an attempted delivery at an unusual hour, as long as it was not agreed upon, is contrary to good faith because it unduly interferes with the creditor's private sphere of life.[20] Hence, Vernon's refusal to accept delivery of the washing machine at three in the morning was justified and he will not be prejudiced by the doctrine of *mora creditoris*.

---

[16] Arts. 1206 ff. c.c.   [17] Galgano, *Diritto civile* (1990) 85 ff.; Bianca, *Diritto Civile IV* 374 ff.

[18] Arts. 1206 ff. c.c. For historical and comparative analysis of this topic see Zimmermann 817 ff.

[19] Arts. 1175, 1375 c.c. and see Cattaneo, Digesto, 4th edn, sez. civ., XI, 1994, 437.

[20] In Italy, behaviour such as this would also contravene local bye-laws which regulate the conduct of business.

THE NETHERLANDS

Delivery at such an early hour can be refused. Such refusal is not against good faith and does not create *mora creditoris*. Where a contractual duty to accept exists, it seems reasonable that performance is offered during the daytime (consequently: this is not a case of non-performance). Where no such contractual duty exists, still the creditor is not compelled to accept the goods. Thus, he is not in *mora creditoris*.

Once again, this is a matter of contractual interpretation. The question is whether a duty to accept has been agreed upon (explicitly or impliedly, based on what good faith requires, cf. art. 6:248 B.W.) and what its contents are (here, too, good faith will play a role). The agreement would normally be that delivery has to occur during daytime. Vernon's refusal to take delivery does not therefore constitute non-performance of any duty to accept the washing machine.

It should be noted that there is a presumption that no such (contractual) duty exists to accept the goods. Non-acceptance can then lead only to *mora creditoris* (arts. 6:58 ff. B.W.), unless there is *force majeure* on the part of the creditor (NB: this is *not* the *force majeure* which might relieve the *debtor* from liability in cases of non-performance of an obligation, as indicated in art. 6:74 B.W.!). The most important legal consequence of *mora creditoris* can be found in art. 6:64 and art. 7:10(2) B.W. The creditor will have to bear the risk that the object of the obligation is destroyed or is diminished in value.[21]

ENGLAND

Given that the contract between the parties is one of sale of goods, the Sale of Goods Act 1979 applies. Section 29(5) provides that '[d]emand or delivery may be treated as ineffectual unless made at a reasonable hour and what is a reasonable hour is a question of fact'. A clearer case of delivery other than at a reasonable hour could hardly be constructed than 3.00 a.m. in what is apparently a domestic context (Vernon is asleep at the premises of delivery). Vernon's refusal is therefore valid as Walter's delivery is 'ineffectual'.

Although this provision does not apply to contracts other than of sale of goods, the same result could and would be achieved as a matter of

---

[21] Questions relating to *mora creditoris* and whether or not *mora creditoris* might also be considered as non-performance of an obligation are of a highly complex and very technical nature. Cf. Asser-Hartkamp, *Verbintenissenrecht I* nr. 278a ff.

construction of any contractual obligation to deliver goods or to perform a service within a particular time-scale. So if, for example, a householder engaged a window-cleaner to clean the windows of her residence in the course of the following week and to allow him access to do so, she would be entitled to refuse any attempt to do the job in the middle of the night, simply on the basis that their agreement should be construed as referring to performance during a time of day which would be reasonable in the context. English courts do not allow the apparent breadth of contractual terms to be interpreted so as to allow an absurd result.

IRELAND

Where no time is specified for the delivery of goods (or the performance of contracts in general) the courts require that delivery (or performance) should be tendered at a *reasonable* hour. This approach is expressly stated in relation to contracts for the sale of goods by s. 29(4) of the Sale of Goods Act 1893. It is a question of fact in each case as to what constitutes a reasonable hour. On the facts of case 8, three o'clock in the morning is clearly an unreasonable hour.

SCOTLAND

The problem here is not that Walter does not perform his obligation under the contract, but rather the manner in which he renders the performance. While he manages to deliver the washing machine in the course of the week, as agreed, the hour of 3 a.m. is both an eccentric and antisocial delivery hour.

Walker[22] indicates that certain contracts are to be performed in a customary manner, whether expressed or implied by the contract terms. Thus performance must be made in the manner customary at the time when performance is due to be made; *Carapanayoti & Co. Ltd v. E. T. Green Ltd.*[23] It appears that no provision has been made for the exact time of delivery in the agreed week. Where no provision is made in the contract for a time for performance, it is implied that each party will perform his part within a time which is reasonable in all the circumstances of the case; *MacBride v. Hamilton.*[24]

---

[22] *The Law of Contracts and Related Obligations in Scotland*, at § 31.7.   [23] [1959] 1 QB 131.
[24] (1875) 2 R 775.

Statute may also cover this scenario. The Sale of Goods Act 1979 does specify certain rules about delivery. In a sale of goods, demand or tender of delivery may be treated as ineffectual unless made at a reasonable hour. What is a reasonable hour is a question of fact. So, if it were the norm for such deliveries to be made at 3 a.m., it would be deemed reasonable and Vernon should not try to prevent Walter from fulfilling his obligation. Where performance by one party requires the permission or co-operation of the other party, e.g. by allowing the first party entry to the other's land, the latter must permit or co-operate in the former's attempt to make performance.

However, as normal business hours extend between 9 a.m. and 5 p.m., it seems highly improbable that the hour could be considered anything but unreasonable. Hence Vernon can refuse to take delivery, and can either insist on performance at a suitable hour, or he can reject the washing machine and recover the price he paid for it. It would probably not be worth his while to sue for damages.

DENMARK AND NORWAY

In West Nordic law the facts of this case will be judged according to precisely the same principles as those applied in resolving case 6. This is again a question of whether the buyer is under a duty to assist in taking delivery of the object. The formal justification for the buyer's duty to assist can today be found in the joint Nordic Sale of Goods Act of 1988 (s. 50(b) of which provides that the buyer shall 'take over the object by collecting or receiving it'). As mentioned above[25] Denmark has retained the Nordic Sale of Goods Acts of 1905–7 for national sales of goods; the Danish law does not have an express provision concerning the buyer's duty to take delivery of the goods, but the rule is nevertheless the same.[26]

The imprecise wording in the Norwegian Act fails to resolve the problem. For want of other points, it would perhaps be said here that the buyer must at the outset be prepared to accept the object during normal business hours. If it is a purchase outside a business relationship, which is what the text appears to suggest, delivery may also be possible, for example, in the evening. But it cannot be said, without any basis in the agreement to this effect, that the buyer is under a duty to take delivery at three o'clock in the morning.

---

[25] See the Danish/Norwegian report to case 6 above.   [26] Nørager-Nielsen/Theilgaard 631.

SWEDEN

There is no legislation or case law concerning delivery at odd times, but I assume that Vernon can refuse to take delivery at three o'clock in the morning.

FINLAND

Once woken up, Vernon cannot refuse to accept the machine. See the Sale of Goods Act of 1987, s. 50: 'the buyer shall co-operate in the sale in such a manner as may reasonably be expected of him in order to enable the seller to fulfil the contract'. Of course, Vernon could from the beginning refuse to accept delivery at an inconvenient time, and if the delivery was then made, he could bluntly refuse to accept it.[27]

Editors' comparative observations

All the legal systems under consideration, except for Finnish law, come to the same result here, so that Vernon would be entitled to reject the tender of performance by Walter at this unreasonable hour, in spite of the fact that it appears to come within the express terms of the contract. The doctrinal bases for this can be grouped into three.

(i) English, Irish and Scots law have special legislative provisions governing the contract of sale of goods to deal with this particular point.

(ii) Many of the other systems (Dutch, Belgian, Spanish and French law) rely on interpretation, usually with reference to trade custom in the context, and this would also be true of English and Scots law outside the particular context of sale of goods.

(iii) German law considers this as a prime example of the application of the general requirement of good faith found in § 242 BGB, though in fact special legislation confirms this in the context of commercial transactions. A number of other legal systems would also rely on good faith (particularly Greek and Italian law), some of them in conjunction with, or as an alternative to, interpretation (Spanish and French law).

---

[27] I have, incidentally, personal experience of waiting for the delivery of a washing machine which eventually arrived after midnight. The manufacturers had had difficulties at previous places on their delivery route.

Case 9: Uniformity of outfit

Case

Kim is employed as a kitchen help in Larry's restaurant. According to her employment contract, Kim has to wear, for reasons of hygiene, a cap as supplied by her employer. These caps, however, turn out to contain material that leads to an allergic irritation on Kim's skin. She therefore buys a cap herself that is made of another material and looks slightly different. Larry objects to Kim wearing her own cap and insists, for the sake of uniformity of the outfit of his employees, on Kim wearing the caps supplied by him.

Discussions

GERMANY

Only the scope and nature of employment are normally agreed upon in a contract of service. The employee's ancillary duties are usually not specifically mentioned. But the employer's right to instruct the employee as to how to carry out the services puts flesh on the skeletal duties of the employee. The legal basis of this right of instruction is seen to be the employment contract in conjunction with § 315 BGB (I: 'If performance is to be determined by one of the contracting parties, it is to be presumed, in case of doubt, that the determination is to be made in an equitable manner.' II: 'The determination is made by declaration to the other party.' III: 'If the determination is to be made in an equitable manner, the determination made is binding upon the other party only if it is equitable. If it is inequitable the determination is made by court decision; the same applies if the determination is delayed.').

Apart from the contract this right of instruction may be limited by statute and by the requirement that determination of the performance

331

has to be made in an equitable manner (*billiges Ermessen*: § 315 I, III BGB).[1] § 315 BGB is one of the general clauses through which the fundamental rights as set out in the Basic Law (*Grundgesetz*) permeate private law (horizontal operation of the constitutional rights).[2] Thus, what constitutes determination 'in an equitable manner' may often be influenced by the fundamental rights of the employee.[3]

In the present case, the solution is straightforward in that the BGB contains a rule specifying the way in which the employer's equitable discretion has to be exercised.[4] For according to § 618 I BGB an employer 'has to set up and maintain rooms, equipment and apparatus which he has to provide for the performance of the service, and so to regulate services which are to be performed under his orders or his direction, that the employee is protected against danger to life and health as far as the nature of the service permits'. No matter which of the two alternatives applies here ('equipment . . . which he has to provide',[5] or 'so to regulate services . . .'): Larry must not expose his employees to materials which cause health problems. 'The nature of the service' clearly does not require Kim to wear this specific type of cap (as long as the cap that she does wear takes care of the hygienic concerns). § 618 I BGB may be seen as a special, statutory emanation of the ancillary duties arising, in terms of good faith, under a contract of employment.[6]

If the Code were not to have contained a special rule covering the present situation, a limitation on the right of instruction would probably have been deduced from § 315 BGB read in conjunction with Art. 2 II GG (the right to bodily integrity). However, the evaluation of the fundamental right of Kim is only one of the issues that will be taken into account in determining the equities for the purposes of § 315 BGB. A comprehensive balancing of interests is required.[7]

For this process of balancing it is essential to know whether the employee at the time of conclusion of the contract must have contemplated that his services might affect his fundamental rights.[8] In the present situation that does not seem to be the case. Moreover, the cap only

---

[1] *Münchener Handbuch zum Arbeitsrecht*/Blomeyer § 46, nn. 29 ff.
[2] Cf. generally Dürig, in: *Festschrift Nawiasky* 158 ff.; Hager, JZ 1994, 373 ff.; Currie 181 ff.
[3] Cf. BAG AP n. 27 (p. 694) on § 611 BGB (*Direktionsrecht*).
[4] See *Staudinger*/Oetker § 618, n. 168.
[5] The term 'equipment' applies to all objects which have to be used, whether for legal or factual reasons, in the course of performing the services and which are supplied by the employer; see, e.g., *Staudinger*/Oetker § 618, n. 123.
[6] *Staudinger*/Oetker § 618, n. 13.   [7] Cf. BAG AP n. 27 (p. 694) on § 611 BGB (*Direktionsrecht*).
[8] Cf. Ibid.

differs marginally from those prescribed by the employer. The interests of the employer therefore do not carry much weight when compared with the infringement of the employee's bodily integrity. The instruction to wear the original cap would therefore also, according to general principles, not constitute an equitable exercise of his discretion. Under § 315 III 1 BGB, Kim is not bound by it.

There is no need to invoke § 242 BGB in this type of case.[9]

GREECE

Article 662 of the Greek Civil Code provides that 'an employer shall be bound to make such arrangements concerning the conditions of work, the premises in which it is carried out and the abode, the installations, machines or implements as are necessary to protect the life and the health of the employee'. It follows from this article that the employer is obliged to make the necessary provision to protect his employees' health and life. Thus, there is no need to turn to arts. 57, 59, 281 and 288 Gr. C.C. or to art. 5 of the Greek Constitution: art. 662 Gr. C.C. regulates the matter specifically. It constitutes *jus cogens* and may be seen as a special emanation of good faith and the protection of the employee's personality.[10]

The caps, as supplied by the employer, contain material leading to an allergic irritation on Kim's skin. Kim therefore has the right to buy for herself another cap to protect her health; since this new cap looks only *slightly* different, Kim has not breached the contract and the employer has no right to dismiss her.

It is generally accepted in Greek law that, where there is a special provision applicable in a certain situation, recourse to the general clauses is unnecessary. If, nevertheless, Kim were to rely on art. 281 Gr. C.C. in the present case, she would have to prove the requirements of this article, which are more strict than those laid down in art. 662 Gr. C.C.[11]

AUSTRIA

Under § 1157 ABGB, an employer owes a duty to take care that the life and health of his employees are protected as far as possible.[12] On the facts of case 9, while it is true that the danger to Kim's health is a slight one, it is

---

[9] Ibid., at 693.   [10] Cf. Stathopoulos, in: *Astikos Kodix II* art. 288, no. 34.

[11] Spiliopoulos, in: *Astikos Kodix III* art. 662, nos. 1–24, pp. 510–16; Androulidakis-Dimitriadis, *Ypochreoseis* 154 ff.; Areopagus 1227/1993 EllDni 36, 849.

[12] Cf. Kramer, *Verbindlichkeiten, passim*; Tomandl, *passim*.

also true that Larry's interest in having his employees wear caps which he has supplied would be considered to be of very low importance. In the result, therefore, Larry has a duty either to supply caps made of another material or to allow Kim to wear her own cap, even though it is slightly different from the others. If he fails to do either, Kim is entitled to ignore the order to wear the cap which is harmful to her health.[13]

FRANCE

In the absence of an internal regulation in the company (which in French law is usually supposed to have rules relating to safety and hygiene) about the obligation to wear caps at work supplied by the employer, Kim and Larry's dispute will be governed by special employment legislation concerning individual or collective rights and obligations at work. Under art. L. 120.2 of the Labour Code (Code du travail) 'no person can restrict the right of persons and individual and collective liberties which are not justified by the nature of the function nor proportional to the desired objectives'. It appears that Larry and Kim's dispute comes within these provisions of the Code. It may also be possible for Kim to exercise her right to withdraw her services under art. L. 231.8 al. 2 of the same Code on the ground that her working conditions create a situation which is harmful to her health and, if this were the case, she would be entitled to stay away from work on full pay. However, the risk caused to her skin by wearing the cap may not justify such a measure.

In the result it is necessary to consider whether or not Larry's demand that Kim wear the cap supplied by him is justified.

(i) In reply to Larry's allegation that she is not performing her contractual obligations and that her refusal to wear his cap is an act of insubordination which constitutes a fault on her part, Kim may be able to rely on art. L. 120.2 of the Labour Code and argue that Larry's own conduct is unjustified. To do so Kim will argue that the purpose of wearing the cap is for Larry to maintain a certain standard of hygiene in the kitchen: while she cannot object to this end, she may argue that the means proposed by Larry are disproportionate to this end where his cap causes her to contract a skin allergy. In order to rebut any allegation of her own bad faith, it would be advisable for Kim to consult a doctor for medically related employment problems (a *médecin de travail* who supervises the health of

---

[13] Cf. Krejci, in: *Rummel, ABGB I* § 1157 n. 49.

employees in every place of work but is independent of both employer and employee) and obtain from him a medical certificate indicating that she does indeed have a skin allergy and that it is caused by the material of the cap supplied by Larry which he is obliging her to wear. If Larry were presented with such a certificate, his refusal to accept the evidence would be considered an act of implicit bad faith on his part.

Nevertheless, it is possible to imagine a situation in which Larry persists in insisting that Kim wears the cap. Indeed, if Kim remains recalcitrant, Larry may decide to dismiss her. Should he do so, Kim could argue (a) that the dismissal is unjustified[14] or (b) that it is void as it constitutes an infringement of a fundamental right. It is unnecessary, in the present context, to consider the details of these provisions any further.

(ii) In the event that Larry can prove that he is justified in insisting that Kim should wear the cap, on the basis that it is necessary for hygienic purposes and that his solution is proportionate to this objective (regardless of the fact that this argument seems rather difficult to maintain on the facts), he could oblige Kim to comply, failing which he may allege a fault, or breach of Kim's obligations at work. He could then attempt to dismiss her. As we can see, it seems unlikely that this argument would be successful on the facts.

It may be added more generally that an inability to perform an obligation at work which is justified for medical reasons would not give rise to a failure to perform on the part of the employee so as to enable the employer to take disciplinary action or the more extreme measure of dismissal. In the event that the inability is medically justified, it is considered inappropriate to reason in terms of breach of contract and, therefore, the question of the employee's good faith in performing his obligations does not arise. In fact, questions of health and safety come within another dimension of the employment contract where the power relationship between employer and employee comes to the fore. It is for this reason that in relation to his powers of management and control, the employer is sometimes referred to as the *chef d'entreprise* and not as an employer to emphasise this more institutional aspect of the employment relationship.

Thus, despite the fact that the contract of employment may be seen as the archetype of a contract which requires both loyalty and co-operation from its parties, and that these requirements are the most important features of the duty of good faith in performance, the latter general

---

[14] Under art. L. 122.14 al. 3 C. trav. a dismissal must be made for 'a real and serious cause'.

principle is rarely explicitly invoked in the context of health and safety. Several explanations are possible for this. First, the employment relationship has given rise to more and more detailed and specific legislation, with the effect that any general principle is supplanted by specific regulation. Thus, for example, the detailed provisions examined in the present case refer not to the conduct of either party in terms of good faith, but rather to the question whether or not the measures imposed by an employer are justified. In fact, the justification for particular measures is implicitly evaluated by reference to a notion of fair dealing. For example, if it is proven that Kim's skin allergy is not caused by the cap Larry supplied, wearing another cap would be considered to be an act of insubordination, in breach of her contractual obligations. Good faith is therefore not explicitly invoked here. Similarly, Larry's behaviour is subject to a criterion of justification: underlying this test is an implicit idea of fair dealing, first cousin to the idea of good faith, from which is derived the test of proportionality of means and end.

On the other hand, it may be argued that labour law is designed to regulate and protect the positions of employers and employees and that the measure of protection given to each is a question of political and economic considerations which vary according to the nature of the government which introduces the legislation. In this respect, although the employment relationship appears to be paradigmatic of the duties of loyalty and co-operation, it is by no means typically contractual, the courts having to consider aspects of the relationship other than the contractual ones. This could be explained by the fact that the difference between an employer and employee's economic power is too wide, that this inequality of power requires the law to introduce protective measures and that this policy of protection may sometimes prevail over other underlying influences in the employment relationship, such as good faith.

BELGIUM

The solution to this case is not really doubtful. For this reason – and also in view of certain practices occurring in the field of industrial relations (collective bargaining, intervention of trade unions, etc.) – such a case will rarely come to court.

(i) According to art. 20, 2° Labour Contracts Act of 1978, the employer is obliged to take care that his employees can perform their jobs in circumstances which are fit for the health of the employees. This rule was originally developed by case law as an additional obligation on the basis of the nature of the contract (art. 1135 C.C.), more specifically as an *obligation de sécurité*. Application of this rule alone will probably lead to the result that Larry may not insist on Kim wearing the caps supplied by him. There may even be specific regulations forbidding the use of such materials for the manufacture of working clothes in this sector.

(ii) Even if art. 20, 2° does not prevent Larry from insisting on Kim wearing the cap, the industrial doctor[15] can prohibit the employer and the employee from working in circumstances which are injurious to the health of the employee.[16] Kim's allergy would then have to be considered as an 'incapacity' or 'disability'. As a result, the employer would be obliged either to modify these circumstances (and thus permit Kim to wear her own cap) or to offer another, equivalent job to Kim, unless this is absolutely impossible. It is most improbable that any Belgian judge would accept it to be impossible for Larry to let Kim work under conditions not injurious to her health.

(iii) Apart from these more precise rules of labour law, the behaviour of Larry could be qualified, under general contract law, as an abuse of right (acting against good faith), on the basis of the principle of disproportionality. There is indeed a disproportion between the small advantage gained by the employer (precise uniformity of outfit) and the disadvantage suffered by the employee because of the adverse effects of the materials on her health.

(iv) Two further remarks may be made. First, labour law has become a field with so many specific regulations that the general notion of good faith was, until recently, rarely resorted to. Only recently has it regained interest among labour lawyers.[17] Second, there may be a temptation to elevate the present issue to the level of human rights. Such a line of argument, however, would not appear to be called for, given the various rules provided by private law.

(v) Concerning remedies, the fact that Larry may not require Kim to wear the cap supplied by him, does not help Kim as long as she can be dismissed for not wearing that cap. Most labour contracts are contracts for an indeterminate period, and termination periods for manual labourers are short under Belgian law (the general rule being about one month). But

---

[15] Every employer has to organise a medical service or be affiliated to one.
[16] See here the *Algemeen Reglement Arbeidbescherming*, or ARAB, i.e. the General Labour Protection Regulations, especially art. 146 *ter*.
[17] See especially Van Eeckhoutte, TPR 1990, 971 ff.

if the employee maintains that the dismissal is 'arbitrary', the employer has to prove that it was motivated by the performance or behaviour of the employee, or by the requirements of the organisation of the firm. He will otherwise be liable to pay an indemnity corresponding to six months' pay (see art. 63 of the Labour Contracts Act of 1978).

(vi) The notion of a unilateral determination of the performance – which is known in Belgium and will be explained in the Belgian report to case 15 – will not be used in a case like this. The requirement that Kim wears a cap supplied by the employer will normally form part of the labour regulations, which have to be drawn up in each firm, by the Labour Council. These regulations automatically form part of the contract (unless there is a written contract deviating from this): see art. 4 of the Labour Regulations Act of 8 April 1965. The notion of a unilateral determination by the employer can only play a role in those aspects of employment relations which have not been specifically regulated but have been left to the discretion of the employer (*ius variandi*).

SPAIN

There are three aspects to this case.

A first question is whether Kim is under an obligation to perform her employment contract in the terms under which it was agreed, despite the health problems that this performance would cause her. Under arts. 1105 and 1184 of the Civil Code, a party to a contract is exempted from liability for 'objective non-performance' if this is due to circumstances which are not imputable to his own conduct. On the facts, this means that Kim would not be liable in damages for not wearing the cap which Larry supplies.

A second question is whether a creditor (Larry) may rescind the contract when the debtor (Kim) 'objectively' fails to perform an obligation, if as a result of this non-performance the contractual interest of the creditor is frustrated, whether or not the debtor is at fault in failing to perform. As regards contracts of employment, the answer to this question is not doubtful, since arts. 20 and 50 of the Contract of Employment Act of 24 March 1995 entitle an employer to rescind the contract if his employee 'objectively' becomes unable to fulfil the requirements of the workplace.

Finally, however, the case may be looked at in terms of the requirements of good faith in relation to the creditor's conduct. For Larry may be said to act in a manner contrary to these requirements by insisting that Kim should wear the cap which he has supplied, given that the material of the cap which Kim herself has bought is of such slight difference that it would not affect the uniformity of the commercial image of the firm required for Larry's ordinary commercial purposes. Spanish case law makes clear that in such cases one should balance the firm's right to settle the conditions of work against the employee's rights to privacy or health. The Constitutional Court applies a three-stage test. It should be determined (i) whether the limitation on the employee's interest (his 'image', privacy or health etc.) which is at issue is to be deemed to be covered by the contractual framework which has been freely accepted by the parties; (ii) whether the limitation on this interest is necessary for the legitimate purposes of the firm; and (iii) whether the employee's burden is proportionate to such a purpose, that is, whether the interest of the firm cannot be achieved by means of a less restrictive or harmful measure.[18]

ITALY

Larry does not have the right to compel Kim to wear a cap which leads to an allergic irritation on her skin.

For reasons of hygiene Kim's employment contract obliges her to wear a cap as supplied by her employer,[19] but the facts of the case are not entirely clear as to whether or not the contract obliges Larry's employees to adopt a uniform outfit at the workplace as well.[20] On the assumption, however, that the contract is so to be interpreted, both the decisions of the courts and the opinions of jurists in Italy suggest that such a contractual requirement, which attempts to restrict an individual's rights to his or her own life-style, should be subject to close scrutiny.[21] Thus, while

---

[18] See the Constitutional Court judgements in 107/1987, BOE 9 July 1987 (in which a firm prohibited its waiters from wearing beards) and 99/1994, BOE 17 May 1994 (in which an employee refused to participate in a publicity photograph for the firm's products).

[19] Indeed, in Italy a kitchen help's duty to wear such a cap is of legislative origin. To comply with the legislation in question the employer must provide caps and see that the employees wear them. See d.p.r. 30 Mar. 1980, n. 327, *Regolamento di esecuzione della l. 30 aprile 1962, e successive modificazioni, concernente la disciplina igienica della produzione e della vendita delle sostanze alimentari e delle bevande, art. 42.*

[20] If such duty does not flow from the contract, the employer can take measures concerning employees' outfits solely where they are necessary for reasons of decency or hygiene: Cass., 9 Apr. 1993, n. 4307, Riv. giur. lav., 1994, II, 226, obs. Bellavista; Dir. prat. lav., 1993, n. 20, 1341, obs. Mannaccio (a case affirming the right of a male worker to wear shorts rather than trousers while working in the defendant's factory).

[21] Cass., 9 Apr. 1993, n. 4307, Riv. giur. lav., 1994, II, 226; Bellavista, Riv. giur. lav., 1994, II, 226, esp. 231. For a general perspective on the power of the employer over the employee at the workplace: Mengoni, in: *Diritto* 387.

contractual terms such as these are in principle lawful, this is true only where they are strictly related to the proper performance of the contract: a capricious term, motivated merely by some general company policy would be considered void. The facts of case 9 do not reveal any circumstances which would support Kim's having to respect a dress code, as they do not indicate that she works in an area of the restaurant where she can be seen by the company's customers or by the public more generally. Thus, in the circumstances, the term in case 9 would not pass the scrutiny which Italian law imposes.

Moreover, even if the contractual term providing for the dress code were to pass the 'strict scrutiny' test and be considered effective generally,[22] the employer's instruction concerning the wearing of the cap is subject to a paramount norm requiring him to protect the health of those working at the workplace. The policy expressed in this rule (and by similar rules enacted by subsequent legislation) has constitutional foundations (arts. 32, 41 of the Constitution of the Italian Republic). Accordingly, Kim may legitimately refuse to wear a cap causing irritation to her skin.[23] If Larry were to insist that she must do so, he would commit a breach of his contractual obligation to safeguard her health. Such a breach obliges him to pay damages. On the basis of art. 1460 of the Civil Code which provides for a defence for one party based on the other's non-performance (a defence termed the *exceptio non adimpleti contractus*, which operates in accordance with good faith) Kim may also legitimately refuse to work in Larry's restaurant until he supplies her with a cap that does not damage her skin.

THE NETHERLANDS

This question would be governed by special rules in the area of labour law and the law on working conditions.

ENGLAND

While Kim is under a contractual obligation to wear a cap as supplied by her employer for reasons of hygiene, this obligation must be seen in the

---

[22] Bellavista, Riv. giur. lav., 1994, II, 226.

[23] In more general terms, this could be considered as a case of impossibility to compel the debtor to exact performance of the obligation. The theory supporting this approach is based on the German doctrine of *Unzumutbarkeit der Leistung*, in contrast with the good faith requirement.

wider context of the relationship of employment. In particular, given the effect of wearing the cap on Kim is to cause her an allergic irritation, it should be noted that at common law employers owe their employees a duty that they be reasonably safe in the doing of their work, this duty being reflected contractually in an implied contract term and tortiously in a duty of care in the tort of negligence.[24] It is clear that the employer's obligation extends to the items put at the disposal of the employee, such as tools or clothing. The primary significance of these obligations is, of course, that where they are broken, the employee may sue the employer for damages, whether these be for breach of contract or the tort of negligence (it not usually being of significance how the claim is put, though it is usually put in tort). However, the employer's obligations as to the employee's safety may also have an impact on the proper interpretation of an *employee's* duty. A good example of this may be found in the decision of the Court of Appeal in *Johnstone v. Bloomsbury Health Authority.*[25] There a junior hospital doctor who worked under a contract of employment which stipulated a working week of forty hours and provided for a possible forty-eight additional hours' availability for work claimed a declaration that he should not be required to work more than seventy-two hours a week on the basis that working longer than this had affected his health. His employer countered that any implied term which it owed relating to its employee's health must take second place to the express term in the contract as to the length of working hours. A majority of the Court of Appeal gave judgement for the employee. *Stuart-Smith* L.J. held that as a matter of construction the express terms of the contract did not attempt to exclude the effect of the implied one.[26] Rather more convincingly, Sir *Nicolas Browne-Wilkinson* V.-C. held that the clause in question did not impose an absolute obligation on the employee to work the extra hours, but rather gave the employer a discretion as to the number of extra hours to be worked, a right which should be considered subject to the employer's implied obligation as to the safety of the employee.[27]

Thus, an English court could take the view that Larry's contractual right to require the wearing of a cap of his choice should be read subject to the implied term as to his employee's safety, with the effect that Larry would be contractually entitled to require her to wear a cap only if the latter does not cause her any injury or illness. If this analysis were accepted, then the significance of Kim's wearing a cap of her own purchase may be seen as

---

[24] *Davie v. New Merton Board Mills Ltd* [1959] AC 604 (negligence); *Matthews v. Kuwait Bechtel Corporation* [1959] 2 QB 57.   [25] [1992] 2 QB 334.   [26] Ibid., at 343.
[27] Ibid., at 350–1.

fulfilling her own *implied* contractual obligation to come to work suitably dressed to do the job which she is employed to do, which, given her working at a restaurant, would include wearing a suitable cap. In the result, if Larry wishes to ensure uniformity of the outfit of his employees, he must provide a cap in this uniform style which does not cause irritation.

Finally, Larry's insistence on Kim wearing the caps supplied by him given that they cause her allergic irritation may give rise to her 'constructive dismissal' for the purposes of unfair dismissal legislation and redundancy payments legislation. Thus, where the employer's conduct amounts to a fundamental breach or repudiation of the contract of employment, the employee may treat this as 'constructive dismissal' and terminate the contract with or without notice.[28] One of the obligations which the courts have recognised as lying on employers in this context has been one to preserve the trust and confidence in their employees.[29] Kim could well argue that Larry's insistence has fundamentally breached this obligation.

IRELAND

The analysis concerning English law holds good for Irish law.

SCOTLAND

This is a contract of employment. Like other contracts, the terms and conditions may be express or implied. The express term of note here is the work rule regarding the dress code, and the question is whether by not observing this rule, Kim is in breach of contract. Concomitant to that is the question of whether Larry has a right to force Kim to adhere to the rule, and whether her continued breach of the rule could warrant her dismissal.

In contracts of employment, the legal significance of work rules is a question of fact to be determined by the circumstances of each case. A work rule is an instruction by the employer on how to do the job. Such instructions must be reasonable *vis-à-vis* the particular employee. The fact is that Kim will not wear the uniform cap because of her allergic reaction to it. However, she has used her initiative and improvised by providing her own cap which surely fulfils the same objective. It is unlikely that Larry

---

[28] Guest, *Chitty on Contracts* § 37–135.   [29] Ibid., § 37–105.

could argue that by wearing her own cap Kim cannot perform her duties. As she works in the kitchen it is less likely that she will be seen by the restaurant customers, so Larry's argument about conformity seems futile, and it is unreasonable for him to insist on her adherence to his instruction in the circumstances.

Bearing all this in mind, it is necessary to look at some of the principles of employment law. While it is certainly the case that where an employee is in breach of a contractual term this could be a ground for dismissal, it has been held that contract terms must be applied reasonably and not literally; *United Bank v. Akhtar.*[30]

As well as the express terms of the contract of employment, the law infers certain implied terms or duties on the employer and employee. Relevant here is the implied duty upon the employer of mutual respect; that is, a legal duty to treat his employees with due respect and consideration, mindful of their needs and problems, and sympathetic to their difficulties. Larry would seem to be breaching this implied duty. Furthermore, in *Akhtar*[31] it was also held that employers will not, without reasonable cause, conduct themselves in a manner calculated or likely to destroy or seriously damage the relationship of confidence and trust between employer and employee.

An implied duty incumbent on the employee is a duty to obey lawful and reasonable orders, i.e. a duty of obedience and respect to the employer. Was the instruction reasonable? An employer cannot lay down rules and act on them in an autocratic manner. The courts and tribunals will use the test of reasonableness to circumscribe employer's policies. It is not necessarily the case that a breach of an order will merit dismissal, as dismissal depends on whether the misconduct is minor or amounts to gross misconduct. Yet, a refusal to wear the appropriate clothing required for the job has been held to warrant a dismissal; *Atkin v. Enfield Hospital Management Committee.*[32] But, in that case the nursing sister had refused to wear the uniform provided for her by the hospital authorities for a period of four years. She had no reason, e.g. an allergic reaction to the fabric, for such a refusal (unlike Kim). In connection with acceptable standards of dress and hairstyle, industrial tribunals are reluctant to recognise that the employer has the right to require conformity unless there is a safety factor involved and the acceptable standard is clearly specified; *Talbot v. Hugh Fullerton Ltd.*[33] It seems unlikely that Kim's refusal to wear the cap

[30] [1989] IRLR 501, EAT.   [31] Ibid.   [32] [1975] IRLR 217.   [33] [1975] IRLR 52, IT.

provided amounts to a safety hazard because she has provided her own cap which performs the same function. While a breach of hygiene rules constitutes misconduct, her improvisation means that the health and safety rules are still being adhered to. The *de minimis* qualification appears to operate here. Kim's performance of her job is not defective owing to her wearing a different style of cap, and it would be deemed unreasonable of Larry to enforce his work rules to the detriment of her health.

If Kim faces dismissal there are principles that Larry should consider before making a hasty decision. Reasons for dismissal must not be 'whimsical or capricious . . . which no person of ordinary sense would entertain'[34] and they should not be 'trivial or unworthy'.[35] If he dismisses her, it is submitted that the dismissal will amount to an unfair dismissal; ss. 54–65, Employment Protection (Consolidation) Act 1978 as amended by the Employment Acts 1980–1990 and the Trade Union Reform and Employment Rights Act 1993. Every employee to whom the Act applies has a right not to be unfairly dismissed. The question of whether the dismissal is unfair is assessed in two stages. First, the tribunal will evaluate the way in which the decision to dismiss the employee was reached. If the employer fails to follow a fair procedure, he must show that none the less he acted reasonably on the basis of the information at his disposal, otherwise the unfair procedure will result in the dismissal being unfair at this stage. Secondly, if the first hurdle is passed, the further test is: 'did the employer act reasonably?', or 'what would the reasonable employer have done?'. This is a question of fact and depends on the circumstances of the individual case.

If Kim herself terminates the contract owing to Larry's unreasonable conduct there is a case for constructive dismissal because, although she has resigned, it is the employer's conduct which constitutes a repudiation of the contract and the employee is deemed to accept that repudiation by resigning; *Western Excavating (E.C.C.) Ltd v. Sharp*.[36] The test for constructive dismissal is to be determined by the contract, i.e. did the employer's conduct amount to breach of contract which entitled the employee to resign? The breach must be significant and go to the root of the contract. There is no unreasonable conduct test for constructive dismissal; the fact that there is constructive dismissal does not necessarily mean that the dismissal was unfair. If, however, it is found to be constructive dismissal and

---

[34] *Harper v. National Coal Board* [1980] IRLR 260, EAT *per* Lord McDonald.
[35] *Gillian v. Kent County Council (No. 2)* [1985] ICR 233, [1985] IRLR 18, CA *per* Griffith L.J.
[36] [1978] QB 761, [1978] ICR 221, [1978] IRLR 27, CA.

the employer can offer no reason for dismissal then it must automatically be unfair; *Derby City Council v. Marshall.*[37]

DENMARK AND NORWAY

This problem may be viewed from two angles. First, it may be seen as raising a more general problem of contract law as to how far obligations extend. Secondly, in view of the fact that it concerns a matter of employment law, it may be discussed, in fairly specific terms, under the employment law legislation which is implemented everywhere in the Nordic region. Concerning the latter, it is difficult to envisage that an employer, by virtue of his right to issue instructions, may impose on an employee a duty of this kind when it entails a health hazard, and when it is of no decisive importance for the fulfilment of the tasks allocated to the employee.[38] Taken to its extreme, the employer rather than the employee would here have a problem under the rules of West Nordic employment law.

If the problem is seen from the point of view of general contract law, the starting point under West Nordic law will probably be that, in determining the obligations of the parties in a complex contractual relationship such as this, it is difficult to refer to absolute obligations in a field other than distinctly commercial contracts concluded between professional parties. West Nordic law will, to a large extent, determine the substance of an obligation in cases like the present one, by interpreting its reasonableness.[39] Under West Nordic law there is a close correlation between the interpretation of reasonableness and the above-mentioned general clause in s. 36 of the Contracts Act; cf. e.g. Rt. 1991, p. 22.

SWEDEN

The interest of the employer is to meet the hygienic standards required in the kitchen. If Kim can meet these requirements by wearing her own cap, she would probably be entitled to wear it, since she had health problems with the cap supplied by her employer. Section 36 of the Contracts Act gives a foundation, but one might come to the same conclusion according to general principles in labour law.[40]

---

[37] [1979] ICR 731, [1979] IRLR 261.   [38] Jakhelln 470.
[39] Selvig 536 ff.; Andersen/Madsen/Nørgaard 378 ff.
[40] In Schmidt 160, the employee's duty to take orders is said to be limited to what is reasonable.

FINLAND

In the Finnish view this is a case where mandatory rules regarding work security and health are applied. This makes the case rather clear. Since the caps supplied by the employer cause Kim an (albeit individual) allergic irritation, the employer is, according to the Work Safety Act of 1958 (Ty 401), s. 20, obliged to provide *personal protection*, which implies that he has to (i) either give Kim a new cap made of another type of material or (ii) accept Kim's cap. There is in Finnish labour law a principle that the employer has a 'right of direction' concerning the work to be done, although its limits are unclear; it is, however, generally recognised that this right has to be used in a fair manner.

Editors' comparative observations

All the legal systems under consideration come to the same result, that is, that the employer was not entitled to require Kim to wear a cap which irritated her skin. However, a number of approaches are found in the legal systems studied.

(i) A variety of legal systems (Germany, Greece, France, Belgium, the Netherlands, the West Nordic countries, Finland) possess special legislative provisions assisting the employee in cases like the present one. In this respect, some systems (for example, French and Belgian law) limit the employer's power to restrict an employee's personal rights and liberties to cases where this is justified by the nature of the employee's function and in proportion to the purpose to be achieved. A similar balancing of interests is undertaken in Austrian and Italian law.

(ii) English, Irish and Scots law, as well as the West Nordic legal systems, rely on the interpretation of the contract, a combination of the construction of express and the finding of implied terms in the contract.

(iii) In terms of general contract law, Belgian law looks to good faith, here preventing the employer from abusing his right under the contract. Spanish law, too, relies on the requirement of good faith in evaluating the employer's conduct. The German solution revolves around a general provision enjoining the employer to determine the conditions of work 'in an equitable manner'. For other legal systems (Scotland, West Nordic, Sweden) the notion of 'reasonableness' plays a crucial role.

(iv) In their decision as to what 'equity' or 'good faith' mean Spanish law and, generally, also German law take into account the protection given by their *constitutional* law to the employee's rights. In this respect, as in French law, Spanish law focuses both on the legitimacy of the employer's action for its purposes and the proportionality of the measure in question. The Italian approach, too, has constitutional foundations.

(v) Assuming that the clause in her contract of employment applies as a matter of its proper construction, Italian law then subjects such a clause which attempts to restrict an individual's 'right to his or her own life-style' to close scrutiny to see if they are justified in the context. Moreover, even if the clause passes this test, the employer could not invoke it to justify conduct which constitutes a breach of his contractual obligation to safeguard his employee's health, an obligation which is a 'paramount norm' and which possesses foundations in constitutional law.

Case 10: Dissolution of partnership

Case

Anton and Barry have formed a partnership. They have agreed that either one of them may request dissolution of the partnership, if the annual profit is less than DM 40,000. In 1991 the profit amounts to only DM 25,000. The reason is that one of the employees has been guilty of embezzlement. The embezzlement was only possible because Barry (who was responsible for keeping the books) had grossly violated his duties of supervision. May Barry demand dissolution of the partnership?

Discussions

GERMANY

It is assumed that Anton and Barry have not concluded a civil partnership (*Gesellschaft bürgerlichen Rechts*) for an indeterminate time. For then the partnership could be terminated at any time even if the parties agree otherwise (§ 723 I 1 BGB; this rule does not constitute *ius dispositivum*: § 723 III BGB). The premise here will be that the contract may only be terminated if profit is less than DM 40,000.

This requirement has been met. But that it has been met is due to a gross breach of duty on the part of Barry. The exercise of a right will be regarded as abusive if it has been acquired by behaviour which is immoral, illegal or in breach of contract.[1] In the present case, therefore, the termination is barred by the defence of abuse of right, as recognised under § 242 BGB. Ultimately it is the general maxim *nemo auditur turpitudinem suam allegans*[2] that is today generally taken to have been absorbed in § 242 BGB.[3]

---

[1] *Jauernig*/Vollkommer § 242, nn. 44 ff.; *Palandt*/Heinrichs § 242, n. 43.
[2] Cf. the references in Zimmermann, *Obligations* 865 f.
[3] Wieacker 30 f.; *Jauernig*/Vollkommer § 242, n. 45.

GREECE

According to art. 767 Gr. C.C., the dissolution of a partnership for an indefinite time does not depend upon the existence of an important reason. If, however, the notice of dissolution is untimely, the person giving notice is liable for any loss caused to the other partners. Good faith and business usage determine whether or not a notice of dissolution is untimely.

In the case in question, it has to be assumed that the contract may only be terminated if the profit is less than DM 40,000. However, Barry cannot demand dissolution because the fact that this requirement is met, is due to a gross breach of duty on his part (cf. art. 281 Gr. C.C.), and *nemo auditur turpitudinem suam allegans*.

Thus, the notice of dissolution by Barry would be invalid because it constitutes an abuse of right. The partnership continues to exist.[4]

AUSTRIA

The conditions as agreed upon for exercising Barry's right to dissolve the contract of partnership appear to be satisfied, but the question arises whether this apparent right is affected by Barry's gross negligence in relation to the partnership's drop in profits.

Although it is true that the Austrian Civil Code does not contain a rule similar to that found in § 162 II of the German Civil Code (BGB), the legal fiction which is established in that provision has also been accepted by the Supreme Court[5] as a matter of Austrian law. In the result, a condition will be deemed not to have been fulfilled where its fulfilment has been brought about by one of the parties to the contract in a way that the other party cannot possibly have expected according to the whole purpose of the contract.[6] This is seen not as a sanction for negligent conduct, but rather as a special case of supplementary interpretation of the contract[7] and in this regard, good faith and generally accepted standards of behaviour are taken into account.[8] Applying this rule, Barry may not demand dissolution of the partnership as this right depends on the fulfilment of the condition.

The same result may be reached following a different line of reasoning. For since Barry has grossly violated his duties of supervision and, in so

---

[4] See Liakopoulos, in: *Astikos Kodix IV* art. 767.   [5] OGH in GlUNF 6838.
[6] OGH in JBl 1991, 382; Rummel, in: *Rummel, ABGB I* § 897 n. 7.
[7] Knütel, JBl 1976, 613 ff.; Rummel, in: *Rummel, ABGB I* § 897 n. 7; OGH in JBl 1991, 382; cf. also OGH in JBl 1990, 37.
[8] OGH in JBl 1991, 382; Rummel, in: *Rummel, ABGB I* § 914 n. 17.

doing, made the embezzlement possible, he must compensate the loss which he thereby caused to the partnership. Once he has paid damages, the partnership's profit will exceed DM 40,000 and, as a result, the condition will not be fulfilled and Barry will not, therefore, be able to claim dissolution.

FRANCE

It is first necessary to determine which type of association between two or more partners (*société*) is the French equivalent of Anton and Barry's partnership because different legal rules apply depending on this preliminary question.

(i) It is possible that under French law Anton and Barry's partnership would be comparable to a *société en participation*. In this case, the partners are free to organise their partnership as they wish and their relationship is based on trust *intuitu personae*. A *société en participation* has no distinct legal identity except in its dealings with third parties. Such a partnership is governed by arts. 1871 ff. of the Civil Code. In the event that Anton and Barry's partnership is of an uncertain duration it can be dissolved at any moment by notice given by one of the partners to the others and it is provided that notice must be given in good faith and not in the context of a dispute.[9] It is open to debate whether Barry's behaviour constitutes bad faith for this purpose. Dissolution would not be awarded if Barry was entirely responsible for the situation, by analogy with the general rules governing the dissolution of companies (i.e. *sociétés* as defined by arts. 1832 ff. of the Civil Code, all of which possess legal personality).

(ii) In the event that the partnership is governed by the general rules in the Civil Code relating to companies, art. 1844-7 8° may apply allowing dissolution as provided in the company's articles. However, as under (i), the fact that the loss of profits is due to Barry's own negligence may well prevent him from invoking this text successfully, for if Barry was in gross breach of duty and asked for the partnership to be dissolved, it is arguable that he is in constructive bad faith, since he would be in bad faith by attempting to benefit from the consequences of his act. In this context we should recall the adage that *faute lourde* (which would include a gross breach of duty) is equivalent to *dol* and that bad faith is an inherent characteristic of *dol*. Such a line of reasoning would lead to treating Barry's

[9] Art. 1872-2 C. civ.

behaviour and subsequent wish to dissolve the partnership as constituting bad faith.

(iii) In the event that dissolution is refused upon the terms originally agreed by Barry and Anton, it is possible to imagine that the company would be dissolved by court order. Article 1844-7 5° provides for dissolution to be pronounced by the court at the demand of one partner 'for justifiable reasons and particularly in the event of breach of a partner's obligations, or a misunderstanding between the partners which paralyses the working of the company'. It is suggested that as *ius fraternalis* governs a company, behaviour of a partner which renders future collaboration impossible would suffice to justify termination. However, in one case before a court of appeal,[10] dissolution was refused the partner who had demanded it since he alone was at fault. *A contrario*, if a partner was not the only one at fault, dissolution may be awarded by the court. It is arguable that Barry was not solely at fault here. It is also clear that Barry's negligence may render future collaboration difficult or impossible.

(iv) A brief word should be added for the situation where the partnership does not correspond to any of the legal entities set out in the Civil Code and is therefore subject to the general rules of contract law. In this event the possibility of asking for the partnership's dissolution would be analysed as an express termination clause (*clause résolutoire expresse*), as governed by arts. 1183 and 1184 of the Civil Code. Reference to case law concerning the use of termination clauses in bad faith in the context of leases has already been made in the discussion of case 7. If Anton resists dissolution (which is difficult to imagine), he may ask for damages under art. 1184 of the Civil Code. It is arguable that Barry's bad faith would prevent him, in any event, from claiming restitution of investments made under the contract, pursuant to the principle *nemo auditur propriam turpitudinem allegans*. However, this principle would in all probability be considered inapplicable to a case where a party's disloyal behaviour has not given rise to the nullity of the contract, but simply to the potential application of a termination clause. In practice, however, practical reasoning would probably be in favour of allowing the partnership to be terminated (despite Barry's lack of good faith) in order to avoid an unhappy result, if it is established that Barry and Anton are unable to work together any longer. The economic considerations which argue for this solution will

---

[10] Paris 20 Oct. 1980, JCP 1981.II.19602 note F. Terré, D 1981.44 concl. M. Jéol, Rev. sociétés 1980.774 note A. Viandier (which held that a partner could not rely on a dissolution clause where he had himself created the 'partnership troubles' in question).

ultimately prevail. Partnerships are economically viable only if the partners are willing to carry on business as co-owners. If this is not the case, the partnership must be dissolved. Although it may be unjust to allow bad faith as a means to get out of a partnership, economic considerations will prevail over equitable or moral ones, since if the purpose of the contract can no longer be achieved, imposing duties of co-operation and loyalty between the partners makes no sense.

This case raises the interesting question whether good faith in specific and detailed rules of the Code relating to *sociétés* bears the same ramifications as the general principle set out in art. 1134 al. 3 of the Civil Code. It would seem that a higher standard of good faith is perhaps required in the context of dissolution of partnerships. This is because French law is biased against unilateral termination and relies more on judicially awarded termination than does, for example, English law. This bias is designed to prevent parties from escaping too easily from their obligations: *pacta sunt servanda*. Even if this rule is mitigated in the context of dissolution, moral and equitable arguments suggest that it should not be at the expense of good faith. This seems to be particularly true when the very nature of partnership requires a high level of co-operation and loyalty. Just as these duties should be respected during the partnership, it would be contradictory not to consider them when the partnership is dissolved. However, these arguments must be counterbalanced by other non-legal considerations.

Finally, it is sometimes said that a partnership in England is like a marriage, being paradigmatic of a contract which requires good faith. It seems appropriate to quote *Carbonnier's* ironic comment on the expansion of the duty of good faith in French contract law in general that 'when marriage is transformed into a contract, others dream of transforming contracts into marriage'.[11]

BELGIUM

The solution to this case depends first of all on the terms, under which the partnership was formed.

(i) If a partnership is formed for an indeterminate period, every partner can terminate the contract at any moment, provided he does so 'in good faith' (art. 1869 C.C.). According to article 1870 C.C. termination is not in good faith when a partner intends to obtain for himself profits which

---

[11] Carbonnier, *Les obligations* 195.

would otherwise be shared by the partners. But this is seen only as an example of termination against good faith. Case 10 could be considered to constitute another example. If the termination is contrary to good faith, Anton may claim continuation of the partnership for a reasonable period. But Anton will probably not be eager to continue the partnership with a grossly negligent partner such as Barry. Normally, therefore, he would claim damages for the loss caused by Barry's negligence, as well as for the loss caused by the untimely termination of the partnership.

(ii) Where the partnership is for a fixed period of time or a specific undertaking, an earlier termination of the partnership is possible only for a legitimate reason (such as non-performance by another partner). Apart from that, a clause such as the one in the present case is perfectly valid as an explicit ground for termination. May Barry thus terminate the partnership on the basis of such a clause? Several arguments could be invoked against the possibility of termination by Barry.

First, one might argue that in a partnership for a fixed period of time, termination must *a fortiori* take place in good faith.

Secondly, another argument could be based upon the adage *nemo auditur turpitudinem suam allegans* which is often applied in Belgian law.[12] This rule is usually not understood as an application of good faith, but both notions can overlap. *Nemo auditur* is used especially in the case of positions acquired by acting *contra bonos mores*, but sometimes also where a position was acquired by acting contrary to good faith.

A third argument could be found in art. 1178 C.C., according to which a debtor who has bound himself conditionally (here: to remain in partnership under the condition that the annual profit remains at least DM 40,000) cannot rely on non-fulfilment of the condition, where such non-fulfilment has been caused by his own fault (including negligence). The notion of condition is understood in a wide sense in Belgian law.[13] A condition must not necessarily have automatic effect; it is quite possible to have a resolutive condition which merely gives one party a right to terminate.

Finally, some of these arguments might also be used to say that the annual profit within the meaning of the present clause has to be

---

[12] It is not generally accepted that this rule forms part of Belgian law (for a negative view, in the context of different cases, see, e.g., Kruithof/Bocken, TPR 1994, 426); but case law seems to confirm that it does (see, e.g., Cass. 13 Apr. 1984, Arr. n° 474).

[13] Compare, however, the facts of case 30, where a Belgian lawyer would probably not apply this rule, considering that case 30 is a problem of non-performance.

calculated without deduction of the loss caused by the embezzlement. This reasoning would, however, be unusual in Belgian law.

Apart from these considerations regarding the possibility of termination by Barry, Barry will be liable for the harm he caused to Anton by his negligence. This liability is a contractual one, and Anton can claim damages for losses incurred as well as for lost profits. Moreover, Anton may terminate the partnership because of Barry's negligence. Again, as under (i), Anton will not probably be eager to continue the partnership.

SPAIN

In Spanish law this case does not need to be analysed in terms of the general requirements found in arts. 7 and 1258 of the Civil Code, as art. 1119 specifically provides that a condition of an obligation is deemed in law to be fulfilled where the debtor intentionally prevents such fulfilment. In this respect, for a debtor to be held to act 'intentionally' it is not necessary that he deliberately aims at the particular result which is the subject matter of the condition (viz. on the facts of case 10 that the profits should be low): it is enough that this result can be traced to his own voluntary action.[14]

There is in Spanish law another route to the same result. Article 1306 of the Civil Code follows Roman law in providing that *nemo propiam turpitudinem allegare potest* (no one may rely on his own wrongdoing). This rule makes clear that Barry is not entitled to rely on the partnership's lack of profit, where this was caused by the grossly negligent breach of his own duties. On the facts of case 10, therefore, a Spanish court would hold that a partner cannot seek the dissolution of the partnership on the basis of the failure of some requirement for which he himself was responsible.

ITALY

A refusal to allow Barry to obtain dissolution of the partnership would rest on two arguments, but in Italian law both of these must be weighed against a general policy favouring dissolution of a partnership where relations between the partners have deteriorated to the point that they can no longer work together.

The dissolution of partnerships is governed in general by art. 2272 of the Civil Code which provides (*inter alia*) that they are dissolved for any cause expressly provided by the contract of partnership itself. A first approach

---

[14] See Morales, 35 ADC 1982, 602.

to the facts of case 10 therefore would be to consider the partnership contract as being subject to a 'resolutive condition' which is satisfied if the
annual profit is less than DM 40,000. Owing to Barry's gross negligence,
this financial condition was satisfied, but art. 1359 of the Civil Code prevents Barry from relying on it.[15] To be sure, the words of art. 1359 relate to
suspensive conditions, but leading scholars and the courts interpret the
provision liberally, seeing it as a particular manifestation of the duty to
perform obligations and contracts in good faith.[16]

A second approach to the problem raised by case 10 would start from
one of the general principles governing the termination of contracts for
non-performance, viz. that a party to a contract who is liable for its breach
cannot rely on that breach to free himself from his contractual obligations.[17] Under this approach, clearly Barry would be unable to insist on dissolution of the partnership.

Finally, if future collaboration between the partners becomes impossible due to their differences, the partnership may be dissolved whatever
the outcome of the foregoing discussions. For the provisions of art. 2272
of the Civil Code have been supplemented by the courts (following the
opinions of leading jurists) so as to allow the dissolution of a partnership
where the partners are no longer able to work together. In such a case,
unless Barry is expelled or resigns from the partnership, such an example
of the supervening impossibility of the contract of partnership causes its
termination.[18] Should Barry indeed cease to be a partner, Anton has six
months to find another partner before dissolution of the partnership
occurs by operation of law.[19]

THE NETHERLANDS

No answer can be given with certainty. Whether termination would be
against good faith depends, in particular, upon the wording of the dissolution clause and on the meaning which that clause has in the circumstances of the case (art. 6:248 B.W.). Barry's role as to creating the

---

[15] Art. 1359 c.c.: 'A condition is considered fulfilled when it fails for a cause imputable to
the party who had an interest contrary to its fulfilment.'

[16] Arts. 1175, 1375 c.c., and see Sacco/De Nova, in: *Trattato Sacco II* 156; Cass., 17 Sept. 1980,
n. 5291, Giur. it., 1983, I,1, 345; Cass., 6 Jun. 1989, n. 2747.

[17] This rule is enacted by art. 1453 c.c. with reference to synallagmatic contracts. The
partnership contract does not belong to this *genus*. Yet, the rule in question could be
applied to the present case by analogy.

[18] See Di Sabato 159–60. Among the latest cases adopting this approach, see Cass., 28 May
1993, n. 3779; App. Milano, 24 Oct. 1992, Società, 1992, I, 1073, obs. Morano.

[19] Art. 2272, n. 4 c.c.

opportunity for embezzlement is of relevance here, albeit not of decisive relevance.

ENGLAND

As a general rule, the parties to a contract of partnership are subject to a requirement of good faith in relation to dealings with each other in the course of the performance of the contract.[20]

The possibility of dissolution of partnership depends on whether the partnership was for a fixed period or otherwise[21] and, in principle, partnerships other than for a fixed period or particular project may be terminated by notice by either party at will. As regards contracts of partnership for a particular period or project, the courts possessed the power at common law to dissolve the partnership on the application of a partner either on the ground of the alteration of the circumstances in which the partnership worked or of the conduct of the parties.[22] However, in the latter type of case, as Sir *John Romilly* M.R. accepted in 1856, 'no party is entitled to act improperly, and then to say that the conduct of the partners, and their feelings towards each other, are such that the partnership can no longer be continued, and certainly this Court would not allow any person so to act, and thus to take advantage of his own wrong'.[23] This approach was retained by the Partnership Act 1890, s. 35(d) in relation to dissolution by the court.

This legal position as regards judicial termination of fixed-term partnerships would no doubt colour the approach of a court to the exercise of an express provision for the termination of a contract of partnership and according to a leading work on the subject, 'while the point is not entirely free from doubt, the current editor takes the view that a partner must display good faith when he seeks to dissolve the firm by notice, whether pursuant to an express power in the agreement or the provisions of the Partnership Act 1890'.[24] In case 10, Barry has grossly violated his duties of

---

[20] L'Anson Banks (*Lindley & Banks on Partnership*, 17th edn) § 16–01; *Blisset v. Daniel* (1853) 10 Hare 493; *Floydd v. Cheney, Cheney & Floydd* [1970] Ch 602, at 608. The first edition of *Lindley* attributed this rule to C. 4, 37, 1, 3: N. Lindley, *A Treatise on the Law of Partnership*, vol. I (1st edn, 1860), at 492.   [21] Partnership Act 1890, s. 32.

[22] *Harrison v. Tennant* (1856) 21 Beav 482.   [23] Ibid., at 493–4.

[24] L'Anson Banks §15–07. The same work later distinguishes between a requirement of good faith in the exercise of the power of dissolution so as to prevent its exercise *mala fide* or for an improper purpose, and a requirement of reasonableness in the exercise of the power, the latter requirement not being made by English law: § 24–13.

supervision (sc.: under the contract of partnership) and for this reason, he would not be entitled to invoke the express contractual power to dissolve the partnership as to do so he would have to rely on his own breach of duty.

While these rules are clearly particular to the law of partnership, they are reflected more generally in judicial approaches to the exercise of contractual rights which have arisen though a party's own wrongdoing, though this has been varyingly expressed as being the result of a rule of law and a rule of construction. Thus, in 1821 in *Doe d. Bryan v. Bancks*[25] Best J. stated (in the context of leases) that 'I take it to be an universal principle of law and justice, that no man can take advantage of his own wrong.' More recently, though, in *Alghussein Establishment v. Eton College*,[26] while the House of Lords recognised the existence of a principle that a party in default under a contract cannot take advantage of his own wrong, it considered that 'in general the principle is embodied in a rule of construction rather than in an absolute rule of law'.[27] In that decision itself, the result of this rule of construction was the denial of the exercise of a contractual right arising in particular circumstances, where those circumstances had arisen from the breach of contract of the person seeking to exercise the right. The difference between placing the principle on the basis of a rule of construction rather than a rule of law is that the former makes clear that it can be ousted by contrary intention, though the speech of Lord Jauncey in *Alghussein Establishment v. Eton College* suggests that very clear contrary intention will be required.[28]

IRELAND

Partnership law is one of the few areas in Irish law in which courts have explicitly recognised a duty on the parties to act in good faith.[29] Notwithstanding the arguments of the English commentator, *l'Anson Banks*,[30] it is the authors' opinion that Irish courts would not apply the requirement of good faith in the context of the dissolution of partnerships at will. The courts are reluctant to force parties together, except where the partnership was agreed for a fixed period or for a single adventure and then only to a limited extent.

Under the Partnership Act 1890 a partner may dissolve a partnership of

---

[25] (1821) 4 B & Ald 401, at 409.   [26] [1988] 1 WLR 587.
[27] Ibid., at 595, *per* Lord *Jauncey* of Tullichettle.   [28] Ibid.
[29] *Blisset v. Daniel* (1853) 10 Hare 493.
[30] *Lindley & Banks on Partnership* § 15.07; and see the English report above.

undefined duration ('partnership at will') except to the extent that the partnership agreement otherwise provides. On the facts of case 10, the right to dissolve is restricted rather than abrogated, and in so far as the factual preconditions for its dissolution exist, a partner (here, Barry) may dissolve notwithstanding any *mala fides* or culpable negligence.

The position would be different if the partnership were either for a fixed duration or for a single venture or undertaking, for in these circumstances Barry would have to request dissolution of the partnership from the court. The grounds for such a termination would be those found in s. 35(d) of the Partnership Act 1890, viz., that the actions of the other party to the contract no longer made the partnership arrangement practicable. Dissolution, when it is requested of the court, is not granted as of right and the court would be reluctant to accept arguments of the impracticability of the continuance of the relationship from a person whose questionable action has given rise to the impracticability in question.

Anton's only source of relief would be on the winding-up of the partnership, at which stage he may argue that he should be indemnified against, or that account be made for, the loss attributable to Barry's action. For such an account to be made, Barry's action would have to be fraudulent or culpably negligent (which seems to be the case on the facts of case 10). Anton would not however receive compensation in relation to any future lost earnings or profits which he might have made had the conditions for dissolution not appeared.

SCOTLAND

Partnership is based on a consensual contract which may be express or implied. While the partnership agreement is often exercised in the form of a deed, in the absence of an express agreement, the agreement may be implied by the conduct of the parties having regard to the rules contained in s. 2 Partnership (Scotland) Act 1890. So, the rights and obligations of the partners between themselves will be governed essentially by the partnership contract or, where there is no written contract of co-partnery, will be implied by the provisions of the 1890 Act.

Partners owe each other a duty to take care and exhibit the diligence in the firm's business which they do in their own affairs. They must employ the highest standards of honour in dealing with each other and with the firm; *Cassels v. Stewart*,[31] *Trimble v. Goldberg*.[32] Barry is in breach of this duty.

There is authority, particularly in England, that a partnership is a con-

[31] (1881) 8 R (HL) 1, 6 App Cas 64.   [32] [1906] AC 494, PC.

tract *uberrimae fidei*. It is less certain that this is so in Scots law, but there is no doubt that a partnership is a relationship of good faith, even if not requiring *uberrima fides*, and it is clear that partners are regarded as being in the position of fiduciaries towards the firm and each other, both when negotiating for a partnership and during the subsistence of the partnership.[33]

With regard to dissolution of the partnership, the agreement may specify (as in this case) that certain events will give rise to a dissolution, or partners may mutually agree to a dissolution. While a partner may give notice of dissolution under the terms of the partnership agreement, if he is in material breach of the contract, he may be prevented from exercising a contractual right to dissolve the partnership; *Hunter v. Wylie*.[34] In this case, partners acting in breach of the terms of the partnership agreement withdrew capital without the consent of the other partners and they sought to exercise a contractual right to dissolve the contract. It was held that there was a *prima facie* case that the partners who had withdrawn the capital had done so in material breach of the partnership contract and accordingly were not entitled to exercise their contractual rights to dissolve the contract. Barry's negligent supervision of the member of staff means he has breached the partnership contract. It follows then that he cannot rely on his own breach to enforce another term of the contract; *Graham v. United Turkey Red Co.*[35]

DENMARK AND NORWAY

Under West Nordic law, an agreement of this nature needs to be laid down in writing. According to the wording of the agreement, co-operation may be terminated if the annual profit is less than DM 40,000. This wording, and the fact that this is a business agreement, will naturally weigh heavily. But presumably we are not dealing here with a major commercial agreement. When the profit is less than DM 40,000, but the reason for this is that one party has grossly violated his duties under the partnership contract, it will be held under West Nordic law that that party may not request the partnership to be dissolved. The outcome will probably be based on an interpretation of the actual agreement; its words cannot be taken to cover a case such as the present one.[36]

---

[33] See ss. 28 and 29, Partnership (Scotland) Act 1890.   [34] 1993 SLT 1091, OH.
[35] 1922 SLT 406, 1922 SC 533.
[36] See the very open approach by the Norwegian Supreme Court in Rt. 1980 p. 610. Andersen/Madsen/Nørgaard 379 comment that this case is consistent with Danish law.

SWEDEN

Barry cannot demand dissolution of the partnership. The condition would probably be interpreted so as not to apply to this particular case. Another possibility is to adjust the term under s. 36 of the Contracts Act of 1915, although this is seldom done in a contract between business parties of equal strength.[37] In this special case, where Barry grossly violated his duties, I nevertheless believe s. 36 could be applied.

FINLAND

A partnership is *in any case* terminable at will (six months' notice), if there is no fixed term (Partnerships Act of 1988 (Yr 101), 5:2). If there is a fixed term, Barry cannot refer to loss of profit caused by his own negligence (Partnerships Act 5:5 *e contrario*).

Editors' comparative observations

All legal systems except for Irish law would probably disallow Barry from claiming the dissolution of the partnership. The doctrinal bases of this were as follows (a number of legal systems adopting alternative analyses).

(i) Interpretation of the contract. While English law takes a special approach to the termination of *partnerships*, outside this context, it is a rule of interpretation that a party should not be able to exercise a right which has arisen though his own wrong. Scots law, West Nordic and Swedish law, and Dutch law also take an interpretative approach here.

(ii) Good faith. For German law, the facts of case 10 would be seen as a case of a potential abuse of rights (here by Barry), in that Barry's right to terminate has arisen through his gross breach of duty. Greek law follows the German position. French, Belgian and English law would also see the facts of case 10 as involving an issue of good faith; English law, however, considers contracts of partnership as special in this respect.

(iii) Condition prevented from materialising. Closely related is an approach adopted in Austrian, Belgian, Spanish and Italian law: a condi-

---

[37] Section 36 of the Contracts Act of 1915: 'A contract term or condition may be modified or set aside if such term or condition is unconscionable having regard to the contents of the contract, the circumstances at the time the agreement was entered into, subsequent circumstances, and circumstances in general. Where a term is of such significance for the agreement that it would be reasonable to demand the continued enforceability of the remainder of the agreement with the terms unchanged, the agreement may be modified in other respects, or may be set aside in its entirety.'

tion is deemed to have been fulfilled if fulfilment has been prevented by the party to whose disadvantage it would operate. This is an old rule based on Roman law; it may be seen as an emanation of good faith.

(iv) *Nemo auditur.* A number of legal systems (particularly Spanish and Belgian law) apply the adage *nemo auditur turpitudinem suam allegans* (nobody will be heard [in court] if he has to plead his own turpitude) whether it be laid down in the civil code, or applied as a general principle. In Germany (and Greece), it has been absorbed into the general good faith principle. A very similar idea can be found in the Italian, English and Scots legal systems.

Thus, while there are clearly contrasts in the ways in which the legal systems justify or legitimate their solutions, the above observations show that they possess a common thread in the idea that a person should not be allowed to exercise a right which has been acquired by wrongdoing. Irish law, on the other hand, would be more likely to allow termination on the ground that the parties should not be forced to continue to operate together. This is a consideration which is also raised, on the facts of the present case, in a number of other reports (France, Italy) as being important though not decisive. Other legal systems would, for this very reason, grant Anton (rather than Barry) the right to demand dissolution of the partnership.

Case 11: Untested motors working

Case

Jim purchases a machine from Kerry who asserts that the motors running the machine have been thoroughly tested. This is, however, not the case and Kerry is aware of that fact. The motors turn out to function smoothly. May Jim (who in the meantime regrets the purchase) rescind the contract?

Discussions

GERMANY

A right to demand cancellation (*Wandelung*) of the contract under §§ 459 I, 462 BGB (*actio redhibitoria*) on account of a latent defect is not available to Jim since the machine is free from defects which diminish its fitness for use.

A right to cancellation may, however, flow from §§ 459 II, 462 BGB, if a promised quality in the thing sold is absent. Kerry promised that he had tested the motors. But the interpretation of this assurance has to be determined, under §§ 133, 157 BGB, in accordance with the principle of good faith and taking due cognisance of general trade practices. According to this interpretation the assurance was merely designed to assure the other party that the motors do not have any negative qualities that would have become apparent during testing. In fact, the motors do not have any such defects. The assurance would have to be interpreted differently where failure to test affects the usability of the article sold, or any other interest of the purchaser, e.g. where a promised MOT test, without which even a properly operating vehicle may not go on the road, has not been made.

Jim may, however, have a right to rescind the contract on the basis of §

119 II BGB (error as to those characteristics of a thing which are regarded in business as essential). But this rule is excluded by the application of the rules relating to liability for latent defects (§§ 459 ff. BGB):[1] *lex specialis derogat legi generali.* § 123 I BGB ('Whoever has been induced to make a declaration of intention by fraud may rescind the declaration') seems to be applicable since the requirements for this remedy are met. Kerry intentionally misled Jim and the misrepresentation was causally related to the conclusion of the contract. However, rescission under § 123 BGB is also subject to good faith (*Treu und Glauben*). It would constitute an abuse of right if a contract is rescinded on the basis of a misrepresentation that has not impaired the legal position of the misrepresentee.[2]

Jim has no right to rescind.

GREECE

A right for Jim to demand dissolution of the sale under arts. 534, 540 Gr. C.C. (*actio redhibitoria*) on account of a defect, which destroys or substantially diminishes the value or the usefulness of the machine, does not exist on the facts.[3]

The next question is whether Kerry's promise that he tested the motors renders him liable under art. 535 Gr. C.C. ('lack of agreed qualities'). But the meaning of 'agreed qualities' is not certain and has to be determined in accordance with art. 173 Gr. C.C. ('interpretation of a declaration') and art. 200 Gr. C.C. ('interpretation of contracts'), i.e., according to the requirements of good faith taking into consideration business usage. According to such an interpretation, Kerry's promise was merely designed to assure Jim that the motors of the machine did not have any negative qualities that would have become apparent during testing.[4] Even if the fact that no tests regarding the motor have taken place can be interpreted as a lack of an agreed quality, Jim's attempt to rescind the contract might, under the given circumstances, be regarded as abusive (art. 281 Gr. C.C.), since the motors turn out to function smoothly.[5]

Does Jim have the right to annul the contract on account of art. 142 Gr. C.C. ('error as to essential characteristics of a thing')?[6] Greek courts

---

[1] *Palandt/*Thomas, Vor § 459, n. 9.

[2] BGH WM 1977, 343 (344); *Münchener Kommentar/*Kramer § 123, n. 23.

[3] Cf. Doris, in: *Astikos Kodix III* arts. 534–5; Vogopoulos, in: *Astikos Kodix III* art. 540.

[4] Cf. Doris, in: *Astikos Kodix III* arts. 534–5, nos. 20–2.   [5] Cf. ibid., at arts. 534–5, no. 19.

[6] Annulment of the contract as a result of error requires a court decision (art. 154 Gr. C.C.). Greek law, in so far, differs from German law.

and legal writers differ on this point. Most authors take the view that annulment on account of error is excluded by the application of the rules relating to liability for latent defects or lack of agreed qualities (arts. 534–5 Gr. C.C.).[7] It is clear, however, that arts. 534–5 Gr. C.C. do not stop the purchaser from suing the seller for fraud (arts. 147 ff. Gr. C.C.) or under the provisions of the law of delict (arts. 914 ff. Gr. C.C.).[8]

If Kerry intentionally misled Jim, Jim might have the right to apply for the annulment of the contract under art. 147 Gr. C.C. But this remedy is also subject to good faith since art. 148 Gr. C.C. orders that 'if the error caused by the deceit is not substantial and the other party has accepted the declaration of will as intended by the victim of the deception, the Court may decide not to annul the act'. In this case the misrepresentation has not impaired the legal position of Jim, because the motors turn out to function smoothly.[9]

For the above reasons, Jim has no right to rescind.

AUSTRIA

Kerry has misled Jim by making false assertions about the machine's motors. First, the question arises whether Jim may rescind the contract for fraudulent misrepresentation under § 870 ABGB. Secondly, though, if Kerry's assertion is interpreted as a specific contractual warranty, Jim's mistake, which was caused by Kerry, would also qualify as a 'mistake as to the content of (Kerry's) declaration' so as to entitle Jim to avoid the contract on the ground of mistake under § 871 ABGB.

Whichever was the basis of Jim's claim, rescission of the contract depends on Jim's mistake having caused the conclusion of the contract.[10] This causal requirement would not be satisfied if Jim would have purchased the machine in the knowledge that the motors had not been tested.

It is to be noted, however, that Jim could in principle rescind the contract on the ground of fraudulent misrepresentation under § 870 (but not under § 871) ABGB even if his mistake was not on a 'material point'. Consequently, Jim could claim rescission of the contract even if he had concluded the contract only on the basis of circumstances which affected

---

[7] Cf. Filios § 6 D III 2, pp. 55 ff. (56); Doris, in: *Astikos Kodix III* arts. 534–5, no. 46; *contra*: Areopagus 706/1985 EllDni 27, 92.   [8] Filios § 6 D III 2, p. 56.
[9] Cf. Simantiras § 41, no. 761, pp. 564–5.
[10] Cf. Rummel, in: *Rummel, ABGB I* § 870 n. 3, § 871 n. 4.

the price at which the contract was concluded (i.e. that a contract for a machine with an untested motor would bear a lower price). According to the convincing view held by *Iro*,[11] a claimant of rescission for fraudulent misrepresentation must also establish that it is unreasonable for him to continue to be bound to the fraudulent party and thereby be exposed to the other's dishonesty. It would seem that this requirement for rescission would probably not be satisfied on the facts of case 11 as the subject matter of the contract is free of defects and because Jim wishes to free himself from the contract for reasons which have nothing at all to do with the other party's fraudulent conduct. Jim would not, therefore, be allowed to rescind the contract.

Reduction of the purchase price could only be claimed by Jim, on the analogy of § 872 ABGB, if he had been willing to purchase an untested machine at a lower price than a tested one.

It might also be possible that Jim had possessed no intention at all, at the time of making the contract, to purchase an untested machine because, for example, he wished to avoid the trouble of possible defects occurring later. If that were to have been the case, his mistake would qualify as one on a 'material point' and he would be entitled in principle to rescind the contract both under § 870 (fraud) and § 871 (mistake) ABGB. However, the view prevails in Austrian law that rescission is not possible if the mistaken party is subsequently restored to the same position in which he would have been in the absence of his mistake. Furthermore, rescission is not allowed if the circumstance which the party mistakenly assumed to be the case actually comes true at a later stage. In both situations, a claimant for rescission would fail for lack of a legitimate interest in bringing a legal action. Such lack of interest is apparent in the present case, for since the machine works smoothly, Jim is in the same position in which he would have found himself had its motors been tested before conclusion of the contract. On the other hand, Jim could possibly claim that the contract be modified by reducing the purchase price as long as he can show that untested machines of the type in question are sold on the market at a lower price than tested ones.

Similar results would probably be achieved by applying the warranty provisions contained in §§ 922 ff. ABGB. Thus, if Kerry had guaranteed that the motors had been tested, the fact that they had not could be thought of as a defect in the subject matter of the contract of sale at the time of delivery, so as to attract a claim for breach of warranty. However, since in

---

[11] JBl 1974, 234 f.

fact they possess no defect which cannot be remedied and since the usual and agreed use of the goods is possible, Jim is not entitled to rescind the contract under § 932 ABGB but can, at most, claim a reduction of the price.

FRANCE

On these facts, it is to be discussed whether Jim may claim: (i) annulment of the contract on the ground of *dol* (fraudulent misrepresentation) under art. 1116 of the Civil Code, and (ii) damages under art. 1382 of the Civil Code.

(i) Kerry knowingly lied to Jim and thereby vitiated his consent. The conditions necessary to invoke *dol* have already been explained in relation to case 2. Jim must first adduce evidence of the fraud (the material element of manoeuvres etc. and the intentional element). Case law has determined that 'fraudulent manoeuvres' (which are included in the definition of *dol* pursuant to art. 1116 of the Code) include lies, whether they be written[12] or oral, even if they are not reinforced by external acts.[13] The intentional element of *dol* is not at issue here as Kerry knowingly and wilfully lied to Jim. Jim must also prove that the fraudulent misrepresentation induced him to enter into the contract.

As a rule of law, the presence of a loss is neither a necessary nor a sufficient condition for requesting annulment of a contract on the grounds of a vitiating factor, such as *dol* or mistake. Moreover, in French law a person who has concluded a contract as a result of fraud by the other party may not simply rescind the contract by notice, but must apply to the court for it to annul the contract.[14] In this respect, Jim may be held to fall foul of the general requirement in art. 31 of the New Code of Civil Procedure (*Nouveau Code de procédure civile*) that any person bringing a claim must possess an *intérêt à agir*. This may be doubted where, as on the facts of case 11, Jim has not been prejudiced by Kerry's fraud.

(ii) It is absolutely clear that Jim could not claim damages from Kerry on account of his fault prior to concluding the contract, under art. 1382 of the Civil Code. This claim would fail as Jim would be unable to satisfy the conditions of having suffered a direct, real and certain loss.[15]

---

[12] Req. 6 Feb. 1934, S 1935.1.296.
[13] Civ. (3) 6 Nov. 1970, JCP 1971.II.6942 note Ghestin: 'a simple lie, not supported by external acts, can constitute a fraud'.
[14] Art. 1117 C. civ. (which applies to all cases of the vitiation of consent).
[15] Civ. 24 Nov. 1942, GP 1943.1.50.

BELGIUM

(i) According to arts. 1641 ff. C.C., the *actio redhibitoria* or *actio aestimatoria* requires that the machine sold has a defect which makes it improper for its intended use. When the motors function smoothly, it is very improbable that a Belgian judge would consider them defective, even if they were not tested.

(ii) Things might be different if, according to the contract, the seller had to deliver a certificate of testing and is not able to produce this. Even in that case, the sanction would normally be that Jim can refuse to accept delivery of the machine as long as the certificate is not presented, and he can terminate the contract for non-conformity of delivery if the certificate is not produced within the required time.

After delivery, the buyer can terminate the contract of sale for non-conformity only if (a) there is a hidden defect, or (b) the machine does not conform to a specific contractual warranty. It is not clear whether the assertion by Kerry should be considered as an explicit warranty. Modern law shows a tendency to interpret statements relating to the object of the sale as contractual warranties.

If Kerry's assertion were to be treated as a contractual warranty, the falseness of the statement in itself would not be sufficient for termination. Termination requires a fundamental breach of contract. As the contract is not of a kind which requires further co-operation between the parties, the seller should normally get an additional period of time to comply with his warranty, by testing the machines. If the seller offers to test the machines within the appropriate period of time, and to compensate the harm Jim might suffer as a result of the delay, Jim cannot terminate the contract.

(iii) Rescission of a contract for fraud is possible only where a party would not have contracted at all if he had known of the incorrectness of the assertion, i.e., in the present case, that the motors had been thoroughly tested (cf. art. 1116 C.C.). As the contract is not of a kind which requires further co-operation between the parties, the factor determining Jim's consent will normally be the quality of the motor itself, rather than the question as to whether it had been tested. It will be difficult to argue that the issue of testing, as such, was the determining factor for him. The burden of proof on this issue rests on Jim.

Where the party would have consented to the contract, though under different conditions (*dolus incidens*), he cannot avoid the contract but may only claim damages. It is, however, difficult to see what harm Jim has suffered in this case. One might perhaps argue that the price of a tested machine is higher than the price of an untested one, and that Jim would not have offered the same price for the machine had Kerry not asserted that the motors had been thoroughly tested.

Moreover, it is not certain whether Kerry's behaviour would be considered fraudulent. Fraud requires an intention to deceive. Depending on the circumstances, there is a possibility that Kerry's behaviour might be considered *dolus bonus*, a normal exaggeration by a seller. In a certain sense, one might even say that the rules on fraud are not really relevant here, because Kerry's assertion either constitutes *dolus bonus*, or it constitutes a statement amounting to a contractual warranty, and there is simply non-performance.

(iv) The rules relating to error are not relevant here, since error cannot give Jim more rights than fraud.

(v) It is to be noted that, for the above-mentioned reasons, the question as to whether it would be abusive for Jim to rescind the contract is not relevant. If, however, we suppose that it is relevant, we may note that the doctrine of abuse of right (restrictive function of good faith) in principle also applies to rights such as the one to rescind or terminate a contract. If a party has suffered no harm or only very minor harm, there would be a disproportion[16] between it and the rescission or termination of the contract. The fact that Jim would only obtain damages can also be seen as a consequence of the idea that no one should be able to use remedies in cases for which they are not made. The possible use of the doctrine of abuse of right, or good faith, in order to prevent Jim from rescinding the contract has nothing to do with a difference between moral and legal rules, but it rather demonstrates that good faith is a device which works in all directions: good faith imposes a *devoir de modération* on *both* parties. This duty also applies to the use of remedies which are regarded as sanctions for behaviour in bad faith by the other party. Even in the case of intentional non-performance, the other party may not use disproportionate reme-

---

[16] Instead of speaking about disproportion, we might also say that Jim has no sufficient interest in, assuming there is harm, obtaining rescission instead of damages. But this absence of interest has nothing to do with the notion of interest used in civil procedure (art. 17, Belgian Judiciary Code). 'Sufficient interest' as a condition for being heard by the judge is an interest related to the object demanded. This has to be judged independently from how well founded the claim may be. A party claiming payment of BF 1,000,000 always has a sufficient *interest* to claim the money, even if he has no *right* to do so. If Jim regrets the purchase, he evidently has an interest in the procedural sense to start proceedings in order to obtain rescission.

dies.[17] This reasoning is also related to the rule in Belgian law that the reaction to an abuse of right must not overshoot the mark, i.e., it must not lead to the loss of the right in cases where a restriction to its normal, 'non-abusive' ambit would be sufficient.[18]

SPAIN

Kerry's conduct would be considered to constitute deception or fraudulent misrepresentation. Under art. 1269 of the Civil Code, a person who has been induced to enter a contract through deception by the other party has the right to be discharged from the agreement, as long as he would not have entered that contract had the true circumstances been known to him. However, although on the facts there is deception in the seller, and although according to the Civil Code deceit renders the contract voidable 'even if no harm was caused' to the buyer,[19] Spanish law requires that the deception be serious in order to have this result.[20] Where this is not the case, the party deceived is entitled only to claim damages which he may have suffered *in contrahendo*.[21] In case 11, the deception does not seem to be serious nor does the buyer seem to have suffered any harm despite the falseness of the seller's assertion as to the motors. Finally, this is not the sort of case in which a buyer can recover damages for non-pecuniary losses which he may have suffered from the deception.

ITALY

This case may have different solutions depending on how Jim frames his claim against Kerry.

Kerry lied to Jim about the testing of the motors. Assuming that this lie influenced Jim's decision to buy the machine, he may rescind the contract pursuant to the Civil Code rules on fraud.[22] In principle, the victim of fraud does not have to show damage to obtain rescission of the

---

[17] But possibly this is not completely correct. In Cass. 13 Apr. 1984, Arr. n° 474, the defence of abuse of right invoked by a party intentionally acting in an illicit manner was rejected on that ground (cf. *nemo auditur turpitudinem suam allegans*). However, the case did not concern the non-performance of a contractual or precontractual obligation, but the (intentional) infringement of a property right.

[18] Cass. 16 Dec. 1982, *du Moulin v. nv Sarma*, Arr. 518. Cf. also the discussion in the Belgian report to case 4 above. [19] Art. 1300 C. civ. [20] Art. 1270 I C. civ.

[21] Art. 1270 II C. civ.

[22] Arts. 1439–40 c.c. On the questions relating to causality see, in general, Sacco/De Nova, in: *Trattato Sacco I* 440–2.

contract,[23] but this point is not entirely free from doubt. Some court decisions maintain that there is no fraud where the false statement is a mere
puff (*dolus bonus*).[24] Supposing that the testing of the motor was not something on which the value of the machine depended, or for which Jim contracted, it could be argued that Kerry's statement was indeed a mere puff,
that was not apt to deceive anybody.[25] How, though, one can reconcile this
supposed 'doctrine of the mere puff' with the requirement of good faith
in precontractual negotiations, or with the Code's provisions on fraud, is
a mystery. The better view is that where the 'puff' induces the contract the
aggrieved party should indeed be able to rescind the contract for fraud.[26]

On the other hand, if Kerry's statement were interpreted as a contractual warranty concerning the good functioning of the motors, the fact
that the motors function smoothly anyway will bar rescission, because the
buyer may rescind the contract for lack of the promised quality only
where this has consequences of some importance according to the usage
of the trade of those goods; otherwise, he may only ask for a reduction of
the price.[27]

Slight variations of the factual situation reveal other consequences of
Kerry's deceitful statements. Assuming that Kerry was in the business of
selling motor cars, competitors in the same field could sue him for unfair
competition (art. 2598, n. 3 c.c.). Furthermore, if the sale of tested motor
cars was advertised, Kerry could be fined for misleading advertising, and
enjoined from propagating the lie.[28]

THE NETHERLANDS

As there is no non-performance whatsoever, Jim has no legal ground for a
claim. This could be different if a reasonable fear might exist that problems could arise in the future.

Compare the position under arts. 6:80 and 6:83 (c) B.W. If a creditor has
reasonable grounds to fear that non-performance might take place at any

---

[23] Cass., 8 Jan. 1980, n. 140. This decision is approved by Sacco/De Nova, in: *Trattato Sacco I*
442, according to whom the contract vitiated by fraud is in any case beneficial to the
party committing fraud (because it fulfils his needs) and prejudicial to the victim of the
fraud (whose freedom of choice was impeded).   [24] Grisi 102.

[25] Cass., 12 Jan. 1991, n. 257; Cass., 6 Feb. 1982, n. 683.

[26] Sacco/De Nova, in: *Trattato Sacco I* 440 ff.; Cass., 29 Aug. 1991, n. 9227, Foro it., 1992, I, 767.

[27] Art. 1497 c.c.; Cass., 10 Jan. 1981, n. 247.

[28] D.lgt. 25 Jan. 1992, n. 74, *Attuazione della direttiva (C.E.E.) n. 450/84, in materia di pubblicità
ingannevole.*

future date, he can ask the debtor by written notice to declare within a stated period that the latter will indeed perform. If no such declaration is made by the debtor, the creditor may consider the obligation as not having been performed, even before any time period within which the debtor should act has lapsed (art. 6:80, sec. 1, c B.W.).

It could perhaps also be argued that providing wrong information either leads to error or, when it is done deliberately, constitutes fraud (cf. art. 6:228 and art. 3:44, sec. 3 B.W.). I doubt, however, if annulment of the contract on these grounds is possible, if there is no apparent damage on the side of the buyer. The seller could invoke good faith to argue that, since no damage has arisen as yet, it would be unreasonable to allow Jim to rescind the contract simply because he regrets the purchase. See also art. 6:230 B.W., which limits the power to annul the contract on the basis of error.

ENGLAND

Kerry's assertion that the motors running the machine have been thoroughly tested when they have not is a misrepresentation of fact. A party to a contract who has been induced to enter it by a material misrepresentation of fact may choose to rescind the contract or affirm it at his option. The right to rescission exists whether the misrepresentation was made fraudulently, negligently or purely innocently.[29] However, the misrepresentation must have 'induced' the contract, in the sense that it must have affected the misrepresentee's decision whether or not to enter the contract, but it is not necessary for the misrepresentation to be the sole cause of entry to the contract. Thus, where a false statement has been made which was likely to induce the contract and the misrepresentee actually entered the contract, then an inference of fact arises that he was influenced by the statement.[30] On the facts of case 11, it is clear that the statement about the testing of the motors of a machine was likely to influence Jim's decision to purchase and that it did indeed do so.

At common law (as distinct from by statute) once the right to rescind the contract arises, the fact that the falseness of the representation has not caused the misrepresentee any prejudice (as on the facts of case 11) is irrelevant to its exercise. Rescission for fraud was available at common

---

[29] *Redgrave v. Hurd* (1881) 20 Ch D 20.
[30] Guest, *Chitty on Contracts* § 6-019-020; *Edgington v. Fitzmaurice* (1885) 29 Ch D 459; *Smith v. Chadwick* (1884) 9 App Cas 187, at 196.

law, but even in respect of rescission in equity for innocent misrepresentation the prevailing view is that the equitable nature of the remedy did not lead to general considerations of fairness or equitableness being taken into account by a court in deciding whether or not to allow a party to rescind.[31]

However, by the Misrepresentation Act 1967, s. 2(2), '[w]here a person has entered into a contract after a misrepresentation has been made to him otherwise than fraudulently, and he would be entitled, by reason of the misrepresentation, to rescind the contract, then, if it is claimed, in any proceedings arising out of the contract, that the contract ought to be or has been rescinded, the court or arbitrator may declare the contract subsisting and award damages in lieu of rescission, if of opinion that it would be equitable to do so, having regard to the nature of the misrepresentation and the loss that would be caused by it if the contract were upheld, as well as to the loss that rescission would cause to the other party.'

Thus, if Kerry's assertion about the motors had been honest (even if negligent), the court could in its discretion in effect deny Jim's exercise of his normal right to rescind and award him damages instead, the court expressly being required to take into consideration in its decision the relative loss to be caused by rescission or its refusal on the parties. If, therefore, Kerry's assertion had not been fraudulent, then the fact that it has caused Jim no harm would be a factor in the court's discretion. However, as we have noted, Kerry's representation was fraudulent and this rules out any exercise of the judicial discretion under s. 2.

A second possible bar to rescission may be affirmation of the contract by Jim. The facts do not make clear how long Jim has known that Kerry's statement was false and of his consequent right to rescind the contract,[32] but if he has done some act inconsistent with an intention to rescind on his part, such as using the machine, then this will be treated as affirmation and he will lose his right to rescind.[33]

In the absence of such an affirmation, Jim is entitled to rescind the con-

---

[31] Cf. the observations of Roch L.J. in TSB Bank plc v. Camfield [1995] 1 WLR 430, at 438–9 ('The court is not being asked to grant equitable relief; nor is it, in my view, granting equitable relief to which terms may be attached') with the earlier ones of Lord Wright in Spence v. Crawford [1939] 3 All ER 271, at 288, which referred to the 'discretionary powers' of equity courts in deciding whether or not to rescind the contract (in the context of deciding how strictly to apply the requirement of restitutio in integrum). As Treitel remarks, the idea that rescission is a discretionary remedy is hard to apply where rescission is (as in misrepresentation) the act of a person rather than the court: Treitel 334, n. 54.   [32] Peyman v. Lanjani [1985] Ch 457.   [33] Guest, Chitty on Contracts § 6–077.

tract. He could also recover damages in the tort of deceit in respect of Kerry's fraud, although on the facts he has suffered no loss and therefore no damages would be awarded. The fact that his motive in exercising this right has nothing to do with the misrepresentation is here irrelevant.

IRELAND

The onus is on Jim to prove the materiality of the misrepresentation (i.e. that but for the representation he would not have entered into the contract on the terms to which he in fact agreed) in order to have the contract rescinded in equity. Proof of loss or injury is not formally a component of this right of action, but rescission is a discretionary remedy and may be denied if its claimant were held to be acting in an unconscionable or inequitable way.[34] On the other hand, as the seller's misrepresentation would be considered to have been fraudulent as it was made with knowledge of its falsity, this fraud would probably overcome any judicial reluctance to grant rescission for lack of any damage suffered by the misrepresentee.

It is important that Jim is not seen to have affirmed the contract and affirmation could be found by his retention of the motors once he became aware of the misrepresentation.[35] It is similarly important that *restitutio in integrum* be possible, i.e. that both the parties can be returned more or less to their position before the contract was made. The facts as outlined do not allow a firm conclusion to be reached on either point.

Finally, it must be added that in relation to contracts for the sale of goods, this position has been altered by statute, a court there enjoying a power to grant damages in lieu of rescission, though this power is restricted to cases where the misrepresentation was made 'otherwise than fraudulently'.[36] On the facts of case 11, this proviso applies and so the court would have no power to award damages in lieu of rescission.

The law of misrepresentation is one of the areas in Irish law in which purchasers have not always been adequately protected. Rescission was available for an innocent misrepresentation, but the 'right' to rescission might be lost, through affirmation, lapse of time or if *restitutio in integrum* were not available. If rescission were not granted, it would not be possible

---

[34] Keane § 17.01. (Although Mr Justice *Keane* does not expressly address the point in this problem he does stress the equitable nature of the remedy of rescission. Being an equitable remedy it would be subject to the equitable maxims that 'he who seeks equity must do equity' and that 'he who comes to equity must come with clean hands': ibid., §§ 3.07–3.08.)   [35] Cf. *Luton v. Saville Tractors Ltd* [1986] NI 327.

[36] Sale of Goods and Supply of Services Act 1980, s. 45(2).

to claim damages unless the representation had been deemed to be incorporated into the contract as a warranty or unless the representation were fraudulent, in which case an action in tort of deceit would lie.

SCOTLAND

Kerry has lied to Jim; the machine has not been tested and Kerry is aware of this fact. His statement is a fraudulent misrepresentation. For a misrepresentation to amount to a fraudulent one, the person making it must know that what he is representing is false or be in ignorance as to its truth or falsehood; *City of Edinburgh Brewery Co. v. Gibson's Trustee.*[37] If Jim was induced to buy the machine because of this misrepresentation, he can rescind the contract. And as victim of such a misrepresentation he can also claim damages in delict for loss or damage sustained by him through the other party's fraud; *Bryson & Co. v. Bryson.*[38]

The misrepresentation must be material in the sense that it was the factor, or one of the inducing factors, which caused Jim to assume the obligation; *National Exchange Co. of Glasgow v. Drew & Dick.*[39] Jim must prove the inducement otherwise the action will fail. How would Kerry's statement impress the reasonable person? It is irrelevant that Jim suffered no loss; if fraudulent misrepresentation is demonstrated, Jim can rescind the contract and seek repetition for the price.

However, what if Kerry's misrepresentation was not an inducement, and that in fact the misrepresentation had no bearing on Jim's decision to purchase the machine? The machine operates smoothly and thus fulfils the subject of the contract. Why does Jim regret the purchase? Is it just a change of mind on his behalf? If Jim was not under any misapprehension when he purchased the machine and the subject of the contract is satisfied, then he has no basis upon which to rescind the contract. Each contracting party must be on his guard and look after his own interests; he must satisfy himself as to the nature, qualities and value of the subject of the contract and the other party is under no duty to prevent him making a bad bargain. His error would only invalidate the contract if induced by the misrepresentation. 'The notion that a party . . . is entitled to get free on the ground that he was in error, that he found he had made a bad bargain where he intended to make a good one, is so utterly preposterous as to be undeserving of any attention.'[40]

---

[37] (1869) 7 M 886.   [38] 1916 1 SLT 361.   [39] (1860) 23 D 1.
[40] *Forth Marine Insurance Co. v. Burnes* (1848) 10 D 689, *per* Lord *Fullerton* at 700.

Therefore Jim can only rely on the misrepresentation if it was a factor which influenced him to purchase the machine. An incorrect statement by one party, even if deliberate, does not automatically or *per se* affect the validity of the contract: 'The alleged false statement must have been relied on, and formed the reason for the pursuer entering into the transaction. If the pursuer relied on his own judgements, there was no case.'[41] A party cannot challenge a contract even if there was a misrepresentation by the other party, if he was not induced thereby to contract, or where the misrepresentation did not come to his attention, or his judgement cannot be shown to have been influenced by it.

DENMARK AND NORWAY

The agreement relates to a purchase, and under the joint Nordic sale of goods law (s. 39(1) of the Norwegian Sale of Goods Act of 1988) a purchase cannot be cancelled because of defects unless they amount to a 'material breach of contract'. Although the seller is in breach of his duties under the purchase agreement, and has acted in bad faith, there is probably no breach of contract on his part significant enough to entitle the buyer to cancel.

The case relates to a request for rescission, i.e. a claim to invalidate the agreement because one party has been in breach of his contractual obligations. Legislation as well as legal usage lay down as a main rule that rescission requires a material cause, so that only the more significant breaches of contract provide a ground for rescission. The requirement as to material cause presupposes an overall evaluation in which not merely the deviation from due performance is relevant.[42] Acting in bad faith would in many instances constitute a fundamental breach. When, as in the present case, we are faced with a contract which does not entail a close relationship between the parties, and a breach of contract which is altogether insignificant, it must be concluded that there is no right to rescind.

SWEDEN

According to s. 17 of the Sale of Goods Act of 1990 the goods are defective since they were not tested as asserted (being tested, or 'being of the same brand as Björn Borg plays with', etc. is probably a quality of the goods).

---

[41] *McLellan v. Gibson* (1843) 5 D 1032, at 1034.   [42] Cf. e.g. Rt. 1923 I, p. 468.

However, cancellation requires that the breach is material/fundamental (s. 25). This does not seem to be the case, since the machine runs smoothly (and, it can be assumed, will continue to run smoothly). The ratio of the rule was, according to the preparatory works of the previous Sale of Goods Act of 1905, that a buyer should not be able to cancel a purchase that he regrets due to reasons other than the non-conformity. This reasoning has been used in case law, and it probably constitutes a good argument *against* cancellation also according to modern law. The preparatory works of the 1990 Sale of Goods Act refer to objective standards, also with the result that the non-conformity in the present case is not material.

A problem is, however, that the case could also be regarded as one concerning fraud. If the fraud caused the other party to conclude the contract, the contract is void. According to s. 30 of the Contracts Act of 1915 it has to be presumed that an established fraud has indeed caused the promisee to conclude the contract.

If Kerry cannot prove that Jim would have bought the machine even if Kerry had not asserted that it had been thoroughly tested, the question arises whether the legislation on fraud is restricted by the legislation on sale. In principle the answer is no. Before it is possible to apply the legislation concerning sale, there has to be a valid contract. Even if it is proved that Jim now wants to cancel only because he regrets the purchase for other reasons, I doubt whether one should complicate the legal system by restricting the application of the fraud rule, especially since there is a general interest to prevent fraudulent assertions. But the answer can probably be disputed.

FINLAND

The question is not whether or not the motors have been tested but whether they are *defective* or not.

Whether tested or not, since the motors do not actually have any defects, Jim cannot rescind the contract (Sale of Goods Act of 1987, ss. 17 and 18). Kerry's assertions about tests – albeit groundless – are of interest for Jim only in so far as the functioning of the machine is concerned. See also s. 33 of the Contracts Act of 1929: Kerry is not dishonest in wanting the contract to hold, since the motors actually function well. Here as elsewhere one is employing the criterion of 'material importance'. This is so (i) for the question concerning validity, and (ii) with regard to remedies, such as damages or price reduction. A misrepresentation regarding testing is immaterial, since the motors are not in fact defective.

Moreover, a Finnish court would probably reason as follows. The assertion that the motors have been tested is intended as *evidence* for their being in order. The real issue, the *evidentiary theme*, is the functioning of the machines. What counts is not evidence but the truth. And, finally, a Finnish court would probably consider the fact that the buyer did not require any documentation regarding the alleged test. For these reasons the court would refuse to consider invalidity, even if it might be said that the seller used a fraudulent assertion in order to bring about the contract.

Editors' comparative observations

This case gives rise to very considerable diversity of result as well as of approach. All the legal systems take as their starting point that a party who has been induced by the fraud of the other party to enter a contract may rescind it (or seek rescission of it from a court). Disagreement then arises as to what qualifications apply to this right.

(i) English law and Scots law would both allow rescission of the contract by Jim on the ground of fraud, despite the absence of any loss caused to him as a result of the fraud. Interestingly, in a case of an *honest* misrepresentation inducing a contract English (but *not* Scots) law would give a court a discretion to deny rescission by the misrepresentee, this discretion specifically including the relative loss to be caused to the parties by either rescission or upholding the contract. Swedish law would also not place any equitable restrictions on the right of rescission for fraud under its Contract Act in a case like the present one.

(ii) The greater number of legal systems, however, would not allow Jim to rescind the contract. A variety of reasons are advanced for this result.

(a) Irish law apparently differs from English and Scots law in that it would consider the equitable nature of the remedy of rescission to be a basis for its denial in the present circumstances.

(b) German law refuses to allow Jim to exercise his right of rescission since, by exercising it, he would not be acting in good faith. German law thus resorts to the notion of good faith in its specific emanation of preventing the abuse of a right. The Greek, Dutch and Belgian solutions are very similar (the latter, however on a hypothetical basis since, according to Belgian law, Jim does not have a right of rescission anyway).

(c) The Austrian and French solutions turn around the lack of legitimate interest, on the part of Jim, in bringing a legal action.

(d) Some legal systems refuse to grant a right of rescission on the basis that the deception was not serious enough (Spain) or immaterial

(Finland), that the consequences of the deception were not sufficiently important (Italy) or that there was no material breach of contract on the part of Kerry (West Nordic and Swedish law in terms of their sales legislation).

(e) Italian courts have, on occasion, had recourse to denying a right of rescission by holding the dishonest statement to be a mere 'puff', not apt to deceive anyone. In other legal systems, too, there are indications that the courts might be disinclined to find that the fraud had induced the contract where on the facts it had caused no prejudice to the misrepresentee. Such an approach assumes a willingness to manipulate the 'determining' nature of fraud.

Case 12: No use for borrowed motor bike

Case

Verulam lends his friend Woodrow his expensive motor bike for a weekend trip from Thursday to Monday. On Friday morning, Woodrow suffers a severe wrist injury which makes it impossible for him to ride a motor bike. He therefore cancels the weekend trip. When Verulam hears about Woodrow's misfortune on Saturday, he goes to Woodrow's house, but does not meet him there. However, he finds his beloved motor bike and decides to take it back with him since it is no longer of any practical use to Woodrow. He leaves a note telling Woodrow that he has taken back the motor bike. Woodrow comes home some hours later, reads the note and gets angry with Verulam's high-handed action. He requests Verulam to return the bike to him until Monday. Verulam objects on the ground that on Monday, Woodrow has got to give the bike back anyway.

Discussions

GERMANY

In principle, Woodrow may claim that the bike be given back to him on the basis of a contract of loan for use (§ 598 BGB).

In the present case, however, it has to be established whether Verulam might not perhaps counter this claim on the ground that its exercise constitutes an abuse of right as recognised under § 242 BGB. If Verulam were forced to hand the motor bike over until Monday, Woodrow would only have the bike for a short time during which he would not be able to use it anyway. On Monday, he would have to return it to Verulam by reason of § 604 I BGB ('The borrower is bound to return the thing lent on the expiration of the time fixed for the loan'). Woodrow has no reasonable interest

379

that would be worthy of protection in having the bike handed back to him. His request, therefore, constitutes an abuse of right, as specified in the maxim *dolo agit, qui petit quod statim redditurus est*.[1]

His contractual rights being barred, there is nevertheless another way how Woodrow can recover the motor bike. For although Woodrow was no longer entitled to keep the motor bike in his possession, Verulam was not allowed to take it high-handedly without Woodrow's consent since this amounted to an unlawful interference with Woodrow's possession (*verbotene Eigenmacht*, § 858 I BGB). According to § 861 BGB, Verulam is thus liable to return the bike to Woodrow. As to this claim, Verulam cannot raise the *dolo agit* defence.[2] § 863 BGB provides that a claim will lie merely because of the unlawful infringement of Woodrow's possession, irrespective of the fact that Verulam was entitled to claim restitution of his property.

GREECE

The agreement that has been concluded between Woodrow and Verulam constitutes a gratuitous loan for use. It is regulated by arts. 810–21 of the Greek Civil Code.

In the case under consideration, Woodrow's demand to take the motor bike back from Verulam is abusive within the meaning of art. 281 Gr. C.C. Although the specific time for the loan that has been fixed by the parties has not yet expired, Woodrow cannot take the bike back from Verulam since, as a result of his injury, he has no use for it.[3] The principle of good faith (art. 281 Gr. C.C.) prevails.

The owner of an object (Verulam) has not, of course, the right to take it back arbitrarily, and without the consent of the other party (Woodrow), before the time agreed upon under the contract has expired.

AUSTRIA

Verulam lent the motor bike to Woodrow for a weekend trip and the parties agreed also on a period of time for the loan (Thursday to Monday). § 976 ABGB determines that a gratuitous lender of a piece of property cannot demand it back before the expiry of the time agreed upon and before the borrower has finished using it. However, it is generally accepted

---

[1] Cf. *Jauernig*/Vollkommer § 242, n. 39; *Palandt*/Heinrichs § 242, n. 52.
[2] *Staudinger*/Bund § 863, n. 4.
[3] See Court of Appeal Athens 9740/1981 Dni 23, 11; Zepos, *Enochikon* 290.

that for the purposes of this provision the borrower has to return the object which has been given to him as soon as he has finished using it, even if the parties have fixed a longer period of time.[4] It is submitted that this view is correct. If the parties, as in case 12, fix both a period of time for the loan of the property as well as a particular use for it, they thereby limit the loan in two distinct and different ways: the question then arises as to which of these two limitations is decisive. Since the loan in question is gratuitous, according to § 915 ABGB, preference must be given to that solution which is favourable to the lender.

In the result, therefore, since Woodrow is no longer able to use the motor bike, Verulam was entitled to demand its restitution and is therefore not obliged to return the bike to Woodrow. One final difficulty should, however, be mentioned. For even if Verulam were entitled to claim restitution of his property, he would not be allowed to take it away highhandedly, for this would constitute an unlawful interference with Woodrow's possession. However, it has been said that the possessor of property cannot bring an action against such an 'intruder' if the latter reasonably assumed that the possessor consents to the interference.[5] Thus, as Verulam rightly thought that the motor bike was of no use to Woodrow, any assumption on Verulam's part that Woodrow would have consented would indeed have been reasonable and, this being so, Woodrow could not sue Verulam on this ground.

FRANCE

Verulam's loan of his motor bike to Woodrow is a gratuitous loan for use for a fixed period (*commodat*) as provided for by arts. 1875 ff. of the Civil Code. This kind of contract, characterised by art. 1876 as 'essentially gratuitous', is subject to special legal rules which have been devised to correspond to this type of contractual arrangement frequently used between friends, as is the case here. In accordance with art. 1888 of the Civil Code, Verulam cannot in principle recover the bike before the end of the weekend as the term of the loan is fixed.

In addition, art. 1888 states that in the absence of agreement as to the term, the lender may recover only once the loan has served its purpose. Although it is clear that Verulam and Woodrow have fixed a period for the loan for use, Verulam may be able to rely on art. 1889 of the Code which

---

[4] Von Schey 228; Stanzl, in: *Klang, Kommentar IV/1* 686; Schubert, in: *Rummel, ABGB I* § 976 n. 1.
[5] Spielbüchler, in: *Rummel, ABGB I* § 339 n. 5.

provides an exception, so that where 'during the period of loan or before the borrower's need has ceased, the lender has an urgent and unforeseeable need for the thing he has lent, in this case the judge may, depending on the circumstances, oblige the borrower to return it to him'. It may be possible for Verulam to argue in the circumstances, by combining the aim of these two articles, that as Woodrow can no longer use the bike, he is entitled to recover it and that Woodrow cannot force him to wait until the end of the term. In other words, as Woodrow has no further need of the loan, it would be difficult for him to insist on keeping the bike until Monday. However, it should be pointed out that Verulam's remedy is subject to the court's equitable discretion and strictly speaking, in order to obtain restitution of the bike, he needs to go to court to obtain a court order. This solution seems to abide by the spirit of the special rules relating to *commodat*. There is however very little case law on the subject, which is not really surprising for the following reasons.[6]

Commodat originates from a Roman law contract and was and is based on an amicable arrangement between friends. Since this type of contract is essentially gratuitous and for the sole benefit of the borrower, it is difficult to imagine the courts insisting on construing such a contract to the letter, being considered the sort of arrangement where to do so would be an invasion of an area which overlaps with that of extra-legal relations. Moreover, as it is for the sole benefit of the borrower, it is understandable that the borrower's rights should be subordinated to those of the lender, particularly if the reason why the loan was made no longer exists. Here, the standards of behaviour which the law sets between contracting parties in other contexts are inappropriate. Is this because a person is assumed to behave in good faith towards his friends? Can Woodrow really claim that Verulam's high-handed behaviour constitutes bad faith when he no longer has any use for the loan which has generously been made to him? This kind of contract, nicknamed a 'small contract' by works of authority, represents a 'fringe' contract where general legal rules are inapplicable.[7]

---

[6] For recent case law relating to the loan of residential accommodation between members of the family, see Civ. (1) 3 Feb. 1993, Bull. civ. I, no. 62, JCP 1994.II.22239 note V. Mogand-Cantegrit; Civ. (1) 8 Dec. 1993, D 1994.248 note A. Bénabent (loans made by parents to children who subsequently divorce: should the daughter-in-law be entitled to continue to live in the accommodation lent?); Civ. (1) 19 Nov. 1996, D 1997.145 note A. Bénabent (in which the heirs of the lender of a flat lent to the deceased's brother were held unable to reclaim it as no evidence of an urgent and unforeseeable need by the lender had been adduced as is required by art. 1889 C. civ.).   [7] Carbonnier, *Flexible droit* 331 ff.

BELGIUM

The case does not appear to be very practical. Pertinent case law does not exist.

A first question is whether we are dealing with a binding contract, or merely a social arrangement between friends which is not binding ('gentlemen's agreement'). Nowadays, such an agreement is understood as a binding contract though one of a less binding nature than contracts based on consideration. This is apparent from art. 1889 C.C.: the lender may take the object back if he needs it urgently, despite any period of time or purpose agreed upon with the borrower.

In the type of contract presently under consideration the object may only be used for the purpose agreed upon by the parties (art. 1880 C.C.). Thus, Woodrow may not use the motor bike for another purpose. Moreover, apart from art. 1889 C.C., the lender may take the object back (only) when the period agreed upon has expired and, where no period has been agreed upon, when it has served the purpose agreed upon (art. 1888 C.C.). One might deduce from this rule that Verulam was not allowed to take back the motor bike before Monday. However, even if art. 1888 C.C. might have to be interpreted in such a way, Woodrow is presently acting contrary to good faith. According to Belgian case law, a party acts contrary to good faith when claiming performance of a contract or clause which has lost its justification.[8] This is not usually seen as a rule of interpretation, but rather as an application of the corrective function of good faith. It may be compared with the notion of 'frustration'.

Belgian law does apply, in some cases, the maxim *dolo agit, qui petit quod statim redditurus est*, though not, probably, in the present case in which the time period is quite considerable.

SPAIN

First, Spanish law follows Roman law in recognising the maxim *dolo facit qui petit quod statim redditurus est* (a person acts in bad faith by demanding what must immediately be returned), even though there is no legal provision specifically to this effect. The recognition of this maxim means that Woodrow's conduct clearly falls within the prohibition on the abuse of

---

[8] Cass. 21 Sep. 1979, *Post v. Locabel*, Arr. 92 – *in casu* a dollar clause had been inserted in a contract in view of the fact that a party was owned by an American company; the clause was, however, invoked later, when the party was owned by a purely Belgian company.

rights contained in art. 7 of the Civil Code.[9] Moreover, other aspects of the case point in the same direction. For it would clearly be an abuse of Woodrow's right to possess the motor bike, which has been lent to him, to insist on repossession where he can no longer himself enjoy any benefit from that possession. Indeed, on the facts, one could go further and question whether any reason could be found for Woodrow's attempted exercise of his right to repossession other than a desire to harm Verulam, this being supported by the fact that Woodrow has not paid for his use of the motor bike. Such a malicious exercise of a right is expressly stated as an abuse of a right under art. 7.

Second, quite apart from any application of the doctrine of good faith and the rule prohibiting the abuse of rights, on these facts Woodrow no longer has a legal right to possession of the motor bike. This results from art. 1749 of the Civil Code, which provides that a person who lends property gratuitously to another for the latter's use can recover it once that use has come to an end. This appears to be the case here since Woodrow can no longer make use of the motor bike in the way which was envisaged by the parties.

ITALY

The contract concluded between Woodrow and Verulam is one of loan for use, or *comodato*. The Civil Code defines this contract as one 'by which one party delivers a movable or immovable thing to another for a specified time or for a specified use, with the obligation to return the thing received'.[10] Traditionally, *comodato* belongs to the category of real contracts, i.e. contracts which are made by delivery of the thing.[11] In the absence of such delivery there is no contract: an agreement between the parties to deliver the property is not enforceable either by specific performance or damages.[12]

In our case the loan for use has two express terms. The first relates to the period of the loan ('from Thursday to Monday'), while the second relates to the purpose of the loan ('a weekend trip'). The parties in the present case would probably interpret these terms, and their relationship,

---

[9] See the Spanish report to cases 3 and 6 above.   [10] Art. 1803 c.c.
[11] On the Roman law background to this contract: Zimmermann 188 ff.
[12] See on this point, Sacco/De Nova, in: *Trattato Sacco I* 712–13; Gorla 174 ff., 365 ff., 383 ff. In both cases, the above scholars note the similarity with the common law rules concerning gratuitous bailment.

differently. Thus, Woodrow would argue that the loan was agreed for a certain time, the weekend trip being merely a motive of the contract, which is, in itself, irrelevant;[13] Verulam, on the other hand, may well counter that the purpose of their contract should be seen as controlling its duration, the term as to the latter having been fixed solely for his convenience. In these circumstances, if there is no other way to resolve the ambiguity in the contract, the interpretation advanced by Verulam will prevail by way of application of art. 1371 of the Civil Code which requires interpretation in cases of obscurity in favour of the debtor of the gratuitous obligation.

Assuming, therefore, that the contract of loan for use did indeed come to an end when the weekend trip became impossible, the mere fact of this termination did not authorise Verulam (to enter Woodrow's premises and) to take the motor bike home. For if Woodrow did not consent to such an act by Verulam it would constitute an unlawful interference with Woodrow's (albeit wrongful) detention of the motor bike. Woodrow could therefore initiate a possessory action to recover the motor bike from Verulam.[14] Italian law does not allow title to the property as a defence to possessory actions.[15] Nevertheless, Woodrow's action for possession could be dismissed on two grounds: Verulam could successfully defend himself by invoking the personal right to obtain restitution of the motor bike,[16] or he could invoke the old maxim *dolo petit qui petit quod statim redditurus est.*[17] The first defence will probably be more successful than the second one, because our courts are slow to recognise the need to restrict the protection of possession where it clashes with title to the property.

If the loan for use had not yet come to an end, i.e. if Woodrow's argument as to the interpretation of the contract prevailed, he would have a contractual right to keep the bike until Monday. Possibly, however, the *dolo petit* maxim would here apply, too, because the *comodato* would terminate on Monday anyway. But it is hard to tell whether this reasoning would persuade an Italian court. Our courts are accustomed to enforce the letter of

[13] See, by way of exception, the provision relating to gifts, art. 787 c.c.
[14] The action in question would be the 'reintegration action', governed by art. 1168 c.c.
[15] Art. 705 c.p.c., which forbids the defendant in a possessory action to initiate a 'petitory action' (i.e. one asserting title) until the judgement on the possessory action is enforced. The validity, as a matter of constitutional law, of this prohibition in the Code against setting up title as a defence to an action for possession is doubtful whenever this rule unduly restricts a person's constitutional right to defend himself: Corte cost., 3 Feb. 1992, n. 25, Foro it., 1993, I, 616, obs. Proto Pisani; Giur. it., 1992, I,1, 1634, obs. Chianale.
[16] Cf. Cass., 26 Jan. 1980, n. 635; Cass., 30 Jul. 1984, n. 4524. Sacco, in: *Trattato Mengoni* 264.
[17] Sacco, in: *Trattato Mengoni* 260 fn. 130.

art. 705 of the Code of Civil Procedure, even where it would be wise to depart from it.[18]

THE NETHERLANDS

It is uncertain if this would be considered a true contract or only a social agreement between friends without any legal consequences. If it were a true contract, Woodrow – under the present circumstances – no longer has any interest in keeping the motor bike. Although Verulam's action is not really how parties to a contract should behave towards one another, still Woodrow cannot reclaim the bike. Asking for performance of the contract would be against good faith (cf. art. 6:248 B.W.).

ENGLAND

In English law, the gratuitous loan of a chattel (i.e. corporeal property) by a person to another for the latter's use does not give rise to a contractual relationship, as *ex hypothesi* no consideration is given.[19] However, a relationship of bailment is said to arise, a relationship which sits uncomfortably astride, and to an extent beyond, the larger categories of contract and tort. Bailment may be said to arise 'whenever one person ("the bailee") is voluntarily in the possession of goods belonging to another person ("the bailor")'.[20] A bailee holds a possessory right under the bailment, a right which may be protected against third parties by the tort of interference with goods (formerly known as the tort of conversion), a wrong which is actionable in damages in tort. While a bailee of property under a *contract* may, depending on its terms, be able to protect himself against a claim for possession by the bailor himself,[21] this is not true of gratuitous loans for use, where the bailee possesses the chattel 'at will'. In the result, the borrower is liable to the owner of the goods if he detains them after the agreed time for their return *or after they have been demanded* by their owner even before the (non-contractual) time for their return.[22]

This means that on the facts of case 12, Verulam had the right to demand the return of his bike at any time, there being no requirement of

---

[18] Ibid.   [19] Palmer, *Bailment* 26–31.   [20] Palmer/Powell, in: *Halsbury* § 1801.
[21] *Roberts v. Wyatt* (1810) 2 Taunt 268.
[22] Palmer/Powell, in: *Halsbury* § 1830. But cf. Palmer, *Bailment* 658 ff. who in a context of 'remarkably little authority' discusses the possible bases on which a gratuitous bailor could be prevented from going back on a grant of possession for a fixed term.

reasonable notice. Thus, he was entitled to write to Woodrow terminating his right to use the bike and retaking possession of it (though there would be a distinct question of trespass to Woodrow's land in entering his premises without permission to take the bike if that is what he did).

IRELAND

The loan of the motor bike between friends is a gratuitous bailment, which is normally revocable at will. Here, there is also an implied promise by Verulam not to revoke the bailment before Monday. This promise does not give rise to any contractual consequences because it is made without consideration (i.e. there is no counterpart obligation undertaken by Woodrow). Voluntary promises are matters for honour only, and not matters on which the courts are generally prepared to act.

A limited exception to this unenforceability of voluntary promises may be found in the doctrine of promissory estoppel.[23] However, there are several grounds for thinking that this doctrine would be of no use to Woodrow on the facts of this case. First, for estoppel to apply, the promisee must have relied to his detriment on the promise so as to make it inequitable for the voluntary promisor to rely on his strict legal right; in this case there appears to be no detrimental reliance. Secondly, and more controversially, it is still probably the case that promissory estoppel does not give rise to a separate cause of action (in the jargon, it is 'a shield, not a sword'): promissory estoppel must be pleaded within an existing cause of action. Thus, Woodrow might have been able to plead an estoppel if Verulam had commenced proceedings to recover his bike, but he could not use estoppel to compel Verulam to make good his promise to allow him to retain the bike, when as in the present case Verulam has recovered it.

SCOTLAND

Like Roman law, Scots law identifies two distinct types of loan: (i) *mutuum*: a loan for consumption; and (ii) *commodatum*: a loan for use. The loan in this case is *commodatum* which is defined as a gratuitous loan for use for a stipulated time or purpose, the thing lent to be returned after use in the same condition in which it was lent. *Commodatum* is regarded as a *bonae fidei* contract; therefore the question of liability is determined with regard to the requirement of good faith.

---

[23] *Central London Property Trust Ltd v. High Trees House Ltd* [1947] KB 130.

The essential elements of *commodatum* are the agreement of the lender and the borrower, and delivery to the borrower of the thing lent for a stipulated time or purpose for use gratuitously, with an obligation on the borrower to restore the thing in the same condition in which it was lent. The contract is not complete until the thing lent has been delivered. Delivery to the borrower gives only detention and not ownership.

Properly the contract of *commodatum* should specify the time or purpose for which the thing is lent. One of the obligations on the lender is that he will be liable for wrongfully taking back the thing before the expiry of the loan or for otherwise interfering with its use.[24] This principle will make Verulam liable for taking the bike early.

However, one could argue that the contract has been frustrated. The doctrine of frustration applies on the occurrence of some event which the law recognises as excusing further performance of those obligations laid upon the parties by their contract. The purpose of the loan was for Woodrow to take the bike on a trip but owing to his wrist injury the purpose cannot be fulfilled. Therefore the contract has become frustrated. Where you cannot foresee an event which makes performance of the contract more difficult or even impossible, the contract is deemed to be frustrated. Verulam could therefore argue that as the purpose of the contract has been frustrated and is impossible to perform, he is excused from his obligation not to remove the thing lent before the specified period of loan has expired.

DENMARK AND NORWAY

This problem is quite special because apparently it concerns a gratuitous loan. It is possible to point at least to two grounds on account of which the borrower may not object to the object having been retrieved by the lender. First, the agreement has to be interpreted. Given that it is a loan between friends where the borrower does not have to pay consideration for the use of the bike, the agreement will be subjected to a fairly wide interpretation in terms of its reasonableness. If the borrower has suffered a physical injury preventing him from making any use of the bike, it is obvious that there is no ground entitling him to keep the bike during the period initially agreed upon. Second, it will also be possible to argue that the loan has been terminated because of a breach of an implied condition. The subsequent development having led to a position where the borrower no longer has any use for the bike, it has removed the basis for the agreement

---

[24] Morrison, in: *Stair Memorial Encyclopaedia* § 1788.

between the parties. Given that it is a gratuitous loan it will be deemed to have lost its effect. Thus, the owner may retrieve his bike.

The present type of agreement (a gratuitous transaction between friends) has to be interpreted in a way entirely different from commercial agreements. Also, it will be much more readily accepted that it has ceased to exist because of changed circumstances.[25]

Inspired by German law, Nordic law has, since the end of the last century, recognised a doctrine of incorrect presuppositions.[26] It entails that if there are material changes in the circumstances, the agreement may be amended or may cease to exist altogether. The doctrine of incorrect presuppositions has played quite an important role in theory and legal usage in the West Nordic countries.[27] Following the introduction of the general clause in s. 36 of the Contracts Act, its place has, however, become more modest.

SWEDEN

Without express provision to the contrary, Woodrow was not entitled to let another person use the bike, and the purpose of this contract was that Woodrow was going to use it, not only look at it. Admittedly, Verulam is bound by a loan contract (although it was without charge) since the bike was handed over to Woodrow (see the 1936 Act on Some Gratuitous Promises, in terms of which gratuitous promises must be made in written form, or with the intent to become publicly known, or be fulfilled, in order to be binding before delivery). But in view of the fact that it was a gratuitous agreement, it would probably be interpreted as a loan-and-use contract, and not a loan-and-look contract. Apart from that, the doctrine of incorrect presuppositions, according to which the risk of a mistaken assumption is usually placed on the promisee in cases of gratuitous promises, may lead to the same result. Finally, Woodrow should not be encouraged to bother the courts with a complaint like this.

FINLAND

This case is somewhat problematic. I think that a Finnish court would view it in the first place as a tort case: Verulam was not entitled to take his bike back without Woodrow's consent. If this has caused economic loss,

[25] Andersen/Madsen/Nørgaard 390.
[26] On which, see Zimmermann 581 f. with references.
[27] Augdahl 142 ff.; Andersen/Madsen/Nørgaard 220 ff.

Woodrow might sue for recovery. A loan is gratuitous, and for this reason Woodrow's claim regarding *praestatio in natura* is probably excluded in this case. Due to the amicable nature of the contract a Finnish court would apply here 'soft law' instead of strict contractual norms and principles. A judge would even perhaps say: 'Get out of here – we have business to do.'

Editors' comparative observations

All the legal systems under consideration reach the same result in so far as Woodrow is no longer entitled to keep the motor bike in his possession. However, different analyses are advanced to reach this result. This does not mean that Verulam was entitled to act as he did; cf., e.g., the German, Austrian and English reports concerning remedies based on unlawful interference with Woodrow's possessions and trespass.

(i) A number of legal systems appeal to good faith, either *simpliciter* (Dutch law) or in more specific terms. According to Belgian law, a party would be acting against good faith if he claimed performance of a contract which had lost its point. Greek law considers Woodrow's behaviour to constitute an abuse of right. German law applies the venerable maxim of *dolo agit qui petit quod statim redditurus est*, which pinpoints a specific instance of abusive behaviour. The same maxim is applied in Spanish and Italian law.

(ii) Austrian law, French law, West Nordic and Swedish law and, by way of alternative analysis, Spanish and Italian law take an interpretative approach to the original contract of loan holding that its purpose (riding by Woodrow) rather than the time period agreed upon is its significant element. Given that this purpose has been frustrated, these systems hold that the owner is entitled to claim back and keep the motor bike. Closely related is the Scots approach, which relies on the doctrine of frustration. Its functional equivalent is the presupposition doctrine which is applied, by way of alternative analysis, in West Nordic and Swedish law. In the Nordic systems, particular emphasis is placed on the fact that we are dealing here with a gratuitous agreement which is interpreted much more leniently than a commercial contract.

(iii) English and Irish law deny the original loan of the bike the status of contract (owing to the lack of any counterpart for Verulam's promise of loan) and therefore allow him to take back the bike and keep it at will. Some of the other legal systems (French law, Belgian law) also consider the possibility that the present arrangement might not be classified as a contract but as a merely social arrangement between friends.

Case 13: Inspecting the books

Case

Cameron has sold to Dorian a quarry. The price, *inter alia*, consists of Dorian having to pay Cameron for a period of ten years 10 per cent of his gross turnover. Dorian has granted Cameron the right to inspect the books of his business. After three years, Cameron purchases a new quarry and requests Dorian to show him his books. He wants to know the names of Dorian's business customers in order to establish his own sales network.

Discussions

GERMANY

Courts have held repeatedly that a contractual duty to supply information is subject to the principle of good faith of § 242 BGB.[1] A duty to supply information will be regarded as inappropriate if there is a danger that it might be used for purposes that are foreign to the contract; and this is especially so if it might be used for the purposes of competition. Good faith allows Dorian to refuse disclosure of the information.[2] He does, however, have to disclose it to a person who has a professional duty to keep it confidential, such as a solicitor.[3]

Dorian is also not obliged to open the books of his business to Cameron but he will have to allow inspection to a third party who may disclose to Cameron information about turnover but not about customers' names.

---

[1] RGZ 127, 243 (245); BGHZ 10, 385 (387); OLG Koblenz VersR 1991, 1191 (1192).
[2] Cf. RGZ, 127, 243 (245); BGHZ, 10, 385 (387); BGH NJW 1966, 1117 (1119); OLG Koblenz VersR 1991, 1191 (1192); *Palandt*/Heinrichs § 261, n. 24.
[3] BGH LM § 260 n. 6; OLG Koblenz VersR 1991, 1191 (1192); *Palandt*/Heinrichs § 261, n. 24.

GREECE

Cameron's demand to inspect Dorian's books in order to be informed about his customers and his sales network is not based on good faith. On the contrary, his behaviour is opposed to good faith and business decency as far as he does not confine himself to the ascertainment of Dorian's gross turnover, but demands to know more about his business for his own purposes.

Dorian's business secrets and confidentiality must be protected. This right derives, *inter alia*, from art. 288 Gr. C.C., which refers to good faith. *Prima facie*, Cameron has the right to inspect the books in order to establish the gross turnover. However, this right terminates where the other party's right of protection regarding his business secrets begins. The demand for disclosure of confidential matters is abusive and Dorian may use art. 281 to protect his business secrets.[4]

Cameron may, therefore, inspect the books but only on condition that he will not use the customers' names. A Greek judge would recommend that a third party should check the books in pre-trial proceedings. If, therefore, Dorian were to refuse to accept Cameron's suggestion of resort to a third party, then Cameron could go to court which would order the appointment of such a third party.

AUSTRIA

As Cameron has now set up in competition with Dorian, Dorian has a reasonable interest in preventing Cameron from discovering the names of his business customers. I consider that Dorian is in principle entitled to prevent Cameron from inspecting the books of his business. This follows from the implicit basis of the contract which Dorian and Cameron concluded, viz. that the latter would no longer possess a quarry and that, therefore, he would not compete with Dorian. On account of the purchase of a new quarry by Cameron, Dorian is entitled to an action which invokes a change of circumstances and can also lead to a modification of the contract.[5]

On the other hand, account must be taken of the fact that, putting aside his illegitimate wish to know the names of Dorian's business customers, Cameron has a reasonable interest in checking Dorian's gross turnover. This being the case, I consider that Dorian is only entitled to an order pre-

---

[4] Cf. Georgiadis, in: *Astikos Kodix I* art. 281, no. 25.
[5] Cf. the Austrian report to case 25 below.

venting Cameron from inspecting the books personally, leaving the possibility of him demanding that the books should be inspected by an independent third party who would be under an obligation of confidentiality as to any information acquired in the process.

FRANCE

Cameron and Dorian have concluded a contract of sale, and their agreement is therefore governed by special provisions in the Civil Code relating to sale, and in particular, those relating to their respective obligations as set out in arts. 1602 ff. Under the sale Cameron has impliedly undertaken to grant Dorian quiet enjoyment of the quarry pursuant to arts. 1625 ff. of the Civil Code (under the *garantie de l'éviction*). Article 1626 of the Code states that the seller is legally obliged to guarantee quiet enjoyment of the whole or part of the subject matter of the sale and the courts have interpreted this to mean that a seller cannot by his own act harm the normal use of the thing sold in so far as this use results from the conditions of sale.[6] Article 1626 must be read together with art. 1628 which imposes absolute liability on the seller for his own acts interfering with the buyer's right to quiet enjoyment. Case law is firmly established that any interference in the form of setting up in competition subsequent to the sale of a business comes within the guarantee of quiet enjoyment pursuant to these articles.[7] The *Cour de cassation* has clarified that although in principle the seller is entitled to set up business again, he must not cause loss to the buyer by interfering with the goodwill of the business sold.[8] In another case, very similar to the facts of case 13, it was held that the mere fact that the seller of a business sets up in business again in proximity to the business sold is not sufficient to constitute breach of the obligation to grant quiet enjoyment 'in the absence of disloyal movements and interfering with the goodwill'.[9]

In this respect, it is arguable that Cameron's behaviour did indeed constitute such disloyal behaviour and he would therefore be in breach of his obligation. To establish Cameron's disloyalty, Dorian may rely on art. 1134 al. 3 of the Civil Code. Although Cameron has a right to inspect the books, this right is linked to Dorian's obligation to pay 10 per cent of his gross turnover, since it enables him to check that the correct amount has been

---

[6] Civ. (1) 29 Nov. 1955, Bull. civ. I, no. 417, p. 335.   [7] Civ. 11 May 1898, S 1898.1.265.
[8] Req. 29 Jul. 1908, DP 1909.1.281 note Lacour; Com. 14 Apr. 1992, Bull. civ. IV, no. 160.
[9] Com. 16 Jun. 1969, D 1970.37.

paid to him. Cameron is not, however, entitled to exploit this right for his own purposes, particularly if by so doing, he interferes with Dorian's right to quiet enjoyment of the property which has been sold to him.

The solution to this case provides another illustration of the bilateral role which good faith is considered to play in the performance of the contracts since both debtor and creditor are expected to conform to the same standard of fair dealing and loyal behaviour.[10] Moreover, there seems to be an overlap between the concepts of good faith and the theory of an abuse of rights in this case.[11] However, it is submitted that a more restrictive conception of good faith in performance may suffice to reach this result on the facts of this case, a conception which links its impact to the process of interpretation of the contract, rather than requiring an independent and clearly normative duty to perform in good faith to be imposed on all parties to contracts.

Clearly, the extent to which a legal system allows or prevents free competition is explained by the balance of conflicting considerations, whether economic (the free running of the market), moral (fair and loyal dealings between parties to contracts) or based on individual rights (for example, freedom to work). In this respect, French law at present has a tendency to 'moralise' the behaviour of contracting parties and this explains the increasingly expansive role played by good faith. Moreover, the issue of good faith is a question of fact and so lies within the purview of the lower courts where the judges have a 'sovereign power' to evaluate questions of fact. In contrast, however, the theory of the abuse of rights is a question of law which can be controlled by the *Cour de cassation*.[12] In allowing more room for the duty of good faith in contracts, French law accepts a degree of casuistry so as to allow the individual circumstances of the case to influence the decision. The concept of good faith produces a dialectic between an external standard of fair dealing between contracting parties and an internal standard applicable to the particular facts of the case.

BELGIUM

In a case like this there will probably be a duty of non-competition (for a certain period within the relevant market) on the side of Cameron. Such a duty is recognised in the case of the sale of a firm, even where it is not

---

[10] See here the references to legal literature on this question in the French report to case 8 above.   [11] See the French report in case 14 below.

[12] See e.g. Com. 5 Oct. 1993, JCP 1994.II.22224 note Ch. Jamin; Com. 5 Apr. 1994, JCP 1994.I.3803 obs. Ch. Jamin; RTDCiv 1994.603 obs. J. Mestre; Com. 4 Jan. 1994, *Sté Fiat Auto France c/ Cachia*, JCP 1994.I.3757 nos. 10 and 11, obs. Ch. Jamin.

expressly provided. This can be seen as a case of supplementary interpretation.

Apart from this additional aspect of the case, it is obvious that Cameron may not abuse his right to inspect the books. Where a right can be exercised in different ways, one of which is detrimental to the other party without procuring for the party exercising the right an additional, legitimate benefit, pursuit of the latter alternative constitutes an abuse of right. The detriment, in the present case, consists in the disclosure of business secrets.

Cameron's legitimate interest would be satisfied equally well, where the inspection takes place by a third party, who informs Cameron only of the turnover, without disclosing the names of the customers. Dorian therefore has the right to refuse inspection of his books by Cameron if he offers to pay a third party (normally a professional accountant) to inspect the books and to inform Cameron of the turnover without disclosing the names of the customers.[13]

Such a result is in conformity with art. 22 of the Commercial Code regarding the inspection of books in general. The legal basis for the refusal on the part of Dorian would thus be good faith in relation to business secrets, combined with art. 22 of the Commercial Code.

SPAIN

First, there is no legislative provision in Spanish law specifically imposing on a seller of a business any duty not to compete with its buyer. Nevertheless, such a duty is seen as a consequence of the seller's implied obligation to make it possible for the buyer to obtain the intended benefit of the property sold which is found in art. 1258 of the Civil Code, as well as of the seller's duty not to hinder the buyer's effective running of the firm which he has bought.[14]

Second, however, to the extent to which Cameron exercises his right to check the books with a purpose other than the one envisaged by the contract so as to attempt to hinder the commercial opportunities of the other party, he would be held to act in breach of the rule of good faith and fall foul of the prohibition on the abuse of rights found in art. 7 of the Civil Code.

---

[13] For further discussion, see M. E. Storme, in: *De behoorlijke beëindiging* 57–109.

[14] High Court judgement of 6 April 1988 (RJA 1988, 3111). Nevertheless, such an implied duty has been rejected in sales cases, unless the parties explicitly assume this duty (Judgement of 25 June 1970, RJA 1970, 3117).

ITALY

On the assumption that Cameron has the right to check the books of Dorian's business solely for the purpose of knowing the exact amount of its turnover, it follows that he cannot inspect them with an eye to the development of his own sales network. In Italian law any different conclusion would be contrary to the interpretation of the contract consonant with good faith as required by art. 1366 of the Civil Code, as well as contrary to art. 2598, n. 3 of the same Code which forbids unfair competition.

Dorian may therefore object to the inspection of the books by Cameron. On the other hand, if required by Cameron to do so, Dorian must show the books to an independent third party, who has a professional duty to keep confidential any information other than that which relates to the gross turnover of the business, so that Cameron may know the exact amount of the money which Dorian owes him.[15] If Dorian were to oppose this request, Cameron could obtain a court order appointing a person to inspect the books in question.

Finally, it is to be noted that in order to prevent this type of controversy, art. 2557 of the Civil Code forbids a person who sells his business to set up a competing business for a period of five years from the date of the sale. This provision would apply to the facts of our case unless there was express provision in the contract to the contrary.[16]

THE NETHERLANDS

This request is for a purpose other than the one for which the right to inspect the books has been given. Cameron cannot solely for this reason ask for inspection of the books. That would be against good faith. If, however, the reason mentioned in the case has become an extra reason for inspection of the books, Dorian might make an application in court to have the terms of the contract modified, based on a change of circumstances. (An example of this would be asking the court to allow the information which Cameron acquires by inspecting the books only to be used for calculating the 10 per cent turnover.) The doctrine of changed circumstances is a specific application of what good faith requires with respect to the parties' behaviour (cf. art. 6:258 B.W.).

Another approach could be that Cameron is seen as abusing his right of

---

[15] Cass., 27 Feb. 1995, n. 2250; Cass., 27 Feb. 1995, n. 2251. Cf. Baldi 190–2.

[16] The possibility of derogating from art. 2557 c.c. by way of contract is not disputed: Colombo, in: *Trattato Galgano* 176.

inspection (art. 3:13 B.W.). However, the inspection will now have a double purpose (checking the accounts and getting information about customers). The first mentioned purpose is completely lawful, the second one unlawful. This would make it difficult to apply art. 3:13 B.W. to this case. The problem here is not so much one of the abuse of a right, but the abuse of information acquired by exercising that right.

ENGLAND

This case would be analysed by an English court in terms of the confidential nature of the information relating to the names of Dorian's business customers. The English law regarding the protection of confidential information has developed since the middle of the nineteenth century, and while it has a certain 'autonomous' or distinct nature (notably, meriting protection outside contractual relationships or situations where the information is protected by the law of property), this is not to say that a very important example or series of examples of its application is not to be found in relation to parties to contracts.

Here, it is clear that the information relating to the customers' names is confidential as it satisfies the conditions of limited public availability and specificity in character.[17] The legal basis for its protection by Dorian may be put in three ways.

First, technically, when looking at the books, Cameron would become bailee[18] of them and it is established that an obligation of confidence arises on a bailee where he derives information from the possession of another's goods, since such a person may deal with that information only in a manner expressly or impliedly stipulated by the terms of the bailment.[19] Here, it is clear that the books are to be inspected only for the purposes of establishing the gross turnover of the business so as to verify the proper price. This protection operates independently of the contract of sale which is at the origin of Cameron's right to inspect the books.

The second and third bases will run together in practice. For while trade practices are protected independently of contract, they may also influence the way in which obligations relating to them will be implied in contracts.[20] So, the contractual right to inspect the books is itself to be

---

[17] Hudson/Palmer, in: *Halsbury* § 409; *Robb v. Green* [1895] 2 QB 1, 315 (list of customers confidential to employer so that former employer in breach of confidence by using them).   [18] See the English report to case 12 above for a definition of bailment.
[19] Hudson/Palmer, in: *Halsbury* § 467.   [20] Baker/Langan 684.

interpreted as limited to the particular contractual purpose envisaged (verifying the price) with the result that use of any information found there for any other purpose would in principle be in breach of an implied term to this effect.[21] It would therefore clearly be a breach of confidence for Cameron to misuse the information in the way in which he wants. How can Dorian prevent this?

First, it could be argued that any contractual right in Cameron to inspect the books should be construed as ceasing where it can be established by Dorian that Cameron intends to exercise the right only to gain knowledge of and to misuse the confidential information to which he would thereby gain access. However, this is difficult to argue as a matter of construction of the contract and particularly so because in practice it would be difficult to show that Cameron intended to act only from his improper motive (to gain and misuse confidential information) rather than at least in part to act to protect his legitimate interest in verifying the price to be paid.

A second approach would be for Dorian to apply to the court for a *quia timet* injunction. Such an injunction is available to order a person not to do something in breach of a duty (including one of confidence) where its applicant can show that there is a danger of substantial damage being suffered by him if no injunction were granted, even where no breach of duty has yet been committed.[22] It would seem likely that Dorian would be able to satisfy this test and so obtain a court order forbidding Cameron from misusing any information gained by inspecting the books, on pain of contempt of court. In practice, the sensible route would be for Dorian's solicitors to request Cameron's solicitors that some independent third party, such as a chartered accountant, be asked to inspect the books to verify the gross turnover instead of Cameron, this request being backed up by the threat of an application for an injunction which, if granted, could be damaging for Cameron's business reputation.

IRELAND

A first question which arises in relation to these facts is whether any use of the books by Cameron for the purposes of promoting the competing business would constitute a breach of their contract, and if so, what relief could Dorian invoke. In this respect, it is to be noted that Cameron is not in a fiduciary relationship with Dorian; he is not Dorian's partner,

---

[21] *Robb v. Green* [1895] 2 QB 1, 315.   [22] Baker/Langan 651.

nor is he Dorian's agent or employee. Accordingly, in principle he is not precluded from competing with Dorian. However, he is probably under a duty of confidence in relation to the information furnished to him under the contract and this duty of confidence would prevent him from using the information for purposes other than those for which it was provided. Thus, in case 13, Cameron would be prevented from using the information as a springboard for commercial benefit at the expense of its provider. The leading Irish case in this respect is *House of Spring Gardens Ltd v. Point Blank Ltd.*[23] Although this duty of confidence is normally implied in employment contracts, it can, in appropriate circumstances, be extended to commercial relationships. Where, as here, the information is clearly intended for a restricted purpose, the courts would find no difficulty in holding that a duty of confidence exists. If use of the information for competitive purposes were to constitute a breach of contract in Cameron, then damages could be recovered if loss had occurred, or alternatively, anticipatory (or *quia timet*) injunctive relief might be sought.

A second question which arises is whether Dorian's refusal to show Cameron the books would constitute a breach of contract, and if so, to what relief, if any, would it give rise. As we have noted, the right of Cameron to obtain and, conversely, the duty of Dorian to disclose, the books of the business will probably be interpreted as being impliedly limited, so that Dorian's refusal in circumstances where there is good reason for him to expect misuse of the information would not constitute its breach. But even if Dorian were in breach of the contract in failing to show Cameron the books, it is unlikely that an Irish court would compel him to do so. Specific performance is discretionary relief and will not be granted when the person seeking it is himself in breach of contract, is acting unconscionably or where the result of granting it would be to produce an inequity. Since the obvious purpose of the contractual provision in question is to enable Cameron to ensure that he is getting his correct payment, the court would not decree specific performance if Cameron's purpose was not the one envisaged by the contract (and *a fortiori*, if this purpose involved a breach of contract). Similarly, even if the nondisclosure did constitute breach of Dorian's obligations, it is unlikely that any damages recovered would be anything other than nominal as no interest intended to be protected by the contract has been prejudiced by nondisclosure.

---

[23] [1984] IR 611.

SCOTLAND

We must look to the contract terms in this case. Dorian has granted Cameron the right to inspect the 'books of his business'. Does this include information relating to his business clients? This is a matter of interpretation.

Where an express term of a contract is silent as to an important point, the courts are obliged to give effect to the presumed intention of the parties by implying the appropriate term. How are the terms of the contract to be construed? There are some basic rules of construction (as opposed to rules of substantive law). Words should be given their ordinary English meaning. The contract should be construed as a whole; *North Eastern Railway Co. v. Lord Hastings*.[24] The courts will not construe a contract or one of its terms in a way which would lead to an absurdity, i.e. if it would be deemed absurd for any business to give access to its client base to a competitor, then perhaps the word 'books' would not be held to include such information. Where the question of construction is open, as could be the case here, the courts will adopt the meaning which is more likely to be intended by the reasonable (business)man; *Commercial Union Assurance Co. Ltd v. Hayden*.[25] Would the reasonable businessman intend the term to cover such information?

Another rule of construction which might apply in this instance is the rule that where a term is ambiguous it should be construed *contra proferentem* i.e. any ambiguity in a contract term should be construed against the *proferens*. Is Cameron the *proferens*? Did he draft the term in the contract which he is now seeking to rely on? In *Birrell v. Dryer*[26] the House of Lords held that the rule could only apply where the party against whom the rule was sought to be invoked had put forward the term. Where the clause was truly the result of mutual agreement between the contracting parties, the rule would not apply. In *G. A. Estates Ltd v. Cariapen Trustees Ltd (No. 1)*[27] Lord *Coulsfield* adopted the view of *Gloag*: '[I]n order to admit the construction *contra proferentem*, there must be a *proferens*, and in ordinary contracts where the parties are contracting on an equal footing it may fairly be assumed that the ultimate terms are arrived at by a mutual adjustment, and do not represent the language of one more than the other.'[28]

If Dorian was in agreement as to the contractual terms with Cameron, the *contra proferentem* rule will not apply. However, it is submitted that the

[24] [1900] AC 260.   [25] [1977] QB 804, [1977] 1 All ER 441, CA.   [26] (1884) 11 R (HL) 41.
[27] 1993 SLT 1037, OH.   [28] Gloag 401.

right to inspect the 'books of business' would only allow Cameron the right to check the turnover/accounts of the business and would not include Dorian's existing client base.

DENMARK AND NORWAY

Since it has to be accepted as a starting point that the seller wants to review the buyer's books in order to gain an overview of the latter's customers so as to establish his own sales network, there will probably not be much doubt, under the Nordic law, that the right of inspection cannot be invoked. This result can be based on several observations. First, the substance of the agreement needs to be more firmly determined. When a contractual right is invoked with disloyal intent, it will be easy to conclude, by way of interpretation, that it does not extend that far. Another possibility would be to apply s. 36 of the Contracts Act. The doctrine on the abuse of rights in a contractual relationship, which had hitherto not been codified, has been further developed in practice on the basis of this legislative provision.[29] Two rulings from the Danish *Højesteret* may be mentioned, namely U 1981, p. 300 H (refusal by the holder of a mortgage to have his security exchanged, mentioned above in the Danish/Norwegian report to case 6) and U 1987, p. 526 H and p. 531 H. In the latter case, the Danish *Højesteret* set aside a provision in a contract involving petrol stations that the tanks sunk into the earth continued to belong to the supplier and could only be used for his products when, after termination of the contract, the dealer was prepared to take over the tanks against due consideration. The supplier had no real need for the tanks, and digging them out would have entailed a considerable waste of time. Nevertheless, the supplier had a legitimate interest in preventing a situation where the tanks could be used by rival suppliers. Still, in the opinion of the court, the clauses constituted undue interference with the free conduct of business, and the claim to have the tanks handed over was not heard. Both these rulings signify a considerable extension of the notion of abuse of rights since it is not ill will which is of decisive importance, but the fact that the other party is subjected to unreasonable pressure. Nevertheless, Nordic law continues to accept that less noble motives do not generally prevent a contractual right from being exercised. In case 13, however, the limits appear to have been exceeded by far.

---

[29] Gomard, *Almindelig kontraktsret* 185.

SWEDEN

When Dorian granted Cameron the right to inspect his books, the agreement rested on a joint presupposition that they were not going to be competitors. Therefore, Cameron's right to be permitted to inspect the books of Dorian himself is now invalid.[30] The inspection term should, however, be adjusted in terms of s. 36 of the Contracts Act of 1915 in the way that Cameron has to rely on an auditor, who may not disclose the names of the customers.

FINLAND

The inspection clause may be adjusted (s. 36 of the Contracts Act of 1929), because Dorian might find the clause unconscionable, since the information obtained may obviously be abused for competition purposes. This is a question of fact, as is Dorian's interest in keeping his clients secret. I have not found the situation presented in case 13 to have been treated in Finnish legal literature or judicial practice. But clauses like the present one would, in court practice, be interpreted in such a way that the party having the right to inspect the other party's documents is required to employ a chartered accountant who is under an obligation not to reveal business secrets.

Editors' comparative observations

All legal systems under consideration protect the interests of Dorian in relation to his business customers, though in none of them does this lead to Cameron being prevented from gaining access to the *information* available in the books. The great majority of legal systems allow the contract to be modified so as to permit a third party (who is subject to a duty of confidentiality) to look at the books on behalf of Cameron. There are several doctrinal bases for the protection of Dorian's interests.

(i) English law and Irish law (but not Scots law) recognise the special status in law of confidential information and protect it by means of a special legal doctrine of breach of confidence, this doctrine being either dependent or independent of the contract from which it arises on the facts of case 13.

---

[30] Cf. NJA 1949, p. 134.

(ii) Most legal systems (German, Greek, French, Belgian, Spanish, Dutch and West Nordic law) apply the general principle of good faith and/or the doctrine of abuse of right (which, in a number of legal systems, is regarded as a specific emanation of that principle).

(iii) A number of legal systems (Italy, Scotland, Norway, Finland) rely on interpretation of the contract to restrict Cameron's right to inspect the books to the figures needed to calculate and verify the price. In some of these systems (particularly Italy) such interpretation is guided by the notion of good faith. In other legal systems (e.g. Germany) the application of good faith in this type of situation is very close to interpretation.

(iv) Austrian and Swedish law invoke specific doctrines turning around the notion of change of circumstances and an erroneous presupposition respectively.

Case 14: Producing new bumpers

Case

Hamish produces cars. He concludes a contract with Ian for the delivery of bumpers. Ian has to produce these bumpers for a specific new car manufactured by Hamish. This requires him to set up a new line of production which involves considerable expense. After seven months, Hamish gives notice to terminate the contract as he is entitled under the relevant legislative provision (which provides for a notice period of six weeks).

Discussions

GERMANY

The right to terminate the contract may be limited by § 242 BGB if Hamish has engendered reasonable reliance on the basis of which Ian has organised his affairs. Hamish must have known that Ian would have had to incur considerable expense in order to make performance possible. Thus Hamish has engendered reasonable reliance that the contract would at least be continued for some time. The premature termination is not in accordance with the reliance engendered and this constitutes *venire contra factum proprium* (going against one's own action). The notice period has to be determined in a manner corresponding to the reliance engendered by Hamish. The termination, therefore, only becomes effective after the lapse of the minimum period for which contracts of this kind are normally concluded.

GREECE

In this contract for the successive delivery of bumpers between Hamish and Ian, no provision is made for notice of termination. Thus, the question arises whether the notice to terminate by Hamish is valid even if it was given after a period of only seven months.

We have to assume that the notice of termination was not expected and that the contract may be described as one for successive delivery. Nevertheless, the notice of termination is valid, because Hamish cannot be forced to receive products (bumpers) from Ian, and to continue to manufacture cars, but he can be obliged to compensate Ian for the untimely notice of termination. The most suitable basis for a claim for compensation will be abuse of right (art. 281 Gr. C.C.) in combination with the provisions of arts. 914 and 932 Gr. C.C. (law of delict). It should be noted that the notice of termination may be untimely but none the less valid. As a result the contract will be terminated but a claim for compensation may arise.

If Hamish continues to manufacture that specific new car with bumpers by other producers rather than with those produced by Ian, the notice of termination may be regarded as invalid (art. 281 Gr. C.C.) and Hamish may be obliged to buy for a reasonable period of time from Ian.

The solution of this case is thus based on the notions of good faith and business usage, which govern contractual rights and obligations.[1]

AUSTRIA

Even if the parties have not expressly modified the period of notice of termination of the contract which results from the legislative rule, 'supplementary interpretation' of the contract may have the effect of restricting Hamish's right to terminate the contract with Ian. According to § 914 ABGB, every contract has to be interpreted according to the *Absicht der Parteien* (intention of the parties) and to the *Übung des redlichen Verkehrs* (practices of honest business dealings). Thus, the central question is what honest and reasonable parties would have agreed upon if they had considered the problem in question.[2] In this regard, courts refer very often to the notions of *Treu und Glauben* (good faith).[3]

The crucial factor in establishing the hypothetical intention of the parties is that Ian has had to set up a new line of production in order to perform his side of the contract and that this has involved considerable expense. Indeed, on the facts as they appear from the case, from Ian's

---

[1] Simantiras no. 324, p. 231; Areopagus 289/1974 NoB 22, 1279.
[2] OGH in SZ 49/86 (1976); JBl 1986, 197; Rummel, in: *Rummel, ABGB I* § 914 n. 12.
[3] SZ 45/11 (1972); SZ 60/50 (1987); JBl 1990, 105.

point of view, these expenses are reasonable only if the contract continues for a period of time in the course of which he would be able to cover
them through what he earns under the contract with Hamish. These
circumstances are capable of being appreciated by Hamish; indeed they
are obvious. Therefore, Hamish must be considered to understand that Ian
necessarily relies on the continuation of the contract for a reasonably long
period of time. This lends support to the hypothesis that the parties have
agreed that, during such a period as is usually needed for recovering the
expenses, Hamish is entitled to terminate the contract only if he can give
good reasons. The Supreme Court, on one occasion, took the view that a
party's exercise of a right of termination of a contract may be *sittenwidrig*
(immoral) and, therefore, ineffective under § 879 sec. 1 ABGB.[4] *Mader,*
however, has pointed out that the more appropriate approach is to rely on
a process of interpretation of the contract in such a way that it does not
allow any abuse of a contractual right to occur.[5]

Another possible approach to this kind of problem would be to establish Hamish's liability in damages for unreasonable termination of the
contract, rather than to restrict Hamish's right to terminate. In my view,
however, it would be illogical to give Hamish the right to terminate with
one hand and then to impose liability if he exercises that right with the
other.[6] Indeed, if Hamish is entitled to terminate the contract, it would
not be unlawful for him to do so and unlawfulness is a pre-condition for
the imposition of liability (§§ 1294, 1295 ABGB).

FRANCE

Ian and Hamish have concluded a contract for the sale of bumpers and for
the supply of services to produce them. The contract is primarily a sales
contract, governed by arts. 1582 ff. of the Civil Code. However, it might be
analysed as a *contrat cadre,* fixing a general framework for subsequent
detailed sales contracts. It is not clear from the facts if the contract has
been concluded for a fixed term or not. This factor may affect Ian's
contractual expectations. Ian has set up a new line of production at considerable expense. It is not known following what period of time he was
expecting this expenditure to become profitable, assuming the contract
continued. In addition, it could be helpful to ascertain whether Ian has
concentrated all his production into making bumpers for Hamish, as this

---

[4] SZ 56/72 (1983).   [5] *Rechtsmißbrauch* 132 ff.
[6] Cf. Avancini/Iro/Koziol, *Bankvertragsrecht II* n. 1/51.

could be another determining factor for the courts. These factual considerations may well influence Ian in his decision whether or not to bring a claim against Hamish.

As Hamish has respected the legislative notice period, Ian cannot claim that his termination constitutes a breach of contract, but he may want to argue that the exercise of Hamish's contractual rights has caused him a loss. In French law the courts are sometimes persuaded by this type of argument on the basis of the theory of an abuse of rights (*abus de droit*). This theory, which was invented by the courts with the backing of the jurists, has been applied to contractual rights and in particular to the unilateral termination of long-term contracts, including contracts of distribution.[7] The case law is at present in a state of flux. In one case decided in 1993, the *Cour de cassation* considered that such a unilateral termination was 'abusive', even though it complied with the notice period,[8] since the licensee of the distribution licence in question had been encouraged to incur investments which would not depreciate during the notice period. However, this case law was overturned by a case in the following year,[9] although its facts were not strictly applicable nor even analogous to those of case 14 since that case concerned non-renewal rather than termination.

To succeed in such an action for the abuse of rights Ian would not have to prove that Hamish was deliberately trying to harm him but would have to convince the court of the significance of his losses arising out of Hamish's unexpected termination.[10] Ian appears to have a claim on this legal basis but the ambiguity in the facts of case 14 makes it difficult to evaluate the success of his claim for two reasons. First, it is not clear that Hamish and Ian's contract falls within the accepted category of distribution contracts: will a contract of sale be treated in the same way by analogy? In this respect it is essential to have more details concerning the duration of the contract. Such an analogy might be possible if, according to the 'framework contract' analysis, it could be shown that Ian and Hamish's contract envisaged a continuity of sales over a long period. If this were the case, it might just be possible for the courts to imply a duty of co-operation between the parties (under art. 1134 al. 3 of the Civil Code)

---

[7] Com. 15 Dec. 1969, Bull. civ. IV, no. 384.

[8] Com. 5 Oct. 1993, JCP 1994.II.22224 note Ch. Jamin; Com. 5 Apr. 1994, JCP 1994.I.3803 obs. Ch. Jamin, RTDCiv 1994.603 obs. J. Mestre.

[9] Com. 4 Jan. 1994, RTDCiv 1994.352 obs. J. Mestre.

[10] Com. 8 Jan. 1968, D 1968.495; Amiens 13 Dec. 1973, D 1975.452 note Rolland; Paris 27 Sep. 1977, GP 1978.1.110 note Guyénot, D 1978.690 note Souleau; Com. 20 Oct. 1982, GP 1983.1.Pan.jur.124 note Ph. Le Tourneau.

in order to make the operation economically viable. Secondly, it is unclear whether Ian's contractual expectations and the expenses which he incurred were justified. For example, if Hamish could prove that he had terminated the contract because of Ian's inefficiency, Ian's claim would be unfounded.[11] Ian's claim appears to be a borderline case.

In any event, were he to succeed, Ian's damages would be on a delictual basis, despite the fact that the 'abuse' occurred within the context of a contractual relationship,[12] and this would mean that he could obtain full compensation for the expenses incurred in setting up the new production line.

The theory of the abuse of a right is an elastic notion used in a diversity of situations. As stated above, its incidence is a question of law and its application is therefore subject to control by the *Cour de cassation*. Its flexibility has given rise to scholarly criticism. In a contractual context, the use of this notion conflicts with the courts' traditional reluctance to interfere in the working of the contract, thus illustrating the eternal conflict between art. 1134 al. 1 and arts. 1134 al. 3 and 1135 of the Civil Code.

BELGIUM

The case is difficult to judge if one does not know what the relevant legislative provision is (and thus for what type of contract it was intended, etc.). The fact that there is such a provision shows that the contract is a contract for an indeterminate period of time. More information on the relevant legislative provision could enable one to argue whether the provision is really to be applied to this type of transaction or not.

Moreover, the case is quite improbable: no manufacturer will set up a whole new line of production which can be used only for one specific customer, without stipulating a minimum number of products to be purchased. The case does not give an idea of how many bumpers have been purchased by Hamish in seven months and six weeks, and whether this number was sufficient in relation to the investment. I assume it was not. The normal life of an automobile model, and thus of a bumper model, is indeed some years.

Given the legal provision mentioned in the case, the question to be asked under Belgian law is whether Ian could argue that Hamish abused his right to terminate the contract and thus acted contrary to good faith. The fact that there is such a legislative provision does not exclude

---

[11] Paris 13 Oct. 1967, GP 1968.1.36.   [12] Soc. 11 Jun. 1953, Bull. civ. IV, no. 443, p. 322.

the possibility of an abuse of right in specific cases. Whether the termination would be considered abusive, depends on the context of that provision. The test of disproportionality, which usually serves to determine abuse of right, is not very helpful in this case. Evaluation will thus depend on the behaviour of the parties. Did Hamish hold out false hopes to Ian? Did he delude him? But, overall, it appears improbable that the termination would be considered abusive under Belgian law.

Should termination, however, be considered abusive, the question of remedies arises. Theoretically, Hamish could be obliged to continue the relationship for a period which would make termination no longer abusive. However, Belgian case law often refrains from ordering specific performance in such cases, and will normally grant damages.

As the abuse of right (assuming there is one) relates to a contractual relationship, damages would be contractual rather than delictual. Thus, the measure for damages is, in principle, the positive interest (expectation interest) based on the period of time for which Hamish should have continued the relationship without abusing his right to terminate.[13]

Finally, depending on the behaviour of Hamish at the time of conclusion of the contract, the rules on fraud and/or abuse of circumstances might also be relevant.[14] If, for example, Hamish had fraudulently asserted that the legislative provision provided a notice period of one year, and that it was thus not necessary to state this in the contract, Ian could rescind the contract on the grounds of fraud and claim damages (negative interest only).

SPAIN

The contract dealt with in this case is one of supply. It is clear that according to Spanish law Ian is not entitled, on these facts, to complain about Hamish's action since the latter was entitled to act as he did. Any contractual advantage of Hamish's position is considered to arise from his stronger bargaining power, rather than from any abuse of his contractual rights.

ITALY

In order to be able to answer the questions posed by this case according to Italian law, it is necessary to draw some distinctions.

---

[13] See e.g. *Hof van Beroep* (Appeal) Antwerpen 28 Oct. 1996, AJT 1996–1997, 531.
[14] See the Belgian report to cases 2 and 4 above.

A legislative period of notice of six weeks would be a serious obstacle to any claim by Hamish against Ian where the rule created by the legislation is viewed as *ius cogens*. It seems unlikely that such a legislative provision could be successfully challenged on the basis that it violates the constitutional principles of solidarity or equality, or that it operates against undue interference with private economic initiatives[15] since the Italian Constitutional Court's review of the exercise of legislative power in such matters stops short of evaluating the merit of the legislative choices made as long as they are not manifestly unreasonable or discriminatory. Moreover, any attempt to limit the exercise of a legislative right to terminate the contract by resorting to the doctrines of the abuse of rights or of good faith would be novel in this context.[16]

On the other hand, if the rule enacting the right to terminate the contract were viewed as *ius dispositivum,* the parties may well be considered to have tacitly excluded it even though the contract is silent on this point. Two provisions of the Civil Code are particularly relevant in this respect: art. 1362 which requires that contract terms must be interpreted according to the intention of the parties, taking into account their behaviour, even if this is subsequent to the conclusion of the contract, and art. 1366 which requires that contracts must be interpreted according to good faith. Ian could invoke these principles in order to argue that the contract should have effect for a time-span equal to that necessary to cover Hamish's foreseeable needs at the time at which the contract was concluded.[17]

Finally, the case should be considered where the contract gives express contractual support for the legislative period of notice which is itself considered to be *ius dispositivum*. Assuming that the parties have not tacitly modified the terms of the contract on this point, the question arises whether Ian can still claim that the six weeks' notice to terminate is too short because it does not allow him to cover the costs of setting up the new line of production. The doctrines of good faith or of the abuse of rights, read in conjunction with the Civil Code's provision prohibiting unfair competition,[18] might come into consideration here,[19] but it must be said that Italian courts have not routinely censored behaviour which in French

---

[15] Arts. 2, 3 and 41 of the Constitution of 1948 respectively.

[16] The doctrine of abuse of rights is not codified in Italy. Its practical significance is limited, though the doctrine is far from unknown: Gambaro, in: *Enciclopedia, passim;* Patti, Digesto, 4th edn, sez. civ., I, 1987, 1; Rescigno, Riv. dir. civ., 1965, I, 205.

[17] Cf. Cass., 15 Nov. 1976, n. 4228, Giust. civ., 1977, I, 470.

[18] Art. 2598, n. 3 c.c.   [19] See the Italian report to case 23 below.

or in German law is considered contrary to good faith or an abuse of rights.[20] Indeed, the problem which underlies this case – i.e. the fairness of a contract which induces one party to incur special expenditure which would not be recovered if the contract were terminated – poses controversial policy issues, which are addressed by a bill curbing the abuse of economic dependency which was under consideration by the Italian Parliament[21] when the answer to this case study was adopted. By way of postscript it may be mentioned that the case is now governed by l. 18 June 1998, n. 192, *Disciplina della subfornitura nelle attività produttive*.[22] Article 6 of this law declares void any contract term which would allow one party to terminate the contract without giving reasonable notice (*un congruo termine di preavviso*). Accordingly, termination of the contract operates only after the lapse of such a reasonable period of time, which may be fixed by the judge in case of controversy between the parties. The producer of the bumpers has a case against the manufacturer under this provision. The period of time to be fixed by the judge should take into account the expense involved in setting up a new line of production and the minimum period for which contracts of this kind are normally concluded. The new law probably applies also to contracts which are automatically renewed from year to year, such as that of case 23. It may also apply to contracts which, though not automatically renewed, are repeatedly concluded for consecutive periods of time as in case 24. Where one party is economically dependent on the other, the arbitrary breaking off of existing commercial relationships by the stronger party is always considered abusive according to art. 9 of the new law, which sanctions the abuse of economic dependency.

THE NETHERLANDS

Although the termination may be lawful, good faith may still require Hamish to pay damages. So-called 'postcontractual' liability is governed by the same basic principles as precontractual liability: the parties have to

---

[20] See the discussion in Baldi 102 ff.

[21] *Camera dei deputati, proposta di legge n. 3509 di inziativa dei senatori Wilde e al.* The considerations of policy which must be balanced here are the need to safeguard competition and to promote an efficient market (which would argue for the timely termination of contracts which are not competitive) on the one side, and the need to curb unfair practices on the other. See Pardolesi, in: *L'artigianato* 133 ff.

[22] G.U., n. 143 of 22 June 1988. For comments see Caso, Riv. crit. dir. priv., 1998, 243; Bortolotti, *passim*.

behave in good faith and should take account of each others' legitimate interests.[23]

ENGLAND

English law does not in general provide one or other parties to a contract with the right to terminate it by notice, though exceptions are made as regards particular types of contract, such as employment or lease. No such right to terminate would apply to a contract like the one in case 14, which is either one of sale or for work and materials. Thus, in the absence of express provision for termination, Hamish would not be entitled to terminate on notice and his attempt to do so would be treated as a repudiatory breach. In consequence, on the facts, Ian could either claim damages (based either on his expected profits to be made in the deal or his wasted expenditure) or even, if he has a 'substantial or legitimate interest' in doing so and if he can do so without Hamish's co-operation, carry on performance, produce the bumpers and then sue Hamish for the contract price.[24]

On the other hand, if Hamish's purported termination of the contract is effected by the exercise of a legislative power attaching to the contract or, as more typically, by the exercise of a power expressly provided for by the contract, then for Hamish this is an effective termination of the contract and he clearly commits no breach of contract by doing so. 'In principle, since the parties are free to incorporate whatever terms they wish for the termination of their agreement, no question arises at common law whether the provision is reasonable or whether it is reasonable for a party to enforce it, unless the situation is one in which equity would grant relief against forfeiture.'[25] In the absence of any breach of contract, there would be no contractual liability in Hamish for terminating the contract; nor can there by any liability in tort for doing so as no tort exists which would cover these circumstances, even if (which is distinctly arguable) Hamish can be said to be at fault in terminating the contract.

---

[23] Cf. *Hoge Raad* 9 December 1955, NJ 1956, 157 (*Boogaard v. Vesta*) and *Hoge Raad* 21 June 1991, NJ 1991, 742 (*Mattel v. Borka*); the second decision is, however, a case about termination of a long-standing relationship which may have influenced the outcome.

[24] *White & Carter (Councils) Ltd v. McGregor* [1962] AC 413.

[25] Guest, *Chitty on Contracts* § 22–043 citing *Financings Ltd v. Baldock* [1963] 2 QB 104, at 115, and *China National Foreign Trade Transportation Corporation v. Evlogia Shipping Co. S.A. of Panama* [1979] 1 WLR 1018, at 1032.

IRELAND

It is very rare in Irish law for *statute* to allow a party to terminate a relationship or a contract by the giving of notice. A distant (and clearly distinguishable) analogous case to the present one may be found in s. 182 of the Companies Act 1963, which allows companies by ordinary resolution to dismiss directors. Companies may not contract out of this provision. Although use of the power to dismiss has been curtailed in certain specified circumstances,[26] *bona fides* or an adequate reason are not required by the statute nor have these been implied by the courts. None the less, s. 182(7) of the 1963 Act confirms that this facility for dismissal does not affect any liability that would otherwise exist and accordingly, where there is anything in a director's service contract which is inconsistent with this peremptory right of dismissal, a breach of contract may still be found.

Instead, in Irish law termination is left to the terms of the contract. Assuming the existence of an express term allowing Hamish to terminate the contract, in principle Ian may recover compensation for wasted expense only if the contract so provides or if the termination was done in breach of the contract. However, as will be seen in greater depth in relation to case 23, Irish courts have recently begun to protect long-term contractors (specifically, distributors) from disadvantageous termination of their contracts by implying a limited duty of good faith into contractual termination procedures. Thus, in *Fluid Power Technology Co. v. Sperry (Ireland) Ltd.*[27] the High Court held that an express power to terminate a contract was subject to an implied obligation to exercise it in a *bona fide* manner, i.e. for what the defendant (rather than the court) regarded as a good reason.

Assuming that the contract is silent as to the issue of termination, the courts would imply a right to terminate on giving reasonable notice.[28]

However, as Irish law stands there is no statutory provision allowing termination by the giving of six weeks' notice and if one were enacted many of the questions raised by this case would depend on the interpretation of the particular provision. Clearly, though, if Hamish were found to have terminated the contract lawfully pursuant to any such statute, Ian would have no recourse.

---

[26] See the Companies Act 1963, s. 205.   [27] Unreported, 22 February 1985.
[28] *Irish Welding v. Philips Electrical (Ireland) Ltd* (unreported, High Court, 8 October 1976) in which nine months was considered reasonable.

SCOTLAND

At common law, once the parties to a contract have reached agreement on the essentials and other specified terms of their contract, and have satisfied any formalities requisite for its formation, they have created and are bound by their obligations, and unless there is a further agreement, neither party can withdraw or cancel the contract.

A withdrawal or cancellation amounts to a breach of contract; *White and Carter (Councils) Ltd v. McGregor.*[29] However, any contract may include a term entitling a party in stated circumstances and possibly subject to conditions, to cancel the contract. There is no breach of contract if a party has a legal right to terminate a contract and has validly exercised that right.

Is Hamish in breach of contract or has he validly terminated the contract with Ian? He has given six weeks' notice, as provided for under legislation, so it would seem that he is fully entitled to cancel the contract despite the great expense that Ian has incurred. Unless their contract specified otherwise it would appear to be a case of 'tough luck Ian'.

If their contract is silent as to duration, at common law the implication is that it is a contract at will which continues indefinitely but may be terminated at any time by any party; *Dunlop v. Steel Co. of Scotland.*[30] Where, however, inconvenience or difficulty would be caused to any other party by immediate termination, the party terminating is bound to give reasonable notice of his intention to do so to all other parties; *Morrison v. Abernethy School Board,*[31] *Stevenson v. North British Railway Co.*[32] Hamish has given the notice required.

Could there be a case of unjustified enrichment here? Unjustified enrichment exists where, at another's expense, one has become the owner of the other's money or property or has used that property or otherwise benefited from his actings or expenditure in circumstances which Scots law regards as actionably unjust and so requiring the enrichment to be reversed. The obligation is obediential and arises by operation of law. Where the case involves the defender benefiting unjustifiably from the expenditure or actings of the pursuer (or from the use of his property), as could be argued in this case, the action is dealt with under the heading of *recompense; Morgan Guaranty Trust Co. of New York v. Lothian Regional Council.*[33] Recompense is properly applicable either to cases where there is no contract between the parties or to cases where work has been done under a contract in circumstances which preclude any direct contractual claim.

[29] 1962 SC (HL) 1.   [30] (1879) 7 R 283.   [31] (1876) 3 R 945.   [32] (1905) 7 F 1106.
[33] 1995 SLT 299.

The limits of the plea of recompense are stated by the maxim *nemo debet locupletari ex aliena jactura* (no one should be enriched by another's loss).[34] Five elements must occur. (i) The pursuer must have suffered loss and it must consist of expenditure which has not met with the expected return or is work or service for which no payment has been received. Note that even where loss of this kind is incurred, there may be no remedy of recompense as there is no doctrine in the law of Scotland that every person who has profited by work done under a contract is to be liable for that work; *Cran v. Dodson*.[35] (ii) The pursuer must have had no intention to make a gift to the defender. (iii) The pursuer must not have carried out the operation for his own benefit. (iv) The pursuer must have no other legal remedy (there are special exceptions here). (v) The defender must have gained as a result of the pursuer's loss. And this is where the action will fail because Hamish is not *lucratus*. He has not gained as a result of Ian's loss. Even if Hamish knew of Ian's vast expenditure there would be no claim for recompense, and this is perhaps an inadequacy in the current Scots law of unjustified enrichment.[36]

DENMARK AND NORWAY

At the outset, the agreement will have to be applied in accordance with its wording. The seller has entered into a contract for the delivery of bumpers which he has to produce. The agreement appears to have been concluded on the basis that it may be terminated, enabling each of the parties to terminate it by giving the statutory period of notice. An agreement thus terminable is subject to a degree of uncertainty arising from the right to terminate.[37] Although the seller has had to make substantial investments to carry out the production of the bumpers, it must initially be said that he made those investments at his own risk. It is assumed here that the party placing the order did not withhold any relevant and material facts on concluding the contract, and that the termination was not made on entirely illegitimate grounds. But one may possibly go further and require the buyer to give the seller a reasonable chance to make an alternative offer if the reason for the termination was merely a wish for a change of manufacturer in order to obtain more favourable terms.

Furthermore, it appears obvious from the facts of the case that this is a commercial agreement between essentially equal parties. Where the

---

[34] Wilson/Forte § 29.13.   [35] (1893) 1 SLT 354.
[36] See *Watson v. Shankland* (1871) 10 M 142, aff'd (1873) 11 M (HL) 51.
[37] See also cases 23 and 24.

agreement is terminable, it would clearly be said that the manufacturer has taken a calculated risk as regards termination.[38] That the termination is inconvenient and causes the other party considerable loss, cannot in itself be seen to be a sufficient ground for setting aside the agreement.

If the facts are changed slightly so that the termination by the buyer was not the result of pure market evaluations, etc., but had definite overtones of disloyalty, it is not impossible that the courts might set aside the termination under s. 36 of the Contracts Act. If the buyer has failed to inform the manufacturer/seller early enough, he might also become liable for compensation, even if the termination is upheld.[39] The assessment would also be different for parties of unequal bargaining power, i.e. where the manufacturer is clearly the less powerful party within the relationship.

SWEDEN

This is a general supplier's contract. General suppliers do not have a mandatory protection in Swedish law entitling them to a certain period of notice, or to compensation for investments, etc. Such a regulation exists only in favour of commercial agents selling in their principal's name and on his behalf (Commercial Agency Act of 1991, following the Directive 86/653/EEC), and consignees selling in their own name but on behalf of their principal (Consignment Act of 1914, amended in the 1970s). There is no case law in which these Acts have been applied *per analogiam*. The point of departure is, therefore, that the supplier acts at his own risk. If the relevant legislative provision provides for a notice period of six weeks (as stated in this case), the notice period cannot be extended by application of s. 36 of the Contracts Act of 1915, since that provision is able to modify only contract terms, not legislative rules. Ian will probably not be entitled to any compensation for his investments.[40]

FINLAND

The termination clause might be adjusted on grounds of unconscionability (s. 36 of the Contracts Act of 1929), depending on evidence regarding the intentions and assumptions of the parties and the amount of the expenses involved.

---

[38] Hagstrøm, *Lov og Rett* 1994, 131 ff., 158 ff.   [39] See Rt. 1988, p. 1078 at p. 1084.
[40] Cf. the answers given in the Swedish reports to cases 23 and 24 below.

Editors' comparative observations

Analysis of this case is complicated by the fact that reference is made to a legislative right to terminate the contract by notice, a type of provision which does not apply (either generally or to facts such as are found in case 14) in a number of countries. Thus, some reporters explained the position on the assumption that the right to terminate the contract arose from a provision in the contract itself. Moreover, some legal systems distinguish between (a) whether and, if so, under what circumstances the contract may be terminated, i.e. the duration of the contract and (b) which notice period applies *if* the contract is terminated, i.e. when a notice of termination becomes effective, once it has been established that it may be given. Other legal systems do not appear to draw this distinction. Finally, the case does not say why Hamish has terminated the contract. According to some legal systems, his reasons may, however, be relevant in determining whether the contract may be terminated and/or whether damages have to be paid.

With all the caution which is due as a result of these complications it may be said that three different solutions are advocated: (i) termination is regarded as premature and thus ineffective; the contract must be allowed to continue for a reasonable period of time; (ii) the notice of termination is valid but Hamish has to compensate Ian for his expenses; and (iii) no relief for Ian at all. These solutions cut across the civil law/common law line.

(i) The first solution is the one adopted particularly clearly in German, Austrian and Italian law. The premature termination of the contract, according to German law, is not in accordance with the reliance engendered and is therefore seen to constitute *venire contra factum proprium* under the general good faith clause. Austrian law arrives at the same result by way of interpretation; the interpretation is, however, also guided by the notion of good faith. In Italy, the case is now governed by legislation focusing on the notion of abuse of economic dependency. Greek law and Belgian law could, under certain circumstances, also see their courts adopting a similar solution, both under the auspices of the doctrine of abuse of right. Finnish law would adjust the termination clause on grounds of unconscionability. Strikingly, while Irish law's starting point is the same stark denial of relief as is found in English law, a developing case law may be discerned which recognises the existence of an implied duty of good faith in the exercise of a right to terminate a long-term contract such as the one found in case 14.

(ii) French courts are open to persuasion that termination in the present case may be abusive but the result would be liability in damages in delict. Greek law would also normally adopt such an approach and so would Belgian law (though with the proviso that damages would be contractual). Dutch law grants a claim for damages on the basis that Hamish has not behaved in accordance with the precepts of good faith.

(iii) The third solution ('tough luck Ian!') is found in legal systems which formally deny any general principle of good faith (English and Scots law) but also in Spanish law which does indeed recognise such principle. West Nordic and Swedish law take the same position.

Case 15: Two cracks in a shed

Case

Eduard asks François to build a shed. In terms of the contract, Eduard is under no duty to pay unless François' workmanship meets the approval of a designated employee in Eduard's firm whose decision 'in aesthetic matters shall be final'. After the shed has been completed, the designated employee withholds his approval because the material used for building the shed contains two cracks which do not in any way impair the use of the shed and which are invisible to the naked eye except under close inspection in bright sunlight.

Discussions

GERMANY

The parties to a contract may leave determination of the performance to a third party. Where they do so it is to be presumed that the determination shall be made in an equitable manner (§ 317 I BGB). If the third party has to make the determination in an equitable manner, it is not binding upon the contracting parties if it is manifestly inequitable (§ 319 I 1 BGB).[1] Thus, the decision of Eduard's employee would not be binding if it has to be considered to be manifestly inequitable (§ 319 I 1 BGB).

François and Eduard have not left determination of the performance (i.e. the building of the shed) to the third party, as envisaged in §§ 317 I, 319 I 1 BGB. They have only left it to him to evaluate the quality of the

---

[1] If the parties have agreed that the third party may determine the performance at his discretion, any determination is valid as long as it is not illegal or immoral (§§ 134, 138 BGB).

performance. However, §§ 317 I, 319 I BGB are taken to apply *a maiore ad minus*. § 319 I BGB may be excluded by agreement.[2] The parties may, therefore, agree that the decision of the third party shall be final even if it turns out to be manifestly inequitable. But the parties have to make their intention absolutely clear, and they have to do so in the knowledge that the BGB does not normally countenance manifestly inequitable determinations.[3] This requirement is not met in the present case, even though the parties have declared the third party's decision to be final.

Eduard's employee has rejected the work although the cracks do not impair the use of the shed and are hardly visible. It is manifestly inequitable to reject the work on this basis and the decision of the employee is therefore not binding upon the contracting parties. It will have to be made by court decision (§ 319 I 2 BGB).

It is, however, questionable whether determination of the quality of performance, in the present case, was left to a third party or whether we are not rather dealing with a case of § 315 BGB: determination of the performance by one of the parties to the contract.[4] Whether an employee of the creditor has to be regarded as a third party has not yet been authoritatively decided. Formally, of course, he is since he is not a party to the contract. Substantially, however, he is not for he is clearly 'in the camp' of the creditor. In legal literature it is often merely asserted, without further comment, that anybody must be regarded as a third party for the purposes of § 317 BGB who is not a party to the contract.[5] The Federal Labour Court, on the other hand, has held § 315 rather than § 317 BGB to be applicable where determination of performance in an employment contract is left to the employers' association.[6] This decision is clearly based on the consideration that the employers' association is on the employer's side and can hardly be regarded as impartial and objective. The position of a third party for the purposes of § 317 BGB thus appears to require some measure of neutrality and independence.[7]

If one were to follow this view (which, indeed, appears to be preferable) § 315 BGB would have to be applied in the present case. As a result, the determination must be made in an equitable manner (§ 315 I BGB); if it is inequitable it is not binding upon the other party (§ 315 III BGB). Since,

---

[2] *Münchener Kommentar/Gottwald* § 319, n. 4 with further references.
[3] *Münchener Kommentar/Gottwald* § 319, n. 4.
[4] On § 315 BGB, see the German report to case 9.
[5] See, e.g., *Staudinger/Mader* § 317, n. 5.   [6] BAG, Der Betrieb 1988, 1273.
[7] See also BAG, Der Betrieb 1996, 2670 and the comments by *Münchener Kommentar/Gottwald* § 317, n. 10.

however, it has been stated above that the decision, in the present case, is *manifestly* inequitable, it also fails in terms of the less stringent standard of § 315 BGB. Again, therefore, the decision will have to be made by court decision (§ 315 III 2 BGB).

GREECE

In Greek law the contract between Eduard and François is characterised as a contract for work (arts. 681–702 Gr. C.C.). Thus, the work has to be approved by Eduard (art. 692 Gr. C.C.). Such approval has, as far as aesthetic matters are concerned, been entrusted to a designated employer in his firm. This means that determination of the performance has been entrusted to a third party. According to art. 371 Gr. C.C. '[i]f the determination of a performance has been entrusted to one of the contracting parties or to a third party it is in case of doubt considered that the determination must be made by reference to equitable criteria. If the determination was not based on equitable criteria or has been delayed it shall be made by the Court.' Equitable for the purposes of art. 371 Gr. C.C. means according to good faith and business usage. Here there is no need for a direct application of the general clauses for good faith and abuse of rights, since art. 371 Gr. C.C. constitutes a *lex specialis*.

The criteria used by Eduard's designated employee are not in accordance with good faith and business usage, since neither the use nor the general aspect of the shed are impaired. The very minor defect does not justify rejection of the work. It merely leads to a claim for a proportional reduction of the remuneration under art. 688 Gr. C.C.

Greek courts might apply art. 207 Gr. C.C. in the present situation, according to which 'a condition shall be deemed fulfilled if its fulfilment was impeded contrary to the requirements of good faith by the person who would have suffered a prejudice from its fulfilment'.[8] This rule constitutes a special expression of good faith in contractual relations. François would thus have the right to claim payment though possibly reduced according to art. 688 Gr. C.C. It has been maintained by the courts that for the application of art. 207 Gr. C.C. the requirements for abuse of right have to be present.[9] This would, however, appear to be the case as the refusal by Eduard's employee to approve the work is completely unjustified.

---

[8] For the respective rule in German law, see § 162 I BGB.
[9] See Simantiras no. 907, p. 673; Areopagus 899/1980 NoB 29, 284; Areopagus 1178/1980 NoB 29, 540.

Article 371 is one of a number of general clauses contained in the Greek Civil Code where the judge is enjoined not to decide according to his subjective perceptions but on the basis of generally accepted values in society at large and in business life.[10]

AUSTRIA

The present case raises the same problem that we find with regard to warranty claims for latent defects in contracts of sale. The arguments used in that context are, in my opinion, also decisive for interpreting the terms of the contract in the present case (even though we are dealing here with a contract for work). As mentioned earlier,[11] under § 914 ABGB a contract has to be understood in a way that corresponds to the *Absicht der Parteien* (intention of the parties) and *Übung des redlichen Verkehrs* (practices of honest business dealings).

According to § 932 II ABGB a buyer cannot avail himself of the warranty claims provided under the law of sale if the value of the object of the sale is only insignificantly reduced. This rule, however, is applicable only after the object of the sale has been delivered. In the present case Eduard did not accept the shed. But the opinion has been advanced that, as far as rejection of goods is at stake, the position must be the same as after delivery has taken place.[12] Thus it has been argued[13] that the buyer has no right to reject the goods if the defect is so insignificant that it hardly reduces their value. However, I think that § 932 II ABGB only concerns the right of reduction of the purchase price and not the right to demand repair,[14] since there is no reason why the buyer should not be able to demand delivery strictly according to the contract. Therefore, I would suggest the following distinction: the buyer has no right to reject the goods only in cases where repair of the defect is impossible or unreasonably expensive; otherwise he may reject them and demand their repair.[15]

Of course, if the defect cannot be qualified as insignificant and if repair is possible and not unreasonably expensive, the right to reject and

---

[10] Doris, in: *Astikos Kodix II* arts. 371–3, no. 17; Papantoniou, *Genikes Arches* 123–4; Stathopoulos, in: *Astikos Kodix II* art. 288, no. 60; Simantiras nos. 907–9, pp. 672–6; Papantoniou, *Kali Pistis* 194; Areopagus 98/1960 NoB 8, 634; Areopagus 794/1983 EEN 1984, 272; Areopagus 385/1978 EEN 1978, 589.   [11] See the Austrian report to case 14.
[12] Apathy, JBl 1975, 577; Bydlinski, in: *Klang, Kommentar IV/2* 158 ff.; Wilhelm, JBl 1975, 121 f.
[13] Apathy, JBl 1975, 577.   [14] Cf. Koziol, ÖJZ 1985, 742 f.
[15] In this case the question arises whether the buyer is entitled to withhold the entire price (OGH in JBl 1990, 248) or only part of it (Koziol, ÖJZ 1985, 743 ff.).

to demand repair, according to the general view, also exists (§ 1413 ABGB).[16]

Some would hold that the buyer has the right to reject even if repair is impossible or unreasonably expensive.[17] But, once again, one has to distinguish: only if the defect is *wesentlich*, i.e. so serious that the object is of no use to the buyer, does Eduard have that right and is not obliged to pay anything. Since, however, in the present case the shed does not suffer from such a serious defect, Eduard has no right to reject it and may only demand reduction of the price (cf. § 920 ABGB).[18]

FRANCE

Under art. 1174 of the Civil Code, a 'potestative condition from the point of view of the debtor' is one which leaves performance conditional on an event the occurrence of which is within the power of the debtor and such a condition renders the contract a nullity. French law would consider the clause which makes Eduard's duty to pay the price for the shed subject to approval given by his own employee as a 'purely potestative' condition for this purpose, and this therefore entails the nullity of the contract itself. Indeed, Eduard's performance is due only if he himself (through his own employee) so decides, in accordance with purely subjective criteria. The fact that approval may well have been withheld here in bad faith would certainly go to confirm the court's assessment of the 'potestativity' inherent in Eduard's promise, but it should be stressed that, under art. 1174, the mere risk of such a decision would suffice.

The effect of art. 1174 is to disqualify as a contract any agreement by which the promisor may withhold performance of such an essential obligation at will, thereby giving a mere appearance of consent to an obligation. Although such a provision has obvious links with the requirement of good faith, it is also considered as giving expression to the more general notion of coherence (compare the adage *donner et retenir ne vaut* . . . : one cannot give with one hand what one withholds with the other). A similar idea appears in art. 1178, which provides that a valid condition is deemed to be fulfilled whenever it is the promisor's own action (or inaction) which prevents its fulfilment.

Finally, it should be noted that this extreme result of rendering the

---

[16] Reischauer, in: *Rummel, ABGB I* vor §§ 918–33 n. 10; Koziol, ÖJZ 1985, 742.
[17] OGH in EvBl 1970/77; Adler/Höller, in: *Klang, Kommentar V* 397; Mayrhofer 357.
[18] Koziol, ÖJZ 1985, 742; Reischauer, in: *Rummel, ABGB I* vor 918–33 n. 10.

contract a nullity could be tempered by allowing recovery by the builder for any work done on the basis of *enrichissement sans cause*. In practice, though, in the context of building contracts and in the absence of an express stipulation determining the question of 'formal acceptance' of the building work (*réception*), art. 1792–6 of the Civil Code sets out how the question of completion of the work should be determined (with or without reservations, at the request of the 'most diligent party', either with or without the intervention of the courts and in all cases in the presence of both parties (*contradictoirement*)).

BELGIUM

Although the rules are to a large extent the same, it is first of all necessary to judge whether the decision of the designated employee is to be considered (i) as a determination by a party to the contract or (ii) as a third party determination.

(i) As the decision is made by an employee of Eduard's firm, it will normally be considered a determination of Eduard's firm itself.

The first question is then whether Eduard has already undertaken to buy the specified type of shed. It is certainly possible to conclude a contract under a suspensive condition such as a sale *ad gustum* (see art. 1587 C.C.). Such a contract is not binding as long as the shed has not been approved by the buyer. François would, in this case, deliberately take the risk of building the shed although Eduard is not at all bound to buy it. Such cases certainly exist, e.g. where Eduard asks several parties to build a shed, stating explicitly that he will buy only one of them according to the preference of his designated employee. In such a case, there are no contractual remedies for François. There may, of course, be precontractual remedies, if François can prove fraud, misrepresentation, etc.

It does not seem, however, that the contract between Eduard and François can be classified in this way. Indeed, in similar cases Belgian law has regarded the contracts involved as valid and binding.[19] Moreover, there is sufficient similarity with some cases explicitly regulated by statute law (especially art. 1854 C.C.). The contract concerned a specified type of shed, and thus clearly had a subject matter that is certain. The des-

---

[19] See especially the examples cited by M. E. Storme, TPR 1988, 1259 ff. at 1282 n° 22. See further Ronse, TPR 1977, 211 ff. Cf. also Cass. 19 Sept. 1983, *Fiat Auto locomotion*, Arr. 52 = RW 1983–1984, 1482 (concerning a contractual *ius variandi*).

ignated employee had to judge the shed according to a certain criterion, albeit a very vague one (namely from the point of view of aesthetics). Under these circumstances, the condition cannot be considered to be a potestative condition. Interpretation according to good faith leads to the conclusion that whilst the designated employee has a margin of appreciation, he may not abuse the power given to him. In the case of an abuse, the other party is not bound by his decision. In assessing whether the decision was abusive or not, the judge may not take a decision himself. He merely checks whether the employee remained within his margin of appreciation. Parties can give a person a wider or narrower margin, but they cannot exclude this judicial control altogether. The disproportionality test will certainly play a role in determining whether the decision was 'manifestly unreasonable' or not. In our case, the decision will normally be judged manifestly unreasonable.

(ii) If the intervention of the employee were held to be a third party determination, the validity of the contract and the clause is not in doubt. However, a similar control as the one sketched above will be exercised.[20] Whilst this control will probably be less strict than in the case of determination by one of the parties, the result in case 15 may well be the same. The decision of the designated person will thus be set aside.

SPAIN

This case raises an issue of fact rather than of law. The question which must be posed is whether the two cracks should be considered to constitute a breach of contract, given that their importance is very small in proportion to the volume of the work and to the size of the contractual price, bearing in mind the considerations discussed in terms of the abuse of rights in relation to case 7.

Article 1598 of the Civil Code provides that parties to a building contract may agree that the work is to be done according to the decision and judgement of the commissioning owner of the property. However, if the parties so agree, the owner's right to approve or disapprove of any work done may not be exercised in an arbitrary fashion nor does the decision rest exclusively on his judgement alone. Thus, where the owner does not approve of work done, the builder may appeal to the adjudication of an expert, in whom then rests the ultimate decision as to whether the work

---

[20] See Storme/Storme, TPR 1985, 713 ff.

has been done in accordance with the requirements and the purpose of the contract.[21]

ITALY

In Italian law it would be tempting to argue that any term by which the parties attempted to give to Eduard's employee an unlimited discretion (based on a purely subjective evaluation) in 'aesthetic matters' is simply null and void. Such an argument would rest on art. 1355 of the Civil Code, which strikes down any contractual term which allows a debtor of an obligation to withhold performance at will and thereby make his obligation illusory.[22] Indeed, some courts and scholars favour this approach with regard to cases like the one under consideration.[23]

However, it should be noted that on the facts of case 15 François (i.e. the debtor) did not reserve a power to withhold performance at will: for it was Eduard (i.e. the creditor) who reserved to himself the right to reject the shed for a failure to achieve the aesthetic result required, as certified by his employee.[24] Clearly, if Eduard's employee were considered to be a third party to the contract for this purpose, the solution to this case would be straightforward since by art. 1349 of the Civil Code parties to a contract may indeed leave to a third party the determination whether performance has been made. And while Eduard and François did not entrust to Eduard's employee the task of determining *performance*, but rather that of judging its *quality*, this provision would be considered as applying *a fortiori* to this situation. Unless the parties have agreed otherwise, any decision made under art. 1349 has to conform to the requirements of equity, and therefore can be challenged only on the ground that it is clearly mistaken or unfair. On the facts of case 15, the parties have agreed that the employee's decision should be final and in these circumstances the decision-maker's discretion is even wider. He may rely purely on his own judgement, provided that it is not tainted by bad faith, such as malice, corruption or the desire to make a sensational choice.[25] Given the trifling significance of the defect in case 15, it is likely that François would be able to establish bad faith on the facts under this test.

---

[21] High Court judgement of 1 April 1971 (RJA 1971, 1480).
[22] Art. 1354 c.c.: 'The transfer of a right or the assumption of an obligation subject to a suspensive condition which makes it depend on the mere will of the transferor or of the debtor is void.'   [23] Galgano, *Diritto civile* (1993) 229 ff.; Cass., 8 Sept. 1988, n. 5099.
[24] Cf. Sacco/De Nova, in: *Trattato Sacco II* 152–3.   [25] Ibid., at 135.

In the result, therefore, Eduard's refusal to accept the shed is not jus-tified. This results from the provision in the *codice civile* on the *exceptio non adimpleti contractus* which expressly states that this defence cannot be allowed where it is contrary to good faith.[26] On the other hand, Eduard may demand that the defect be repaired, or that the price be reduced pro-portionately. He will also obtain damages for any loss caused by the cracks in the building if he shows that they were due to François' negligence.[27]

THE NETHERLANDS

The decision (a so-called 'party decision') has to be made in good faith. Since the problem in the present case was a very minor one, approval cannot be refused.[28] This result could be different if the aesthetic aspects of the shed are an essential feature of the contract, thus leading to non-performance of the contract because of a matter which, in terms of the agreement, would then not be insignificant.

Pre-existing case law has been codified in art. 7:904 B.W., albeit with one important difference. Under the old Civil Code the consequences of acting contrary to good faith were also governed by good faith. Under the new Civil Code a decision by a (third) party as in the present case can be avoided[29] if its binding nature would be against good faith because of its contents (substantive defects) or the way in which it was reached (proced-ural defects). This article is also applicable when one of the parties to a legal relationship or a third party is allowed to supplement or change the rules governing that relationship.[30]

Articles 7:904 and 7:906 B.W. belong to Title 15 of Book 7, which contains special provisions on the 'contract of assessment', i.e. a contract by which parties wish to avoid or end a conflict as to what is legally binding upon them.

ENGLAND

A contracting party's duty to pay the price depends on a distinction between entire and severable obligations. Accordingly, if a party's obliga-tion is entire, he can recover payment only if it has been completely

---

[26] Art. 1460 c.c.   [27] Art. 1668 c.c.
[28] Cf. *Hoge Raad* 9 February 1923, NJ 1923, 676 (*Artist de Laboureur*) and *Hoge Raad* 12 September 1997, RvdW 1997, 171 (*Confood Diepvries v. Zürich Verzekeringen*).
[29] Cf. arts. 3:49 ff. B.W.   [30] Art. 7:906.

performed: part or even substantial performance is not enough.[31] Thus, notably, if a builder agrees to build a house for a lump sum, he can receive no payment if it is not completed, even if a very considerable amount of work has been done.[32] However, a party's obligation is said to be severable where payment is due from time to time as performance of specified parts of the contract is rendered.[33] In general, as has been indicated, an obligation to build a shed for a lump sum (assuming this to be the case in case 15) is entire, but the builder's obligations as to its quality or aesthetic appeal are severable,[34] though the cases which are used to support this proposition are sometimes instead treated as authority for a doctrine of 'substantial performance' according to which the price may be recovered as long as the promisor has received 'substantial performance'. However, it is clear that a contractual provision can validly stipulate that payment may arise only on the exact performance of any type of obligation, including one as to the quality or aesthetic appeal of the result.[35]

Indeed, it is usual in a building contract of any size for payment to be due only on the certification of work having been done to specification and to the required standard in the opinion of some person other than either of the contracting parties and this type of provision is in principle effective. Such a certifier is not without more to be treated as an arbitrator in a technical sense[36] so as, for example, to attract an arbitrator's immunity from liability for negligence in the conduct of the arbitration,[37] but he must nevertheless act in a 'fair and unbiased manner' and must 'reach [his] decisions fairly, holding the balance between his client and the contractor'.[38] Moreover, where a certifier fails to show that 'attitude of judicial independence' required of him, even though this failure does not consist of fraud or collusion with the other party, then his decisions cease to bind and a party to the contract can apply to the court to instruct an independent referee to decide the issue of his liability to make payment.[39] Such a failure to act properly according to the special position 'completely annuls' the contractual requirement.[40]

It would, therefore, be for François to show that the withholding of approval of the building by Eduard's employee reflects his failure to act impartially and independently, acting instead in the interests of his

---

[31] *Cutter v. Powell* (1795) 6 TR 320.   [32] *Sumpter v. Hedges* [1898] 1 QB 673.   [33] Treitel 699.
[34] Treitel 701, so interpreting *Hoenig v. Isaacs* [1952] 2 All ER 176.
[35] *Hoenig v. Isaacs*, [1952] 2 All ER 176, at 180–1.
[36] *Northampton Gas-Light Co. v. Parnell* (1855) 15 CB 630.
[37] *Sutcliffe v. Thackrah* [1974] AC 727.   [38] Ibid., at 737 *per* Lord Reid.
[39] *Hickman & Co. v. Roberts* [1913] AC 229.
[40] *Kimberley v. Dick* (1871) 13 Eq 1 *per* Sir John Romilly M.R.

employer, Eduard. Such a failure may be inferred from the circumstances, as was the case in *Hickman & Co. v. Roberts*, where an architect's 'entirely unexplained delay in giving his final certificate' showed that he was still under his employer's influence. In case 15, a decision by Eduard's employee to withhold payment on the basis of some trifling aesthetic defect in a building such as a shed where perfection would hardly normally be required may well be enough to raise such an inference. If it were shown, François can sue for the price on the ground that the work has been done (having performed his entire obligation to build the shed) and apply to the court for the appointment of an independent referee if Eduard argues that his liability is contingent on a particular degree of workmanship being achieved.

This law is long established in the context of building contracts, but it would seem to be reflected more generally in judicial attitudes to cases where some right or liability in one party to a contract is contingent on the decision of an employee or agent of the other party. For example, in *Cobelfret N.V. v. Cyclades Shipping Co. Ltd (The 'Linardos')*,[41] a charter-party provided that the ship's master's 'notice of readiness' to receive cargo would, after a delay, start 'notice time' running so as to allow its owner to claim demurrage, even though a port marine surveyor later declared that it was unready (as insufficiently clean). *Colman J.* observed that 'a notice of readiness proved to be given by the master or chief officer with knowledge that it was untrue, that is to say in the knowledge that the vessel was not then ready would be ineffective to start time running. There must by implication be a requirement of good faith.'[42] Here, though, it is to be noticed that the significance of good faith is the imposition of a requirement of honesty, whereas in the building contract cases, the certifier is held to the much more demanding standard of fairness, of 'holding the balance' between the two parties in question.

IRELAND

The English law analysis holds good for Irish law.

SCOTLAND

If the contract is written the courts will look to the terms of the contract contained in the writing. Once ascertained, the terms demarcate the amount of the parties' respective contractual obligations. The courts must

---

[41] [1994] 1 Lloyd's Rep 28.   [42] Ibid., at 32.

determine the exact import of the terms. The contract term here allows Eduard to withhold payment if his employee is not satisfied as to the aesthetic quality of the shed. The contract is thus subject to a condition. Eduard has a future obligation by the terms of the contract in that his performance (the payment) cannot be called for until the occurrence of the event which must happen – the aesthetic quality of the shed must be approved. Although Eduard's obligation exists from the moment of the formation of the contract, enforcement of this obligation is suspended until the condition is satisfied.

Has the condition been satisfied? According to Eduard's employee, the condition has not been satisfied, and therefore Eduard need not pay. The terms of the contract stipulate that his decision shall be final. This would indicate that even in the event of experts disagreeing with his decision regarding the aesthetic quality of the shed, his decision will stand. Matters of aesthetics are subjective, thus it may be hard to argue that the employee's decision is unreasonable. The courts are reluctant to decide matters of architectural taste; *Duke of Buccleuch v. Edinburgh Magistrates*.[43] And as François is mutually in agreement with Eduard, that his employee shall have the final say, then even although the cracks are virtually invisible to the eye, because of this clause, François has no comeback.

However, François has provided a benefit, the shed, under the mistake that he will get the contract price. There is therefore a case that while he cannot sue for the full contract price, Eduard has become unjustifiably enriched[44] at François' expense and therefore *prima facie* Eduard must disgorge the benefit, i.e. pay François to the extent that he has benefited, which may well be less than the contract price. Again the action falls under the heading of recompense. The action is open to François because as he is in breach of contract, contractual remedies are unavailable/exhausted; the case is a typical one of recompense where a party has supplied goods under a contract but has departed from the contractual terms so that a claim for the contract price is excluded. So, where a builder produces a building which is materially different from what is ordered, he may have no claim directly under his contract, but if the employer does not choose to reject the building, he is at least liable *quantum lucratus*; *Ramsay v. Brand*.[45] *Quantum lucratus* is measured and limited by the advantage which the services have produced to the recipient; *Landless v. Wilson*.[46] In this case, Eduard is *lucratus*. The alternative claim is for *quantum meruit* which applies if the contract is void/voidable (which is not the case here),

---

[43] (1865) 3 M 528.   [44] See the Scottish report to case 14 above.
[45] (1898) 25 R 1212, (1898) 35 SLR 927.   [46] (1880) 8 R 289.

and which is measured by the market value of the services rendered and maintainable whether they have proved beneficial or not.

DENMARK AND NORWAY

It is difficult to see that a case of this nature could raise the question as to whether an absolute obligation in contract law exists. Although the contract specifies that the decision of the appointed person 'in aesthetic matters shall be final', this can hardly be taken to entail a right to refuse to take delivery without legitimate grounds. After all, the words and phrases contained in the contract must be determined by interpretation. In this respect, it must be taken into account that this is a contract for a shed, not a commission for a work of art. Thus, it does not make sense that refusal to take delivery should be possible merely because of two insignificant cracks which do not impair the use of the shed and which are invisible to the naked eye, except under close inspection in bright sunlight; see Rt. 1980, p. 610 regarding the broad interpretation of a contract couched in absolute terms.

SWEDEN

In the preparatory works to s. 36 of the Contracts Act of 1915, clauses giving one party (or his employee) a discretionary right to decide in contractual matters are especially mentioned as being liable to be set aside if they are applied unreasonably.[47] There may be cases where individual taste is of such importance that a customer can validly lay down a condition that he may refuse to take delivery on subjective grounds. A contract to build a shed is hardly such a case. As the defects are insignificant both as far as its use and appearance are concerned the buyer can, according to s. 36 of the Contracts Act, be forced to take delivery.[48] The buyer may be entitled to a small price reduction.

FINLAND

The principles of the Sale of Goods Act of 1987 might, in principle, be applied *per analogiam* to construction work, although there are no statutory provisions in this respect. In practice, however, a set of general

---

[47] See Proposition 1975/76:81 p. 118.
[48] Cf. NJA 1983, p. 332 denying a bank reliance on a discretionary right to change a letter of credit.

conditions is always used, and they are considered to constitute *customary law*.[49] The buyer is only entitled to disapprove the delivery, if it is *objectively* defective, and the defect is of *material importance* (see ss. 17–18 of the Sale of Goods Act). This is presently not the case. A condition allowing the buyer to reject the delivery *at will* would in any case be considered as unconscionable.

Editors' comparative observations

All legal systems accept that François is entitled to be paid for his work, whether by way of receiving the price agreed upon (which may have to be slightly reduced in view of the cracks) or by being entitled to bring a claim for unjustified enrichment.

(i) The majority of legal systems would not accept the designated employee's decision as binding because it is manifestly inequitable, abusive, unreasonable, unfair, or does not conform to the standards of good faith (Germany, Greece, Belgium, Spain, Italy, the Netherlands, England, Ireland, Sweden, Finland). Some of the codifications contain special provisions to this effect, other systems rely on their general provisions or refer to general principles. English law is interesting in that on the facts of case 15 it refers to a requirement of good faith in the exercise of a contractual power. This special solution may, however, be related to a more general approach. The West Nordic countries would also not accept the decision of the employee, but they adopt an interpretative approach.

(ii) French law denies that the agreement is a contract in view of the fact that performance is made conditional on an event the occurrence of which is within the power of the debtor (who, therefore, cannot seriously be taken to have bound himself). French law then, however, allows Eduard remuneration for the work which he has done on the basis of *enrichissement sans cause*. Scots law, on the other hand, upholds the decision of the employee with the result that Eduard cannot recover under the contract for the work that he has done. Like French law, however, it allows recovery on the basis of unjustified enrichment.

(iii) The Austrian solution turns around the analogous application of a provision in the code, according to which warranty claims are excluded, if the value of the object sold is only insignificantly reduced. Whilst a number of legal writers would not be prepared to accept the employee's decision in view of the insignificance of the cracks, the Austrian reporter

---

[49] See Laine 3 ff.

argues that the decision must depend on whether it is possible and not unreasonably expensive to repair the shed and, where it is impossible or unreasonably expensive to do so, whether the cracks are serious or not. In view of the fact that the cracks are not serious and, supposing that repair is impossible or unreasonably expensive, the Austrian reporter would also accept that Eduard has no right to reject the shed. As a result, therefore, François would receive the price agreed upon, but Eduard may demand a (slight) reduction.

Comparative excursus

MORIN BUILDING PRODUCTS COMPANY, INC. V. BAYSTONE CONSTRUCTION, INC., 717 F.2D 413 (7TH CIRCUIT 1983), PER POSNER, CIRCUIT JUDGE

Subcontractor, which installed aluminium exterior siding for walls of a factory, brought suit against the general contractor, seeking to recover balance of contract price. The United States District Court for the Southern District of Indiana, Indianapolis Division, S. Hugh Dillin, J., entered judgment in favor of plaintiff, and defendant appealed. The Court of Appeals, Posner, Circuit Judge, held that although contract provided 'that all work shall be done subject to the final approval of the Architect or Owner's authorized agent, and his decision in matters related to artistic effect shall be final', and that 'should any dispute arise as to the quality or fitness of materials or workmanship, the decision as to acceptability shall rest strictly with the Owner', the artistic effect and quality fitness clauses in the form contract were not intended to cover the aesthetics of a mill-finish aluminium factory wall; accordingly, the jury was properly asked to decide whether a reasonable man would have found that plaintiff used aluminium sufficiently uniform to satisfy the contract's matching requirement. Affirmed.

POSNER, Circuit Judge.

This appeal from a judgment for the plaintiff in a diversity suit requires us to interpret Indiana's common law of contracts. General Motors, which is not a party to this case, hired Baystone Construction, Inc., the defendant, to build an addition to a Chevrolet plant in Muncie, Indiana. Baystone hired Morin Building Products Company, the plaintiff, to supply and erect the aluminium walls for the addition. The contract required that the exterior siding of the walls be of 'aluminium type 3003, not less than 18 B & S gauge, with a mill finish and stucco embossed surface texture to match finish and texture of existing metal siding'. The contract also provided 'that all work shall be done subject to the final approval of the Architect or Owner's [General Motors] authorized agent, and his decision in matters relating to artistic effect shall be final, if within the terms of the Contract Documents'; and that 'should any dispute arise as to the quality or fitness of materials or workmanship, the decision as to acceptability shall rest strictly with the Owner, based on the requirement that all work done or materials furnished shall be first class in every respect. What is usual or customary in erecting other buildings shall in no wise enter into any consideration or decision.' Morin put up the walls. But viewed in bright sunlight from an acute angle the exterior siding did not give the impression of having a uniform finish, and General Motors' representative rejected it. Baystone removed Morin's siding and hired another subcontractor to replace it. General Motors approved the replacement siding. Baystone refused to pay Morin the balance of the contract price ($23,000) and Morin brought this suit for the balance, and won.

The only issue on appeal is the correctness of a jury instruction which, after quoting the contractual provisions requiring that the owner (General Motors) be satisfied with the contractor's (Morin's) work, states: 'Notwithstanding the apparent finality of the foregoing language, however, the general rule applying to satisfaction in the case of contracts for the construction of commercial buildings is that the satisfaction clause must be determined by objective criteria. Under this standard, the question is not whether the owner was satisfied in fact, but whether the owner, as a reasonable person, should have been satisfied with the materials and workmanship in question.' There was much evidence that General Motors' rejection of Morin's exterior siding had been totally unreasonable. Not only was the lack of absolute uniformity in the finish of the walls a seemingly trivial defect given the strictly utilitarian purpose of the building that they enclosed, but it may have been inevitable; 'mill finish sheet' is defined in the trade as 'sheet having a nonuniform finish which may vary from sheet to sheet and within a sheet, and may not be entirely free from stains or oil'. If the instruction was correct, so was the judgment. But if the instruction was incorrect – if the proper standard is not whether a reasonable man would have been satisfied with Morin's exterior siding but whether General Motors' authorized representative in fact was – then there must be a new trial to determine whether he really was dissatisfied, or whether he was not and the rejection therefore was in bad faith.

Some cases hold that if the contract provides that the seller's performance must be to the buyer's satisfaction, his rejection – however unreasonable – of the seller's performance is not a breach of the contract unless the rejection is in bad faith. See, e.g. *Stone Mountain Properties, Ltd v. Helmer*, 139 Ga.App. 865, 229 S.E.2d 779, 783 (1976). But most cases conform to the position stated in section 228 of the Restatement (Second) of Contracts (1979): if 'it is practicable to determine whether a reasonable person in the position of the obligor would be satisfied, an interpretation is preferred under which the condition [that the obligor be satisfied with the obligee's performance] occurs if such a reasonable person in the position of the obligor would be satisfied'. See Farnsworth, Contracts 556–9 (1982); Annot., 44 A.L.R.2d 1114, 1117, 1119–20 (1955). *Indiana Tri-City Plaza Bowl, Inc. v. Estate of Glueck*, 422 N.E.2d 670, 675 (Ind. App. 1981), consistently with hints in earlier Indiana cases, see *Andis v. Personett*, 108 Ind. 202, 206, 9 N.E. 101, 103 (1886); *Semon, Bache and Co. v. Coppes, Zook and Mutschler Co.*, 35 Ind. App. 351, 355, 74 N.E. 41, 43 (1905), adopts the majority position as the law of Indiana.

We do not understand the majority position to be paternalistic; and paternalism would be out of place in a case such as this, where the subcontractor is a substantial multistate enterprise. The requirement of reasonableness is read into a contract not to protect the weaker party but to approximate what the parties would have expressly provided with respect to a contingency that they did not foresee, if they had foreseen it. Therefore the requirement is not read into every contract, because it is not always a reliable guide to the parties' intentions. In particular, the presumption that the performing party would not have wanted to put himself at the mercy of the paying party's whim is overcome when the nature of the performance contracted for is such that there are no objective standards to guide the court. It cannot be assumed in such a case that the parties would have wanted a court to second-guess the buyer's rejection. So 'the reasonable person standard is employed when the contract involves commercial quality, operative fitness, or mechanical utility which other knowledgeable persons can judge . . . The standard of good faith is employed when the contract involves personal aesthetics or fancy.' *Indiana Tri-City Plaza Bowl, Inc. v. Estate of Glueck, supra*, 422 N.E. 2d at 675; see also *Action Engineering v. Martin Marietta Aluminium*, 670 F. 2d 456, 460–1 (3d Cir. 1982).

We have to decide which category the contract between Baystone and Morin belongs in. The particular in which Morin's aluminium siding was found wanting was its appearance, which may seem quintessentially a matter of 'personal aesthetics', or as the contract put it, 'artistic effect'. But it is easy to imagine situations where this would not be so. Suppose the manager of a steel plant rejected a shipment of pig iron because he did not think pigs had a pretty shape. The reasonable-man standard would be applied even if the contract had an 'acceptability shall rest strictly with the Owner' clause, for it would be fantastic to think that the iron supplier would have subjected his contract rights to the whimsy of the buyer's agent. At the other extreme would be a contract to paint a portrait, the buyer having reserved the right to reject the portrait if it did not satisfy him. Such a buyer wants a portrait that will please him rather than a jury, even a jury of connoisseurs, so the only question would be his good faith in rejecting the portrait. *Gibson v. Cranage*, 39 Mich. 49 (1878).

This case is closer to the first example than to the second. The building for which the aluminium siding was intended was a factory – not usually intended to be a thing of beauty. That aesthetic considerations were decidedly secondary to considerations of function and cost is suggested by the fact that the contract specified mill-finish aluminium, which is unpainted. There is much debate in the record over whether it is even possible to ensure a uniform finish within and among sheets, but it is at least clear that mill finish usually is not uniform. If General Motors and Baystone had wanted a uniform finish they would in all likelihood have ordered a painted siding. Whether Morin's siding achieved a reasonable uniformity amounting to satisfactory commercial quality was susceptible of objective judgment; in the language of the Restatement, a reasonableness standard was 'practicable'.

But this means only that a requirement of reasonableness would be read into this contract if it contained a standard owner's satisfaction clause, which it did not; and since the ultimate touchstone of decision must be the intent of the parties to the contract we must consider the actual language they used. The contract refers explicitly to 'artistic effect', a choice of words that may seem deliberately designed to put the contract in the 'personal aesthetics' category whatever an outside observer might think. But the reference appears as number 17 in a list of conditions in a general purpose form contract. And the words 'artistic effect' are immediately followed by the qualifying phrase, 'if within the terms of the Contract Documents', which suggests that the 'artistic effect' clause is limited to contracts in which artistic effect is one of the things the buyer is aiming for; it is not clear that he was here. The other clause on which Baystone relies, relating to the quality or fitness of workmanship and materials, may seem all-encompassing, but it is qualified by the phrase, 'based on the requirement that all work done or materials furnished shall be first class in every respect' – and it is not clear that Morin's were not. This clause also was not drafted for this contract; it was incorporated by reference to another form contract (the Chevrolet Division's 'Contract General Conditions'), of which it is paragraph 35. We do not disparage form contracts, without which the commercial life of the nation would grind to a halt. But we are left with more than a suspicion that the artistic-effect and quality-fitness clauses in the form contract used here were not intended to cover the aesthetics of a mill-finish aluminium factory wall.

If we are right, Morin might prevail even under the minority position, which makes good faith the only standard but presupposes that the contract conditioned acceptance of performance on the buyer's satisfaction in the particular respect in which he was dissatisfied. Maybe this contract was not intended to allow General Motors to reject the aluminium siding on the basis of artistic effect. It would not follow that the contract put Morin under no obligations whatsoever with regard to uniformity of finish. The contract expressly required it to use aluminium having 'a mill finish . . . to match finish . . . of existing metal siding'. The jury was asked to decide whether a reasonable man would have found that Morin has used aluminium sufficiently uniform to satisfy the matching requirement. This was the right standard if, as we believe, the parties would have adopted it had they foreseen this dispute. It is unlikely that Morin intended to bind itself to a higher and perhaps unattainable standard of achieving whatever perfection of matching that General Motors' agent insisted on, or that General Motors would have required Baystone to submit to such a standard. Because it is difficult – maybe impossible – to achieve a uniform finish with mill-finish aluminium, Morin would have been running a considerable risk of rejection if it had agreed to such a condition, and it therefore could have been expected to demand a compensating increase in the contract price. This would have required General Motors to pay a premium to obtain a freedom of action that it could not have thought terribly important, since its objective was not aesthetic. If a uniform finish was important to it, it could have gotten such a finish by specifying painted siding.

All this is conjecture; we do not know how important the aesthetics were to General Motors when the contract was signed or how difficult it really would have been to obtain the uniformity of finish it desired. The fact that General Motors accepted the replacement siding proves little, for there is evidence that the replacement siding produced the same striped effect, when viewed from an acute angle in bright sunlight, that Morin's had. When in doubt on a difficult issue of state law it is only prudent to defer to the view of the district judge, *Murphy v. White Hen Pantry Co.,* 691 F.2d 350, 354 (7th Cir. 1982), here an experienced Indiana lawyer who thought this the type of contract where the buyer cannot unreasonably withhold approval of the seller's performance.

Lest this conclusion be thought to strike at the foundations of freedom of contract, we repeat that if it appeared from the language or circumstances of the contract that the parties really intended General Motors to have the right to reject Morin's work for failure to satisfy the private aesthetic taste of General Motors' representative, the rejection would have been proper even if unreasonable. But the contract is ambiguous because of the qualifications with which the terms 'artistic effect' and 'decision as to acceptability' are hedged about, and the circumstances suggest that the parties probably did not intend to subject Morin's rights to aesthetic whim.

AFFIRMED

Case 16: Drug causing drowsiness in driving

Case

Tancred is a doctor who treats Sean for a severe back injury. He prescribes a medication which considerably slows down Sean's reactions and thus impairs his ability to drive a motor vehicle. He forgets to tell Sean about these effects of the drug. After Sean has taken the drug, Sean causes an accident whilst driving his motor car which is attributable to his poor reaction. Can Sean institute a claim against Tancred?

Discussions

GERMANY

The contract between Tancred and Sean for the treatment of Sean's back injury is a contract for services (§§ 611 ff. BGB).[1] Tancred does not only have a duty to treat Sean in the narrow sense but he also has ancillary duties such as to inform his patient about side-effects of medication that he prescribes.[2] These kinds of ancillary duties are not confined to contracts with doctors but can arise in all contractual relationships. Unless they are specifically laid down in the Code or another piece of legislation, their doctrinal home is invariably taken to be § 242 BGB.[3]

If one assumes that the accident has resulted in injuries to Sean and damage to his vehicle, he may claim damages for positive breach of contract (*positive Vertragsverletzung*) of the contract of services from Tancred. 'Positive breach of contract' is a specific type of breach of contract which

---

[1] Medicus, *Schuldrecht II* nn. 348 ff.; *Jauernig*/Schlechtriem, Vor § 611, n. 21.
[2] BGH NJW 1982, 697; *Palandt*/Heinrichs § 823, n. 21.
[3] *Jauernig*/Vollkommer § 242, n. 16; *Palandt*/Heinrichs § 242, nn. 23 ff.

supplements the system of remedies provided in the German Code. Concentrating on delay of performance and (supervening) impossibility, the draftsmen of the BGB had, apparently, forgotten to deal with these cases, a gap which was 'discovered' by *Hermann Staub* as early as 1902. The courts immediately set about providing legal protection and today 'positive breach of contract' is generally recognised as a judge-made institution *praeter legem.*[4] It covers, *inter alia*, cases of deficient performance of a main obligation[5] and infringements of ancillary obligations,[6] and it is based on fault.

Moreover, Sean can claim his damages in delict under § 823 I BGB (injury to bodily integrity and to property), since failure to disclose the information has caused the accident. Compensation for pain and suffering may be claimed by way of application of § 847 BGB.

GREECE

There are two possible legal bases for Sean to claim against Tancred, i.e. (i) under the provisions of arts. 914 ff. Gr. C.C., provided there is an unlawful act, and (ii) in accordance with the provision of art. 330 Gr. C.C., a claim based on the medical contract between Tancred and Sean. Article 330 Gr. C.C. provides that '[s]ubject to any differing provision a debtor shall be responsible for any non-compliance with his obligation caused by his own intentional or negligent behaviour or by that of his legal representative. Negligence is present in every case, where the care required in the carrying out of business is not observed.'

The doctor's obligations under a contract for medical services[7] are not limited only to furnishing medical treatment. This is a contractual relationship *sui generis* which gives rise, apart from the main obligations, also to ancillary obligations. Thus, the debtor (Tancred) is bound to take every possible precaution in order to protect his patient (Sean) from dangers which derive from the medical treatment. Ancillary obligations such as these essentially derive from art. 288 Gr. C.C.[8] In medical law the doctor's

---

[4] BGHZ 11, 80 (83 ff.); *Münchener Kommentar/*Emmerich, Vor § 275, nn. 218 ff.; for the background, see Zimmermann, *Obligations* 813 ff.; Lorenz, (1997) 1 *Edinburgh LR* 317 ff.; Ebke/Steinhauer, in: *Good Faith* 172 ff.

[5] As far as these do not fall under the special rules provided, e.g., in the law of sale for liability for latent defects (§§ 459 ff. BGB). Delimitation of §§ 459 ff. BGB and positive malperformance belong to the thorniest questions in the German law of obligations.

[6] *Jauernig/*Vollkommer § 276, nn. 52 ff.; Medicus, *Schuldrecht I* nn. 414 ff.

[7] On the qualification of the legal relationship between Tancred and Sean, see Androulidakis-Dimitriadis, *Ypochreosi enimerosis* 106–16.   [8] Ibid., at 114.

obligations are extended even beyond the medical contract itself to include the obligation of informing the patient, since medical treatment concerns the life and personality of the patient. Sean, therefore, who has not been informed properly of the effects of the drug, has a right to claim compensation from Tancred.

The ancillary obligations in the field of medical liability, such as the duty of the doctor to inform his patient, basically derive from good faith; they have been recognised for a long time in Greek law, though there is not yet a special court decision in point.[9]

AUSTRIA

As has already been explained in relation to case 1, it is generally accepted in Austrian law that special duties of care arise between the parties from the beginning of their precontractual contact with each other and that these duties continue after conclusion of the contract.[10] Breach of one of these duties of care is usually termed positive breach of contract (*positive Vertragsverletzung*).[11]

These duties of care require that parties to a contract must actively safeguard each other from harm. Therefore, Tancred should have informed his patient Sean of the particular effect of the medication which he prescribed for him. Moreover, while these duties of care are concerned with protecting the safety of the persons or property of the parties from physical damage, they are also concerned with safeguarding the purely economic interests of parties to a contract from prejudice.[12] As a result, Tancred would be liable in damages to Sean, even if Sean were not himself injured in the accident, but simply found himself liable to compensate harm caused to a third party involved in the accident.

FRANCE

There are two legal bases for Sean to recover damages. Not only can he bring a claim against (i) Tancred his doctor but also against (ii) the manufacturer.

---

[9] Androulidakis-Dimitriadis, *Ypochreosi enimerosis* 362–6; Androulidakis-Dimitriadis, *Ypochreoseis* 96, 121, 149 ff.; Zepos/Christodoulou ch. 6, no. 67, p. 33.

[10] Cf. OGH in JBl 1985, 239; JBl 1991, 457; Schlesinger, ZBl 1926, 721; Koziol/Welser, *Bürgerliches Recht I* 194 f. and 268 with further references.

[11] Disapproved by Reischauer, *Entlastungsbeweis* 147 ff.   [12] Cf. Koziol, ZEuP 1995, 360 ff.

(i) Sean can bring a claim against Tancred by joining him as a 'third party' to the claim against Sean arising out of the motor car accident. According to French courts, the relationship between a doctor and his patient is based on contract.[13] Case law decided in the 1930s that a contract is formed between a doctor and his patient under which the former has a duty to treat the patient in the most attentive and conscientious way (this being an example of an *obligation de sécurité*). If this obligation is not performed, the doctor is held liable; there is a breach of contract.[14] As contractual liability, it is governed by art. 1147 of the Civil Code, but French courts have accepted a distinction according to the nature of contractual obligations arising under this text. According to the object of the obligation in the contract, there can be either an *obligation de moyens* or an *obligation de résultat*. The main difference is as to the burden of proof. The *obligation de moyens* is based on the idea that its debtor will do as much as he can in order to perform.[15] Even if he fails to perform he will not be held liable as long as he tried to perform by all reasonable means. The plaintiff must prove that the other party failed to fulfil this duty to take care. In contrast, the *obligation de résultat* implies that the promisor will perform his undertaking whatever may happen, subject only to a defence of *force majeure*.[16] He is in breach as soon as the result sought is not obtained. There is no need for the other party to prove any fault.

French case law decided that a doctor has a duty to take reasonable care (*obligation de moyens*) towards his client. He undertakes that he will do his best to treat the latter, making use of the 'medical data available at the time'.[17] Therefore, the patient who believes that his doctor did not perform his contractual duty to take care must prove that he made a professional mistake. This classification finds an exception in the case of simple operations where a doctor may be held to the stricter obligation

---

[13] For a discussion of the contractual relationship between doctors and their patients, see Le Tourneau/Cadiet no. 2025. Where a doctor provides public health care, liability is considered to be a matter of administrative law and for the jurisdiction of the administrative courts. The most recent approach of the *Conseil d'Etat* has been to subject a claim by a patient receiving public health care simply to proof of ordinary fault (*faute simple*) rather than gross fault (*faute lourde*): CE 10 Apr. 1992, JCP 1992.II.79027 note J. Moreau, Leb. 1992.171 concl. Legal.   [14] Civ. 20 May 1936, DP 1936.1.88.

[15] Art. 1137 C. civ.

[16] Art. 1147 C. civ. states that '[a] debtor of an obligation is to be condemned, where appropriate, to the payment of damages, whether by reason of the non-performance of the obligation or by reason of delay in performance of the obligation, in all circumstances in which he does not show that the non-performance results from a *cause étrangère* which is not attributable to him, as long as there is no bad faith on his part'.

[17] Civ. 20 May 1936, DP 1936.1.88.

which requires no proof of fault (*obligation de résultat*). Thus the difficulty of establishing breach depends on the way in which the actual type of medical treatment is classified in law.

In addition to the requirement of using one's best endeavours, the courts have decided that doctors have a duty to inform or advise their patients about the treatment prescribed. They must be told the risks they will run and the possible consequences of such treatment. While this duty is particularly stringent as far as surgery is concerned, this kind of information is also required when non-surgical treatment is highly risky.[18] The advice need not be written. In the circumstances of case 16, the medication prescribed to Sean satisfies the condition of being risky in that it slows down patients' reactions and impairs their ability to drive. The risk associated with the treatment intensifies Tancred's duty to inform Sean of the medication's possible side-effects. In the result, the doctor's duty to inform forms part of his general duty of care and so if a patient proves that his doctor did not perform this obligation, the doctor is in breach of contract.

The burden of proof will therefore lie on Sean to prove that, despite his duty to do so, Tancred did not inform him of the effects which the prescribed drug might cause. He must also prove the chain of causation between the damage he caused while driving and Tancred's breach of his duty to inform him about the effects of the medication. This may raise a question of remoteness of damage. Moreover, in view of the fact that Sean has a severe back injury, it may not be unreasonable to infer that he should not, in any event, be driving a motor car, and therefore cannot hold Tancred liable for the consequences of his decision to do so. Finally, and crucially, Sean also had a duty to read the instruction notice included with the drug (assuming that such a notice existed). In French law, such a duty to keep oneself informed is a corollary of the duty on the part of a 'professional' (or the better informed party) to inform his less informed co-contractor. The level of duty which lies on each party is a question of fact and depends on the status of the parties, their relative degree of knowledge and the technicality of the knowledge or information in question.

Although it is clear that Tancred owes a duty to advise Sean, it is difficult to evaluate its extent. Perhaps Sean's duty to obtain information, i.e. to read the instruction notice, would be held to be a contributing factor, and thus lead to an apportionment of liability, with a consequential

---

[18] Civ. (1) 29 May 1984, D 1985.281 note Bouvier, D 1985.I.R.368 obs. Penneau.

reduction in damages recoverable by Sean against Tancred in respect of his own injury.

(ii) A claim by Sean against the manufacturer?

Sean has no direct action against the manufacturer on the basis of the drug's 'latent defects' nor for any failure to perform an *obligation de renseignement* owed by the manufacturer. However, a manufacturer must take proper care in respect of the safety of the product as a matter of the general law of delictual liability for fault, and a direct action by Sean against the manufacturer could lie if fault were shown (notably based on a failure to provide proper warnings with the product).[19]

(iii) If the manufacturer did include a notice indicating the risk associated with the treatment, Sean may nevertheless have a claim against the immediate seller, the dispensing chemist (*pharmacien*), if he can prove that the chemist did not comply with his duty to draw the buyer-patient's attention to this risk. The chemist's duty is, here again, a product of case law.

More generally it can be seen that the approach of the courts to these sorts of questions reveals a change in their approach to the effects of contracts. The courts used to hold that contractual obligations consisted only of those which were specially and deliberately included in the agreement and the parties had a duty to obtain their own information. Therefore, a lack of knowledge of one party (most of the time the weaker party) did not lead to a breach of contract. Some French judges referred to the adage *emptor debet esse curiosus*. Nowadays, by contrast, the courts interpret contracts more widely. They consider that apart from the express obligations, there are others which the parties must perform. These ancillary obligations, distinct from the principal explicit obligations, are based on art. 1135 of the Civil Code according to which the parties to contracts are bound to 'all the consequences which fairness (*équité*), custom and the law itself (*la loi*) give to the obligation according to its nature'. The duty of disclosure is an example of an ancillary obligation created by case law interpreting this statutory provision. In addition, it is arguable that art. 1134 al. 3 forms the basis of the obligation to inform which lies increasingly on the contracting party who possesses the more specialised knowledge. This principle of good faith or of loyalty encourages the parties to inform one another. Here the content of the information, the side-effects of the

---

[19] In the absence of implementation of the E.C. Council Directive on Product Liability, 85/374, see the discussion in Viney, JCP 1997.I.4025. The directive was implemented in French law by the *loi* no. 98–389 of 19 May 1998, inserting new provisions at arts. 1386–1 ff. C. civ.

medication, is linked to contractual performance. Even under a strict interpretation of art. 1134 the parties must perform their obligations in good faith. It is considered fair that the onus of the obligation lies on the party who is in possession of the relevant information to inform the uninformed party, provided that a limit is placed on this duty.

In the result, the imposition of a duty to inform is aimed at the protection of the weaker party (the non-professional) against the economic and intellectual power of professionals. The reasons for this protection are based on policy considerations, both moral and economic. The limit to be placed on the protection of the 'weaker' or less informed party is said to be justified by the latter's legitimate ignorance. Other jurists insist on the fact that this does not release either party from his obligation to obtain his own information about matters which he could know relatively easily.[20] On the facts, Sean's case highlights the difficulty of where to fix the limits. Another academic suggestion as to how to solve this kind of difficulty would be to create an autonomous category of professional liability, which would be distinct from contractual or tortious liability, but this may not actually solve the difficulty of where to fix the limits of protection.

BELGIUM

Medical doctors, just as other professionals, are under a duty to warn the other party about the possible dangers arising from their performance, treatment, etc. This includes a duty to warn and to inform their patients of the risks inherent in an operation or associated with the taking of some medication.[21] Such duties are now more prominent than in the past.[22] Only in exceptional cases will there be no duty to inform, e.g. with regard to effects which the patient evidently should have known himself.

Such ancillary obligations are often seen to be based on the 'complementary function' (*ergänzende Funktion*) of good faith. They could, however, also be based on art. 1135 C.C.

The claim for damages against the doctor will be of a contractual nature. There is no claim in tort, unless the behaviour of the doctor is also

---

[20] See, notably, Jourdain, D 1983.Chron.139 and Le Tourneau, D 1987.Chron.101.

[21] Cf. in general, e.g., Cass. 28 Feb. 1980, *pvba Gymnastiekwerktuigen international v. asbl Arts & métiers d'Erquelinnes, asbl Centre intercommunal de loisirs actifs d'Erquelinnes v. Picart*, JT 1981, 241 note M. Fallon, RCJB 1983, 228 note J. L. Fagnart. As to medical doctors, see Military Court 4 Apr. 1962, RW 1962–1963, 900; Vansweevelt, *Aansprakelijkheid, passim*; Vansweevelt, TPR 1991, 320 ff. no. 49.

[22] For this general tendency, see the Belgian report to case 1.

a criminal offence (which will probably be the case if the patient suffers corporeal damage).

The patient will not obtain full compensation for those injuries or losses to which his own negligence has contributed. If the patient is held liable towards third parties (victims of the accident) on the basis of the general liability rules (i.e. not on the basis of strict liability alone), this will necessarily imply contributory negligence. The patient (or his insurer) will then not be able to claim a 100 per cent indemnity in respect of the amount he has to pay to the victims, unless there is an explicit clause, agreed upon between the doctor and the patient, to the effect that the doctor will indemnify the patient against his liability towards third parties.

The duty to inform the patient of the effects of a drug is so essential that an exclusion clause would probably be invalidated.

SPAIN

This dispute is quite easily solved in Spanish law. Under the rule laid down in a decision of the High Court in 1995,[23] confirming its own earlier decisions in the matter, the doctor is held to owe an obligation to inform the patient of those matters which concern any treatment to be undertaken and its expected effects, and would be held liable in damages for any harm which results from its breach. The source of this liability is either a breach of a legal duty which arises from the requirement of performance of the contract in good faith, or delictual fault under art. 1902 of the Civil Code; and the courts allow an injured party to opt freely upon which of these two legal bases to proceed. More generally, both commentators and courts have accepted the existence of duties to inform and to disclose in contracts in which one party puts at risk a significant personal interest (such as his health) and the other party is a 'professional'.[24]

ITALY

Under Italian law, medical patients have the right to be informed of the risks involved in medical treatment, a right which enjoys constitutional protection,[25] and doctors are under a corresponding duty to provide such

---

[23] Judgement of 25 May 1995 (39 CCJC 1995, 1063).   [24] Gomez Calle 88 ff.
[25] Arts. 13 and 32 of the Italian Constitution are invoked in this respect: Cass., 15 Jan. 1997, n. 364, Foro it., 1997, I, 773, obs. Palmieri (this is the most recent of many cases in the same sense); for a general treatment of the issue of informed consent, see Monateri, in: *Trattato Sacco* 760; De Vita, in: *Rapports* 118–19 ff.

information. Doctors who prescribe medicines must choose the best treatment for their patients, taking into consideration their health, any hypersensitivity to certain drugs, the concurrent use of other drugs, etc., as well as their duty to reduce the risk of harm connected with the use of the medicines in question. They must certainly inform their patients of the possible side-effects of drugs which they prescribe to them, so that the patients themselves can adjust their behaviour accordingly.

Within this general framework, the Code of Conduct of the medical profession, which was adopted on 24–25 June 1995, specifies further the duties of doctors in relation to the prescription of medicines.[26] According to this Code, doctors must have adequate knowledge of the nature and effects of the drugs which they prescribe, of their indications and contraindications, interactions and foreseeable individual reactions. Medical prescriptions themselves 'must be supplied with all the adequate information in understandable terms; as far as possible, doctors must ensure the correct execution of their prescriptions . . .'.

Certainly, these rules of conduct do not have the force of law, being contained in neither primary nor secondary legislation, but they are relevant to the question whether or not a doctor has acted diligently, in accordance with the standard of care required by the professional performance of his contractual obligations relating to the type of activity in question, and in accordance with the duty of good faith in the performance of obligations and contracts.[27] Claims by patients against their doctors which are brought on the basis of the general provision imposing liability for delictual fault will be decided on the same basis.[28] As regards both contract and delict, art. 2236 of the Civil Code provides some special protection for members of liberal professions who undertake the performance of obligations involving the solution of technical problems involving special difficulties. On the facts of case 16, though, Tancred's failure to warn Sean about the side-effects of the drug which he has prescribed to him seems

[26] Introna/Colafigli/Tantalo, *passim.* The citations concerning the Code in the text refer to arts. 12 and 18.
[27] Art. 1176.2 c.c.: 'In the performance of obligations inherent in the exercise of a professional activity, diligence shall be evaluated with respect to the nature of that activity.' The relevant provisions on good faith are arts. 1175, 1375 c.c. Apparently, there is only one legislative norm expressly stating the prescribing doctor's duty to inform patients of the warnings supplied by the pharmaceutical producer together with the drug. This norm deals with drugs which diminish one's appetite, and which have insidious effects. See d.m. 13 Apr. 1993, *Divieti e limitazioni nella preparazione di medicinali concernenti sostanze anoressizzanti.*
[28] Medical liability in Italy sounds in contract and in delict; it is the typical case of a complex liability: cf. Carlo Rossello, Contr. e impr., 1996, 664; Monateri, *Cumulo* 171 ff.

to be a glaring failure to take proper care[29] and would not come within the protection of art. 2236. On the other hand, if a patient was in fact fully aware of the side-effects of the drug prescribed to him, any omission of the prescribing doctor to inform him would not be considered causally relevant to the patient's injury.[30] Moreover, if a patient were to have had *some knowledge* of the side-effects of the drug (independently from any medical advice) then any award of damages which he could otherwise recover could be reduced proportionately to his share in the causation of the damage.[31] The burden of proof as to the injured party's lack of care for his own safety rests upon the defendant.

THE NETHERLANDS

Sean can indeed institute such claim. This is non-performance of the medical treatment contract (arts. 7:446 ff. and 6:74 ff. B.W.). The doctor should have warned the patient of this risk.

The medical treatment contract has only recently (in 1995) been added to the Civil Code. Its purpose is the protection of the patient by giving him, *inter alia*, mandatory rights as to information. Moreover, the provisions on the medical treatment contract 'channel' liability. Alongside the person with whom the medical treatment contract has been concluded the hospital in which any treatment takes place is also liable 'as if it were itself a party to the contract' (art. 7:462 B.W.). Thus, the medical treatment contract is part of a trend, which is characteristic of the new Civil Code, to protect consumers.

ENGLAND

A doctor owes his patient a duty of care, this being imposed as a matter of the general law by way of the law of torts (the tort of negligence) and existing independently of contract,[32] though this does not mean that a private patient may not claim instead on the basis of an implied term in the contract of the same content as the tortious duty.[33]

---

[29] Cf. Cass., 11 Jan. 1978, Gandini, Riv. pen., 1978, 767. According to this decision, the doctor's failure to read the written warnings provided by the producer of the drug and to pass on to the patient the relevant information about the period of rest recommended after treatment with the drug amounts to negligence.

[30] Bussani 215 ff.; Cafaggi, *passim*.   [31] Art. 1227 c.c.

[32] *Pippin v. Sheppard* (1822) 11 Price 400; *Gladwell v. Steggall* (1839) 5 Bing NC 733.

[33] See the discussion in *Thake v. Maurice* [1986] 1 QB 644.

The standard of care required of doctors is the exercise of a reasonable degree of skill and knowledge and a reasonable degree of care. Where there is more than one view as to the proper diagnosis or treatment of particular symptoms, to show negligence a patient must establish that no reasonable doctor of ordinary skill would have acted in the way in which he did.[34] On the facts of case 16 can Sean establish a lack of reasonable care in relation to his prescription of the drug in Tancred's failure to warn him of its side-effects? Evidence would have to be adduced as to the usual professional practice in relation to warnings concerning the use of prescribed medicinal products. For, it may be argued that doctors in general (properly and reasonably) leave the giving of warnings concerning use of the drugs which they prescribe to the manufacturer or supplier of the drug (the latter being the 'dispensing chemist' or pharmacist). On the other hand, it could instead be argued that where (as here) a very simple warning concerning a drug's effect could prevent a life-threatening accident, then (following general principles which balance the cost of precautions against the magnitude of harm and degree of risk of injury) a duty to warn should be imposed. On the other hand, if it is shown that in general it is not normal practice for doctors to warn about the effects of drugs so that Tancred is under no duty to do so, in principle the fact that he himself 'forgets' to do so is irrelevant: but, *forensically*, it would surely be difficult for a doctor who admits to forgetting some aspect of health care which he normally performs to escape an imputation of negligence.

Whether the source of Tancred's duty is the contract or the tort of negligence, if breach of a duty to warn is established, there would be no problem on the facts with establishing a causal relationship between this breach and Sean's injuries as this sort of consequence is indeed its natural and probable consequence. However, Sean's ultimate recovery against Tancred may depend on whether the drug itself carried a sufficiently clear warning about its effects and against driving etc. If it did, then Tancred could raise the defence of contributory negligence in Sean in failing to take proper care of his own safety by reading the drug's warnings or taking notice of them, this defence leading to a reduction in any award to him under the Law Reform (Contributory Negligence) Act 1945, s. 1. The size of the reduction is a matter for the discretion of the court, 'having regard to the claimant's share in the responsibility for the damage'.[35] In

---

[34] *Bolam v. Friern Hospital Management Committee* [1957] 1 WLR 582; *Bolitho v. City and Hackney Health Authority* [1998] AC 232.   [35] Law Reform (Contributory Negligence) Act 1945, s. 1.

the particular circumstances of case 16, this defence would apply to a claim brought for breach of contract as much as one brought in the tort of negligence.[36] If the drug did not bear the proper warnings, then a range of defendants including its manufacturer or supplier could be liable as a result, whether in the tort of negligence or under the Consumer Protection Act 1987, Part I (which implements into English law the E.C. Directive 85/374 concerning liability for defective products). However, any liability in a third party to Sean in respect of the same harm which Tancred's breach of duty had caused would not affect Tancred's liability to Sean: in such a case, the third party and Tancred would be 'joint tort-feasors' and liable as regards their victim in full, their relative responsibility arising only as regards any claim for an indemnity *inter se* under the Civil Liability (Contribution) Act 1978.

IRELAND

In this case Sean would have claims in tort and in contract against Tancred. Either claim, if successful, would yield the same damages on the facts, i.e. all reasonably foreseeable damages.

First, then, the claim in tort will be one of alleged negligence, namely, that Tancred failed in a duty of care to Sean. The essence of such a claim is that Tancred, as a reasonable professional, should have appreciated both the effects of the prescribed treatment and the likelihood that his patient might want to drive whilst under treatment. Accordingly, he should have appreciated the risk to his patient in failing to warn him of the resultant impairment of his driving ability. However, the question of Sean's contributory negligence could be raised, it being asked whether a reasonable patient of normal experience and intelligence should have appreciated the slowness of his reactions and/or should have enquired as to the effects of his own medications. Any award of damages to Sean would be reduced by the relative extent to which he is adjudged to be at fault. It is, however, unlikely that Irish courts would accept that Sean was at fault *vis-à-vis* a prescribing doctor.

A substantially similar claim could be made by Sean in contract. Normally, a contract for the provision of specialised or professional services will be construed as implying a contractual duty to act with due care, due care being construed in the same way as under the law of tort. This

---

[36] *Forsikringsaktieselskapet Vesta v. Butcher* [1988] 3 WLR 565 (see the English report to case 1 above).

position is now reinforced by s. 39 of the Sale of Goods and Supply of Services Act 1980, according to which a supplier of a service in the course of his business must supply the service with due skill, care and diligence. As we have noted in relation to case 1,[37] a defence of contributory negligence would be available against Sean even if he claimed for breach of contract, though on the facts of case 16 it is unlikely that he would be found to have been negligent.

Any person who suffers injury in Sean's accident could sue Tancred in the tort of negligence, as Tancred should reasonably have foreseen the possible effect on a third party that his failure to warn Sean might have. Such a person may also sue Sean if he were found negligent in relation to his failure to appreciate his own slowness of reaction. If this were the case, but only Tancred were sued, then the latter (or his insurer) could claim an indemnity against Sean under the law governing joint tortfeasors.

SCOTLAND

This case raises the issue of professional liability, specifically medical negligence; that is, the principles applicable to the liability of doctors in delict for their negligent acts or omissions. Furthermore, the problem would seem to raise two lines of inquiry depending on how it is interpreted: (i) Assume that Sean has been injured in the accident. What is the position regarding liability? Or, (ii) assume that Sean has not been injured in the accident, but has injured others. What is now the position regarding liability? Each line of inquiry shall be dealt with in turn.

(i) If Sean has been injured in the accident the question is whether Tancred is liable. The general principles of the Scots law of negligence apply. Therefore a doctor is liable in delict if the harm done to his or her patient is the result of a breach of a duty of care. The *Donoghue v. Stevenson*[38] neighbourhood principle applies. There would seem to be no problem in establishing that a doctor owes his or her patients a duty of care. The duty is imposed by law when the doctor undertakes the task of providing advice, diagnosis or treatment. It is irrelevant who called the doctor to the patient or who pays. In the case of private treatment a term will be implied into the contract that the treatment will be performed with reasonable care and skill. The standard of care required to satisfy this obligation is the same as in the delict of negligence and therefore for most practical purposes there is no difference between the position of a private patient who

---

[37] See the Irish report to case 1 above.   [38] 1932 SC (HL) 31, 1932 SLT 317.

sues a doctor in contract and a National Health Service (NHS) patient who sues a doctor in the delict of negligence.

The question here is whether Tancred has breached the duty of care owed to Sean. Has his conduct fallen below the standard of skill/care expected of him? The leading Scottish case on medical negligence is *Hunter v. Hanley*[39] in which Lord *Clyde* states the following: '[T]he true test for establishing negligence in diagnosis and treatment on the part of a doctor is whether he has proved to be guilty of such failure as no doctor of ordinary skill would be guilty of if acting with ordinary care.'[40] Thus a doctor is judged by the standard of care expected of the doctor of ordinary skill in the medical profession. This standard includes a duty to give the patient instructions, in comprehensive terms, making sure that he or she understands the instructions and the importance of adhering to them. Therefore it can be negligent to give no warning about the side-effects of a drug; *Crichton v. Hastings*.[41] The standard of care is a duty to take certain precautions but not all precautions. The law does not demand an individual to be able to foresee all consequences of his actions/omissions, only what is *reasonably* foreseeable; *Margrie Holdings Ltd v. City of Edinburgh District Council*.[42] The doctor's actions are measured against the objective hypothetical doctor who is expected to foresee which risks ought to be guarded against. The danger must be reasonably foreseeable; *Overseas Tankship (UK) Ltd v. Morts Dock & Engineering Co. Ltd (The Wagon Mound No. 2)*.[43] Was it reasonably foreseeable that Sean would drive a car?

Furthermore, it must be established that there was a causal link between the breach of duty (if it is established that the duty has been breached) and the damage sustained by Sean. The 'but for' test applies, i.e. but for Tancred's failure to tell Sean not to drive while on the medication, would Sean have had the accident? If there is found to be any *novus actus interveniens* which breaks the causal chain then Tancred may not be liable, or only partly liable.

Tancred's actions will therefore be measured against the conduct of the hypothetical reasonable doctor. Cases of medical negligence almost invariably turn on expert evidence. Expert views of other members of the medical profession will be sought as to whether Tancred's conduct was reasonable in the circumstances. While the common practice of the medical profession is evidence, it is not conclusive as to whether the

---

[39] 1955 SC 200, 1955 SLT 213.   [40] Ibid., at 204 and 217 respectively.
[41] (1972) 29 DLR (3d) 692.   [42] 1993 SCLR 570, 1994 SLT 971.
[43] [1961] AC 388, [1961] 1 All ER 404, PC.

expected standard of care has been breached; that said, it is very rare for the courts to declare the common practice itself as negligent.

The burden of proof rests with the patient, Sean, and he must prove that *no* reasonable doctor exercising his ordinary skills would have acted as Tancred did in the circumstances of his particular case. This is a very heavy burden to displace. Cases of gross negligence apart, invariably some responsible body of medical opinion will regard the doctor's decision/conduct as reasonable in the circumstances.

(ii) If Sean has not been injured but has caused injury to others in the accident he will face a claim for damages from the injured parties. Thus Tancred's negligence has only caused Sean economic loss. Can Sean sue Tancred for his economic loss?

Scots law, as a general rule, does not allow recovery in delict where the pursuer only suffers economic loss as a result of the defender's careless conduct. In the area of liability in delict for pure economic loss, the concept of a duty of care is employed extensively by the courts as a threshold device and, where the pursuer has suffered pure economic loss, the courts have been reluctant to impose a duty of care. Although reasonable foreseeability of pure economic loss is not sufficient to impose a duty of care, the courts have in certain situations been prepared to hold that a duty of care does exist. There must be additional factors which show that there is a sufficient degree of proximity between the parties for a duty of care to be inferred. Thus the courts have developed certain areas where liability in delict for pure economic loss will be found.

For example, careless misrepresentations; in this case Tancred owes Sean a duty of care if it is reasonably foreseeable that Sean will suffer physical injury or damage to his property if Tancred's statement is made carelessly. If Sean suffers pure economic loss, the answer depends on whether Tancred owes a duty of care not to make careless statements which cause Sean pure economic loss. The criteria for the existence of this duty were laid down by the House of Lords in *Hedley Byrne v. Heller.*[44] It was held that the defendant owed a duty of care to the plaintiff if the defendant had undertaken responsibility for the accuracy of the statement and knew or ought to have known that the plaintiff would rely on that statement. If the duty broken was a result of the statement being made carelessly, the defendant could be liable for the plaintiff's pure economic loss. Lord *Devlin* said that the plaintiffs had to show that the defendants owed the plaintiffs 'a special duty' to take care.[45] Categories of relationships where

---

[44] [1964] AC 465, [1963] 2 All ER 575, HL.   [45] [1963] 2 All ER 575, at 610.

this duty arose were not limited to contractual relationships or fiduciary relationships.

The limitations of *Hedley Byrne* were recognised in *Caparo Industries plc v. Dickman*[46] where the issue was whether the careless auditor owed a duty of care to existing and potential shareholders of the company. The answer was 'no', based on the premise that while the losses were reasonably foreseeable, the auditor owed no duty of care to the shareholders as relationships were not sufficiently proximate.

The relationship of doctor/patient surely infers the necessary proximity of relationship between the parties so that as Sean's doctor, Tancred owes Sean a special duty. This coupled with the fact that it is foreseeable that Sean would rely on Tancred's statements (or lack of statements), and that it is within Tancred's knowledge that information will be used by Sean in a particular way, will surely infer Tancred's liability for the economic loss that Sean has suffered (assuming we can establish negligence).

If the accident is attributable to both Sean and Tancred, there is a case of joint and several liability. Joint and several liability arises where harm caused to the pursuer(s) is a result of the conduct of more than one defender. Before joint liability is established, each breach of duty must have materially contributed to, or materially increased the risk of the *same* delict to the pursuer. If Sean and Tancred are jointly liable, the pursuer(s) may sue Sean or Tancred or both. This entitles the pursuer(s) to obtain all the damages from either Sean or Tancred. If Sean pays all the damages, the court can apportion the damages between them, and if Tancred is not sued in the original action, Sean can nevertheless recover from Tancred the proportion of the damages which the court deems attributable to Tancred's conduct.[47]

DENMARK AND NORWAY

Under West Nordic law the attending doctor in a case such as this would, at the outset, have to be held liable to pay compensation for the loss incurred if there has been incorrect treatment resulting from negligence. The failure to warn against the serious side-effects of the medication used will readily be regarded as negligent, and, consequently, the attending doctor will be liable for the loss.

In West Nordic law, no sharp distinction is made between liability

[46] [1990] AC 605, [1990] 1 All ER 568, HL.
[47] Section 3, Law Reform (Miscellaneous Provisions) (Scotland) Act 1945.

within and outside a contractual relationship. It is recognised that even where there is a contractual relationship, the damage or injury may lie on the borderline.[48] A typical example is damage or injury occurring during various forms of treatment. Obviously, there is a contractual relationship between the doctor and his patient, and with regard to certain issues, e.g. the doctor's claim for his fee, the rules of contract law will apply. Where injury to the patient is concerned, including injury resulting from failure to warn about side-effects of medication, the general rules concerning compensation (i.e. the law of tort) will usually be applied.[49] Whether a contractual or a tortious perspective is adopted normally does not matter, as far as the requirements of liability are concerned. Only in relation to specific rules such as the limitation provisions will the classification be of direct relevance.

The problem posed in this case is hardly very practical in the Nordic countries in view of the fact that a mandatory road traffic insurance scheme in favour of victims of traffic accidents has been implemented. The insurers are under a duty to pay compensation the moment a motor car has caused damage or injury, i.e. irrespective of the question of guilt on the driver's part.[50] The liability of the attending doctor will therefore only be relevant in relation to the right of recourse by the insurer.

SWEDEN

I deal with this case as if there was no insurance for injuries caused by car accidents. I also disregard the insurance afforded patients treated by public hospitals.

A doctor failing ('forgetting') to give important and known (to doctors) information regarding the side-effects of certain drugs is negligent and would, in terms of the applicable (non-statutory) contract law, and also in tort, be liable to pay damages for impaired health and injuries suffered by the patient.[51] Consequently, Tancred will be liable to pay damages if Sean was injured in the car accident. The same applies to damage to Sean's property (cf. s. 32 of the Consumer Services Act of 1985, in terms of which a person who, in the course of business, undertakes work on a consumer's property is liable for any damage caused by negligence in relation to other property belonging to the consumer). If another person were injured or if that person's property were damaged in the accident, Sean would be liable

---

[48] Gomard, *Obligationsret* 2 139 ff.   [49] Nygaard 461 ff.

[50] Nygaard 287 ff.; Von Eyben/Nørgaard/Vagner 155 ff.   [51] Tort Act of 1972, ch. 2, sec. 1.

towards that person only if Sean were negligent, which does not seem to be the case. Hence, the question of an indemnity for Sean's liability towards a third party does not arise.

FINLAND

Here, again, the Finnish solution to the case is connected to public law regulation (as in case 1). Tancred's failure to warn is irrelevant in the causal chain. According to Finnish law, the packages of medicines which affect the ability to drive should contain a warning (a red triangle plus instructions). The doctor is responsible for the failure to warn only if he knew that this particular medicine was sold without such a warning, and thus contrary to the norm. He may also be held responsible if there were special circumstances regarding his patient's personal condition (back injury) which rendered him prone to the sedative effects of the medication.

Thus, we are dealing here not so much with an issue regarding ancillary obligations as with a problem of causation. Even if the doctor failed to warn the patient, and the patient then got a package of medicine lacking the statutory warning, it is at least arguable that the causal chain between the doctor's fault and the accident has been broken.

In Finland liability for harmful effects of medicines is, incidentally, governed by a special Patient Damages Act of 1986 (Si 302) which is based upon a mandatory insurance scheme. Physicians are, as a rule, not responsible if the medicine as such was properly chosen but nevertheless caused harmful individual effects.

Editors' comparative observations

The result reached by all legal systems is the same: the doctor has a duty to take reasonable care in informing his patient of the risks of the drugs which he prescribes. Some commentators raise the possibility of a reduction of the damages to be awarded to Sean on the basis of his own contributory negligence, either in relation to any knowledge as to the effects of the drug which he may have had, or in relation to driving when aware of being drowsy. The doctrinal bases for the imposition of liability in Tancred are as follows:

(i) German and Greek law rely on the general principle of good faith found in § 242 BGB and art. 288 Gr. C.C. as the legal basis for the acceptance of ancillary obligations such as the one of a doctor to inform his patient about the effect of the drugs. Spanish and Italian law also resort to the notion of good faith. So do French and Belgian law but only in addition to arguing that an obligation to warn must be imposed on the doctor in terms of 'equity' or fairness.

(ii) Austrian law is prepared to impose special duties of care on the basis of the lawful contact that arises between parties when they negotiate a contract and that continues to exist once the contract has been concluded.

(iii) English, Irish and Scots law treat the obligation to warn as flowing from the interpretation of the contract.

(iv) The relatively recent Dutch Civil Code makes special provision for the contract concerning medical treatment, as a result of which the doctor would, in the present case, be liable for a contractual non-performance.

(v) Danish, Norwegian and Swedish law simply accept that a doctor who fails to warn his patient of the adverse effect of drugs acts negligently.

(vi) Most legal systems allow the patient to sue for any personal injuries which he has himself incurred not only in contract but also in delict. French law, and partly also Belgian law, form an exception which is based on their general principle of *non-cumul*. The Nordic legal systems do not distinguish sharply between liability in delict and in contract.

Case 17: Bank miscrediting customer

Case

Douglas owns a bank and Eugene is one of his long-standing clients. One day Eugene notices that his bank account has been credited with $8,000. He realises that this must be due to a mistake. Does he have to inform Douglas about that mistaken transfer?

Discussions

GERMANY

A duty to disclose the information about the mistaken transfer exists for Eugene if Douglas could reasonably expect it in terms of the principles of good faith (§ 242 BGB). A contract between banker and client establishes a long-term business relationship from which an ancillary duty arises on the part of the customer to avoid damage to the bank. The customer must accordingly disclose mistaken transfers to the bank.[1] A claim for the recovery of damages based on positive breach of contract[2] will arise when this duty is breached. §§ 812 ff. BGB, on the other hand, allow a claim for restoration of the money; since Eugene has known about the mistaken payment, he will not be able to plead loss of enrichment (§§ 818 III, 819 I BGB).

Eugene will, therefore, have to inform Douglas of his mistake.

GREECE

Eugene is obliged, according to art. 288 Gr. C.C., to inform Douglas that his bank account has been credited with $8,000 due to a mistake. This is

---

[1] BGHZ 72, 9 (14); OLG Frankfurt WM 1972, 436 (438); *Münchener Kommentar*/Roth § 242, n. 242; *Soergel*/Hefermehl, Vor § 275, n. 525.   [2] On which see the German report to case 16.

an ancillary obligation (*Nebenpflicht aus Treu und Glauben*), arising under the contract between Eugene and Douglas. It requires parties to long-term contractual relationships not to disappoint the trust they reasonably place in each other.[3]

AUSTRIA

As a result of the special duties of care between the parties to a contract which were mentioned in relation to cases 1 and 16, Eugene must inform Douglas about the mistaken transfer of funds to his account in order to protect Douglas from suffering financial harm (arising, e.g., from liability which Douglas might incur, as a result of his mistake, towards the proper recipient of the money).

It is to be noted, moreover, that in any event Eugene is not allowed to spend the $8,000, as the money in the bank account is not his property.[4]

FRANCE

According to art. 1235 of the Civil Code, 'every payment implies a debt: anything which has been paid without being due must be repaid'. Article 1376 explains further that 'a person who receives, by mistake or knowingly, something to which he is not entitled is obliged to restore it to the person from whom it was unduly received'. Thus, Douglas' mistaken payment entitles him to claim restitution of the money from Eugene (*répétition de l'indu*). This action arises when a payment is made without a legitimate cause, as is the case here.[5] As long as the payment made is not due (by any person to the payee, this being called an 'objectively undue' debt), the person who made the mistaken payment (the *solvens*) can claim restitution without evidence of his own mistake.[6] Nevertheless, the burden of proof lies on Douglas to prove that the payment was not due in this sense.[7]

But does Eugene have to tell Douglas spontaneously about the mistaken transfer? Can he not wait until Douglas reclaims the $8,000, perhaps even making use of the money in the meantime? Under art. 1378 of the Civil Code 'if the receiving party was in bad faith, he must restore not only

---

[3] Stathopoulos, in: *Astikos Kodix II* art. 288, nos. 46, 47; Androulidakis-Dimitriadis, *Ypochreoseis* 96, 121, 149.

[4] Cf. Koziol, in: *Avancini/Iro/Koziol, Bankvertragsrecht I* n. 6/74 and 87.

[5] Civ. (3) 2 Jul. 1970, D 1971.41.

[6] Ass. plén. 2 Apr. 1993, D 1993.373 concl. Jeol, D 1994.Somm.14 obs. Aubert.

[7] Civ. (1) 13 May 1986, Bull. civ. I, no. 20.

the capital but also the interest or fruits arising from the date of the payment'. Thus, if Eugene tells Douglas of his mistake, he will be held to be in good faith and will be obliged to repay $8,000 without interest, but silence on Eugene's part will be taken as a sign of bad faith. It will be up to Douglas to establish Eugene's bad faith since under art. 2268 of the Civil Code, good faith is presumed. Moreover, art. 1378 must be read in combination with art. 1153 concerning the date from which interest runs. If Eugene is held to be in good faith, he must repay the $8,000 from the date of the demand, whereas, on the contrary, if he is held to be in bad faith, he will be liable to pay interest from the date of the mistaken payment.[8] The judges cannot make interest run from the date of the mistaken payment without investigating whether the debtor was in good or bad faith.[9] If Eugene fails to tell Douglas that he has received the money and is held to be in bad faith as a result, Douglas need not prove that he has suffered a particular loss in order to claim the backdated interest.[10]

In conclusion, it can be seen that in French law the level of behaviour required of the creditor in the case of a mistaken payment is explicitly set out in the Civil Code. Mistaken payment is often explained as an example of unjust enrichment.[11] This explanation confirms why explicit mention is made of bad faith. Sanctioning the creditor's bad faith goes hand in hand with preventing the creditor being unjustly enriched at the expense of the debtor. It is a kind of double sanction. However, the existence of special provision in the Civil Code for this situation in its provisions on *répétition de l'indu* has the effect of ruling out recourse to the law of contract, despite the presence of a contract between the parties.[12] This means that French law would not impose a duty on the holder of the account by application of the principle of good faith in the performance of contracts.

BELGIUM

First of all, Eugene will have to pay back the $8,000 to Douglas as an unduly received payment. Moreover, he will have to pay interest on that sum from the day when he gets to know of the payment and that it was

---

[8] Civ. (3) 12 Feb. 1985, Bull. civ. III, no. 30.   [9] Civ. (1) 14 Oct. 1988, Bull. civ. I, no. 273.
[10] Civ. (1) 8 Jun. 1983, Bull. civ. I, no. 172, RTDCiv 1985.168 obs. Mestre.
[11] Malaurie/Aynès 537–8.
[12] The foundation of art. 1376 C. civ. is the subject of debate, but according to the classification in the Civil Code, the action for restitution comes within the category of *quasi-contrats*, which are an autonomous source of obligations: art. 1370 C. civ. and see Carbonnier, *Les obligations* no. 306.

not owed to him. These obligations arise as a matter of law and are unrelated to the contractual relationship. Collecting the money could even under certain circumstances be considered criminal fraud (art. 496 of the Criminal Code).

That there is an obligation to pay back the money (possibly with interest) does not exclude the possibility of there being, in addition, a duty to inform the bank about the mistaken transfer. Such a duty can, again, be seen as an application of the 'complementary function' of good faith, or it may be based on art. 1135 C.C. However, such a duty is only relevant if its violation causes a loss which is not yet compensated for by the interest to be paid, i.e. a damage different to the one caused by any delay in making restitution of the money.

SPAIN

A duty to inform the bank arises on the facts of this case directly from art. 1258 of the Civil Code, which provides that a duty to perform a contract must be interpreted not only according to its express terms, but also according to all the terms to be implied under the requirement of good faith. This legal duty to inform arises from the contractual relationship of the parties and its breach may therefore give rise to liability in damages. Quite apart from any contractual relationship between the parties, Eugene would be liable to make restitution of the money as *accipiens indebiti* (receiver of what is not due) by way of application of the rule in art. 1896 of the Civil Code.

ITALY

There are two approaches to this case in Italian law. The first one focuses on the law of restitution and leads to a fairly settled and predictable result, having been tested in similar cases. The second approach involves the application of the principle of good faith in the performance of obligations and contracts[13] which in this context could be considered innovative.

First, if the problems raised by this case were analysed in terms of the law of unjust enrichment, there is no doubt that the bank has the right to recover its mistaken payment. The only question is whether or not the client's liability towards the bank is limited to the sum to which his

---

[13] Arts. 1175, 1375 c.c.

account was mistakenly credited. In this respect, the Civil Code provides that if Eugene was in good faith when the bank transferred the money to him he must repay merely the amount transferred without interest.[14] In this context 'good faith' means 'honesty' rather than 'fair dealing', and good faith in a recipient of money or other property is presumed unless the transferor proves fraud or gross negligence.[15] On the other hand, a recipient in bad faith must restore the amount received plus interest from the date of the receipt.[16] Finally, a recipient who was in good faith at the time of receipt nevertheless incurs the same liability as a recipient in bad faith after the transferor demands the return of the money, since from this date he too must pay the capital plus interest.[17]

Having said this, the question arises whether Eugene owes Douglas a duty to inform him about the mistaken transfer. If he were to do so when he becomes aware of the mistake, he would be considered to be in good faith and would merely have to repay the $8,000 without interest. On the other hand, if he were to keep silent he would probably be exposed to the more stringent liability to which recipients in bad faith are subject.

It should be added that a person to whom money is owed may claim compensation for the harm which he has suffered from the date of his *demand*, on top of any interest.[18] Here, then, the measure of the liability of a recipient in bad faith is not restricted by the rules of the law of restitution which would limit any restitutionary claim to the value which the recipient received plus interest. Note also, that while a recipient in good faith cannot set up a defence of change of position under the Civil Code rules relating to the payment of money,[19] special legislation relating to pensions payments adopts a more lenient approach so as to give special protection to pensioners (and their successors in title!) who receive mistaken payments in good faith.[20]

Secondly, we should examine the case from the point of view of the possible application of the principle of good faith in the performance of obligations and contracts, according to which it would seem that Eugene should tell Douglas about the mistaken transfer of money to his account. In Italian law, the standard approach to the good faith requirement in the performance of contracts attaches to it a reciprocal duty in the other party to draw attention to mistakes or misapprehensions from which the other

---

[14] Art. 2033 c.c.   [15] Cf. art. 1147 c.c.

[16] The rate of interest relevant for the purposes of making restitution is fixed by law (*tasso legale di interesse*). See art. 1284 c.c.   [17] Art. 2033 c.c.   [18] Cass., 4 Nov. 1992, n. 11969.

[19] Art. 2033 c.c.

[20] Cf. l. 23 Dec. 1996, n. 662, art. 260. This is the latest in a series of legislative provisions of the same kind.

party may suffer.[21] On the facts of case 17, Eugene has failed to comply with this duty and for this reason he must pay Douglas the $8,000 plus damages. While this conclusion is relatively clear, no Italian jurist or court has previously considered the impact of the general duty of good faith in relation to cases such as this one. Moreover, from a practical point of view, it is hard to tell whether analysis of the case in terms of good faith would lead to results substantially different from those flowing from the traditional approach based on the law of restitution.

THE NETHERLANDS

Good faith demands from Eugene that he inform the bank about the mistaken payment. The client is the party who can more readily notice this kind of mistake.

The acceptance of a duty of disclosure is not based on any special relationship between customer and bank, but on the general duty that a contract has to be performed in good faith (art. 6:2 jo. 6:248 B.W.). This is one of those areas where the duty of disclosure, as originally developed in the area of mistake, is now also applied.

ENGLAND

It is clear law that where a person pays money to another under a mistake of fact, then in principle it may be recovered from that person under the law of restitution.[22] Case 17, however, differs from this ordinary case in that it relates to the running of a bank account, the miscrediting occurring, therefore, in the course of the performance of a contract between the parties.

English law has long taken the view that the nature of the contract between the parties to a bank account is simply one of debtor and creditor. Thus, when the account is in credit, the bank is the customer's debtor; when the account is in debit, the customer is the bank's debtor.[23] The general rule applicable to current accounts (which it will be assumed is the case in case 17) is that the bank is entitled to rectify any errors in the running of the account by reversing the entry.[24] Clearly, this cannot be done until the bank is aware of the mistake. Given the nature of the relationship between parties to a bank account, until Eugene withdraws the

---

[21] Benatti, Digesto, 4th edn, sez. civ., VII, 1991, 221; Castronovo, in: *Enciclopedia, passim.* Cf. Cass., 11 Dec. 1995, n. 1267, Foro it. 1996, I, c. 544. [22] Burrows 95 ff.
[23] *Foley v. Hill* (1848) 2 HLC 28. [24] Ellinger/Lomnicka 168–9.

money, Douglas does not suffer any loss (so as to found any claim for breach of contract if there were one) nor is Eugene *actually* (as opposed to potentially) enriched: for even if interest is added to the miscredited account, Douglas simply becomes a creditor to Eugene to this further enhanced amount. Thus, if the bank discovers its mistake before Eugene has withdrawn the money, then it is in principle entitled to reverse the entry; if after he has done so, it may still reverse the entry, this having the effect of making Eugene debtor to the amount in question. There is, therefore, no need to resort to the general law of restitution where the bank has a (contractual) power to remedy its own mistake.

However, a customer who has been miscredited with an amount may have two defences against the exercise of the bank's power of reversal. First, and rarely in practice, the bank may have 'stated an account' with its customer so as to bind it to the amount which it has stated as holding. Secondly, the bank may be estopped from relying on its own mistake in crediting the account: for where a customer has changed his position to his detriment, the bank may be precluded from reversing the credit entry. This means that if Eugene has noticed the miscrediting some time after it occurred and after having relied to his detriment on his balance as an accurate one, then the bank will not be able to rectify its error.

Finally, the question is posed at the end of case 17 whether Eugene owes Douglas any duty to inform him of his mistake. There is no authority directly on this point, but an analogy may be made with the position as regards a customer's other duties in respect of the running of the account. For it is established that while a customer owes his bank no duty to take reasonable care in the running of the account, he must inform the bank of any fraud or forgery committed by third parties in relation to the account, such as forgery of his signature by his wife or employee.[25] However, this analogy is not complete as in the situation of case 17, any duty to inform imposed on the customer would be to his prejudice, whereas his duty as to third party fraud does not in principle prejudice the customer, though it helps to protect the bank.

IRELAND

It is probable that in Irish law Eugene would owe no duty to inform Douglas of the mistaken crediting of his account, since a party to a con-

---

[25] *Greenwood v. Martins Bank Ltd* [1932] 1 KB 371; *Tai Hing Cotton Mill Ltd v. Liu Chong Hing Bank Ltd* [1986] AC 80.

tract cannot be expected to inform the other party that a cause of action may have accrued against him.[26]

On the other hand, if Eugene were to withdraw and use the money in any way he would be liable under a restitutionary claim for an action of money had and received together with simple interest of 8 per cent from the time of the accrual of such action,[27] this being set probably at the date of use of the money. It is unlikely that Eugene would be able to raise any argument based on an estoppel in order to resist Douglas' claim on the facts.

If Eugene did not use the money in any way, Douglas' claim is somewhat less clear. He may resist any claim by Eugene to enforce payment of the amount. He may also, on the same basis, resist a claim by Eugene for any interest which might notionally have arisen on the falsely credited account. Less clear is whether Douglas has any claim against Eugene relating to interest or lost earnings on the miscredited money. It is unlikely that a mere accounting mistake in which one account is credited with a sum, which is not subsequently used, would give rise to a restitutionary claim as the money might not properly be described as 'had and received' to the account-holder's use, nor any 'benefit' received by payment. Accordingly, as no cause of action has accrued by the accounting error, simple interest would not be payable.

SCOTLAND

The relationship of banker and customer is principally a contractual one. The relationship was examined in *Royal Bank of Scotland v. Skinner*[28] which declared the nature of the contract to be one of creditor and debtor. In the English case of *Joachimson v. Swiss Bank Corporation*,[29] it was held that as the elements of the contractual relationship vary from case to case, it goes beyond the creditor–debtor relationship. Given that the relationship between a banker and his customer is contractual, it will begin when the parties reach agreement. A course of dealing becomes the accepted and contractually binding arrangement. Written contracts covering every aspect of the relationship are rare.

A customer has two duties to his bank: (i) to notify the bank when he discovers that someone has forged cheques on his account; *Greenwood v.*

---

[26] Cf. Breslin, *passim*, who accepts that a bank's customer's duties are very restricted.
[27] Courts Act 1981, s. 22.   [28] 1931 SLT 382.   [29] [1921] 3 KB 110, CA.

Martins Bank Ltd;[30] (ii) to take reasonable precautions to prevent the fraudulent alteration of cheques drawn; *London Joint Stock Bank Ltd v. MacMillan & Arthur.*[31] The courts are reluctant to extend these duties and create extracontractual obligations. If the bank so desires to extend these duties it must inform its customer; *Tai Hing Cotton Mill Ltd v. Liu Chong Hing Bank Ltd.*[32] In this case the Privy Council stated the law of the relationship between banker and customer; it is contractual and it was up to the bank to impose more rigid conditions than were recognised by the law if it so wished, but the banker would have to make these conditions known to the customer. The question whether a customer owes a duty of care to the bank seems to have been dealt with in this case; the decision removed the possibility of establishing a duty of care between customer and bank and made it clear that however negligent the customer may be, unless there is a binding contractual term to the contrary, he will have no duty to examine his bank statements or query them.

It follows then that unless an agreed contractual term exists between Douglas and Eugene which imposes a duty on Eugene to reveal errors etc. in his bank statements, then Eugene is under no contractual obligation to tell Douglas of the bank's error. But there is an obligation on Eugene to inform the bank of the overpayment based on the ground that he has become unjustifiably enriched.[33] The plea of repetition will allow Douglas to recover the money as it has been paid in circumstances where it would be unjust for Eugene to keep it. The plea for recovery of the money will be based on the *condictio indebiti* (a claim for recovery of a payment which is not due). The essentials of the *condictio indebiti* are that the sum which the pursuer paid was not due and that payment was made in error; *Morgan Guaranty Trust Co. of New York v. Lothian Regional Council.*[34] Clearly if Eugene spends the money he is liable for unjust enrichment, unless it was done in good faith in which case he can rely on a change of position defence.

DENMARK AND NORWAY

The case raises two issues. One is the problem of whether the customer is obliged to notify the bank of the incorrect entry crediting his account with $8,000. The other question is whether a customer may found a claim on the fact that in his statement of account he has received incorrect notification.

---

[30] [1933] AC 51, HL.   [31] [1918] AC 777, HL.   [32] [1986] AC 80, [1985] 2 All ER 947, PC.
[33] See the Scottish reports to cases 3, 4, 14, 15 and 26 above and below.
[34] 1995 SLT 299.

Considering the latter issue, it must be asked whether this type of statement of an account on the part of the bank constitutes merely a notification for information (which may give rise to liability for misleading the customer), or a promise which obliges the bank irrespective of the underlying circumstances. Here the answer will probably be that the statement is deemed to be a notification for information only.[35] If the customer is aware of the facts, it cannot mislead him. Thus, it is not possible that he can have incurred a loss, for which he may be allowed to claim damages.

The question of whether the customer has any duty to notify the bank must be viewed against this background. In a relationship between a bank and a customer, the point of departure must be that the bank has to protect its own interests, and that it is not the customer's business to call the bank's attention to the existence of any accounting errors. It will be a different matter where the customer attempts to withdraw funds on the basis of the incorrect entry in the account. At that stage the customer would indeed have a duty to inform the bank. When a customer withdraws more than the sum to which he is entitled under the prevailing circumstances, a claim arises, on the part of the bank, for repayment of the amount paid in excess (according to the doctrine of *condictio indebiti*;[36] cf. Rt. 1985, p. 290 where it is stated that '[i]t is a fundamental feature of the *condictio indebiti* doctrine that each instance must be evaluated concretely and with due account taken of reasonableness').

As long as no dispositions have been made concerning the account, the main rule will be that the customer has no duty to inform the bank. Exceptions may be imagined in the case of sensationally large amounts of money which have clearly gone astray.

SWEDEN

According to case law, a person who receives a payment not owed may sometimes retain it, provided he had no reason to realise the mistake, and especially if the payment was a settlement of a disputed amount or he subsequently acted in reliance on the payment.[37]

In this case, Eugene realised that his account was, by mistake, credited with $8,000. Thus, he has to repay the amount, with interest, if the balance falls below $8,000. He is not entitled to interest on the amount credited by mistake. On the other hand, Eugene, a private individual, hardly has a duty to inform Douglas, a banker, of the mistake as such.

---

[35] Hagstrøm, *Lov og Rett* 1995, 375 ff.   [36] Gomard, *Obligationsret 3* 171 ff.; Krüger 309 ff.
[37] See, for instance, NJA 1933, p. 25, NJA 1961, p. 18, and NJA 1970, p. 539.

Consequently, I doubt that Eugene would be liable to compensate Douglas for any costs incurred in his search of the amount.

FINLAND

According to Finnish law Eugene does not have any positive obligation to inform the bank about the mistake. On the other hand he is, of course, not entitled to use the money that was mistakenly transferred to him. There are criminal cases where the courts have convicted the customer of embezzlement, in similar situations, where he had used the money. I have found no pertinent private law cases – apart from certain instances where a bankrupt estate was held bound to return money that had mistakenly been paid into the bank account of the debtor. I think that a Finnish judge would, at most, consider the analogous application of the Hidden Property Act of 1988 (Si 512), s. 4, which imposes upon the finder a general duty to take care of hidden property and report it to the police. It would probably not be viewed as an obligation ancillary to the contract concerning the bank account. But in this respect this is a borderline case the solution of which would have certain implications also with regard to interest when Eugene is obliged to pay back the unjust enrichment.

In this context it should be remarked that although loyalty is recognised as a general principle of Finnish contract law,[38] its scope in judicial practice is unclear. Loyalty is usually referred to in *rationes decidendi* as a supporting argument, not as the main argument which directly justifies a certain pattern of behaviour as a contractual norm.[39]

Editors' comparative observations

While all legal systems agree in principle that Eugene cannot simply draw out and retain the money miscredited to him by Douglas' bank, they differ as to whether Eugene has any duty to inform Douglas of the mistake.

(i) Many legal systems (Germany, Greece, Belgium, Spain, Italy and the Netherlands) accept that there is clear duty on the customer to reveal the mistake to his bank, this being a clear consequence of good faith. The

---

[38] See above all Taxell 78 ff.
[39] See e.g. KKO 1980 II 70, KKO 1983 II 79 where loyalty was used as an argument for imposing a duty duly to inform the other party; in other situations where reference has been made to loyalty the courts have held one party to be under an obligation to take care of the interests of the other according to good commercial usage (KKO 1982 II 128, KKO 1985 II 29).

result of this conclusion is the imposition of liability in damages: Eugene, the customer, has to make good any loss which the bank may suffer as a result of its mistake (such as its failing to credit another customer). Austrian law reaches the same conclusion under its doctrine of special duties of care arising from lawful contractual contact.

(ii) There is clearly no duty to inform the bank of the mistake in French law. Recourse to the law of contract is ruled out in view of the fact that the situation is covered by the rules relating to unjustified enrichment. Interestingly, while the Belgian and Italian reports take the same starting point in their analysis of the problem as does French law, both the Belgian and Italian reporters do not rule out recourse to the law of contract and see it as a distinct possibility that a duty to inform the bank of its mistake could be imposed on the basis of their principles of performance in good faith, though there is no direct authority to this effect in either system. Although their starting point is not the same, the Nordic legal systems and Irish law take the same view as the French and deny the existence of any duty of disclosure in this situation.

(iii) In English and Scots law it is *arguable* that a duty to disclose the mistake exists (by analogy with knowledge of another's fraud) but this is by no means clear.

Finally, it was noted by the Scots reporter at the Regensburg symposium that in practice in Scotland the contract under which the bank operates will normally contain an express provision requiring the customer to disclose mistakes of the type found in the present case.

Case 18: Access to medical records

Case

Clement has, for a long time, been Donovan's doctor. As a result of a dispute between the two, Donovan decides to consult another doctor from now on. Does Clement have to hand over to Donovan the data on the latter's health that he has on his files and the X-rays he has made?

Discussions

GERMANY

The doctor is bound under the contractual relationship with his patients (which has to be classified as a contract for services) to treat them properly. This includes an obligation to keep proper records of the treatment.[1] These records should always be available, even to a successor of the original doctor whom the patient may wish to consult. For a patient must always be free to choose a doctor in whom he has confidence. The Federal Supreme Court has therefore allowed a claim by a patient for delivery of the records by one doctor to his successor.[2] The basis for the claim has again been found in an ancillary duty derived from § 242 BGB.[3]

Nevertheless, inspection of the records by the patient himself (and thus also the right to claim their delivery) has been limited by the Federal Supreme Court. The patient may not inspect the records if there are therapeutic reasons for withholding them. In the present case there is no sign of any need for any such qualification and Donovan will therefore have a

---

[1] BGHZ 85, 327 (329).
[2] BGHZ 85, 327 (327). For further details see, e.g., *Münchener Kommentar*/Keller § 260, nn. 22 ff.   [3] Cf. BGHZ 85, 327 (331 f.).

claim based on an ancillary obligation which is, in turn, deduced from § 611 (contract for services) read in conjunction with § 242 BGB. Alternatively such claim may also be seen to be derived from the constitutional right to personal integrity and human dignity (Arts. 2 I, 1 I GG).[4] Yet, the fundamental rights only operate indirectly in private law: the general provisions contained in the BGB provide the most convenient port of entry for the evaluations contained in them. The latter approach will therefore also lead via § 242 BGB. Clement has to hand the records (and the X-rays) over to Donovan.

It may be noted that in most cases today, patients in Germany receive treatment on the basis of health insurance certificates (*Krankenscheine*). There is a complex web of public law regulation concerning the relationships between the patient and his social health insurance, the social health insurance and the association of panel doctors and the association of panel doctors and the individual panel doctor administering the treatment. Somewhat surprisingly, perhaps, § 76 IV SGB V determines that, as far as the rights of the patient against his doctor are concerned, contract law (i.e. the normal private law regime) is applicable.[5]

GREECE

Donovan has the right to receive all data concerning his health from Clement. Clement's obligation to hand over the medical data is of an ancillary nature, and it arises from the contractual relationship between patient and doctor[6] in conjunction with the precepts of good faith (art. 288 Gr. C.C.)

AUSTRIA

The Austrian Supreme Court[7] has allowed claims by patients against their doctors to inspect their own medical records and to make copies of them. The Court has also accepted that doctors are bound to hand over the results of any tests undertaken on their patients, e.g. electrocardiograms.[8] Doctors are held to be under an ancillary contractual obligation to deliver

---

[4] Ibid.   [5] For a brief and concise overview, see Medicus, *Schuldrecht II* n. 355.
[6] On the *sui generis* nature of that relationship, see Androulidakis-Dimitriadis, *Ypochreoseis* 99 and *Ypochreosi enimerosis* 117; Stathopoulos, in: *Astikos Kodix II* art. 288, nos. 63, 64.
[7] SZ 57/98 (1984); cf. also Giesen nn. 429 ff.; Krejci, in: *Rummel, ABGB I* §§ 1165, 1166 n. 17; Krückl, ÖJZ 1983, 281.   [8] JBl 1964, 515; cf. also SZ 57/98.

to their patients all material which they make on their behalf and at their expense.

As a result of this position, Clement must either hand the files over to Donovan or give him the opportunity to copy them. He must also hand over to Donovan the X-rays which he has taken of him.[9]

FRANCE

Under art. 77 of the law of 18 January 1994 codified in the Public Health Code (*Code de la santé publique*),[10] a patient's medical files are recognised as being his personal property. Pursuant to art. L. 145–7 of this Code, a patient is entitled to have a choice concerning his doctor, free access to his files and, upon changing doctors, the former doctor is bound to transfer all the contents of the file to the new doctor who has been chosen by the patient.

It follows, therefore, that Clement is obliged to hand over to Donovan's new doctor the data and the X-rays on Clement's files. The relevant legislative provision states that all the elements of the file must be handed over. It is, however, not clear whether Clement is obliged to give the actual file physically to Donovan himself.

The overall purpose of this recent law is to improve co-ordination and continuity of care between doctors and patients.[11] In other respects doctors must respect ethical principles laid down in the Public Health Code. As the doctor/patient relationship is a contractual one,[12] and the obligation to transfer the patient's file a legislative one, it is possible to envisage that Donovan could specifically force Clement to hand over the files under art. 1184 of the Civil Code (which provides for court orders for performance of contractual obligations).

BELGIUM

It is disputed under Belgian law whether the medical file is the 'property' of the patient or not. Most modern authors consider that, in principle, a medical file belongs to the patient.[13] But it is rather an attribute of his per-

---

[9] The patient may demand delivery of the documents to himself (JBl 1964, 515). An exception is made where there are therapeutic reasons against this way of proceeding (SZ 57/98).   [10] Art. L. 145–6 ff. of the *Code de la santé publique*.
[11] *Décret* no. 95–1000 of 6 September 1995, art. 45 als. 3 and 4.
[12] See the French report to case 16 above.
[13] For example, Lambert 161; Dalcq, in: *Liber amicorum Krings* 502; Schutyser, RW 1984–1985, 3044.

sonality right than a property right in the strict sense of the word. As to certain contents of the file (e.g. photos for which he has paid), these may be property of the patient even *sensu stricto*. It is generally accepted that the doctor must hand over to the patient at least the objective results contained in the files,[14] unless this would be harmful to the patient (the so-called therapeutical exception).[15]

Even if (on the basis of an archaic and paternalistic view of the so-called 'medical confidentiality' as a professional privilege of the doctor) one were to see this differently, the patient may certainly require the first doctor to hand over the files to his new doctor. This is explicitly provided for by legislation (art. 13 of Royal Decree No. 78 of 10 November 1967); non-compliance leads to disciplinary sanctions (apart from the civil law remedies).

Donovan's claim against Clement will normally be a contractual one. If it is accepted that the file is the patient's 'property', Donovan also has a claim based on his property right.

SPAIN

Clement ought to hand over to Donovan all the relevant information so that the latter may choose the doctor whom he likes for his future health care. The source of this duty is again to be found in art. 1258 of the Civil Code,[16] this sort of case being seen as an example of a 'post-contractual duty'. The only limit on this duty lies in Clement's right to keep his own professional secrets.

ITALY

In Italian law, Donovan has a right to obtain the information contained in the medical records and the X-rays which Clement keeps.

The contract between the parties will normally be the source of this right, though there is good reason to consider that, quite apart from any contract, an identical right arises from either the constitutional norm which protects peoples' health[17] or from data protection legislation giving patients control over information concerning their own health.[18]

---

[14] See e.g. Civ. Brussels 11 Apr. 1962, JT 1962, 603.
[15] See Vansweevelt, TPR 1991, 366 ff. no. 110 ff.   [16] See the Spanish report to case 17.
[17] Art. 32 *Constituzione della Repubblica Italiana.*
[18] L. 31 Dec. 1996, n. 675, *Tutela delle persone e di altri soggetti rispetto al trattamento dei dati personali, art.* 22.3. The prohibition covers data recorded both with and without the use of electronic devices (art. 5).

Not surprisingly, therefore, art. 64 of the Code of Conduct of the Italian medical profession expressly states that all medical records concerning patients must be put at their disposal or at the disposal of persons designated by the patients. This article also safeguards a patient's right freely to choose his own doctor. Article 65 of the same Code specifies that this rule of free choice also applies if a patient decides to seek medical advice against the wishes of his attending doctor. For while in this case the doctor already in attendance on the patient can properly refuse to work together with any new doctor so brought in, he must hand over to the latter all medical information concerning the patient which he possesses, including the medical records which he keeps.

THE NETHERLANDS

Clement has to hand over the data and the X-rays. There is no justifiable interest on the part of Clement to refuse Donovan's new doctor the medical file. Such a refusal would therefore be in contravention of good faith. Although the article does not apply directly to this case, a statutory argument can be found in art. 7:456 B.W. (medical treatment contract), which gives the patient a right to see what is in his file.

ENGLAND

Where private health care is provided the relationship between a doctor and his patient can be analysed as a matter of contract, but the vast majority of health care is provided in the United Kingdom without charge by the National Health Service and this rules out the existence of a contract between the doctor, or other provider of care, and the patient for lack of consideration. Not surprisingly, however, the courts have shown themselves hostile to distinctions being drawn between public and private health care as regards the rules to be applied, notably but not exclusively, to the standard of care required of doctors with respect to their patients.[19]

The common law dealt inadequately with the question of access by patients to their medical records. For access to the documents themselves could be denied in the vast majority of cases on the basis that the paper etc. on which they had been written was owned by the doctor or other health professional in question, and the common law failed to develop an

---

[19] Cf. *Naylor v. Preston Area Health Authority* [1987] 2 All ER 353, at 360 *per* Sir *John Donaldson* M.R.

idea of a right to the information itself (as distinct from the documents in which it was contained), whether as a matter of implied term in any contract or otherwise.[20]

In 1990, parliament intervened by the Access to Health Records Act which generalised the protection given to patients and others in relation to data stored electronically provided by the Data Protection Act 1984. The 1990 Act may be seen to reflect both a developing general concern for rights of access to information which affects individuals and, specifically in the medical context, a growing sense of the importance of informed decision-making by individuals about their own health care. Thus, by s. 3 of the 1990 Act a patient may apply for access to a health record to its holder and the latter must give such access within twenty-one days of the application in respect of records made within the previous forty days, and within forty days in any other case. Access relates only to health records made after the commencement of the provisions of the Act (in November 1991).[21] Access to the record may be given by allowing its inspection or by provision of an extract from it and copies may be required (though the cost of these and postage may be charged).[22] The 1991 Act makes exceptions to disclosure by the holder of a record, notably where he or she thinks it or part of it would cause serious harm to the physical or mental health of the patient or where it would contain information relating to someone other than the patient applying.[23]

Thus, Clement does have to provide access or photocopies of the files and X-rays relating to Donovan which he holds, subject to these conditions.

IRELAND

No litigation has occurred in Ireland on the ownership of documents arising from medical consultations and there is no specific statute in Irish law governing general access by patients to medical records, although patients do benefit from the protection of information stored in computers etc. as against 'data controllers' under the Data Protection Act 1988.

Despite this absence of specific authority, the authors of the leading Irish textbook on medical law[24] accept that ownership of the material on which medical data is recorded probably resides in the doctor, clinic, hospital or health authority as the case may be, but they also take the view

---

[20] Kennedy/Grubb 610–12.   [21] Access to Health Records Act 1990, s. 5(1)(b).
[22] Ibid., s. 3(4)(b).   [23] Ibid., s. 5(1)(a).   [24] Tomkin/Hanafin 52–3.

that there is probably an implied term in the contract between patient and the provider of health care to the effect that 'a patient has a right of access or possession, should the patient need the records for further health care, for example, to change doctors'.[25] Furthermore, a distinction could be drawn between doctors' records on the one hand and images or test results (here, an X-ray) on the other, if those images or results are specifically paid for by the patient: for if a patient has to pay a hospital doctor a separate fee for the taking of an X-ray (quite apart from its analysis or examination), the patient might well be held to own it.

In the result, though, on the facts of case 18 it would seem that the doctor would be obliged to hand over the records and X-rays, or copies of them, to his patient, though where the patient is in arrears of payment, in principle the doctor could assert a lien on them for any amounts outstanding even though it would be difficult to imagine such a lien being asserted in practice.

SCOTLAND

Patients are entitled to expect their doctors' confidentiality regarding their health, but can doctors keep secrets from their patients, i.e. can a patient such as Donovan compel his doctor to give him information or let him see his records?

The obligation on the doctor is to give the patient any information necessary to ensure that the patient has adequate health care. Where the records kept are computerised, since November 1987, a patient can invoke his right as a 'data subject' under the Data Protection Act 1984 to demand a copy of any information held about him in computerised form. So, if Clement holds Donovan's records in computerised form, Donovan has a statutory right to get a copy of them. But the majority of health records are not held on computer (the cynic might argue that this is owing to the 1984 Act).

From November 1991, further rights have been granted to the patient by the Access to Health Records Act 1990. The Act applies to patients treated in the private sector as well as National Health Service patients. Under the Act, patients may apply for access to their 'health records' but only records compiled after November 1991. Health records include any information relating to the patient's physical or mental health made by or on behalf of a health professional in connection with the care of that individual. In

---

[25] Ibid., at 52.

Donovan's case, this would include both the data and the X-rays *post* November 1991. However, the legislation merely affords the patient access (the patient may take a copy or an extract of the information) and not possession of the records.

Access to health records is not unlimited. It may be wholly excluded if the holder of the record believes that the patient is incapable of understanding the nature of his application for access.[26] It may be partially excluded where the holder of the record believes either that (i) the relevant information is likely to cause serious harm to the physical or mental health of the patient, or that (ii) the information includes information regarding someone other than the patient.[27] In deciding whether to refuse access, health professionals are required to consult the health professionals currently responsible for the patient's care.[28]

Unless Clement can assert the above objections, Donovan will have a right to gain access to his medical records by virtue of the 1990 Act. However this does not entitle him to acquire possession of them.

DENMARK AND NORWAY

Under West Nordic law the question of patients' case files and other information concerning the patient which the attending doctor possesses will not be one of contract law, since a comprehensive set of rules exists concerning the disposal of case files, etc., as a matter of public law. I presume that these regulations will be of fairly limited interest in the present report. Suffice it to say that under the Norwegian law on doctors (Act No. 42 of 13 June 1980, § 45) a doctor is obliged to provide a copy of the case files where this is necessary for the treatment of the patient.

Should the question be viewed in terms of contract law, it is not so obvious that the patient has a right of disposal of the files in the attending doctor's possession. In view of possible future claims that might be brought against him, for instance, for incorrect treatment, the attending doctor may have a legitimate interest for retaining documentation concerning former patients. On the other hand, regard for the patient and the best possible treatment by another doctor clearly demands that the patient and his new doctor must not be precluded from access to the information which is in the possession of the former doctor. On the basis purely of contract law it could, under West Nordic law, presumably be said that the patient is entitled, against reimbursement of all costs, to receive

---

[26] Section 4, Access to Health Records Act 1990.   [27] Section 5, ibid.   [28] Section 7, ibid.

copies of all files and any other material, but cannot demand that these materials have to be handed over to him and thus be removed from the former doctor.

SWEDEN

Under s. 16 of the Patient Files Act of 1985, a patient is entitled to read or copy his file, unless the treatment requires that the patient not be informed. Since the patient Donovan paid for treatment by Clement, Donovan ought also from a contractual point of view to have access to copies of the files (against reimbursement of costs). Doctors are supposed to be obliged to give information from the files, on the patient's demand, to third parties (such as insurance companies), and Clement's interest in preventing Donovan from going to another doctor does not deserve to be protected.

FINLAND

According to case law, now codified in the instructions of the Medical Board,[29] a patient has the right to obtain copies of his files and X-rays. Hospital doctors have the right to keep the originals (with the view to a possible malpractice claim or something similar). In Finnish law, this is a clear case.

Editors' comparative observations

All the legal systems give the patient access to the information contained in the doctor's records. The doctor has to hand over the records in his possession either to the patient himself or to the second doctor or he has, at least, to make them available for the purpose of copying. The legal bases for this obligation differ.

(i) Many legal systems possess special legislation providing for patients to have rights of access to the information contained in their own patient records (France, Belgium, England, Scotland, Denmark, Norway, Sweden, Finland).

(ii) In the absence of either legislative or judicial authority, it is argued

---

[29] In Finnish, *Lääkintöhallitus*; it is now known as the Social Board (*Sosiaalihallitus*). At present, amendments and new instructions are issued by another body known as *Terveydenhuollon oikeusturvakeskus*.

in Ireland that the patient has the right to the information on the basis of an implied term in the contract under which treatment is given.

(iii) A number of systems rely on the notion of an ancillary duty arising under the contractual relationship between doctor and patient (Germany, Greece, Austria, Spain). In German, Greek and Spanish law, these ancillary duties are related to good faith. Dutch law, too, invokes the principle of good faith. Italian law, in turn, derives the doctor's duty simply from the contract. Leaving special legislation aside, the contract would also provide a suitable point of departure in the West Nordic and Swedish legal systems.

(iv) Belgian lawyers might also resort to proprietary claims.

This case is of considerable interest as an example of the way in which different legal systems have reacted similarly to a changing perception as to a particular type of relationship, a change in perception which can broadly be characterised as one from paternalism (in the doctor towards his patient) to an approach which centres on the patient's rights. One of the reflections of this is the recognition by all legal systems of a right in a patient to the information acquired or held by his doctor, the most important purpose of which is to enable the patient to assess the proper course of his own treatment, thus enhancing his own autonomy (though this purpose is not really the one for which the information is required on the facts of case 18). A broad division may be seen in the reactions of the legal systems to this shift in perception: while some of them feel able to achieve the recognition of the patient's rights of access by development of traditional legal (contractual) techniques, be they implied term, good faith or the imposition of ancillary obligations, others have resorted to special legislation, permitting a detailed regulation of the conflicting considerations in this area.

The case is also a good example of the way in which the domain of (the private law of) contract is subject to the institutional mechanisms surrounding the particular context. In some countries, the provision of health care remains paradigmatically one for contract law. This may be true even in countries which operate extensive social insurance schemes, such as Germany. German law, therefore, continues to make use of its private law principle of good faith to determine the patient's rights against his doctor. This does not, however, mean that public law is excluded from this field: the present case demonstrates that the values entrenched in the constitution may support access by a patient to his records (cf. also the reference to constitutional law in the Italian report). A contrast here may be made with English law, for since the establishment of the National Health Service in the late 1940s, the provision of health care is paradigmatically non-contractual, the patient benefiting from a public service. This has meant that, while contracts between doctors and patients may still arise in the private health sector, clearly one of the reasons why it would have been unsatisfactory for English courts to have developed contractual techniques for dealing with such matters as access to patient records is that they simply would not work at a technical level for the vast majority of cases.

Case 19: Doctors swapping practices

Case

Richard and Spencer both practise as medical doctors, the one (Richard) in Castle Combe, the other (Spencer) in Lintz. Since Richard wants to move to Lintz and Spencer to Castle Combe, they agree to swap their practices. A year after they have effected the transfer, Spencer realises that he does not like to live in Castle Combe. He lets Richard know that he wishes to return to Lintz and that he is going to set up a new practice in the neighbourhood of his old one. Richard asks the court to issue an order restraining Spencer from carrying out his plan.

Discussions

GERMANY

Any right, on the part of Richard, to restrain Spencer from opening a practice in his neighbourhood can only be based upon the contract. However, the contract contains no provision directly dealing with the situation that Spencer wishes to return to Lintz. When they concluded their contract, neither Richard nor Spencer contemplated the possibility that one of them might give up his practice in order to return to his earlier residence. Thus, the contract contains a lacuna which may, however, be filled by 'supplementary interpretation' (*ergänzende Vertragsauslegung*) according to the principles contained in §§ 133, 157 BGB.[1] It has to be determined what the parties would have intended, had they foreseen that this situation might arise and had they been guided by the precepts of good faith and business

---

[1] Cf. BGHZ 16, 71 (76). See generally on 'supplementary interpretation' *Jauernig/*Jauernig § 157, nn. 2 ff.; *Palandt/*Heinrichs § 157, nn. 2 ff.; Medicus, *Allgemeiner Teil* nn. 338 ff.

mores (§ 157 BGB). Had Richard and Spencer foreseen the prospect that Spencer might wish to return to Lintz before long, they would have taken into consideration that a doctor who takes over someone else's practice is not likely, within a short period, to consolidate the relationship with his patients to such an extent that his predecessor's return would not result in a significant loss of income. The return by either of them to his old place of residence was therefore going to defeat the purpose of the contract to a considerable extent and that should reasonably have induced them to agree upon a clause, in terms of which the other party was not allowed to return to his old place of residence for at least two or three years.[2] This is how the lacuna in the contract has to be filled.

Richard will therefore succeed in his application and the court will issue the order as requested.

GREECE

The agreement between Richard and Spencer to swap their practices is valid. A problem arises from the moment when Spencer realises that he does not like to live in Castle Combe, since if the contract would have to be understood in the way that he could not move back to Lintz, it would be contrary to the basic right of free movement.

Freedom of movement is enshrined in art. 5 of the Greek Constitution which also applies to private agreements (*Drittwirkung*). An agreement to the effect that Spencer would have to stay in Castle Combe even if he does not like it would be invalid, since such restriction on his freedom to move would also be contrary to arts. 178–9 Gr. C.C., and arts. 57–9 Gr. C.C.[3] Thus, a Greek court would not be able to prohibit Spencer's return to Lintz. It can, however, prohibit him from setting up his new practice in a neighbourhood so close to his former practice, for to do so would constitute an abuse of his right to set up practice anywhere in the country which is prohibited by art. 281 Gr. C.C. He is not allowed to act in a way which would result in his old patients coming back to him.[4]

If there has been fault on Spencer's part and if Richard has suffered loss, Spencer can be held liable to pay compensation to Richard (arts. 914, 919 Gr. C.C.) or will even have to pay reparation in money for the immaterial loss which Richard has suffered as a consequence of Spencer's unlawful act (art. 932 Gr. C.C.).

---

[2] Cf. BGHZ 16, 71 (77 ff., 81).
[3] Cf. Androulidakis-Dimitriadis, in: *Festschrift Karakatsanes* 35–42.
[4] See Simantiras no. 324, p. 231; Papantoniou, *Kali Pistis* 172–5.

AUSTRIA

It is generally thought that a party to a contract owes special duties of care to the other party even after performance of the contract has been completed.[5] The Supreme Court has on occasion justified this position by reference to the notion of good faith,[6] but in my opinion it is more convincing to rely on all the arguments which are normally adduced for establishing special duties of care between the parties from the very beginning of their coming into contact with a view to contract.[7]

In relation to the case in point, if Spencer were to set up a new practice in Richard's neighbourhood, it would endanger Richard's practice much more than if anyone else did so, since the practice's patients would be likely to return to the doctor whom they have been used to for many years. If this occurred, the value of the practice to Richard and, therefore, the value of the benefit accruing to him from Spencer's performance of the contract to swap practices would be much lower than he (Richard) was entitled to assume. In the result, the particular risk of causing special loss to Richard which setting up practice locally would entail justifies the imposition on Spencer of a special duty of care to avoid such a loss.[8] Richard can, therefore, indeed ask the court for an order against Spencer restraining him from carrying out his plan to set up practice in the neighbourhood.

FRANCE

In French law, Richard may have difficulty obtaining a court order restraining Spencer from setting up his practice again in Lintz. In order to succeed, he will first (i) have to prove that the swap arrangement was valid, and then (ii) that Spencer was under an implied restrictive covenant not to set up a practice in Lintz again within a given time.

(i) A medical practice is considered to be a 'civil practice' as opposed to a 'commercial' one.[9] This is based on the idea that the practice itself is inseparable from the doctor's personal qualities and attributes. Each contract made between a doctor and his patient is *intuitu personae*, made in consideration of the trust and services expected of a particular doctor. Article 1128 of the Civil Code prohibits contracts which concern things which are 'not part of commerce', and French law considers that since a

---

[5] Cf. OGH in SZ 60/50 (1987); RdW 1990, 374; ÖBA 1991, 535; RdW 1992, 239.
[6] SZ 60/50.   [7] See the Austrian reports to cases 1, 16 and 17.
[8] Cf. Gschnitzer/Faistenberger/Barta/Eccher, *Schuldrecht* 51.
[9] These terms translate as *clientèle civile* and *clientèle commerciale* respectively.

person may not be the object of commerce, so neither may a 'civil practice', which is an extension of physical personality. It is indeed firmly established in case law that the clientele of a practice of a 'liberal profession' is not 'part of commerce'.[10] Arguably, therefore, any arrangement to assign or to swap a civil practice is void.

However, certain exceptions to the principle laid down in art. 1128 of the Civil Code have been admitted; for example, the assignment of a professional's right to present his successor to his clients has been held valid,[11] though the case law is conflicting.[12] Moreover, Richard and Spencer have not actually assigned their respective practices and no money has changed hands. A 'swapping arrangement' is arguably less likely to offend art. 1128 than others involving an implicit sale of the practice. In this respect, the fact that there is case law upholding the validity of a contract for a medical replacement may be a useful analogy.[13]

Even if Richard may well be able to show that the swap was valid, the next obstacle may be more difficult to overcome.

(ii) In order to prevent Spencer from setting up a new practice, Richard will need to rely on a restrictive obligation to the effect that it was part of the arrangement that the doctors would not return to the original place of practice within a given time. As nothing is mentioned about the duration of the swap, it is assumed that this matter was not expressly dealt with by Richard and Spencer. Richard will therefore need to plead that such an obligation is to be implied in their contract. In order to do so, it would be necessary to draw an analogy from the swap contract to a sale and argue that Spencer as a seller is subject to the obligations set out under arts. 1625 ff. of the Civil Code in relation to the quiet enjoyment of his buyer. A seller is personally liable to guarantee quiet enjoyment, and if Spencer sets up practice again in Lintz, this could constitute a breach of Richard's right to quiet enjoyment.[14] Nevertheless, it is felt that this reasoning by analogy is too tenuous to be upheld.

In the absence of an express or implied restrictive obligation limiting

---

[10] In relation to doctors, see e.g. Trib. civ. Seine 27 Jun. 1956, JCP 1956.II.9624 note J. Savatier.

[11] Civ. (1) 29 Apr. 1954, JCP 1954.II.8249 note Bellet (surgical dentists); Civ. (1) 5 May 1993, JCP 1994.II.22279 note Mémeteau, RTDCiv 1994.639 obs. Zenati (medical practice).

[12] Civ. (1) 17 May 1961, Bull. civ. I, no. 257 (which allowed a doctor's heirs to sell the deceased's former practice); Lyon 13 Jan. 1983, D 1983.490 note Landraud (which held a contract for the sale of the right of presentation null and void as contrary to public policy).   [13] Civ. 16 Mar. 1943, JCP 1943.II.2289 obs. Voirin.

[14] Cf. what has been said in relation to case 13.

Spencer from returning to the area of his previous practice, Richard could rely on a moral obligation binding Spencer (as part of medical deontology set out in art. L. 162.2 of the Public Health Code (*Code de la santé publique*)) which, however, is not in itself legally binding. On the other hand, it may be that Spencer's return could constitute a breach of his duty to perform the contract in good faith.[15] If this were so, then Richard may be able to claim damages (assessed in the same way as in other cases of direct interference with goodwill). It is more doubtful whether he could obtain an order restricting Spencer from returning to Lintz in the absence of an implied obligation not to return.

BELGIUM

First of all, there is no reason to doubt the validity of a contract whereby medical doctors 'swap' their practices. Secondly, the sale of a firm or practice in principle implies an obligation on the seller not to compete with the buyer within a reasonable period of time and within a reasonable distance.[16] This can be seen as a case of supplementary interpretation. The clientele is regarded as an essential element of a firm or practice, and the absence of any duty of non-competition would imply that this element is not transferred to the buyer. The parties may specify this duty, but in the absence of such specification, the duty exists for a reasonable period within a reasonable area (relevant market). Although most of the case law deals with commercial firms, the same rule applies to liberal professions, such as medical doctors. Case 19 does not deal with a sale, but with an exchange; this does not, however, change anything as to the obligations of the parties (see art. 1707 C.C.).

Remedies: Richard can obtain an order from the court restraining Spencer from competing in the neighbourhood for a reasonable period.

SPAIN

In a decision of the High Court in 1988,[17] it was held to be contrary to good faith for a lessor of a public house to open a new public house in close

---

[15] Art. 1134 al. 3 C. civ.
[16] Cf. Cass. 2 Jun. 1959, Pas. I 1004; Cass. 24 Sep. 1968, Pas. I 92. See also Neels, RW 1980–1981, 2133; Bouckaert 39 ff.
[17] Judgement of 6 April 1988 (RJA 1988, 3111). But see the High Court judgement of 17 June 1970 (RJA 1970, 3117).

proximity to the other, the possession of which he had transferred to the lessee, provided that both the number and the kind of customers of the first establishment were considered important factors in fixing its price. This approach would be applied to the facts of case 19, because in Spanish law the rules that govern contracts of lease also apply to contracts of exchange.[18]

ITALY

Richard will be able to obtain a court order restraining Spencer from carrying out his plan to set up a new practice in the neighbourhood of his old one.

Under Italian law, the legal position of a doctor, just like that of any other member of a liberal profession, differs from that of a trader (*imprenditore*).[19] For this reason the present case is not covered by the letter of art. 2557 of the Civil Code, which obliges the seller of a *business* to refrain from competing with the buyer for a five-year period after the sale. However, the distinction between the legal position of the member of a liberal profession and that of a trader has been declining in practice.[20] Therefore, if Richard and Spencer's medical practices are organised in such a way that the element of capital can be said to prevail over that of personal work, their case will be governed by analogy with the rule contained in art. 2557.

Moreover, it is clear that even if the facts of case 19 do not support the analogous application of this provision, Spencer should be enjoined from setting up a new practice in the neighbourhood of his old one. For by transferring his practice to his colleague and by leaving Lintz, Spencer has made clear his intention to abstain from interfering with Richard's own activity in the town in which he was formerly based. This conclusion follows from an interpretation of the contract passed between them in a way consonant with good faith.[21]

---

[18] Arts. 1541 and 1553 C. Civ.

[19] Compare arts. 2229–38 c.c. (on the liberal professions) with arts. 2082–5 c.c. (on the *imprenditore*).

[20] The latest manifestation of this trend is the abrogation of the statute prohibiting members of the liberal professions from setting up business entities to carry on their professions: l. 7 Aug. 1997, n. 266, art. 24.1.

[21] De Nova, Giur. it., 1974, I,1, 2045. De Nova cites in support the *Bundesgerichtshof* (BGH) judgement of 18 Dec. 1954, BGHZ 16, 72. On similar facts, the BGH ruled in favour of the doctor seeking enforcement of the agreement in accordance with the good faith principle.

There is certainly no reason why the contract between Richard and Spencer should be held invalid: it is not contrary to public policy nor related to a subject matter which is not within the course of trade (*res extra commercium*).

From a different point of view, it is worth noticing that the usual difficulty of estimating the value of an intangible like a clientele is enhanced by the recent data protection legislation forbidding disclosure between the parties to the contract of the patients' files without their consent.[22]

THE NETHERLANDS

Under Dutch law there is an element of (public) competition law involved here, since the right to establish a general medical practice is limited. Looking at the facts from a strictly private law point of view it would probably be against the intentions of the parties and the economic background of the contract to allow Spencer to return to Lintz. This would seriously harm Richard's economic interests. It is likely that a court would consider the re-establishment of Spencer's practice as breach of his obligation under the contract and would compel Spencer not to re-open a practice in Lintz.

This approach could either be defended as being the result of interpretation in good faith of the contract or on the basis of the supplementary role of good faith. In both views the contract could be said to imply a negative covenant not to return to the place where the practice had originally been established.

The restraining order could also be based on violation of a duty of care (tort of negligence) that Spencer owes Richard. This delictual duty would, however, exist independently from the contractual duty not to return to Lintz.[23] In any case (whether based in contract or tort) a possible damages claim would be governed by arts. 6:95 ff. B.W.; the right to performance of any duty (contractual, delictual or *sui generis*) can be found in art. 3:296 B.W.

ENGLAND

In the absence of any express stipulation by way of restrictive covenant, a vendor of a business (including a professional practice) which includes the element of 'goodwill' owes no obligation not to set up a competing

---

[22] See the Italian discussion to case 18 above, and the reference to l. 31 Dec. 1996, n. 675.
[23] See HR 3 May 1946, NJ 1946, 323 (*Staat der Nederlanden v. Degens*).

business.[24] However, the vendor is not allowed himself or through agents to solicit his former customers, even though he may advertise publicly in the locality of his former business in general terms and he may take on former customers if they come to him.[25] Whether this duty of non-solicitation is 'to be regarded as based on the principle that he [the vendor] is not entitled to depreciate that which he has sold, or as arising from an implied contract to abstain from any act intended to deprive the purchaser of that which has been sold to him and to restore it to the vendor', the obligation may be enforced by injunction in equity.[26] For Lord *Macnaghten*, it is 'not an honest thing to pocket the price and then to recapture the subject of sale'.[27] This means that while Richard would not be able to prevent Spencer from setting up a new practice in the neighbourhood, he could apply for a *quia timet* injunction to prevent him personally from soliciting his former patients if he could establish a danger of substantial damage being suffered by him if one were not granted.

It should be noted that the English law position denying any *implied* terms as to non-competition has meant that it has long been very common for parties to contracts to make express provision as to restrictions on setting up a rival business. Such terms however are 'in restraint of trade' and are, therefore, *prima facie* illegal and ineffective, being valid only if 'reasonable' and not contrary to the public interest.[28] (There is a further requirement that the parties must have an interest in the stipulation which merits protection, but in the case of sale (and, presumably, exchange) of a business, this is satisfied by the purchaser's 'proprietary interest' in the goodwill of the business he has bought.[29]) The requirement of 'reasonableness' is decided according to the character of the business to be protected, the extent of the area of operation of the restrictions and the duration of the restrictions.[30]

IRELAND

On the sale (and presumably, also the exchange) of businesses or practices together with their goodwill, Irish courts would not imply a condition preventing the seller from subsequently competing with the purchaser, but they would imply certain other obligations on the part of the seller, in par-

---

[24] Whish, in: *Halsbury* § 11; *Trego v. Hunt* [1896] AC 7, at 20.   [25] Ibid.
[26] *Trego v. Hunt* [1896] AC 7, 21 *per* Lord *Herschell*.   [27] Ibid., at 25.
[28] Guest, *Chitty on Contracts* § 16–066 ff.; and see *Esso Petroleum Co. Ltd v. Harper's Garage (Stourport) Ltd* [1968] AC 269, esp. at 295.   [29] Treitel 414.   [30] Treitel 417 ff.

ticular that he should not directly or through agents solicit his former customers, clients or patients.[31] The legal basis for such an obligation not to solicit former customers is derived from the notion that a seller of goodwill cannot derogate from what he has sold.[32] It should be noted, however, that there is an argument which has not been tested before the courts, that any such obligation of non-solicitation does not, and indeed cannot, exist in perpetuity, an analogy being drawn with covenants in restraint of trade which must be reasonably limited in time to be effective.[33] Even if such an argument were accepted, it is unlikely that an obligation of non-solicitation would be limited to a period of a year.

More generally, the attitude of the courts to the interpretation of an agreement such as the one found in case 19 would be influenced by common practice in which those purchasing businesses will, if properly advised, limit any competition that may emanate from the seller of the business by seeking a specific restrictive covenant.

SCOTLAND

What are the terms of the agreed swap? As a general rule contracts which involve an undue interference with personal liberty are void as being oppressive. This is qualified to the extent that it may be lawful, if certain conditions are satisfied, to secure freedom from competition by contracts, usually termed restrictive covenants, under which a party undertakes not to carry on a particular trade or profession. Unless there is a restrictive covenant in the contract, i.e. a clause which aims to limit a party's liberty to practise his trade or profession, then there is nothing that the courts can do to protect Richard's interests.

Such clauses have presented difficulties for the courts because on the one hand the courts wish to uphold contracts; they are reluctant to release a party from an obligation freely entered into. But, on the other hand, they also wish to uphold individual liberty, e.g. a person's right to have a livelihood. The Scottish courts' approach to restrictive covenants is as follows. Restrictive covenants are *prima facie* void and unreasonable. They will only be upheld if reasonable (i) between the parties, and (ii) in the public interest. They are most readily enforced in contracts for the sale of a business (we can liken the swap to a sale). The restriction must go no further than is reasonably required.

---

[31] *Trego v. Hunt* [1896] AC 7, as applied and extended in Ireland by *Gurgan v. Rustle* [1931] IR 152.   [32] Clark 336.   [33] *Nordenfelt v. Maxim Nordenfelt* [1894] AC 535.

While *prima facie* void, it is relatively easy to prove that the restrictive covenant is reasonable. The test is whether the agreement is *reasonable* as between the parties and consistent with the interests of the parties. In contracts for the sale of a business, the courts will enforce a restrictive covenant provided it protects a legitimate interest; *Deacons v. Bridge.*[34] However, while it is open to the purchaser to restrict competition by the seller, the converse does not hold; *Giblin v. Murdoch.*[35] In this instance we have a swap, so who is the hypothetical seller or purchaser? It is likely that had there been a restrictive covenant in the swap agreement it would have placed a restriction on both parties.

If there is no such clause then the courts will not interfere with the liberty of a person to work. Starting from the premise that restrictive covenants are *prima facie* void and unenforceable, a court would not write one into a contract.

DENMARK AND NORWAY

In the case in point it has to be decided whether the swap entails that the doctor who now wants to move back has bound himself to abstain from setting up a competing practice, or whether his subsequent action may merely be regarded as the breach of an implied condition entitling the other party to terminate the contract.

There is a ruling by the Norwegian *Høyesterett* in a case which is not entirely dissimilar.[36] Doctor A sold his real property and various chattels in order to move out of the district. He sold the chattels to his rival doctor B who paid a high price, precisely in order to induce doctor A to move. When a short while later A moved back and resumed his practice, doctor B refused to pay the purchase price for the chattels. The *Høyesterett* held that doctor A had not undertaken any duty to abstain from resuming a practice in the district. However, the precondition for doctor B's purchase of A's chattels ceased to exist when A resumed his practice, and for that reason B was held to be in a position to request the sale of the chattels to be cancelled.

There is no reason, *per se*, why an agreement to swap practices should not entail a prohibition on starting competing activities in the same place. Nevertheless, West Nordic courts of law would probably still require such a restrictive covenant to follow fairly clearly from the agreement, especially where the liberal professions rather than typical commercial

---

[34] [1984] 2 All ER 19.   [35] 1979 SLT (Sh Ct) 5.   [36] Rt. 1898, p. 135.

businesses are concerned.[37] In keeping with the old ruling from Norway's *Høyesterett* in Rt. 1898, p. 135, the presumption here must be that no agreement exists concerning non-competition.

However, according to West Nordic law it is often difficult to decide which considerations may still be said to form part of the agreement, and which of them merely constitute a prerequisite, or presupposition, of the agreement. In the one case we would be dealing with a contractual obligation which may or may not have been breached, in the other with the basis for the agreement which may or may not have ceased to exist.[38] This delimitation depends on the facts of each case. In the present case, which raises the problem of non-competition, we are dealing with a contractual obligation which ought to have been evident from the agreement itself and cannot merely be deduced from the parties' assumptions on entering into the agreement. The attitude to the issue in this case is probably predetermined by the fact that it relates to the freedom to practise a liberal profession rather than to a typical restraint of trade between professional businessmen.

SWEDEN

The two doctors did not expressly agree not to move back and compete. Hence, the question is whether this was an implied condition, sanctioned in such a way that Spencer could be prohibited, by court order, from moving back his practice for a reasonable period of time. As far as I know there is no case law on this point. Presumably restraint of competition clauses, sanctioned by prohibitions, are not easily implied. (Clauses in restraint of competition can be adjusted under s. 38 of the Contracts Act of 1915 if they are too burdensome.)

Another question is whether Richard may terminate the swap contract on the basis of incorrect presuppositions, or whether he may be entitled to a reduction of the price, here converted to money as a return of a part of his practice in Castle Combe is not practical. A right to termination or price reduction is probably available, especially if Spencer treats his old patients, since both parties acted in the belief that they would not compete, and since it was within Spencer's control to stay or move.[39]

---

[37] Andersen/Madsen/Nørgaard 413 f.

[38] Gomard, *Forholdet* 140–50; Hagstrøm, *Fragmenter* 38 ff.

[39] Cf. NJA 1949, p. 134, where an employer was entitled to cease paying a severance allowance when the former employee started to compete; no petition was lodged so as to order the employee to stop competing.

FINLAND

As there was no provision limiting competition in the swap agreement, Richard cannot get a court order to prevent Spencer from carrying out his plan. Finnish law is reluctant to recognise limitations on competition even where agreed upon (they may be adjusted to be 'reasonable'; see the Contracts Act of 1929, s. 38). To read such limitations into the contract as implied conditions would be alien to Finnish legal thinking.

Editors' comparative observations

Here, there are differences of result among the legal systems, some accepting a duty not to set up in competition, others denying it.

(i) In the absence of express stipulation, there is *no* duty not to set up a competing business in French law, English and Irish law, Scots law, West Nordic law and Finnish law. However, this general position is nuanced in some of the systems, so that, for example, in English law Spencer is not entitled to solicit his former patients and in French law the right to compete is qualified to the extent that Spencer may not engage in disloyal behaviour or interfere with the 'goodwill' of the medical practice.

(ii) Other systems (German, Greek, Austrian, Belgian, Spanish, Italian, Dutch law) do indeed deny that Spencer has the right to set up in the same town for a reasonable period after the swap. This result is usually based on a (supplementary) interpretation of the contract, guided by the precepts of good faith. This approach would typically result in Richard being granted the restraining order which is mentioned in the case itself.

(iii) Swedish courts might well resort to the doctrine of incorrect presuppositions which may lead either to termination of the contract or to a reduction of the purchase price.

Case 20: Prescription I

Case

Geoffrey has a claim in damages against Hugh which is about to prescribe. Geoffrey therefore requests payment and threatens to sue Hugh. Hugh requests some more time for considering the matter and for consulting his legal advisers about some issues concerning the claim. He communicates his intention to Geoffrey not to raise the defence of prescription. Some months later, Hugh informs Geoffrey that he is not prepared to pay. Geoffrey thereupon sues Hugh. The latter raises the defence of prescription.

Discussions

GERMANY

In German law, a claim is not extinguished on account of the expiry of the relevant prescription period. The debtor is merely granted a peremptory defence: he is entitled to refuse performance.[1]

Delictual claims prescribe in three years (§ 852 I BGB), contractual claims sounding in damages prescribe, as a rule, in thirty years (§ 195 BGB). Whatever the prescription period applicable to the present case may be, it may have been interrupted or suspended. If prescription is interrupted, the time which elapsed before the interruption is not taken into account; if the cause of the interruption ceases to exist, prescription begins to run anew (§ 217 BGB). Suspension of prescription, on the other hand, merely has the effect that the period during which prescription is

---

[1] Cf. generally Zimmermann, in: *German National Reports XIVth Congress* 153 ff.

suspended is not counted; when the cause of suspension ends, it is therefore the old prescription period that continues to run (§ 205 BGB).

Acknowledgement of the claim by the debtor *vis-à-vis* his creditor interrupts prescription (§ 208 BGB). On the assumption that Hugh does not merely want to consult his legal advisers about the extent of the damages but rather about whether he is liable to pay or not, and that his declaration to Geoffrey has to be interpreted accordingly, there is no acknowledgement of the claim on the part of Hugh.

Prescription may, however, have been suspended during the negotiations about the claim by way of application of § 852 II BGB ('Pending negotiations between the persons bound to make compensation and entitled to receive compensation concerning the compensation to be paid, prescription is suspended until the one or the other party refuses to continue the negotiations'). This rule applies directly only to delictual claims but it is held to be applicable by analogy to contractual damage claims.[2] The rule today contained in § 852 II BGB is regarded as a special manifestation of the principle of good faith (*Treu und Glauben*)[3] and was recognised as such by the courts before its enactment in 1978.[4] Similar rules exist in §§ 14 StVG (Road Traffic Law), 39 LuftVG (Air Traffic Law), 11 HaftpflG (Legal Liability Law), 32 AtomG (Atomic Energy Law), 3 Nr. 3 PflVersG (Compulsory Insurance Law).

The term 'negotiation' in § 852 II BGB has to be interpreted extensively.[5] Any exchange of opinion is covered which may reasonably lead the claimant to believe that his claim has not been finally rejected by the other party.[6] In the present case, this requirement is met since Hugh has indicated that he wants to think the matter over again. The defence of prescription can only be raised successfully if the claim would have prescribed even after the period of negotiation has been taken into consideration in calculating the period of prescription.

GREECE

On the facts of case 20 the defence of prescription which Hugh raises contradicts the notion of good faith, but in Greek law the law of prescription is a matter of the public interest (art. 275 Gr. C.C.) and for this reason a general legislative provision such as the one concerning the abuse of a

---

[2] *Münchener Kommentar*/Mertens § 852, n. 64.   [3] BGH NJW-RR 1990, 664 (665).
[4] *Münchener Kommentar*/Mertens § 852, n. 64.   [5] *Palandt*/Thomas § 852, n. 18.
[6] *Münchener Kommentar*/Mertens § 852, n. 65; *Palandt*/Thomas § 852, n. 18.

right (art. 281 Gr. C.C.) cannot be applied. However, a part of Greek juristic opinion[7] accepts that resort to a defence of prescription may constitute an abuse of right in circumstances where there is an *obvious* breach of good faith, unfairness or behaviour *contra bonos mores*. On the facts of case 20, this would be the case as the situation results from Hugh's own previous behaviour. If this position were followed then Geoffrey could object to the defence of prescription on the basis of an abuse of right with the result that the court would reject this defence.

An earlier decision of the *Areopagus*[8] held that the defence of prescription should be suspended only in the context of art. 255 Gr. C.C., namely, in the situation where the person who wishes to rely on it maliciously prevented the claimant from bringing his claim within the last six months of the prescription period, a circumstance which is clearly not present on the facts of case 20. However, other cases[9] have simply accepted that reliance on the defence of prescription may constitute an abuse of right.[10]

AUSTRIA

Under § 1502 ABGB, before a period of prescription has expired a debtor is not able to waive the defence of prescription nor to extend the period, though such a waiver of the defence is effective after the period has expired.[11] On the facts of case 20, therefore, Hugh's statement that he intends not to rely on a defence of prescription does not extend the prescription period and he could therefore, in principle, subsequently rely on such a defence.

However, in Austrian law it is generally agreed that where a prescription period is just about to expire it is reasonable to expect the parties to come to an extra-judicial settlement of their dispute rather than be forced to go to law. Courts and scholars have indicated several ways in which this expectation may be prevented from being disappointed. We will examine them in turn and see whether they help Geoffrey.

First, a teleological approach is sometimes adopted, according to which negotiations towards reaching a settlement have the effect of suspending the running of any prescription period.[12] As a result the creditor may still

---

[7] See Simantiras no. 1075, p. 774.   [8] 882/1983 EEN 51, 348.
[9] Areopagus 673/1974 NoB 1975, 285; Court of Appeal Piraeus 928/1994 EllDni 37, 377.
[10] Areopagus 693/1992 EllDni 34 (1993), 1282.
[11] OGH in SZ 47/104 (1974); SZ 50/110 (1977).
[12] Bydlinski, JBl 1967, 130; OGH in JBl 1989, 460.

sue, even if negotiations ultimately fail after the normal period of pre-scription has elapsed. However, this approach requires that the parties carry on specific negotiations concerning proposals for a settlement of their outstanding points of difference. In the case in hand this require-ment is not satisfied.[13]

Secondly, it is widely held that, where a debtor pleads a defence of pre-scription having previously declared his intention not to do so, a creditor will be granted an *exceptio doli* (defence of bad faith).[14] This approach to the problem is based on the *natürlichen Rechtsgrundsatz* (principle of natural law, in terms of § 7 ABGB) that no one should gain a legal advantage by acting in bad faith. Applying it to the facts of case 20, one would have to conclude that Geoffrey would enjoy the protection of an *exceptio doli* if Hugh were to raise the defence of prescription. However, it should be noted that some scholars consider it doubtful that a person can be consid-ered 'in bad faith' if he simply invokes the protection of a binding legisla-tive provision.[15]

Thirdly, some authors argue that, by way of application of § 1502 ABGB, a waiver of the defence of prescription is effective not only if it has been declared after the prescription period has expired; even before its expiry a debtor may waive his right to rely on those parts of the prescription period which have already elapsed.[16] According to this view, Hugh could also not successfully raise the defence of prescription since he waived his right to rely on prescription immediately before expiry of the period. Thus, he has waived almost the entire period of prescription.

FRANCE

Geoffrey may try to counter Hugh's defence of prescription on the basis that he acted in bad faith in stating that he was not going to raise the defence of prescription and then, nevertheless, raising it. He could do so either on the basis (i) that Hugh's behaviour amounted to an acknowledge-ment of a debt under art. 2248 of the Civil Code; (ii) that Hugh and Geoffrey had reached an agreement suspending the prescription period under art. 2220 of the Civil Code, or (iii) on the grounds of fraud.

(i) Under art. 2248 of the Civil Code a period of prescription is inter-rupted once a debtor acknowledges his debt. In acknowledging his debt,

---

[13] OGH in SZ 62/64 and 150 (1989).
[14] OGH in SZ 48/79 (1975); ZVR 1991/38; Schubert, in: *Rummel, ABGB II* § 1501 n. 2.
[15] Mader, JBl 1986, 1; Koziol/Welser, *Bürgerliches Recht I* 190.   [16] Ibid.

even partially, the debtor is deemed to waive the defence of prescription. No formalities are required in order to acknowledge a debt. Such an acknowledgement can be express or implied, such as by asking for extra time to pay[17] or for a reduction[18] or by any other acts or attitudes which the courts deem indicative of such an acknowledgement, provided that it is unequivocal.[19] Whether an acknowledgement has taken place is a question of fact which is for the judges of the lower courts to determine.[20]

If Hugh's behaviour is considered to amount to an acknowledgement of his debt, this interrupts the prescription which starts running again as soon as Geoffrey sues him. The issue here therefore turns on a question of fact: is Hugh's behaviour sufficiently unequivocal for Geoffrey to rely on art. 2248 of the Civil Code? The request for more time could be taken as an implicit acknowledgement when coupled with the act of taking legal advice, but it is a borderline case.

(ii) Article 2220 of the Civil Code states that it is not possible to waive the defence of prescription before it has been acquired. It is worth noting, however, that in a case of anticipatory waiver, the *Cour de cassation* has held this provision not to prevent the parties from agreeing to suspend the prescription period provided that the agreement is concluded after the obligation has arisen and before the period of prescription expires.[21] This fairly recent case confirms an older one decided by the *Cour de cassation*[22] where it was held that when a debtor has asked that the prescription be stayed, and the creditor has accepted this request, prescription cannot run in favour of the debtor during the suspension which he requested. This situation is comparable to the one on the facts of case 20. Thus, Geoffrey could argue that he and Hugh concluded an agreement to suspend the prescription period until he had taken time to consider the matter and until he had taken legal advice, this agreement taking effect as an enforceable contract (known as a 'tolling contract'). In the present case, Geoffrey will be able to claim the benefit of the prescription running afresh from the moment Hugh announced that he was not going to pay.

(iii) Thirdly, in a recent case on similar facts to those found in case 20, the *Cour de cassation*[23] held that an insurance company had, by 'fraudulent

---

[17] Montpellier 15 May 1872, DP 1874.2.165.   [18] Ass. plén. 27 Jun. 1969, JCP 1969.II.16029.
[19] Civ. (1) 25 Jan. 1954, S 1954.1.199; Civ. (3) 24 Oct. 1984, JCP 1985.IV.6; Civ. (1) 22 May 1991, Bull. civ. I, no. 164, p. 109.
[20] Civ. (3) 20 Feb. 1969, Bull. civ. III, no. 158; 29 Apr. 1986, Bull. civ. III, no. 54, RTDCiv 1987.763 obs. Mestre; 17 Jan. 1996, Bull. civ. III, no. 15.
[21] Civ. (1) 13 Mar. 1968, JCP 1969.II.15903 note Prieur.   [22] Civ. 28 Nov. 1865, D 1867.1.225.
[23] Civ. (1) 28 Oct. 1991, Bull. civ. I, no. 282.

manipulations', committed an abuse against the beneficiary of a contract of insurance and that this fraud prevented it from invoking the defence of prescription. The insurance company had dragged things out under the pretext of waiting for a criminal investigation and had subsequently attempted to raise prescription as a defence. In a similar way, Hugh keeps Geoffrey waiting and asks for more time to consider the claim. Hugh's dilatory and contradictory behaviour could be interpreted as acting in bad faith.

BELGIUM

According to contemporary Belgian law, waiver is a unilateral act, which is binding without acceptance by the beneficiary. This corresponds to the general rule in Belgian law, that unilateral promises for which the promisor does not require acceptance are binding without such acceptance.[24] This would appear to be appropriate since there is no obligation on the part of the promisee. Also, it follows from the letters of art. 1106 C.C., which requires only the consent of the party who binds himself, not that of the other party.

Moreover, although a debtor cannot normally waive his right to invoke the defence of prescription before the period of prescription has elapsed, the courts have allowed him to do so with regard to the *time* that has elapsed:[25] prescription then simply starts to run again. Acknowledgement of the debt is a sufficient, but not a necessary condition for such a waiver.

Thus, since Hugh has communicated his intention to Geoffrey not to raise the defence of prescription, the case is simple under Belgian law. The communication of intention is a unilateral legal act which is binding, and the prescription period simply starts to run again from that moment. Whether this communication of intention by Hugh was followed by an acceptance by Geoffrey is irrelevant.

SPAIN

In Spanish law, the type of issue raised by these facts has attracted the application of a well-known set of rules which the courts have constructed in developing the principle of good faith found in art. 7 of the Civil Code. Under the 'rule of previous conduct', a person who has a right is bound by

---

[24] This follows from Cass. 9 May 1980, Arr. 1132 and 1139; Cass. 3 Sep. 1981, T. Aann. 1982, 131.   [25] See Cass. 23 Oct. 1986, TBBR 1988, 209 note A. van Oevelen.

his own conduct in relation to the exercise of the right where (i) this conduct was *concluyente*[26] and (ii) it has created in another person the legitimate confidence that the right will be exercised in a certain way and (iii) that other person has relied on the conduct in such a way that it would be inequitable for the first person to go back on it and exercise his right in a different manner. It is not necessary for a person's earlier 'clear conduct' to amount to a contractual promise.[27] According to the Constitutional Court, the 'rule of previous conduct' 'finds its ultimate foundations in the protection which confidence seriously placed on other people's conduct deserves and in the rule of good faith, which requires a person's conduct to be consistent, and thereby limits the exercise of his rights'.[28]

ITALY

According to art. 2936 of the Civil Code any agreement intended to modify the legal rules governing extinctive prescription is void. A corollary of this rule is the provision contained in art. 2937 of the Civil Code according to which a debtor may waive the defence of prescription only after expiry of the period of prescription. Articles 2941–2 of the Civil Code list the circumstances which suspend the running of any limitation period, but none of them apply to the facts of case 20. Under these auspices, then, Hugh's declaration of intention not to raise the defence of prescription is null and void, being contrary to *ius cogens*.

Nevertheless, though Hugh's promise has no effect as such, his conduct may be taken as an acknowledgement of Geoffrey's right and such an acknowledgement interrupts the running of a prescription period.[29] Italian courts and legal scholars adopt a liberal interpretation of the concept of 'acknowledgement' of a right in this context and so a reassuring communication addressed by a debtor to his creditor stating that 'there is no reason to worry about the running of the prescription period' would be held to amount to an acknowledgement of the other party's right.[30] Nevertheless, on several occasions, the *Corte di Cassazione* has

---

[26] See the Spanish report to case 22 below.
[27] See, *inter alia*, the High Court judgement of 21 May 1982 (RJA 1982, 2588).
[28] Judgement 73/1988 of 21 April 1988 (BOE 5 May 1988).   [29] Art. 2944 c.c.
[30] See Cass., 27 Jun. 1996, n. 5939; Cass., 21 Jan. 1994, n. 576. In both cases the communication was addressed by the *Ente Ferrovie dello Stato* to its employees; it concerned the remuneration of overtime work that should have been financed by the legislature. See also: Cass., 15 Feb. 1992, n. 1866. Legal scholars adopt the same approach, see, e.g., Geri/Breccia/Busnelli/Natoli 400 ff.

denied that negotiations with a view to settlement imply any such recognition of the creditor's right.[31]

All in all, Hugh's declaration of intention will probably be interpreted as an acknowledgement of Geoffrey's right because he has implicitly recognised the existence of the claim by asking for some more time for considering the matter and for consulting his legal advisers 'about some issues concerning the claim'. But a word of caution is necessary: one would get the opposite outcome should the issues in question concern the very existence of the claim.

The Italian approach to this type of case is influenced by two factors. First, the *Corte di Cassazione* refrains from interfering with the lower courts' findings that on the facts an acknowledgement of the plaintiff's right has occurred and this means that the *Corte di Cassazione* need not declare that any given set of facts entails the recognition of the claimant's rights *as a matter of law*. Secondly, by holding that statements and acts which do not necessarily express an intention to acknowledge the other party's right constitute an 'acknowledgement' of that right, this traditional approach protects the creditor in this sort of circumstance without openly acknowledging the possibility of relaxation of the strict legislative rule on the basis of the requirement of good faith. Thus, an equitable doctrine inspired by the need to deter fraud and to protect good faith thrives in disguise under the heading of a debtor's acknowledgement of his creditor's rights.[32] The ultimate explanation for this apparent rather than real deference to the debtor's intention lies in the difficulty of fully accepting the idea of a creative or corrective role of interpretation, which is itself the legacy of a positivistic idea of the Civil Code as a manifestation of legislative *imperium*.[33]

THE NETHERLANDS

Waiver of a right (here: the defence of prescription) has to be expressed very clearly. This has not happened here. However, under the circumstances of cases 20 and 21, both parties are aware of the prescription

---

[31] Cass., 7 May 1982, n. 2482; Cass., 27 Apr. 1973, n. 1149. See, however, Cass., 12 Aug. 1992, n. 9539: if the negotiations between the parties abort because they do not agree on the value of their claims the lower court can nevertheless find that each party recognised the other party's right.   [32] Cf. Ranieri, Digesto, 4th edn, sez. civ., VII, 1991, 328.

[33] See, on this point, Gambaro, in: *Enciclopedia* 6; Ranieri, Digesto, 4th edn, sez. civ., VII, 1991, 330–1. The traditional attitude mentioned in the text has come under attack in recent years.

period running. Given the acts of Hugh, he cannot now raise the defence of prescription. This would be against good faith.[34]

ENGLAND

English law provides by statute that rights of action are limited in time, this being found in relation to contractual remedies principally in the Limitation Act 1980, though equitable remedies, such as the action for specific performance, are governed by the equitable doctrines of laches (delay) and acquiescence. It is to be noted that statutes of limitation bar the remedy, rather than extinguishing the right, and therefore create a defence available to a party to litigation.

Various ways exist of countering the defence of prescription. First, where a party has acknowledged the debt, under s. 29 of the Limitation Act 1980 the limitation period starts running again from the time of acknowledgement. However, there is no such acknowledgement on the facts of case 20, for the statute requires that it be in writing and signed by the person making it and that the amount of the debt, if not stated in the acknowledgement, must be capable of being ascertained by other means.[35]

Secondly, a contract by a person with another not to rely on a defence of limitation is valid and binding on that person.[36] In case 20, it is said simply that Hugh 'communicates his intention' to Geoffrey regarding the defence, and this would not be enough without more to constitute a contract not to do so as contract requires the agreement of both parties and consideration. As to the latter, while Geoffrey's forbearance to sue Hugh is detrimental to him (Geoffrey), this would not constitute consideration moving from him as there is no evidence that this was done as the *price* of Hugh's promise not to rely on the defence of limitation.[37]

Thirdly, Geoffrey may be able to rely on the equitable doctrine of promissory estoppel (sometimes known as 'forbearance in equity'). According to this doctrine, where a person promises not to enforce a legal right against another person and the latter relies on this promise to his detriment, then the court may, if it is equitable to do so, prevent the promisor from going back on the promise.[38] This doctrine has been applied to the

---

[34] Cf. *Hoge Raad* 10 February 1967, NJ 1967, 212 (*De Zaan v. Intercoal*).

[35] Guest, *Chitty on Contracts* § 28–072; *Jones v. Bellgrove Properties Ltd* [1949] 2 KB 700.

[36] *Lubovsky v. Snelling* [1944] 1 KB 44.   [37] *Combe v. Combe* [1951] 2 KB 215.

[38] *Hughes v. Metropolitan Rly Co.* (1877) 2 App Cas 439.

situation where a person promises not to rely on a defence of limitation of action[39] (and indeed on the facts of the case in question there was no express promise, the fact that the defendant had made an admission of liability being treated as having the same import). It is submitted that Geoffrey will in principle be able to rely on this doctrine of promissory estoppel so as to prevent Hugh from relying on the defence of limitation.

IRELAND

In Irish law, periods of prescription of contractual causes of action for damages are generally governed by the Statute of Limitations 1957, and in particular s. 11 thereof.

The application of statutory limitation periods is moderated by the equitable doctrine of estoppel under which the courts do not allow a person who makes a representation to resile from it where to do so would prejudice the person to whom the representation was made.[40]

It is clear from the judgement of the Supreme Court in *Doran v. Thomas Thompson and Sons Ltd*[41] that Hugh would not be able to resile from his clear undertaking not to rely on the defence of prescription, though it should be noted that if Hugh had merely requested time to consider his position, it would be less likely that an estoppel would be found.

SCOTLAND

The principle of prescription in relation to contractual and related obligations is that after the lapse of a certain period of time the obligation is extinguished. Thereafter, performance of the obligation cannot be enforced and there will be no claim for damages for non-performance.

The particular form of prescription we are concerned with here is negative prescription; the right/liability is extinguished by lapse of time. The principle is stated in *MacDonald v. North Bank of Scotland*: 'The principle clearly emerges that the non-enforcement by a creditor of a contractual right for the prescriptive period infers an irrebuttable presumption that the right has been abandoned, and therefore that the correlative obligation has been extinguished.'[42]

---

[39] *Wright v. John Bagnall & Sons Ltd* [1900] 2 QB 240.
[40] The leading Supreme Court cases in this area are *Doran v. Thomas Thompson and Sons Ltd* [1978] IR 223 and *Boyce v. Brady* (unreported, 4 July 1986), and see Brady/Kerr 171 ff.
[41] Above.   [42] 1942 SC 369, at 373; 1942 SLT 196, at 202 *per* Lord Justice-Clerk *Cooper*.

The rules regarding both long and short negative prescription are stated in the Prescription and Limitation (Scotland) Act 1973 (as amended). This case is probably one of short negative prescription. Section 6 of the 1973 Act states that if after the appropriate date, an obligation to which s. 6 of the Act applies has subsisted for a continuous period of five years (i) without any relevant claim having been made in relation to the obligation, and (ii) without the subsistence of the obligation having been relevantly acknowledged, then as from the expiration of that period the obligation will be extinguished. It is the right that prescribes, not the remedy. It is not permitted to contract out of negative prescription whether long or short.[43] Consequently, the defence of prescription will stand even though Geoffrey and Hugh might have agreed otherwise (assuming that the prescriptive period has passed).

However, Geoffrey is afforded protection by the *caveat* to s. 6 which states that in the computation of the period for prescription one must disregard any period during which the creditor was induced to refrain from making a relevant claim in relation to the obligation by reason of fraud on the part of the debtor or any person acting on his behalf, or error induced by words or conduct of the debtor or any person acting on his behalf.[44] This means that from the moment that Hugh told Geoffrey that he would not raise the defence of prescription (and possibly from the moment Hugh told Geoffrey that he wished to seek legal advice regarding the claim), the clock will stop, and this will probably mean that Geoffrey's claim for damages will not be time-barred. The period would not be disregarded if Geoffrey could with reasonable diligence have discovered the true facts.

For the purposes of this exercise I have assumed that the claim for damages is one of the thirteen obligations which the 1973 Act covers regarding short negative prescription.

The common law plea of personal bar is unlikely here given the statutory protection afforded by s. 6(4)(a), but the principle is worthy of mention. There is no formal or general Scottish definition of personal bar. *Rankine*[45] cites English authority as a good explication: '[T]he rule of law is clear that, where one by his words or conduct wilfully causes another to believe the existence of a certain state of things, and induces him to act on that belief, so as to alter his own previous position, the former is

---

[43] Section 13, Prescription and Limitation (Scotland) Act 1973, as amended by the Prescription and Limitation (Scotland) Act 1984, s. 6(1), Sch. 1, § 5.

[44] Section 6(4)(a), Prescription and Limitation (Scotland) Act 1973.

[45] *A Treatise on the Law of Personal Bar in Scotland*, at 2.

concluded from averring against the latter a different state of things as existing at the same time.'[46] In *Gatty v. Maclaine*,[47] Lord Chancellor *Birkenhead* explained the premise of the plea of personal bar by representation as follows: 'Where A has by his word or conduct justified B in believing that a certain state of facts exists, and B has acted upon such belief to his prejudice, A is not permitted to affirm against B that a different state of facts existed at the same time.'

Therefore, personal bar is different from contract. It is an equitable doctrine which operates by intercepting or shutting out all contrary pleas and proof. The party who pleads personal bar must show that in reliance on the other's words or acts he has altered his position and altered it to his disadvantage. So at common law, if Geoffrey could demonstrate that he had altered his position to his detriment because of Hugh's statement or conduct, then Hugh would be personally barred from asserting his rights.

DENMARK AND NORWAY

The rules concerning prescription, or limitation of claims, are laid down by legislation in all the Nordic countries. In this area there is no West Nordic uniformity of law, since details such as the length of the period of limitation and the starting point from which that period is to be calculated vary. The basic structure of the limitation legislation is, however, the same. Limitation is only interrupted when an action is brought or on acknowledgement of the claim. An acknowledgement is only seen to exist if the debtor has made a statement which may fully constitute a new basis for a claim according to Norwegian law,[48] whereas the Danish rules seem less strict.[49] In Norway, the requirements as to acknowledgement are thus very strict. It is a well-known phenomenon in Norwegian law that a party may 'negotiate himself into limitation'. It is not unusual that a claim is filed, e.g., with an insurance company, that negotiations are subsequently held to determine the amount of damages, and that the party liable finally invokes limitation in spite of the discussions which may have gone on for several years. Norwegian law, at least, does not in principle prevent the debtor from invoking prescription. The matter would be different if one were to assume that the debtor has accepted a suspension of the period of limitation while negotiations are under way. This, however, presupposes

---

[46] *Pickard v. Sears* (1837) 6 Ad & El 469, *per Denman* C.J., at 747.   [47] 1921 SC (HL) 1.
[48] Cf. Holmboe s. 143; for a less strict view, see Kjønstad/Tjomsland 106 ff.
[49] Gomard, *Obligationsret* 3 234.

an agreement; the *travaux préparatoires* of the Norwegian statute on limitation[50] seem to indicate that such an agreement must be express, and
may not be implied.[51] Alternatively, it may be argued that the defence of
limitation has been waived. Such an approach may commend itself in
cases where negotiations continue beyond the time when, in the opinion
of the debtor, limitation has occurred. Danish law seems to have a less
strict approach. In U 1963, p. 87 the Danish Supreme Court held that a
mere stipulation in a company's published accounts was sufficient, under
the circumstances, to interrupt the period of limitation.

Regarding case 20 itself, it is stated that 'Hugh requests some more time
for considering the matter and for consulting his legal advisers about
some issues concerning the claim.' This is obviously not an acknowledgement of the claim. Basically, therefore, the limitation period continues to
run. It is then stated that '[Hugh] communicates his intention to Geoffrey
not to raise the defence of prescription.' This would be deemed to be a sufficient basis for asserting that the limitation period has been waived in
Danish law, and possibly even in Norwegian law.

SWEDEN

Provided that Geoffrey did not request payment in writing, no interruption of the limitation period has taken place with the effect that a new
limitation period of ten years would have started since Hugh did not
admit his indebtedness, not even orally (Limitation Act of 1981, s. 5).
However, if the alleged debtor promises the creditor not to invoke limitation during negotiations, the limitation is suspended.[52] The same probably applies as soon as the debtor expresses himself in a way that could
reasonably be understood as temporary waiver. In this case Hugh communicated his intention to Geoffrey not to raise the defence of prescription.
Whether this amounts to a binding promise is a question of interpretation
(cf. comfort letter cases such as *Kleinwort Benson Ltd v. Malaysia Mining
Corp.*[53] etc.). According to Swedish case law concerning comfort letters, the
expressed intention to supply the subsidiary company with sufficient
capital is equivalent to a promise.[54] Consequently, Hugh would not be permitted to rely on limitation, if Geoffrey requests payment in writing or
sues him shortly after the negotiations have broken down.

---

[50] *Lov om foreldelse av fordringer av 18. mai 1979 nr. 18.*   [51] Hagstrøm, *Lov og Rett* 1997, 385 ff.
[52] NJA 1971, p. 429. This case was decided before the new legislation but should still be
relevant.   [53] [1989] 1 WLR 379.   [54] NJA 1995, p. 586.

FINLAND

According to the Finnish law of obligations the mere *request* by Geoffrey interrupts the prescription of his claim in damages (Prescription Act of 1868 (Si 715), s. 1). For this reason it is irrelevant whether or not Hugh has promised not to invoke prescription. (An effect similar to the creditor's request may, at least under certain circumstances, be given to the debtor's admission that there may be a certain debt and that the issue will be investigated further.) Both the existence of a request and of an admission are, of course, questions of evidence.

There are, however, special claims in damages (e.g. in labour law) where, in the place of the normal ten-year prescription period, shorter statutory prescription periods are applicable. Here the claim must, as a rule, be brought before the court within the relevant period. In such situations promises concerning the intention not to invoke prescription might be relevant.

Generally speaking, prescription periods rely on unilaterally mandatory norms in such a manner that they may be *shortened* from the beginning (but not in an unconscionable manner). They may, however, not be contractually *extended ab initio*.[55] These rules are not based upon statutes or judicial practice but on legal literature.

In any case, a promise given by the alleged debtor *after* the damage has occurred is fully valid, since whether he wants to invoke the defence of prescription is in the debtor's discretion. The question in the present case, however, is whether there is only a declaration of intention or a binding promise. There is no rule which is directly applicable, and cases from judicial practice are extremely scarce, too. As for legal literature, one may refer to the recent treatise by *Hemmo*.[56] He relies on the general principle in the Contracts Act of 1929 of protecting reliance: if the addressee could with good reason regard the declaration by the debtor as binding, the binding effect should be recognised. But even here one should stress the relevance of a holistic assessment of all the relevant circumstances. The Supreme Court has in a recent decision accepted a binding tender to have been made, where, although the decision had been taken by a municipal board rather than the municipal executive board, the addressee could reasonably conclude from the discussions with the chief engineer of the municipality that the approval by the executive board was not needed and that the construction work was to begin as soon as possible.[57]

[55] See Halila/Ylöstalo, *passim*.   [56] *Sopimusoikeus* 77 ff., esp. at 81.   [57] See KKO 1996:84.

In the present case, a Finnish court would obviously rule that Hugh has in a binding manner promised to abstain from invoking the defence of prescription should the case be dealing with shorter statutory prescription periods which are usually only interrupted by the commencement of a lawsuit.

Editors' comparative observations

These may be found, together with those relating to case 21, at the end of the next section (p. 513).

Case 21: Prescription II

Case

The situation is as in the previous case, but this time Hugh has left no doubt that he does not consider Geoffrey to be entitled to claim damages from him; he has, however, given Geoffrey to understand that he would not invoke the defence of prescription.

Discussions

GERMANY

Hugh has left no doubt that he did not consider Geoffrey to be entitled to his claim. He only expressed his intention not to raise the defence of prescription. § 852 II BGB (as extended by analogy) cannot be applied since no negotiations about the claim have been conducted.

The right to invoke the defence of prescription may not (as in the present case) be waived before the claim has prescribed.[1] Such waiver is invalid; this is usually deduced from § 225, 1 BGB ('Prescription may neither be excluded nor made more onerous by legal transaction'). Nevertheless, according to general opinion invocation of the defence of prescription may, under circumstances such as in the present case, be regarded as an abuse of right (§ 242 BGB) on account of *venire contra factum proprium* (going against one's own action) on the part of Hugh. The debtor is barred from relying on the defence of prescription for the period that he has delayed enforcement of the claim.[2] If Hugh had intended, from the

---

[1] The position would have been different if the waiver had taken place after the claim had prescribed: *Palandt*/Heinrichs § 222, n. 5.

[2] Cf. BGH WM 1991, 739; BGH NJW 1998, 902 (903); *Palandt*/Heinrichs § 225, n. 2; *Staudinger*/Schmidt § 242, n. 598.

outset, to deceive Geoffrey, the same conclusion can also be reached along a different route. Hugh has brought about prescription by way of breach of an obligation arising from a special relationship[3] which, at the same time, constitutes a delict (§§ 823 II BGB, 263 StGB, 826 BGB) and he owes Geoffrey restoration in kind (§ 249, 1 BGB). Hence, Geoffrey must be placed in the same position as if the claim had not prescribed.[4]

As a result, therefore, Geoffrey can still bring his action. Hugh is barred from invoking the defence of prescription.

GREECE

In case 21, Hugh has declared to Geoffrey that he rejects the existence of any debt, but nevertheless renounces any future reliance on the defence of prescription. According to art. 276 of the Greek Civil Code, renunciation of the defence of prescription in advance is invalid.[5] Furthermore, as long as Hugh is not deliberately protracting the period of negotiations, there will be no question of his abusing his right to rely on the defence of prescription. The matter is different where there is an *obvious* breach of good faith.

AUSTRIA

On these facts it is clear that no negotiations between the parties have taken place with a view to a settlement. Nevertheless, I think that the Austrian courts would allow Geoffrey an *exceptio doli* even in these circumstances.[6] As in case 20, Geoffrey might also invoke Hugh's waiver in respect of the period of prescription which had already run out.

FRANCE

The same arguments apply to this case as to case 20. Here, though, it seems that Hugh's position is unequivocal because he states clearly that he does not consider that Geoffrey is entitled to payment. He therefore expressly

---

[3] The special relationship arises from the delict, or breach of contract, which Hugh has committed and on account of which he is now under an obligation to pay damages to Geoffrey. Hugh and Geoffrey are thus in a debtor–creditor relationship *vis-à-vis* each other, as envisaged in § 241 BGB. The claim for damages as a result of a breach of obligation arising from this debtor–creditor relationship is usually based on 'positive breach of contract' (on which cf. the German report to case 16). This demonstrates that the term 'positive breach of contract' is imprecise; contract is just the paradigmatic case of a special relationship.   [4] See *Staudinger*/Schmidt § 242, n. 594.

[5] See also Areopagus 634/1954 EEN 21, 1125.

[6] Cf. Schubert, in: *Rummel, ABGB II* § 1501 n. 2. See also the Austrian report to case 20 above.

asserts that he is not liable and it may be indeed difficult to hold that an explicit denial of the debt is equivalent to acknowledging it! Geoffrey would, however, be able to rely on a suspension of the prescription period on the basis of the arrangement (the 'tolling contract') which he reached with Hugh. Here it seems that the facts are even more conclusive in favour of the parties having agreed, since Hugh has made it quite clear that he intends to defend the claim and that he will not invoke the defence of prescription.

The defence of prescription must be invoked specifically by the claimant; unlike the immense majority of the rules of the Civil Code, a prescription point may not be raised by the court of its own motion[7] which may explain why the courts are relatively flexible in allowing a temporary suspension or waiver of the prescription period. Furthermore, the acceptance of arrangements by which prescription is put on ice may be a convenient way of encouraging the parties to settle their disputes out of court. These provisions in the Civil Code do not explicitly take into account the parties' behaviour, but indirectly prevent a 'blowing of hot and cold air'; such contradictory behaviour is hard for any legal system to swallow and the result here is similar to promissory estoppel under English law. It is interesting to note that in one recent and analogous case,[8] which was considered partly under special rules relating to insurance, the court took the parties' behaviour into account in determining whether or not the defence of prescription could be invoked. This solution would suggest that French law may be moving towards an estoppel-based remedy although it would be hasty to draw general conclusions from one isolated case.

BELGIUM

The solution would be the same as in case 20. In order to distinguish both cases, it is assumed that Hugh has not communicated his intention to Geoffrey not to raise the defence of prescription but simply requests more time for considering the matter and for consulting with his legal advisers.

If there is no waiver, because there is no communication of intention, it may still be abusive to invoke prescription. Raising the defence of prescription could be considered abusive especially if the debtor has caused the creditor not to interrupt prescription (by suing the debtor, the credi-

---

[7] Art. 2223 C. civ.   [8] Civ. (1) 28 Oct. 1991, Bull. civ. I, no. 282.

tor would have interrupted prescription). This is occasionally accepted by Belgian case law.[9]

Specific statutory provisions can be found, for example, in insurance law. According to art. 25 § 3 Land Insurance Contracts Act of 1992, prescription is interrupted by a request for payment by the creditor to the insurer and runs again only from the moment at which the insurer expressly refuses to pay. For other claims, a request for payment is normally insufficient to interrupt prescription.

SPAIN

Spanish law would treat these facts no differently from those in case 20.

ITALY

For the reasons explained in relation to case 20, on the facts of case 21 Hugh can still invoke his defence based on prescription since he has left no doubt that he contests Geoffrey's right to be compensated.

THE NETHERLANDS

The solution is the same as for case 20.

ENGLAND

The fact that Hugh denies liability does not affect the possibility of Geoffrey's raising the estoppel as in case 20 though, as has been said, in the absence of an admission of liability no promissory estoppel would be raised without a clear promise by Hugh not to rely on the defence of limitation.

IRELAND

Although many of the estoppel cases in relation to the defence of limitation involve defendants who have not made clear to the plaintiff whether or not they accept or reject liability (as in *Doran v. Thomas Thompson and Sons Ltd*[10]), the doctrine of estoppel may equally apply to a case where a

---

[9] See, e.g., *Hof van Beroep* (Appeal) Gent 8 Apr. 1982 and Cass. 8 Apr. 1988, both in the case of *Neirynck v. Verstraete, Eurogas,* Arr. n° 482.   [10] [1978] IR 223.

defendant has made clear his position regarding liability, but where he represents to the plaintiff that he will not raise a defence of limitation. Accordingly, if Hugh has 'given Geoffrey to understand' that he will not do so, then he will not be able to resile from this undertaking, even though he has made clear that he intends to contest liability. However, as Hugh's undertaking is not express, Geoffrey's inference of an undertaking not to rely on the defence must be a reasonable one in the circumstances.

SCOTLAND

The rules stated in the Scottish report to case 20 will apply. Geoffrey should have raised his claim from the moment Hugh informed him that he considered that Geoffrey had no case. As you cannot contract out of prescription the right has prescribed, but Geoffrey may try to rely on s. 6(4)(a), based on the argument that Hugh misled him. Alternatively, Geoffrey could raise the common law plea of personal bar because Hugh has led him to believe that he will not raise the defence of prescription.

DENMARK AND NORWAY

Given the starting point outlined above,[11] it is difficult to see that cases 20 and 21 can be distinguished from each other in any point that would be relevant for the solution. In particular, it is of no consequence to the assessment that in case 20 the debtor does not dispute the claim, while in case 21 he disputes it the moment it is advanced. Obviously, there is no acknowledgement in this case, but there may be a waiver.

SWEDEN

If Hugh made clear that he does not consider Geoffrey to be entitled to a claim, the mere fact that Hugh listens to Geoffrey's claims does not suspend limitation.[12] However, Hugh gave Geoffrey to understand that he would not invoke limitation; see therefore the Swedish report to case 20.

---

[11] See the discussion in the first paragraph of the Danish/Norwegian report to case 20 above.

[12] Cf. NJA 1993, p. 436 where a seller was allowed to defend himself with the submission that the buyer had in fact been too late in notifying the seller of a non-conformity, although the seller for some period had listened to the buyer's complaints but without admitting any responsibility.

FINLAND

See the Finnish report to case 20 above. This is also a clear case.

Editors' comparative observations

All legal systems protect Geoffrey in case 20; all of them, except for Italian law, also protect him in case 21. The following bases for granting such protection are advanced.

(i) English and Irish law would invoke their equitable doctrine of promissory estoppel, which is based on the idea of it being unfair for someone to be allowed to go back on a representation as to the non-exercise of a right where a person has relied on that representation. Scots law is similar here in that it possesses an equitable doctrine of personal bar that would cover cases 20 and 21 but for the fact that in the context of prescription there are special legislative provisions protecting Geoffrey. These provisions may be regarded as a statutory version of personal bar.

(ii) The analysis in German and Spanish law, too, is very similar. Both legal systems resort to the general notion of good faith since Hugh's behaviour constitutes *venire contra factum proprium*, i.e. a case of acting against his own previous behaviour which has engendered reasonable reliance in Geoffrey. (For case 20, German law has a provision in the code specifying this idea.) Hugh's inconsistency of behaviour is, probably, also what motivates Dutch and Greek law to apply their principles of good faith and abuse of right, and it certainly explains Austria's recourse to the *exceptio doli*.

(iii) Closely related is the analysis in terms of a (unilateral) waiver of the defence of prescription advocated in Belgian, West Nordic, Swedish and Finnish law, and partly also in Austrian law. French law protects Geoffrey on the basis that he and Hugh have reached an agreement (a so-called 'tolling contract') under which Hugh is precluded from invoking the defence of prescription.

(iv) An alternative analysis would focus on the notion of 'acknowledgement'. Whilst most legal systems recognise that an acknowledgement, on the part of the debtor, interrupts prescription, only French and Italian law would consider that Hugh's action in case 20 might be taken to constitute an acknowledgement. But however liberally one is prepared to interpret this notion, it cannot be applied in case 21. This is why Italian law is unable to grant any protection to Geoffrey in that case. The Italian commentator notes, however, that the traditional attitude (denying the possibility of open recourse to the notion of good faith in cases of this kind) has come under attack in recent years. On the other hand, however, a certain reluctance is also apparent in other legal systems (notably in Greek and Norwegian law) to tamper with prescription rules under the auspices of good faith, or abuse of right: such interference might obviously undermine the policy of these prescription rules.

Case 22: Sitting on one's rights

Case

Lessee Lester has to pay to his landlord Mark a monthly rent of DM 1,000. Since he regards the rent as too high, he pays only DM 900. The landlord does not protest. Three years later, however, he demands payment of the remaining DM 100 per month for the past three years. (The prescription period for these kinds of claims has not yet expired.)

Discussions

GERMANY

The claim of Mark would be unfounded if the parties had implicitly changed the amount of rent required. But the first payment of DM 900 does not yet constitute an offer by Lester to change the contract. From the point of view of the recipient, it may as well have appeared as an error on Lester's part.[1] At least the second payment of only DM 900 does, however, constitute an implied offer to change the agreement. But Mark has not accepted the offer. His silence in principle constitutes neither an acceptance nor a rejection. Silence can only be regarded as a legally relevant declaration in exceptional cases, e.g. where the parties agreed that it would have this effect or where this is determined by statute.[2] The present case does not reveal any such exceptional circumstances.

Likewise, there has been no waiver (§ 397 I BGB). For on the one hand, there are insufficient indications that by not exercising his right to claim

[1] Cf. Werner BB 1984, 221 (222) (concerning the analogous problem of paying too much or too little under a contract of sale).
[2] Medicus, *Allgemeiner Teil* nn. 345 ff.; *Palandt*/Heinrichs, Einf. v. § 116, nn. 7 ff.

the full rent Mark can be taken to have intended to waive his right to the remaining amount.[3] On the other hand, the waiver of a claim requires a contract[4] which has not been concluded in the present case, not even tacitly.

Nevertheless, Mark may have lost his right to payment of the arrears. Loss (*Verwirkung*) in these kinds of cases is based upon an abuse of right in the specific form of *venire contra factum proprium*.[5] It constitutes a subcategory of behaviour not in accordance with the requirements of good faith and requires, firstly, that the creditor does not exercise his right for a relatively long period of time. The length of time must be determined by reference to the circumstances of the specific case; particularly the extent to which the debtor deserves protection has to be taken into account.[6] In the present case, the amount of rent was obviously of considerable importance to Lester, and Mark should therefore not be allowed to keep him in the dark for three years. Thus, the time requirement appears to be met.

Apart from the time factor, however, loss of a right requires something more: there have to be additional factors inducing the objective observer to regard the delay in the exercise of the right as a hardship which is contrary to good faith. This circumstantial requirement will, as a rule, be satisfied if the debtor has already organised his patrimonial affairs on the supposition that the right will not be exercised.[7] In lease relationships it can be accepted that it will constitute an economic hardship for the lessee if the unpaid amounts which have been piling up are later claimed. If the rent had been claimed in time, Lester could have adjusted his life-style accordingly.[8] The circumstantial requirement is therefore also met on the facts.

Mark has forfeited his claim to the arrears. Of course, he can claim the sum originally agreed upon for the future.

Loss of right on account of lapse of time is of practical significance particularly where claims are subject to a very long prescription period (cf. the regular prescription period of thirty years according to § 195 BGB).

---

[3] Waiver requires conduct which may be interpreted as a declaration of will, i.e. a declaration communicating the will to waive the right in question; see, e.g., *Palandt/Heinrichs* § 242, n. 89. As usual, of course, a tacit declaration is sufficient.

[4] I.e. acceptance of the declaration of intention mentioned in the previous footnote; cf., e.g., *Münchener Kommentar/von Feldmann* § 397, n. 1.

[5] Cf. *Jauernig/Vollkommer* § 242, nn. 53 ff.; *Palandt/Heinrichs* § 242, nn. 87 ff.; *Münchener Kommentar/Roth* § 242, nn. 360 ff.   [6] Cf. *Palandt/Heinrichs* § 242, n. 95.

[7] *Palandt/Heinrichs* § 242, n. 95.   [8] Cf. *Palandt/Heinrichs* § 242, n. 95.

GREECE

The issue to be considered in the present case is whether Mark, who did not protest when Lester only paid DM 900, made Lester believe that he had accepted a rent of DM 900 rather than DM 1,000. The answer would probably have to be that a period of three years seems too short to apply the doctrine of deactivation of rights as recognised under art. 281 Gr. C.C. The principle of deactivation of rights (forfeiture, equitable estoppel, *Verwirkung*) which has been developed in Germany has been also accepted in Greek law. The acceptance has, however, been rather hesitant since Greek courts fear that the principle might undermine the prescription periods. Under Greek law, Mark's claims would be barred after a period of five years (art. 250 Gr. C.C.).

The principle of deactivation of rights may only be applied if the creditor has failed to exercise his right for an inordinately long time under conditions that have led the debtor reasonably to believe that the right would not be exercised. Moreover, enforcement of the right would have to render the condition of the debtor especially onerous.[9]

AUSTRIA

Quite apart from the limitation of actions, in Austrian law a creditor may lose a right by doing nothing as long as this inaction is to be interpreted as an implicit[10] waiver of the right in question.[11] Therefore, loss of a legal right by a creditor occurs only if the debtor reasonably infers from the behaviour of the creditor that the latter will no longer assert his claim. In Austrian law, such a loss of a right is subject to the law relating to legal transactions and that is why (in contrast to German law) a creditor is allowed to rescind the 'loss of his right' (*Verwirkung*) on the ground of mistake.[12]

The different positions reached in Austria and in Germany can be explained by the fact that the Austrian Civil Code gives much greater legal significance to a person's reliance than does the German Civil Code. One result of this is that the need in Austrian law for a special legal doctrine of *Verwirkung* is much less pressing. The Austrian approach has two

---

[9] See, among others, Simantiras nos. 329–93, pp. 236–9; Symeonides, in: *Introduction* 61; Areopagus 295/1987 EEN 55, 35.   [10] See § 863 AGBG.
[11] OGH in JBl 1989, 649; ÖRZ 1993/17; Kramer, JBl 1962, 540; Bydlinski, *Privatautonomie* 184 ff.
[12] Cf. Bydlinski, *Privatautonomie* 184 ff. at 189.

particular consequences. First, it is generally held that it is the *objective* meaning of a statement which is of decisive importance and that, therefore, a declaration of intention is effective even if the person who appears to be making it is not conscious of making a legally relevant declaration of intention (if, in other words, he has no *Erklärungsbewußtsein*).[13] Secondly, rescission on the ground of mistake is only permissible if the other party to the transaction does not deserve the law's protection.[14] The other party will be considered undeserving in this context if he himself caused the other's mistake, should have recognised it or was informed of it before he arranged his affairs in reliance on the existence of the contract.[15]

The question whether in Austrian law Lester can plead waiver by Mark of his rights to the rent in case 22 depends on several factors. First, it must have been reasonable for a person in Lester's position to interpret Mark's behaviour as an implicit waiver of these rights, and in deciding this issue it must be taken into account that in the course of business activities it is unusual for a legal right to be given up without recompense. The yardstick in judging any conduct so as to imply such an intention must therefore be a very strict one.[16] On the other hand, the Austrian Supreme Court has accepted the existence of waiver in a case in which a landlord collected the same rent as before even though he was entitled to a higher rent,[17] though the court restricted the effect of this waiver to the landlord's accrued claims for rent and found no waiver as to his future claims.[18]

Even if it is accepted that Mark has waived his rights in the present case, Mark may be able to avoid the effect of any such waiver if he can show that he was mistaken about the significance of Lester's inaction. Thus, for example, if Mark was mistaken as to the real amount of the rent because Lester had carried on paying DM 900 month by month, then any 'implicit declaration' of waiver which he is taken to have made was made under a mistake as to what was owing. Since in this example, Lester can be said to have caused Mark's mistake, Mark is entitled to avoid the effects of his waiver by way of application of § 871 ABGB. By contrast, if Mark did indeed know the correct amount of the rent which had been agreed upon and was mistaken only as to the meaning of Lester's behaviour, then Lester would not be said to have caused his mistake.

---

[13] Cf. Koziol/Welser, *Bürgerliches Recht I* 94.   [14] § 871 ABGB.

[15] According to the Supreme Court (e.g. SZ 67/136 = JBl 1995, 48) the prerequisites provided in § 871 ABGB must also be present if a gratuitous contract (*unentgeltlicher Vertrag*) is rescinded for mistake in motive; disapproved by Koziol/Welser, *Bürgerliches Recht I* 127.

[16] OGH in JBl 1993, 592.   [17] OGH in MietSlg 19.099 (1967).

[18] OGH in RdW 1985, 75.

Finally, it should be noted that a person may lose a right not only by waiver (which requires a declaration of intention even if implied), but also by simple inactivity over a period of time.[19] This position may be derived from § 418 ABGB,[20] which concerns the situation where a person by mistake builds on another's land. However, the general rule is kept within narrow limits in Austrian law. A first requirement is that the person against whom the holder of the right asserts the right in question be honest, in the sense that he neither knew nor ought to have known of the right. Secondly, there must have been a risk that the inactivity of the holder of the right would cause harm to the other party. And thirdly, the holder of the right must have been 'knowingly inactive', i.e. he did not take any action whatsoever even though he knew of his rights and realised that the other party would be prejudiced by his behaviour. If these three requirements are fulfilled, the effect of the application of the doctrine is to prevent the holder of the right from exercising it. However, the 'honest defendant' does not acquire these assets for nothing, but has to pay compensation.

Applying these rules to the facts of case 22, it is clear that Lester does not deserve the protection which they offer as he knew that his creditor, Mark, was entitled to DM 1,000 per month. Furthermore, any loss by Mark of his claim to the outstanding DM 100 per month would lead to a gratuitous transfer of property and this is precisely where § 418 ABGB would not give protection.

FRANCE

The tenant Lester cannot claim that the lease has been varied under French law, since a lease must be varied in writing.[21] In fact Lester may not be able to prevent Mark from claiming the arrears of rent unpaid over the last three years, though he might be able to prevent him from claiming it all at once.

Under French law there is insufficient evidence here to suggest that Mark has really reduced the rent and given satisfaction for the debt. It would be necessary to adduce evidence of an agreement between the parties as to the waiving of rent and the mere fact that Mark does not

---

[19] E.g. if his behaviour has to be interpreted as a mere *Wissenserklärung* (declaration of knowledge).   [20] See Bydlinski, *Privatautonomie* 192 ff.
[21] L. no. 89–462 of 6 July 1989, art. 3 amending L. no. 86–462 of 23 December 1986. This law applies to all types of leases.

protest when Lester pays less rent would probably be insufficient. The courts require that the creditor expresses an unequivocal desire to release the debtor.[22] Tacit acceptance by the debtor may constitute an agreement that the debt had been satisfied, but it is unlikely that it can be deduced from the creditor's silence.

While Mark has the right to exercise his contractual rights, the tension between art. 1134 al. 1 and art. 1134 al. 3 is illustrated here again. Thus Lester could perhaps protest if Mark were to attempt to recover the arrears all at once. An analogy can be drawn with the case law concerning land-lords abusively invoking forfeiture clauses[23] and particularly the decisions of the *Cour de cassation* concerning a lessor's failure to demand arrears of rent over a long period.[24] Moreover, there is an analogy in a recent case in which an agreement made by lender and borrower to suspend interest for late payment of a loan was subsequently disregarded by the lender and the *Cour de cassation* criticised the lower court for omitting to take into account this bad faith on the lender's part.[25] Lester may well be able to show that Mark is in bad faith in demanding all the arrears in one go and if the *juges du fond* are convinced by this argument, they might award extra time to Lester to pay (a *délai de grâce* under art. 1244–1 of the Civil Code) and order Mark to recover the arrears in instalments, obliging him as a creditor to act in good faith.[26]

BELGIUM

Such cases are highly debated in Belgium. Litigation is common. Given the political sensitivity surrounding conflicts in the field of housing, legislation with respect to such contracts is frequently changed.

Most case law concerns situations where the landlord has a right to adapt the rent every year ('indexation') and forgets to do so. In 1983, a prescription period of one year was introduced for such cases (this prescription only concerns the top-up amount and only relates to past amounts; it does not prevent the landlord from asking that in future the rent be calculated as if it had been adapted every year). Case 22, however, is not a

---

[22] Versailles 20 May 1994, RTDCiv 1994.863 obs. J. Mestre.
[23] See the French report to case 7 above.
[24] Com. 7 Jan. 1963, Bull. civ. IV, no. 16, p. 14; Civ. (3) 8 Apr. 1987, Bull. civ. III, no. 88, p. 53.
[25] Civ. (1) 31 Jan. 1995, D 1995.389 note Jamin.
[26] Cf. the French reports to cases 6, 8 and 13 above for an explanation of the application of art. 1134 al. 3 C. civ. to *creditors*.

problem of non-indexation. As to the rent itself, the prescription period is normally five years (art. 2277 C.C.). We will have to discuss (i) waiver and (ii) abuse of right in the form of *venire contra factum proprium*.

(i) As in case 20, the solution is simple if the conduct of the landlord may be interpreted as waiver. Waiver requires communication of intention; it does not require acceptance. Silence as such does not constitute a communication of intention; only under specific circumstances can it acquire such significance.

A Belgian judge will probably find that the facts of case 22 do not constitute a sufficient indication of waiver, and not even of a temporary waiver (i.e. for the past only). This, at least, would be the position of the *Hof van cassatie*. Judges of lower courts tend to accept waiver more readily. Thus, it may not be excluded that, depending on the surrounding circumstances, such behaviour might be interpreted as waiver.

It is much debated in Belgium whether legal acts, including waiver, require a 'real' intention (established *a posteriori* by the judge), or whether it is sufficient that the other party could legitimately deduce such an intention from the circumstances at the time of the communication of intention. The latter view seems to be gaining ground.[27]

(ii) The doctrine of abuse of right (good faith) could apply to cases where one party tolerates a certain interpretation of the contract by the other for a lengthy period of time. It is not necessary that the other party legitimately believed the landlord to have waived his right to the full rent of DM 1,000. But the behaviour of the landlord must be manifestly unreasonable.

The *Hof van cassatie* accepts the doctrine of *venire contra factum proprium* (*rechtsverwerking*) only in cases where the behaviour of the creditor is manifestly unreasonable, i.e. abusive. Judges of lower courts, again, tend to be more flexible and regularly accept it in cases like the present one.[28] As the *Hof van cassatie* wants to see one of the specific formulas for abuse of right it has coined (disproportionality, or a manifest excess of the limits of normal use), lower court judges will normally dress up their acceptance of *venire contra factum proprium* by using one of these formulas.

Where, however, a landlord does not protest for thirty-six months

---

[27] For an example, see *Hof van Beroep* (Appeal) Brussel 26 May 1992, *ARCO*, TBBR 1993, 333 ff.; for a recent discussion, see M. E. Storme, in: *Vetrouwensbeginsel passim*.

[28] Cf. also *Hof van Beroep* (Appeal) Gent 12 Apr. 1995, TBH 1996, 737 (terms of payment granted, without interest, for twenty years).

against the fact that the tenant pays a lower rent than the one provided by the contract, this will often be accepted as evidence that he has agreed on a rent reduction. But it must be doubted whether the tenant could legitimately believe that the landlord really accepted such rent reduction.

SPAIN

In Spanish law, silence or even forbearance by the holder of a right is not taken to mean that he thereby gives it up, as long as the right has not expired as a result of lapse of time (prescription) and as long as there has been no genuine (*concluyente*[29]) renunciation of it. As regards the latter, the High Court has held that a renunciation cannot be inferred from silence alone.[30] Nevertheless, in circumstances where the prescription period is considered to be too long (the general prescription period in Spanish law being fifteen years[31]) and where the silence of the holder of a right has been *very prolonged*, the courts usually find that the right has been renounced on the facts.[32] However, in the present case the time during which Mark has not insisted on his full rent does not appear to be quite long enough to support such an inference of a renunciation on his part, especially because Lester has not incurred any expense by placing confidence in his landlord's conduct. Therefore, it follows on the facts of case 22 that the contractual rent is still owed.

It is to be noted that Spanish courts, unlike their German counterparts, have not yet developed a clear juristic approach to the relationship between the extinction of legal rights by prescription and (unilateral) unfair delay in the exercise of those rights, even though the approach of legal scholars in this area has been directly influenced by the doctrine of *Verwirkung* in German law.[33] The High Court has on one occasion adopted this doctrine, but it did so in a case which is better explained in terms of other legal rules.[34]

---

[29] *Concluyente* is to be contrasted with 'presumed' (*presunto*) rather than 'silent' (*tácito*) and may in this context signify a real or genuine intention.

[30] See the High Court judgement of 4 March 1988 (RJA 1988, 1551), confirming many earlier decisions.   [31] Art. 1964 C. civ.

[32] See the High Court judgement of 19 June 1985 (RJA 1985, 3298).

[33] For example, Miquel, in: *Comentario, sub* art. 7.

[34] High Court judgement of 13 June 1986 (RJA 1986, 3549). In this case, a husband and wife had agreed to separate and had lived independently of each other for thirty years without any judicial order or divorce. After the husband's death, the wife claimed from his heirs the rights to his estate which would be accorded in Spanish law to a widow, but her claim failed on the basis of the doctrine of *Verwirkung*.

ITALY

Lester must pay Mark the arrears, but if sued for them by Mark a court may give him extra time to pay under special legislative rules applicable to residential leases in order to avoid hardship.[35]

It is to be noted that Italian law has not developed a doctrine of *Verwirkung* ('sitting on one's rights') along the lines of German law,[36] though in certain areas of the law sitting on one's rights may indeed bar their enforcement, a result which is usually justified in terms of a tacit renunciation of the right in question.[37] On the facts of case 22, however, it seems difficult to resort to this technique, because silence by the creditor in itself does not warrant the inference that he has decided to give up his right.

THE NETHERLANDS

It is a principle, deduced from settled case law, that not acting on one's right cannot, on its own, lead to a good faith defence that the right has been given up. Something more is needed. In this case it could be argued that the landlord should have realised that he received DM 100 less than he was entitled to. The period of three years is long enough to react and protest. Waiting for so long and then suddenly demanding payment might therefore be considered to be against good faith. (Although a judge may not dismiss the whole claim, but only a part of it, given that Lester knowingly paid less than the rent he owed and that he must have known that he violated clear contractual rights of the landlord.)[38]

ENGLAND

English law takes a bifurcated analysis of these sorts of facts.

At common law, the rule is that part payment of a debt is not full discharge and that a promise to accept a lesser sum in full discharge is not binding.[39] This second proposition remains the case even if (which does

---

[35] L. 27 Jul. 1978, n. 392, art. 55.   [36] See the German report on this point.

[37] Once more, Italian law sides with French rather than with German law. On this subject see Ranieri, *Rinuncia, passim*; Ranieri, in: *Mélanges Bastian* 427; Ranieri, Digesto, 4th edn, sez. civ., VII, 1991, 311.

[38] Cf. *Hoge Raad* 5 April 1968, NJ 1968, 251 (*Pekingeenden*); and see Asser-Hartkamp, *Verbintenissenrecht II* nr. 320 ff.

[39] *Pinnel's Case* (1602) 5 Co Rep 528; *Foakes v. Beer* (1884) 9 App Cas 605.

not appear to be the case on the facts) receipt of part payment constitutes a real or practical benefit to the creditor.[40]

However, equity has since the decision of the Court of Appeal in *Central London Property Trust Ltd v. High Trees House Ltd*[41] applied the doctrine of promissory estoppel recognised in *Hughes v. Metropolitan Rly Co.*[42] to the context of promises to accept part payment of a debt. To attract the application of this doctrine, there must be a promise or representation by the person to be estopped (Mark) that he will accept a lesser sum for his rent, either in full discharge or for the time being. While such a statement need not be express and may in appropriate circumstances be made by conduct, mere inactivity will not normally suffice as it is insufficiently unequivocal. According to *Treitel*, '[u]nless the law took this view, mere failure to assert a contractual right could lead to its loss; and the courts have on a number of occasions rejected this clearly undesirable conclusion'.[43] If, therefore, Mark has simply received the lesser sum without more (for example, by post or in his bank account) this would be insufficient to raise an estoppel. However, if Mark's conduct in the circumstances can be interpreted as representing to Lester that he would not require the balance of rent due and if Lester can establish that he has relied on this to his detriment as a result and that it would be inequitable for Mark to go back on his representation, then an estoppel would be raised and the court would prevent Mark from claiming the balance of rent due until Mark gives reasonable notice that he wishes to return to the contract rent.

IRELAND

In Irish, as in English, common law part payment of a debt does not result in full discharge of the debt.[44] Also, as in English law, Irish law has accepted a similar equitable qualification to this rigid common law rule on the basis of 'promissory estoppel'.[45] According to this equitable doctrine, if the tenant could show that an unequivocal promise or representation has been made to him that the lesser amount would be accepted as a valid discharge of the monthly rent, and, furthermore, if the tenant can

---

[40] *Re Selectmove, The Times* of 13 January 1994, CA.   [41] [1947] KB 130.
[42] (1877) 2 App Cas 439.   [43] Guest, *Chitty on Contracts* § 3–069.
[44] *Foakes v. Beer* (1884) 9 App Cas 605.
[45] *Central London Property Trust Ltd v. High Trees House Ltd* [1947] KB 130 is the leading English decision (see also the Irish report to case 12 above). An Irish example of the doctrine's application may be found in *McCambridge v. Winters* (unreported, High Court, 28 August 1984).

show that he had relied to his detriment on such a promise or representation, then the courts will prevent the landlord from resiling from his representation or promise. However, on the facts of case 22, it is doubtful that the mere inactivity of the landlord can reasonably be construed as a promise not to enforce the full amount of the rent.

However, certain differences may be noted between the Irish and English positions as regards promissory estoppel. Certain English authority suggests that promissory estoppel would only suspend a person's rights, thereby allowing the promisor (typically a landlord) to return to the *status quo ante* by the giving of notice. Irish authority has shown a willingness to extend the application of the estoppel beyond the mere suspension of contractual right so as to prevent a promisor from ever enforcing the entire debt.[46] Another difference between the two systems relates to the growth in Irish law of the notion of a person's 'legitimate expectations' as a ground of action separate from promissory estoppel. In *Kenny v. Kelly*[47] this notion was pleaded as an alternative to contract *and* to estoppel and while estoppel has traditionally placed emphasis on the reliance on promises, the notion of a person's 'legitimate expectations' does not seem to. On the other hand, the leading commentator on Irish contract law sees these developments as most likely to lead to a more expansive doctrine of promissory estoppel than that which obtains in England, a doctrine in which 'injurious reliance' is no longer central to the plaintiff's claim.[48] If this were to occur, then it is possible that it could apply to a situation like the one in case 22.

SCOTLAND

Is Mark personally barred[49] from claiming the rent arrears because he has delayed his claim even though the obligation has not prescribed? The right to enforce his claim may be barred by his acquiescence. His *mora* (delay) is not enough; the true basis of the plea of personal bar in this instance is acquiescence from which consent to the shortfall in rent may be inferred: '[M]ere *mora*, taciturnity, or silence has no legal result (a) where it is not in breach of an express or implied condition of promptness, or (b) where it does not come up to the appropriate statutory period of prescription or to the common law equivalent (in certain cases) of time immemorial.'[50]

---

[46] *Revenue Commissioners v. Moroney* [1972] IR 272.   [47] [1988] IR 457.   [48] Clark 65–7.
[49] See the Scottish reports to cases 20 and 21 above.   [50] Rankine 117.

Mora and taciturnity are merely evidence of acquiescence. The principle of this plea is that because the creditor has done nothing to enforce his claim for a considerable period, an inference may in certain circumstances be drawn that he has abandoned it; *Pearl Mill Co. Ltd v. Ivy Tannery Co. Ltd.*[51] In this case it was held that 'an inordinate lapse of time . . . may . . . give rise to the implication of abandonment'.[52] Delay (short of prescription) will not in itself bar a claim; *MacKenzie v. Catton's Trustees:*[53] '*Mora* is not a good *nomen juris*. There must either be prescription or not. We are not to rear up new kinds of prescription under different names.'[54]

To be effective, delay must at least be accompanied by something which can be described as acquiescence; *Moncrieff v. Waugh.*[55] In *Assets Co. Ltd v. Bain's Trustees*[56] the law is stated in the three propositions: (i) that delay *per se*, so long as it is within the years of prescription, does not bar a pursuer's claim; (ii) that to avail a defender anything it must be delay in prosecuting a known claim – that is, a claim known to the pursuer to exist; and (iii) that the delay has been prejudicial to the defender in depriving him of evidence which would or might have supported his defence. Here the pursuers had 'lain asleep' on their rights for so long that witnesses had died.

So Lester will have to demonstrate that aside from Mark's delay in claiming the rent due Mark has in some other way indicated that he did not object to Lester underpaying him. Delay and taciturnity if combined with other circumstances, i.e. some conduct on the part of Mark, could raise the presumption that Mark had abandoned his claim. Negative actings are not grounds for claiming that the agreement has in any way been varied. For the contract to be varied, there would need to be positive actings, i.e. proof of consent to vary the agreement. If Mark has merely delayed making the claim, because the period of prescription has not lapsed, he will not be personally barred from making the claim.

DENMARK AND NORWAY

In addition to the very strictly formulated rules on extinctive prescription, and the somewhat more discretionary complaints rules, West Nordic law also recognises the non-codified so-called principles of laches which will cause a claim to lapse due to failure by the holder of the right to assert it in time.

---

[51] [1919] 1 KB 78.   [52] At 83, *per* Judge *McCardie*.   [53] (1877) 5 R 313.
[54] Ibid., at 317 *per* Lord *Deas*.   [55] (1859) 21 D 216.   [56] (1904) 6 F 692.

There is a certain parallel to case 22 in a Norwegian ruling by the *Høyesterett* in Rt. 1954, p. 980. The parties to a lease of land, entered into in 1914 for ninety-seven years, had for a number of years performed the contract in such a way that the tenant did not pay the rent of his own accord, as he had to under the contract, but that the owner himself collected the rent at somewhat irregular intervals. After many years, in 1937, the owner wanted to terminate the lease for substantial breach, because the tenant had not of his own accord paid the rent for many years. It was quite clear that the tenant was financially well-off and otherwise met all his obligations. The *Høyesterett* concluded that there was no default on his part. When the landlord had for a number of years accepted an arrangement with regard to payment that was different from that laid down in the contract, he could not, without reasonable notice to the lessee, demand compliance with the agreement. The same attitude is reflected in a lower court decision from Denmark reported in U 1923, p. 348 regarding a purely commercial relationship.

In the light of these and similar rulings it must at least be held that the tenant, in the present case, may not be given notice to leave because of failure to pay rent for three years. Whether the claim for payment should be deemed to have ceased to exist due to the doctrine of laches is an issue which may be open to doubt. Personally I would tend to say that the claim for payment has lapsed.

The doctrine of laches is, as mentioned above, not codified, and whether rights must be deemed to have ceased to exist in terms of it is based on an overall evaluation of all circumstances of the case.[57] This evaluation will very much depend on the area of law concerned. In commercial affairs, a quick reaction is often called for, while, for example, in matters of family law and succession, it will not always be regarded as desirable that rights are enforced with precision and carried to their extreme. Similar reflections may apply in affairs between neighbours, between landlord and tenant, and other, more complex legal affairs. Another important consideration is a comparative evaluation of the detriment suffered by the debtor, if the right could still be enforced, to that of the creditor, if he were to lose his right. Significant weight must also be given to whether it requires little to speak out, compared with the loss the other party might suffer. One example here is a ruling by Norway's *Høyesterett* in Rt. 1902, p. 641. A built a house, but by mistake he built it in such a way that a small part of it stood on the neighbouring land; it occupied a total of 3.10 sq m

---

[57] Arnholm, *Privatrett I* 275 ff.

of that land. The neighbour B had been aware of the violation of his border but had done nothing. When A's house was completed, however, B raised objections and demanded substantial compensation for the infringement of his property if he were to refrain from demanding that the house be pulled down. The *Høyesterett* concluded here that there was blameworthy inactivity on B's part since he had long had the opportunity of taking steps against the construction.

The duration of the inactivity will, of course, also be an important point. Regard must, furthermore, be had to the intentions of the party concerned. If the inactivity is intentionally disloyal, i.e. where a party merely waits in order to attack the other party in due course, the law may react particularly strongly. Here the above-mentioned ruling in Rt. 1902, p. 645 is illustrative.

Finally, the rules on prescription have always had strongly positivistic features in the West Nordic countries. It is characteristic of them that they only apply to loss of so-called mandatory rights. The rules concerning complaints have not had such firm contours, and, moreover, their basis in positive law has been slender. The doctrine of laches has emerged through legal usage. The courts of law have here followed a very casuistic approach. Today, however, as the usage has gradually developed, it is possible to show that true principles of laches do exist in West Nordic law. Inactivity has a double nature: in some instances it expresses a tacit acquiescence. What is characteristic of the principles of laches, in this context, is that the lapse of rights takes effect independently of the wishes of the party entitled to the right.[58]

SWEDEN

There are rules related to specific contractual relationships demanding some activity by the creditor when performance is defective, e.g. in the legislation on sales, consignation and lease of land. According to some of these rules the creditor, after some time, loses his right not only to cancel or terminate the contract but also to demand the quality or quantity of goods originally agreed upon (especially in sales law). The rules demanding some activity after knowledge of the incomplete performance may be applied by analogy though, presumably, limitation rules which may already be applicable after the lapse of a certain period of time cannot be extended to this case.

---

[58] Gomard, *Obligationsret 3* 227 ff.

Now the issue in the present case is whether the landlord Mark may, a long time after the lessee Lester has paid the lesser sum, demand that the missing amount be paid. The case does not seem to be solved by legislation or by an easily comparable Supreme Court precedent. However, in the literature there are statements to the effect that, as a general principle, a right may cease to exist, should the creditor not take action within a reasonable time of receiving a performance which he realises is defective. In this case, where the amount paid was nine-tenths of the full amount, I suppose that the debtor can after a while rely upon the landlord being satisfied, and consequently the tenant is discharged as far as the past is concerned (cf. the reverse case of *condictio indebiti* and the duty of a purchaser to complain 'as to non-conformity' within a reasonable time if it can be presumed that the seller thinks he has delivered in full; s. 43, Sale of Goods Act of 1990). It is also possible, but unlikely, that the contract is changed for the future and that it has to be terminated for the purposes of re-negotiation, if the landlord wishes to return to the rent originally agreed upon. This could only be assumed, if the landlord had, in a manifest way, created the impression of being satisfied with the lower amount also for the future.[59]

FINLAND

This is really a matter of evidence, but usually a Finnish court would not interpret the failure by Mark to protest as a tacit approval of a lower rent than that agreed upon.[60] The preconditions for accepting such approval are clearly not met in this case, since the amount of the rent was in no way ambiguous according to the contract.

As mentioned above[61] Finnish law, generally speaking, employs very liberal prescription periods, and for this reason it is understandable that passivity is only reluctantly interpreted as waiver of rights, where the existence and content of these rights is in no way disputed or questionable.

The outcome might be different if Lester, when he began to pay a lower

---

[59] Somewhat similar cases are discussed by Karlgren 11 ff.

[60] See Telaranta 165 ff.: 'Being silent may as earlier stated only be considered as a declaration of will, if the requirements concerning consciousness of declaration and contractual will have been fulfilled. As for the subjective requirement it is necessary that the party is conscious of the fact that he, being silent, gives the other party legally relevant information . . . he is aware of the fact that the information is equivalent to legal regulation, normally an approval' (my own translation from the Finnish).

[61] See the Finnish report to case 20 above.

rent than that agreed upon, clearly informed the landlord about his posi-tion (i.e. that the rent was, in his view, ambiguous or too high) and the landlord did not protest. In that case Lester's conduct might be under-stood as an offer – perhaps to avoid litigation regarding the reduction of rent (this is possible) – and Mark's failure to protest could be accepted as an approval. But in order to predict the possible outcome of the case in a Finnish court one would need more information about the circum-stances, e.g. the relationship existing between Mark and Lester, whether they were in continuous contact with each other, etc.

Editors' comparative observations

This case gave rise to considerable differences both in result and analysis. While all legal systems under consideration possess mechanisms for the protection of the reasonable reliance of a debtor in situations similar to the present one, only a few of them would be prepared to hold that Lester may defeat the claim for the arrears by Mark. At the same time, however, it is generally agreed that sitting on one's rights as such, i.e. mere inactiv-ity on the part of the creditor, does not lead to a loss of right.

(i) The most generous approach is the one adopted in the West Nordic countries, in Sweden and in the Netherlands. Here it is accepted that a right may cease to exist, should the creditor not take action within a rea-sonable time after he has received a performance which is in some ways defective. The decision must be based on an overall evaluation of all the circumstances of the case. The length of time during which the creditor remained inactive is a very important factor but it is not decisive on its own. The West Nordic countries, in this context, apply the doctrine of laches, Dutch law resorts to the notion of good faith.

(ii) German law would come to the same result on the basis of its doc-trine of *Verwirkung*. Mark's sudden demand for the outstanding amount, after having accepted, on no less than thirty-six subsequent occasions, a sum amounting to nine-tenths of the rent originally agreed upon, is seen to constitute an abuse of right in the specific form of *venire contra factum proprium*. The doctrinal home of the doctrine of *Verwirkung* (which is of practical significance in cases where the statutory prescription periods are insufficiently short) is the good faith clause of § 242 BGB.

(iii) Some legal systems have, under the influence of German law, accepted the notion of *Verwirkung* but apply it more restrictively. This is true, particularly, of Greek and Spanish law. Both legal systems do not regard the time that has passed as long enough to accept a loss of Mark's right to claim the full rent, even for the past. Belgian law is similar in that it would also turn to its notion of good faith in its more specific form of the prohibition of *venire contra factum proprium*. Belgian judges (particularly those in lower courts) might well consider the lessor's demand, in the present case, to be abusive.

(iv) Both Spanish and Belgian law would also ask whether the landlord may have tacitly waived his right to receive the rent originally agreed upon. The notion of a tacit (or implicit) waiver is also the focal point in the Austrian and Italian analyses. It is widely held (though not necessarily in Belgian law) that there are insufficient indications, in the present case, to accept a waiver.

(v) English and Scots law both rely on the idea of a representation of intention by the landlord which would (coupled with other factors, notably, reliance) effectively prevent the landlord from claiming this contract rate at least until he gave reasonable notice to the tenant to return to it. The idea is expressed in English law by the doctrine of equitable or promissory estoppel and in Scots law by the common law doctrine of personal bar. On the facts of case 22, neither of these doctrines help the tenant as there is no representation by the landlord.

(vi) Interestingly, while Irish law has accepted English law's doctrine of promissory estoppel, recent judicial developments have added a further and distinct doctrine based on a person's 'legitimate expectations' which does not include any element of injurious reliance. This doctrine may well apply to a situation like the one in case 22.

(vii) The approach of French law is most restrictive in that a waiver of right would have to be based on an agreement between the parties. However, Lester may, in the present case, be able to prevent Mark from claiming all arrears at once. Italian law, too, possesses rules enabling the courts to grant the lessee extra time to pay the arrears, in order to avoid hardship.

Case 23: Long-term business relationships I

Case

Oliver is a car manufacturer in London. He appoints Rodney his sole distributor of automobiles for Cornwall. The contract takes effect on 1 January 1950, and runs for one year. It provides that Oliver may give Rodney one month's notice if he does not wish to renew the contract. One-year contracts are issued by Oliver and signed by Rodney during the following years. In 1992, however, Oliver decides that he does not wish to renew the contract for 1993. He so informs Rodney on 30 November 1992. Does the contract come to an end? Is Rodney entitled to claim damages?

Discussions

GERMANY

The renewal of the contract for the following year can, according to the wording of the contract, be refused one month before the end of each year, at the latest. Oliver has complied with this period of notice. But the fact that the contract has been renewed every year for more than forty years, and that therefore an expectation of continued renewals has been engendered, may affect the validity of Oliver's notice of termination.[1] For the exercise of a right will be regarded as an unacceptable *venire contra factum proprium* under § 242 BGB if a reasonable expectation has been engendered by one party's behaviour and if the other party has organised his affairs on the basis of this expectation.[2]

---

[1] The rules concerning so-called chain 'employment relationships' (*Jauernig*/Schlechtriem § 620, nn. 5 f.) do not apply in the present case since Rodney is not an employee but an independent, authorised dealer.   [2] *Palandt*/Heinrichs § 242, n. 56.

In the present case, however, it has to be taken into account that a new contract has been concluded every year and that in each of these contracts the possibility of terminating the relationship was expressly provided for. A reasonable expectation cannot be engendered under such circumstances. Oliver has not acted in breach of his contractual duties. No claim for damages can be brought.

Moreover, as an authorised dealer Rodney has a claim to be compensated for advantages that Oliver obtains from availing himself of the business network that Rodney has built up (§ 89 b HGB *per analogiam*[3]). Hence there is no need for limiting Oliver's possibility to terminate the contract on the basis of § 242 BGB.[4]

GREECE

Greek law could look at these facts either (i) simply in terms of good faith, or (ii) as an example of a situation analogous to partnership and therefore governed by rules analogous to those found in relation to partnership.

(i) The fact that Oliver and Rodney have signed one-year contracts continuously for forty-two years, from 1950 until 1992, indicates that the two contracting parties do not wish to be bound in a long-term relationship. Thus, the doctrine of deactivation of rights (*Verwirkung*)[5] cannot be applied in this situation. However, because the relationship, regardless of the fact that the contracts were renewed every year, has lasted for so many years and Rodney has every right to believe that it will continue, the notice of termination given by Oliver on 30 November 1992 (though conforming to the letter of the contract) is obviously contrary to good faith.

(ii) On the other hand, if here we regard the relationship between Oliver and Rodney as a *de facto* partnership, art. 767 Gr. C.C. could be applied by analogy.[6] According to this article: '[a] partnership constituted for an indefinite period shall be dissolved by means of a notice given by a partner at any time. If a partner gave notice at an inappropriate time and with no serious ground justifying the inappropriate notice, he shall be liable for the loss caused to the other partners by the dissolution.'[7] The application of art. 767 Gr. C.C. means that the untimely nature of the notice of

---

[3] For details on the analogous application of the law concerning commercial agents to authorised dealers, see Baumbach/Hopt § 84, nn. 12 ff.   [4] Cf. Baumbach/Hopt § 89, n. 16.
[5] See the Greek report to case 22.   [6] Court of Appeal Athens 1381/87 EED 1989, 673.
[7] See Simantiras no. 324, p. 231; Areopagus 1671/1983 NoB 32, 1531; cf. MonProt Athens 12796/1987 EllDni 32, 843.

termination cannot oblige Oliver to sign a new contract or to extend the contract which already exists, because that contract has a specific date of expiry. However, Oliver will be obliged to compensate Rodney for the damage he has suffered as a result of the untimely notice of termination of their contract.

Article 767 Gr. C.C. which is applied here by analogy, focuses on two notions, i.e. 'serious ground' and 'untimely'. These notions are relative and they are closely related, though not absolutely identical, to 'good faith', *boni mores*, 'business usage' and 'abuse of rights'. The notions 'serious ground' and 'untimely' must be interpreted according to the intensity and the specific features of the relationship between the parties and the expectation engendered between them. Oliver has to pay compensation to Rodney because, whilst he has exercised his legal right of termination, such an exercise was unfair to Rodney and resulted in loss suffered by him. Rodney may also be able to request compensation for advantages that Oliver obtains from availing himself of the business network that Rodney has built up.[8]

In conclusion, a Greek court is likely to accept the second of these routes to the solution of this sort of case, preferring to rely on a specific legislative provision rather than a principle as general as good faith, even though the specific provision is applicable only by analogy.

AUSTRIA

The distribution contract is terminated, as the notice not to renew it has been given by Oliver in accordance with its terms and in due time. There is no reason to suppose on the facts that the parties have changed the terms of the contract governing its renewal by any conduct implying an intention to do so,[9] since each year Oliver and Rodney concluded only a contract for one year and, therefore, acted within the framework originally established by them.

Moreover, a claim for damages by Rodney against Oliver must also be ruled out. For while it is true that there is a possibility of liability being imposed on a similar basis to the principles developed for the situation of the unreasonable breaking-off of contractual negotiations,[10] a

---

[8] On the possibility of the application of the law concerning commercial agents, see the Greek L.D. 219/1991 arts. 8 and 9; cf. Georgiadis, *Nees Morphes* 233, 237, 238. Regarding case law, see MonProt Athens 12796/1987 EllDni 32, 843.   [9] § 863 ABGB.
[10] Cf. the Austrian report to case 3 above.

prerequisite for any such liability would be that Oliver induced Rodney to rely on the continuance of their contractual relationship. It is clear that the facts of case 23 give no indication of any such an inducement, for the fact that over the years Oliver entered only one-year contracts was a clear indication to Rodney that he did not want any longer term engagement.

FRANCE

In order to claim damages for the non-renewal of the successive one-year exclusive distribution contracts he has made with Oliver for forty-two years, Rodney will have to claim that Oliver has abused his right not to renew the contract, which is tantamount to a claim for the wrongful termination of the contract.

Case law has firmly established that a long-term contract of exclusive distribution is not to be treated as a *mandat d'intérêt commun* (agency contract of common interest) under which an automatic right to damages arises in the agent upon termination by the principal.[11] It follows therefore that a short-term contract of exclusive distribution does not come into this category either.

Thus, Oliver has a right to put an end to the contract provided that he respects the notice period (which is the case on the facts), this being a straightforward application of the principle of the binding force of contracts under art. 1134 al. 1 of the Civil Code. Where a contracting party is entitled to put an end to the contract, it has been held that such a termination does not require justification[12] nor does it give rise to a liability in damages.[13] Moreover, the courts have held that the contracting parties have no right to a renewal.[14] On the other hand, various decisions have had recourse to the theory of the abuse of rights in situations where the distributor had a legitimate reason to believe that the contract would be renewed and had made investments as a result of this belief, to the knowledge of the other party; it is true, however, that the majority of the case law is against the application of this theory in circumstances such as

---

[11] Com. 12 Feb. 1968, Bull. civ. IV, no. 68, p. 59; followed in Com. 13 May 1970, Bull. civ. IV, no. 161, p. 144 and consistently thereafter; for a categorical refusal to extend the category of agency contracts to other contractual relationships, see Com. 30 Nov. 1982, Bull. civ. IV, no. 383, p. 320.   [12] Com. 6 Jan. 1987, Bull. civ. IV, no. 7, p. 5.
[13] Com. 4 Jan. 1994, *Sté Fiat Auto France c/ Cachia*, JCP 1994.I.3757 nos. 10 and 11, obs. Ch. Jamin.
[14] Com. 4 Feb. 1986, D 1988.Somm.19; Com. 4 Jan. 1994, *Sté Fiat Auto France c/ Cachia*, JCP 1994.I.3757 nos. 10 and 11, obs. Ch. Jamin.

appear from the facts of case 23.[15] In the result, it would be difficult to maintain this argument.

There is no evidence of an implicit agreement to renew the contract, unless on the grounds that it has been renewed for the last forty-two years. Moreover, there is case law which suggests that just because an agreement has been renewed previously, this does not give rise to a right to damages.[16]

Therefore, in the absence of 'fraudulent or disloyal manoeuvres' on the part of Oliver, to which there is no allusion on the facts,[17] Oliver is entitled to give notice to end the contract with impunity. In the circumstances, this looks like a case which marks the limit of the extension of the principle of good faith, as set out in art. 1134 al. 3 of the Civil Code. Even though Rodney, as an exclusive distributor of cars, belongs to a category of contracting parties which has sometimes benefited from a degree of protection by the courts (so as to prevent an abuse of economic power), this protection is not systematic. Indeed, the *Cour de cassation* has recently affirmed the principle of freedom of contract so as to enable a party to put an end to contractual relations, thus marking a limit to a certain amount of protection given where one party was considered economically dependent and subject to abuse by the other.[18] Has the moralisation of contractual relationships played out its role?

BELGIUM

The Belgian discussion of case 23 may be found together with the one of case 24, below, p. 549.

SPAIN

In Spanish law, there are no legal provisions which specifically concern contracts of exclusive distribution such as the one found in this case, but in several respects the courts apply by analogy rules found in the Agency Contract Act of 27 May 1992, the distributor's position being seen as similar to that of an agent, the manufacturer's to that of a principal. According to the view taken by the High Court, where a contract of exclusive distribution is not expressed to continue for a specific duration, in

---

[15] Com. 6 Jan. 1987, Bull. civ. IV, no. 7, p. 5; Com. 30 Nov. 1982, Bull. civ. IV, no. 392, p. 326; *contra* in favour Com. 9 Feb. 1981 (réf. 1057) GP 1981.Pan.jur.234.
[16] Com. 3 Jan. 1980, GP 1980.Pan.jur.224 and cf. Com. 22 Jan. 1980, GP 1980.Pan.jur.215.
[17] Com. 5 Oct. 1993, *Renault c/ Rouvel Automobiles*, JCP 1994.II.22224 obs. Ch. Jamin.
[18] Virassamy, *passim*.

principle either party to the contract may terminate it unilaterally. On the other hand, if the *manufacturer* terminates the contract, he must compensate the distributor where (i) he did not give the latter any previous warning as to the future termination; (ii) his termination of the contract is contrary to good faith; *or* (iii) he will in future enjoy the benefit of the clientele resulting from the efforts of the distributor.[19]

However, the fact that the contract is expressed to be renewable from year to year unless one of the parties gives notice of his intention to terminate does not mean that the contract is to be treated to be of indefinite duration. This is the reason why art. 28 of the Agency Contract Act, which gives agents rights of compensation, should not be applied by analogy to this particular type of distribution agreement, despite the occasional confusion between agency and distribution agreements in some decisions.[20]

According to these criteria, on the facts of case 23 the contract of distribution does indeed come to an end and Rodney has in principle no right to recover damages from Oliver in respect of any losses which he may have suffered in consequence of the termination of the contract. Indeed, on similar facts, the High Court has found occasion to observe that in a free market every party to a contract may make use of his bargaining power in order to achieve his own best economic advantage in respect of any renewal of the previous contractual relationship.[21]

ITALY

The answer to the questions raised by this case must be somewhat nuanced. The outcome of the dispute between the parties is straightforward only where Oliver's refusal to enter a new annual contract is clearly in conformity with his duties to negotiate and to perform the contract in good faith.[22] For if Oliver does not violate either of these duties the contract does indeed simply expire and Rodney has no claim against him,

[19] High Court judgements of 17 December 1973 (RJA 1973, 4788), 22 March 1988 (RJA 1988, 2224).

[20] See, e.g., the High Court judgement of 8 November 1995, criticised by Bercovitz, 41 CCJC 1996, 530 ff.

[21] Judgement of 23 May 1995 (RJA 1985, 4257). See also Judgement Audiencia Provincial La Coruña 2 February 1998 (*Aranzadi Civil* 1998, n⁰ 442).

[22] Arts. 1337, 1375 c.c. The answer is given on the assumption that the car manufacturer does not have a dominant position in the market. If the opposite were true his refusal to renew the contract would be controlled either by the competition law of the E.C. Treaty (art. 86) or by the corresponding Italian legislation (art. 3, l. 10 Oct. 1990, n. 287, *Norme per la tutela della concorrenza e del mercato*). For an up-to-date review of this law, see Coraggio, Nuova giur. civ. comm., 1997, II, 179.

apparently not even for the advantages that the latter obtains from himself exploiting the business network which was built up by his former co-contractor.[23] On the basis of the bare facts mentioned in case 23, this would appear to be the result.

However, the conclusion would be different if Oliver were in breach of his duties of good faith. A typical example of such a breach which is discussed by Italian scholars may be found in the situation where a party to a contract who wishes to terminate it induces the other party to make investments which cannot be amortised within the time-span of the contract.[24] In these circumstances, the aggrieved party may obtain damages equal to its reliance interest in relation to the contract. Furthermore, if the distributor has bought from the manufacturer goods in such a quantity that they cannot be resold within the stipulated duration of the contract, the manufacturer having given him the impression that their relationship was going to last longer than this period, then the distributor may be authorised by the court to sell on the stock within a certain period of time, despite the fact that the contract of distributorship with the manufacturer has come to an end.[25]

Postscript: See now l. 18 June 1998, n. 192, *Disciplina della subfornitura nelle attività produttive*, as discussed in the Italian contribution to case 14, text after n. 21.

THE NETHERLANDS

The Dutch discussion of case 23 may be found together with the one of case 24, below, p. 552.

---

[23] Independent distributors have argued that they are entitled to the same protection granted by the law to commercial agents in the case of termination of the contract (cf. art. 1751 c.c., amended by d.lgt. n. 303/1991, art. 3, implementing E.C. Council Directive 86/653/EEC on self-employed commercial agents), but the majority of scholars and one *Corte di Cassazione* decision reject their approach. Cass., 21 Jun. 1974, n. 1888, Giur. it., 1975, I,1, 1290 (termination of contract concerning a gasoline station); Pardolesi, *Contratti* 339, 343; Cagnasso/Irrera 66 ff. In practice, distributors act in their own name and on their own account (hence the clients they contact are their own), while commercial agents act in the name and on behalf of the principal. But this reasoning holds only in so far as the distributor is not bound to the manufacturer by a contractual term restraining competition even after termination of the contract: Pardolesi, *Contratti* 348 ff.

[24] Pardolesi, *Contratti* 323, 331 f. See also Vettori 215 ff., at 217–18, with reference both to art. 1375 c.c. and to the general provision against unfair competition enacted by art. 2598 n. 3 c.c.; Frignani 113 ff.; De Nova, Digesto, 4th edn, VI, 1991, 100 ff.

[25] Cf. the interim measure granted by Pret. Roma, 11 Jun. 1984 (ord.), Giur. it., 1985, I,2, 711, obs. Aldo Frignani, *Quando il giudice ordina la prosecuzione di un rapporto di Franchising*.

ENGLAND

English law does not recognise any special concept of a 'long-term contract' or 'relational contract' and instead leaves it to the parties to make their own appropriate provision, in particular for any changes which may be needed owing to circumstances changing over time.[26] As a result, the contract between Oliver and Rodney takes effect according to its terms. Here, Oliver fulfils the conditions for the exercise of his option not to renew the contract between them and thereby brings the contract to an end. Rodney may not claim damages as no breach of contract has been committed by Oliver; nor is there any tortious ground of recovery on these facts.

These facts illustrate the general position in English law according to which a party to a contract is entitled to exercise the rights which he possesses under the contract in his own interest and without reference to any criterion of good faith. It is to be noted, however, that in some contexts, modern legislation has affected the extent to which a party to a contract can refuse to renew a contractual arrangement with the other party, even though the contract on its terms has come to an end, for example in relation to contracts of employment (where the employee may gain rights against dismissal on the expiry of the 'fixed term' of his contract)[27] or business leases (business tenants having a statutory right of renewal of the lease which may be opposed by the landlord only on various particular grounds).[28]

IRELAND

For Irish law, two principal questions arise on these facts: first, whether Oliver's option not to renew the contract is an absolute one, and, secondly, if so, whether Rodney is entitled to compensation for work commenced before the end of the contract but which inures to the benefit of Oliver after its termination.

While until recently Irish law would have regarded such an option of non-renewal as absolute, there is a movement in the interpretation of long-term relationships towards implying some requirements of good faith. In *Fluid Power Technology Co. v. Sperry (Ireland) Ltd*,[29] the High Court held that an express power in a contract to terminate the contract was subject to an implied obligation of exercise of the right of termination in

---

[26] McKendrick, in: *Good Faith*, *passim*.
[27] See Guest, *Chitty on Contracts* §§ 37–153, 37–155 ff.
[28] Landlord and Tenant Act 1954, ss. 24 and 30.   [29] Unreported, 22 February 1985.

a *bona fide* manner. Specifically, there was an implied obligation to state the reasons for the termination and a requirement that the terminating party must honestly believe these reasons to be valid. It is probable that Irish courts would extend this requirement of *bona fides* to the exercise of an option not to renew a yearly contract which has been running for some time because in such a context non-renewal is equivalent to termination. Accordingly, Oliver would have to be able to state his reasons (which he must believe genuine) for the non-renewal for it to be effective.

As to the second question regarding any recovery of compensation on effective termination of the contract, it is unlikely that it will be payable unless the manner in which the contract was terminated constituted a breach of contract or unless the contract provided some mechanism for the ascertainment of commission etc. attributable to the efforts of the former agent: it is unlikely that an Irish court would imply a term regarding the payment of commissions accruing after termination but attributable to the period before termination. Here, the policy of the law is not to substitute its own bargain for the one agreed by the parties: if the parties are short-sighted or allow for a compensation package that is incomplete or even partially unfair, this is no concern of the courts. Thus, Irish law deals with concerns about legitimate expectations of the parties in this sort of context by the interpretation of and application of procedures for termination, rather than by the implication of new terms dealing with the consequences of such a termination.[30] Furthermore, as yet no claim in unjustified enrichment has been attempted by an agent whose distributorship has been lawfully terminated and it is generally considered that where there is a valid contract between the parties only that contract should govern remuneration: actions in quasi-contract (i.e. restitution) lie only where the contract is voided. On the facts of case 23, the agent received the commission for which he bargained and therefore has no grounds for complaint. In all, therefore, if the non-renewal of the contract were held to be valid then no compensation would be payable to Rodney.

SCOTLAND

In legal form this is simply a series of individual contracts with no ongoing relationship between the parties. Yet, the reality is otherwise, i.e. there may be little difference between a series of individual contracts and

---

[30] Cf. *Irish Welding v. Philips Electrical (Ireland) Ltd* (unreported, High Court, 8 October 1976, *per* Finlay P.).

a single contract which is stipulated to last for a considerable time. But this contract expressly provides for the contract to last for a period of one year, and that one month's notice is sufficient to cancel the contract. So despite the fact that the contract is renewed yearly over a long period of time, the fact that Oliver fulfils the terms of the contract in giving one month's notice not to renew the contract means that the contract comes to an end and Rodney cannot claim damages.

The courts are reluctant to interfere with parties' freedom to contract, and will not imply terms into a contract which contradict its express terms; *Cummings v. Charles Connell & Co. (Shipbuilders) Ltd.*[31]

However, it is worth noting that in some cases the principle of *tacit relocation* applies. The principle operates where there is a contract which has been made initially for a fixed period, but neither party has before the date of expiry given the other due notice of intention to terminate the contract at its date of expiry. The contract is held to be extended by the presumed consent of the parties, if originally for a year or longer for a further year, and if originally for a shorter period for the same duration again, and in all respects on the same terms and conditions as originally agreed. This principle only operates in contracts of lease, contracts of employment and contracts of partnership.

This is probably a case of 'tough luck Rodney!' There appears to be no evidence of variation of the contract. Has Rodney acted in reliance and knowledge owing to something that Oliver has said? Is there a tacit understanding that the contract will be continually renewed? If, for example, Oliver had told Rodney that he would always renew the contract then he may be personally barred from cancelling the contract.[32] Has Oliver acquiesced in the alteration of the contract? To amount to such a licence, in effect to alter the terms of the contract, an agreement for such an alteration, though it may be verbal, must be proved.

DENMARK AND NORWAY

In order to solve this case, some points need to be made clear at the outset. I take the text as relating to a dealer relationship, i.e. the intermediary is selling in his own name and for his own account and thus has no right of return of the property to his 'principal'. The alternatives would be either a relationship of agency where the agent merely receives orders which he forwards to the principal, or a commission business where the commission

---

[31] 1968 SC 305.   [32] See the Scottish reports to cases 20, 21 and 22 above.

agent is selling in his own name but takes no financial risk in view of the fact that he has a full right of return to his principal.

In the West Nordic countries the most common form of distribution in such matters as are raised in the present case is the dealer contract. The dealer contract was made for a period of time that was not specified; it may be terminated by giving notice. That such notice may be harsh for the dealer since he may, for instance, have created a market for the product, is not enough to set aside the notice of termination. Also, in general, it is not possible to award damages to the dealer if the notice is lawful. In a ruling in Rt. 1980, p. 243, the *Høyesterett* explicitly rejected a submission to apply by analogy the rules concerning commission agents, which at the time applied both to agents and commission agents, to sole distributorships. Of course, there may be cases in which damages may have to be awarded to the dealer, also in respect of a lawful termination. This will apply particularly in cases where the dealer is strongly dependent on his client and requires to be protected against a notice of termination which is given when the dealer has carried out his job to the satisfaction of the producer and the latter deems it appropriate that he himself should now reap the benefits in a market that has been well prepared. In Rt. 1980, p. 243 the *Høyesterett* opened up the possibility of damages to dealers 'in special cases where otherwise the outcome would have an extremely low degree of reasonableness'. The situation seems to be the same in Denmark, although no Supreme Court decision supports that view.[33]

It will have been seen that under West Nordic law it is necessary to make a fundamental distinction between agents who do not trade in their own name and only accept orders for their principal, commission agents trading in their own name, but enjoying full rights of return of the goods, and dealer relationships. As far as the two first groups are concerned, there is, in keeping with the E.C. Council Directive 86/653/EEC of 18 December 1986, legislation which contains rules about remuneration on termination of the relationship.[34] The condition for such remuneration is that the intermediary has created a market from which the principal continues to benefit.

As pointed out already, the most important intermediary in the retail trade is the dealer. A characteristic feature of dealer relationships in West Nordic law is that the contracts usually run on a terminable basis, with all

---

[33] Wegener, *Juristen* 1992, 361 ff.; Wegener, U 1994 B, 20 ff.; Wegener, U 1994 B, 350 ff.; Borcher, U 1993 B, 97 ff.; Svendsen, U 1993 B, 227 ff.; Svendsen, U 1994 B, 252 ff.
[34] *Agenturloven av 19. juni 1992 nr. 56.*

the ensuing uncertainties. Furthermore, only to a very small degree is it possible to pay compensation for notice of termination. Although the problems have been well known for many years, and discussed in the West Nordic countries, no rules of law have been introduced which may protect the dealer. The lack of initiative regarding legislation may partly be explained by the fact that dealers constitute a very diverse group. In a number of instances, the dealer will not need to depend on the principal in the same way as, for instance, the agent or the commission agent. Dealers in the West Nordic countries on average hold a position of considerable importance in the market, for instance dealers for the major motor car companies. The notion here has probably been that these dealers must protect their own interests in the distribution contracts on the basis of which they operate.

SWEDEN

In Swedish law there is legislation (Commercial Agency Act of 1991) on commercial agents, who sell in the name of a principal and on his behalf. Under this legislation, the agent has a mandatory right to terms of notice which are determined in proportion to the time for which their contract was in force, and to compensation if the contract comes to an end without cause (cf. Directive 86/653/EEC). A sole distributor, selling in his own name and on his own behalf, is not protected by legislation. There are some vague statements in the preparatory works of the legislation on commercial agents that its rules could be applied by analogy. Since the reasons for a term of notice are the same, no matter whether a person sells in his principal's or his own name and on his principal's or his own behalf, and especially if Rodney was prohibited from representing other principals and is obliged to invest in personnel, marketing measures etc. to meet the demands of Oliver, there are good reasons why Rodney should enjoy the same term of notice as a commercial agent and why Oliver ought to be liable in damages, if he does not comply with that term of notice.

Under s. 25 of the 1991 Commercial Agency Act a contract for a definite period of time becomes a contract for an indefinite period of time if the parties continue their relationship after the original period has ended. The notice period should then be calculated according to the total time for which the relationship has existed. As, in the present case, it has lasted for more than six years, Rodney would as a commercial agent be entitled to a period of notice of six months, although the parties had agreed otherwise (s. 24). The same rule would probably be applied in favour of a distributor.[35] If Oliver does not grant Rodney his full notice period, Rodney is entitled to damages. Oliver would, of course, try to argue that there is no mandatory legislation applicable to a distributor (in contrast to a commercial agent) and granting him a minimum period of notice and that, therefore, the contract term ought to be upheld. However, a contract term can be set aside in favour of supplementary general principles under s. 36 of the Contracts Act of 1915.[36]

As to economic compensation when the relevant period of notice is observed, the point of departure must be that the distributor is not entitled to more than that for which he has contracted. No general legal principles apply affording a party compensation for frustrated investments or for the other party's enrichment when a contractual relation ceases to exist. The preparatory works of the 1991 legislation on commercial agents give some, but only vague, support for an enrichment action by way of analogy[37] provided, presumably, the distributor supplies the manufacturer with the names of his buyers and possibly also refrains from competing for some years (for what would otherwise be the enrichment?). It can be assumed, however, that the courts would be more reluctant to grant economic compensation after a reasonable time of notice than they are prepared to grant such reasonable term of notice. No Supreme Court cases exist. It might be mentioned that on the basis of the same point of departure the *Sø- og handelsret* (Commercial Court) in Copenhagen has granted some compensation,[38] while the Supreme Court of Norway, with the bench divided three against two, has denied it.[39] My guess is that the Supreme Court of Sweden would not grant compensation for enrichment without any support for such ruling in the contract.

The reasons why distributors were not covered by the same protective rules as commercial agents are (i) because the E.C. Directive does not cover them, (ii) because the Danish legislation on commercial agents preceding the Swedish one did not cover distributors, and (iii) because it had been agreed in the law commission preparing the legislation on commercial

---

[35] In Norway, the Oslo District Court afforded a distributor in 1978 (that is, before the commercial agency legislation was enacted in the Scandinavian countries) a notice period of one year where the contract had been renewed every year for twenty-three years.

[36] The *Sø- og handelsret* (Commercial Court) in Copenhagen (Denmark) has ruled that a distributor is entitled to a reasonable period of notice, but in the case at hand it accepted the six months which had been provided for in the contract; U 1980, p. 42.

[37] *Statens Offentliga Utredningar* (SOU) 1984:85 pp. 72 ff. and 185 ff., and Proposition 1990/91:63 p. 22.   [38] U 1988, p. 264, but contrast U 1980, p. 42.   [39] Rt. 1980, p. 116.

agents to keep distributors outside the scope of the legislation, if the organisations representing the parties involved were to draft a standard agreement containing the same protection as for commercial agents. This was done just before the commission presented its proposal, but the standard agreement is never used without alteration.[40]

FINLAND

The Finnish discussion of case 23 may be found together with the one of case 24, below, p. 554.

Editors' comparative observations

These may be found, together with those relating to case 24, at the end of the next section (p. 554).

[40] Answers to an inquiry from eighty lawyers specialising in this field of law; see here Håstad, *Den nya köprätten* 292 fn. 6.

Case 24: Long-term business relationships II

Case

Boris supplies Cary with replacement parts for the cars which the latter produces. The contract between Boris and Cary has been concluded on 1 January 1950. According to its terms the contract shall in the first place run for one calendar year from the date of contract and shall be renewed from year to year unless one or other party shall give notice to the other of his intention to terminate for the successive year. It further provides that this notice must be given at least a month prior to the end of the calendar year. For more than forty years Boris and Cary work together smoothly. On 30 November 1992, however, Boris gives notice to terminate the contract by the end of the year. Does the contract terminate? May Cary claim damages?

Discussions

GERMANY

In this case the contract was not renewed every year. Contrary to case 23 a reasonable expectation in the continuation of the contractual relationship could therefore be engendered in Cary. Boris behaves inconsistently, if after forty years of smooth co-operation he suddenly terminates the contract by availing himself of the short period of notice of one month. Moreover, Cary is not protected, in this case, by the analogous application of § 89 b HGB. A limitation of the right to terminate the contract based on § 242 BGB is therefore justifiable.

This may not, however, lead to the conclusion that the termination is invalid for it would then become impossible to terminate long-term contracts. Cary's reasonable expectations should rather be taken account of by lengthening the period of notice so as to give him the opportunity to adjust and reorganise his affairs. A notice period of about one year appears to be appropriate. Thus, the contract will only come to an end on 30 November 1993. Up to this time, Boris will have to supply the spare parts if he does not want to lay himself open to a claim for damages.

GREECE

The difference between case 23 and case 24 is that the contract between Boris and Cary shall, according to its terms, in the first place run for one calendar year but that it shall be renewed from year to year, unless one of the parties gives notice to the other of his intention to terminate the contract for the successive year. This means that the parties have not agreed to be bound by a long-term contract: they have left open the following year's renewal of the contract. Their contract also provides that notice to terminate must be given at least one month prior to the end of the calendar year. The contract has been renewed for forty-two years. On the basis of these facts, the notice by Boris on 30 November 1992 to terminate the contract by the end of the year may be considered invalid as being abusive, on the presupposition that it was not expected (art. 281 Gr. C.C.).[1]

If the court decides that the notice of termination is invalid as being abusive, the contract between Cary and Boris will continue for a reasonable time. Thus, Cary will have the opportunity to adjust and reorganise his business.[2] But the court has a discretionary power to order compensation instead.

The case does not attract application of the rules on deactivation of a right (*Verwirkung*).[3]

AUSTRIA

On these facts, as in those of case 23, one first has to consider whether the parties have implicitly varied their original agreement in relation to the termination of the contract. In this respect, though, merely to continue a contractual relationship is not a sufficient indication of a tacit waiver of a right to terminate the relationship within a short time. In Austrian law

[1] Cf. Georgiadis, in: *Astikos Kodix I* art. 281, no. 24.
[2] Cf. PolProt Athens 10104/1995 EED 96, 607 ff.
[3] On which, see the Greek report to case 22.

it is generally accepted that the mere non-use of a right does not lead to its loss.[4] For as a rule in these circumstances there is no intention to undertake any contractual commitment and, therefore, there can be no declaration of intention.

On the other hand, it is more likely on the facts of this case than on those in case 23 that a claim for damages will succeed. For Boris and Cary did not explicitly conclude a short-term contract from year to year (as did the parties in case 23) and the long duration of their mutual dealings and the steadiness of their co-operation suggest that Cary could rely on their contractual relationship being continued. Therefore, if Boris was able to appreciate that Cary relied on the continuation of their dealings and has arranged his affairs as a result, then Boris would have to give Cary proper notice of their termination, and any negligent failure to do so would attract liability in damages. Here, again, the principles of liability based on an unreasonable breaking-off of contractual negotiations are applicable by analogy.[5]

At first sight, it may seem illogical that Cary is not protected by contract law but only under the law of delictual liability. But this can be explained by the fact that any change in the terms of the contract requires a declaration of intention, whereas the weaker protection which is provided by imposing liability in damages is attracted by the engendering of reliance.

FRANCE

Cary and Boris have made a series of short-term contracts of sale for the supply of replacement parts for cars, renewed annually by tacit agreement. It is not known if Boris is Cary's sole supplier, nor if Boris supplies car parts to other persons.

If Cary wants to claim damages from Boris for his termination of the contract, he could argue that their one-year contract, renewed tacitly year by year, has been converted into a long-term contract of no fixed duration, support for this being found in the lack of any limit fixed on the number of renewals. This solution has been adopted by the courts with respect to contracts of employment[6] and agency contracts.[7] However, this argument may backfire on Cary, rather than protect him, as contracts of no fixed duration are terminable at will. On the basis that the contract of sale

---

[4] Cf. Rummel, in: *Rummel, ABGB I* § 863 n. 24.   [5] See the report to case 3.
[6] Civ. (1) 31 Mar. 1924, GP 1924.2.15.   [7] Civ. (1) 12 Jan. 1988, Bull. civ. I, no. 3, p. 2.

becomes a long-term contract, Boris is entitled simply to give notice to terminate with impunity, unless it can be shown that he has committed an abuse of his right to do so.[8] The same arguments apply here as are set out in the French discussion in relation to case 23.

In order to come to a view as to whether any abuse has taken place, it would be necessary to have clarification about the respective independence of the parties. There is thus insufficient evidence on the facts to hypothesise about the parties' potential bad faith. It is also assumed for the purpose of this analysis that Cary was not in breach nor in any way the cause of Boris' giving notice. In the result, on the facts as given, Boris could terminate the contract and Cary may not claim damages.

BELGIUM

The structure of the answer to cases 23 and 24 is somewhat complicated, because under Belgian law it is highly relevant whether the contract is (i) one of sole distributorship (as in case 23) or (ii) another type of supply contract (as in case 24). The differences between the solutions to cases 23 and 24 are mostly based on this aspect of the facts, rather than on whether the contract was renewed every year or had been concluded for an indeterminate time.

(i) Sole distributorships give rise to much litigation in Belgium. Termination of a sole distributorship is governed by a specific statute in Belgian law (Act of 27 July 1961 on sole distributorships). It applies in cases of sole distributorship and also in some cases of distributorship which place the distributor in an analogous position.

According to arts. 2 and 3 of the Act, a sole distributorship for an indeterminate period can only be terminated (except for fundamental non-performance) by observing a reasonable period of notice or by providing equitable compensation. Further, the distributor has to be compensated also for the goodwill he has created (in favour of the manufacturer), for other costs incurred from which the manufacturer benefits, and for the compensation due to employees who are to be dismissed. Belgian case law tends to grant very high compensation and to require a period of very long notice. For terminating a distributorship which has lasted forty-two years, as in this case, a notice period of several years, or an equivalent compensation, is required.

For the solution to cases 23 and 24 it is important to note that,

---

[8] Com. 16 Oct. 1967, D 1968.193 note R. Plaisant.

according to art. 3 *bis*, any distributorship to which the Act applies, and which is concluded for a fixed period of time, (a) can only be terminated by way of notice given at least three months prior to the end of the term, and (b) automatically becomes a contract for an indeterminate period, subject to arts. 2 and 3, following a second renewal.

Although in case 23 the contract would come to an end under Belgian law, Rodney is entitled to a considerable amount of compensation, as described above.

Even under general contract law, i.e. if the 1961 Act were not applicable, Rodney would be entitled to some compensation, at least for the goodwill he has created. Such a protection for sole distributors is understandable, precisely because they create a market (something which is not done in supply contracts as in the one in case 24). It is true that commercial agents also create goodwill, and are less protected (according to the E.C. Directive on commercial agents[9]), but the economic risk taken by an agent is much smaller than that taken by a sole distributor, who himself has to invest and who buys and sells the products in his own name and on his own behalf (account).

(ii) For other supply contracts, there are no specific statutory rules and thus the general contract law applies. Termination of the contract must be done in good faith. This normally requires a notice of reasonable length, but case law has not required periods of comparable length for cases of sole distributorship. It is usually held to be abusive (i.e. contrary to good faith) to terminate such a relationship without a reasonable period of notice. Clearly, in cases such as 23 and 24, where the relationship has lasted for forty-two years, notice of one or some months will be insufficient under Belgian law. Certainly, the case would be even clearer if Cary attempted to terminate such a contract, as it is generally thought to be easier to find a new supplier rather than a new regular customer. According to the test of disproportionality, a judge will take account of the advantages and disadvantages created by the termination; one of the elements may be the degree of dependency of one party (Cary) on the other (Boris).

Theoretically, a judge may decide that the contract was not lawfully terminated and oblige Boris to continue to supply Cary for a reasonable period (which is sufficient in order to find a new supplier under normal market conditions). However, it is disputed whether such an injunction

---

[9] 86/653/EEC of 18 December 1986.

can be given in summary proceedings (which is the only way to provide a remedy within a short time, i.e. a remedy which is effective).

Since any abuse of right would relate to a contractual relationship, damages would sound in contract rather than in delict. Thus, the measure for damages is, in principle, the positive interest (expectation interest) calculated on the basis of the period of time which Boris should have respected when terminating the contract.[10]

If the supply contract were a one-year contract, which had been renewed annually for forty-two years, the solution would normally be the same. This does not make a real difference for the application of the doctrine of abuse of right (good faith) which requires, in principle, notice of reasonable length or equivalent compensation.[11] But there may be circumstances where it is not abusive to refuse to renew the contract, such as where there has been a call for tenders every year.

SPAIN

For Spanish law, the facts of case 24 attract the same legal approach as do the facts of case 14 (that is, the case concerning the production of new bumpers), and for the reasons which are stated in relation to that case the contract is indeed terminated and Cary is not entitled to recover damages from Boris.

ITALY

From the point of view of an Italian lawyer, it is difficult to distinguish the issues raised by case 24 from those discussed in relation to case 23. However, it is arguable that the term of the contract which provides for renewal of the contract from year to year is more apt to generate reliance on the continuation of the relationship than is the consecutive conclusion of contracts year by year. If this argument were accepted, then a court would be more likely to hold Boris to have been in breach of his duties of good faith, with the consequences which we have already described in relation to case 23.

Postscript: See now l. 18 June 1998, n. 192, *Disciplina della subfornitura nelle attività produttive*, as discussed in the Italian contribution to case 14, text after n. 21.

---

[10] See, e.g., *Hof van Beroep* (Appeal) Antwerpen 28 Oct. 1996, AJT 1996–1997, 531.
[11] Ibid.

THE NETHERLANDS

These cases are considered from a strictly private law point of view, leaving aside the aspects of public competition law which may be involved. The legal consequences of Oliver and Boris' acts will have to be assessed in very much the same way as indicated in the Dutch report to case 14. Given that this is a long-term relationship and that termination is really at the last possible moment, a court will probably award Rodney and Cary a substantial amount of damages or might even order them to start negotiations on how to terminate in a less abrupt manner.

ENGLAND

The English law approach is the same as in case 23. The contracts take effect according to their terms, under one of which Boris has (validly) terminated the contract. The fact that the parties have worked together for forty years is irrelevant. Again no damages are due from Boris.

IRELAND

No Irish decision exists on the special problems arising from long-term supply contracts, but it may be supposed that, as in the interpretation of exclusive agency contracts,[12] the courts would be sensitive to the legitimate expectations of parties who have incurred significant costs. However, there is an important difference between the two types of contract. For in the case of long-term supply contracts termination of the agreement by one party does not lead to the enrichment of that party at the expense of the other, whereas in exclusive agency contracts the former 'principal' will benefit from the agent's pre-termination efforts. However, it is not at all clear whether an Irish court would use this difference to distinguish its approach to exclusive agency contracts.

It is submitted that, as in all cases of implied terms, much will depend on the context. Would the termination by the supplier render production impossible and cause a loss of all the costs incurred by the manufacturer of the assembled product? If that were the case, the court might be prepared to moderate the seemingly absolute right to terminate the contract with an implied duty of good faith such as was found in *Fluid Power*

---

[12] See the Irish report to case 23 above.

Technology Co. v. Sperry (Ireland) Ltd.[13] If the parts were available elsewhere, albeit at a higher price, then it is unlikely that any restriction on the right to terminate would be found. Again, though, as in case 23, if the termination of the contract were valid, then no compensation would be payable in respect of the other party's costs.[14]

SCOTLAND

The answer to this problem mirrors case 23. Boris has fulfilled the terms of the contract which required him to give one month's notice to terminate the contract. The fact that they have been contracting for over forty years is irrelevant; there is no evidence of variation of the terms of the contract. The contract terminates and Cary has no claim for damages.

This case, and case 23, are clear examples of the absence of good faith in the Scots law of contract.

DENMARK AND NORWAY

At the outset the position in this case is not different to that in case 23, except we are not dealing here with dealership. Commercial agreements concluded for an indefinite period of time continue until notice of termination. The termination may, of course, affect the other party in an unexpected manner and entail hardship. Nevertheless, it must be said that this is an uncertainty inherent in the actual contractual relationship, and does not provide any justification for the courts to interfere by setting aside the notice of termination. Unless it is a case where the parties are of significantly unequal bargaining power, so that there would be a strong dependency on the part of the vendor, the termination will generally have to be respected. However, the courts may find by way of interpretation that termination requires a 'good reason'.[15]

SWEDEN

As stated above,[16] there is no legislation concerning the long-term rights of a supplier. In principle there is freedom of contract. There probably

---

[13] Unreported, High Court, 22 February 1985. See also the Irish analyses to cases 14 and 23 above.   [14] See the Irish report to case 23 above.   [15] Gomard, *Obligationsret 1* 27.
[16] See the Swedish report to case 14 above.

exists a general supplementary rule, however, that contracts for an indefinite period can be terminated (only) under a reasonable period of notice (cf. the 1991 Commercial Agency Act, the 1914 Consignment Act and the 1970 Real Estate Code on lease). Since the contract between Boris and Cary is a contract for an indefinite period, Cary has a good chance of having the agreed notice period of only one month declared unreasonable for the purposes of s. 36 of the Contracts Act of 1915. A notice period of at least six months ought to be given, or damages ought to be paid. However, no Supreme Court case exists and, therefore, the situation is somewhat uncertain.

Remuneration for any enrichment as a result of a market position created by the supplier cannot be granted. Only compensation for investments that have not yet been amortised may be contemplated. However, it is very difficult to find a basis for such a claim.

FINLAND

Even here, with respect to long-term relationships, Finnish law only reluctantly recognises facts as contractual norms.[17] It is a different matter, of course, that business practices between parties may have the effect that, as courts often say, something is 'to be considered as agreed upon'. The cases here (cases 23 and 24) are not of such a type.

With respect specifically to cases 23 and 24, the long duration of a contractual relationship does not *per se* affect the termination (at will) at the end of the one-year period. Rodney (case 23) and Cary (case 24) cannot claim damages, but the condition of one month's notice might be adjusted (s. 36 of the Contracts Act of 1929). This is, again, a matter of evidence.

Editors' comparative observations

The responses to these cases of the legal systems under consideration may be tentatively grouped into six.

(i) At the one end of the spectrum are Swedish, Finnish and Belgian law. Swedish and Finnish courts would probably regard the notice periods in both cases (23 and 24) as unreasonable and adjust them under s. 36 of the Contracts Act (which allows the adjustment of any contract term which is considered unreasonable). In Belgium, too, the period of notice would be

---

[17] See the Finnish report in case 22 above.

regarded as unreasonable in both cases. However, protection is not granted, normally, by regarding the notice of termination as invalid, or by adjusting the period of notice, but by awarding a substantial amount of damages. This result is reached in case 23 through special legislation applicable to contracts of sole distributorship and in case 24 on the basis of the good faith requirement of general contract law.

(ii) Greek and Dutch law are similar in granting protection to both Rodney and Cary. Greek law regards the notice of termination in case 24 as abusive and thus invalid. In case 23 it grants a claim for damages on the basis of an analogous application of a rule of partnership law. In the absence of this rule, it would, however, also have considered the notice of termination in case 23 as being contrary to good faith. Dutch courts would probably (on the basis of the general notion of good faith) award a substantial amount of damages to both Rodney and Cary or even require negotiations on how to terminate the contracts in a less abrupt manner.

(iii) Perhaps somewhat surprisingly in view of the diametrically opposite position taken by English and Scots law, Irish law might also be prepared to moderate both the option not to renew the contract in case 23 and the seemingly absolute right to terminate the contract in case 24 with an implied duty of good faith, though this would result merely in an implied obligation on the person purporting to exercise his right to state the reason for which it is done and a requirement that the terminating party must honestly believe these reasons to be valid.

(iv) Some legal systems distinguish between the two cases and are prepared to protect Cary (case 24) but not Rodney (case 23), or at least not to the same extent. This is the position in German law. Whereas Rodney has no legitimate expectations of a continued contractual relationship since his contracts with Oliver require renewal from year to year, Cary does have such expectations as the contract is renewed automatically (though subject to notice of termination). Good faith (§ 242 BGB) does not, however, require that Boris' termination is held ineffective, but rather allows a court to lengthen the period of notice so as to allow Cary to adjust his affairs. Some measure of protection is, however, also granted to Rodney in the form of a claim for compensation. It is based on the analogous application of a rule concerning commercial agents (the same analogy is proposed in Swedish law). Austrian law also distinguishes between the two cases. But while it does not grant Rodney any protection at all, it would probably award damages to Cary on a basis similar to that in cases of the abrupt breaking-off of negotiations. Italian law inclines in the same direction; it would contemplate a claim for damages more readily in case 24 where Boris may be seen to have been in breach of his duties of good faith.

(v) At the other end of the spectrum there are those systems which protect neither Rodney nor Cary. This is true, in particular, of English, Scots and Spanish law: they deny any protection to a person whose contract has been terminated according to its terms. In English and Scots law this is seen as reflecting the binding force of the terms of the contracts and the absence of any general principle such as good faith tempering the exercise of any right arising from these terms. For Spanish law, which does possess such a principle, the High Court has ruled that such an outcome merely reflects the parties' use of their bargaining power to their economic advantage.

(vi) According to the West Nordic legal systems, too, the risks inherent in contractual relationships such as those in cases 23 and 24 must be borne by the parties exposed to a rather sudden and unexpected notice of termination. In both cases the termination is taken to be valid and no claim for compensation is granted (except in special cases 'where otherwise the outcome would have an extremely low degree of reasonableness'). The same is true of French law since, in the absence of 'fraudulent or disloyal manoeuvres', the notice to terminate, or not to renew the contract, cannot be regarded as abusive. In view of the exceptions mentioned, the West Nordic and French legal systems seem to adopt a somewhat more lenient approach than English, Scots and Spanish law.

Case 25: Effect of inflation

Case

A long-term lease provides for the supply of steam for heating purposes at a fixed price. The price reflects the market value of the steam. Due to 'normal' inflation the price becomes derisory (7 per cent of the market value). Can the supplier of the steam demand a higher price than the one originally agreed upon? Would your answer differ if the price becomes derisory owing to a dramatic and unforeseeable inflation as a result of post-war economic difficulties?

Discussions

GERMANY

This case concerns the adjustment of a contract on the basis of the doctrine of the collapse of the underlying basis of the transaction (*Wegfall der Geschäftsgrundlage*), as developed under cover of § 242 BGB.[1]

The basis of the contract consists of those circumstances which (i) the parties have presupposed at the time of conclusion of their contract, which (ii) are so important to one of them that he would not have concluded the contract, or would have concluded it differently and (iii) the importance of which the other party would have had, in good faith, to acknowledge.[2] If circumstances of this kind have fallen away, an adjustment or, if need be, even the termination of the contract, is both justified and required.[3]

---

[1] Cf. *Jauernig/*Vollkommer § 242, nn. 64 ff.; *Palandt/*Heinrichs § 242, nn. 110 ff.
[2] Cf. Medicus, *Bürgerliches Recht* n. 165 a; § 306 I KE-BGB (Draft of the Commission charged with the reform of the law of obligations).   [3] *Palandt/*Heinrichs § 242, nn. 130 ff.

Presently, one of the circumstances fundamental to the contract may be seen to be the expectation that the value of money would not substantially change. This was indeed so important to the seller that he probably would not have concluded the contract or would have concluded it differently, had he foreseen such change. Yet foreseeable changes do not lead to the collapse of the underlying basis of the transaction.[4] Normal inflation therefore does not justify invocation of § 242 BGB. This would run counter to the principle of nominal value which is fundamental to German private law.[5]

However, the contract may be amended if the price becomes derisory as a result of dramatic and unforeseeable inflation in times of crisis. The balance in value between performance and counter-performance must have been disturbed to such an extent that the change of circumstances can no longer be regarded as being covered by the normal contractual taking of risks, and that the interests of one party to the contract are gravely jeopardised.[6] The creditor would clearly not undertake to carry the risk of a dramatic and unforeseeable inflation. His interest is gravely jeopardised if the price is only 7 per cent of the market value. Hence, the doctrine of the collapse of the underlying basis of the transaction is applicable. As a result, the price has to be adjusted so as to take account of the inflation.

Adjustment of a contract on account of the collapse of the underlying basis of the transaction is a well-established feature of the modern German law of obligations. It constitutes a particularly prominent example of judge-made law, under the auspices of a general clause, within a codified legal system.[7] Paul Oertmann in a monograph from 1921 laid the doctrinal foundations[8] which have since been elaborated in countless books and articles.[9] Some of the birth pangs could have been avoided had the draftsmen followed Bernhard Windscheid's advice not to jettison the clausula rebus sic stantibus (or, indeed, his own presupposition doctrine).[10]

GREECE

The increase of the market price due to 'normal' inflation does not allow the supplier of the steam to demand a higher price than the one originally

---

[4] Palandt/Heinrichs § 242, n. 128; Münchener Kommentar/Roth § 242, n. 543 (prevailing opinion).   [5] For details see Staudinger/Karsten Schmidt, Vorbem. zu § 244, nn. 20 ff.
[6] BGHZ 77, 194 (198 f.); Palandt/Heinrichs § 242, n. 137.
[7] See, e.g., Zimmermann, in: Introduction 16 ff.; Zimmermann/Jansen, in: Essays Fleming 296 ff.   [8] Die Geschäftsgrundlage: Ein neuer Rechtsbegriff.
[9] Cf., e.g., Larenz, passim; Diesselhorst, in: Rechtswissenschaft 153 ff.
[10] For details, see Zimmermann, Obligations 576 ff., 581 f.

agreed upon, because it is an ordinary event which is quite foreseeable.[11] However, the second situation will be judged according to art. 388 Gr. C.C.[12]

Article 388 Gr. C.C. provides as follows: 'If, having regard to the requirements of good faith and business usage, the circumstances on which the parties had mainly based the conclusion of a bilateral agreement have subsequently changed on exceptional grounds that could not have been foreseen and if because of this change the performance due by the debtor has become excessively onerous, taking also into consideration the counter-performance, the court may, at the request of the debtor, and according to its own discretion reduce the debtor's performance to the appropriate extent or determine the dissolution of the contract in its entirety or with regard to the part which has not been performed. If the dissolution of the contract has been ordered the obligations to perform arising from that contract shall be extinguished and the contracting parties shall be reciprocally obliged to restore the performances which they have received, in terms of the provisions on unjustified enrichment.'

Under this article, the supplier of the steam has the right to ask for a higher price than that originally agreed upon, because there was a change in the circumstances, the change had occurred after the conclusion of the contract, and it was caused by a dramatic and unforeseeable inflation as a result of post-war economic difficulties. The adjustment of the contract to the appropriate extent, namely determination of a higher price, has to be ordered by the court and does not follow *ipso iure*.[13]

Article 388 Gr. C.C., which is a special expression of the principle of good faith (art. 288 Gr. C.C.), is one of the most fundamental and forward-looking provisions to be found in the Greek Civil Code. It expresses a combination of views and criteria which are drawn from classical contract theory, emphasising the need for a balance between performance and counter-performance, on the *clausula rebus sic stantibus*, the German doctrine of the collapse of the underlying basis of the transaction (*Wegfall der Geschäftsgrundlage*) and the French theory of the unforeseen (*théorie de l'imprévision*).

The solution provided by art. 388 Gr. C.C. could also be achieved by way of application of art. 288 Gr. C.C.[14] Nevertheless, in practical terms, the

---

[11] Areopagus 509/62 NoB 11, 159; Areopagus 399/61 NoB 10, 83; Stathopoulos, in: *Astikos Kodix II* art. 388 no. 2.

[12] Cf. Papantoniou, *Kali Pistis* 172 ff.; Sakketas, in: *ErmAK II* art. 388, nos. 28 ff.; Areopagus 676/1994 NoB 43, 825.

[13] Stathopoulos, in: *Astikos Kodix II* art. 388, nos. 20, 22, 26; Sakketas, in: *ErmAK II* art. 388, no. 60.   [14] See the German approach which is based on § 242 BGB.

adoption of this special provision is useful, since it gives a clearer and more specific expression to the will of the legislator and motivates the judge to overcome any doubts which he might have in the application of the general 'good faith' provision.

An action brought under art. 388 Gr. C.C. is not one for compensation. The rule aims at the restoration of a balance between performance and counter-performance to the extent that it will correspond to the requirements of good faith; it does not aim at making good any loss. A basic difference between art. 388 Gr. C.C. and art. 288 Gr. C.C. is that determination under the former rule is made by judicial decision, whereas in the case of art. 288 Gr. C.C. the consequences follow *ipso iure*.[15]

AUSTRIA

The parties have agreed on a fixed price for their contract rather than on a price which may increase according to changes in market value. As a result, in Austrian law the supplier of steam has no contractual claim to any higher price even if the contract price becomes derisory due to inflation. Nor can the supplier demand a higher price on the basis of any alleged mistake, for while a party's mistake may indeed lead to a modification of the contract in terms of § 872 ABGB, this is the case only where the normal criteria laid down in § 871 ABGB have been met. A mere error in motive is irrelevant except in case of fraudulent behaviour by the other party (§ 870 ABGB).

Another possibility would be for the supplier of the steam to bring an action invoking a change of circumstances fundamental to the contract.[16] From various provisions in the ABGB *Pisko*[17] derived the principle that a party to a contract enjoys protection if a fundamental change of circumstances leads to a serious disturbance of the balance between performance and counter-performance.[18] However, a party to a contract cannot rely on this principle if the facts in question arise within his own sphere of

---

[15] Stathopoulos, *Contract* nos. 291–7, pp. 192–6; Chiotellis, *passim*; Fragistas, in: *Festschrift Wolff* 64–5; Stathopoulos, in: *Astikos Kodix II* art. 388, nos. 1–31, pp. 365–74 (see at pp. 365–74 the selected bibliography of Greek authors writing in the Greek language); also Papanikolaou, *Peri ton orion* 111–17; Papanikolaou, *Katapleonektikes Dikaiopraxies, passim*; Georgakopoulos 163–4.   [16] Koziol/Welser, *Bürgerliches Recht I* 133.
[17] Pisko, in: *Klang, Kommentar II/2* 348 ff.; in the same sense Gschnitzer, in: *Klang, Kommentar IV/1* 334 ff.; OGH in ÖBA 1991, 759; ÖRZ 1992/40. Rummel, JBl 1981, 7 ff. considers that this is a question of interpretation of the contract.
[18] Koziol/Welser, *Bürgerliches Recht I* 134.

responsibility[19] or if they were foreseeable at the time of entering into the contract.[20] Thus, in Austrian law the supplier of steam in case 25 has no claim if the contract price becomes derisory merely as a result of normal, foreseeable inflation, but in the case of dramatic, unforeseeable inflation, he may demand that the price be modified.

FRANCE

In order to ask for the revision of a price fixed by a long-term contract, the supplier of steam would have to base his claim on the theory of 'modification on the ground of unforeseeability' (*révision pour imprévision*). Various explanations for the theory of revision for unforeseeability have been put forward. Thus, it has been said that contracts are deemed to contain an implied clause of *rebus sic stantibus* according to which if unforeseeable circumstances appear, the contract is void, a theory which suffers from artificiality. Other authors have resorted to the theory of *la cause*. Thus, once a contract has been entered into and the balance of the obligations are broken, the obligation undertaken by one party no longer has any cause because the performance of the counter-obligation would not be its equivalent. Finally, authors have relied on the theory of *force majeure* to free the debtor of his contractual obligations, for 'no one can be bound to something which was unforeseeable and impossible' (*à l'impossible, nul n'est tenu*).

However, in 1876 the *Cour de cassation* clearly rejected the theory of *imprévision*,[21] holding that 'in no case is it up to the courts, no matter how equitable their decision might appear, to take time and circumstances into consideration in order to modify private contracts and substitute new clauses for the ones which have been freely accepted by the contracting parties'. This principle, constantly reaffirmed by the civil courts,[22] means that the courts cannot modify the price to be paid in long-term contracts unless the parties have included contractual terms so providing.

By analogy, if the fall in value of a contract price is due to normal inflation, the supplier cannot ask for its modification. This rule is based on a strict application of the principle of the binding force of contracts found

---

[19] OGH in JBl 1989, 650; JBl 1994, 260.
[20] Cf. OGH in SZ 59/17 (1986); JBl 1979, 651; Ertl 235.
[21] Civ. 6 Mar. 1876, *Canal de Craponne*, DP 1976.1.193 note A. Giboulot.
[22] Civ. 4 Aug. 1915, DP 1916.1.22; Civ. 10 Mar. 1919, S 1920.1.105 note E. Naquet, and more recently e.g. Com. 3 Jan. 1979, GP 1979.1.Pan.jur.214.

in art. 1134 al. 1 of the Civil Code. The *Cour de cassation* has held that equitable considerations cannot, in this instance, prevail over the primacy of the contract.[23] It is interesting to note that decisions of arbitrators follow the line taken by the civil courts in this respect,[24] although some authorities suggest that recently they have started to recognise the implied clause *rebus sic stantibus*.

However, the French civil and administrative courts differ in their positions as to the theory of *imprévision*, the administrative courts accepting that it may apply in certain circumstances to the 'administrative contracts' which come before them. In a famous judgement given on 30 March 1916,[25] the *Conseil d'Etat* held that due to unforeseen circumstances arising from the war, a supplier of gas in a locality was not bound to continue to supply gas at the original contract rate, as long as the abnormal situation created by the First World War in relation to the prices of their own supply of fuel continued. The *Conseil d'Etat* therefore sent the parties back to the lower court in order to come to an agreement as to higher rates for the gas to be supplied, taking into account this difficulty but also the residual risk that the supplier must bear in relation to an increase in prices. This principle has been reapplied in relation to various administrative contracts including the supply of services.[26] It is clear that the administrative courts accept this theory on the ground of ensuring the continuance of a 'public service' which is in the public interest.[27]

It is unclear whether the lease in case 25 concerns the supply of steam for heating purposes as part of a 'public service' and thus whether the contract would come within the jurisdiction of the administrative courts. If it did so, and if the change of price was due to unforeseeable inflation due to post-war economic difficulties, the steam supplier's claim might be admitted by the administrative courts. As we have noted, if such a claim were admitted, the judges ask the parties to renegotiate the contract price, though if they are unable to agree, they fix an indemnity. If this were the case, the steam supplier would be obliged to continue the supply. If the contract does not concern the supply of a public service and therefore does not fall within the jurisdiction of the administrative courts, then, in the absence of express contractual provision, the steam supplier will have no chance of succeeding with his claim for a higher price.

---

[23] Com. 18 Dec. 1979, Bull. civ. IV, no. 339, p. 266.   [24] Kassis, *passim*.
[25] CE 30 Mar. 1916, *Gaz de Bordeaux*, Leb. 125 concl. Cardenet.
[26] CE 8 Feb. 1918, *Gaz de Poissy*, Leb. 122 concl. Corneille.
[27] See the *conclusions* of Comm. gouv. *Cardenet*, in CE 30 Mar. 1916 above.

The approach of French private law to *imprévision* reflects the primacy given by both jurists and the courts to the principle of the binding force of contracts: the moral rule *pacta sunt servanda* prevails over economic considerations. Moreover, legal literature suggests that good faith cannot be invoked in this context, for while this principle may be used to determine the scope of the parties' obligations, it may not determine their existence. Nor should 'equity' be allowed to supplant, nor be used as a pretext to override, the express terms of the agreement. French private lawyers are swayed by the arguments that revision would require judicial intervention of a type for which they do not have authority and that it would deny the primacy of party autonomy. This inflexibility is criticised by the majority of jurists on the basis that it means that French law is unable to compete with remedies offered by other legal systems in international commerce.[28]

BELGIUM

(i) Belgian law is very restrictive in admitting a modification or termination of the contract because of changed circumstances. This is especially the case when the changed circumstances result from any depreciation in the value of money or from macro-economic reasons, because a change of circumstances of this kind is usually not unforeseeable (for the principle of monetary nominalism see, e.g., art. 1895 C.C.). Moreover, the parties to a contract can easily include in it an adjustment clause to take account of inflation. Such clauses are very common especially in lease-type contracts (in some leases, indexation even takes place by operation of law, without the need for a specific clause[29]).

If we look at the facts of case 25, which refer to normal inflation causing the price to become only 7 per cent of the market value, this presupposes

---

[28] Ghestin/Jamin/Billau nos. 303 ff.

[29] Variation is often tied to an index of prices established by the government (e.g. rent variation control – art. 1728 *bis* C.C. concerning variation of rent for immovables; interest for certain credits – art. 9, Mortgage Credit Act of 4 August 1992), or only a certain portion thereof; economic legislation has also restricted the possibility of adapting prices. For example, art. 57 of the Act of 30 March 1976 provides that industrial and commercial prices and tariffs (excluding rent for immovables, wages and salaries, and tariffs of the liberal professions) in contracts concluded between Belgian residents and to be performed in Belgium cannot be linked to the general development of prices ('indexation'), but only to the specific costs of performance, and even here only up to 80 per cent. Sometimes, variation is simply forbidden (instalment sales to consumers and consumer leasing: art. 30, Consumer Credit Act of 12 June 1991).

a contract for a very long period (some twenty or thirty years) which must have been concluded for a fixed period of at least this length (if the contract is a contract for an indeterminate period, it can be terminated at any moment by giving notice of reasonable length). It is very improbable that a supplier would bind himself for such a long period without any possibility of terminating the contract or adapting the price.

Even in the case of dramatic and unforeseeable inflation due to post-war economic difficulties, Belgian case law remains very restrictive. This is considered a matter for parliament which has, indeed, intervened on several occasions (for example, after the First World War and, to a lesser extent, after the Second).

(ii) Where, however, the change of circumstances does not concern the value of money but rather the difficulty of performing itself, Belgian case law is a little less restrictive.[30] Although, in principle, termination is possible only in the case of 'absolute impossibility' of performance, it has also been allowed in cases where performance has become fundamentally different due to a change of circumstances. In some specific cases (of long-term contracts), it was considered an abuse of right by the creditor to insist on further performance of the contract and to refuse to accept termination and a reasonable amount of damages.[31] The rule, mentioned previously,[32] that a party acts contrary to good faith when claiming performance of a contract or clause which has lost its justification,[33] might also help in some cases of changed circumstances. But mere 'equity' is certainly an insufficient ground for the modification or termination of a binding contract[34] – a more specific rule or ground is always necessary. Moreover, a judge will never modify the terms of the contract himself; he will either grant termination of the contract, or decide that a refusal to terminate the contract is abusive if the other party offers a reasonable adaptation.[35]

Adjustment clauses, as has been mentioned, are not rare in important contracts. But they are not accepted as implied terms. Only in some types

[30] See, in general, Philippe, *passim*. See e.g. Comm. Brussel 16 Jan. 1979, JT 1980, 461.
[31] Cass. 16 Jan. 1986, *Le Hardy v. Derouaux*, Arr. 683 = RW 1987–1988 note A. van Oevelen; Cass. 22 Nov. 1996, *WE Belgium v. Camaieu*, Arr. 1996–1997.
[32] See the Belgian report to case 12 above.
[33] Cass. 21 Sep. 1979, *Post v. Locabel*, Arr. 92 (cited also in the Belgian report to case 12 above).
[34] See e.g. Cass. 1 Oct. 1987, RW 1987–1988, 1506; Cass. 14 Apr. 1994, Arr. n° 177.
[35] See again Cass. 16 Jan. 1986, *Le Hardy v. Derouaux*, Arr. 683 = RW 1987–1988 note A. van Oevelen.

of contracts concluded with public authorities is a kind of *clausula rebus sic stantibus* recognised as an implied term in favour of the public authority.[36]

SPAIN

The Spanish High Court has for some fifty years accepted that a party to a contract who is affected by a change in circumstances may seek to rescind the contract by way of application of the rule known as *rebus sic stantibus*, but the lack of legislative basis for this rule is considered by that court a reason for taking a restrictive approach to its interpretation and application. Accordingly, a party to a contract may bring an action to change or to rescind the contract only if all the following conditions are fulfilled: (i) it is a long-term contract; (ii) an extraordinary change of circumstances has occurred since the contract was made; (iii) this change of circumstances results in a very considerable disparity in the respective duties of the parties; (iv) the change in circumstances was not foreseeable at the time the contract was made and (v) there is no other route for relief for the claimant which would allow him to avoid any harm which would otherwise result from the change of circumstances.[37]

The High Court has not yet allowed a party to a contract to rely on the rule *rebus sic stantibus* so as to avoid the disastrous effects of inflation in relation to long-term contracts. In the view expressed by that court, parties to a contract *ought* to foresee such a situation and provide themselves against it by the terms of the contract which they conclude.[38] The decisions in which this view was taken concerned cases of dramatic changes of circumstances and economic difficulties which arose in Spain after the Civil War, in which the High Court did not normally accept the application of the rule so as to give relief. However, in the present writer's view, the courts' approach to the conditions for the application of the rule *rebus sic stantibus* is currently more flexible than in the past, and this would mean perhaps that a different result would be reached if the contract price 'becomes derisory owing to a dramatic and unforeseeable inflation as a result of post-war economic difficulties' (the second question posed in

---

[36] For example, 'concessions' of public services to private parties (for a determinate period) can be terminated because of changed circumstances, even if this is not explicitly provided for in the contract – see Cass. 31 May 1978, RW 1978–1979, 1229.

[37] High Court judgements of 14 December 1940 (RJA 1940, 1135), 17 May 1941 (RJA 1941, 632), 27 June 1984 (RJA 1984, 3438).   [38] Judgement of 19 April 1985 (RJA 1985, 1804).

the case scenario). Since, however, there are no actual Spanish cases dealing with such a dramatic inflation no final view may be offered for this hypothesis.

ITALY

Although inflation has dramatically altered the relationship between the market price and the contract price for supply of the steam, the supplier cannot obtain a price higher than the one to which he originally agreed.

Article 1467 of the Civil Code, which introduces the general rule governing the situation where contracts have become excessively onerous for one party due to change of circumstances, applies only when extraordinary and unforeseeable events have taken place.[39] The same requirement may be found in art. 1664 of the Civil Code which allows revision of the terms of a contract like the one in discussion, where a change in circumstances has altered the proportion between the obligations of the parties by at least one-tenth.[40] On the facts of case 25, the assumption is that the rate of inflation is 'normal' and this means that the contract must be performed without taking into account the effects of inflation.[41]

Clearly, though, the answer given by Italian law to this case would differ if the price of the steam had become derisory due to a 'dramatic and unforeseeable inflation'.[42] Here, then, the supplier could insist on a modification of the price which had originally been agreed upon.

THE NETHERLANDS

In both situations presented art. 6:258 B.W. will apply. A court could order that the contract be modified or set aside, even with retroactive effect, upon the demand of one of the parties.

Article 6:258 contains a rule that was already applied by the *Hoge Raad* before the enactment of the new Civil Code.[43] It was clear that, given the ever widening ambit of good faith generally, the legal consequences of changed circumstances should be looked at from the point of view of both parties: the party who benefited from the new situation and the one to

---

[39] For comparative analysis of Italian law on this point see Gallo, *passim*; Philippe 406 ff.
[40] Art. 1664 c.c.
[41] Terranova, in: *Il codice civile* 140; Gabrielli, Giur. it, 1986, I,1, 1717–18; Lipari, Giust. civ., 1985, I, 2803. Cass., 9 Jul. 1969, n. 2518; Cass., 9 Oct. 1971, Riv. not., 1972, II, 562; Trib. Roma, 7 Mar. 1969, Riv. not., 1971, II, 287.
[42] Rubino/Iudica, in: *Commentario Scialoja-Branca* 306–7.
[43] *Hoge Raad* 27 April 1984, NJ 1984, 679 (*Nationale Volksbank v. Helder*).

whose detriment it operated. The new Civil Code, in this respect, adopted the following approach. If the circumstances, which arose after the conclusion of the contract, were taken into account by the parties when they made their contract, they have become part of the parties' assessment of the risks. In such a case there can be no intervention in terms of good faith. Otherwise (and this means that the parties may well have realised what might happen, but did not take account of it in their assessment of the contractual risks), the consequences must be governed by good faith. In such a situation a court may, at the request of one of the parties, (completely or partially) dissolve the contract even with retroactive effect (art. 6:258 B.W.). It may also attach to its decision certain conditions (art. 6:260, 1 B.W.), such as the payment of an amount of money.

From the *travaux préparatoires* it becomes clear that art. 6:258 should be applied with extreme caution. The *Hoge Raad* has reiterated this.[44]

ENGLAND

First, in principle, changes of circumstances subsequent to contract do not affect the parties' obligations, the only general exception to this being termination of the *contract* under the doctrine of frustration.[45] The test for frustration is whether the supervening event or circumstances make performance of the contract radically different from that undertaken by the parties.[46] While this test may be satisfied in circumstances other than of impossibility of performance, it is clear that a contract will not be frustrated simply on the ground that its performance becomes more onerous or expensive. Obviously, therefore, the contract between the parties to the lease is not frustrated in the present case since the supplier of the steam (whom we must presume also to be the landlord) can supply it, only at an amount hugely more expensive than was originally envisaged. In principle, it would not matter how 'dramatic or unforeseeable' was the increase in cost of the supply of the steam.

Secondly, though, having said this, the courts have on occasion managed to avoid unduly harsh or unfair consequences caused by changes in circumstances in long-term contracts with no fixed duration by implying a term in the contract providing for termination by notice.[47]

---

[44] See further Asser-Hartkamp, *Verbintenissenrecht II* nr. 329 ff.
[45] *Davis Contractors Ltd v. Fareham Urban District Council* [1956] AC 696.   [46] Ibid.
[47] Bell, in: *Contract* 206–7; and see e.g. *Staffordshire Area Health Authority v. South Staffordshire Waterworks Co.* [1978] 1 WLR 1387.

Thirdly, modern well-drawn leases, especially those which are for longer terms of years, contain express provision for the revision of terms which may be unduly affected by changes either in market values or the value of the currency. In the case of commercial premises, some kind of rent review clause is 'almost invariably included'.[48] Moreover, where, as in case 25, a separate sum is charged for the provision of services by the landlord, which are known as 'service charges', 'the almost invariable practice is to stipulate that the service charge is to be paid by reference to a formula, which usually imposes on the tenant liability for a fixed percentage, or a fair proportion to be determined pursuant to a special procedure, of the cost to the landlord of providing the relevant services'.[49] On the facts of case 25, therefore, contractual practice regulates the problem.

IRELAND

This problem must be analysed under two quite different legal bases, namely, frustration and implied rights of termination.

As to frustration, the leading English case of *Davis Contractors Ltd v. Fareham Urban District Council*[50] is regarded as good law in Ireland.[51] Accordingly, any obligation to continue performance will be discharged if, due to unanticipated difficulty, the contract as performed would be something fundamentally different from that envisaged by the parties on contract.

However, a number of difficulties stand in the way of the tenant in relying on frustration in case 25. The first is that courts have traditionally been reluctant to declare that a lease is frustrated, because a lease confers not only contractual rights, but also an interest in land, which should endure, though this reluctance is abating in both Irish and English law.

The second difficulty relates to whether the supervening events in question were capable of being anticipated, as frustration will rarely be decreed in these circumstances. While dramatic post-war inflation might be unanticipated, the same cannot be said of the cumulative effects of normal inflation in long-term contracts. Indeed, the real value of rent in long-term leases is very often rendered nominal, and this has never been thought a ground for claiming frustration.

The third, and most substantial, difficulty for the tenant is that the courts have generally not allowed claims of frustration to succeed where

[48] Colyer, in: *Halsbury* § 261.   [49] Ibid., § 287.   [50] [1956] AC 696.
[51] *Mulligan v. Browne* (unreported, Supreme Court, 23 November 1977).

the supervening events merely make performance more expensive. While there is some authority that a contract might be frustrated where prices had been driven to 'unheard of levels',[52] it is better explained as being concerned with the interpretation of express contractual provisions of the contract in question. The courts would probably take the view that parties should take care to protect themselves against inflation or the devaluation of the currency of payment, and that it is not for the courts to invent protection themselves, though it has been said that 'the possibility that extreme (as opposed to merely severe) inflation may be capable of frustrating a contract cannot be wholly ruled out'.[53] It should be noted that if frustration of the contract were indeed applied, it would probably have the effect of discharging the whole contract, and not merely the obligation to supply the steam.

Secondly, English courts have provided some relief to those in long-term contracts of indefinite duration by implying a right in the parties to terminate by the giving of reasonable notice.[54] It is likely that this sort of approach would be followed in Ireland, but it would not apply to the facts of case 25 if the lease were for a fixed period, as is more likely than not to be the case.

SCOTLAND

In a perfect situation the terms of a contract would provide for every contingency which might occur. However, it is rare for the parties to a contract to have either the time or prescience to provide for every foreseeable possibility in the contract. So, what happens after the contract is made could well be an occurrence which the parties failed to foresee.

Looking at the terms of this contract, it would appear that from the outset a bad bargain has been made. The law will not interfere with a bad bargain *per se*. The scope of the contract is deemed to reflect the intention of the parties, and the courts will not infer an implied term which directly contradicts an express term; *Cummings v. Charles Connell & Co. (Shipbuilders) Ltd.*[55] It thus follows that while the price of the steam has become no longer economically viable owing to normal inflation, the courts will not interfere with the agreed price in order to give the contract business efficacy. Only the parties to the contract can alter its terms in this situation.

---

[52] *Tradax Export SA v. André & Cie SA* [1976] 1 Lloyd's Rep 416.   [53] Treitel 783.
[54] *Staffordshire Area Health Authority v. South Staffordshire Waterworks Co.* [1978] 1 WLR 1387.
[55] 1968 SC 305.

Neither party may unilaterally vary the contractual terms, but both by agreement could do so.

In the latter scenario presented by the problem, the question is whether supervening events which alter the value of the contract will allow the terms of the contract to be varied to make it economically viable. The proposition that the price should be altered would be based on the principle of frustration[56] whereby a contract may be discharged because of a change of circumstances, or a change in the law, which either renders performance illegal, impossible, or so alters the conditions that should the contract be performed it would be a substantially different contract from that to which the parties agreed.

However, the principle of frustration is limited. It does not apply to a change in economic conditions which renders the contract more onerous than had been contemplated. The fact that supervening events or a change in the law have made the contract more burdensome or less profitable is irrelevant; *Holliday v. Scott*.[57] And the fact that the contract has become more expensive or commercially less attractive for one party than anticipated is not enough to bring about a frustration of the contract; *Wilson v. Tennants*.[58] Inflation *per se* does not constitute frustration; *Wates Ltd v. Greater London Council*.[59] Scots law does not recognise the defence of 'commercial impossibility' and will not release one party from a bad bargain; *Hong-Kong and Whampoa Dock Co. Ltd v. Netherton Shipping Co. Ltd*.[60] It is for the legislature to provide for exceptional circumstances where a change in conditions would make the performance of certain contracts economically disastrous.

The Scottish cases cited here are very old and hence a view of the English position may be worthwhile. The leading case is *Staffordshire Area Health Authority v. South Staffordshire Waterworks Co.*[61] A hospital had in 1919 agreed to give up its right to take water from a well to the waterworks company and the company had in return promised that it would 'at all times hereafter' supply water to the hospital at prices fixed in the contract. By 1975 the cost to the company of supplying the water had risen to over eighteen times the contract price, and the company gave seven months' notice to the hospital to terminate the contract. The Court of Appeal held that the notice was effective but its members differed in their reasons for this result.

Lord *Denning* held that although the contract on its literal construction

[56] See the Scottish report to case 12 above.   [57] (1830) 8 S 831.   [58] [1917] AC 495.
[59] (1983) 25 BLR 1 (CA).   [60] 1909 SC 34, 16 SLT 417.   [61] [1978] 1 WLR 1387.

meant that it was intended to continue 'in perpetuity'[62] it had ceased to bind because 'the situation has changed so radically since the contract was made'.[63] This seems to mean that he had regarded the contract as having become frustrated by the change of circumstances which had taken place.

Lord Justices *Goff* and *Cumming-Bruce* based their decision on different grounds; namely, that the words 'all times hereafter' were not to be taken literally and that the agreement on its true construction was intended to be one of an indefinite (rather than one of perpetual) duration, and that the case fell within the general principle that in commercial agreements of indefinite duration, a term is often implied entitling either party to terminate by reasonable notice.

English authority seems to be opposed to the view that a party can rely on inflation as a ground for discharge merely because it has reduced, in real terms, the benefit that he expected to gain under the contract; *Wates Ltd v. Greater London Council*.[64] *Treitel*[65] proposes that from English case law it seems that nothing short of an extreme depreciation of currency would be regarded as sufficient to discharge a contract. Where inflation is not of the extreme kind, it would be likely to be within the contemplation of the parties, or to be dealt with by the terms of the contract, e.g. 'index-linked' payments. If inflation is so extreme that the currency collapses then there would probably be legislation regarding its effects on contracts.

Note that parties can include a *force majeure* clause in the contract which enables them to provide for a discharge, or some other form of relief, on the occurrence of an event which but for the provision would have no effect on their legal rights and duties, because the change of circumstances brought about by the event was not sufficiently serious or fundamental to discharge the contract under the general common law doctrine, e.g. provide relief for non-frustrating events.

DENMARK AND NORWAY

Price rises are a familiar problem, also in West Nordic law, and the courts have for a long time revised contracts where an unexpected price rise has overturned the preconditions for the agreement. A formal justification in law for a revision of the agreement exists today in s. 36 of the Contracts Act.

---

[62] Ibid., at 1394.   [63] Ibid., at 1398.   [64] (1983) 25 BLR 1 (CA).   [65] § 6-041.

As has been pointed out before, there is a gradual transition between the interpretation of reasonableness and the use of s. 36 of the Contracts Act. It cannot be excluded that an agreement such as this one will be interpreted to mean that the energy for heating is to be supplied at cost price.[66] Both the fact that it is a long-term agreement, and that the agreed price appears to reflect the market price at the time the agreement was concluded, appear to suggest this interpretation.

The question as to what economic sacrifices a party to an agreement may be expected to make will often raise doubts. But, in principle, it is not sufficient for a revision of an agreement that the agreement no longer covers costs,[67] or that performance has become significantly more expensive than expected. The main rule must still be that when a contract is made at a fixed price, the parties have to carry the risk of an unexpected price increase themselves. Cost increases may, however, be so massive that performing the agreement inflicts a burden on one of the parties which is, objectively speaking, outside what the parties can be taken to have contemplated when concluding an agreement of that nature. Early in this century, the West Nordic courts of law were rather hesitant in recognising price rises as giving rise to relief, so that only 'an altogether exorbitant loss which performance of the contract would entail' was taken into account.[68] The change in Norwegian legal usage occurred in Rt. 1935, p. 122, and also in a decision from 1941, included in Rt. 1951, p. 371, and as a result of the way in which these decisions were perceived at least by some authors. For while some of them saw these rulings as relating specifically to long-term delivery agreements under which the seller had the position of an intermediary rather than a straightforward commercial role, others emphasised the more lenient approach, accommodating the seller, of which the rulings were an expression. By the time when s. 36 of the Contracts Act was introduced, and the two plenary rulings in Rt. 1988, p. 276 and p. 295 were handed down, this more liberal view concerning price rises and issues relating to inflation had clearly gained more general acceptance.

The decision as to whether a financial difficulty exists which may lead to a revision of the agreement rests on a fairly complex evaluation. Consideration must be given, for example, as to whether it is a long-term delivery agreement or an agreement which involves only one performance, whether the goods concerned are usually subject to price

---

[66] Cf., in this direction, Rt. 1991, p. 22.   [67] Cf. Rt. 1918, p. 475.
[68] Cf. Rt. 1919, p. 167 at p. 169.

fluctuations or not, whether the price increase was caused by a sudden change of circumstances, such as the outbreak of a war, or was due to ordinary price rises, or whether the seller has taken a genuine commercial risk, or rather occupies the position of an intermediary. In any event, however, the disadvantage caused to one of the parties must be of a certain size.[69]

Thus, as was pointed out above, a development has taken place in the West Nordic countries as to whether price rises may justify a revision of a contract. In the time between the wars, the courts were rather restrictive, and the solutions had to be found essentially in the doctrine of breach of implied conditions, etc. A more liberal view has gradually won through, and today there is formal justification in law in s. 36 of the Contracts Act for revising a contractual relationship.[70]

SWEDEN

The general principle is still *pacta sunt servanda*, but terms may be adjusted according to s. 36 of the Contracts Act of 1915 (amended in 1976) or according to the doctrine of incorrect presuppositions. Some guidelines are given in the preparatory works prior to the enactment of s. 36. First, long-term contracts may be terminated by application of s. 36. Secondly, price or escalation clauses may be adjusted, also in favour of a party of superior bargaining power. According to the commission report, contracts with a fixed price may become unreasonable after some years; the commission did not require that the inflation was unexpected.[71] In the bill preceding the Act, the secretary of justice agreed. He added that an adjustment was justified more often in long-term contracts and that the possibility of foreseeing the change was of importance. Furthermore, '[i]f the parties have taken account of the changed conditions and agreed who shall carry the risk for unforeseen changes, the contract shall normally not be adjusted, especially not if the party at risk was compensated'.[72] If the parties have tried to adjust the price to inflation by using an index, but the index term is not effective, s. 36 affords a possibility of adjusting the index term, provided the term was not individually negotiated in a contract between businessmen.[73]

---

[69] Hagstrøm, *Fragmenter* 22 ff.; Mestad, *passim.*   [70] Andersen/Madsen/Nørgaard 254.
[71] *Statens Offentliga Utredningar* (SOU) 1974:83 p. 164.
[72] Proposition 1975/76:81 p. 127; my own translation from the Swedish.
[73] *Statens Offentliga Utredningar* (SOU) 1974:83 pp. 166 f.

One should also look at s. 23 of the Sale of Goods Act of 1990. According to this provision, the seller need not perform when performance would entail (physical or economic) sacrifices which are not reasonable, taking due consideration also of the buyer's interest in performance. In terms of the bill which preceded the Sale of Goods Act, when goods sensitive to economic fluctuations have been bought or when the seller deliberately took a risk, the section can be applied only in extreme cases. It was added that a general change in the price level does not normally create the disproportion presupposed in the provision. Furthermore, according to this bill, there is no room for applying s. 36 in the Contracts Act alongside s. 23 of the Sale of Goods Act.[74] This may be doubted; obviously the two bills do not correspond entirely, which makes the interpretation of both acts somewhat uncertain in the respect discussed.

In case law, real estate lease prices were sometimes adjusted due to unexpected cost increases during the Second World War. On the other hand, a forty-year-old contract from 1904 to provide transport by railway at a fixed price for an indefinite period of time could not be terminated in the 1940s despite the effect of high inflation.[75] However, this decision is probably superseded by the new s. 36 of the Contracts Act. In NJA 1979, p. 731, a rent fixed at 50 crowns per year for a lease of land for forty-nine years, made in 1960 well after inflation resulting from the Korean War and at a low price originally (but agreed upon, none the less, without any undue influence), was not increased to market value (around 400 crowns) but only to the level of 150 crowns, which was conceded by the tenant in order to make, at least, some adjustment for general price increases (of 155 per cent). The lack of an index clause was not ruled to be unreasonable. It is an open question whether and, if so, to what extent an adjustment would have been made, had the defendants not agreed to the increase of 100 crowns. In another case,[76] also concerning the lease of land, which was concluded in 1950 for forty-nine years, half of the rent was indexed to the price of wheat (equivalent to 31 crowns in 1949), with the other half (30 crowns) fixed in cash without reference to an index. The purpose was to compensate the landlord for inflation. The rent was originally fixed at market value. However, the result did not prove satisfactory for the landlord. The rent had become remarkably low (altogether equivalent to 85 crowns whereas an application of the consumer price index would have

[74] Proposition 1988/89:76 p. 101.
[75] NJA 1946, p. 679, with a majority of three to two in the Supreme Court.
[76] NJA 1983, p. 385.

resulted in 265 crowns; consequently the rent was now only 32 per cent of the market value). In view of this development and because of the limited experience available in 1950 regarding index clauses, the Supreme Court ruled that the landlord could not have been expected to foresee that the clause might be ineffective. Hence, the rent was adjusted according to the general consumer price index, with respect both to the part of the rent which had been poorly indexed and the part that had not been indexed at all. In the latter respect, the Supreme Court referred to the fact that the contract had been concluded thirty-three years ago. In RH 1980, no. 14, an appellate court adjusted, somewhat astonishingly, a contract to take care of the garbage in a town, entered into for five years and won on tender, when the index clause (a reference to the consumer price index) used in the contract did not reflect increases in costs and caused loss to the entrepreneur, who was dependent mainly on this contract.[77]

I assume that the contract in case 25 was concluded for a long but definite period of time. Otherwise the supplier would no doubt be entitled to terminate the contract with a reasonable period of notice. In the case of a fixed period of time, the question arises whether the duration may be adjusted under s. 36 of the Contracts Act, or whether the price may be adjusted under that provision or s. 23 of the Sale of Goods Act. If the increase in the market value for steam was due to dramatic and unforeseeable inflation, the price would definitely be adjusted according to s. 36, or the supplier might also terminate the contract. As to normal inflation, concerning a contract concluded originally at market price and with no index clause, the precedent to be found in NJA 1983, p. 385 is of interest. Also with regard to the part that was not indexed (50 per cent), the rent was adjusted by reference to the full consumer price index, although some inflation must have been expected. But this was not done until thirty-three years had elapsed, and the parties seem to have intended the indexed part to take care of all inflation. In NJA 1979, p. 731 the lack of an index clause was not deemed to be unreasonable, but experience regarding inflation had improved (as is the case today), and the landlord had been fully compensated for the inflation. Neither according to the preparatory works prior to s. 36 of the Contracts Act nor according to those relating to s. 23 of the Sale of Goods Act does the inflation have to have been unexpected, although the latter contain a statement to the effect that a

---

[77] There is a statement in *Statens Offentliga Utredningar* (SOU) 1974:83 p. 166 to the effect that a negotiated index clause in a contract between businessmen should not be adjusted, but that an unsuitable index chosen without reflection might be adjusted.

general change in the price level does not normally create the presupposed disproportion. Even expected inflation seems to allow for adjustment, if the effect of the inflation is unreasonable and the parties have not specifically negotiated the issue. Therefore, a decrease to 7 per cent of the market value may, as such, justify an adjustment, especially if many years have elapsed since the conclusion of the contract, or many years remain until the end of the contract, or the supplier was not well experienced in matters like this. However, for lack of good precedent, the answer is uncertain.

FINLAND

This is a case where adjustment of the price under s. 36 of the Contracts Act of 1929 is obvious, irrespective of the causes of inflation.[78] As for delivery of electricity, there is a case, viz. KKO 1990:138, where the Finnish Supreme Court adjusted a long-term contract on the grounds of unconscionability – inflation was not, however, at issue.

Editors' comparative observations

This case distinguishes between the situation of price changes owing to 'normal' inflation and those owing to 'dramatic and unforeseeable inflation', such as occurs after a major war. The responses can be divided into three groups. While some legal systems would give no legal remedy to the tenant in either case (i), others would give remedy in both cases (iii). A third group of legal systems distinguishes between the two situations and would grant relief only in the case of 'dramatic and unforeseeable' inflation (ii).

(i) Protagonists of the first approach are English, Irish and Scots law. Here it is clear that a change in circumstances such as the one envisaged in the case scenario would not, in principle, constitute a frustration of the contract of lease. However, it is noted in the Irish report that the possibility that extreme inflation may be capable of frustrating a contract cannot be wholly ruled out. And the English report observes that the courts have, on occasion, managed to avoid harsh consequences caused by a change in circumstances in long-term contracts with no fixed duration by implying a term providing for termination by notice.

French and Belgian law, too, are not prepared to grant relief to the

---

[78] Contracts Act, Amendment Bill 247/1981, p. 15; Wilhelmsson 87; see KKO 1981 II 126.

landlord, both denying as a matter of *private law* any revision of contracts on the ground of supervening unforeseeable circumstances not amounting to *force majeure*. In both countries, however, the matter would be different if the supply of steam had constituted a 'public service', for a theory of *imprévision* is applied to 'administrative contracts'.

(ii) German, Greek, Austrian, Italian and Spanish law take a differentiated approach. Courts and legal writers in Germany have developed, on the basis of § 242 BGB, the doctrine of *Wegfall der Geschäftsgrundlage*, a modern version of *Windscheid's* presupposition doctrine (and a substitute for the *clausula rebus sic stantibus* which was rejected by the draftsmen of the BGB). This doctrine allows adjustment of the contract in the second case but not in the first. Greek law possesses a codified version of this doctrine. Italian law comes to the same conclusion on the basis of two provisions in the code which grant a right of dissolution where long-term contracts have become excessively onerous as a result of change of circumstances and allow adjustment where a change of circumstances has altered the proportion between the obligations of the parties by at least one-tenth. In Austria, legal scholars have developed a doctrine protecting the disadvantaged party in case of fundamental change of circumstances. Spanish law, too, has long possessed a doctrine of change of circumstances but it has not as yet been applied to the disastrous effect of unforeseeable inflation.

(iii) The Dutch, West Nordic, Swedish and Finnish legal systems would give a remedy in both cases. The Nordic countries usually rely on s. 36 of the joint Nordic Contracts Act, according to which 'an agreement may be set aside wholly or in part or may be amended in so far as it would seem unreasonable or in conflict with good commercial practice to invoke it'. A West Nordic judge might even adopt an interpretative approach. In the Netherlands, art. 6:258 B.W. allows modification of a contract in view of an unforeseen change of circumstances. Strikingly, the Swedish report makes clear that s. 36 of the Contracts Act has been used even where the parties have agreed to a particular type of indexation clause to govern the price payable over a period of years, where the type of index chosen is not considered appropriate to the actual changes in cost in this context.

(iv) It was noted in the English, Belgian and Swedish reports that on the facts of case 25 (i.e. in residential leases), but also in other practically important situations, express contractual provision would usually allow adjustment to take account even of ordinary inflation. The same would presumably apply in a number of other countries.

Case 26: 'Sale' of soccer player

Case

Two soccer clubs agree upon the transfer of a player for a price of DM 900,000. Neither of the clubs knows that some months earlier, and on the occasion of a league match against a third club, that player had accepted a bribe. Some time after the transfer has been effected, the bribery scandal is uncovered. The national soccer association withdraws the player's licence to play professional soccer. His new club thereupon terminates the contract. Is the new club entitled to claim back the transfer sum from the club for which the player had previously played?

Discussions

GERMANY

A right to claim back the transfer sum could, in the first place, be based upon §§ 323 III, 818 I, II BGB. Implementation of a reciprocal obligation would then have to have become impossible. The old club's obligation, however, consisted in the transfer of the player to his new club. That this player has a licence is not part of the agreement, but constitutes a tacit presupposition common to both parties.

In the second place, it could be argued that the transfer sum has to be returned by way of application of §§ 346, 1; 467; 465; 462; 459 I BGB *per analogiam* (cancellation of a contract of sale as a result of latent defects in the object sold). It has been argued that the contract between the two clubs concerning the transfer of the player constitutes a sale.[1] In

---

[1] Cf. the references and the discussion in Wertenbruch, NJW 1993, 182. The transfer of players is governed by regulations of the German Soccer Association. These regulations used to require a certificate releasing the player from the old club before he was allowed

general parlance these types of transactions are indeed usually referred to as *Spielerverkauf* (sale of a player). The Federal Supreme Court in the decision on which the present case scenario is based also uses language pointing in the direction of the aedilitian remedies: the player, as a result of his entanglement in the bribery scandal, is defective; and as a result of the 'personal defect' he has become 'objectively worthless'.[2] But the Federal Supreme Court has not in fact classified the transaction as a contract of sale. According to the prevailing opinion we are dealing here with a contract *sui generis* to which the aedilitian remedies cannot be applied.[3]

If the old club has infringed a precontractual duty to inform the new club about the player's involvement in the scandal, it would be liable under the rules relating to *culpa in contrahendo*. In the present case, however, the old club does not seem to have been at fault.

A fourth possibility would be a claim based on § 812 I 1, first alternative BGB (unjustified enrichment resulting from a transfer without legal ground). If the new club were entitled to rescind the contract with the old club on account of either mistake (§ 119 BGB) or fraud (§ 123 I BGB), the transfer would indeed have happened without legal ground (§ 142 I BGB: 'If a transaction liable to be rescinded is rescinded it is deemed to have been rescinded from the outset').[4] There was, however, no fraud on the part of the old club. On the other hand, the new club was labouring under a mistake but not one that would be relevant for the purposes of § 119 BGB. More particularly, the mistake did not relate to 'a characteristic of a

to play for the new club. This certificate was only granted when the transfer sum agreed upon between the clubs had been paid. This system was struck down by the Regional Labour Court of Berlin (NJW 1979, 2582 ff.) by way of application of Art. 12 GG (free choice and exercise of profession) in conjunction with § 134 BGB (illegality of contracts) and was subsequently changed. Even without the co-operation of the old club the player is now allowed to change clubs. The new club is still, however, obliged to pay the transfer sum, as negotiated between the clubs. For details, see Westermann, JA 1984, 394 ff. In the meantime, however, the new system has also been struck down, this time by the Federal Labour Court: BAG NZA 1997, 647 (concerning a regulation of the German Ice Hockey Federation, in terms of which a transfer sum may be claimed after the time for which the contract between the player and his old club has expired: § 138 I BGB (provisions *contra bonos mores* are invalid) in conjunction with Art. 12 GG). As a result of this ruling, transfer sums are today no longer paid for players whose contract has expired. It is assumed, therefore, that the contract between the player and the old club had not yet expired; in cases like that transfer sums are still today agreed upon and are generally held to be valid. It is also assumed that we are dealing with a purely national transaction and that the *Bosman* judgement of the European Court of Justice (ECJ NJW 1996, 505) is not, therefore, applicable.   [2] BGH NJW 1976, 565 ff.
[3] *Palandt*/Heinrichs, Einf. v. § 433, n. 20; *Münchener Kommentar*/H. P. Westermann § 433, n. 21.
[4] Rescission is effected by declaration to the other party (§ 143 I BGB).

person . . . which is regarded as essential in business' (§ 119 II BGB). Having accepted a bribe from another club is not a 'characteristic' of a player.[5] The underlying character defect on which this behaviour is possibly based may be regarded as a 'characteristic' but hardly one that 'is regarded as essential in business': it is not a factor which normally determines the appreciation of a professional soccer player in transfer negotiations.[6]

Thus, there is finally the option of a claim based upon § 812 I 2, first alternative BGB (*condictio ob causam finitam*). The legal reason for the payment of the DM 900,000 has subsequently fallen away, if the withdrawal of the licence has led to a collapse of the underlying basis of the transaction (*Wegfall der Geschäftsgrundlage*). The requirements of this doctrine, which applies, *inter alia*, to cases of mutual mistake,[7] have been sketched above.[8] In the present case, both clubs have presupposed the continued existence of the licence when they concluded the contract. The licence is so important that the new club would not have concluded the contract had it known about the player's involvement in the bribery scandal and the resulting danger of the licence being withdrawn. Also, according to the Federal Supreme Court – and this is the crucial point upon which the decision hinges – the withdrawal of the licence cannot be regarded as falling within the sphere of risk of the new club. The act which led to the withdrawal of the licence was committed at a time when the player was still active for the old club and is thus intimately related to his professional activities in the old club's services.[9] The principle of the collapse of the underlying basis of the transaction, therefore, applies. On the assumption that the player's services have not yet significantly been used by the new club, an adjustment cannot sensibly be made and the contract will therefore have to be dissolved. Dissolution does not take place *ipso iure*; rather, the disadvantaged party has to be given a right to terminate the contract.[10] If the new club exercises this right, the legal ground for payment of the transfer sum falls away; the latter can consequently be reclaimed under § 812 I 2, first alternative BGB (not § 346 BGB[11]).

---

[5] For the standard definitions of this term, see *Jauernig*/Jauernig § 119, n. 13; *Palandt*/Heinrichs § 119, n. 24.   [6] Cf. Dörner, JuS 1977, 226.
[7] See, e.g., *Jauernig*/Vollkommer § 242, nn. 80 ff.; *Palandt*/Heinrichs § 242, nn. 149 ff.
[8] See the German report to case 25 above.
[9] BGH NJW 1976, 565 ff. This decision has not universally been approved: for a critical discussion, see Dörner, JuS 1977, 225 ff. Cf. further, approving the decision, Wertenbruch, NJW 1993, 181 ff.; Medicus, *Bürgerliches Recht* n. 165 b.
[10] *Palandt*/Heinrichs § 242, n. 132; *Staudinger*/Schmidt § 242, n. 950; BGH NJW 1987, 2674 (2676) describes this as the 'general view'.   [11] Cf. *Palandt*/Heinrichs § 242, n. 132.

GREECE

The transfer of players is valid according to the regulations of L. 1958/1991 regarding the relationship between players and soccer clubs. The player is allowed to change clubs and the new club is legally obliged to pay to the old club the transfer sum, as negotiated between the clubs. The transfer price is a matter of negotiation.[12]

Thus, in the present case, we have a valid contract. But is it a contract of sale within the meaning of arts. 513 ff. Gr. C.C., so that cancellation as a result of latent defects in the object sold (arts. 534, 540 Gr. C.C.) may be possible? The object sold in this case is not the player himself but his abilities as a player. Thus, it might be argued that from the moment of his entanglement in the bribery scandal, the object of the sale, i.e. his ability to play, is 'defective'. Nevertheless, since the player is not an 'object', a *res* in the classical sense of the word, it seems preferable to refer to a new kind of contract *sui generis*, with respect to which the aedilitian remedies of arts. 534 ff. Gr. C.C. cannot even be applied by analogy.[13]

A second possible legal basis for a claim could be substantial error (art. 142 Gr. C.C.). The application of the provisions concerning mistake (arts. 140 ff. Gr. C.C.) could give the right to the second soccer club to rescind the transfer contract. For the application of art. 142 Gr. C.C. it is necessary to prove that the qualities of a person are of such importance for the transaction, taking into consideration the agreement of the parties or the requirements of good faith and business usage, that the person in error would not have concluded the contract if he had been aware of the truth. Thus, the second club would have to show that they would not have concluded the transfer contract had it been known that the player had such character defects that he might be involved in a bribery scandal. The transfer contract could then be nullified by the courts and the claims of the second club would be based on arts. 904 ff. Gr. C.C. (unjustified enrichment). On the other hand, the first club may, under art. 145 Gr. C.C., claim any damages that may have arisen as a result of the annulment of the contract.[14]

More suitable for the second club would seem to be the possibility of claiming under art. 388 Gr. C.C., because the circumstances on which the clubs had based their agreement, taking into consideration good faith and business usage, have subsequently changed for exceptional and

[12] Regarding specialised literature, see Papaloukas, *passim*.
[13] Doris, in: *Astikos Kodix III* arts. 534–5, nos. 6 ff.; cf. Stathopoulos, *Contract* 217–18, no. 337.
[14] Simantiras nos. 719–50; Symeonides, in: *Introduction* 58–9.

unforeseeable reasons and because as a consequence of this change the performance due by the second club has become excessively onerous. The real basis of this claim is not the player's reputation but his licence which was a presupposition common to both parties. But since the contract between the first and the second club has already been performed, art. 388 Gr. C.C. can be applicable only in exceptional cases, in particular if the contract has not yet been performed for very long.[15]

If the court decides in favour of the dissolution of the contract under art. 388 Gr. C.C., the first club will be obliged to return the sum received under arts. 904 ff. Gr. C.C. (unjustified enrichment) in the form of the *condictio ob causam finitam*.[16]

AUSTRIA

Before the new soccer club can claim restitution of any unjust enrichment from the old club, the contract between them must be set aside. Setting aside a contract may take one of two forms in this sort of context: the contract may be *cancelled* on the ground of breach of an implied warranty or it may be *rescinded* on the ground of the new soccer club's misapprehension.

As to cancellation of the contract, it is clear that the transfer agreement between the two clubs has as its purpose the receipt of the right to deploy the player in return for payment. Since the player cannot be deployed owing to his 'qualities' existing at the time of the transfer, performance of its obligation by the transferring club would be considered defective. This defective performance gives to the new club a claim based on breach of a warranty (§§ 922 ff. ABGB). And as the defect prevents his 'use' and cannot be remedied, the new club may rescind the contract of transfer (§ 932 ABGB). It has to be noted, in this context, that §§ 922 ff. ABGB do not only refer to contracts of sale but to all contracts under which a performance has to be paid for.

Secondly, and in the alternative, the new club may rescind the contract on the ground of its mistake as to important qualities of the subject matter of the contract (§ 871 ABGB). For the transfer agreement relates to a player who at the time of the contract possessed a licence, but who was already at risk of a subsequent withdrawal of this licence owing to his involvement

---

[15] See mainly Stathopoulos, in: *Astikos Kodix II* art. 388, no. 18; also Spyridakis, in: NoB 25 (1977) 762; cf. Stathopoulos, *Contract* 192–6, nos. 291–8.
[16] Stathopoulos, *Contract* 192–6, nos. 295–6.

in bribery. This being the case, performance which was due by the old club lacked the characteristics which are taken for granted in this type of transaction. However, under Austrian law[17] a contract may only be rescinded on account of mistake, if the other party either caused the mistake or ought to have realised it (as we have seen in relation to case 2). These conditions for rescinding the contract on the ground of mistake are not fulfilled on the facts of case 26. Moreover, the mistaken party may rescind the contract only if he brings his mistake to light in good time (*rechtzeitig*), i.e., before the other contracting party arranges his affairs in reliance on the existence of the contract.[18] This requirement is not satisfied if the transferor has spent the money which he received, though according to *Bydlinski*,[19] in a case of a serious disturbance of equivalence in the effect of performance of the contract, rescission should be allowed as long as the party rescinding the contract compensates the other party for any prejudice which this may cause. Furthermore, according to the prevailing opinion, rescission of a contract on the ground of mistake is always available where both parties entered the contract under a mistake.[20]

Finally, if the view were taken that the new club's mistake does not relate to important qualities of the subject matter of the contract, it is possible that it could instead bring an action by invoking a fundamental change of circumstances underlying the contract, this doctrine being discussed earlier in relation to case 25.

FRANCE

The new club (the 'transferee' club) may be able to claim back the transfer sum from the club which transferred the player (the 'transferor' club) by bringing an action to annul the transfer agreement. (It is assumed that the transferee's termination of the contract refers to the fact that it terminates the player's contract of employment, since it cannot terminate the transfer agreement as it has already been discharged by performance.) In order to succeed with this claim for annulment and thereby recover the sum which it paid by way of restitution on the return of the parties to the *status quo ante*, the transferee club may proceed on two distinct legal bases: (i) mistake as to the 'essential qualities' of the player or (ii) mistake as to or absence of *cause*.

---

[17] See § 871 ABGB.   [18] OGH in SZ 42/121 (1969).   [19] *Privatautonomie* 180 ff.
[20] OGH in SZ 61/53 (1988); Gschnitzer, in: *Klang, Kommentar IV/1* 133 f. *Contra* Rummel, JBl 1981, 7; Koziol/Welser, *Bürgerliches Recht I* 129.

(i) In a claim for annulment for mistake under art. 1110 of the Civil Code the transferee club must show that it was mistaken about the essential qualities of the subject matter of the contract, i.e. the quality of the player, including his licence to play professional soccer. Article 1110 states that 'mistake is a cause for annulling the contract only when it concerns the very substance of the thing which is the subject matter of the contract', but interpreting this widely the courts annul contracts for a mistake about substantial qualities and not just about the substance of the subject matter of the contract.[21] The transferee club must prove also that the player's qualities were a determining factor and induced its consent to make the contract, that is to say, that if it had been aware of the reality of the situation (i.e. that the player had taken a bribe and would consequently be barred from playing professional soccer) it would not have entered the contract. This kind of mistake is categorised by leading writers as a case of mistake about the aptitude of the subject matter, as it turns out that the player is not able to play for the transferee club since his dishonesty disentitles him to a soccer licence. In addition, neither club knew about the player's inaptitude at the time the contract was made. This means that they were both of good faith. Where this is the case and where the defendant also knew of the importance which the plaintiff attached to the quality, there is what is called a 'common mistake' (*erreur commune*). Normally the existence of such a common mistake makes it more likely that the contract will be annulled.[22]

(ii) It may also be possible for the transferee club to ask the court to annul the contract for 'absence of *cause*' or 'false *cause*' under art. 1131 of the Civil Code. In fact, this remedy may, in certain cases, offer an advantage as to what needs to be established over a remedy for mistake (as well as a longer period of limitation, though this is the subject of academic controversy), although this is not the case here since there is a common mistake. The remedy is identical, namely, the contract is annulled with consequential restitution. To obtain annulment for absence of *cause* or false *cause*, the transferee club would have to show that the *cause* of the transferor's obligation to pay the money was its ability to use the services of the player and that since the player has taken a bribe and cannot actually play football for the club, this *cause* of the contract is false. Case law has held that a *cause* is defined as false when the person believes in its reality, i.e. that the player is honest and can play for the tranferee's club,

[21] Rouen 19 Mar. 1968, D 1969.211; Com. 20 Oct. 1970, JCP 1971.II.16916 note J. Ghestin.
[22] See Paris 13 Dec. 1856, DP 1857.2.73.

whereas the *cause* does not exist as the player is dishonest.[23] Moreover, *cause* is evaluated at the time the contract is formed; here the player had already taken the bribe before the contract, so the reason for making the contract was in fact false at the contract's beginning.

Since neither party knew of the player's dishonesty when the contract was made, it might be argued that one party should not be protected any more than the other. It is evident from the foregoing that French law has developed rules on mistake which are protective of the mistaken party even where the mistake is unilateral. An identical solution could be reached on the basis that the contract was made on a false *cause*, although in the circumstances this presents no procedural advantage. Annulment of the contract on the latter basis shifts the focus onto more objective grounds (a lack of correspondence between the reality and the belief) whereas annulment for mistake implicitly takes into consideration moral and subjective grounds, the behaviour of the parties, good faith etc. When the parties are of equal good faith, these legal rules cannot be justified on economic grounds, but simply by a dogmatic insistence on adherence to the positive law. Jurists have criticised extending the notion of a false *cause* on the grounds that multiplying the functional definitions of the notion of *cause* leads to confusion and a dissipation of the doctrine as ill-defined.[24]

BELGIUM

First of all, the new club is in any event probably entitled to claim back the transfer sum, because the contract concluded between both clubs is illegal. It certainly is in transfers between different countries of the European Community (*Bosman* case, CJEC 15 Dec. 1995).

Secondly, apart from the problem of legality, this case would, under Belgian law, probably be dealt with as a case of error (mistake). The fact that the player had accepted a bribe is a past circumstance, and not being corrupt is probably a substantial characteristic of a player for any soccer club. The mistake is shared by both parties. Each of them can thus rescind the contract if the supposition that the player is not corrupt was a determining factor for its consent. There is also no (gross) negligence on the side of the new club, which could prevent it from rescinding the contract.

Moreover, the new club can certainly rescind its contract with the player (on the ground of mistake and even for fraud) and/or terminate that

---

[23] TGI Seine 19 Mar. 1963, GP 1963.2.18.   [24] Ghestin no. 860, p. 861.

contract (for non-performance, in view of the fact that the action of a third party, the national soccer association, was caused by the fault of the player himself).

Thirdly, although error (mistake) would be the normal pigeonhole for classifying the problem in this case, it cannot be excluded that the contract might be interpreted as implying an obligation on the old club to transfer a player who has not been involved in bribery. As in other legal systems, there is a tendency in Belgian law to treat information provided with regard to the object of a contract as an implied warranty as to the correctness of this information. In so far as the old club has given information about the qualities of the player, this rule could apply. Furthermore, the rules on 'latent defects' in the law of sale are often applied by analogy to other contracts. These rules have been discussed in case 1. They can apply only if the fact of having been bribed may be considered a latent defect. The withdrawal of the licence cannot constitute a latent defect, because it took place after the transfer of the player. Such withdrawal will therefore only constitute non-performance in so far as there had been a specific (normally express) warranty that the player would remain licensed to play during a certain period.

Finally, this case would, under Belgian law, probably not be seen as a case of changed circumstances. Belgian law, as was noted in case 25, adopts a restrictive approach in this respect. One of the few cases where termination for changed circumstances is accepted is the situation where the performance, which still has to be rendered, is fundamentally different from the performance as foreseen by the parties when concluding the contract. However, in the present case, there is no problem as to a performance which still has to be rendered. It is not a case of collapse of the underlying basis of the transaction (*Wegfall der Geschäftsgrundlage*), but rather of frustration of purpose (*Zweckwegfall*). Termination would here require, in principle, an implied resolutive condition; this is rarely accepted, unless there are specific indications that both parties intended to make their contract dependent on such a condition.

SPAIN

It is difficult to give a response to these facts from the point of view of Spanish law. If the contract of transfer could be seen as analogous to one of sale or hire, the bribery scandal could perhaps be considered as the equivalent of a latent defect in the property which is the subject matter of the contract (the player) for which a seller or hirer is liable and for which the transferring club would therefore also be liable. However, it is submitted that such an analogy would not accepted by Spanish law and there is no sufficient reason, in the present case, to make the player's former club bear the risk of the effects of his conduct, especially because on the facts as presented in the scenario it was apparently not aware of the problem. Nor would this position be affected by appeal to the principle of good faith contained in art. 1258 of the Civil Code. The effect of the bribery scandal is a risk, not something to be attributed to any fault in the transferring club. This is indeed the difference between a contract concerning a soccer player and one concerning goods. The facts of case 26 are, therefore, analogous to a case where a person sells a valuable old picture to a dealer, the picture later proving to be a fake: here too, there is no good reason to impute the risk of this transpiring to the other party and so *casum sentit dominus* (the loss lies with the owner). Indeed, even if recourse were made to any special customs or usages in the contract of transfer of the soccer player by way of interpretation of the contract, these would lead to the same result: for at least in the Spanish football business, all parties assume that the high losses or high gains which *suddenly* occur in the course of a player's professional career should be considered as *casus fortuitus*, taken by his club for the time being. In the result, therefore, the player's second club may not recover the transfer sum.

ITALY

The outcome of this case is quite clear: the new club may recover the sum which it has paid to obtain the right to employ the corrupt soccer player. On the other hand, the legal route by which this result is reached is open to argument.

First of all, though, it may be remarked that this case offers a good example of metaphor casting its shadow over reality, for it is absolutely clear that the rules concerning latent defects in relation to contracts of sale cannot be applied to the facts of case 26. For professional soccer players are employees of soccer clubs and even though in common parlance phrases concerning the 'sale' or 'purchase' of soccer players are often heard, they should be understood merely as shorthand expressions for more accurate descriptions of those transactions. In Italian law, the basic effect of the sum paid by the 'transferee' club to the 'transferor' is that it renders lawful what would otherwise be an act of unfair competition, a typical case of wrongful interference with the contract of employment between the soccer player and the club that first hired him.[25] However, if the national soccer association withdraws the player's licence to play professional soccer as a consequence of a bribery scandal any payment of the above-mentioned sum loses its justification and may therefore be recovered in accordance with the rules on restitution of payments 'without a cause'.[26]

Secondly, though, a more traditional analysis of the case would hold any contract between the two clubs void because of its invalidity according to the national soccer league rules. These rules forbid the employment of corrupt soccer players. For this purpose, it is irrelevant that neither club realised that the football player had accepted a bribe. True, the national soccer league's rules do not have legislative status, but are based on contract.[27] Yet, the contract not conforming to those rules cannot operate between the parties because they are both bound by the league's rules. This is why its cause could be considered to be defective.[28]

However, in a case like this we have too many doctrines chasing the same problem: for one could also argue that the contract between the clubs was void because its object was originally impossible,[29] or that it was voidable, being affected by an essential mistake,[30] or that the basic assumption shared by the contracting parties collapsed when the national soccer league revoked the player's licence to play.[31] All these arguments lead to the conclusion that the club may recover the money paid to enlist the corrupt football player in its team.

THE NETHERLANDS

This is not so much a case about change of circumstances as about (mutual) error. Therefore art. 6:228 B.W. applies, making it possible to

---

[25] The law on the employment contract of professional athletes is l. 23 Mar. 1981, n. 91. Article 3 of this text expressly provides that professional athletes are employees of their clubs. Note, however, that sometimes even the *Corte di Cassazione* talks of the 'sale' and 'purchase' of professional athletes. Coming to the point raised in the text, to my knowledge, students of the economic analysis of law have devoted little attention to schemes that involve payments of money between clubs in order to acquire the right to employ players coming from other clubs. This is surprising, because these schemes provide excellent examples of how competitors may share the surplus produced by soccer players' (efficient) breaches of contract. By their very nature, however, these arrangements come under scrutiny where they unduly restrict competition and freedom of contract.   [26] Art. 2033 c.c.   [27] Sanino, in: *Enciclopedia* § 4.2.

[28] Those who are familiar with the French notion of *fausse cause* will recognise the same notion disguised under the pretentious sentence 'inidoneità funzionale della causa': Cass., 28 Jul. 1981, n. 4845, Giust. civ., 1982, I, 2411. See also: Cass., 5 Jan. 1994, n. 75, Rass. dir. civ., 1996, 185, obs. Vitale.   [29] Arts. 1346, 1418 c.c.   [30] Arts. 1428, 1429, n. 2 c.c.

[31] On the Italian reception of the German theories of *Voraussetzung* and *Wegfall der Geschäftsgrundlage* see Sacco/De Nova, in: *Trattato Sacco I* 443; Bessone, *passim*.

avoid the contract. See for a further elaboration as to error the Dutch report in case 2 above.

ENGLAND

There are three ways in which this case could be analysed: under the law of mistake, the law of frustration, and by implication of a term in the contract.

What is the nature of the contract under which the 'transfer' has been made? In English law, an employer cannot simply assign to another person his rights against his employee.[32] This means that the contract of transfer must essentially be one of novation, i.e. a contract under which the two contracting parties (the first club and the player) agree that a third (the second club) shall with its consent stand in the relation of either of them to the other.[33] The effect of novation is to extinguish the first contract and to replace it with another; here, extinguishing the first contract for services between the first club and replacing it with a second contract for services between the player and second club.

With this in mind, at first sight, the facts of case 26 seem to attract the general law governing supervening events in English law in that the withdrawal of the player's licence could be said to be a supervening event of a type which might attract the doctrine of frustration. It has been noted that the test for frustration is whether performance of the contract is radically different from that undertaken by the contract.[34] However, it is clear that the doctrine of frustration operates only so as to terminate contracts which are at least in part executory, whereas the contract in case 26 between the two soccer clubs is executed: the first club has given up its rights against the player in return for payment of the sum of DM 900,000. The fact that the rights against the player have become less valuable after the contract has been performed cannot entail the frustration of the contract since the contract has been performed.

Can the facts be analysed instead as one of mistake? Such an approach would look to the mistake of the two soccer clubs that the subject matter of their contract (the right of the first club to the player's professional soccer services) was fundamentally different from what they had thought, in that the player had behaved in a manner which (at most) is likely to lead to his licence to play professional soccer being withdrawn. However, as has

---

[32] *Nokes v. Doncaster Amalgamated Collieries Ltd* [1940] AC 1014, at 1018.
[33] See Guest, *Chitty on Contracts* § 19–050.   [34] See the English report to case 25 above.

already been mentioned,[35] English law takes a very narrow view indeed of relief on the ground of common mistake, this being restricted to cases where the subject matter is so fundamentally different that it was essentially different from the thing as it was supposed. In the leading case of *Bell v. Lever Bros. Ltd*,[36] two directors of a company engaged for five years (under a 'service agreement') entered into an agreement (called by the parties a 'compensation agreement') on its reorganisation under which they gave up their rights in consideration for the payment of a lump sum totalling £50,000. Unknown to the company, the directors had committed breaches of their service contract which would have entitled it to have dismissed them without compensation. Nevertheless, the House of Lords held that the company's mistake in entering into the compensation agreement was *not* sufficiently fundamental to make it void: the company had obtained what it bargained for, viz. the surrender by the directors of their extant (if voidable) rights against it under the service agreement. There is a close parallel here with the facts of case 26, for it can be said that the second club received exactly what it contracted for, viz. the rights of the first club in respect of the services of the player. These rights *did* exist at the time of the contract of transfer, even though they were likely to be rendered worthless by the revocation by the soccer association of his licence to play.

It should be noted, however, that a more liberal doctrine of fundamental mistake was promulgated by the Court of Appeal in *Solle v. Butcher*,[37] being formally reconciled with the House of Lords' decision in *Bell* on the basis that the latter had been decided 'at law' whereas its own approach was based on equitable principle. According to the more liberal doctrine, where both parties to a contract enter into it under a mistake which is both causal and very serious, then the contract will be voidable in the sense that it may be set aside by the court in equity on such terms as it thinks fit (which would include return of some if not all the money paid). It could well be said that the parties to the contract in case 26 have entered into it under such a mistake. However, this equitable doctrine is of uncertain authoritative status and has been very little applied by the courts.[38]

A final way of looking at the case would be to ask if any term should be implied into the contract of transfer as to the availability of the player to play professional soccer. The test for the implication of terms is one of necessity rather than of reasonableness.[39] There would certainly be a

---

[35] See the English report to case 2 above.   [36] [1932] AC 161.   [37] [1950] 1 KB 671.
[38] Guest, *Chitty on Contracts* § 5–068.   [39] *Liverpool City Council v. Irwin* [1977] AC 239.

strong argument for saying that it was an implied term of the contract that the player should be entitled to play professional soccer at the time of the formation of the contract (this being practically necessary for the 'business efficacy' of the contract).[40] It would, however, be more difficult to establish an implied term to the effect that the player had not behaved in such a way that his licence to play would not at some later date be withdrawn.

In conclusion, it is doubtful whether the second club will be able to claim back the transfer sum from the first club. It should be added that the player himself would not be held to have owed the second club a duty to disclose his past conduct: *Bell v. Lever Bros. Ltd.* However, his first club would be entitled to recover either damages for breach of his contract with it in accepting the bribe or (more likely) the bribe itself[41] as he was its servant or agent at the time.

IRELAND

The English law analysis holds good for Irish law.

SCOTLAND

There are possibly three contracts to consider here: (i) the contract for the transfer of the player between the two clubs, (ii) the contract between the player and the club he has transferred to, and (iii) the contract between the player and the selling club.

Regarding the first contract, because the contract has been performed, i.e. executed, the doctrine of frustration does *not* arise.[42] Frustration only operates to relieve the parties from performing any obligations which were outstanding at the time of the frustrating event. However, at the time of the formation of the contract, *both* parties were unaware that the player had accepted a bribe. In Scots law, the parties' error as to the quality of the subject matter of a contract can render the contract null, provided that that quality is the essence of the contract, i.e. error *in substantialibus*.[43] While it can be argued that a player without a licence is fundamentally different from a player with a licence, i.e. the error as to the quality goes to the root of the contract, the difficulty in this case is that the player lost

---

[40] '*The Moorcock*' (1889) XIV PD 64.
[41] *Boston Deep Sea Fishing & Ice Co. Ltd v. Ansell* (1888) 39 Ch D 339.
[42] See the Scottish report to case 25 above.   [43] See Bell § 11.

his licence *after* the contract was formed. Moreover, it is not clear that withdrawal of the licence was an automatic sanction or whether the association had a discretion: indeed, we are not told for how long the licence has been withdrawn. It is submitted that only if the loss of the licence was automatic and for a long period would the error go to the root of the contract rendering the contract null.

The question of whether the club may recover the price paid rests on whether the law would consider that the selling club has become unjustifiably enriched[44] at the other club's expense and so require the enrichment to be reversed. The obligation does not depend on contract but is obediential and arises by operation of law. The buying club would have a plea of repetition which allows for the recovery of money which has been paid in circumstances where it would be unjust for the defender to keep the money. The plea applies to a number of cases which reflect its Roman law origins. The plea for repetition here would fall under the heading *condictio causa data causa non secuta*. The selling club may set off that proportion of the fee which represents the services of the player which the club enjoyed before he lost his licence.

If the contract is not rendered null as a result of the doctrine of error, the buying club would be able to obtain damages only if the selling club had warranted that the player's licence was not vulnerable. Unless there was an express term to that effect, it is doubtful whether the court would imply such a term.

However, the selling club would have a remedy against the football player who is himself in breach of contract with the club as he has incapacitated himself from performance of the contract. *Walker* submits that a football player who engages in a risky pastime before the season opens and breaks a leg for example, could well be in breach of contract with his club.[45] He was also in breach of his contract with the selling club when he accepted the bribe, and in this sense could possibly be sued for material breach of contract.

DENMARK AND NORWAY

The fact that a fundamental precondition of the agreement ceases to exist, viz. that the player loses his licence to play professional soccer, will very likely be seen as a breach which is so essential that it causes the agreement to cease to exist. As a result, the price will have to be repaid. It is

---

[44] See the Scottish reports to cases 3, 4, 14, 15 and 17 above.   [45] § 32.8.

important to point out that the circumstances in question must be of such a nature that the parties, when concluding their contract, could not reasonably have taken them into consideration, and that one party is completely deprived of all its interest in the agreement.

The abnormal development consists in the fact that the rights for which payment is made are no longer of economic value. It might thus be said that an essential defect has arisen in the interest which one of the parties has in the contractual relationship. This kind of breach of an implied condition belongs traditionally to those acceptance of which has been particularly difficult. However, now and again, on grounds of reasonableness, a party to a contract may be rendered assistance because due to subsequent events, he no longer has a need for the performance. If the facts of the so-called 'coronation cases'[46] had arisen in this country, it is probable that the failure of the implied conditions would have been taken account of. This may be seen if we look at two textbook examples which are frequently discussed in Nordic literature. For if a steamship company advertises an extra departure from Oslo to Kristiansand on the occasion of the forthcoming national choral convention at Whitsun, and the convention is subsequently cancelled, it would seem fairly obvious that the disappointed singers should not need to pay for the tickets they have ordered. Or: A has hired, for a high price, a window seat in order to watch a procession that is supposed to pass the street. The procession is then cancelled, or its route is changed, so that it does not pass along the window. Here A should be discharged.[47] *Arnholm* is of the same opinion: 'The man who buys the trousseau for his daughter's wedding, cannot be released from the purchase if the wedding plans flounder – even if the other contracting party is fully aware that the purchase has its grounds in the approaching marriage and would not have been made, had the purchaser known that it would come to nothing. And this is the way the case will in reality need to be resolved if the motive is of a more general nature . . . It may be a different matter if subsequent events rob the consideration of its objective value. Somebody booking window positions to watch a festive procession in the street should presumably not pay for them if the procession comes to nothing. But it is probably not possible to move very far in that direction. Somebody renting a cottage for Easter cannot refuse to pay because the weather turned out so bad that it was no use thinking of doing an Easter trek.'[48]

---

[46] Cf., e.g., *Krell v. Henry* [1903] 2 KB 740.   [47] Augdahl 154.
[48] Arnholm, *Tre utsnitt* 40 (my own translation from the Norwegian).

Also in Danish law, *Ussing* in his classic work supposes that the principle of the 'coronation cases' must apply: 'Thus, somebody having at a high price hired a window position or a room in order to watch a forthcoming procession from there, must be able to rescind the agreement if the procession comes to nothing. In a similar manner there may, in other instances where the consideration is of value because of general demand, be grounds for giving relevance to the precondition when an unexpected event causes the consideration to lose its value to all and everybody or even loses a particularly high value which was founded on an intended use which has now been prevented.'[49]

SWEDEN

The bribed soccer player ought to be compared to any other goods, which cannot be used for their normal and intended purpose because of a restriction ordered by an authority, as a result of a circumstance existing before the contract was made, and referring to the individual goods. In these cases the seller probably bears the risk, no matter whether he was innocent and ignorant (cf. ch. 4, s. 18 of the Real Estate Code of 1970).[50] Reference can be made to restrictions concerning the use of property bought as a restaurant, as a hotel etc. and caused by the quality it had when the contract was made. The outcome ought to be the same, no matter whether the Sale of Goods Act of 1990 is applied by analogy (s. 17) or the doctrine of the lapse of presuppositions is applied. This view is supported by NJA 1961, p. 330 but contradicted by NJA 1991, p. 808, both cases concerning small business enterprises. In the latter case the Supreme Court held that the seller is responsible only when he has warranted the quality, or given the buyer the impression that there is no restriction, or when he knew of the restriction but did not inform the buyer. The answer therefore is uncertain.

FINLAND

Even more so than construction work,[51] sport is in Finland traditionally situated to a great extent outside the legal litigation *system* in the strict sense. The central organisations have arbitration systems of their own, the

---

[49] Ussing 478 (my own translation from the Danish).
[50] See Håstad, *Den nya köprätten* 130 ff., and Hellner, in: *Festskrift* 209 ff.
[51] See the Finnish report to case 15 above.

most important being the central Legal Protection Board for Sport (in Finnish, *Urheilun oikeusturvalautakunta*; this is no arbitration tribunal but in fact a judicial board chaired by a Supreme Court justice, with outstanding lawyers as members). Since the contracts and rules of associations contain arbitration clauses, going to court is usually excluded.

The transfer system has also been a matter for arbitration under the rules of the Finnish soccer (and ice hockey) associations. For this reason there are no court cases on transfer contracts between clubs and very few court cases in general on sports, apart from a few tax law, labour law and accident cases. Also, legal science has for these reasons shown no great interest in the internal rules of sports and in their application by arbitration tribunals. From the information that I have received I have understood that the principle *periculum est emptoris* is largely applied in such situations, although the arbitration awards are not published. For this reason it is rather problematic to speculate over the outcome of the case in a 'normal' Finnish court.

Players are prone to repeated injuries; the buyer can hardly claim the price of such 'slaves' back. The case presented is very problematic indeed and of a special nature, and its solution will largely depend on the specific rules and practices of the football association in question. These rules seem to resemble the Roman rules of *emptio hominis*. In legal science there have been attempts at labelling the entire transfer system (that is, the one applied before the *Bosman* case[52]) invalid, since restrictions regarding re-employment after the contract of services has expired are against good faith (*contra bonos mores*). Cautious recommendations to this effect by legal scholars (*Palmgren, Saarnilehto* and myself) have not been tested before the court. In one case, however, where the arbitration clause happened to be invalid, the Finnish Ice Hockey League and the club KalPa accepted a settlement lifting the ban placed upon their former goalkeeper Mika Rautio by the transfer system. Thus, even this case produced no precedent.

There was a recent case where a player's licence had been withdrawn: he had used drugs (but this did not involve doping). The player sued the Ice Hockey League, but again the case was settled. The relative extraterritoriality of sports continues.

But assuming that this were not a sports case but concerned the hiring of qualified professional services which presuppose a licence or authorisation and assuming further that the qualification of the employee were

---

[52] C-415/93 *Union Royale Belge des sociétés de football association ASBL and others v. Jean-Marc Bosman* (1995), E.C.R. I-4921.

withdrawn, thus preventing the rendering of services, the situation would be that the contract is void or that the new employer is entitled to rescind the contract on grounds of defective performance.

Editors' comparative observations

Nearly all legal systems incline towards the view that the second club may claim back the transfer sum from the first club but quite a few of them make it clear that the solution is rather doubtful. This lack of certainty is due to the fact that in most legal systems there is no precedent, or any other relevant authority, for such a case. Even in Germany where a case like the present one was actually decided, the decision remains disputed. The only legal system which clearly rejects a claim by the second club is the Spanish one. The doctrinal bases advanced are extremely diverse. Some legal systems admit the possibility of more than one way of looking at these facts.

(i) Particularly popular is an analysis in terms of mistake. Here it is usually argued that the second club laboured under an error as to the essential qualities of the player in entering the 'contract of transfer' with the result that that contract may be rescinded and the money returned. It is also often considered to be relevant that we are dealing here with a mistake that was shared by both parties to the contract. In Greece, Austria, France, Belgium, Italy, the Netherlands and Scotland this kind of argument would be acceptable, while it is rejected in German law. The English report makes clear that while the case does not attract application of the doctrine of fundamental mistake as traditionally understood, it might be covered by a more liberal doctrine espoused by the Court of Appeal some time ago.

(ii) Alternatively, it is argued that withdrawal of the player's licence constitutes a fundamental change of circumstances which must lead, in the present situation, to dissolution of the contract and a claim for recovery of the money. This argument would be accepted in Germany (under its doctrine of *Wegfall der Geschäftsgrundlage*, as recognised under the auspices of good faith), Greece (art. 388 Gr. C.C., a codified version of the German doctrine), Austria (theory of fundamental change of circumstances), Italy (under an Italian version of *Wegfall der Geschäftsgrundlage*) and Sweden (presupposition doctrine, a close relative of *Wegfall der Geschäftsgrundlage*). Belgian law would not apply its (very restrictive) doctrine of change of circumstances.

(iii) An English court might have recourse to the implication of a term in the contract to the effect that the player had not behaved in such a way that his licence to play would not at some later stage be withdrawn, though such an implication is not covered by authority. A not dissimilar approach is taken by West Nordic law which holds that the ability of the player to play professional soccer was an essential condition of the contract of transfer. On failure of this condition, the contract is terminated with the result that the second club may recover the price.

(iv) The West Nordic analysis also suggests frustration as a possible basis for recovery. In England and Scotland, however, the doctrine of frustration would not be applied in view of the fact that the contract has been executed.

(v) Yet another approach would focus on the fact that the second club has received a performance which is defective. Austrian law, therefore, allows the second club to cancel the contract on the basis of the aedilitian remedies (which it does not apply only to contracts of sale but to all contracts under which a performance has to be paid for). The application, *per analogiam*, of the rules relating to latent defects in contracts of sale to the present case is held to be possible in the Belgian report, while it is rejected in the German, Greek and Spanish reports and categorically rejected in the Italian report. Under Swedish law, it would be helpful to look at the present transaction as a contract of sale. A similar view is taken in Finnish law where the second club would be entitled to rescind the contract on the ground that the performance was defective.

(vi) French and Italian law accept the possibility of the contract being annulled for failure of the *cause* (or *causa*) of the second club's obligation to pay the money.

Case 27: Disability insurance

Case

Ivory, an insurance company, has concluded a disability insurance with Jacques. The contract contains a forfeiture clause, under which Jacques has to report his disability within two weeks or lose his benefits. As a result of an accident, Jacques is indeed disabled. However, he fails to report his disability (a) because he has become insane, (b) because for four weeks after the accident he was in a coma.

Discussions

GERMANY

In accordance with § 6 III 1 VVG (Contracts of Insurance Act) an insurance company is not released from its obligation to pay out the benefits even though the insured party has failed to do what was incumbent upon him after the event has occurred against which he was insured, if such failure is not due to his gross negligence or intention. This rule is mandatory in so far that it may not be changed to the disadvantage of the policyholder (§ 15 a VVG).

In both cases, Jacques was not at fault when he did not report his disability. Thus, the insurance company still has to pay.

§ 6 III 1 VVG may be regarded as a manifestation of the principle of good faith. For good faith requires that far-reaching and clearly inappropriate consequences do not flow from a minor breach or from a breach which is not attributable to the policyholder.[1]

---

[1] *Palandt*/Heinrichs § 242, n. 53; *Staudinger*/Schmidt § 242, n. 781.

GREECE

The insurance policy between Ivory and Jacques is now regulated by the provisions of L. 2496/1997 (Private Insurance Act). Under art. 10 of this law, Jacques' claims against the insurance company will prescribe after five years, this period running from the end of the year in which the obligation on the part of the insurer arose.

In the present case there is a forfeiture clause limiting the time within which Jacques has to report his disability to two weeks; otherwise he would lose his benefits. However, this clause must be construed as an agreement to abbreviate the period of prescription to two weeks rather than five years. Such an agreement is void under art. 275 Gr. C.C. ('Any legal transaction shall be void which excludes prescription, or provides for a period shorter or longer than the one laid down by law, or generally aggravates or attenuates the conditions of prescription').[2] These provisions are *ius cogens.*

Law 2496/1997 includes also another provision favouring Jacques in the present case, for according to art. 7 I 'the insured is obliged to inform his insurer within eight (8) days, from the day that the accident occurred'. This provision is a 'burden' (*Obliegenheit*) which can result in an obligation on the insured to compensate his insurer for any losses which may have occurred as a result of a lack of information which the insured should have provided. The insured does not lose his claims against the insurance company even if his failure to inform the insurance company is due to his gross negligence (art. 7 II of L. 2496/1997).

Thus, it follows that the forfeiture clause which is included in the disability insurance contract between Ivory and Jacques is invalid under Greek law. Since Jacques was not at fault, the insurance company has to pay and no right of compensation arises in its favour.

It is obvious from the above analysis that Greek law employs clear and specific provisions in this area so that reliance upon the general clauses in the Code is unnecessary. Of course, the reference to 'gross negligence' in art. 7 I of L. 2496/1997 can be interpreted as a special manifestation of good faith.[3]

AUSTRIA

Jacques' obligation in the contract to give notice within two weeks of the occurrence of any insured event corresponds to the obligation to give

---

[2] This is applicable also with regard to commercial contracts; cf. L. 2496/1997, art. 33 I.
[3] Cf. Simantiras no. 328, pp. 235 f.

immediate notice which is incumbent on an insured person by way of application of § 33 of the Contracts of Insurance Act (*Versicherungsvertragsgesetz* = VVG).[4] However, the consequences of failing to report the disability within two weeks which are expressed in the contract in the present case reach far beyond what is specified by § 6 sec. 2 VVG and this provision is mandatory, i.e. it cannot be the subject of an agreement to the contrary. § 6 sec. 2 VVG itself provides that where a contract of insurance excludes a benefit or benefits which would have accrued to the insured person in the event of breach of any of the latter's obligations relating to matters after occurrence of the insured contingency, this exclusion will only take effect where breach of one of these obligations resulted from the insured person's intended act or omission or gross negligence. Clearly, in the case of either his subsequent insanity or his entering a coma, Jacques was not at fault[5] and this means that any contractual attempt to exclude his benefits will not take effect.[6]

This legislative provision in the VVG is based on the idea that the imposition of a sanction for breach of an accessory contractual obligation should correspond as far as possible with established principles of liability law[7] (notably, whether or not the person in question was at fault) and the general liability law has already worked out which are the important factors in deciding whether there are sufficient reasons for the imposition of sanctions for breach.

FRANCE

Jacques is under an obligation to report his disability to Ivory in order to prevent the forfeiture clause from operating, but he is unable to comply with this obligation. In principle in French law the time to notify the other party of a claim does not start to run until the insured has knowledge of an accident likely to involve the insurer's liability. Nevertheless, an insured who knows that the accident has occurred may be in a position where it is impossible for him to give notice of a claim. Article L. 113–2 of the Insurance Code (*Code de l'assurance*) states that when a clause provides that the right to an indemnity may be repudiated, the insurer cannot rely on it 'in any case where the delay is due to an accident or an act of *force majeure*'. In addition, in French law the insurer cannot rely on a forfeiture

---

[4] In the version BGBl 1994/509. Cf. Schauer 258 ff.
[5] Fault has to be judged by a subjective yardstick; cf. Koziol, *Haftpflichtrecht I* nn. 5/35 ff.
[6] The question regarding whether Jacques' legal representative might have been at fault need not, probably, be discussed here.   [7] Jabornegg 41.

clause unless he can prove that any failure to notify him of the claim within the indicated time limit caused him damage.

An insured's inability to act is a question of fact and so the lower courts must assess whether it possessed the characteristics of an act of *force majeure*. The judges evaluate the relevant allegation of the insured in relation to the facts of each case. So, for example, it has been held that the insured was not in a condition of total prostration so as to attract the excuse of *force majeure* where he had taken various steps relating to the accident before notifying the insurer of his claim.[8] On the other hand, such an inability may result from a physical trauma 'coupled with an important psychological trauma which meant that he was unable to look after the medical–legal consequences of the accident immediately'.[9] Applying this approach to the particular circumstances of case 27 would lead to the following results. (i) When Jacques has become insane he must be considered unable to notify the insurer of his claim as a result of the accident within the meaning of art. L. 113–2 as above. Ivory cannot therefore rely on the forfeiture clause. (ii) When Jacques has been in a coma for four weeks following the accident he would also be under such inability. Time starts running with respect to notification of the claim from the date on which he becomes sufficiently conscious to carry out the obligation.

Thus, in French law the facts of case 27 do not raise an issue of good faith under art. 1134 al. 3 of the Civil Code between the parties, but are rather the subject of detailed legislative provisions which govern the parties' behaviour and restrict the insurer's ability to repudiate the insurance if the insured's failure to give notice of a claim is due to circumstances which make it impossible for him to do so.

BELGIUM

In non-transport insurance, art. 19 § 1 of the Belgian Land Insurance Contracts Act of 1992 provides that an insurer cannot invoke the failure to respect the contractual period within which to report, if the report has been made as soon as was reasonably possible. This provision is mandatory in favour of the insured party. Thus, under this Act, Jacques will not lose his benefits in either case (insanity or coma).

On the assumption of there not being such a clear and specific rule in insurance contracts (e.g. in transport insurance contracts, governed by the

[8] Civ. 28 Feb. 1944, Rec. gén. des ass. terr. 163 note A. Besson.
[9] Civ. (1) 1 Dec. 1969, no. 68–12.562, no. 671, Rec. gén. des ass. terr. 1970.514 note A. Besson.

old Act of 11 June 1874, or in some other type of contract), Jacques would not lose his benefits if he could invoke *force majeure*. Indeed, reporting the disability would not be considered a 'condition' in the strict sense of the word, but an additional duty (*Nebenpflicht*) (or, perhaps more correctly, a 'burden' in the sense of *Obliegenheit*) of the insured party. Thus, he would not incur any sanction in the case of an impossibility to report which is not due to his own fault. Both cases (i.e. insanity and four weeks in a coma) will normally be accepted as *force majeure* in relation to this duty.

Moreover, it would constitute an abuse of right by the insurer to invoke forfeiture because of a failure to respect the contractual period within which to report if he has suffered no loss or if that sanction is in some other way disproportionate to the failure to report on the part of the insured party.

SPAIN

In both cases (a) and (b) the policyholder, Jacques, has failed to communicate his disability as required under the contract for reasons which he could not influence. This means that such a failure will not constitute 'contractual fault' on his part and he will, therefore, be relieved of the duty to report his disability and will not suffer any disadvantage from failing to do so. These consequences are based on arts. 1105 (no liability for unforeseeable and inevitable consequences) and 1184 (no liability in cases of impossibility) of the Civil Code.

ITALY

If the insured person negligently fails to report the accident to the insurer, under art. 1913 of the Civil Code the insurer has the right to reduce the indemnity correspondingly.[10] This provision of the Code cannot be derogated from by the parties in a way favourable to the insurer.[11] Since Jacques either became insane or fell into a coma, he could not be considered to be at fault in relation to his reporting of the insured event and so the forfeiture clause will not take effect.

THE NETHERLANDS

In both situations the insurance company probably cannot invoke the forfeiture clause. In a case decided in 1949 the *Hoge Raad* ruled that an insu-

---

[10] The same rule applies to disability insurance.   [11] Art. 1932 c.c.

rance company could not refuse payment on account of the fact that the premium had not been received in time. (This late payment of the premium was due to the situation in the Netherlands at the end of the Second World War.) The *Hoge Raad* refused to accept a literal application of the policy, referring to customs within the insurance industry and the meaning of the policy in the light of what good faith under specific circumstances demands of the parties to an insurance policy.[12]

ENGLAND

The terms of contracts of insurance which stipulate conditions as to recovery of sums under them are valid at common law. Indeed, from the eighteenth century, stringent conditions were considered both prudent and reasonable for insurers to require, given the great risk of fraudulent claims to which they were exposed.[13] In the absence of express provision as to the effect of a failure to comply with a condition for recovery, the courts have construed them as conditions precedent to recovery so that no claim can be maintained unless the condition is fulfilled.[14] The approach of the common law courts in the eighteenth and nineteenth centuries can be seen at its most strict in a decision in which it was said that the fact that an insured person's inability to fulfil a condition was due to circumstances beyond his control would not excuse a failure to comply.[15] And in *Cassell v. Lancashire & Yorkshire Accident Insurance Co. Ltd*,[16] it was held that a claimant who was ignorant of the fact of the injury or death throughout the period for giving notice of a claim, had none the less failed to do what he was required to do in order to recover under the contract. This very strict approach is all the more striking given that it had been declared that contracts of insurance were of the utmost good faith, but what this was understood to mean was that the parties to them had duties of disclosure of circumstances material to the risk.[17]

However, while this law still remains good in principle,[18] it has been overtaken or may be circumvented in several different ways.

First, in the particular circumstances of Jacques' mental incapacity (whether through insanity or being in a coma), provision exists for an

---

[12] *Hoge Raad* 20 May 1949, NJ 1950, 72 (*Rederij Koppe*).
[13] *Worsley v. Wood* (1796) 6 TR 710, at 718 *per* Lord *Kenyon* C.J.
[14] *Roper v. Lendon* (1859) 1 E & E 825.
[15] *Worsley v. Wood* (1796) 6 TR 710 (where the condition required a certificate of the loss to be made by the local minister and church wardens, who refused to do so).
[16] (1885) 1 TLR 495.   [17] *Carter v. Boehm* (1766) 3 Burr 1905.
[18] See Ivamy, in: *Halsbury* § 482; Guest, *Chitty on Contracts* § 39–057.

application to be made to the court for the latter to take over the management of Jacques' property and other affairs.[19] While in principle the court
needs to be satisfied that Jacques is a 'mental patient' within the meaning
of the legislation, there is provision for an emergency application to be
made pending determination of the question of capacity.[20] There is little
doubt that if Jacques' 'next friend' applied to the court within the period
required by the contract of insurance, the court would exercise its jurisdiction in the management of his affairs by giving notice of his disability.
Perhaps an even simpler route would be for a relative or friend of Jacques
to give the requisite notice on Jacques' behalf, leaving it to the court to
ratify this action under the legislative powers described above.

Secondly, it has been said that 'the manifest hardship . . . produced by
[the rule in *Cassell's* case] has produced both a reluctance on the part of the
judges to construe such a provision as a condition and, in the United
States, an inclination to imply a term as to the possibility of performance'.[21] While the first of these possibilities is not open to the court in
case 27, the second one is. The exact technique would perhaps depend on
the specific terms of the condition. So, for example, if it required 'notice'
of the disability to be given, 'notice' could itself be interpreted as requiring in the person notifying knowledge of the circumstances giving rise to
the claim. Then it could be said that such a person could not 'know' of
circumstances where he was mentally or physically incapable in the way
Jacques is on the facts.

Thirdly, the position at common law has been significantly altered by
the Unfair Terms in Consumer Contracts Regulations 1994,[22] themselves
implementing the Directive on Unfair Terms in Consumer Contracts
1993.[23] Unlike the Unfair Contract Terms Act 1977, the 1994 Regulations
in principle apply to contracts of insurance, though not as regards those
elements going to the definition of the insured risk.[24] The 1994
Regulations apply only to contracts between business suppliers of property or services (here, the financial service of taking a risk by insurance)
and consumers. It would seem clear that Ivory is such a business supplier
and that Jacques is a consumer within the meaning of the Regulations.
Jacques could, therefore, challenge the validity of the condition regarding
the reporting of his disability on the basis that 'a contractual term
which has not been individually negotiated shall be regarded as unfair if,
contrary to the requirement of good faith, it causes a significant imbal-

---

[19] Mental Health Act 1983, Part VII.   [20] Ibid., s. 98.   [21] Ivamy, in: *Halsbury* § 419.
[22] SI 1994/3159.   [23] E.C. Council Directive 93/13/EEC.
[24] See the preamble to the Directive, ibid.

ance in the parties' rights and obligations arising under the contract, to the detriment of the consumer'.[25] To the extent to which the condition in case 27 is interpreted as requiring the reporting of Jacques' disability when Jacques is physically or mentally incapable of doing so, it would seem highly likely that the term would be considered unfair and therefore not bind Jacques.

Quite apart from these recent changes to the law, the strict position at common law does not represent the position in practice. For, the Association of British Insurers and Lloyd's of London have issued Statements of Practice, to which their members are expected to adhere, with a view to mitigating the severity of the obligations in the case of private policies. Thus, in the case of policies taken out by individuals in a private capacity, the Statement of General Insurance Practice, paragraph 2 (a) provides that a policyholder should not be asked to do more than report a claim and subsequent developments as soon as reasonably possible, except in the case of legal processes, and claims where a third party requires the policyholder to notify within a fixed time where immediate advice may be required. Although provisions in this Statement do not have the force of law, they bind the Insurance Ombudsman or any arbitrator appointed under the Personal Insurance Arbitration Scheme.[26]

IRELAND

In Irish contract law stipulations regarding the time for performance of obligations are first analysed to see whether time is considered by the parties as being 'of the essence' and therefore the fulfilment being a 'condition precedent' to liability. In the commercial context, and particularly in the context of insurance, time will be regarded as being of the essence: it is felt reasonable that an insurance company would wish to know as soon as possible of potential claims, so that it might fully verify claims and, more generally, so that it might take suitable steps in making provisions for its liability, future underwriting and pricing of policies. Here, although not formally described as a 'condition' of the insurance contract, it is clear that the intention of the parties was to make time of the essence. It is unlikely that the insanity or temporary unconsciousness of the insured would excuse breach of his obligation to report the disability within the period of a fortnight.

Two decisions throw light on the facts of case 27, namely, *Gamble*

---

[25] Directive, ibid., art. 3; cf. Unfair Terms in Consumer Contracts Regulations 1994, SI 1994/3159, ss. 3(1) and 4(1).   [26] Statement of General Insurance Practice, § 6.

v. Accident Assurance Co.[27] and *Patton v. Employers Liability Assurance Corporation.*[28] These cases establish that where the time for reporting an insurance claim is considered a condition precedent to the insurer's liability, as appears clear in the current context, then it is immaterial that any failure to give notice is due to circumstances outside the control of the insured, or person claiming on his behalf. It seems that even the death of the insured is not an excuse for breach of such a condition, neither is ignorance of the existence of the policy on the part of those claiming under a life policy. It is also immaterial that the insurer would not be specifically prejudiced by any failure by the insured to give timely notice.[29]

Finally, for insurance contracts concluded after 31 December 1994 by consumers, the fairness of the clause would have to be established, pursuant to the E.C. (Unfair Terms in Consumer Contracts) Regulations 1995.[30] These regulations represent Ireland's implementation of the Unfair Terms in Consumer Contracts Directive.[31]

SCOTLAND

The forfeiture clause in this insurance contract imposes a condition on Jacques which has become impossible to fulfil. Like an exclusion clause, the forfeiture clause seeks to absolve one party (the insurance company) from a liability (paying up the insurance) which would otherwise arise under the contract. Although some contracts are protected against exclusion clauses by the Unfair Contract Terms Act 1977, it does not apply to contracts of insurance. However, the Unfair Terms in Consumer Contracts Regulations 1994,[32] which came into force on 1 July 1995, do cover contracts of insurance and will be discussed below.

As a general rule, if a party binds himself by contract to do anything he is bound to do it, notwithstanding any accident, because he ought to have guarded by his contract against it; *Clark v. Glasgow Assurance Co.*[33] Should or could Jacques have guarded against such a predicament as this? He has failed to fulfil the terms of the condition by not reporting his disability within the time limit. Whether owing to his insanity or his being in a coma, he is unable to perform his part of the contract and thus relieves Ivory of its liability to pay up.

---

[27] (1869) IR 4 CL 204.   [28] (1887) 20 LR Ir 93.
[29] *Pioneer Concrete (UK) Ltd v. National Employers Mutual General Insurance Association* [1985] I Lloyd's Rep 274.   [30] SI No. 27 of 1995.   [31] 93/13/EEC.
[32] SI 1994/3159. The regulations implement E.C. Council Directive 93/13/EEC.
[33] (1854) 1 Macq 668.

However, the general rules of law also recognise certain excuses for non-performance, in particular kinds of contracts and certain other excuses, as applicable to all, or at least most kinds of contracts. An example is the death or permanent incapacity of either party to a contract involving *delectus personae*, and also inability to perform by reason of illness; *Robinson v. Davidson*.[34] A contract which involves *delectus personae* is a contract where one party entered into the contract in reliance on the qualities possessed by the other, e.g. where a party agrees to do something which involves a personal skill. No one can take Jacques' place. It follows then that Ivory will not be able to rely on the provisions of the forfeiture clause, circumstances making its condition impossible to fulfil.

But Jacques' best defence lies in the Unfair Terms in Consumer Contracts Regulations 1994. The regulations essentially subject terms in consumer contracts to a fairness test, and a term will be considered unfair when 'contrary to the requirement of good faith' it 'causes a significant imbalance in the parties' rights and obligations under the contract to the detriment of the consumer'.[35] Where the term is held to be unfair it is not binding on the consumer but the contract shall continue to bind the parties if it is capable of continuing in existence without the unfair term. The regulations only apply to consumer contracts between 'a seller or supplier and a consumer'.[36] Regulation 1 defines a 'consumer' as 'a natural person who in making a contract to which these regulations apply, is acting for purposes which are outside his business'.

The regulations apply to any term in a consumer contract which has not been 'individually negotiated'.[37] The assessment of the unfair nature of the term 'shall be made taking into account the nature of the goods or services for which the contract was concluded and referring, as at the time of the conclusion of the contract, to all the circumstances attending the conclusion of the contract on which it is dependent',[38] and to determine whether the term satisfies the requirement of good faith, regard shall be had to the matters specified in Schedule 2 of the Regulations.[39] Regard shall be had in particular to: (i) the strength of the bargaining positions of the parties, (ii) whether the consumer had an inducement to agree to the term, (iii) whether the goods or services were sold or supplied to the special order of the consumer, and (iv) the extent to which the seller or supplier has dealt fairly and equitably with the consumer. Bearing all this

---

[34] (1871) LR 6 Ex 269.
[35] Reg. 4(1), Unfair Terms in Consumer Contracts Regulations 1994, SI 1994/3159.
[36] Reg. 3(1), ibid.   [37] Reg. 3(1), ibid.   [38] Reg. 4(2), ibid.   [39] Reg. 4(3), ibid.

in mind it is submitted that the exclusion clause will be struck down as an unfair term in this consumer contract.

DENMARK AND NORWAY

This is a so-called 'claims made' clause which at West Nordic law would probably be enforced with great leniency outside strictly commercial insurance agreements, such as marine insurance. Clauses of this kind, particularly in an insurance agreement for a private individual, will hardly be taken by their letter, regardless of any legislation protecting the insured party. There is therefore, in my opinion, no great difference between failure to report a claim because the policyholder has become insane and because for four weeks after the accident he has been in a coma. But these questions have long been regulated by statute. According to the Insurance Act of 16 June 1989 § 13–11, the claim shall be made without undue delay. A similar rule applies in Denmark according to § 21 of the Insurance Act, no. 129 of 15 April 1930.[40] Such elastic rules will not preclude Jacques' claim in the present case.

There are probably a number of aspects on account of which a clause of this type would not be upheld by courts of law. First, such a brief period fixed in an agreement concerning insurance of a private individual will encounter considerable opposition by the courts. Second, it is regarded as essential that the right-holder must not be unable to report his claim for reasons beyond his control.

Of course, it does not follow from the above that every term and condition in an insurance agreement will be struck down by the courts. By way of example, a ruling by the Danish *Højesteret* in U 1988, p. 449 H, may be mentioned where a condition in an export credit agreement, in terms of which the seller's claim against the buyer had to be evidenced by a court decision or an arbitration award, was not set aside under s. 36 of the Contracts Act, regardless of the fact that the information available as to the particular circumstances of law in Libya (the buyer's domicile) made it not very tempting for the seller to bring an action against the buyer in that country.

Freedom of contract does not fully prevail with regard to insurance contracts in the West Nordic countries, since the legislation concerning insurance agreements contains extensive mandatory protection for policyholders.

---

[40] Selmer 255 ff.; Lyngsø 190 ff.

SWEDEN

According to a Scandinavian Act on Insurance Agreements from 1927 (still in force in Sweden), s. 21, the insurance company may stipulate that the insured without delay has to notify the company of an event giving rise to a claim. If the insured should fail to do this, no matter whether he is aware of the event or not, and if it might be assumed that that failure caused a disadvantage to the company, his claim may be reduced or even lapse. Otherwise no sanctions are allowed. Case 27 thus provides a problem only if the insurance company could have taken measures against the disability (or lost an opportunity to invoke reinsurance) if it had been duly informed. If so, the question arises whether the contract clause might be unreasonable and therefore void. Since the clause in the present case more or less conforms with the statute, it will be difficult or even impossible to disregard it. It might be added that according to s. 39 of the Consumer Insurance Act of 1980, which is applicable to insured goods only, it is always sufficient if the consumer takes action within three years.

FINLAND

The two-week term for reporting the injury, as such, is manifestly too short and according to Finnish law the condition is even invalid (Insurance Act of 1994 (Ra 201), ss. 73 and 3: at least one year which cannot be shortened in favour of the insurer where, as in this case, the insured is a consumer). Even if the reporting-time were not unconscionable, non-compliance with the clause is excused on grounds of sickness, especially if it is connected with the disability covered by the insurance in question.

Editors' comparative observations

All legal systems would protect Jacques in the circumstances. The reasons for doing so may be broadly categorised in the following way.

(i) Many countries (Germany, Greece, Austria, France, Belgium, Italy, Denmark, Norway, Sweden and Finland) possess special legislation, governing contracts of insurance covering the problem raised in the present case. In some of them, the relevant provisions of this legislation reflect principles existing in the respective legal systems more generally. Thus, German law would prevent forfeiture of Jacques' rights on the basis of provisions seen as a manifestation of the principle of good faith; Austrian law would do so on the basis of provisions corresponding, as far as possible, with established principles of liability law (notably the fault principle); and French and Belgian law would do so on the basis of provisions seen as a special example of the application of a doctrine excusing non-performance of a contractual obligation on the ground of *force majeure*. Interestingly, it is noted in the English report that insurers are expected to adhere to statements of General Insurance Practice according to which policyholders should not be asked to do more than report a claim as soon as reasonably possible. As a matter of contractual practice, therefore, English law reaches very similar results to those which the above-mentioned systems reach under their special legislation.

(ii) In some countries the answer is directly based on more general principles: the notion of 'contractual fault' (Spain), interpretation of the contractual clause according to good faith (the Netherlands) or impossibility as an excuse for non-performance of a contract involving *delectus personae* (Scotland).

(iii) The traditional legal approach in England would be to have recourse to interpretation of the contract so as to deny the exercise of a right of forfeiture by the insurance company on the facts. English courts would feel relieved, however, in being able to avoid straining the terms of the contract through construction and instead to have recourse to legislation implementing the E.C. Directive on Unfair Terms in Consumer Contracts, according to which such a term could be declared ineffective as unfair. That legislation (as implemented in the respective countries) would also provide Jacques' best defence in Scotland and Ireland.

Case 28: Crop destroyed by hail

Case

Jordan has insured his crop with the Insurance Company Illingworth against hail. If the crop is destroyed by hail, according to the contract Jordan has to leave his fields as they are for the next twenty days, in order to allow one of Illingworth's employees to inspect the damage. After Jordan's crop has been destroyed by hail, he ploughs it under without waiting for the damage to be inspected because he has been advised by the state authorities that to leave the field as it is will cause vermin to spread an infectious disease.

Discussions

GERMANY

Jordan was required by the terms of the contract to leave the field untouched for twenty days in order to allow Illingworth to inspect the damage. Yet, under the present circumstances it would clearly be inappropriate for him to do so. The breach is not attributable to his fault. Again, therefore, the insurance company will have to pay (§ 6 III 1 VVG).

GREECE

If Jordan can prove that, by waiting for the next twenty days in order to allow Illingworth Insurance Company employees to inspect the damage, he would expose not only his own field but also other fields to the danger of vermin spreading an infectious disease, he does not lose his right to seek compensation from the insurance company (see L. 2496/1997).[1]

---

[1] Cf. Stathopoulos, *Contract* nos. 177–84, pp. 129 ff.

AUSTRIA

Again, § 6 sec. 3 of the Contracts of Insurance Act (*Versicherungsvertrags-gesetz* = VVG) is applicable with the result that breach of an obligation which has to be performed by an insured person after the occurrence of the insured event leads to the exclusion of benefits only if the breach of obligation resulted from the insured person's intended act or omission or gross negligence. Since Jordan has ploughed his field on the advice of the state authorities in order to prevent the spread of an infectious disease he would not be held to have been at fault, or at least not at gross fault.

Furthermore, the relevant standard terms of insurance applicable in Austria[2] provide expressly that the insured is allowed to change the state of things which have been damaged by an insured event even without the consent of the insurer if such a change is necessary to reduce the damage or is required in the public interest. The measures which Jordan has taken to prevent the spread of an infectious disease were done on the advice of state authorities and were therefore clearly in the public interest. As a result, the insurer is not released from liability even though Jordan has acted in breach of a term of the contract.

Finally, § 6 III sent. 2 VVG provides that if an insured person shows that breach of one of his obligations did not affect establishing the occurrence of the insured event nor that it affected the existence or the scope of the liability of the insurer, then the insurer remains liable to the extent to which this is shown. Evidence to establish any of these matters becomes inadmissible only if the insured person broke the obligation in question with an intention to deceive the insurer.[3]

FRANCE

In principle, it is up to the insured to adduce evidence that the loss has occurred. The disappearance of pieces of the evidence may be due to the insured's own act; in this case the insurer would not be liable. On the other hand, if part of the reason for its non-availability is not owing to an act or omission of the insured, but rather due to the intervention of, e.g., a public authority, such as an administrative authority, the problem may be approached in a different way (although we do not know of any case law on the subject).

---

[2] Art. 5 (1) e of the *Allgemeinen Bedingungen für die Sturmschaden-Versicherung mit Einschluß von Schäden durch Hagel, Schneedruck, Felssturz, Steinschlag und Erdrutsch*, version 1986.
[3] Cf. Schauer 259 ff.

First, it may be possible to take into account the state authorities' knowledge of the accident. Evidence of the insured event may be adduced 'by any means'; testimony by the authorities' agents would be admissible if they have seen the consequences of such an event.

Secondly, while the mere filing of a claim by the insured to this authority does not constitute evidence of the facts which it contains under the general rules of evidence (*droit commun de la preuve*), the inherent difficulty of adducing evidence of certain risks has meant that the courts have relaxed this rule by recognising an evidential role to the mere filing of a claim.[4] Thus, for example, the *Cour de cassation* has recently held that in the absence of an inventory made in the joint presence of the parties of objects left by a guest in the hands of an owner of a hotel, because of the presumption created by the guest's staying in July in a luxury hotel, the fact of the loss of the objects resulting from robbery was established by the declaration of the theft made by their owner at the police station.[5]

Finally, it would be possible to question the good faith of the insurer who repudiates his liability: is it fair for him to make his liability as an insurer (for which he has received a premium) depend on evidence which he knows cannot be adduced because of the very nature of the risk? This situation is analogous to that of an insured who files a claim for theft of his vehicle in circumstances in which there is no trace of the theft (the car is not found, there are no witnesses etc.). In the same spirit, and in similar cases, it has been suggested that one can discern an attempt to use the interpretation of the common intention of the parties to modify the burden of proof and admissibility of evidence by giving a certain evidential value to the filing of a claim of evidence of loss arising from an accident.[6] In this way, the *juges du fond* may consider that the parties had agreed to modify the legal rules of evidence, so as to allow evidence which is based only on the insured's filing of the claim.

If this approach towards this kind of insurance case were accepted, it would be possible to infer that the general principle of good faith, as provided for the general law of contract under art. 1134 al. 3 of the Civil

---

[4] In the case of theft, see Montpellier 29 Jan. 1986, Rec. gén. des ass. terr. 1986.466 and Aix-en-Provence 11 Jan. 1984, Rec. gén. des ass. terr. 1984.440 which admitted as evidence a declaration of theft to the police authorities, but ultimately held that theft had not been proved since the car was found with the anti-theft device intact.

[5] For the decision relating to the civil liability of the hotel owner: Civ. (1) 9 Mar. 1994, no. 91–17.464, no. 407, Rec. gén. des ass. terr. 1994.623 note A. Favre-Rochex.

[6] Civ. (1) 10 Jun. 1992, no. 89–12.513, no. 880, Rec. gén. des ass. terr. 1992.619 note J. Kullman; for an example of a well-known modification, in the area of credit cards, Civ. (1) 8 Nov. 1989, no. 86–16.196, no. 1340, D 1990.369 note C. Gavalda, D 1989.Somm.327 note J. Huet.

Code, also permeates a more specialised set of legal rules, here those relating to insurance. It is interesting to note that the concept of good faith which is applied to insurers follows the modern tendency of imposing a duty of loyalty and co-operation on the creditor as well as on the debtor of an obligation.

BELGIUM

According to art. 56 of the Land Insurance Contracts Act of 1992, Jordan may not modify (without the consent of the insurer) the state of the damaged objects in such a way that it becomes impossible, or more difficult, to determine the extent or causes of the damage.

According to art. 56, sec. 2 and sec. 3 of the same Act, the insurer may completely refuse to pay if the insured party acted fraudulently. In other cases, the insurer may only reduce the benefit in relation to the damage caused to him by the modification. These provisions are mandatory in favour of the insured party. They can be seen as illustrations of the general idea that sanctions may not go further than necessary for the *ratio legis*. This idea is generally not seen as a specific application of the good faith principle, but authors have pointed to an existing affinity.

From this rule, and also from the fact that non-modification is seen as a duty (or rather a burden, i.e. an *Obliegenheit*[7]) of the insured party, it can be deduced that Jordan may modify the state of things in so far as there is a ground of justification for his behaviour. The fact that leaving the field as it is will cause vermin to spread an infectious disease is certainly such a cause for justification ('higher interest'). Although this relieves Jordan from the forfeiture clause (since art. 56 is mandatory in favour of the insured party, the contract may not be stricter than art. 56), this still does not relieve Jordan from the normal burden of proof; he must give sufficient evidence of the damage suffered.

If the information provided by the state authorities is not correct, art. 56 still applies and the question arises whether the interests of the insurer are prejudiced or not. The practical result, however, is merely that the evidence provided by Jordan will be judged more severely; if this is done, the interests of the insurer are not prejudiced and the forfeiture clause does still not apply in this case.

The outcome of the case will thus probably depend on whether Jordan has taken any other initiative to preserve evidence of the damage. Belgian

---

[7] See the Belgian report to case 1 above.

law has appropriate summary proceedings by which a judicial expert can be appointed in cases of urgency. In a case of utmost urgency, it is possible to get a court order immediately (even *ex parte*, without hearing the other party). Furthermore, bailiffs can, on request, report on facts which can be sensorily perceived, and their report will constitute full proof of the reported facts. Jordan might, at least, have taken photographs himself. If Jordan has kept no evidence at all, he has little chance of obtaining the insurance benefit under the contract described in case 28.

Without art. 56 of the Insurance Contracts Act of 1992, the result would be probably the same under general contract law, except that a stricter clause in the contract would not as such be invalid. It would then be necessary to fall back on general doctrines such as abuse of right in order to protect Jordan from forfeiture. Consumer law would not apply, as Jordan is not a consumer in relation to his crop.

SPAIN

The same considerations apply to the facts of case 28 as in case 27 (disability insurance),[8] so that the failure to comply with the condition will also be held not to constitute 'contractual fault' within the meaning of the relevant provisions of the Civil Code. However, the particular facts of case 28 also attract a special rule in Spanish law which leads to the same result. For art. 16 of the Contract of Insurance Act of 8 October 1980 provides that where an insured person has failed to give the insurer information about the harm which he has suffered, he does not lose his right under the contract if this was not due to his own fault.

ITALY

Article 1914 of the Civil Code obliges an insured person to do whatever he can to prevent or mitigate damage to the insured property. Where the insured maliciously or negligently fails to act accordingly, the insurer can refuse payment, or reduce it proportionately to the damage caused by such an omission.[9] On the assumption that on the facts of case 28 the state authorities advised Jordan that he should plough the field in question so as to prevent the spreading of an infectious disease, he can hardly be considered negligent, provided that he promptly communicated to the insurer his intention to follow this advice.

---

[8] See the Spanish report to case 27 above.   [9] Art. 1915 c.c.

Normally, the terms of contracts of insurance in Italy[10] specify the rights and duties of the insured in the case of hail and the standard form of contract in use obliges the insured person to perform all the work which is recommended by good agricultural practice. Furthermore, the insured is not allowed to harvest any products damaged by hail before their inspection by the insurance company, unless they are ripe. In the latter case he may harvest them, but he must warn the insurer of his intention to do so by telegram and he should also leave one strip of the crop damaged by hail on the field, without making any changes to its state.

THE NETHERLANDS

This is a case of *force majeure* as to non-performance of an obligation: art. 6:75 B.W. Jordan is acting on the advice of state authorities and also attempts to avoid an infectious disease. Non-compliance with the clause in his insurance contract can for that reason not be imputed to him. He might, however, in good faith be required to inform the insurance company of his intention. This would allow the latter to make an appointment for inspection at very short notice. Were he not to have informed the insurance company it may be argued that Jordan cannot, in good faith, invoke his *force majeure* defence.

ENGLAND

The first question on these facts would be to determine whether Jordan has in fact broken the condition as to leaving his fields. Although this would appear to be clearly the case, an argument could be made that any such condition should be subject to an implied term that the act of leaving the fields should not cause a legal nuisance. In this respect, it is important to note that the leaving of 'premises in such a state as to be prejudicial to health or a nuisance' is a statutory nuisance which empowers the relevant local public authorities to serve an abatement notice on the person on whose premises the nuisance has arisen that they are to remedy the nuisance.[11] The failure of that person to do so constitutes a criminal offence.[12] The facts of case 28 suggest that the local authority already is interested in the state of Jordan's land and it would be typical of the way of public

---

[10] Insurance companies have agreed on general conditions of insurance for hail: see Bellero, Digesto, 4th edn, sez. comm., I, 1987, 426.
[11] Environmental Protection Act 1990, ss. 69–80.   [12] Ibid., s. 80(4).

authorities working in the fields of public health and environmental protection to offer advice before invoking their legal powers of enforcement. It would be difficult for Illingworth Insurance Company to argue that its conditions validly require Jordan to continue a statutory nuisance.

However, quite apart from this, it could be argued that the condition as to inspection by the employees of the insurance company is not a condition precedent to the company's liability under the policy. This approach has been taken in the case of a person's practical inability to notify a claim.[13]

Finally, Jordan could again wish to rely on the terms of the Unfair Terms in Consumer Contracts Regulations 1994.[14] The only difficult question in attracting the test of unfairness is whether Jordan is a consumer within the meaning of the Regulations (and the 1993 Directive[15]). 'Consumer' is defined by the Regulations as 'a natural person who, in making contracts to which these Regulations apply, is acting for purposes which are outside his business'.[16] Clearly, in insuring his crop, Jordan is acting for the purposes of his own business of farming, but a more liberal interpretation of the ambit of the provisions would be that a person acts as a consumer where he makes a contract for his own business purposes but of a type unconnected with those purposes. Jordan's business is one of farming and vis-à-vis the insurance company he is a consumer. Finally, it should be noted that if Jordan runs his farm through a company then the 1994 Regulations cannot protect him, as the definition of 'consumer' restricts their application to natural persons.

IRELAND

Two important questions arise from these facts: (i) whether Jordan is in breach of contract by ploughing the crop under, and, (ii) if so, is the provision a condition of the insurance contract breach of which would absolve the insurance company from liability?

As to the first issue, it is unlikely that a contractual provision would be found to be broken by action required by law of one of the parties. Accordingly, the question arises as to whether the ploughing under was required to be done to avoid breach of Jordan's public or private duties.

[13] See the quotation from Hardy Ivamy, in: *Halsbury* § 419 cited in case 27 above; and *Stoneham v. Ocean, Railway and General Accident Insurance Co.* (1887) 19 QBD 237.
[14] SI 1994/3159.
[15] E.C. Council Directive 93/13/EEC; see the English report in case 27 above.
[16] Unfair Terms in Consumer Contracts Regulations 1994, SI 1994/3159, s. 1.

Under s. 107 of the Public Health (Ireland) Act 1878 premises must not be kept in such a state as to be a nuisance or injurious to health. Local authorities may serve abatement notices and failure to comply is an offence punishable summarily. Additionally, failure to abate vermin may constitute a private nuisance to adjoining landowners, in that their possession might be interfered with by the unreasonable behaviour of Jordan.

If, though, Jordan's action were a breach of the contract the next question would relate to the consequence of that breach. Is the requirement to leave the fields as they are a condition precedent to the insurer's liability? This is a matter of the construction of the contract.[17] In case 28, the term is not described as a condition nor are specific consequences for breach detailed as in case 27. The clause in question is obviously of importance in relation to the verification of the loss and its causation, and so in the present context, it would be more likely than not that it would be seen as a condition precedent to the insurer's liability.

Finally, it should be noted that the E.C. (Unfair Terms in Consumer Contracts) Regulations 1995[18] would have no application to the facts of this case so as to invalidate the clause on the ground of unfairness, as Jordan is not acting as a consumer for their purposes.[19]

SCOTLAND

Again we have an insurance contract where a condition has not been fulfilled and the insurance company seeks to rely on this to excuse its liability to pay up. The Unfair Terms in Consumer Contracts Regulations 1994 will apply,[20] and if the condition is deemed to be unfair it will be struck down, i.e. Jordan need not fulfil the condition.

At common law we could look to the doctrine of frustration which covers the situation of supervening illegality; if the main object of the parties' contract, or the proposed method of performance, or anything essential for performance, is made illegal after the contract has been made but before performance has been completed, non-performance or cessation of performance is justified, and both parties are discharged from their duty of further performance; *Fraser & Co. Ltd v. Denny, Mott & Dickson Ltd*,[21] *George Packman & Sons v. Dunbar's Trustees*.[22] So, if a change in

---

[17] Cf. *Stoneham v. Ocean, Railway and General Accident Insurance Co.* (1887) 19 QBD 237.
[18] SI No. 27 of 1995.   [19] Ibid., regs. 2 and 3.
[20] See the Scottish report to case 27 above.   [21] 1944 SC (HL) 35.   [22] 1977 SLT 140.

the law renders performance illegal, the contract is discharged on the basis that it is not to be presumed that a man is bound to commit an illegal act.

Therefore, if it is the case that had Jordan ignored the state authorities' warning and not ploughed the field he would be breaking the law, his breach of the condition of the insurance contract is justifiable. Furthermore, Illingworth would have to pay the insurance sum because surely the obligation to pay the insurance arises as soon as the crop is destroyed. The insurance contract contains a suspensive condition; namely, that the obligation of the insurance company to pay the insurance cannot be enforced until the condition that the insurable interest (the crop) is destroyed by hail is purified. The condition has been purified, hence Illingworth must perform its obligation. Jordan will be discharged from his obligation, i.e. he would not have to fulfil an illegal condition.[23]

DENMARK AND NORWAY

Much of what has been said with regard to case 27 also applies to case 28. Nevertheless, there are significant differences here. In this case, the insurer has a justified commercial interest in being able to make an independent assessment of the damage. Although the policyholder has not really acted disloyally, it must be said that, having himself destroyed the evidence, he must to a certain degree bear the risk. These questions are dealt with by § 4–10 in the Norwegian Insurance Act of 16 June 1989; according to this provision the court may, at its discretion, reduce the insured's claim against the insurance company. This is contrary to the solution in § 21 of the Danish Insurance Act, no. 129 of 15 April 1930, which orders the insurance company to be placed in the position in which it would have been if it had been given proper notice.

The problem posed in this case may be taken as a question of loss of evidence and could thereby be said to have a more general implication in contract law. Illustrative here is a ruling in Rt. 1930, p. 257 concerning fungus damage discovered three years after the sale of a tenement block. The buyer claimed that the fungus already existed at the time of sale, but the seller believed that the damage resulted from substantial and protracted roof leakage after the buyer had taken over the block. A majority

---

[23] *Shearer v. Alexander* (1875) 12 SLR 333.

in the *Høyesterett* held that the buyer had not discharged his onus of proof: he had himself significantly weakened his position in that respect since he had performed repairs concerning the fungus damage without having had independent experts inspect the damage, and without having notified the seller prior to commencing the repairs. The ensuing uncertainty had to be to his disadvantage. In other words, failure to secure evidence meant that it could not be ruled out that the damage had occurred subsequent to the transfer of the block of tenements, and, as a result, the requirement concerning evidence had not been met.

SWEDEN

Jordan could probably have delayed acting in the way he did and could probably have told the insurance company that he would plough the crops under after a few days, thereby enabling the company to inspect the damage. Because of the good reason to plough under, the company ought to have inspected immediately, unless it was impossible to do so (e.g. many similar hail storms elsewhere). If the company ought to have inspected immediately, it has probably forfeited its right to rely on the term (see s. 36 of the Contracts Act of 1915) and Jordan's account ought to be accepted unless the company can prove it to be inaccurate. If, on the other hand, the company had a good excuse not to inspect before Jordan ploughed under, and in line with the answer to case 27, Jordan's action would probably deprive him of his insurance benefits if, but only if, it could be assumed that the company after an inspection would have been able to refuse compensation or estimate it at a lower amount.

Regarding cases 27 and 28, reference could be made to NJA 1935, p. 424. According to certain terms in a contract, a doctor's certificate was to be presented within ninety days; otherwise compensation would be forfeited. The term was ruled to be unreasonable, since the omission had presumably been of no importance to the company.

FINLAND

Conditions like this are in Finland interpreted in favour of the insured; the principle *in dubio contra stipulatorem* is largely applied. Inspection by the insurer is not a condition of coverage, but Jordan's conduct will probably put the burden of proving the extent of the damage on him.

Interpretation of insurance policies is to a great extent guided by social considerations favouring the insured:[24] often even clear conditions are 'interpreted' against the insurer.

Editors' comparative observations

On these facts, most of the legal systems protected Jordan from Illingworth's insistence on the strict terms of the contract. The position in the Nordic legal systems is somewhat more nuanced. Of those legal systems which ensured protection, the following points can be made.

(i) Again, as in case 27, many legal systems (Germany, Greece, Austria, France, Belgium and Italy) rely here on special legislative provisions in the field of insurance. In the case of Germany and Austria, these provisions are seen as reflecting the same general legal principles as in case 27, but in the case of France and Belgium, in the circumstances of case 28, they are seen as reflecting a principle of good faith or a doctrine of the abuse of rights rather than *force majeure*.

(ii) Spanish, Dutch and Scots law would, again, rely on more general principles. According to Spanish law failure, on the part of Jordan, to comply with the condition would not be seen as constituting 'contractual fault'. In the Netherlands, Jordan would be given a defence based on *force majeure*. Scots law would, in view of the supervening illegality of complying with the condition, rely on the doctrine of frustration of the contract.

(iii) English law, Irish law and Scots law would see this as a case attracting the application of the E.C. Directive on Unfair Terms in Consumer Contracts. In addition English law would again, at common law, think in terms of interpretation of the contract and might resort to the device of an implied term. An interpretative approach is also adopted in Finnish law.

Finally, the West Nordic systems differ in their approach to this sort of problem, Norwegian law recognising here a discretion in the court to reduce the extent of any indemnity due by the insurer; Danish law providing that the insurer is entitled to be put into the situation in which it would have found itself if proper notice of the insured event had been given. Swedish law takes a similar approach to the Norwegian here, providing that an insurer is entitled to rely on breach of a condition for a claim by the insured but only to the extent to which it has thereby been prejudiced. The main concern voiced in the Nordic reports is that the

---

[24] See Wilhelmsson esp. 63 ff.

insured has to take all reasonable steps, in the circumstances, to allow the insurer to assess the damage. In that sense, even the Nordic systems do not necessarily insist on strict compliance with the contractual clause (ploughing under only after twenty days). But they emphasise that the insured will have to carry the loss if, as a result of his own action, he is no longer able to prove his loss. This point is also raised (or tacitly presupposed) in other reports (e.g. Belgium, Italy). Even in the face of the emergency, the insured must make sure that he remains in a position to prove the damage, and its extent.

Case 29: Divorce settlement

Case

On the basis of a divorce settlement, Lothar may claim from his ex-wife Morena DM 1,000 per month for maintenance until he remarries. After having paid for some years, Morena refuses to continue to pay, because for two years Lothar has lived together with another woman in extra-marital cohabitation.

Discussions

GERMANY

The maintenance agreement is subject to the resolutive condition (§ 158 II BGB) that Lothar does not remarry. According to § 1585 c BGB the partners to a marriage may indeed conclude an agreement for the time after divorce. Here the clause concerning remarriage merely reiterates the content of § 1586 I BGB.

In the present case, however, § 162 I BGB ('If the fulfilment of a condition is prevented, contrary to good faith, by the party to whose disadvantage it would operate, the condition is deemed to have been fulfilled') may affect the relationship between the parties. This rule is an emanation of § 242 BGB in that it wants to prevent a party from deriving a benefit from a behaviour that infringes the precepts of good faith.[1] Morena can refuse to pay maintenance if Lothar has prevented the condition from materialising

---

[1] See *Jauernig*/Jauernig § 162, nn. 3 f.; *Palandt*/Heinrichs § 162, nn. 1, 6. § 162 I BGB derives from Roman law; on the problem of conditions prevented from materialising in Roman law, and for a critical evaluation of the modern German rule, see Knütel, JBl 1976, 613 ff.; Zimmermann, *Obligations* 730 f., 746.

contrary to good faith by living together with another partner. In principle, of course, Lothar cannot be forced to marry. But this cannot lead to
the consequence that Morena remains indefinitely obliged to pay maintenance. Even if the maintenance creditor does not refuse to remarry merely
in order to retain his claim for maintenance, the condition is deemed at
any rate to have materialised, by way of application of § 162 I BGB, if he has
lived together for a number of years (in the case decided by the Regional
Appeal Court Düsseldorf for six years) with a new partner.[2]

It is questionable whether the same already applies if the maintenance
creditor has lived together with his new partner for two years. It would
appear to be important to determine to what extent the new relationship
has been viewed, from the start, as being permanent and to what extent
it has been consolidated. In this context it is interesting to note that the
statutory claim for maintenance after termination of a marriage is taken
to be excluded, by § 1579 n. 7 BGB, after a period of two to three years.[3]

GREECE

In Greek family law, as amended by L. 1329/1983, maintenance after
divorce has certain requirements which are determined in art. 1442 Gr.
C.C. However, because the provisions regarding maintenance after divorce
are *ius dispositivum*, the spouses may validly conclude an agreement deviating from the provisions of art. 1442 Gr. C.C.

In the present case, Morena agreed to pay maintenance to Lothar until
the latter remarries. However, Lothar has lived together with another
woman in extra-marital cohabitation for two years. The problem here is
whether this fact entitles Morena to refuse to continue paying maintenance to Lothar.

According to Greek law (art. 1444 II Gr. C.C.), a claim for maintenance is
discontinued if the ex-husband 'cohabits permanently with someone else
in extra-marital cohabitation'. Strictly speaking, the provisions of this
article apply only to the maintenance awarded by the court under the provisions of art. 1442 Gr. C.C. and not to maintenance claims which were
freely agreed upon by the ex-spouses. Article 1444 II Gr. C.C., therefore,
cannot be applied in the present case. Thus, it will have to be investigated
whether refusal, on the part of Morena, to pay maintenance may be
based on an abuse of right by Lothar (art. 281 Gr. C.C.). The claim for

[2] OLG Düsseldorf NJW 1981, 463; Medicus, *Allgemeiner Teil* n. 835.
[3] *Palandt*/Diederichsen § 1579, n. 39; *Münchener Kommentar*/Richter § 1579, nn. 47 ff.

maintenance, from whichever source, is supposed to cover the necessities of life of the particular person entitled to the claim. If Lothar permanently lives with another person and thus no longer has a need for maintenance from another source, Morena's obligation could be considered terminated by way of application of art. 281 Gr. C.C.

The provisions of art. 1444 II Gr. C.C. concerning cohabitation after divorce are a poor and unhappy special application of art. 281 Gr. C.C. This is why, in the opinion of the present writer,[4] the former article has to be narrowly interpreted. It is not justified by current custom, or by the spirit of Greek law. Moreover, it might also be against the Greek Constitution (namely, arts. 5 and 21, which protect the freedom of a person in matters such as living alone, marriage, cohabitation, divorce, remarriage, etc.). The important point that may concern the ex-spouse, who pays maintenance, relates to the personal needs of the other party.

The matter has been the subject of academic discussion, but there is not yet any case law.[5]

AUSTRIA

If in their divorce settlement the former spouses have mentioned only *remarriage* as a resolutive condition for Lothar's maintenance, then it would appear that the question of the effect of an *extra-marital* cohabitation on that maintenance is one of interpretation of the contract.[6] However, in Austrian law the problem raised by case 29 is not discussed from this point of view at all, but rather in terms of the existence of a gap or *casus omissus* in the legislative provisions governing divorce. For § 75 of the Marriage Act (*Ehegesetz* = EheG) expressly provides that any claim for maintenance by a divorced spouse terminates on remarriage and this provision also applies directly to divorce settlements to the extent that a claim for maintenance is fixed within the same scope as the legislative claim[7] and by analogy to purely contractual claims for maintenance.[8] However, in the absence of any legislative provision specifically governing the matter, the question of the consequence of an extra-marital cohabitation

---

[4] Androulidakis-Dimitriadis, *Exogami symviosi* 200 ff. Cf. Androulidakis-Dimitriadis, in: *Scheidungsfolgenrecht* 186, no. 162.

[5] For literature regarding the case, see: Androulidakis-Dimitriadis, *Exogami symviosi* 200–8; Androulidakis-Dimitriadis, in: *Festschrift Michaelides-Nouaros* 65–85; Skorini, in: *Astikos Kodix VII* art. 1442, nos. 31–5; Androulidakis-Dimitriadis, in: *Astikos Kodix VII* art. 1485–1504, no. 65.   [6] §§ 914, 915 ABGB.   [7] Cf. § 69a EheG; OGH in SZ 55/54 (1982).

[8] Zankl, in: *Schwimann, ABGB I* § 75 EheG n. 2; § 80 EheG n. 16.

on a claim for maintenance remains unanswered. Nevertheless, the arguments which are rehearsed in relation to this problem should also be of importance in relation to the interpretation of the present contract clause.

In the view of the Supreme Court[9] an extra-marital cohabitation entered into by a dependent former spouse leads neither to the forfeiture of any claim for maintenance in terms of § 74 EheG[10] nor to its extinction as provided for by § 75 EheG, but only to its suspension, with the result that it can be enforced again after the end of any period of extra-marital cohabitation. The Supreme Court does not attribute this to the principle of good faith, but argues that during the period of extra-marital cohabitation the enforcement of the claim would be contrary to morality.

However, it is more correct as a matter of legal dogmatics to inquire whether a gap does indeed exist in the law and then to consider how it should be filled. Such a line of approach would force the court to work out the value judgements behind the law as it stands, to consider the differences between remarriage and extra-marital cohabitation in this respect and then to determine the proper legal consequences of the latter.[11] One factor which has to be stressed here is that extra-marital cohabitation should not be favoured above marriage[12] and this certainly suggests that a claim for maintenance of a former spouse should be cancelled on entering into extra-marital cohabitation, as long as and to the extent that the considerations which are relevant to the case of remarriage are also applicable to the case of extra-marital cohabitation. Here, it may be noted that the decisive reason for the definitive expiry of the claim in the case of remarriage is found in the fact that the new marriage itself gives rise to a new claim for maintenance, this time as against the new spouse and even after dissolution of that new marriage.[13]

At this stage it can be appreciated why the approach of the Supreme Court, as noted above, is to be criticised, for in its view a claim for maintenance is suspended irrespective of whether or not the dependent spouse actually receives maintenance from his cohabitee. But since, in contrast to marriage, no new maintenance claim arises as a result of any extra-

---

[9] SZ 27/134 (1954); JBl 1991, 589; cf. Schwind, in: *Klang, Kommentar I/1* 875.

[10] This rule provides that the dependent former spouse is deprived of his claim if he is guilty of serious misconduct with respect to the other party after the divorce, or if he leads a disreputable life.

[11] Regarding the *Prinziplücke* relevant in this case cf. Bydlinski, *Methodenlehre* 474.

[12] Koziol/Welser, *Bürgerliches Recht II* 233.

[13] Cf. Schwind, in: *Klang, Kommentar I/1* 901.

marital cohabitation, juristic opinion in Austria takes the view that extra-marital cohabitation affects any maintenance claim only if the essential needs of the dependant are in fact met by the cohabitee.[14] At the same time, the Supreme Court's position according to which a claim for maintenance does not expire on extra-marital cohabitation, but is only suspended, is accepted in the legal literature[15] on the basis of the differences which exist between marriage and extra-marital cohabitation. For if a dependent former spouse remarries, the law of divorce provides a further claim for maintenance if the new marriage fails; but if an extra-marital cohabitation comes to an end, the former partner enjoys no claim for maintenance from that cohabitation, and must therefore still depend on the claim which arose on his or her divorce which was decreed before entering into that extra-marital cohabitation.

FRANCE

It is inferred from the reference to a 'divorce settlement' that Lothar and Morena have divorced on the basis of a non-contested divorce (by mutual consent), in which case they will have agreed upon the amount of maintenance, and the judge will have subsequently ratified their agreement. Even if this inference is not correct, and Lothar and Morena have divorced on other grounds, provided that the maintenance can be analysed as falling within arts. 270 ff. of the Civil Code and therefore possesses a compensatory nature (*prestation compensatoire*), then the validity of the remarriage clause needs to be discussed, and this is done under (i). However, a distinction may be drawn in the event that the parties have divorced on the grounds of six years' separation and that Morena had deserted Lothar. In this case the maintenance payment would be analysed differently, involving the application of a different set of rules, which expressly provide for the cessation of such payments in the event of remarriage or cohabitation under art. 283 of the Civil Code. Although this latter analysis seems unlikely on the facts, it will be discussed briefly under (ii).

(i) A compensatory maintenance payment is fixed according to the needs of the spouse who stands to benefit from it, and the resources of the spouse making the payment, taking into account the situation at the time of the divorce and its evolution over the foreseeable future.[16]

---

[14] Gimpel-Hinteregger, in: *Familie und Recht* 633; Verschraegen 482 f.
[15] Cf. Pichler, in: *Rummel, ABGB II* § 75 EheG n. 2; Zankl, in: *Schwimann, ABGB I* § 75 EheG n. 7.
[16] Art. 271 C. civ.

Furthermore, a maintenance payment following divorce is classified by art. 273 of the Civil Code as a lump sum payment, and these are not, as a general rule, subject to revision. In addition, art. 276 states that a lump sum may be paid in instalments, and for a period equal to or less than the life-time of the former spouse.[17] Two consequences follow from these legislative provisions. First, a lump sum payment cannot be made the subject of a condition[18] and the cessation of maintenance upon remarriage could be analysed as a condition subsequent. Secondly, these articles are interpreted cumulatively so that until recently the courts held that a payment made for a period less than the life-time of the ex-spouse cannot be made the subject of a condition of remarriage. Such a clause is void.[19] However, this case law has been thrown into disarray by a case in 1985 in which the *Cour de cassation* implicitly recognised the validity of a divorce settlement made between the spouses which included a clause which provided for maintenance to cease upon remarriage or cohabitation.[20] It must be emphasised that the case is not published in the *Bulletin de la Cour de cassation* and does not have the authority of an *arrêt de principe*, since the *Cour de cassation* did not have to pronounce expressly on the validity of the clause but was merely asked to control the court of appeal's 'factual assessment' as to the interpretation of the parties' intention. The *Cour de cassation* did not censure the court of appeal's restrictive interpretation of the clause since it did not come into play on the facts because insufficient evidence of continuous cohabitation was adduced. By inference, the clause appears to be valid only if it has been included at the choice of the parties, since the court has no power to include such a term.

The question of the validity of remarriage clauses has been the subject of academic as well as judicial controversy for some time. In favour of their validity, it has been suggested that in the case of divorce by mutual consent, the intention of the parties is decisive as long as it does not contradict public policy. A distinction has been drawn between the advantages that come from testaments or contracts of employment, which are

---

[17] Art. 276–1 C. civ.
[18] Civ. (2) 5 Nov. 1986, Bull. civ. II, no. 158, p. 107.
[19] Civ. (2) 2 May 1984, Bull. civ. II, no. 76, p. 55, JCP 85.II.20494 note Philippe; Grenoble 20 May 1981, JCP 1983.II.20086 note De La Marnierre; TGI Saint-Nazaire 25 Oct. 1985, D 1987.Somm.45 obs. A. Bénabent. See also TGI La Rochelle 19 Oct. 1977, D 1978.I.R.435 note A. Bénabent, where it was held that to uphold the clause would impose a moral and material constraint on the beneficiary who would thereby be dissuaded from remarrying so as not to lose the benefit of the allowance.
[20] Civ. (2) 16 Jan. 1985, GP 1985.2.Pan.jur.211 note M. Grimaldi.

independent of the marital status of the parties, and maintenance which is based on the condition of celibacy that the spouse is reduced to as a result of his divorce. This distinction militates in favour of admitting that this status might cease. On the other hand, it has been argued that acceptance of a condition of a celibate life as a basis of an obligation of maintenance undermines the idea of unlimited freedom of marriage. Since the 1985 decision of the *Cour de cassation*, scholarly controversy has continued. Although this case has been approved on the basis that it re-establishes parity as to the event of remarriage of former spouses, regardless of the original ground of divorce, and on the basis of human rights (that continuing maintenance payments is undignified for their recipient and the life of the new couple), it has also been criticised on technical grounds in that accepting a remarriage clause introduces an uncertain term as to the time period for performance of the contract,[21] which is contrary to the purpose of the payment, which is essentially a lump sum payment.

On the facts of case 29, the divorce settlement includes an express reference only to Lothar's remarriage. It is highly unlikely that a French court would accept an argument by analogy so as to entitle Morena to stop paying Lothar upon his cohabitation, because such clauses are presently regarded with some hostility by the courts and are thus interpreted strictly. In fact such an argument was raised before the *Cour de cassation*[22] which held that the court of appeal had correctly interpreted a divorce settlement by not extending the cessation-of-maintenance-upon-remarriage clause to the cohabitation of the beneficiary.

(ii) In the event that the maintenance payment could be analysed as a continuation of the obligation to assist one's spouse, as set out in art. 212 of the Civil Code and as extended after the divorce, and if it is based on a separation which lasted for at least six years, it would be categorised differently (as *pension alimentaire* rather than *prestation compensatoire*). Under art. 283 of the Civil Code such a payment ceases automatically upon remarriage or upon cohabitation. On the facts, analysis as *pension alimentaire* seems unlikely. However, if it were accepted, by virtue of a legislative provision, Morena would be entitled to stop paying Lothar the DM 1,000 per month.

Finally, it may be remarked that whatever the position taken by the

---

[21] See arts. 271, 273 and 276–1 C. civ., but cf. Aix-en-Provence 20 Jun. 1995, Jurisdata no. 052178 in which the parties had made a settlement ratified by the court containing a condition as to remarriage (which contains an uncertain element) and which was upheld.

[22] Civ. (2) 19 Jan. 1994, no. 92–14.67, no. 136, unpublished – lexilaser research.

courts regarding the continuance of Morena's obligation to pay, it is clear that in French law this case does not raise a question of good faith under art. 1134 al. 3 of the Civil Code. Instead, the question is subject to specific legislative provisions which are self-explanatory in view of the aims of the 1975 law on divorce, codified in arts. 229 ff. of the Civil Code.[23] Moral considerations come into play here and controversy over the validity of such clauses centres around an implicit public policy dilemma concerning freedom of marriage.

BELGIUM

This type of case occurs rather frequently in Belgium. Its solution depends, first of all, on the type of maintenance involved, i.e. whether it is for the children or for the husband (spouse). In the first case, a change of circumstances can always be invoked in order to try and obtain a modification of the allowance from the judge (see art. 1288, 2 Judiciary Code).

The maintenance allowance in this case, however, is probably not meant for the (education of the) children, but purely for the ex-husband and has been agreed upon between the spouses. Such divorce settlements are valid in Belgian law, and divorce by consent is accepted provided that the parties conclude a complete settlement[24] and have been married for at least two years (art. 276 C.C.). Since 1994, art. 1288, 1, 4° explicitly provides that the parties have to determine, in the case of a maintenance allowance given by one spouse to the other, under which circumstances the maintenance may be modified (the new article is applicable to divorces requested after 1 October 1994).

As to the question whether a clause, which provides that maintenance falls away in the case of remarriage, can also be applied in the case of extra-marital cohabitation, case law in Belgium is divided. The question is normally seen as one of interpretation of the settlement. Most case law applies a rather strict interpretation and orders the continuation of payment in such cases. Appeals to the *Hof van cassatie* have been rejected, both against judgements giving the clause a narrow interpretation and against judgements construing it more broadly. In other words, the *Hof van cassatie* considers this a question of fact. However, 'external elements'

---

[23] L. no. 75–617 of 11 July 1975.

[24] Divorce by consent is not granted on the basis of a partial settlement; see arts. 1287–8 of the Judiciary Code.

as to the intention of both parties must be established in order to give an extensive (rather than a literal) interpretation to a clause.[25]

Except by way of 'interpretation' of the contract, the courts are unwilling to admit a modification on the basis of the good faith principle. It would indeed be difficult to solve this case under the traditional criterion of abuse of right (i.e. disproportionality in the way the right is exercised; or: does a person manifestly exceed the limits of a normal use of his right?). Moreover, the change of circumstances is not unforeseeable.

In a few cases, it has been decided to give a remarriage clause an extensive interpretation on the grounds of public policy, arguing that a strict interpretation would be an incentive for extra-marital cohabitation instead of remarriage. But the argument has been rejected by other judges. The judiciary, and especially the *Hof van cassatie*, seems to be more interested in literal interpretation than in upholding public policy.

One of the reasons for the tendency towards a restrictive interpretation of such a clause is that it might be invalid in cases where, in fact, it constitutes a sanction for remarrying (e.g., where there is a clear disproportion between the maintenance lost in case of remarriage and the improvement or possible improvement of the position of the remarrying party). Providing a sanction for remarrying is contrary to public policy as it is seen as an interference with the freedom to marry. Strictly speaking, this aspect should not be relevant in case 29, but it may help to explain why judges tend to apply such clauses restrictively.

Furthermore, it might theoretically be argued that a party living in extra-marital cohabitation prevents the fulfilment of a resolutive condition. The Belgian Civil Code contains a rule analogous to § 162 I BGB,[26] which is usually taken to cover both the case where the fulfilment of a condition is prevented by the party to whose disadvantage it would operate and where the fulfilment of a condition is brought about by the party in whose advantage it would operate. This rule would not apply to case 29, since art. 1178 C.C. only applies (in both alternatives) where the behaviour of the party preventing, or bringing about, fulfilment of the condition is considered illicit (tortious).[27] Living together in extra-marital cohabitation instead of (re)marrying can certainly not be considered illicit as such. It is also difficult to consider it as a violation of a duty towards the other party (the ex-spouse). One might perhaps argue that while it is not

---

[25] See Cass. 1 Feb. 1980, Arr. 1979–1980, 652 = Pas. I 645; Cass. 5 Jun. 1986, RW 1986–1987, 1478 = Pas. I 1221.   [26] Art. 1178 C.C.   [27] Cass. 5 May 1955, Arr. 739.

contrary to good faith to live together in extra-marital cohabitation, it is contrary to good faith to continue claiming maintenance under these circumstances; but I do not know of any case where this argument has been successfully brought forward.

SPAIN

In Spanish law, this set of facts is governed by a specific legal rule. Article 101 of the Civil Code provides that a former spouse loses any right to receive periodic payments arising on divorce (a 'post-marital pension') where he or she either enters a new marriage or extra-marital cohabitation with another person, no matter whether these payments arise from a court order or from a settlement concluded by the former spouses. This reflects a general position taken by Spanish family law which treats extra-marital cohabitation in the same manner as marriage. The result of the rule found in art. 101 is that Lothar will no longer be entitled to recover the maintenance payments from Morena.

It is to be noted, though, that a similar conclusion could be reached by interpretation of the terms of the contract and focusing on the real or presumed intentions of the parties at the time when the contract was made.

ITALY

Morena and Lothar's divorce settlement is within the scope of the legislative regime concerning maintenance allowances on divorce to the extent and whenever Lothar's means of livelihood are not 'adequate', nor can become 'adequate' for 'objective reasons'.[28] The exact meaning of these somewhat oracular formulae is controversial.[29] The *Corte di Cassazione* supports the thesis that the allowances on divorce should reflect the life-style of the couple during marriage.[30]

The fact that the settlement in question in case 29 terminates on

---

[28] Divorce was reintroduced in Italy by l. 1 Dec. 1970, n. 898, *Disciplina dei casi di scioglimento del matrimonio*. This law was amended in 1978 (l. 1 Aug. 1978, n. 436) and in 1987 (l. 6 Mar. 1987, n. 74). The exact words of the article cited in the text are: 'quando quest'ultimo non ha mezzi adeguati o non può procurarseli per ragioni oggettive' (l. n. 898/1970, art. 5.6).

[29] Cf. Bonilini/Tommaseo, in: *Il codice civile* 457 ff.

[30] The text of l. n. 898/1970, art. 5.10, as amended in 1987 supports this interpretation, because it considers the duration of marriage as one of the factors to be taken into account in order to fix the amount of the divorce allowance. See, on this point, Bonilini/Tommaseo, ibid., at 486.

remarriage corresponds to the position under the legislative regime.[31] Moreover, under this regime, the courts have the power to vary divorce settlements provided that there are 'sufficient reasons' to do so.[32] For this purpose, however, the mere fact that Lothar has lived for two years together with another woman in extra-marital cohabitation does not *per se* affect Morena's obligation to pay the divorce allowance: to obtain variation of her obligation Morena must prove that Lothar receives financial support on a regular basis from his cohabitee.[33] If she can do so, Morena's duty to pay maintenance to Lothar is correspondingly reduced or suspended. Extra-marital cohabitation differs from marriage in this respect because the former does not support a claim for maintenance.[34] The simple fact that Lothar is living or has lived together with another woman in extra-marital cohabitation is therefore of no legal consequence.

Finally, it should be noted that a contract falling outside the scope of this legislation would be possible.

THE NETHERLANDS

Article 1:160 B.W. states that a duty to pay maintenance ends when the ex-spouse who is entitled to payment either remarries or lives together with someone else as if they were married. See also art. 1:159 B.W. which gives a court the power to modify a contract to pay maintenance because of changed circumstances, even where this is contrary to a specific provision in the contract which excludes modification.

ENGLAND

The modern approach to financial provision for former spouses on divorce contains within it a central tension. For while private arrangements or settlements providing for lump sums or periodic payments are generally encouraged, it is clear that they may not oust the court's power under

---

[31] L. 1 Dec. 1970, n. 898, art. 5.10.

[32] L. 1 Dec. 1970, n. 898, art. 9, speaks of *giustificati motivi*. According to art. 5.8 of the same law, the court has no power to alter settlements that stipulate the payment of a lump sum, but will not approve them if they are 'inequitable'.

[33] The latest case confirming this solution is Cass., 5 Jun. 1997, n. 5024, Fam. dir., 1997, 305, obs. V. Carbone. For commentary, see Bonilini/Tommaseo, in: *Il codice civile* 557 ff.

[34] Hence, it is well established that it is not possible to establish an analogy between a new marriage and an extra-marital cohabitation: Cass., 30 Oct. 1996, n. 9505, Fam. dir., 1997, 29, obs. Ferrando.

legislation to make alternative arrangements. In modern practice, the 'divorce settlement' agreed to by Lothar and Morena in case 29 could take one of two forms.

First, it could take the form simply of an agreement between the parties. While such an agreement is in principle binding on its terms, it is clear that either party may nevertheless apply to the court for an order containing financial arrangements.[35] In making an order, the court would look to the circumstances obtaining at the time of application in deciding what sums should be payable to Lothar.

Secondly, and more commonly, the agreement could be made the subject of a 'consent order'. Under this procedure, the parties to the voluntary settlement submit it to the court for the latter's approval and to give to it the force of an order under its jurisdiction to make financial provision. Once the subject of such an order, the settlement takes its binding force as a court order rather than as a contract.[36] Interestingly, when an obligation to make a *periodic* payment to a former spouse is contained in a court order (whether 'by consent' or contested), remarriage by the beneficiary of the obligation automatically terminates the obligation.[37] While subsequent cohabitation does not have this drastic effect, it may constitute a change of circumstances so as to allow the party obligated to apply to the court for a variation of the order under s. 35 of the Matrimonial Causes Act 1973 to the extent that it has financial consequences.[38] However, it has been said that the courts are not too free in varying settlements contained in consent orders for fear of discouraging their use.[39]

IRELAND

The legislative background to maintenance of spouses is s. 5 of the Family Law (Maintenance of Spouses and Children) Act 1976, under which maintenance may be ordered where there is a failure adequately to provide for the needs of the other spouse. One among many criteria is the fact that the spouse seeking support is cohabiting with another person.

Separation agreements which provide for maintenance cannot prevent the maintained spouse from applying to court under s. 5 should the payments agreed upon subsequently prove inadequate. Moreover, it is common for such agreements to have variation clauses, and indeed for

---

[35] Matrimonial Causes Act 1973, s. 34(1).   [36] Cretney/Masson 399.
[37] Matrimonial Causes Act 1973, s. 28(1).
[38] *Hepburn v. Hepburn* [1989] 1 FLR 373, at 376.   [39] Dewar 343.

such agreements to stipulate that an obligation to pay money is terminated if the maintained party remarries or cohabits as spouse for a particular period. However, in the absence of such an express provision, the courts do not imply them.[40] The fact that the maintained spouse (or ex-spouse) is receiving more than he would have received under a maintenance order does not, in any way, alter his rights under the contract.

In the case under consideration, Morena's payment obligation will only be suspended if Lothar actually remarries: the fact that Lothar's principal motivation for not remarrying might be to continue to receive maintenance payments is irrelevant. First, given the status attached to marriage under the Irish constitution, courts would hardly find Lothar in breach of any contractual obligation by not marrying. Secondly, as mentioned above, the courts will not imply terms which the parties could have agreed, and indeed often do agree but have not in fact agreed.

It should be noted that in practice in Ireland separation agreements are made 'rules of court'.[41] Being made a rule of court does not affect the agreement's identity and enforceability as a contract; it merely adds to the available means of enforcement and so allows easy enforcement by the maintained spouse, particularly by the attachment of earnings or by proceedings for contempt of court. If the agreement in this case had been made a rule of court, Lothar might have difficulty persuading the court to commit Morena for contempt if she stopped paying or to continue any attachment of her earnings.[42] None the less, he would be able to enforce his rights by the normal procedures for contract, i.e. action for debt.[43]

In fact, though, Morena's best claim might be against her legal advisers on grounds of negligent advice. A competent solicitor should at least have warned Morena about the deficiencies of the settlement, particularly in the light of common practice in Ireland of the insertion of variation clauses and termination clauses upon lengthy cohabitation on the part of the maintained spouse.

SCOTLAND

The divorce settlement between Lothar and Morena stipulates that the periodic payment should continue until Lothar remarries not cohabits. The law does not regard cohabitation to be the equivalent of marriage in

---

[40] Cf. *O'S. v. O'S.* (unreported, High Court, 18 November 1983) and *J.D. v. B.D.* [1985] ILRM 688.
[41] Family Law (Maintenance of Spouses and Children) Act 1976, s. 8.
[42] Cf. *J.D. v. B.D.* [1985] ILRM 688.   [43] Shatter 212.

Scotland, thus the rights and obligations accorded to a married person are quite different to those afforded to a cohabitee.

Financial provision on divorce is governed by the Family Law (Scotland) Act 1985. On the divorce of a married couple, s. 8(1) gives the court the power to make one or more of the following orders: (i) an order for the payment of a capital sum or transfer of property; (ii) a periodic allowance; (iii) incidental orders. The ethos of the legislation is to encourage a 'clean break', hence orders for financial provision should preferably take the form of a capital sum payment or for the transfer of property, rather than a periodic payment. Thus s. 13(2) states that a periodic allowance will be awarded only if the court is satisfied that the payment of a capital sum or the transfer of property is inappropriate or insufficient in the circumstances. The aim is to ensure that spouses are no longer economically dependent on each other after divorce. The Lothar/Morena situation would be unusual, as only in exceptional circumstances are orders for periodic allowances made.

Orders for periodic allowances can be for a definite period or until the happening of a specified event,[44] and the periodic allowance ends with the death or the remarriage of the payee.[45] So, it could have been specified in the agreement that the periodic payments should cease on the event of Lothar cohabiting with a new partner. However, as the agreement only provides for the payments to stop on the remarriage of Lothar, Morena is in default and has no right to cease making the payments. A consideration of Lothar's new circumstances may be worthwhile because if there has been a material change of circumstances, a periodic allowance can be varied or recalled. So for example, if Lothar is being financially supported by his new partner to a significant extent this may mean that Morena's payments will be reduced or it may well be deemed no longer necessary for Lothar to receive the payments. Note that it is only if the court ordered the agreement in the first place that the court can do this. If the court did not order the agreement, i.e. if it is a self-regulated agreement made between the spouses without the aid of the court, then the court only has limited powers, by virtue of s. 16, to set aside or vary the agreement. And any term in an agreement relating to the payment of a periodic allowance may only be varied or set aside provided there is an express term in the agreement to this effect.[46] While the courts have the power to police such agreements to ensure they are 'fair and reasonable',[47] they can only do so at the time

---

[44] Section 13(3), Family Law (Scotland) Act 1985.   [45] Section 13(7)(b), ibid.
[46] Section 16(1)(a), ibid.   [47] Section 16(1)(b), ibid.

when they were made, because the power can only be granted when granting the decree for divorce. It is worthy of note that the court's discretionary power to make orders accorded by s. 8(2) is limited by s. 9 which sets out the principles to be considered when making such orders. Orders must be reasonable having regard to the resources of the parties.

NB: Morena may argue that Lothar and his new partner have married according to an irregular form of marriage still recognised in Scots law; marriage by cohabitation with habit and repute.[48] But if they deny this, she will have no case.

DENMARK AND NORWAY

Opinions may be divided as to the treatment of this case: it is an agreement in family law which is not subject to the same rules as agreements in patrimonial law. In principle, this kind of agreement is subject to a possibility of revision when circumstances change, so that the old doctrine of *clausula rebus sic stantibus* applies. Agreements concerning maintenance require very little in order to be retried. At the same time, cohabitation is so widespread that, if the parties had intended the maintenance to stop as soon as a cohabitation had been established, they ought to have said so in their agreement. Moreover, there is no information on the background relating to the maintenance agreement made in the present case.

Thus, the agreement on maintenance would probably be applied according to its letter, so that the condition concerning remarriage should not be extended to cases of cohabitation.

Agreements in family law are regarded, in West Nordic law, as different in nature from ordinary agreements in patrimonial law. The joint Nordic Contracts Act of 1918 relates only to the latter. For instance, when the general clause of s. 36 of the Contracts Act was introduced, it was stated explicitly that it could not be directly applied to agreements in family law.[49] In certain respects, such agreements will be treated more leniently than agreements in patrimonial law. Change of circumstances may, for instance, lead to a revision of an agreement to a greater extent than in business life. In other respects the tendency is more restrictive, especially in questions concerning defects in conclusion of the agreement.

---

[48] The logic behind this form of marriage is that if a man and woman cohabit as husband and wife and are generally held and reputed to be husband and wife and are free to marry each other, they will be presumed to have tacitly consented to be married, and if this presumption is not rebutted will be legally married.   [49] Bull 251 ff.

SWEDEN

According to Swedish law, maintenance for an ex-spouse cannot be imposed for a longer period, unless that spouse has difficulties in supporting himself or herself after a long marriage, or unless there are other special reasons. If the conditions have changed, maintenance under a contract or a judgement may be lowered (but rarely increased); see ch. 6, s. 11 of the Code on Marriage of 1987. In this context, a new marriage and extra-marital cohabitation are normally regarded as being equivalent.

In this case, Lothar and Morena have agreed on maintenance until Lothar remarries. In this situation one would ask why they did not mention extra-marital cohabitation, as would have been natural to do. Hence, it is possible – but far from evident – that extra-marital cohabitation would be treated in the same way. According to oral information from the leading specialist on family law in Sweden, Professor *Anders Agell*, no standard interpretation exists.

If we assume that the contract would not be interpreted in the way that views both situations as equivalent, it would be difficult to use the discretionary power to adjust the contract contained in ch. 6, s. 11. (If Morena's economic situation is impaired or Lothar's is improved, it could be considered that Morena's promise was generous compared to that required by the law.)

The Supreme Court in NJA 1987, p. 553 tried a case where two persons had bought a prefabricated building for erection but were entitled, under a standard term, to resile from the purchase in case of divorce. The court held that this clause could not be applied when their cohabitation broke up. One important reason was that the seller had offered an escape, not provided in the law. In case 29, Morena offered maintenance that Lothar normally would not be entitled to. This might be a reason to treat her more favourably.

FINLAND

This is a question of evidence related to the interpretation of the maintenance agreement. The starting point in maintenance issues is that marriage is marriage, and extra-marital cohabitation is not the same thing. It is, however, possible that the parties may have intended something else. The other starting point is the well-known principle of *pacta sunt servanda*. Nevertheless, adjustment of such an agreement, or a court verdict on grounds of unconscionability, is even here possible, especially if the circumstances have changed. See the Marriage Act of 1929 (Si 201), s. 51, par. 3. Extra-marital cohabitation might, in this case, justify such an adjustment.

Editors' comparative observations

Most legal systems possess mechanisms by which Morena's obligation to pay maintenance to Lothar might fall away, or be varied, in the present situation. While it is widely regarded as doubtful whether these mechanisms would cover the present case, most reporters incline to the view that they would.

(i) In German law, this is seen as resulting from the application of a rule in the code concerning resolutive conditions (condition prevented from materialising) which has an ancient pedigree and is regarded as an emanation of the precepts of good faith. In Belgium, the same analysis would be 'theoretically possible'. In Greece, Lothar's behaviour might be considered abusive.

(ii) Spanish law comes to the same result by applying a special rule concerning 'post-marital pensions'.

(iii) In Austria, the divorce settlement would be interpreted so as to allow suspension of the payments to Lothar during the period of cohabitation.

(iv) An interpretative approach is also adopted in Belgium and in Finland.

(v) In a number of countries it is possible for the divorce settlement to be varied by the court depending on the change of circumstances under special legislation (Italy, the Netherlands, England, Scotland, Sweden) or according to general principle (West Nordic countries).

(vi) The only legal systems which unequivocally adopt the view that Morena still has to pay are the French and Irish ones. In France this is based on the hostility with which remarriage clauses contained in divorce settlements are viewed traditionally. The Irish reporter drew attention to the fact that since it was sufficiently common practice for divorce settlements to include an express clause dealing with subsequent cohabitation, its omission could be said to constitute negligence in the lawyer who drew up the contract for the 'paying' spouse. In the result, Morena would still have to pay Lothar, but could sue her lawyer!

Case 30: Penalty for late delivery

Case

Audrey is under an obligation to deliver 100 personal computers to Bartholomew. Should the computers not be delivered, for whatever reason, by 10 October, Audrey has promised to pay a fixed sum of £3,000. When Audrey tries to deliver the computers on 10 October, Bartholomew refuses to accept them since, he says, he cannot remember having concluded a contract with Audrey. A week later, he requests delivery and demands payment of the fixed sum.

Discussions

GERMANY

Audrey and Bartholomew have agreed on a conventional penalty. Penalty clauses are valid according to German law. If the penalty is disproportionately high, however, it may be reduced to a reasonable amount by court decision on the application of the debtor.[1] In principle, the penalty is payable if the debtor is in default (§ 339 BGB), and default (*mora debitoris*) requires fault (§ 285 BGB). But the requirement of fault may, as in the present case, be excluded by agreement between the parties.[2] As a result, Audrey is therefore bound, in principle, to pay Bartholomew £3,000 as she has not delivered the computers by 10 October.

A penalty clause constitutes a condition. According to § 162 II BGB, a condition is deemed not to have been fulfilled if its fulfilment has been

---

[1] For background discussion, see Zimmermann, JZ 1995, 483 with further references.
[2] *Palandt*/Heinrichs § 242, n. 3. The fault requirement can only, normally, be excluded by means of an individually negotiated term.

brought about, contrary to good faith, by the party to whose advantage it would operate. Just as in § 162 I BGB, this rule wishes to prevent a party from deriving a benefit from behaviour that infringes the precepts of good faith.[3] The requirements of § 162 II BGB appear to be met in the present case. Apart from that it is generally recognised that if the creditor has either provoked the debtor's breach of contract, or has himself been in breach, claiming the penalty would constitute an abuse of right.[4] The operation of conventional penalties has to be scrutinised particularly carefully in terms of the precepts of good faith.[5]

Bartholomew may therefore not claim £3,000 from Audrey.

GREECE

Penalty clauses are usually valid in Greek law (arts. 404–9 Gr. C.C.).[6] Article 407 Gr. C.C. provides that if a penalty has been agreed for the case of an improper, and more particularly of a delayed, performance the creditor shall have the right to claim, apart from the penalty, that performance be rendered. He shall also be entitled to claim damages in respect of any additional loss that he may be able to establish as flowing from the improper performance. But Bartholomew contradicts his previous behaviour (*venire contra factum proprium*) by demanding the fulfilment of Audrey's performance and invoking the penalty clause, even though the latter is not in default. Bartholomew has acted against good faith (art. 288 Gr. C.C.). As a result, Bartholomew must be considered to be in *mora creditoris* (art. 349 Gr. C.C.). Audrey may therefore either rescind the contract or deliver the computers without Bartholomew being able to claim the penalty.[7]

AUSTRIA

A first possible approach to the facts of this case is to analyse the default of the debtor. Audrey has promised to pay £3,000 if she does not deliver the computers by 10 October and this term should be interpreted (§ 914 ABGB) to mean that Audrey has to pay if she fails to do whatever she could reasonably be expected to do, i.e. to tender delivery by the agreed date in the proper manner (§ 918 ABGB). As Audrey did indeed tender the computers

---

[3] See the German discussion to case 29 above.
[4] BGHZ 82, 398 (402); *Münchener Kommentar*/Gottwald § 339, n. 22.
[5] *Münchener Kommentar*/Gottwald § 339, n. 20.
[6] Stathopoulos, *Contract* nos. 162–8, pp. 121 ff.
[7] Cf. Stathopoulos, in: *Astikos Kodix II* art. 288, no. 12.

in due time according to the terms of the contract, she is not in default and, therefore, the condition for paying the sum of £3,000 is not fulfilled. Also, Bartholomew failed to take delivery when it was tendered by the seller and, therefore, in Austrian law must take certain 'unfavourable consequences' of his default in acceptance (§ 1419 ABGB).[8] It may be concluded that Bartholomew must also not gain any advantage from his delay. In the result, Bartholomew has no claim to the sum of £3,000, but he does have a claim to delivery of the computers as his delay in accepting performance does not release Audrey from her obligations.

The second possible starting point for analysing this case is to be found in the law of conditions. As mentioned already in relation to case 10, the legal fiction contained in § 162 I of the German Civil Code (BGB) is accepted by Austrian law and accordingly the fulfilment of a condition will be deemed to have occurred if one of the parties to the contract affected the condition in a way which the other party could not possibly have expected, given the purpose of the contract. This rule is understood to be concerned not with the sanctioning of wrongful conduct but rather with the supplementary interpretation of the particular contract in question.

On the facts of case 30, the crucial issue is the effect of Bartholomew's default in acceptance of performance tendered by the other party, Audrey, known as *mora creditoris*. This is a very general problem and not one for resort to any possible supplementary interpretation of the particular contract in question. It is dealt with by general rules of the law of contract, rules which are 'dispositive' in the sense that they may be ousted by contrary expression. This being the case, I prefer to analyse a problem like the one arising from case 30 in terms of *mora creditoris* rather than in terms of interpretation.

FRANCE

Audrey and Bartholomew have included a penalty clause of £3,000 if delivery does not take place by 10 October. Can Bartholomew rely on this clause if he has prevented Audrey from fulfilling her obligations? In addition, Bartholomew has requested delivery of the computers (specific performance) and payment of a fixed sum of damages. However, he may not be able to combine these remedies under arts. 1228 and 1229 of the Civil Code, which set out the rules relating to penalty clauses.

[8] Cf. the Austrian report to case 8 above.

Article 1228 of the Civil Code states that, instead of claiming the penalty, the 'creditor' of a penalty clause can request specific performance of the obligation which has not been performed. According to art. 1229, a penalty clause provides compensation for damages which the creditor suffers from failure to perform the principal obligation, and the creditor may therefore not claim for specific performance and for damages at the same time. But to this rule there is an exception for the case where the penalty clause applies to cases of mere delay, where both may indeed be requested. It is arguable that a penalty clause payable if delivery does not take place 'by 10 October for whatever reason' falls within this exception and covers mere delay.

However, in order to rely on the penalty clause, Bartholomew must show that Audrey's failure to deliver is imputable to her.[9] This has been interpreted to mean that non-performance must be due to the debtor's own acts, rather than to *force majeure*, an act of a third party, or an act of the other contracting party. On the facts of case 30, Bartholomew would not be able to discharge this onus since he himself prevented Audrey from delivering the goods. Audrey would be able to prove not only that she offered to perform, but that it was impossible for her to deliver. This impossibility was not due to an act of *force majeure* but to Bartholomew's refusal to take delivery. In the circumstances, Bartholomew would not be entitled to rely on the penalty clause; that clause cannot operate if he himself has caused Audrey's failure to perform. The only argument that Bartholomew could raise would be for an extremely wide construction of the phrase 'for whatever reason' to be adopted so as to include Bartholomew's obstructive behaviour, but it is extremely dubious whether such an argument would find favour with a French court, since a party cannot waive good faith.

It would be possible to arrive at the same solution by an extensive interpretation of art. 1134 al. 3 of the Civil Code. A creditor cannot rely on the exercise of his strict contractual rights by acting in bad faith. The facts illustrate clearly an application of this rule in a particular context.

BELGIUM

Bartholomew will certainly not receive payment of the fixed sum in this case. Several arguments may be used.

(i) Although the doctrine of *mora creditoris* is underdeveloped in Belgian

---

[9] Art. 1230 C. civ.

law,[10] it is generally accepted that a party cannot invoke non-performance by the other party to the extent that he has caused such non-performance himself. This is usually based on the principle of good faith (art. 1134, 3 C.C.) which implies a duty to co-operate. In the case of sale, a duty to accept delivery is seen as an obligation (or rather as a burden, i.e. *Obliegenheit*) of the buyer, even if this is not explicitly provided by the Code (it is implied in art. 1657 C.C.).

(ii) Such clauses, as used in the present case and normally called penalty clauses, are illegal (i.e. contrary to good morals and public policy) in so far as they would allow the creditor to speculate on non-performance by the other party. This is especially the case if the sum of the penalty is higher than the possible damage that could be foreseen at the time of conclusion of the contract.[11] But the rule may also apply to the situation in case 30.

(iii) Theoretically, art. 1178 C.C. could also apply. Article 1178 C.C. provides that a debtor who has bound himself conditionally cannot rely on the non-fulfilment of a condition, if the non-fulfilment has been caused by his own fault. Although the provision only refers to the debtor, it would apply also to the creditor, at least in bilateral contracts, where Bartholomew is under an obligation to pay the price of the computers. The requirement of fault (negligence)[12] is fulfilled, as the behaviour of Bartholomew constitutes a violation of a contractual duty (burden) to receive the goods.

It must be added, however, that such a case is generally not seen as a problem involving a conditional obligation, but as a problem of non-performance, *in casu* non-performance by the buyer of his obligation (burden) to receive the goods.

SPAIN

The Spanish Civil Code contains several provisions which impose on the creditor of an obligation a duty to co-operate with the debtor in performing the obligation of the latter. Where a creditor fails in this duty of co-operation, he is prevented from complaining about the debtor's failure to perform.[13] The High Court holds that a creditor who unlawfully refuses to accept the fair performance tendered by the debtor thereby incurs *mora creditoris* (delay of the creditor). When a creditor is in *mora*, any loss caused by the delay in performance cannot be imputed to the debtor who, there-

---

[10] See M. L. Storme, in: *Op de grenzen* 231.   [11] Cass. 17 Apr. 1970, Arr. 654 = Pas. I 711.
[12] See the Belgian report to case 29 above.   [13] See arts. 1452, 1505, 1589, 1590 C. civ.

fore, does not incur liability. The duty of co-operation in a contractual relationship arises directly from the duty of good faith imposed by art. 1258 of the Civil Code on both the creditor and the debtor of an obligation.[14]

ITALY

Bartholomew has no right to recover the £3,000, but he may still insist on delivery of the computers one week later.

According to the terms of the contract, Audrey has an obligation to pay £3,000 to Bartholomew if she does not deliver the computers by 10 October. As she does indeed *tender* delivery on the agreed date she is not in default in performing this obligation, with the result that Bartholomew cannot insist on payment of the £3,000. If Audrey had tendered delivery in the presence of a public officer (usually a court official or a notary) Bartholomew's failure to accept it without reasonable excuse[15] would mean that he must suffer any unfavourable consequences which result from this, in accordance with the rules on *mora creditoris*.[16] Nevertheless, he may still insist on performance until Audrey is released from her obligations.[17]

Finally, it should be noted that in Italian law the law governing conditions is not involved in the discussion of a situation such as is found in case 30. The contractual obligation to deliver the computers is not a condition in the technical sense because it does not depend on an uncertain future event.[18] Therefore, the legal fiction contained in art. 1359 of the Civil Code according to which a condition is deemed to be fulfilled when it fails for a cause imputable to the party to whose disadvantage it would operate is not relevant to the solution of this case.[19]

THE NETHERLANDS

This is a case of *mora creditoris* (art. 6:58 ff. B.W.). As a result, there is no non-performance on the side of Audrey; consequently the clause to pay a fixed sum cannot be invoked. See for further elaboration the Dutch report to case 8 above.

In case the clause could be invoked (i.e. in different circumstances from

---

[14] See the High Court judgement of 30 May 1986 (RJA 1986, 2835). More decisions can be found in Cabanillas, 40 ADC 1987, 1342–52.   [15] Cf. art. 1220 c.c.
[16] Arts. 1206 ff. c.c.   [17] Arts. 1210–11 c.c.   [18] Art. 1353 c.c.
[19] On art. 1359 c.c., see the text at the first footnote in the Italian report to case 10 above.

in the present case) art. 6:94 B.W. (see also art. 6:91 B.W.) allows a court to modify its consequences for reasons of equity (good faith). This is mandatory law (cf. art. 6:94, par. 3 B.W.). The court may not, however, award the creditor less than the reparation of damage due in law for failure to perform the obligation.

ENGLAND

The first point which arises here is whether the clause to pay a fixed sum on failure to deliver at the appointed time is valid. In this respect, English law distinguishes between penalty clauses, which are invalid, and 'liquidated damages clauses' which are valid. In deciding whether a clause is penal or not, the modern courts look at a variety of factors, the essence of their approach being that 'a penalty is a payment of money stipulated as *in terrorem* of the offending party; the essence of liquidated damages is a genuine pre-estimate of damage'.[20] On the facts of case 30, it is not clear whether or not there are any circumstances from which Bartholomew can argue that the fixed sum was a genuine pre-estimate of the loss which Audrey's failure to deliver the computers would cause him. As barely stated, the clause looks like a classic penalty clause. (On the facts, the clause is unlikely to be vulnerable to attack under the Unfair Terms in Consumer Contracts Regulations 1994[21] as it would appear that Audrey is not dealing as a consumer for the purposes of those provisions, though the same doubt arises as has been discussed in relation to case 29.)

Assuming, however, that in principle the clause is not struck down as a penalty or under the 1994 Regulations, the question arises as to the effect on it of Bartholomew's rejection of Audrey's tendering of the goods at the stipulated time. First, his rejection of the goods was wrongful, in breach of his duty to accept them.[22] On the facts of case 30, Bartholomew's wrongful rejection of the goods also constitutes repudiation of the contract by him. This gives Audrey an option. She may 'accept the repudiation' and thereby terminate the contract. This would have the effect of terminating her obligations under the contract prospectively and she could not therefore be held liable for any subsequent failure to perform.[23] If, on the other

---

[20] *Dunlop Pneumatic Tyre Co. Ltd v. New Garage and Motor Co. Ltd* [1915] AC 79, at 86–7 *per* Lord Dunedin.   [21] SI 1994/3159.

[22] Sale of Goods Act 1979, s. 27 (his supposed reason in not remembering the contract is wholly irrelevant).

[23] Guest, *Benjamin's Sale of Goods* § 9–016; *Gill & Duffus S.A. v. Berger & Co. Inc.* [1984] AC 382, at 395–6.

hand, Audrey chooses to keep the contract alive, then it will remain valid for both parties. However, as Lord *Ackner* has observed 'it is always open to A, who has refused to accept B's repudiation of the contract, and thereby kept the contract alive, to contend that in relation to a particular right or obligation under the contract B is estopped from contending that he, B, is entitled to exercise that very right or that he, A, has remained bound by that obligation. If B represents to A that he no longer intends to exercise that right or requires that obligation to be fulfilled by A and A acts upon that representation, then clearly B cannot be heard thereafter to say that he is entitled to exercise that right or that A is in breach of contract by not fulfilling that obligation.'[24]

Thus, even if Audrey had elected to keep the contract alive she could argue that Bartholomew is estopped from complaining of her failure to deliver the goods at the originally stipulated time (and from recovery under the 'penalty clause', assuming the latter to be valid).

IRELAND

As regards the payment of the fixed sum, the question to be posed in Irish law, as in English law, is whether the sum in question is a genuine estimate of liquidated damages or a penalty. If it is a penalty the clause will be invalid. The English case of *Dunlop Pneumatic Tyre Co. Ltd v. New Garage and Motor Co. Ltd*[25] is accepted as being the leading case in the area.[26] Accordingly, the question to be put is whether the sum of £3,000 is so extravagant as to be beyond the greatest loss that could conceivably be proved to follow from the breach. However, where there is difficulty in putting a figure on loss, the courts are ready to defer to the agreement of the parties.[27] In this case the burden is on Audrey to prove that the clause is an invalid penalty.

Although the clause requires the payment of the sum where delivery fails for 'whatever reason', no Irish court would interpret this expansive phrase to include situations where the failure was caused by Bartholomew, and *a fortiori* where the failed delivery is due to wrongful rejection of the goods by Bartholomew.[28] Accordingly, Bartholomew's claim for any stipulated sum would be unenforceable. Finally, Audrey

---

[24] *Fercometal S.A.R.L. v. Mediterranean Shipping Co. S.A., 'The Simona'* [1989] AC 788, at 805; and see Guest, *Benjamin's Sale of Goods* § 9–018.   [25] [1915] AC 79.   [26] Clark 49.

[27] *Smith v. Ryan* (1843) 9 ILR.

[28] Cf. Sale of Goods Act 1893, s. 27 (purchaser's duty to accept delivery in accordance with contract).

need not be under any obligation to tender delivery when requested to do so a week later. She may, at her discretion, treat the first refusal as repudiating the contract, thus freeing her of further obligations and allowing her to sue for any loss.

SCOTLAND

Audrey's performance of her obligations under the contract requires the co-operation of Bartholomew; Bartholomew, however, thwarts her attempt to deliver the computers.

While performance of the obligation was impossible, this is not a case of frustration. The doctrine of frustration[29] holds that the change of circumstances in question which is the cause of the frustration, must have occurred from some cause independent of the volition of the contracting parties. An act or omission by a party to a contract which is intended to engineer a frustrating event amounts to a material breach of contract and bars the plea of frustration; *Joseph Constantine Steamship Line Ltd v. Imperial Smelting Corporation Ltd, The Kings Wood*.[30]

It is a principle of Scots law that where the performance of a contract by one party requires the permission or co-operation of the other party, for example, by allowing the first party entry to the other's land, the latter must permit or co-operate in the former's attempt to make performance. Bartholomew cannot rely on the contract of which he himself is in breach; *Graham v. United Turkey Red Co. Ltd*.[31]

This contract is probably protected by the Sale of Goods Act 1979 which states that when a seller is ready and willing to deliver the goods and requests the buyer to take delivery, and the buyer does not within reasonable time after such request take delivery of the goods, he is liable to the seller for any loss occasioned by his neglect or refusal to take delivery and also for a reasonable charge for the care and custody of the goods, but without prejudice to the seller's rights where the buyer's neglect or refusal amounts to a repudiation of the contract.[32]

Furthermore, the contract contains a 'penalty clause' – if the computers are not delivered, for whatever reason, by the due date then Audrey must pay the fixed sum. At common law, penalty clauses are unenforceable as they are regarded as a method of frightening the other party into

---

[29] See the Scottish reports to cases 12, 25, 26 and 28 above.
[30] [1942] AC 154, [1941] 2 All ER 165, HL.   [31] 1922 SLT 406, 1922 SC 533.
[32] Section 37, Sale of Goods Act 1979.

performance. Penalty clauses are distinguished from 'liquidated damages clauses', and whether the clause is one or the other is a matter of construction of the contract, as a whole, at the time of making the contract. A clause which is intended to secure performance of the contract by means of a penalty in the event of non-performance will be struck down, but a clause which is intended to fix in advance the amount of damages payable on breach will be upheld and enforced.

Tests to aid construction of the clause were laid down by Lord *Dunedin* in *Dunlop Pneumatic Tyre Co. Ltd v. New Garage and Motor Co. Ltd*:[33] (i) It will be held to be a penalty if the sum stipulated is extravagant and incomparable in amount to the greatest loss that could conceivably be proved to have followed from the breach. (ii) It will be held to be a penalty if the breach consists only in not paying a sum of money, and the sum stipulated is greater than the sum which ought to have been paid. (iii) There is a presumption that it is a penalty when 'a single lump sum is made payable by way of compensation, on the occurrence of one or more or all of several events, some of which may occasion serious and others but trifling damage'. On the other hand: (iv) It is 'no obstacle to the sum stipulated being a genuine pre-estimate of damage that the consequences of the breach are such as to make precise pre-estimation almost an impossibility. On the contrary, that is just the situation when it is probable that pre-estimated damage was the true bargain between the parties . . .'

It is submitted that the clause in this problem is a penalty clause, and that Bartholomew will be barred from enforcing it as it will be struck down.

It is unlikely that the Unfair Terms in Consumer Contracts Regulations 1994[34] will apply, although they recognise penalty clauses as unfair,[35] because the regulations only apply to consumer contracts and this is not a consumer contract. Bartholomew is not a 'consumer' because in making the contract with Audrey he is not 'acting for purposes which are outside his business'.[36]

DENMARK AND NORWAY

In West Nordic law, this case causes no problems. It will never constitute a breach of contract if failure to perform is caused by the creditor or

---

[33] [1915] AC 79, HL, at 86–8.   [34] See the Scottish reports in cases 27 and 28 above.
[35] Reg. 4(4), Sch. 3, 1(e), Unfair Terms in Consumer Contracts Regulations 1994, SI 1994/3159.   [36] Reg. 1, ibid.

results from factors for which he carries the risk; cf., e.g., the explicit regulation in s. 22 of the joint Nordic Sale of Goods Act of 1988.[37] On the contrary, the situation will then be one of *mora creditoris* (delay in accepting)
which precludes liability on the part of the debtor.

The agreement to pay a so-called penalty will never be taken to cover
cases of non-performance caused by the creditor himself. Apart from that,
penalty clauses in Nordic law are valid, even if the party entitled to the
penalty suffers no financial loss. However, application of s. 36 of the
Contracts Act may result in a reduction of the sum claimed when there is
a completely unreasonable imbalance between the amount of the penalty
and the financial loss suffered by the party entitled to it.

SWEDEN

Since the delay was caused by Bartholomew's refusal to take delivery, he
is not entitled to the penalty, as he would not have been entitled to other
remedies (s. 22 of the Sale of Goods Act of 1990).

Generally speaking, penalty clauses, or liquidated damages clauses, are
in principle valid. Contrary to ECE 188 article 7.3,[38] there is no general
requirement that the seller must have suffered some loss (see also article
13 of Orgalime S 92,[39] copied almost verbatim from the corresponding
Nordic standard terms NL 92[40]). Liquidated damages can, of course, be
adjusted under s. 36 of the Contracts Act of 1915 if they are unreasonable,
especially if the parties' bargaining powers differed. Between commercial
parties, however, this rule is not normally applied. One fundamental idea
behind penalty clauses is that the party entitled to the penalty should not
have to prove his damages; moreover, the penalty is supposed to prevent
default of performance.

FINLAND

Bartholomew's refusal to accept the computers is a breach of contract that
does, however, not as such terminate the contract (Sale of Goods Act of

---

[37] Hagstrøm, *Fragmenter* 11 ff.

[38] General Conditions for the Supply of Plant and Machinery for Export, issued in Geneva
in March 1953.

[39] General Conditions for the Supply of Mechanical, Electrical and Associated Electronic
Products, issued by the liaison group of the European mechanical, electrical, electronic
and metalworking industries, Brussels, October 1992.

[40] Issued in 1992 by the industrial (metalworking) organisations of Denmark, Finland,
Norway and Sweden.

1987, ss. 51 and 53), and is a unilateral withdrawal from the contract which frees Audrey from any liability for delay. For this reason Audrey (i) may choose to deliver (Sale of Goods Act, s. 53), or (ii) may treat the contract as terminated (without notice, since the buyer has claimed that there is no contract at all; see Sale of Goods Act, s. 55). In both cases she may claim damages, e.g. under alternative (i) for the second delivery (transport costs, insurance, etc.) and, under alternative (ii), also for possible loss of profit (if she has sold the computers to someone else at a price lower than that agreed upon with Bartholomew). See Sale of Goods Act, ss. 67–8.

Editors' comparative observations

All the legal systems under consideration agree that Audrey does not have to pay the fixed sum in these circumstances.

(i) For English, Irish and Scots law, Audrey would owe no obligation under such a clause as it would probably be considered a penalty clause and thus be ineffective at common law. In the other legal systems, penalty clauses are valid, in principle, though they may be the subject of control on the basis that the sum stipulated is disproportionate to the other party's loss.

(ii) Assuming the validity of the penalty clause, the following approaches were adopted in order to argue that Audrey does not have to pay.

(a) Bartholomew did not accept performance when it was duly tendered by Audrey; he was in *mora creditoris*. As a result, he cannot invoke the penalty clause (Greece, Austria, Spain, Italy, the Netherlands, Sweden, West Nordic countries).

(b) A condition is deemed not to have been fulfilled if its fulfilment has been brought about, contrary to good faith, by the party to whose advantage it would operate (Germany; a similar approach, turning around fictional fulfilment, or non-fulfilment, of conditions is regarded as a possible alternative in Austria and Belgium but is rejected in Italy).

(c) Failure to deliver is imputable to Bartholomew, not to Audrey (France, Sweden).

(d) Belgian law derives the solution from the general principle of good faith (which is also seen to provide the background to the French solution and is relevant in Greek law, too). Good faith, in the present context, entails a duty of the creditor to co-operate (cf. also the Spanish report on the duty to co-operate).

(e) Finally, if (which is highly unlikely on the facts of case 30) for English law the clause were held effective (on the basis that it can be construed as a liquidated damages clause), Audrey would still not be liable to pay on it either on the basis that Audrey has terminated the contract or on the basis that Bartholomew is estopped from claiming on it.

Coming to terms with good faith

SIMON WHITTAKER AND REINHARD ZIMMERMANN

I. Harmony and dissonance

In drawing more general conclusions about the responses of the legal systems which have formed part of this project, one is first struck by the considerable degree of harmony as to the results reached on the particular facts of many of the cases. Thus, of the thirty cases, eleven led to the same result in all the legal systems considered;[1] nine led to the same result in the majority of legal systems but not in one or two ('cases of general but imperfect harmony');[2] and ten led to a considerable variety of result among the legal systems.[3] In all, therefore, twenty of the thirty cases led either to the same result in all the systems or the same result in all the systems bar one or two. This degree of harmony is particularly remarkable in view of the fact that many of the situations included in the study are recognisably 'hard cases'.

However, as we have seen, harmony of result is by no means to be equated with harmony of analysis or technique; as the comparative observations at the end of each case reveal, the legal systems employ a wide variety of legal doctrines to reach these results, some relying on the idea of good faith, on a combination of this idea with others or on other clearly distinct legal doctrines or techniques. It is, moreover, important to note that while in the

---

Note: This chapter was drafted by *Simon Whittaker* on the basis of joint discussions between himself and *Reinhard Zimmermann* undertaken principally in Regensburg in spring 1997. It was amended to take account of the refinements made by contributors to their reports after the meeting at Regensburg in July 1997, and of suggestions made by *Reinhard Zimmermann*.

[1] These are case 1 'Courgettes perishing'; case 7 'Late payment of rent'; case 9 'Uniformity of outfit'; case 12 'No use for borrowed motor bike'; case 13 'Inspecting the books'; case 15 'Two cracks in a shed'; case 16 'Drug causing drowsiness in driving'; case 18 'Access to medical records'; case 20 'Prescription I'; case 27 'Disability insurance'; case 30 'Penalty for late delivery'.   [2] See II.1. below   [3] See II.2. below

cases of harmony or near harmony of result *on the particular facts* of the cases which have been chosen the same results would be reached, this is not to say that if a particular element within those facts were changed then one or more legal systems would not diverge from the pattern: given that the elements of the various legal techniques used differ, it would be very surprising if this were not the case.[4] On the other hand, however, it is equally true that a minor change in the facts of a case would sometimes also make a legal system fall into line with the majority approach.[5]

Quite apart from our central concern with the significance of good faith in the contract laws of the legal systems under consideration, a range of other similarities and differences has emerged, both at the level of style of analysis and use of sources and at the level of the substantive law. An example of the latter may be found in the very considerable divergence in the formal requirements applicable to contracts involving the transfer of land and in the effects of their non-compliance: thus, while in Austria they do not have to comply with any special form at all, in Spain they require notarial authentication but its absence does not lead to the contract's invalidity, in English law they have to be contained in writing on pain of nullity and in Germany they are invalid but for notarial authentication.[6] Other examples may be found in the fact that the Nordic legal systems often do not find it necessary to distinguish between contractual and delictual liability[7] and that the law of Scotland recognises marriage by cohabitation with habit and repute as an irregular form of marriage.[8]

At a more general level, the patterns of relationship between the private laws of some of the legal systems studied seem to be changing. Thus, while the Italian reports do cite French decisions[9] and still side at times with French rather than with German law,[10] they sometimes show the influence of German doctrine;[11] Belgian law sometimes adopts significantly different solutions to the problems posed from French law, despite sharing the same legislative framework in their civil codes;[12] the enactment of a new civil code in the Netherlands makes clear its emancipation

---

[4] See, e.g., case 1 'Courgettes perishing'.   [5] See, e.g., case 3 'Breaking off negotiations'.
[6] See above, pp. 261, 267, 272–3, 258 respectively.
[7] See above, pp. 202 (case 1 'Courgettes perishing'), 454–5 (case 16 'Drugs causing drowsiness in driving').   [8] See above, p. 637 (case 29 'Divorce settlement').
[9] See above, p. 189 (case 1 'Courgettes perishing').
[10] See above, pp. 546–51 (case 24 'Long-term business relationships II').
[11] See above, pp. 246 (case 3 'Breaking off negotiations'), 340 (case 9 'Uniformity of outfit'), 588 (case 26 '"Sale" of soccer player').
[12] See above, pp. 324–5 (case 8 'Delivery at night'), 459–61 (case 17 'Bank miscrediting customer'), 483–5 (case 19 'Doctors swapping practices').

from the *Code Napoléon* and its openness to other (and particularly German) influences; Austrian law, while in many respects closely related to German law, nevertheless differs significantly from it, its civil code placing less emphasis on private autonomy and more on protection of reliance than its more recent German cousin;[13] and Irish law, while often following the English position closely, at other times adopts a less conservative and more flexible approach, notably by protecting the interests of the parties to long-term contracts[14] (though the converse is true in another of the cases which we have considered).[15]

II. Observations on particular cases

We shall look first at those cases where there was a general but imperfect harmony and then at those where there was a wide divergence of result.

1. Cases of general but imperfect harmony of result

It may have been thought (perhaps particularly by civil lawyers) that the common law systems would, owing to their lack of acceptance of a principle of good faith, quite frequently be found out on a limb as to the result which they reach. However, on the basis of analysis of the particular cases taken by our study this has not proved to be true. In all, nine cases fell into our category of a general but imperfect harmony of result[16] and only one (case 2 'Degas drawing') found English law as the odd man out. Instead, we often find a smaller legal jurisdiction out on a limb, this being particularly noticeable as regards the Nordic legal systems and Irish law.[17] One possible reason for this may be that where a legal system by its size tends to engender less litigation there are fewer occasions on which courts are presented with facts suitable to test or to clarify the application of existing legal rules; and where rules are untested or uncertain, they either remain untempered or are interpreted in a cautious (and therefore often more conservative) way.

---

[13] See, e.g., pp. 517–19 (case 22 'Sitting on one's rights').

[14] See above, pp. 373–4 (case 11 'Untested motors working'), 413 (case 14 'Producing new bumpers'), 525 (case 22 'Sitting on one's rights'), 539–40 (case 23 'Long-term business relationships I'), 552–3 (case 24 'Long-term business relationships II').

[15] Case 6 'One bag too few' (above, pp. 298–300, the result of English legislation).

[16] Case 2 'Degas drawing'; case 3 'Breaking off negotiations'; case 6 'One bag too few'; case 8 'Delivery at night'; case 10 'Dissolution of partnership'; case 21 'Prescription II'; case 26 '"Sale" of soccer player'; case 28 'Crop destroyed by hail'; case 29 'Divorce settlement'.

[17] This is true of cases 3, 6, 8, 10, 28 and, to a more limited extent, case 29.

(a) Case 2 'Degas drawing'

In relation to case 2, English law's stark denial of any claim or ground of vitiation of the contract of sale of a picture at an extraordinary under-value even where the buyer knew that it was by a famous artist may be seen as reflecting a particularly powerful strand in the English approach to the effect of informational imbalance between the parties to a contract. So while a person who positively misleads the other (even if entirely inno-cently and taking all reasonable care) will in principle be faced with res-cission of the contract, a person who says nothing will be secure,[18] a distinction which may itself be seen to reflect a continuing attachment to the distinction between positive action (to which liability may attach) and pure omission (to which no liability will attach in the absence of special circumstances).[19] Before leaving this point, however, it should be noted that, as was made clear in its response to case 1 'Courgettes perishing', where English law sees the circumstances as ones in which one of the parties to the contract is in a position to know of the characteristics of the subject matter of the contract and the other is not, it may simply place the *responsibility* for those characteristics being present on the shoulders of the typically knowledgeable party by means of an implied term.[20] Interestingly, although the other legal systems came to the same result in case 2, they used a wide variety of ideas to do so, concentrating on the quality of the seller's consent, the wrongfulness of the buyer's conduct, the substantive unfairness of the result or simply the requirements of good faith. It should also be remembered that a much more extensive concept of fraud was recognised in early nineteenth-century English law. The quotation from the first edition of *Chitty's* textbook provided above[21] demonstrates that case 2 may well have been decided differently in his day.

(b) Case 3 'Breaking off negotiations'

As to case 3, which involved the (somewhat abrupt) breaking-off of nego-tiations, all legal systems allowed some recourse for the person who had undertaken work (and thereby incurred expense) in reliance on the con-tract going ahead, though they differed considerably as to the juristic

---

[18] See the English law discussion to case 2 'Degas drawing', above, pp. 226–8.
[19] This is clearly seen in the courts' attitude to liability in the tort of negligence: Margaret Brazier (gen. ed.), *Clerk and Lindsell on Torts* (1994) § 1–040.   [20] See above, pp. 194–7.
[21] See above, p. 43.

basis on which they did so. Only Swedish law, and possibly Finnish law, took a different view, denying any recovery for the person undertaking work on the facts, a position which was explained as resting on the idea that, in the absence of an agreement, in a business context the parties are able to safeguard their own interests. Doctrinally, this is reflected in a narrow doctrine of *culpa in contrahendo* in Swedish law and reinforced by its restrictive approach to recovery for pure economic loss caused by negligence. However, even Swedish law recognised the existence of limits on a party's freedom to withdraw from negotiations, accepting that a person who wishes to do so must inform the other party without any delay.[22]

(c) Case 6 'One bag too few'

All the legal systems agreed that in general the tendering of a part performance of an obligation was not effective, but on the facts of case 6, all but Irish law found mechanisms for preventing the creditor of the obligation from refusing delivery of a near complete performance and requiring instead contemporaneous complete performance at a later stage. Here Irish law may be seen to uphold the strict common law position (though this position was put into statute in the Sale of Goods Act), there being no room for the application of the maxim *de minimis non curat lex* on the facts as the shortfall in performance was not sufficiently trivial. English law, on the other hand, has recently tempered this position as regards contracts for the sale of goods to commercial buyers where the shortfall or excess is 'so slight that it would be unreasonable for him to [reject the goods]'.[23]

(d) Case 8 'Delivery at night'

All the legal systems bar the Finnish allow a person to refuse delivery of the washing machine at night (assuming no special circumstances or agreement). Somewhat frivolously it may perhaps be thought that in the land of the midnight sun the distinction between day and night has been blurred. In fact, however, Finnish law is not really quite as out on a limb as the result given by the reporter to these facts suggests as even it would allow refusal to accept delivery at an inconvenient time if this had been made clear at the time of contract.

---

[22] Above, p. 255.
[23] Sale of Goods Act 1979, s. 30 (2A) and (2B), above, pp. 298–300. The position is similar in Scots law, above, p. 301.

(e) Case 10 'Dissolution of partnership'

In relation to case 10, it was the turns of Irish and Italian law to be some-what out on a limb as to the result reached, for all the other legal systems in the study prevent a partner from dissolving a partnership in the circumstances of the case. However, the concern of these two legal systems is that contracts of partnership create a relationship whose nature makes it inappropriate for its continuance to be required against the wishes of the parties and this concern is shared by some of the other legal systems.[24] The difference between their positions and at least these others may be characterised, therefore, as one of degree rather than of kind.

(f) Case 21 'Prescription II'

All the legal systems apart from Italian law protected the person whose claim expired owing to statements by his would-be defendant that he would not rely on his legal rights in relation to prescription, though some of them (such as Norwegian law) hesitated as to whether its strict require-ments for waiver of the defence of prescription had been met on the facts. As to Italian law, the reporter specifically notes that the result described by him has been criticised in recent years; and he regards the traditional approach leading to this result as a legacy of positivistic thinking pat-terns.[25]

(g) Case 26 '"Sale" of soccer player'

Spanish law is out of step with the response of the other legal systems in relation to case 26, being the only system which comes to the clear con-clusion that the transferee club has no ground for terminating the con-tract of transfer and recovering the money which it has paid. The reason given for this position is that there is no sufficient reason on the facts why the transferor club, who were not aware of the 'latent defect' in their player, should bear the risk of what has transpired.[26] However, the case is a particularly hard one for many of the systems in the study, for neither of the parties to the contract can be seen as having behaved badly and it is therefore a genuinely difficult question whether the loss should lie where it falls or be redistributed by law. This is reflected in the fact that

---

[24] Above, pp. 354–5; 357–8 and see e.g. French law (above, pp. 350–2).   [25] Above, p. 500.
[26] Above, pp. 586–7.

even those legal systems which would ultimately grant a remedy see the question as finely balanced.

(h) Case 28 'Crop destroyed by hail'

The Nordic legal systems were somewhat out on a limb as to their results concerning case 28 in relation to a policyholder's inability to preserve the evidence on which to found his claim on a contract of insurance as was stipulated by that contract.[27] Norwegian law recognises here a discretion in the court to reduce the extent of any indemnity due by the insurer; Danish law provides that the insurer is entitled to be put into the situation in which it would have found itself if proper notice of the insured event had been given; and Swedish law takes a similar approach to the Norwegian one. The main concern voiced in the Nordic reports (and also raised in other reports) was that the insured has to take all reasonable steps, in the circumstances, to allow the insurer to assess the damage. In that sense, even the Nordic systems do not necessarily insist on strict compliance with the contractual clause. On the other hand, it should be noted that English and Scots law would until 1994 have taken a very different view of the other insurance case (case 27), for it was only in that year and as a result of implementation of the E.C. Directive on Unfair Terms in Consumer Contracts that the laws of those two systems received rules under which the fairness of these conditions of insurance could be judged.

(i) Case 29 'Divorce settlement'

The divergences both of result and of analysis in this case were for the most part the result of the context of the particular contract in question, viz. divorce. Whatever else can be said, the case illustrates the way in which questions which are for some legal systems simply ones of the general law of contract are in others not merely ones to be governed by special rules pertaining to the particular contract, but ones which reflect strong normative policies (here of family law) which have very little to do with ordinary contract doctrine. Moreover, the two legal systems which unequivocally adopt the view that the former spouse still has to pay maintenance after subsequent extra-marital cohabitation did so for diametrically opposed reasons. For in the case of French law, this stemmed from the traditional

---

[27] Above, pp. 619–20.

hostility with which remarriage clauses are viewed, while in Irish law remarriage clauses are both valid and a matter of common practice, but this common practice means that the courts will not imply them.

2. Cases of significant disharmony of result

The cases in which considerable divergences of result were reached are cases 4 and 5 'Formalities I and II'; case 11 'Untested motors working'; case 14 'Producing new bumpers'; case 17 'Bank miscrediting customer'; case 19 'Doctors swapping practices'; case 22 'Sitting on one's rights'; cases 23 and 24 'Long-term business relationships I and II'; and case 25 'Effect of inflation'. What can be seen to lie behind these divergences?

(a) Cases 4 and 5 'Formalities I and II'

The responses given to these facts are perhaps the most difficult to categorise. A first difficulty stems from the fact that the case as described posits the requirement of a particular form for the contract (notarial authentication), which has not been satisfied. As one would expect, this particular formal requirement is not made throughout the legal systems included in the study, but perhaps more surprisingly, as we have noted, some of the legal systems make *no* formal requirements for contracts for the sale of land. Secondly, even where a legal system does require a specific form for these types of contract, it may take the view that any failure to comply with this requirement does not go to the validity of the contract between the parties (though it may have other effects).[28] Clearly, where a legal system either makes no requirement of form in the particular context or where it does make such a requirement but does not sanction its failure with invalidity of the contract, its response to the 'bare facts' of cases 4 and 5 (i.e. the agreements relating to land concluded informally) would be the same: the agreement is simply enforced as a contract. Some reporters of the legal systems included within either of these categories, helpfully but none the less hypothetically, described what the legal position would

---

[28] The term 'validity' here itself conceals a variety of phenomena. Some legal systems consider that informality renders the contract 'a nullity' (English law, above, pp. 272–3); others that it renders it 'unenforceable' (Irish law, above, p. 276); others that it opens to either one of the parties or any other interested person the possibility of applying to the court for a declaration that the contract be annulled (the question as to who may apply being determined in part by the distinction between 'absolute' and 'relative' nullity): see the discussion of the (hypothetical) Belgian position, above, pp. 264–5.

be according to the general stance taken to requirements of form which do go to validity, some describing the possible application of doctrines which would mitigate the harshness of invalidity in the sorts of circumstances found in cases 4 and 5. Nevertheless, to the extent that one considers the particular context of these cases (viz. contracts relating to land) to be of crucial importance, these observations may be thought to be of somewhat tangential significance.

What certainly can be said is that *all* the systems which hold that requirements of form relating to contracts for the sale of land do go to their validity possess doctrines to deal with the potential hardship which this combination of rules may cause. However, the focus of these doctrines varies: sometimes it is to be found in reliance by one party; sometimes (in relation to case 5) in the enrichment of the other party; sometimes (in relation to case 4) in the wrongful conduct of the other party; sometimes in the otherwise crushing effect of invalidity on a (disadvantaged) party.

(b) Case 11 'Untested motors working'

Case 11 is in some ways pivotal. For this is a case of clear bad faith displayed by one party to the contract however the idea of bad faith is understood, as it involves the making of a statement by one party to the contract which he knows to be false. But does *fraus omnia corrumpit*? Almost all the legal systems[29] would in principle grant a person who has been induced to enter a contract in reliance on the dishonesty of the other party a right to have it set aside (whether this be effected by the party himself or by the court), but the application of this clear law to the facts of case 11 raised more divergence.

For German law, this is a classic case for the application of the requirement of good faith, it being considered *bad* faith for a person to rescind a contract even on the grounds of fraud, where that person's position has not been at all impaired by the fraud.[30] English and Scots law, on the other hand, take a more absolute line: once it has been shown that a fraudulent misrepresentation was 'material in the sense that it was the factor, or one of the inducing factors, which caused [a person] to assume the obligation', then '[i]t is irrelevant that [that person] suffered no loss'.[31] In

---

[29] An exception is found in relation to the law of Denmark and Norway, which view this case rather in terms of the materiality or otherwise of the seller's breach of contract on the ground of defect: above, p. 375.   [30] Above, pp. 362–3.

[31] Above, p. 374 (Scots law) and see, similarly, above, pp. 371–2 (English law). Cf. the similar position in Swedish law, above, p. 376.

principle, once a party possesses a right to rescind a contract on the ground of fraud, then he may do so whatever the effect of such fraud and, indeed, whatever the motivation for rescission of the party possessing that right. Irish law, on the other hand, follows the apparent logic of the equitable nature of the remedy of rescission for misrepresentation and holds that it is 'a discretionary remedy and may be denied if its claimant were held to be acting in an unconscionable or inequitable way', though it is added that the seller's 'fraud would probably overcome any judicial reluctance to grant rescission for lack of any damage suffered by the mis-representee'.[32] There is, though, a divergence between the English and Scots position on similar facts to this case: for if the statement had been made honestly, even if negligently, then in English law a court would by statute possess a discretion to refuse to allow the misrepresentee to rescind and award damages 'if [it is] of opinion that it would be equitable to do so, having regard to the nature of the misrepresentation and the *loss that would be caused by it if the contract were upheld*, as well as to the loss that rescission would cause to the other party'.[33] Here, then, English law accepts a qualification of a legal right to rescind taking into account exactly those circumstances which would weigh with a German court in terms of good faith.

Belgian law's approach to this case differs again. It recognises the vitiat-ing effect of precontractual fraud (*dol*) but subjects this to the condition that it must induce the contract in the sense that without the fraudulent statement, the victim of the fraud would not have entered the contract, all this being law which it shares with France. However, where it departs from the norm is in its attitude to the finding of an inducement for this purpose, as it is concluded that 'the factor determining Jim's consent will normally be the quality of the motor itself, rather than the question whether it had been tested. It will be difficult to argue that the testing, as such, was the determining factor for him.'[34] Here, then, it can be seen how courts may take into account a consideration which some legal systems deal with in terms of good faith by the interpretation of a factual element, here the causal element required for vitiation for fraud. Clearly, this pos-sibility is more open to a legal system such as the Belgian one whose civil judicial institutions distinguish between those lower courts who possess very considerable discretionary power in relation to the finding of facts

[32] Above, p. 373.   [33] Misrepresentation Act 1967, s. 2(2) (emphasis added).
[34] Above, p. 367.

(known as a *pouvoir souverein d'appréciation*), and the highest court (the *Cour de cassation*) whose role in this respect is a restrained one.[35] It is also worthy of note that Belgian law does not appeal here to its very general theory of the abuse of rights in order to curtail the circumstances in which the victim of a fraud may apply for termination of the contract. Clearly, though, given what has been said as to its treatment of the 'inducement' element of *dol*, this is unnecessary. By contrast, it would seem that French law would deal with this case not by interpretation of the facts in relation to the requirement that Kerry's *dol* induced the contract, but rather on the basis that in the absence of any loss suffered as a result Jim would have not an 'interest in suing' (*intérêt à agir*) as is required by the general law of civil procedure.[36]

(c) Case 14 'Producing new bumpers'

All legal systems had in common in their responses to this case that it concerned the exercise by a party to a contract of a right to terminate the contract *which arises from it*, whether as a matter of law or under the terms of the contract (this last feature distinguishing it from case 11, in which any right to rescind the contract or to have it annulled arises as a result of a legal doctrine stemming from facts independent of the contract itself, viz., the fraud). However, their willingness to control the exercise of this right and the effect of any control differed significantly. At one end of the spectrum of control were German and Austrian law, both of which would deny the immediate effectiveness of the purported exercise of the right to terminate the contract.[37] German law is able to base this result simply on its general principle of good faith, but the particular factor which triggers this idea in the case is the reasonable reliance in its continuance by the other party given the nature of the contract. This reliance also determines the effect of the application of the principle, for '[t]he termination . . . only

---

[35] This is not of course to say that the Belgian *Cour de cassation* never intervenes in findings of fact (it clearly does and on grounds which it itself controls), but that the distinction between the roles of the two judicial bodies allows the highest court to let the lower courts give particular solutions to certain types of fact taking into account considerations of fairness, a role which is sometimes acknowledged in the juristic literature as a *pouvoir modérateur* in the lower courts.   [36] Above, p. 366.

[37] Above, pp. 404, 405–6. The Italian position is very similar to the Austrian one; Greek, Belgian, Finnish and Irish law would also, in one way or another, question the effectiveness of termination; see above, pp. 377–8.

becomes effective after the lapse of the minimum period for which contracts of this kind are normally concluded'.[38] Austrian law comes to the
same conclusion, its approach combining reliance on the interpretation
of the parties' intention and reference to considerations of good faith,[39]
but again, it is the reasonable reliance on the continuance of the contract
by one party to the other's knowledge which restricts the latter's right of
termination. In both the German and Austrian laws, the law's refusal to
give effect to the termination until after the other party's expectations as
to its continuance are satisfied allows that other party to continue to
perform and, therefore, to make any profit for which he was hoping under
the contract. Upholding the contract and (implicitly) requiring both
parties to perform gives the best protection to the other party's expectations in relation to their mutual business.

Next on the spectrum comes French law which holds that the termination of the contract is effective, but that this exercise of a legal right must
not be 'abusive'. This allows the courts to investigate whether, under the
circumstances, the termination was illegitimate, taking into account a
range of factors, notably the legitimacy of the other party's expectations
that the contract would be continued, given the nature of the contract
under consideration[40] and the extent of harm which termination would
cause the other party. However, unlike the German and Austrian position,
the practical outcome of a finding that the terminating party has abused
his right would be the imposition of (delictual) liability in damages for the
expenses which the other party has incurred in reliance on the contract.
In general, therefore, it would seem that a French court would *not* allow
the party who expected to make a profit from the continuance of the contract to recover this lost profit by way of damages.[41] The French position is
therefore a compromise.

At the other end of the spectrum lie those legal systems which simply
allow the party who possesses the right to terminate the contract to do so,
viz., Spanish law, English law, Scots law, Danish and Norwegian law. For

---

[38] Above, p. 404.   [39] Above, pp. 405–6.

[40] A distinction perhaps being drawn for this purpose between 'distribution contracts' and
contracts of sale: above, p. 407.

[41] Above, p. 408. It is difficult to be dogmatic on this last point as for the most part French
jurists and courts do not draw a distinction in the types of awards of damages which
common lawyers or German lawyers do in terms of 'expectation and reliance interest'
and because, in principle, the question of how much a person recovers in damages is,
like his loss, one for the 'sovereign power of assessment' of the lower courts.

the two common law systems, at one level this result arises from the very nature of legal rights: if a party has a right to terminate the contract in certain circumstances (which are unqualified by reference to some such notion as reasonableness), then he may do so. In both the English and Scots legal systems, however, this apparently tough approach is also supported by the idea that if the party making expenditure in reliance on the contract had wished to protect himself from losing on an early (but legal) termination of the deal before he could break even, then he could and should have done so. Any unpleasant result is not caused by the other party, but by the terms of the agreement which the parties in fact made. In these circumstances, according to this way of thinking, the law should not protect any *actual* reliance by one party on the continuance of the contract because in the circumstances of the contract as it was made this reliance, even if reasonable, was not legitimate.[42] This is also in substance the position of the Nordic countries, for '[a]lthough the seller has had to make substantial investments to carry out the production of the bumpers, it must . . . be said that he made those investments at his own risk'.[43]

The fact that Spanish law should come to the same result here is particularly interesting, given that it *does* contain a general theory of the abuse of rights which it sees as intimately connected with the idea of the performance of contracts in good faith.[44] On the facts of case 14, though, there is no such abuse, for any contractual advantage which the party terminating thereby enjoys is considered as arising from his stronger bargaining power, rather than from any abuse of his contractual rights.

(d) Cases 23 and 24 'Long-term business relationships'

Very similar divergences appear in relation to this pair of cases as have just been discussed in relation to case 14 ('Producing new bumpers') and, to an extent, case 11 ('Untested motors working'). Again, German law looks to the reliance engendered by the creation and continuing performance of the contracts and asks whether it is worthy of protection; such reliance is not considered legitimate where the contract on its terms requires

---

[42] Above, pp. 412, 414–15. This approach is also taken by Irish law as its starting point, but is subject to a possible qualification based on a line of cases which protects a party's reliance even where the strict terms of a contract are satisfied (implied duty of good faith in the exercise of a right to terminate a long-term contract; above, p. 413).

[43] Above, p. 415 (Danish and Norwegian law). The position is the same under Swedish law, above, p. 416.   [44] Above, pp. 52, 409.

positive renewal for its continuance.[45] French law again looks to the question whether the party's clear rights either not to renew the contract (in case 23) or to terminate the contract (in case 24) have been abused, though on the bare facts as given no circumstances suggest that such an abuse of rights has taken place. Once again, English, Scots, Spanish and West Nordic law find themselves agreeing that any disappointment suffered by the party whose long-term contractual relationship has been terminated stems from the terms of the contract to which he has agreed and must be borne without relief. Once again, it is interesting to note that Spanish law comes to this conclusion even though its code contains two general provisions revolving around good faith; whereas Irish law which does not have any such provision is likely to imply an obligation to state the reasons for the failure to renew the contract, subjecting the option to renew to a requirement of good faith.

(e) Case 17 'Bank miscrediting customer'

While a majority of legal systems saw a duty in a bank customer whose account had been miscredited to inform the bank as resulting from the requirements of good faith, there were exceptions. The common lawyers' hesitation on these facts may be explained by reference to their more general reluctance to impose duties of disclosure as between the parties to a contract, though the actual context of the facts would, in slightly different circumstances, provide an example where such duty would indeed exist.[46] By contrast, the Nordic legal systems and Irish law deny the existence of any duty of disclosure in these circumstances. Here, the result in French law is similar, but this is based on the consideration that analysis in terms of the rules relating to unjustified enrichment allows no room for the application of the contractual principle of good faith.[47] Thus, as soon as the customer is aware of the fact that the payment is not due to him, he will be liable not merely to return the sum which he has thereby received but also to pay interest on it. Clearly, though, denying the existence of a duty to inform the bank means that the latter may not recover

---

[45] Above, pp. 532–3. It must be noted, however, that some measure of protection is also granted to Rodney in case 23 in the form of a claim for compensation. Swedish, Finnish, Belgian, Greek, Dutch, Austrian, Italian and Irish law would also grant protection (either by adjusting the notice period in view of its unreasonableness, or by awarding damages) though opinions differ as to whether such protection must be granted in case 23, case 24, or both.   [46] Above, pp. 463–4. Cf. above, p. 656 (in relation to case 2 'Degas drawing').
[47] Above, pp. 459–60.

any *damages* for other losses incurred in relation to the mistaken payment. Interestingly, Belgian law differs here, its report being prepared to argue for the imposition of such an obligation on the ground of good faith or *équité*. [48]

(f) Case 19 'Doctors swapping practices'

As we have seen, the legal systems represented in this study are fairly equally divided on the question whether the exchange (or sale) of a business entails in itself a duty not to compete with the business for a period.[49] Those legal systems which hold that it does focus on the idea that this reflects the likely intentions of the parties to the type of contract in question and that the opposite position would tend to defeat the point of the contract. The most common doctrinal expression of this idea is, as one would expect, the (supplementary) interpretation of the intentions of the parties to the contract guided by the precepts of good faith.[50] Those legal systems which deny a duty not to compete in these circumstances concentrate on the personal liberty of the transferor to continue the practice of his profession with the result that they therefore require any restriction on this liberty to be expressly stipulated,[51] though some systems qualify this position in certain respects.[52] On the other hand, those legal systems which uphold the duty not to compete also recognise the importance of personal liberty, and private autonomy. Case 19, therefore, can be seen as a case in which the various legal systems give different weight to a particular legal value (liberty of profession or trade) which nevertheless they all share.

(g) Case 22 'Sitting on one's rights'

While it is clear that the various responses which the legal systems offered to this case led to different results, all legal systems possess some mechanism for dealing with similar cases, so that the rate of payment under the contract may be 'disapplied' on the ground of what has been said by one party and done by the other. Clearly French law, which requires nothing

---

[48] Above, p. 461. [49] Above, p. 492.
[50] For Swedish law (which might resort to its presupposition doctrine), see above, p. 491.
[51] See Scots law, above, pp. 489–90; English law, above, pp. 487–8; Nordic law, above, pp. 490–1.
[52] Thus, e.g., English law forbids any direct solicitation of former patients: above, p. 488.

less than agreement, is more concerned to protect the binding force of the contract and (doctrinally) is most wedded to the idea that contractual rights may be modified only by another contract. On the other hand, the doctrines used by the other legal systems all had in common the idea of reliance on either a statement or conduct (including mere inactivity in certain circumstances) of the party holding the right.[53]

(h) Case 25 'Effect of inflation'

There was a variety of legal analyses and results on the facts of this case. All legal systems apply their own particular rules as to the effect of change of circumstances, from the narrowest position in French and Belgian law (resting on *force majeure*), through English, Irish and Scots law's somewhat more liberal law of frustration, through the differentiated approach adopted in German, Greek, Austrian, Italian and Spanish law (focusing on some or other modern version of the *clausula rebus sic stantibus* doctrine[54]) to the very wide and discretionary approach found in the Nordic countries (and also in Dutch law).[55]

(i) Some wider issues

At a more general level, of all these divergence cases, cases 14, 23 and 24 are particularly interesting. For the very considerable differences between the legal systems as to the appropriate result or results cut across the dividing line between civil law and common law. Thus, while party reliance on the continuance of contractual relations is protected in a number of civil law systems, often by reference to good faith and the abuse of rights (as, for instance, in German and Belgian law), this is also true of Irish and East Nordic law. On the other hand, while English and Scots law consider these cases as typical of ones where a principle of good faith is neither recognised nor (generally) desired, the same position is also taken by Spanish law, which does contain principles both of good faith and of the abuse of rights. What these cases therefore illustrate is that the mere

---

[53] For German law, above, p. 516 (as an element within *Verwirkung*); Austrian law, above, pp. 517–18 (reliance relevant to the issue of waiver); English law, above, p. 524 (promissory estoppel); Scots law, above, pp. 525–6 (personal bar).

[54] Greek and Italian law possess codified versions of this doctrine. Germany appears to be the only country where it is historically related to the general notion of good faith (see above, pp. 557–60, 566).   [55] Above, pp. 576–7.

recognition of a principle of good faith (or of the abuse of rights) does not in itself say much about a legal system; it certainly does not *determine* the outcome of particular cases. This outcome, instead, depends on deeper values embraced or policies pursued by the legal system in question, as well as the more general legal background within which a principle of good faith operates (or is not required to operate). This last point appears clearly, e.g., from case 22 'Sitting on one's rights', for the question whether a legal system feels the need to rely on a doctrine such as *Verwirkung* (loss of a right)[56] largely depends on how happy or unhappy it is with its set of rules of prescription or limitation of actions. Thus, in Germany the general prescription period of thirty years is widely regarded as unsatisfactory and the doctrine of *Verwirkung* has to serve the function of a stop gap.[57] Also, it is obvious that whether, and, if so, how widely, a particular legal system employs a notion such as good faith will often depend on the weighing up of competing factors, 'equitable considerations' being balanced against the general desirability of the strict enforcement of the relevant legal rules in the interests of legal or transactional certainty. Such a weighing up of competing factors may also be seen in cases 4 and 5 dealing with formalities in the context of sale of land.

III. More general observations

1. Remedial variety

One noticeable feature of the case studies is that the remedial variety of the doctrines employed could hardly be wider, whether these remedies are put in terms of good faith, interpretation, abuse of rights, reasonableness or any other general notion. The remedial results include the following.

(a) 'True obligations'

At their most demanding, the doctrines can lead to the imposition of a 'true obligation', i.e. one which may be the subject of direct enforcement in kind by its 'creditor', the debtor being required *to do* or *not to do* some-

---

[56] Above, p. 516.
[57] See, e.g., Frank Peters, in: Staudinger, *Kommentar zum Bürgerlichen Gesetzbuch* (13th edn, 1995) Vorbem. zu §§ 194 ff., nn. 17 ff.

thing, rather than merely to pay damages for failing to do or doing something. Examples may be found in relation to cases 4 and 5 'Formalities I
and II' and case 19 'Doctors swapping practices'.[58] This is readily understandable in the formalities cases since the effect of the various doctrines
resorted to (good faith, proprietary estoppel, etc.) is in a sense to cure the
defect of form in the contract so as to allow the enforcement of an obligation directly undertaken by the other party (even though this may not be
put in terms of enforcement of the contract itself). However, this remedial
dimension to case 19 makes the recognition of a duty of non-competition
all the more striking a limit on the personal liberty of the transferor
doctor. It is not merely that he has to compensate the doctor with whom
he should not compete: he may be prevented by injunction from doing so.

(b) Liability in damages

On the other hand, sometimes an obligation is imposed by a legal system,
but its purpose and effect is not truly obligational in the sense that its
creditor may enforce it in kind, but rather it is imposed in order to allow
its non-performance to give rise to an award of damages to the benefit of
the creditor. Examples may be found in case 1 'Courgettes perishing' and
case 16 'Drug causing drowsiness in driving'.[59] While it is clear that the
legal systems are concerned here primarily with compensation, this is not
to deny that the imposition of such an obligation may nevertheless have
a truly normative effect (as may again be seen in case 16, as judicial rulings
on the extent of medical duties of explanation of the characteristics of
drugs to their patients may well affect the doctors' practice in the matter).
It is also clear, though, that these sorts of cases often exist at the borderline of contract and delict, the imposition of liability in damages being, in
principle, equally possible under the latter branch of the law (its actual
incidence being determined by the technical restrictions on liability in
delict existing in a given legal system). It is noteworthy, in this respect,
that on the actual facts of cases 1 and 16 which both concern liability for
physical harm (damage to property and personal injury respectively[60])

---

[58] See above, pp. 290–1, 492 respectively.   [59] Above, pp. 203–7 and 456–7 respectively.
[60] Case 16 may include a liability for economic loss if the patient's accident involves a
third party, for any claim by the patient to be indemnified in respect of compensation
paid out to such a third party is treated as a claim for pure economic loss by some legal
systems: see above, pp. 453–4 in relation to Scots law.

almost all legal systems allow the possibility of a parallel liability in delict, the exceptions being those systems which adopt a strict denial of concurrence of contract and delict in principle.[61] Equally, for some systems the possibility of a contractual route to liability becomes crucial where the harm suffered is 'pure economic loss', for example, if in case 1 the fertiliser were simply ineffective in increasing the market gardener's crop of courgettes.[62]

We should also note here that where the result of the analyses is the imposition of liability in damages, the test for their measure may differ according to the distinction between an injured party's 'positive' or 'negative' interest (*aliter*, 'expectation' or 'reliance' interest) according to the circumstances. In general, though, the effect of the various doctrines applied to our thirty cases is to limit the imposition of liability in damages to recovery of the negative interest, so as to allow 'out of pocket expenses' but to refuse compensation to an injured party for his or her lost expectations as to the contract being made and performed[63] or being continued and performed.[64]

(c) The imposition of a 'burden'

Some legal systems see the effect of a legal doctrine as potentially prejudicing one of the parties, not by way of the imposition of an obligation or liability, but by the imposition of a 'burden' (*Obliegenheit*). We have seen examples of this type of legal response in cases of *mora creditoris*, where the creditor does not owe the debtor any *obligation* to accept tender, but where his failure to do so may result in detrimental consequences, notably as to risk.[65]

(d) Termination of the contract

Sometimes the doctrine used in our cases allows a party (or the court on the party's application) to *terminate* the contract in question, this being illustrated by case 2 'Degas drawing'. Here, most legal systems allow the

---

[61] I.e. French law, above, pp. 441–5, 457 and Belgian law, above, pp. 445–6.
[62] See Austrian law, above, p. 177; English law, above, p. 196.
[63] See case 3 'Breaking off negotiations' for the majority of legal systems, above, pp. 256–7.
[64] See, notably, the French approach to case 14 'Producing new bumpers', above, p. 408.
[65] See, e.g., case 30 'Penalty for late delivery' especially as regards Belgian law above, p. 644.

seller of the drawing to escape the contract where the drawing is later proved to be by a famous artist unknown to the seller, this being reflected in a huge difference in value.[66]

(e) Denial of termination by a party

Conversely, in other circumstances, the effect of the application of the doctrine under consideration is the denial by a court of the effectiveness of the exercise of a right to terminate (see, notably, case 14 'Producing new bumpers' and case 24 'Long-term business relationships II' in some legal systems).

(f) Extra time to perform

In case 7 'Late payment of rent', the effect of the application of the various doctrines (all of which come to the same result) is to give extra time to one of the parties to the contract to perform a contractual obligation.

(g) Modification of the contract for the future

Modification of the terms of a contract may be the consequence, in a number of legal systems, of a fundamental change of circumstances affecting long-term contractual relationships (see case 25 'Effect of inflation'). Moreover, the Nordic legal systems possess in section 36 of their joint Contracts Act (first passed by Sweden in 1915), a very general provision which allows modification of terms, this section stating that '[a] contract term or condition may be *modified* or set aside if such term or condition is unconscionable having regard to the contents of the agreement, the circumstances prevailing at the time the agreement was entered into, subsequent circumstances, and circumstances in general'.[67] Less obviously, the modification of the terms on which the parties deal with each

---

[66] See above, p. 233.

[67] Emphasis added. For use of this provision see case 2 'Degas drawing' (Danish, Norwegian and Swedish law, above, pp. 231–2); case 9 'Uniformity of outfit' (Danish, Norwegian and Swedish law, above, p. 345); case 10 'Dissolution of partnership' (Swedish law, above, p. 360); case 13 'Inspecting the books' (all Nordic legal systems, above, pp. 401–2); case 14 'Producing new bumpers' (Danish and Norwegian law, above, p. 416); case 23 'Long-term business relationships I' (Swedish law, above, p. 544); case 25 'Effect of inflation' (all Nordic legal systems, above, pp. 571–6); cf. case 29 'Divorce settlement' (Danish and Norwegian law, above, p. 637).

other may also be seen as the practical result of the analyses of the majority of legal systems in relation to the actual or threatened abuse of a contractual power in case 13 'Inspecting the books', which required or allowed a third party to inspect the books, and in case 15 'Two cracks in a shed', which required a third party to judge the question of satisfactory performance of the building contract.[68]

(h) The prevention of the exercise of a right

Sometimes the doctrine in question prevents a party to a contract from exercising a right (other than of termination) which otherwise would arise from the contract. This is particularly noticeable as regards the various doctrines discussed in relation to case 22 'Sitting on one's rights', though, as we have noted, under some legal systems the actual facts of this case were rather too weak to attract their application.[69]

(i) The preservation of a right

In cases 27 'Disability insurance' and 28 'Crop destroyed by hail' the operation of various doctrines allows the parties to exercise a right arising under the contracts in question which would otherwise have been excluded as the result of an express provision in the contract. Here, then, a contractual right is preserved despite the apparent intention of one of its particular terms.

2. Contrasts between general and special regulation

The doctrinal responses to the cases revealed a series of contrasts in relation to their reliance on general or special regulation. This itself can be split into a series of further contrasts.

(a) The general law of contract versus the law of special contracts

Most of the legal systems under consideration at one time or another look to their special law of contracts rather than to their law governing contracts in general to deal with the problems raised by the cases. While, therefore, there is no absolute contrast between the systems in this

---

[68] Above, pp. 402 and 432 respectively.   [69] Above, pp. 530–1.

respect, we nevertheless find a noticeable tendency for English and Scots law to rely on special rules to a greater extent than the other legal systems,[70] though some of these special rules are based on the 'implication of terms' which as a technique is general to contract law as a whole.[71]

(b) General law (whether in a code or common law) versus special (modern) legislation

Again, some of the legal systems under consideration deal with the cases through special legislative rules, which (by the nature of such legislation) are often more or less special to the context. This is noticeable as regards the regulation of the employment relationship in case 9 'Uniformity of outfit'; the regulation of patients' rights to their own medical information in case 18 'Medical records' and the regulation by some legal systems of contracts of insurance in relation to case 27 'Disability insurance'. In some of these cases, moreover, it may be thought that the facts in question are not ones (or no longer ones) which give rise to contractual problems at all. From this perspective, case 9 belongs to the law of employment, case 18 to medical law, or even public law more generally. Several of the cases under consideration (or cases which are very like them) give rise, or are capable of giving rise, to regulation stemming from 'consumer law'.[72] In some legal systems these types of categorisation may have legal effects (notably, jurisdictional ones), while in others their significance is more expositional. Of course, sometimes the line between the general law and special legislation is not a sharp one. So, for example, the imposition of liability in English law in case 1 ('Courgettes perishing') by the Sale of Goods Act could be seen as resting on special legislation, but in the context of the particular legal rule in question, this legislation merely confirmed the existing common law approach, itself part of the wider technique of the implication of terms.

---

[70] For the cases in which one or more legal systems rely on the special law of contract, see case 1 'Courgettes perishing' (sale of goods) above, p. 205; case 6 'One bag too few' (sale of goods) above, p. 304; case 7 'Late payment of rent' (lease) above, pp. 320–21; case 8 'Delivery at night' (sale of goods) above, p. 330; case 9 'Uniformity of outfit' (employment) above, p. 346; case 10 'Dissolution of partnership' (partnership) above, p. 360; case 15 'Two cracks in a shed' (building contracts) above, pp. 427–9; case 27 'Disability insurance' (insurance) above, p. 609; case 29 'Divorce settlement' (divorce settlements) above, p. 639.

[71] See, e.g., case 1 'Courgettes perishing', above, pp. 194–7; case 9 'Uniformity of outfit', above, pp. 340–2.

[72] E.g. case 1 'Courgettes perishing' (not involving a consumer contract on the facts); cases 27 'Disability insurance' and 28 'Hail destroying crop' (the latter case arguably involving a consumer depending on the definition given to this term: above, p. 617).

(c) Contract law versus general legal principle

While often the cases are answered by reference to the rules of contract law, sometimes a legal doctrine is used whose domain extends beyond contract law. Two examples of this are particularly prominent: good faith and the abuse of rights. Thus, in German law, for example, the principle of good faith which rests on § 242 BGB is considered a general principle of law, its applications permeating private law in general and even stretching into public law.[73] However, this is by no means a universal attribute of the principle of good faith, which in some legal systems is of much more limited ambit. This is the case in French law, for while the concept of good faith is certainly found outside its law of contract (notably being used in relation to title to movables[74]), we do not find in French treatises on civil law any discussion which shows that these various references to good faith are examples (even disparate ones) of the application of one overarching principle. However, French, Belgian and Spanish law do possess general theories of the abuse of rights, theories which certainly permeate private law as a whole and which go well beyond it, while in the context of contract law often being closely related to the notion of good faith itself. Are the common lawyers out on a limb in this respect? There are no doctrines of good faith or the abuse of rights permeating the law; on the other hand, the historical role of equity was to act as a general corrective of the common law, of potential application throughout the law.[75] Moreover, whether one sees the modern role of equity in English law as vigorous or somewhat etiolated, those equitable doctrines which are accepted in modern judicial practice have a tendency to cut across other legal categories; so we find that in English and Irish law recourse is made to equitable doctrines which apply beyond contract, a notable example being the doctrine of estoppel.[76] It must be said, though, that these doctrines lack the breadth of sweep of the civilian doctrines of good faith or the abuse of rights.

3. Good faith and other doctrines of contract law

It is clear from the various analyses of the cases that there is an intimate relationship in some systems between the idea of good faith and other, more particular and differently focused legal doctrines or ideas.

---

[73] See, e.g., Günter H. Roth, in: *Münchener Kommentar zum Bürgerlichen Gesetzbuch*, vol. II (3rd edn, 1994) § 242, nn. 57 ff.

[74] Art. 2279 C. civ. and surrounding *jurisprudence*. It is also used in the context of the French law of *répétition de l'indu*, see arts. 1378–81 C. civ., on which see above, pp. 459–60.

[75] A qualification on the generality of impact of equity may be found in that it has not been used in the context of criminal law. [76] Above, pp. 273–5 and 275–6 respectively.

The range of doctrines which figure in the reports is very considerable. They include, as regards the civilian jurisdictions, and apart from special legislation: *culpa in contrahendo*; *obligations d'information*; *laesio enormis*; the abuse of rights; personal bar; interpretation of the parties' intentions (whether standard or 'supplementary'); the doctrine of 'lawful contact'; laches; unconscionability; *Verwirkung*; *purgatio morae* and *purgatio poenae*; doctrines of change of circumstances or 'erroneous presuppositions'; the notion of a 'burden' (*Obliegenheit*); *force majeure*; *exceptio doli*; mutual mistake; liability for latent defects; the legal consequences associated with the maxims *nemo auditur turpitudinem suam allegans* and *dolo agit qui petit quod statim redditurus est*; and *venire contra factum proprium*. Quite a number of these doctrines are still regarded (in some systems) as emanations of the principle of good faith. Others are seen to have been linked in this way to good faith historically, but to have 'flown the nest', being now accepted as distinct or 'autonomous' legal doctrines, with their own contours and concerns. Into this last category come *obligations d'information* in French and Belgian law and the doctrines of *Verwirkung* and *Wegfall der Geschäftsgrundlage* in German law. One may also include as an example of such a doctrine the seller's liability for latent defects, which is closely linked historically to the development of good faith in contract law, but which is seen in most legal systems today as a distinct 'legal' basis of liability.[77]

The range of doctrines relied on by the common law jurisdictions, again apart from special legislation, is hardly less varied, reference being made to: the law of implied terms; the doctrine of estoppel (including proprietary estoppel); part performance of a contract in equity; the *de minimis* rule; qualifications of legal rights by reference to the notion of reasonableness; relief against forfeiture in equity; the maxim according to which 'no man can take advantage of his own wrong'; the notion of breach of confidence; the doctrine of fundamental mistake; the law relating to repudiation; and (occasionally) even a rule that a contractual power may only be exercised in good faith.

While certainly remarkable, the breadth of range of these doctrines in the laws of contract which we have studied should not be surprising. For it would indeed be odd if the actual rules governing the making and performance of contracts which have been laid down by legislators, advocated by jurists or constructed by courts were *not* to reflect the idea that contracts should be made and performed by the parties in good faith or,

---

[77] See Schermaier, above, pp. 85–6 (for the Roman law); p. 204.

to put it in terms more familiar to common lawyers, according to the reasonable expectations of honest people. A rule of contract law which was
seen by jurists or judges as out of tune with these very basic precepts
would not last long in any but the most static legal system, or at least, it
would not last long without significant qualification or circumvention.[78]
Indeed, once such a general assumption as to the purpose of contract law
is shared by those active in a legal system, one could go further and assert
that *all* the law governing contracts should either reflect these precepts or
be justified by reference to some other competing or at least differently
focused consideration (for example, the need for legal or transactional certainty), on pain of condemnation. However, if this very general understanding of good faith or the reasonable expectations of the parties is
adopted, then these notions would appear to be very little more than
translations into more familiar terms of the requirements of commutative justice itself. Such a link certainly has its roots in the civilian tradition, in which good faith and equity were at times related to Aristotelian
notions of justice.[79]

All this is not to say that jurists or judges across the legal systems (or
even within any one legal system) necessarily have agreed or do agree as
to what these general standards of good faith or reasonable expectation
require as regards the development of more particular contractual rules.
People differ as to what good faith entails; people's expectations and their
reasonableness may differ or be differently viewed in different legal
systems; in both respects, different views may be taken according to the
different contractual contexts in which they arise within those legal
systems and, indeed, at different times within each legal system's
history. What this does emphasise, however, is that a legal system which

---

[78] One could well see such a tension in the English law of privity of contract. Here, many
judges and commentators have expressed discontent with the denial of a right to a
third party which he is intended to have under a contract, principally on the ground
that it defeats the intentions of the parties without justification. English courts have
nevertheless held to the formal rule denying the possibility of such a right, while
constructing a number of more or less artificial techniques for its circumvention: see
generally, Law Commission, *Privity of Contract: Contracts for the Benefit of Third Parties*, Law
Commission Report No. 242 (1996). At the time of writing, there is a bill before
Parliament which would recognise such a right in a third party overtly: Contracts
(Rights of Third Parties) Bill 1998 (HL Bill 5). Many of those who oppose the creation of
such a right do so on the basis that it would go against the doctrine of consideration,
which they see as the key element in the common law understanding of contract (even
where, one may add, it defeats the reasonable expectations of the parties to the
contract).   [79] See Gordley, above, pp. 106 ff.

is generally at ease with its own legal rules for the creation and regulation of contracts will have very much less of a need to have recourse to a general legal principle such as good faith; if the legal rules are seen as generally good (however this is conceived), there will be no need to correct or to supplement them. On the other hand, even in such a happy legal system, there remains a need for techniques (whether general or special, judicial or legislative) for dealing with cases where a (perfectly good) rule would cause particular injustice on the facts. Of course, a highly formalistic legal system could take the view that, in this type of situation, the law should simply apply its rule: norm is norm. However, none of the legal systems in our study comes into such a category; each possesses one or more techniques by which such a tempering of the stark legal position is achieved, even if it draws the line between certainty and 'individuated justice' differently from the others.

In a sense, then, and at this very general level, the principle of good faith in contract law is potentially related to all or most of the doctrines of modern laws of contract. Having said that, however, it is clear from the present study that in the positive law of the systems under consideration there are four groups of doctrines to which this idea is particularly closely related.

First, as regards some 'precontractual' problems, there is a clear relationship in the modern law between an analysis in terms of the requirements of good faith and one in terms of defects in consent of one party and/or the sanctioning of wrongdoing in the other. This appears from the discussions in relation to cases 1 'Courgettes perishing' and 2 'Degas drawing'. Sometimes the element of wrongdoing is made a *condition* for the exercise of a doctrine based on *bad* faith (as is clearest in relation to *dol* in French and Belgian law[80]). Sometimes, the legal analysis concerns itself wholly (or almost wholly) with the quality of the consent of a party to a contract, particularly where a case may be analysed in terms of mistake.

Secondly, in some cases the legal analyses in one or several legal systems revolve around the wrongful nature of one of the contract's terms or of the behaviour of one of the parties. Thus, a contractual term may be considered *contra bonos mores* or contrary to public policy and invalidated on this ground, rather than on the ground of the good or bad faith of either

---

[80] Above, pp. 216–19 and 219–21 (respectively). Cf. German law's use of the principle of good faith to construct a duty of precontractual disclosure for the purposes of vitiation on the ground of deception by silence: above, pp. 209–10 (case 2 'Degas drawing').

of its parties. An example may be found in the way in which some legal systems held that an employer in case 9 'Uniformity of outfit' could not by a term of the contract require something which would harm the health of his employees.[81] While the cases which have been the object of this study have not given rise to many examples of invalidity of either a contract term or a contract itself on the ground of public policy or public morality, clearly where this is the case the legal system in question has no need to appeal to the idea of a party's bad faith.[82] In other cases, a legal system may simply look to the wrongful conduct of one of the parties. For example, in case 10 'Dissolution of partnership', Belgian and Spanish law see the facts as attracting application of the maxim *nemo auditur turpitudinem suam allegans*, while for German law the idea behind this very maxim has been 'absorbed' into the general principle of good faith.[83] Looking at the wrongful nature of one of the parties' conduct is clearly also the starting point for those systems which recognise doctrines of *culpa in contrahendo* or who see a person's abuse of rights as potentially productive of delictual liability for fault.

Thirdly, there is clearly an intimate relationship in some types of cases between issues of interpretation (whether of express terms or by the implication of terms) and good faith. There are a number of variations on this theme. Thus, some legal systems talk of good faith or equity *in* the interpretation of the contract, an approach which allows the court to take account of the parties' likely expectations as well as of broader normative considerations. Other legal systems look rather to the performance of a contract in good faith or equity as a *supplement to* interpretation of the parties' intentions, a perspective which is adopted, e.g., in French law.[84] For those legal systems which relate the idea of performance in good faith to the interpretation of the intention of the parties, it is sometimes neither immediately obvious nor necessarily legally significant which of the two elements is more dominant in any particular case. Application of the

---

[81] Above, pp. 346–7. On occasion, a legal system combines appeal to *contra bonos mores* with appeal to good faith, e.g. Greek law in relation to case 2 'Degas drawing' above, p. 214.

[82] We noted (above, pp. 27–8) in our introduction that one of the most important applications of the principle of good faith in German law was to control unfair standard contract terms. It is interesting to note that such control had been started by the Imperial Court under the auspices of the *contra bonos mores* clause of § 138 I BGB. Other legal systems have used other techniques: see above, pp. 360–1 in relation to French law.

[83] Above, pp. 36–7.

[84] See above, pp. 29, 33; cf. also the editors' comparative observations to case 19 'Doctors swapping practices', p. 492.

general principle of good faith is sometimes very close to interpretation (especially where such interpretation is also guided by good faith), and is occasionally suggested as an alternative way of looking at a case.[85] It is obvious that the more a legal system allows interpretation to be guided by normative considerations, the less it needs to make recourse to the more openly normative principle such as good faith. Alternatively, it may also be said that recognition of a normative principle of good faith may save a legal system the trouble of trying to impute these normative considerations to the intention of the parties.

This last point is made particularly clear from the approach of the common law to a number of our cases, for our study confirms the role of interpretation here as an alternative technique to resort to a principle of good faith elsewhere. This is achieved in a number of ways. Sometimes, an approach is taken at a high level of generality to construction of the contract with the result that, even for a common lawyer, the difference between a rule of construction and a rule of law proper is a fine one; this may be seen, for example, in English law's treatment of the rule that 'no man can take advantage of his own wrong'.[86] However, even more the present study has emphasised the prominence of implied terms in the modern English law of contract. These may be of two types. The first type consists of terms 'implied in fact' and they are found by applying the so-called test of the 'officious bystander'. '*Prima facie* that which in any contract is left to be implied and need not be expressed is something so obvious that it goes without saying; so that if, while the parties were making their bargain, an officious bystander were to suggest some express provision for it in the agreement, they would testily suppress him with a common, "oh, of course".'[87] Terms recognised under this test are seen as directly related to presumed party intention, though this is determined in a typically objective fashion. Far more important in practice, however, are terms 'implied in law'. While formally these are to be implied in contracts only if they are *necessary* (as opposed to being merely *reasonable*),[88] over the last century and a half the courts have found them in a vast variety of different types of contract and different situations. Moreover, one can discern in recent decisions of the House of Lords a more liberal attitude to the implication of terms, as long as the circumstances in which the term is to be implied can be defined with sufficient

---

[85] See the editors' comparative observations to case 8 'Delivery at night', p. 330 and to case 13 'Inspecting the books', p. 403; cf. also the approach of German, Greek and Italian law as opposed to that of Dutch law in case 6 'One bag too few', pp. 303–4.
[86] Above, p. 357.   [87] See *Shirlaw v. Southern Foundries (1926) Ltd* [1939] 2 KB 206, 277.
[88] The '*Moorcock*' (1889) 14 PD 64; *Liverpool City Council v. Irwin* [1977] AC 239.

certainty.[89] In the result, English courts can be seen to have been active in the regulation of the consequences of particular types of contract (such as leases, contracts of employment, sales of goods etc.) according to the appropriate range of considerations of policy applicable, of which the legitimate expectations of typical parties in the circumstances form an important but not the sole element.[90]

This regulatory function of implied terms in modern English law, bereft as it is both of a principle of good faith and of a broad tradition of the direct legal (but non-legislative) regulation of special types of contract, may explain to continental lawyers the courts' willingness to 'find' implied terms in the absence of any convincing contractual intention as they would recognise it. Moreover, the notion of an implied term was used to provide a juristic basis for the construction of the doctrine of frustration, a doctrine which has allowed the courts to declare that a contract has come to an end on the ground of subsequent (radical) changes in circumstance and which is common to contracts in general.[91] That this basis for frustration was subsequently rejected by the courts as a fiction,[92] serves only to emphasise its flexibility in the hands of the earlier English courts, who clearly did not see this point or (more likely) chose not to see it as long as the result was an appropriate one. Here, the parallels both with the use of a *condicio tacita* as the basis for the *clausula rebus sic stantibus* in continental legal history and the use in German law of §242 BGB as a legal basis for the construction of the doctrine of *Wegfall der Geschäftsgrundlage* are very striking. Also, just as the doctrine of frustration has gained its independence from implied term, so *Wegfall der Geschäftsgrundlage* has gained its independence from good faith for all practical purposes.

Overall, therefore, it is not *simply* that some legal systems have recourse to interpretative techniques in order to achieve the results which others reach by means of a principle of good faith. For in some classes of case,

---

[89] See especially, *Scally v. Southern Health and Social Services Board* [1992] 1 AC 294, 307 *per* Lord Bridge, an approach approved and applied by Lord Woolf in *Spring v. Guardian Assurance plc* [1995] 2 AC 296, 353–4.

[90] For a comparison between the English technique of implying terms into a contract and the German good faith analysis, see Wolfgang Grobecker, *Implied Terms und Treu und Glauben* (1999), concluding that the implication of terms in law widely gives effect to evaluations which a German lawyer would consider under the label of § 242 BGB.

[91] See *Taylor v. Caldwell* (1863) 3 B & S 826. For a general evaluation, in historical perspective, see Reinhard Zimmermann, '"Heard melodies are sweet, but those unheard are sweeter . . .": Condicio tacita, implied condition und die Fortbildung des europäischen Vertragsrechts', *AcP* 193 (1993) 121 ff.

[92] *Davis Contractors Ltd v. Fareham U.D.C.* [1956] AC 696.

good faith may be seen as being concerned with very much the same range of factors, from genuine or typical party expectation to more specifically normative concerns, as are taken into account by others as a matter of interpretation. On the other hand, it is clear that not all the situations which are regulated by means of good faith could be effected simply through notions of interpretation: for an interpretative technique will typically fall down in the face of express contrary intention, whereas the application of a principle of good faith need not do so.[93]

Fourthly, there are links between recourse to ideas of good faith or bad faith and the substantive injustice of the contract more generally. This usually finds its expression as a ground of intervention in the contract where there is a (gross) disparity between what the parties actually have to do under the contract, their 'performances'. Thus, for example, in case 2 'Degas drawing' in order to help the disadvantaged buyer Austrian law looks, in the first place, at the 'objective imbalance between performance and counter-performance' of the parties as regards the sale of a picture worth £85,000 for a price of £1,200. At other times, a legal system will reject the application of a strict rule on wider considerations of fairness. Thus, German law allows the avoidance of invalidity for informality where the economic 'existence of a party would otherwise be destroyed'.[94] West Nordic law is perhaps the widest in this regard as the courts possess a discretion to intervene in the effect of a contract to avoid an extremely unreasonable outcome.[95] The substantive injustice of the outcome may also be seen to be significant in some of the legal systems' responses to case 25 'Effect of inflation'. For while many of them disallow any adjustment of the contract on the ground of ordinary inflation, they do allow such adjustment where the inflation is 'dramatic and unforeseeable' (so that, for example, the nominal price of the other party's performance is only 7 per cent of its market value).[96] This sort of case can be seen, at least in part, as driven by a concern for the huge disproportion which has unforeseeably developed between the parties' performances. Indeed, art. 388 of the Greek Civil Code expressly refers to this idea, dealing with the situation where, owing to a subsequent change of circumstances, 'the performance due by the debtor has become excessively onerous, taking also into consid-

---

[93] It is to be noted, however, that it is not universally true that interpretative techniques fall down in the face of express contrary intention, there being a school of thought in the Netherlands which takes the opposite position.

[94] See above, pp. 259, 281 (cases 4 and 5).   [95] See above, p. 542 in relation to case 23 ('Long-term business relationships I').

[96] Above, pp. 557–8, 577. This is the position taken by German, Greek, Austrian, Italian and Spanish law.

eration the counter-performance'.[97] At the same time, however, it should be noted that a number of legal systems approach the problem of the possible adjustment of grave contractual imbalance under the auspices of their (much stricter) *contra bonos mores* clause rather than in terms of *bona fides*[98] (though control in terms of the *boni mores* may, in the course of time, shade into an inquiry guided by the precepts of good faith[99]).

On the other hand, sometimes the converse of this is also true, so that a legal system may *deny* a party's general right to escape from a contract where the substantial fairness of the contract is not threatened. This may be found in relation to case 11 'Untested motors working', where German law denies to a 'victim' of fraud the right to terminate the contract where it has no prejudicial result; other legal systems would reach a similar result if the party had been the 'victim' of a non-fraudulent misrepresentation.[100] In these types of case, it is the disproportionate nature of the 'victim's' reaction which leads to qualification of the normal legal position.

All this leads us to observe that in some of our cases some of the legal systems under consideration do not need to resort to any general corrective principle such as good faith because they possess instead particular legal doctrines which do the job, whether or not these are considered to be related to any wider principle. This is particularly clear in relation to the effect of changes of circumstances on a contract. It is often dealt with by particular doctrines (notably, the doctrine of frustration and *force majeure*) through which a legal system may establish what it considers to be the appropriate balance of interests between the parties.[101] Neither frustration nor *force majeure* are related to good faith by the systems which embrace these doctrines: frustration is tied by some courts and authors to the construction of the contract (i.e., once again, to interpretation of the intention of the parties), while others simply say it is justified in the interests of fairness, though the latter approach 'does not purport to explain why the courts sometimes abandon the doctrine of absolute contracts: it simply says that they do so';[102] *force majeure* finds its place in the French

---

[97] Above, p. 559; cf. also Art. 1467 *Codice civile*.
[98] The prototype is German law; see the editors' comparative observations (above, p. 234) to case 2 'Degas drawing'; and above, pp. 29–30.
[99] See the German experience concerning the control of unfair standard contract terms: above, p. 28, n. 116.   [100] Above, p. 377.
[101] Above, pp. 576–7. Another example may be found in the acceptance by Austrian law of duties of care arising from the 'lawful contact' of the parties: see above, pp. 176–7 in relation to case 1 'Courgettes perishing'.
[102] Günter Treitel, *The Law of Contract* (9th edn, 1995) 833.

and Belgian civil codes for historical reasons, but it has kept its potency in their modern laws owing to the idea that only where an obligation is impossible should its non-performance be excused, for otherwise the binding force of obligation must prevail.[103]

The existence of various other legal doctrines which 'do the job' of good faith lends support to the view that, at least to an extent and in certain respects, its use in a particular legal system is contingent on the presence of such other, more particular doctrines.

4. Non-contractual legal techniques

We have already noted that some legal systems deal with our cases by reference to legal rules which are not considered to be part of contract law proper. Thus, in particular, the law of delict (or torts) has been at times in evidence. It sometimes acts as an alternative to an analysis based on good faith, so that, for example, the patient in case 16 'Drug causing drowsiness in driving' may usually rely on the law of delict (or torts) in order to win compensation for at least any personal injury or damage to property which he has suffered as a result of the doctor's failure to advise, rather than on any remedy arising from a contract between himself and the doctor.[104] At other times, a particular legal system's law of delict may reinforce and sanction by an award of damages a failure to act in good faith or an abuse of rights, this being particularly clear in French and Belgian law in cases 2 'Degas drawing' and 3 'Breaking off negotiations'.[105]

The role of the law of restitution has been much more restrained in governing the cases in this study. Sometimes, it has been seen to give a remedy in order to deal with an otherwise unsatisfactory legal outcome even at the expense of its own core idea of the reversal of unjust *enrichments* (as may be thought to be the case concerning English law's treatment of case 3 'Breaking off negotiations').[106] In case 17 'Bank miscrediting customer' French law saw the analysis in terms of restitution as *excluding* appeal to its contractual principle of performance in good faith.[107]

5. Contractual practice

On occasion, we have seen that the problems arising from the state of the law in a particular legal system are dealt with (or dealt with to an extent) by the parties including suitable express terms in their contracts. Thus,

---

[103] Above, pp. 561–5 (in relation to case 25 'Effect of inflation').   [104] Above, p. 457.
[105] Above, pp. 218–19 and 239–41.   [106] Above, pp. 248–9.   [107] Above, pp. 459–60.

while English law took a strict view of the effect of inflation on the contract for the purposes of case 25 'Effect of inflation', it is standard practice in the particular context of the case to make express provision according to which the cost of the stipulated service would rise according to changes in a particular index of prices.[108] Another example may be found in Scots law in relation to case 17 'Bank miscrediting customer', where it was reported that the contracts under which banks operate will normally contain an express provision requiring the customer to disclose mistakes of the type found on the facts.[109] It would indeed be surprising if in certain of the types of cases under consideration well-advised parties would not expressly provide for the contingencies arising in the cases. To this extent, it may be thought that where this is the case, a legal system has no need to have recourse to the legal regulation of the situation, whether by a principle of good faith or otherwise.

However, contractual practice is by no means a universal escape route from the problems raised by the cases in our study.

First, while in some of our cases the problems could be dealt with by the inclusion of a suitable express term, the reason why many legal systems instead have recourse to a principle of good faith, the implication of terms or direct legal regulation of the matter is precisely because by no means all parties to the types of contract or in the types of situation in question do in fact make express provision. Dealing with the problem by law, rather than leaving it to be dealt with by the parties, may at times be thought almost a 'word-saving' matter: why should parties clutter their contracts with standard form provisions, when the legal system could conveniently provide a 'default-position'?[110] This sort of idea can certainly be seen to be part of the thinking behind the imposition of 'ancillary obligations', implied terms or *lois supplétives* in case 16 'Drug causing drowsiness in driving'.[111] But this is by no means the complete story. To an extent, it is true, it may be thought that since some parties to contracts are not sufficiently well informed or well advised to include an express term, the law should take the (paternalistic) view that it should make provision for them

---

[108] Above, p. 568.   [109] Above, p. 469.

[110] Cf. the attitude of the French jurist *Laurent* to the regulation of contracts found in the Civil Code: see Gordley, above, p. 116.

[111] Above, pp. 439 ff. A striking example of a historical 'word-saving' provision may be found in arts. 1183–4 of the French Civil Code. In the absence of any legal ground for termination of a contract based on the other party's non-performance, parties to contracts of sale used to include an express provision, known as a *lex commissoria*: Reinhard Zimmermann, *The Law of Obligations: Roman Foundations of the Civilian Tradition* (1990, paperback edn 1996) 737–8. The Civil Code, following *Pothier* in this respect, implies such a term in all synallagmatic contracts.

as though they had been properly advised. Yet it is clear that in many legal systems neither the legislature nor the courts limit themselves to acting as what one could describe as surrogate draftsmen, but, instead, take a specific view of the proper regulation of the relationship which the parties have created, proper according to the considerations of policy which are thought by them to be applicable in the context concerned. Moreover, in many situations, the legal systems under consideration clearly go further and regulate the parties' relationship notwithstanding any expressed contrary intention on their part. This is because it is widely recognised that some contractual relationships are not concluded on the basis of equal bargaining power and/or that some types of legal relationship which have their origin in contract nevertheless attract the application of principles which are 'non-negotiable'.[112] Here, contractual practice may form part of the problem rather than act as a means of achieving a solution.

Secondly, and following on from this, many of the problems arising in the cases which we have included in this study cannot be dealt with by express contractual provision. This is particularly clear in relation to those cases where the 'problem'[113] stems from the exercise of a right which is created by a provision of the contract itself, as in case 10 'Dissolution of partnership' or case 15 'Two cracks in a shed'.[114] Other cases involve problems which arise from the exercise of a right or liberty which the law (as opposed to the terms of the contract) gives to one of the parties, such as the ability to rely on a failure to follow the proper legal form in cases 4 and 5 or a party's right to oppose a defence of prescription as in cases 20 and 21.[115] But the inability of express contractual provision to solve perceived problems also arises in other cases. Case 3 'Breaking off

[112] Thus, to take an obvious example, French law forbids the exclusion of a trader's liability for latent defects arising from a case such as case 1 'Courgettes perishing' (see above, p. 37, n. 184 *in fine*); English law distinguishes in this regard as between consumer and non-consumer buyers: Unfair Contract Terms Act 1977, s. 6. The cases in our study which have attracted (at least for some legal systems) the application of principles or rules which are not capable of being ousted by contrary intention include case 9 'Uniformity of outfit' (which involves employees' rights, above, pp. 346–7).

[113] The use of this term is not intended to insinuate that all legal systems see the circumstances in question as giving rise to a problem, some legal systems seeing the exercise of a right such as that which is found in cases 23 and 24 'Long-term business relationships I and II' as unproblematic.   [114] Above, pp. 348 ff. and 419 ff. respectively.

[115] See above, pp. 258 ff. and 493 ff. respectively. See also case 7 'Late payment of rent', above, pp. 305 ff. and case 11 'Untested motors working', above, pp. 362 ff.

negotiations' could, it is true, be satisfactorily dealt with if the parties had reached an agreement concerning payment for work done in anticipation of the contract; but this rather misses the point, for the parties in case 3 failed to make such a provision precisely because they (or at least one of them) expected that the main contract would go ahead.[116]

6. The significance of general principle

It is clear that a legal system's attitude to either the recognition or use of a general principle of good faith is based, to a certain extent, on its lawyers' juristic taste: here we agree with the received wisdom that at least *European* common lawyers, in contrast to civil lawyers, in general seem more at home with the particular than with the very general. On the other hand, the common law systems, Scots law and the Nordic legal systems which do not accept general principles of good faith are not short of ways in which to deal with many, though by no means all, the situations for which other legal systems invoke good faith. Conversely, acceptance by a legal system of a general principle of good faith does not answer the question whether good faith *requires* a certain type of conduct in a party to a contract or the restriction on the exercise of a contractual right in any particular set of circumstances; indeed, as we have seen, those legal systems which do accept such a principle at times differ as to what good faith does in fact require.[117] In this way, as was suggested earlier, it can be seen that the recognition of a principle of good faith does not require a particular result in the circumstances, it merely allows the possibility of a particular result, leaving the court to decide whether or not it should be brought about.

From this perspective, it could indeed be argued that there would be no *substantive* legal change were English or Scots law to accept a general principle of contractual good faith, as long as such a principle were interpreted merely as providing a certain unity to those doctrines and rules which could (in some way or other) be said already to give effect to good faith. Thus, English law might hold that only dishonest statements (as opposed to mere silence in the knowledge that the other party is labouring under a misapprehension) constituted bad faith, or that it could never be bad faith for a party to rely on the express rights granted to him under

---

[116] Above, pp. 236 ff.
[117] See above, pp. 665–6 in relation to cases 14 ('Producing new bumpers'), 23 and 24 ('Long-term business relationships I and II').

a contract. So conceived, the principle could not be relied upon by a party to negotiations or to a contract so as to gain a particular legal result which could not be obtained under the existing law. However, it is not at all clear what purpose would be served by such a toothless principle, and for common lawyers on both sides of the argument as to the desirability of recognising a principle of good faith in contract law, the main if not the whole point of such a recognition would be the possibility of changing the positive law by reference to the new principle, as well as influencing the way in which future developments occur. As we have noted earlier, where lawyers within a system are relatively happy with the law's existing approach, there is no pressure to recognise or to develop a principle like good faith so as to serve as a vehicle for legal change.

For in practice, the recognition of a principle of the breadth of good faith by a legal system does rather more than merely *allow* a court to decide according to its perception of the proper view of the case; it *invites* a court to do so. Broad principles are attractive and may act as the justification for a wide range of legal developments (as the German experience in particular shows).[118] Now, giving the courts a wide-ranging power to change more particular legal rules or to innovate in unregulated situations may or may not be attractive as a matter of the substantive results which are thereby to be achieved, but such a power is not necessarily one which is welcome (or not equally welcome) to all modern legal systems, either as a matter of constitutional principle or of the practicalities of law reform. For while most lawyers today accept the important role of courts in developing the law, it is still thought to be principally the responsibility of legislatures to make law, as their (typically elected) members are in a better position than are judges to assess and to balance the range of competing policies and, indeed, political considerations in issue. Now, clearly some of the issues raised by our cases are not ones on which it is particularly necessary to have a democratic input, but others could benefit from it and have indeed done so in some of the legal systems under consideration. This may be seen in relation to case 9 'Uniformity of outfit', which a number of legal systems dealt with in terms of specific rules of employment law; case 18 'Access to medical records' which gave rise to difficult questions relating to the right of self-determination of medical patients

---

[118] Here, perhaps an analogy may be drawn with the historical significance of recognition of the 'neighbour principle' in *Donoghue v. Stevenson* [1932] AC 562 in the English tort of negligence which invited future courts to add situations in which previously no duty of care had been recognised.

and its limits; and case 29 'Divorce settlement' where for a number of legal systems any possible contractual analysis of the settlement has to take second place to the policies and principles of family law.[119]

Of course, it may be countered that many European lawyers and, indeed, many European citizens, in fact trust their judges to know how far to go in their law-making, taking into account their traditional role and the balance of powers within their own constitution. However, such an observation acknowledges that the courts in different legal systems may come to different views as to the appropriateness of undertaking judicially a particular legal reform. Where a legal principle (such as good faith) appears to invite a high degree of judicial law-making, it should not be surprising that the courts of those systems which take a stricter view of the proper limits of their own creative potential should shy away from its adoption or its use. In this respect, it must be said that at least in the area of contract law, English courts have proved themselves distinctly and deliberately timid in their law-making. Judicial development has taken place in particular contexts (in particular, through the law of implied terms which is by its nature particular in its application), but more generally common law innovation has been restrained.[120] In this respect, the approach adopted towards the control of unfair contract terms, while not falling within our own thirty cases, is particularly instructive. For German law, this was one of the main areas of operation for the principle of good faith.[121] For French law, the courts accepted that a legislative provision which gave authority to the *administration* to declare certain classes of contract terms unfair, but which had hardly been used, should be accepted as giving them the power to make such a declaration.[122] The House of Lords, on the other hand, steadfastly refused to develop a robust common law technique for the control of unfair exemption clauses in the 1960s and 1970s, at least in part because it was considered to be a matter for Parliament (which indeed eventually

---

[119] Above, pp. 331 ff., 470 ff. and 623 ff. respectively.

[120] Apart from in relation to implied terms, the major judicial innovations in contract law over the last thirty years or so have been the recognition of a law of economic duress, developments in relation to undue influence, and the creation of further circumventions of the doctrine of privity of contract. A striking contrast is to be seen in the courts' attitude to the law of restitution, even where the restitutionary issue arises in a contractual context; see *Lipkin Gorman v. Karpnale Ltd* [1991] 2 AC 548; *Kleinwort Benson Ltd v. Lincoln City Council* [1998] 3 WLR 1095. On the latter case see, in the present context, Reinhard Zimmermann, 'Rechtsirrtum und richterliche Rechtsfortbildung', *ZEuP* 7 (1999) 713.   [121] Above, pp. 27-8.   [122] Above, p. 37.

though only partially dealt with it).[123] Where, then, judges have traditionally shown themselves to be doctrinally conservative in a particular
area of law, they are unlikely to wish to adopt a legal principle which
invites innovation and change.

While such a conservative attitude in the judiciary towards doctrinal
innovation in contract law may occasionally be irritating we do not wish
to give the impression that it is necessarily bad, and that a marked willingness to innovate would be necessarily desirable. It *may* be desirable. We
have seen, for example, that those legal systems which do recognise a principle of good faith in contract law have used it to allow their laws of contract to be suffused with constitutional perceptions of individuals'
rights.[124] However, at times innovation may be substantively misguided or
even corrupting. We should not forget that the German experience of the
application of §242 BGB has not always been a happy one.[125] Legal formalism may seem to be a legal vice, inappropriate in a legal system come of
age; but the legal certainty and respect for legal authority which it
expresses (even if in an exaggerated form) are rather legal virtues, associated with the rule of law itself.

7. The meanings of good faith

We have said that good faith may be seen to require different results in
different legal systems. But it should be said more clearly that the notion
of good faith (or its equivalents in the various languages used by the legal
systems under consideration) actually means different things both *within*
a particular legal system and *between* the legal systems. Moreover, while in
certain types of context, it seems more natural to appeal to what *good faith*
requires, in others it seems more natural to refer to how *bad faith* should
be sanctioned: there are positive and negative ways of expressing the prin-

---

[123] The common law technique was the 'doctrine of fundamental breach', advocated in
particular by Lord *Denning* M.R., but firmly rejected by the House of Lords: see *Suisse
Atlantique Société d'Armement Maritime SA v. N.V. Rotterdamsche Kolen Centrale* [1967] 1 AC 361
(HL); *Harbutts 'Plasticine' Ltd v. Wayne Tank and Pump Co. Ltd* [1970] 1 QB 447 (CA); *Photo
Production Ltd v. Securicor Transport Ltd* [1980] AC 827, especially at 843. Parliamentary
intervention occurred in the Unfair Contract Terms Act 1977.

[124] Of our cases, this was seen in relation to case 9 'Uniformity of outfit', both German law
and Spanish law being able to give effect in contract law to decisions as to employees'
rights taken under their constitutions through the mediation of their principles of good
faith: above, pp. 331–3, 338–9. Cf. also, e.g., the reference to constitutional law in the
Italian report to case 18 'Access to medical records': above, p. 473.   [125] Above, pp. 21–2.

ciple. We shall therefore in the following discussion look sometimes at meanings of bad faith, sometimes of good faith. It is striking how these meanings echo at least some of the significances given to 'good faith' and 'equity' by the tradition of Roman law and Canon law.[126]

For all the systems under consideration, dishonesty constitutes *bad faith*. This is axiomatic in those systems which recognise good faith as a principle, being clearest in the context of precontractual dishonest statements. However, it is also true of the common law systems. This can be seen not so much in the context of fraud (for fraud is fraud rather than bad faith, though it clearly is dishonest), but rather in a context like the one found in case 15 'Two cracks in a shed', where a person's contractual rights are made contingent on a decision of the agent of the other party to the contract. Here, it is clear that such a decision must be made in good faith which means that it must be made with an honest belief in the genuineness of the reasons on which it purports to be made.[127] On the other hand, our legal systems do not agree on the circumstances which should count as dishonesty. Thus, some consider that a failure to disclose significant facts to the other contracting party *may* constitute bad faith (though the details of when it *will* again vary among them), while others (the common law systems and Scots law) do not in general consider such a failure to disclose to be dishonest at all.[128] In this respect, it is interesting to note that in those cases where exceptionally English law does indeed impose precontractual duties of disclosure and even does so in the language of good faith, as in contracts of insurance, even a knowing failure to disclose is not usually classed as fraudulent (and therefore dishonest) but merely as breach of a special duty of disclosure.[129]

A second aspect of good faith which has been found is the idea that it requires a person to keep his word. At one level, a level which has been of the utmost importance historically in the generalisation of contract theory, this may be applied to agreements in general: good faith requires parties to an agreement to keep to its terms; here, then, it acts as a buttress for the principle of the binding force of contracts. However, so stated,

---

[126] See Gordley, above, pp. 94 ff. and 117.
[127] See above, p. 429, especially *Colbelfret N.V. v. Cylclades Shipping Co. Ltd (The 'Linardos')* [1994] 1 Lloyd's Rep 28 at 32 *per* Colman J.   [128] See case 2 'Degas drawing', above, pp. 208 ff.
[129] The fact that the breach of a duty of disclosure in insurance law is not equated with fraud is made clear by English law's denial that breach of the duty gives rise to liability in *damages*: see *Banque Keyser Ullman v. Skandia (UK) Insurance Co. Ltd* [1990] 1 QB 665, affirmed on other grounds [1991] 2 AC 249.

once it has done its job of ensuring that no agreements fall through the net of legal contract,[130] this idea at first seems 'to have done its job', as the older French *doctrine* thought indeed was the case concerning their own principle of good faith: a legal system which recognises all agreements as contracts and gives them the force of law no longer needs any recourse to good faith.[131] However, it can be seen from the present study that even today the idea that a person should keep his word (whether this word is a promise or merely a representation) may, at least when combined with reliance by another, be seen as a consequence of good faith: *ne veneat contra factum proprium*.[132] Interestingly English law, while still denying that all agreements are contracts (owing to the rules of consideration), does possess a doctrine, viz. promissory estoppel, which combines elements of representation and reliance and which is equitable both in the sense that it qualifies the rigours of a general legal rule (consideration itself) and in the sense that it is subject to general considerations of fairness. French law, on the other hand, does not allow a person's contractual rights to be lost in this way: here the binding force of agreements cannot be relaxed on the basis of a mere representation, but only on the basis of a further *consensus ad idem*.[133] In French law good faith does not (at least overtly) refer to combinations of representation and reliance. At the same time, however, the need to protect reliance or a party's expectations beyond the contract becomes an element within good faith for French law (and other systems[134]) in the context of long-term contracts.[135]

A third meaning of *bad faith* shared by several systems is that a party to a contract should not make the other party's position *worse* by behaving in an unreasonable way or without any legitimate interest, this reflecting a duty of contractual loyalty.[136] This is particularly clear in case 3, where the breaking-off of negotiations in a sudden or otherwise

---

[130] This very general statement has to be qualified, for even a legal system such as the French one which defines contracts as agreements giving rise to obligations hesitates to class certain agreements as contracts, for example, those which are made in a purely social context: Philippe Malaurie, Laurent Aynès, *Cours de droit civil, Les obligations* (8th edn, 1998) 201.   [131] Above, pp. 33–4.

[132] See especially case 21 'Prescription II', above, p. 508. The significance of *venire contra factum proprium* is wider, as it may act to prevent someone from acting inconsistently with his own *deed* as opposed to word: see especially German law in case 14 'Producing new bumpers', above, p. 404.

[133] See above, pp. 519–20, 524 (case 22 'Sitting on one's rights').

[134] See especially cases 23 and 24, 'Long-term business relationships I and II', above pp. 554–6.   [135] Above, pp. 535–6 and see also p. 510.

[136] Cf. above, p. 240 in relation to French law.

inappropriate way (often combined with an element of induced reliance) leads to the imposition of liability in damages.[137]

Fourthly, good faith sometimes seems to mean no more and no less than that the parties cannot be allowed to rely on, nor be kept to, an absurdity which appears to follow from their agreement. This is the sense of good faith in cases 6 'One bag too few' and 8 'Delivery at night'. As regards case 15 'Two cracks in a shed', for some legal systems the particular element which attracts intervention in the apparent contractual position lies in the disproportion between the one party's non-performance (two slight cracks in the shed) and the other party's employee's reaction (withholding his approval of the building with the result that no price is payable). Similar to this are those cases where good faith is almost synonymous with fairness. Thus, it would generally be agreed by most non-lawyers that it would be unfair to keep either of the policyholders in cases 27 'Disability insurance' and 28 'Crop destroyed by hail' to the strict terms of their contracts in the circumstances. Even in English and Scots law which before 1994 did indeed keep policyholders to their strict contractual terms in this context, this would not have been considered *fair* (as the codes of practice of UK insurers themselves make clear) and could be justified only on the basis that other competing considerations (such as a fear of fraud or the need for certainty) had to take primacy.[138]

Fifthly, while this aspect has not specifically been the subject of the present study, some systems (the French and Spanish, for example) characterise the deliberate breach of a contract as constituting bad faith, with various legal results, most obviously as to liability in damages. However, for German law a deliberate breach is no different from an 'innocent' breach: breach is breach and good or bad faith does not come into the discussion.[139] In this context, therefore, it is not that the same meaning of bad faith is applied differently in the two systems: the meanings themselves are different. Before moving on, we can note that, unsurprisingly, English law has much in common with the German position, but there is an exception in the case of a deliberate refusal to perform made *before* the time for performance, though not by reference to the language of good faith.[140]

These five paragraphs do not of course exhaust the possible meanings which good faith may bear, even in the cases under our consideration.

---

[137] Above, pp. 236 ff.   [138] Above, pp. 603–5.
[139] See, e.g., Helmut Heinrichs, in: Palandt, *Bürgerliches Gesetzbuch* (57th edn, 1998) Vorbem. v. § 249, n. 6.   [140] Above, p. 41.

Thus, English law's appeal to good faith on the particular facts of case 15 'Two cracks in a shed' refers to a requirement that the person judging the performance of the contract must 'reach [these] decisions fairly, holding the balance between his client and the contractor'.[141] But they make clear that while certain common meanings of the notion of good faith (and its cousin concepts) are to be found within our study, these meanings differ both within and among the particular legal systems.

8. Good faith, legal rights and the abuse of rights

Certain legal systems, most clearly Spanish law, consider the idea of good faith in contract law as closely related to a more general idea of the abuse of rights. Since the Spanish Civil Code was amended in 1975, it has contained a provision in art. 7 which combines the two notions overtly. It states that (i) rights must be exercised in conformity with the requirements of good faith; and (ii) the law will not recognise the abuse of a right nor its anti-social exercise.[142] Again and again, the Spanish response to our cases invoked this provision or its older cousin, art. 1258, which deals with good faith in the performance of contractual obligations.[143]

Other legal systems, notably German law, despite possessing a provision in the code which expressly recognises the idea of the abuse of rights,[144] have preferred not to develop an overarching theory based on this idea;[145] instead, the wider principle is one of good faith, recognised by the Civil Code as applicable only to the manner in which performance is to be effected but interpreted by the courts so as to cover the exercise, and the assessment, of contractual rights in general[146] and even extended far beyond the law of obligations. This does not mean that the notion of the abuse of rights in a more general sense is altogether absent, for in German law it comes in to describe certain *examples* of the application of the principle of good faith.[147] This type of approach does not, therefore, formally need to qualify the concept of an 'individual's right', whether this right

---

[141] Above, p. 428.   [142] For the full text see above, p. 244.

[143] See above, p. 244 for its text. The cases in which art. 7 was invoked were 3, 6, 7, 8, 12, 13, 14 (clearly not an abuse) and 20. Art. 1258 was invoked in cases 8, 13, 17, 18 and 30.

[144] § 226 BGB: 'The exercise of a right is unlawful, if its purpose can only be to cause damage to another.'

[145] Indeed, German lawyers have interpreted § 226 very restrictively so that it is little used in practice. One possible reason for this is a distrust for the investigation of motive which it requires.   [146] For details, see above, pp. 18 ff.

[147] See above, p. 24, n. 94 ('Abuse of a right. . . constitutes a sub-category of cases covered by th[e] general provision [of § 242 BGB]').

arises from the law directly or from the terms of a contract which the law allows him to make, but instead looks to a super-eminent, legally recognised principle, whose impact qualifies the exercise of particular rights in particular contexts.

Other legal systems distinguish between the idea of good faith in contract law (whether in the creation and/or the performance of contracts) and a more general theory of the abuse of rights. Thus, while good faith in the performance of contracts is required by the French Civil Code and, conversely, bad faith (*dol*[148]) is sanctioned either by nullity or more generous damages (depending on the context), by the later nineteenth century French lawyers found little need to resort to the general principle of good faith in their decisions about contracts: consensualism in all its various expressions dominated juristic and judicial thinking.[149] However, we have also seen how from the beginning of this century French lawyers have recognised a role for the abuse of rights in civil law generally[150] and this has had an important impact on contract law itself and on the development of delictual liability between contractors and would-be contractors. These developments explain why argument in modern French discussions often slides effortlessly from the notion of the abuse of rights to that of the requirements of good faith. Indeed, as was pointed out in the course of the French analysis of the cases, in the contractual context, the choice between the two doctrines (of good faith or the abuse of rights) depends (at least in part) on the question whether the *Cour de cassation* desires to keep the matter within its own control or to abandon it to the *pouvoir souverain d'appréciation* of the lower courts.[151] To this extent, the difference between the two doctrines seems no more than one of technique, contingent on an institutional arrangement central but particular to the private law of a particular system.

At a more theoretical level, though, it may be helpful to recall the debate which existed in France especially in the earlier part of this century concerning the significance of the notion of the abuse of rights. For some partisans of the notion, a right could be abused only when its exercise was malicious in the sense of motivated by an intention to harm

---

[148] The translation of *dol* as bad faith may seem at first rather odd, for the general term for bad faith would be *mauvaise foi* rather than *dol*. However, while on occasion *mauvaise foi* is used in French discussions, *dol* is much more frequently used. If nothing else, *dol* can be seen as the primary legal expression of bad faith in French contract law. In practice, *dol* may refer either to dishonest precontractual conduct which induces a mistake in the other party or the deliberate non-performance of a contractual obligation: above, p. 33.   [149] Above, pp. 33–4.   [150] Above, pp. 34–5.   [151] Above, p. 394.

another person. This may be seen as the moralistic (and more narrow) view of the notion. However, the wider position was that the exercise of legal rights should be recognised only where it fulfils their social or economic purpose.[152] As it was later put by admittedly hostile commentators: 'The success of the expression [abuse of rights], and its imprecision, suggested to certain authors the idea of making it an instrument of the socialisation of the law, that is to say of the reduction of the value of rights[153] as the prerogatives of individuals.'[154]

Here, we should return to art. 7 of the Spanish Civil Code, which explains what is to be understood by the abuse of rights, providing that '[t]he law will not recognise the abuse of a right *nor its anti-social exercise. Any action or omission which either in the intention of its author, in its purpose* or in the circumstances in which it occurs manifestly surpasses the normal limits of the exercise of a right, to the prejudice of a third party, shall give rise to an appropriate compensation or to the adoption of judicial or administrative measures to prevent persistence in the abuse.'[155] Here, then, we find explicitly and combined the two theories of the abuse of right: abuse through malice and abuse through exercise contrary to its purpose.

This approach to the exercise of legal rights makes a striking contrast with the English legal tradition. For, as we earlier noted, English law has set its face against any general idea of the abuse of rights.[156] This does not of course mean that English legal rights are unqualified, which would be absurd, but rather that they bear their own limitations, either specific ones expressed in the language of exception or non-application, or by containing within them criteria of reasonableness.[157] Nevertheless, the hostility which a general idea of the abuse of rights has met among English lawyers reflects a considerable attachment, at least within traditional legal thinking (as reflected in the courts), to a particular liberal conception of rights, stressing the importance of free choice in their exercise. One of the points of possessing a right is the freedom of its abuse. As the traditional maxim has it, *neminem laedit qui suo iure utitur.*[158]

While all this is true, there is a central and striking paradox in English law taking such a stand and this lies in the historical and present role of

---

[152] Above, p. 34.   [153] *Droit subjectifs.*
[154] M. Planiol, G. Ripert, *Traité pratique de droit civil français*, t. VI, *Obligations, première partie* by P. Esmein (2nd edn, 1952) 801. As we have noted earlier, both Planiol and Ripert were opponents of this version of the abuse of rights theory.   [155] Emphasis added.
[156] Above, p. 41.   [157] For examples, see above, pp. 298–9, 372 and below, n. 164.
[158] Cf. Gaius D. 50, 17, 55 (*nullus videtur dolo facere, qui suo iure utitur*).

equity. Clearly, the doctrines of equity *do* at times act to control the exercise of legal rights as a matter of conscience or fairness: this is surely (at least originally) the very nature of the equitable jurisdiction. However, as we earlier noted, modern English equitable controls on the exercise of legal rights have been exercised through its own doctrines, doctrines at times every bit as technical and limited as 'rules of law' themselves. Equity was domesticated a long time ago in England, even if traces of its older, wilder nature have become prominent in other Commonwealth jurisdictions.

However, the existence of the historical and jurisdictional equity in the English legal system raises the more fundamental question of the role of a principle such as good faith in contract law as an instrument of equitable correction of the harshness of the law: equity in the Aristotelian sense (*epieíkeia*), or at least, a modernised version of this sense.[159] It is important to distinguish two types of equitable correction. The first may apply where the legal rule in question is itself considered to be *in general* a good rule (according to whatever criteria one cares to apply) but may nevertheless on occasion work injustice. Here, equity corrects the harshness of the strict application of a rule. This may be illustrated at a particular level by the discussions concerning our prescription cases[160] and much more generally by those cases in which it was felt that a particular right arising from a contract should not (for one or another reason) be invoked.[161] On the other hand, equity may be used in a more generally corrective manner in that the effect of a rule is considered to be unjust not only in exceptional situations: here, the rule itself may not be reformed, perhaps for reasons of authority (it is a legislative rule and there is no political will to change it) and so is instead circumvented by appeal to another principle. This sort of correction is perhaps most clearly found in relation to case 25 ('Effect of inflation'), where, by arrogating to themselves the right to adjust the contract, the courts in Germany were also interfering with the law as laid down by the draftsmen of the BGB (though not with any specific legislative rule but rather with a decision *not* to adopt the *clausula rebus sic stantibus*). Here, then, as we have argued earlier, a general principle such as good faith acts simply as a mechanism for the reform of the law.

---

[159] On *epieíkeia*, see Gordley, above, pp. 108 ff. and Schermaier, above, p. 65, n. 9.

[160] Cases 20 and 21.

[161] Cases 13 ('Inspecting the books'); 15 ('Two cracks in a shed'); 22 ('Sitting on one's rights'); 23 and 24 ('Long-term business relationships I and II'); 27 ('Disability insurance'); 28 ('Crop destroyed by hail'); 30 ('Penalty for late delivery').

9. Different conceptions or models of contract?

Do the responses to our cases reflect any more general differences in the *conception* of contract in the various legal systems? Of course, we do not here mean to ask this question at large, for clearly a great deal could be said in answer to it which would not bear on our concerns, including the debates between consensus and bargain theory, the truly binding nature of contract as against *Holmes'* view of the common law position,[162] etc. Here, the question is posed much more specifically in relation to the presence or absence of appeal to the idea of good faith. Our answer, though, is that it would be going too far to characterise the differences between the legal systems as ones of conception, that is, relating to (at least one aspect of) the very nature of contract. It is often said that English law takes as its starting point a commercial model of contract, whereas 'civil law systems' think more in terms of private transactions more generally; and the attitudes visible in Lord *Ackner's* speech in *Walford v. Miles*[163] reflect this view. However, we consider that even in relation to English law, this characterisation is overdone. The responses of English law to the particular cases considered in this study demonstrate a long-standing awareness, on the part of the courts, that all contracts are not charterparties or other 'pure commercial' transactions and that the courts have long been and still are therefore willing to adapt the general doctrines of contract law to the particular situations before them. Even in purely commercial transactions, such as commercial sales of goods, rights are qualified by reference to the criterion of reasonableness.[164] Qualifications on the idea of contract as being about ruthless bargaining and strict performance abound.

---

[162] See O. W. Holmes, *The Common Law* (1881) 301, according to whom the common law leaves a party to a contract 'free from interference until the time for fulfilment has gone by, and therefore free to break his contract if he chooses'. It is to be noted that Holmes' work concerned the *common law*; clearly, the above position must be read subject to the impact in the modern law of the equitable remedies of specific performance and injunction.   [163] [1992] 2 AC 128.

[164] For examples in the present work, see case 1 'Courgettes perishing', above, p. 195 (goods must be '*reasonably* fit for their purpose': Sale of Goods Act 1979, s. 14(3)); case 6 'One bag too few', above, pp. 298–9 (no right of rejection of wrong quantity of goods where the 'excess is so slight that it would be unreasonable for him to do so': Sale of Goods Act 1979, s. 30 (2A)); case 8 'Delivery at night', above, p. 327 (demand or delivery may be treated as ineffectual unless made at a *reasonable* hour: Sale of Goods Act 1979, s. 29(5)). Other examples may be found in Sale of Goods Act 1979, s. 8(2) (if price not fixed, buyer has to pay a *reasonable* price); s. 15A (no right in buyer to reject goods for breach of implied conditions as to title, description etc. if *unreasonable* to do so given the slightness of the breach); ss. 34 and 35 (buyer has a '*reasonable* opportunity' of examining the goods, this forming an element in their 'acceptance').

Very closely related to this line of thought is the idea that good faith reflects a communitarian ideal rather than individualistic values, at least where the parties have entered a relationship (even if not a contractual one). This is perhaps typically seen in cases of duties of precontractual disclosure, but may be seen more generally. However, while there is a certain validity in this contrast, the differences here in practice may again be more a question of which is the rule and which the exception. Let us again take English law. Here, we appear to have the 'robust' model, but we have earlier noted[165] that this model does not apply to a whole range of classes of contractors, notably not to those who are classed as fiduciaries. Conversely, where a general principle of good faith in the creation of contracts exists in a legal system, this leaves open the question whether it requires disclosure in the circumstances.[166] This does not mean that no differences exist between the systems, but the contrast between them is not sharp enough to be considered one of conception, unless conception refers to the way in which lawyers still think about and express the law after it has in fact moved on. For it is clear that acceptance of a principle of good faith does not necessarily mean that a legal system will always take a 'soft' approach to cases where tension exists between the exercise of market power by one party to a contract and a 'fair result' for the other. Here, again, Spanish law's approach is important: as it is said in relation to case 14 'Producing new bumpers', '[a]ny contractual advantage of [one party's] position is considered to arise from his stronger bargaining power, rather than from any abuse of his contractual rights'.[167]

In sum, therefore, good faith is not devoid of meaning, a pious hope or incantation or simply a super-technique waiting to be put to whatever legal end a legal system wishes (though it may act as a super-technique if required). But its meanings do differ within and among the legal systems and even where a particular meaning of good faith is accepted in two systems, this does not entail that they will take the same view of what it in fact requires in any given situation. While, therefore, the differences in results of the analyses of our case studies are fairly restrained, the significance given to a potentially corrective principle such as of good faith, or

---

[165] Above, pp. 46–7.
[166] To take simply one example, in German law there would be no duty on the directors in the famous English case of *Bell v. Lever Bros Ltd* [1932] AC 161 to disclose their earlier breaches of contract: this is not required in good faith of employees.
[167] Above, p. 409 in relation to case 14 ('Producing new bumpers'). Cf. Spanish law's responses to cases 23 and 24 ('Long-term business relationships I and II'), above, pp. 536–7, 551.

of the abuse of rights, may differ widely between the legal systems. There is, then, a certain 'common core' of result, but even if *all* the legal systems included within the study were to accept a general principle of good faith in contracts, this would by no means have the same significance, let alone the same impact, in the context of each legal system. This study also reinforces the perception that legal principles such as good faith and the abuse of rights are only one type of mechanism for the solution of legal problems. Some legal systems prefer, instead, to use more particular techniques, whether these are legal doctrines common to contract law as a whole, or legal rules special to particular contracts; and that the focus of these particular techniques may be very different from the traditional concerns of contract law itself.

Finally, our study emphasises the fact that *all* the legal systems included within our study have moved away or are in the process of moving away from a paradigm of contract which focuses almost exclusively on the autonomy of the parties. Instead, we find a growing significance given to party loyalty, the protection of reliance, (occasional) duties of co-operation, the need to consider the other party's interest or the substantive fairness of the contract, whether or not these are the terms in which this change of emphasis is put in any one system. It is a qualification of the nineteenth-century paradigm of party autonomy (or 'freedom of contract') which may be seen in all the systems, including the common law ones to one degree or another and may be seen to reflect a return (at least in the civilian systems) to an older model of contract which takes a less exaggerated approach to party autonomy.[168]

Each legal system, then, finds the need to strike a balance between party autonomy and wider considerations of fairness and also between the certainty of the law and individual justice. Our study shows very clearly that each legal system has its own range of mechanisms by which these two balancing acts may be achieved. In this respect, it does not matter all that much whether this is done through a general notion like good faith, or the implication of terms, or some other more particular technique. These sorts of legal tools are very malleable and the extent to which a legal system wishes to use them depends on what it considers to be the proper balance in any given situation. To the extent to which that balance is not

---

[168] See, in particular, James Gordley, *The Philosophical Origins of Modern Contract Doctrine* (1991). The extent to which older common law or equitable rules took into account substantive fairness or good faith is less clear, see above, pp. 41–4, especially at note 227.

struck in the same way in which it was struck (at least according to what is usually termed classical contract theory) in the nineteenth century, it may be said that all the legal systems included in our study (including the common law ones) embrace a notion of good faith in contract law; the fact that, for example, English law has not chosen to do so (as yet), says more about its lawyers' juristic taste, the perceptions of judges as to their proper role *vis-à-vis* the legislature and, perhaps, their attachment to a nineteenth-century *model* which has become canonised in the precedents. This is not, of course, to argue that English courts should openly declare a principle of good faith: whether this is, or is not, desirable is a matter for English lawyers to decide and falls outside the purposes of our inquiry.

To reiterate: good faith is a concept which possesses different meanings and is used for a variety of different purposes. It may invite judges to qualify strict legal rules or the terms of a contract but it does not require them to do so. A precise definition is impossible. Even the term as such does not much matter. At the same time, however, it would be both wrong (at the level of legal policy) and incorrect (at a merely descriptive level) to deny the corrective influence of ideas like good faith, or reasonableness, or fair dealing, or equity, in contract law – even in a contract law which may be oriented largely towards a commercial community. For, in the words of *Baldus de Ubaldis*: good faith is much required of those who trade most.[169]

---

[169] 'Unde Baldus noster ... ait bonam fidem valde requiri, in his, qui plurimum negotiantur': Benvenuto Straccha, *Tractatus de mercatura seu mercatore*, Lugduni 1558, as reprinted in *Klassiker des Europäischen Handelsrechts*, vol. II (ed.: Karl Otto Scherner), p. 411; cf. also, for instance, Petrus Santerna, *Tractatus de assecurationibus et sponsionibus*, bound together with Straccha's *Tractatus* in the volume just quoted, p. 567: '... ex bona fide, quae maxime inter mercatores observanda est, cum inter eos non conveniat de apicibus iuris disputare' (also attributed to Baldus by Santerna).

Index

contract (*cont.*)
   reimbursement of costs 280
   taking advantage of 267–8. *See also*
     abuse of rights
   third party involvement 264, 269, 283
  formation
   agreement on essential elements 263
   consensus in idem 251, 692
   offer and acceptance 251
   oral contract 245, 255
   performance 241
   signature, relevance 241
  frustration. *See* **frustration**
  gratuitous. *See* **bailment; gratuitous
   contract; gratuitous loan**
  illegal 276
  implied 251–2
  implied terms. *See* **implied terms**
  impossibility of performance 86, 578,
   588, 602
  innominate. *See* **innominate contracts**
  interpretation. *See* **interpretation of
   contract**
  intuitu personae 483
  'lawful contact'. *See* **'lawful contact'**
  long-term contract 546–56
  loss of right 516, 517
   inactivity 519, 520, 522, 523, 526, 528,
    530, 548, 667–8
   laches 526, 527–8, 530
   See also **Verwirkung**
  malperformance 31, 173
  mistake. *See* **mistake (error)**, effect on
   contract
  modification 134, 135, 137, 402 [3]
   by agreement 569–70
   changed circumstances 396, 557–77
   implicit 515, 521–2, 522, 526, 529,
    529–30, 541
   ius variandi 338
   révision pour imprévision 561–3, 577
  Nichtigkeit 269 n. 37
  novation 589
  nullité absolue 269 n. 37
  nullité relative 216
  nullity 272–3, 285, 423–4, 592
   dol 217
   illicit cause 222
   See also void *below*
  part performance 676
   'integrity of due performance' 296
   right to refuse 292–304, 657; contract of
    sale. *See* **contract of sale**

   See also under failure to comply with
    formalities *above*
  parties' will as basis of obligation 116
  penalty clauses. *See* **penalty clauses**
  performance
   building contracts, determination 424,
    427–8
   determination by court 420, 421 [2]
   equitable requirement 420–1, 421;
    determination by third party 419–21
   good faith requirement 33, 124, 297
   in accordance with customary manner
    328
   legislative provision 419–21, 421
   reasonable man test 435–8
   unilateral determination 331, 338,
    420–38
  performance at unsuitable time
   definition 322–30
   injunction against 325
   right to refuse 322–30, 657
  periculum est emptoris 595
  positive breach 27
  preservation of a right 673
  re 97, 99–100
  real contract
   gratuitous loan 384
  rebus sic stantibus. *See* **clausula rebus sic
   stantibus**
  renewable
   good faith 532–45, 546–56
   implicit agreement to renew 536
   long-term contract distinguished 547,
    548–9
   right not to renew 532–45
  repudiation
   refusal to take delivery as 646, 647–8,
    648
  rescission. *See* **remedies**, rescission of
   contract
  sale of immovable property. *See*
   **immovable property, contract for the
   sale of**
  severability 56 n. 293, 427–8
  standard form 47
  standard terms 27–8, 31
  statu nascendi 172
  stricti iuris. *See* **actiones stricti iuris**
  tacit relocation 541
  termination
   for an important reason 26–7, 32
   at short notice: abuse of right 404–18,
    405, 406, 407–8, 408–9, 410–11, 418,

Printed in the United Kingdom
by Lightning Source UK Ltd.
136199UK00001B/264/P